North Gate to Jerusalem

North Gate to Jerusalem

A HARMONY OF THE GOSPELS
IN MODERN ENGLISH—
The Life of Jesus Christ

By
Fred R. Coulter

Published by
YORK PUBLISHING COMPANY

ISBN 978-0-9675479-1-6
Copyright 2001, 2006
Fred R. Coulter
York Publishing Co.
P.O. Box 1038
Hollister, CA 95024

TABLE OF CONTENTS

I. DIVISIONS OF THE HARMONY

II. COMMENTARIES

CHARTS

ILLUSTRATIONS

MAPS

Other Works by the Author

The New Testament In Its Original Order—A Faithful Version With Commentary is a new translation and is the only English New Testament that has the books arranged in their original order. It retains the grace and grandeur of the King James Version while clarifying many of its problematic Scriptures. Some commentaries answer the questions: What is the New Testament? Who wrote it? When was it written? When was it canonized? Who canonized it? Other commentaries show the history and preservation of the Bible. Appendices contain many detailed studies of controversial New Testament teachings. This 928-page book is an absolute must for all Christians.

The Christian Passover is a book of over 500 pages that details the scriptural and historical truths of the Passover in both the Old and New Testaments, leading the reader step-by-step through every aspect of one of the most vital and fundamental teachings revealed in the Bible. It fully explains the meaning of the Christian Passover—a remembrance of the sacrifice of Jesus Christ the Passover Lamb of God—in a most compelling and inspiring manner. The full meaning of the body and blood of Jesus Christ is revealed, showing the magnitude of God's love for every person.

The Day Jesus the Christ Died—the Biblical Truth About His Passion, Crucifixion and Resurrection is THE ONLY BOOK to present "the rest of the story"—left out by Mel Gibson in his epic movie *The Passion of the Christ*. Without the true historical and biblical facts, no one can fully understand the meaning of Jesus Christ's horrific, humiliating and gruesome death by beating, scourging and crucifixion. The author presents the full biblical account in a most compelling way. As you will see, the truth is more astounding and profound than all of the ideas, superstitions, traditions and misbeliefs of men!

Occult Holidays or God's Holy Days—Which? For centuries leaders of Orthodox Christendom have sold to the masses—Halloween, Christmas, New Years, Easter, etc.—as though they had "Christian" meaning. This book effectively emphasizes that these celebrated holidays are not of God but originate in ancient pagan, heathen religions rooted in satanic occultism, witchcraft, the feminine divine and "New Age" spirituality. Contrary to the fiction of men the true biblical holy days and feasts of God have spiritual meaning and portray God's fantastic plan of salvation for all mankind—past, present and future—as revealed in the Holy Scriptures.

The Seven General Epistles is designed for an in-depth verse-by-verse study of the epistles of James; I and II Peter; I, II and III John and Jude. As part of the living Word of God, these epistles are as meaningful today for personal Christian growth as when they were written.

Lord, What Should I Do? is a book for Christians who are confused and bewildered by the escalating spiritual and doctrinal chaos in Christian churches today, which is undermining the true faith of the Bible. Any religious organization that teaches truths from the Word of God is a target for the forces of evil behind this chaos. This book clarifies the problem and offers the solution.

On-Line studies for the serious Bible student, more written information and in-depth Bible studies in audio format can be obtained at **www.cbcg.org** and **www.biblicaltruthministries.org**.

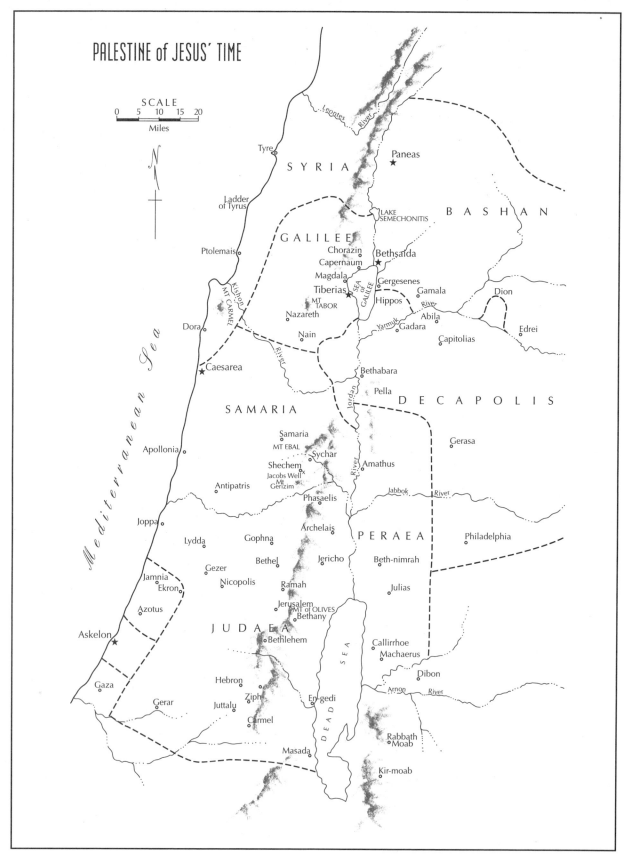

Map – Palestine of Jesus' Time

PREFACE TO THE FIRST AND SECOND EDITIONS
PUBLISHED IN 1974 AND 1975

We have entered the age of the *exposé* and the tentacles of evil and corruption have left few untouched. Immorality and dishonesty have been exposed even among the once trusted political, economic, educational and religious institutions of this world. In some nations the exposure of scandalous conduct on high levels has shaken confidence in governments. The result has been a public demand for a return to morality, ethics and honesty.

On an individual level, the result is that more and more people are seeking a deeper meaning to their personal lives. In their search for greater understanding, many have come to realize that there is a missing dimension in their lives. That missing dimension is a basic spiritual need that cries out to be filled.

In the final analysis that vital spiritual dimension can only be filled by God through Jesus Christ. The beginning step to fill that spiritual vacuum is to understand the life and message of Jesus. That is the reason this book has been written.

In religion also, as in politics, business, and education, people are demanding facts and honesty. This book, *A Harmony of the Gospels in Modern English—The Life of Jesus Christ*, is dedicated to that precept. The true Jesus Christ, His life and message, is presented throughout the pages of this book with clarity and meaning.

Religious myths, superstitions, and traditions of men have not been considered. Rather they have been set aside in order to present the scriptural and historical facts.

As an ordained minister of Jesus Christ, I find that these are the basic questions people ask after studying and investigating the Bible.

"When was Jesus really born?"

"What are the original teachings of Jesus?"

"Was Jesus God or man?"

"Why did Jesus have to die?"

"When was He crucified—Friday, Thursday, or Wednesday?"

"How long was He in the tomb?"

"When was He resurrected?"

"On which day did Jesus keep the Passover?"

The life of Jesus Christ is of paramount importance to all mankind. It is the focal point of history. The Gospels of Matthew, Mark, Luke and John are the fulcrum of the Bible and comprise almost half of the New Testament.

One of the easiest ways to understand the Gospels is to have them compiled into a harmony, which coordinates and blends the events of all four accounts into one synchronized story flow.

Up to the first edition of this book in 1974, there had been no new major work in harmonizing the Gospels in over one hundred and forty years. The first edition has been enthusiastically received. Many thousand of readers have expressed their positive thoughts and reactions.

This second edition has been revised and updated. It has been built on the foundation of the first edition. Every word of the text and commentaries has been revised and re-edited by the most proficient editors obtainable. It is written in modern English, my own paraphrased translation. This makes it the first harmony of the Gospels in recent years to be written in modern English. Twenty pages have been added. Eight maps showing the travels of Jesus have been incorporated in appropriate places. Many photographs have been added making a total of over one hundred. These make a unique combination which captures the flavor of the holy land.

New commentaries have been added—"Jesus' Last Passover, Which Day of the Month—the 14th or 15th?"* All of these additional features make this second edition essentially a new book.

An accurate chronology based on the framework of the Biblical holy days restores and reconstructs the events of Jesus' life. A modern computer was used to accurately coordinate the Hebrew and Roman calendars of Jesus' time. Easy-to-understand commentaries explain and clarify difficult sections. Graphs and charts clearly show when Jesus was born, when He died, how long He was in the tomb and when He was resurrected.

Original art work by Jay Vance and Alfred D'Amelio portray, in detail, the Temple and Jerusalem. The basis for the etchings was the model city of first century Jerusalem.

A Harmony of the Gospels in Modern English—The Life of Jesus Christ has been designed to be used as a study aid, commentary, textbook, and Bible class aid. I sincerely hope that this book will help bring a more profound understanding of Jesus' life to you personally. My personal desire is that this work will help to inspire you to become a better Christian.

---

*Since publishing the first and second editions of the *Harmony of the Gospels*, the author has published a 512-page book, which fully explains the Passover questions in great detail, entitled, "*The Christian Passover,*" 1993, 1999; "*The New Testament In Its Original Order—A Faithful Version with Commentary,*" 2003, 2004, 2006; "*The Day Jesus the Christ Died,*" 2004; and "*Occult Holidays or God's Holy Days—Which?*" 2006.

ACKNOWLEDGMENTS: FIRST AND SECOND EDITIONS

The initial credit and primary acknowledgment for such a work belong to God the Father and Jesus Christ. The spirit of inspiration and understanding imparted throughout the compilation of this work has been evident to me, personally. It is hoped that this same inspiration and understanding will be imparted to you, the reader.

Many people have helped and shared in making the production of this book possible. Without their diligence, kindness and willingness, such an undertaking would have been beyond my abilities as an individual. Appreciation and love go to my lovely, dear wife and family, who have cooperated so wonderfully and encouragingly in sacrificing their time with me during the last three years, while this book was in its final stages. I am deeply thankful and indebted to all who have so graciously helped in making this book a reality. My heartfelt gratitude is extended to all of those who have helped in so many ways: Frank Aloia, Bob Anderson, Evelyn Arnet, Graham Davies, Heather Deininger, Ron Duskis, Bob Ellsworth, Joyce Fenton, Carl and Jeannie Franklin, Barbara Griffin, Bill and Helen Halbe, Evelyn Harford, E. Michael Heiss, David Huyink, Connie Land, John Livingston, Stan and Betty Suchocki, and Marlene Valarde. In addition, many personal friends and acquaintances have given their encouragement and prayers to make this a success.

Frederick R. Coulter

THE NEW FEATURES
OF THE THIRD EDITION

This book, now in the second printing of it's third edition, is the result and accumulation of studies done by the author over the past forty-one years. As a minister of the gospel for over forty-one years, the author can attest to the fact that questions concerning the life of Jesus Christ have repeatedly troubled the minds of many who desire to follow the true teachings of the Savior of mankind. Much of this uncertainty is due to conflicting opinions about who Jesus Christ was. Was He a man, an angel in a human body, or the Son of God—God in the flesh? What was the year of His birth and the length of His ministry? When was He crucified—on a Wednesday, Thursday or Friday? How long was He in the tomb—a day and two nights, two days and two nights, or three days and three nights? When was He resurrected—late on the weekly Sabbath, or early Sunday morning? This book answers those questions with precise accuracy by presenting pertinent Scriptural teachings and historical records that fully establish when these events occurred.

The third edition of *A Harmony of the Gospels in Modern English—The Life of Jesus Christ* is an entirely new book. Each of the commentaries has been expanded to give the reader a more detailed understanding of the teachings of Jesus Christ. Every chart has been updated to precisely reflect the events surrounding the birth, ministry, crucifixion, death and resurrection of Jesus Christ. The first and second editions showed the year of the birth of Jesus Christ to be 4 BC. However, because of additional knowledge and understanding of the Scriptural and historical facts, the time of Jesus' birth has been conclusively established as the fall of 5 BC. This places the beginning of His ministry in the fall of 26 AD, and the date of His crucifixion in 30 AD. He died on the Passover day, Nisan 14, which was Wednesday, April 5, 30 AD. These corrections to the chronology of Jesus Christ's life have been confirmed by many historical facts which were not known thirty years ago when the first and second editions were published *(See Appendix A, p. 348).*

One of the most important new Scriptural understandings that have been discovered since the second edition is that the covenant oath that God made to Abraham, as recorded in Genesis 15, was a foretype of the crucifixion and death of Jesus Christ. This covenant oath was given to Abraham during two days, the 14th and 15th days of the first month, called Abib, and later Nisan. Biblical days are reckoned from sunset to sunset. Nisan 14 is the day that God ordained for the Passover. On the night of Nisan 14, Jesus kept the Passover with His disciples and instituted the New Covenant ceremony consisting of the footwashing, partaking of the bread and wine. On the day portion of Nisan 14, He was crucified and died on the cross. He was put into the tomb just before sunset ending Nisan 14. The night of Nisan 15 was the first of three nights that Jesus was in the tomb. This was the same night that Jesus Christ, as the Lord God of the Old Testament, had confirmed His covenant with Abraham by passing between the parts of the sacrifice. This act was a maledictory oath, a pledge by the Lord God that He would die to fulfill His promises to Abraham. (A detailed account of God's oath and covenant with Abraham is presented in *The Christian Passover*, written by the author and published by York Publishing Company.)

In this third edition, the paraphrased translation of the New Testament Greek that was used in the first and second editions has been replaced with a precise translation of the Greek text. The author recently completed this translation after twenty-seven years of continuous study of New Testament Greek. The translation of the Gospels of Matthew, Mark, Luke and John and for passages cited in the commentaries are from *The New Testament In Its Original Order—A Faithful Version With Commentary* by the author.

The author has been a student of New Testament Greek since 1972. His original tutelage was under Dr. Charles V. Dorothy, PhD, of Ambassador College, Fuller Theological Seminary, and Claremont Graduate School. Although he was the author's mentor in New Testament Greek for many years, the author's translation of the New Testament is solely the responsibility of the author. The author has endeavored to translate the New Testament Greek as accurately as possible in order to bring out the rich teachings that God has inspired for us. The author's translation is based on the Greek text of Stephens, 1550. This is the same Greek text that was used for the translation of the King James Version in 1611.

ACKNOWLEDGMENTS: THIRD EDITION

Initial credit and acknowledgment for this book belong to God the Father and Jesus Christ. Their inspiration and understanding imparted throughout the compilation of this work have been continually evident. It is my sincere hope that this same inspiration and understanding may be imparted to you, the reader.

Appreciation and heartfelt gratitude to my lovely, dear wife, Dolores, who has cooperated so wonderfully and encouragingly in sacrificing her time with me during the writing of this book. I am deeply grateful to Carl and Jean Franklin for their dedication in editing the manuscript for final publication. It was a difficult and tedious task to make such a technical work easy to read. My sincere thanks for the diligent work by John and Hiedi Vogele for the page layout for the third edition. Special appreciation goes to Jim Sorenson for his detailed research and work in order to synchronize the ancient historical records which fully establish the year of the birth of Jesus Christ and the date of His death.

Special thanks are extended to the members of the Christian Biblical Church of God for their love, prayers, encouragement and support in making this vital book possible. Finally, appreciation and thanks go to God and for all the faithful Bible scholars and writers who, in their search for truth down through the centuries, have endeavored to uphold the Word of God.

Fred R. Coulter
First Edition, 1974
Second Edition, 1976
Third Edition, 2001, 2006

WHY THIS THIRD EDITION
WAS PUBLISHED

In the 30 years since the second edition of *A Harmony of the Gospels in Modern English—The Life of Jesus Christ* was published, the world has dramatically changed. All societies have been transformed by the increase of knowledge and technology, affecting everyone in the world. Rapid transportation by auto, train, and airplane has made even the most remote areas of the world accessible to businessmen and tourists. Instant communication through telephone and electronic mail, and on-the-spot news reporting on radio and television, are at one's finger tips daily. Banking and business transactions are conducted around the world using computers that are linked by satellite technology. New inventions and improvements affecting everything in life are continually superseding the old, and even the relatively new, almost as fast as they can be manufactured and sold.

Through the increase of knowledge, men now have the ability to genetically alter the very creation of God. Modern research has unlocked the genetic structure of plants, animals, and human beings. As a result, thousands of plants have been genetically engineered, thereby altering the balance of nature that God has created. Significantly, men of science have also genetically engineered and cloned various animals. And now, scientists claim that they have completely mapped the human genome—the genetic code of human life. Undoubtedly, they will attempt to clone human life in the near future, and may have already begun to do so.

Seemingly awesome miracles have been achieved in medicine. Modern medicines and vaccines have apparently eradicated many diseases. Surgeons can reattach severed limbs and transplant human and animal organs. There appears to be no end to the wonders that man can do. As these human achievements increase and abound, men no longer seem to have need of God or a Savior. Is it any wonder that Jesus Christ asked, "When the Son of man comes [at His second coming], shall He find the *true* faith on the earth?" (Luke 18:8)

Most people do not realize that this tremendous advance in human knowledge and achievements was prophesied thousands of years ago. In the sixth century BC, the prophet Daniel was inspired to write of these days: "But *thou*, O Daniel, shut up the words, and seal the book, *even* to **the time of the end: many shall run to and fro, and knowledge shall be increased**" (Dan. 12:4, *KJV*). Through the centuries, from Daniel's time until now, no one has understood the fullness or the magnitude of this prophecy. Knowledge is not only increasing, but it is multiplying at such a rate that it is nearly doubling every six months—and the end is not yet in sight.

Building Toward One World Government

The rapid growth of technology and communication has broken down political and linguistic barriers between nations. Moreover, because of the dominance of the English-speaking peoples of the world, English is recognized as the universal lan-

1

guage. One can go almost anywhere in the world and find that English is spoken. In addition, an entirely new language, the language of computers, has been created. It is the common language of industry, science and education. As it was at the beginning of human history, a common language is again uniting mankind.

Over four thousand years ago, when all nations spoke one language, they rebelled against God at the tower of Babel. They rejected God and His authority. As in our world today, they had advanced scientific knowledge and were capable of doing anything they imagined to do. The account is recorded in the book of Genesis: "And the whole earth was of one language, and of one speech. And it came to pass, as they journeyed from the east, that they found a plain in the land of Shinar; and they dwelt there. And they said one to another, 'Go to, let us make brick, and burn them thoroughly.' And they had brick for stone, and slime had they for mortar. And they said, 'Go to, let us build us a city and a tower, whose top *may reach* unto heaven; and let us make us a name, lest we be scattered abroad upon the face of the whole earth.'

"And the LORD came down to see the city and the tower, which the children of men builded. **And the LORD said, 'Behold, the people *is* one, and they have all one language; and this they begin to do: and now nothing will be restrained from them, which they have imagined to do**. Go to, let Us go down, and there confound their language, that they may not understand one another's speech.' So the LORD scattered them abroad from thence upon the face of all the earth: and they left off to build the city. Therefore is the name of it called Babel; because the LORD did there confound the language of all the earth: and from thence did the LORD scatter them abroad upon the face of all the earth" (Gen. 11:1-9, *KJV*).

Today, as at the tower of Babel, the world is again becoming "one." We are being globalized. People of the world are coming together in one grand, monolithic civilization. As the globalization of the world continues, the sovereignty of the nations is giving way to regional alliances such as the European Union, soon to expand to twenty-five nations. Trading alliances between North America, Europe, and South America have given way to the World Trade Organization, an international agency which has been given authority to formulate rules, settle disputes and promote the smooth flow of trade between the nations.

At the same time, the United Nations is growing in power and influence over all the nations of the world. It is slowly, but surely, developing into a world government. In conjunction with the development of the UN as the world government, an international criminal court has been organized which will have power to bring individuals from any country to the bar of world justice, regardless of the laws of their native lands. Through all these forces, a modern tower of Babel is being built, which the book of Revelation identifies as "Babylon the Great" (Rev. 17:5).

One World Religion in the Making

The religious organizations of the world have not been left behind in the globalization and unity process. For over forty years, since the historic Vatican II meetings, the World Council of Churches, the Roman Catholic Church, and nearly all the leading Protestant denominations have been busily working to bring all professing Christians together. Currently, their dialogue is reaching out even to non-Christians. In recent years, Pope John Paul II and the Dalai Lama, leader of Tibetan Buddhism, have been working hand in hand to find common ground in their religious beliefs as well as in other religions.

Few realize that the modern ecumenical movement actually began in 1893 in Chicago, Illinois, with the first meetings of the World's Parliament of Religions. At that time, four hundred delegates from many of the world's religions gathered for their first conclave. One hundred years later, in 1993, 3500 leaders from nearly every religion in the world attended the second gathering, again called Parliament of the World's Religions. Their agenda was clearly spelled out, leaving no doubt that they are working toward the unity of all religions under the umbrella of a new world religion: "The Parliament, however, has two specific goals: That top religious leaders adopt a Declaration of Global Ethics [to replace the Ten Commandments of God], and that the delegates set up two ongoing interfaith organizations—a working group in Chicago and an international network as **a kind of religious United Nations**" (*Chicago Tribune* Magazine, August 29, 1993).

In addition to the sweeping efforts of the Vatican and various Protestant churches to bring about full ecumenism, other prominent religious leaders of the world have been busy. At the behest of the Parliament of the World's Religions, they have adopted a Declaration of Global Ethics and are developing a framework for a United Religions organization. As a leading force behind this movement, Episcopalian Bishop William Swing has initiated the United Religion Initiative 2000. He desires to create in the Presidio in San Francisco, California, a forum where the world's religious leaders can meet together. The goal is to unite the world's religions under a global organization affiliated with the United Nations.

Rising from the midst of this broad ecumenical movement is the worship of a mother goddess in various forms and guises. In the environmental movement and modern witchcraft, this goddess is worshiped as Mother Earth, or Gaia. Neo-pagans worship her as the ancient Egyptian goddess Isis. For centuries, Catholics have worshiped the virgin Mary as the queen of heaven and mediatrix between men and God. In recent years there has been a growing movement among the clergy and laity to declare Mary as co-redemptrix, making her equal with her Son.

In concert with the ecumenical movement, the publication in 1997 of *World Scripture—A Comparative Anthology of Sacred Texts* has created a powerful tool to further the uniting of religions. Notice these excerpts from the introduction: "A movement for a 'wider ecumenism' has begun, bringing together for dialogue leaders and scholars from all the world's religions. Theologians of all faiths are affirming the positive worth of other religions and are seeking to overcome the prejudice of an earlier time. It is now widely recognized that humanity's search for God, or for the Ultimate Reality, called by whatever name, is at the root of all religions....Thus the variety of religions would appear to be a testimony to the relativity of human beliefs rather than to the existence of the one Absolute Reality which stands behind all of them" (*World Scripture—A Comparative Anthology of Sacred Texts,* p. 1, International Religious Foundation, New York).

The effect of this book is to reduce God's existence and His inspired Word to the realm of human ideas and thoughts. The Holy Scriptures that God inspired to be written and preserved for humanity, have now been downgraded to the same level as the writings of demon-inspired men and their religions. Instead of upholding the Word of God as the one and only truth, the authors of *World Scripture* boast that there are many paths of truth that lead to the "Absolute Reality": "The passages from diverse scriptures affirm that others who do not share the faith of that scripture are also following the way of Truth. Thus Hinduism, Jainism, and Buddhism understand the various gods to be expressions of a single Absolute Reality, and the various paths to lead to one Supreme God" (Ibid., p. 34).

Contrary to the claim that various paths are leading to the one Supreme God, the result of following the "diverse scriptures" of human wisdom is that people are being drawn away from the true God, Who sent His Son Jesus Christ into the world to bring salvation to all nations.

Scholars Dismantle the Four Gospels

In concert with the ecumenical movement, the divine mission of Jesus Christ, as the Savior of mankind, has been discredited. The true Christ and Messiah, Who was God manifested in the flesh, has been relegated to the role of one among many religious prophets and teachers of wisdom. Two hundred scholars and fellows of the *Jesus Seminar* and *Westar Institute*, located in Santa Rosa, California, have been searching for the "historical Jesus." They are downgrading the inspiration of the Scriptures, which clearly proclaim the divinity of Jesus Christ. To them, these writings are only the works of men, and Jesus was only a man. They are trying to find the historical Jesus by critically dissecting the four Gospels: "The scholarship of the Bible once belonged to the churches. It has now moved out into secular institutions and functions quite apart from, and in some respects in opposition to, the denominations. **The Fellows of the Jesus Seminar approach the Bible, the gospels in particular, as a cultural artifact** rather than as an ecclesiastical handbook. We are interested in assessing the import of the Bible, and of the pioneers and prophets who figure prominently in its story, for the society at large, rather than merely for the churches and their programs" (Funk, *Honest to Jesus*, p. 297, emphasis added).

As stated by Robert W. Funk, the fellows of the Jesus Seminar view the Bible solely as a "cultural artifact"—not as the inspired Word of God. This view is particularly evident in their statements concerning the four Gospels, which they regard not as eyewitness accounts of Jesus' life and ministry, but as a collection of stories based on Old Testament prophecies and later Christian legends. The end result of this view is an outright rejection of major portions of the four Gospels, which they maintain were written at least forty to ninety years after Jesus' ministry and death, and perhaps three hundred years later. They have systematically gone through the four Gospels and have decided by vote which passages to accept as authentic and which passages to reject as myth.

Through this process of voting, they have categorized 82-84% of the Gospel records as partial or complete fiction, and have accepted as authentic, or nearly authentic, only 16% of the events and 18% of the sayings of Jesus as recorded by Matthew, Mark, Luke and John. They expressed their opinions by voting with color codes:

Red: The authentic acts or sayings of Jesus

Pink: A close approximation of what Jesus did or said

Gray: Stories that show minimal historical traces, or probably not what Jesus said

Black: Stories that are improbable events and sayings, or fictive creations of the writers

Based on this voting method, the fellows of the Jesus Seminar have concluded the following concerning the birth and childhood of Jesus: "Jesus was probably born in Nazareth, his hometown. **Later legends** that assign his birth to Bethlehem **were invented to satisfy an ancient prophecy**.

"**Jesus was not born of a virgin**; the Fellows doubt that Mary conceived Jesus without sexual intercourse. Jesus' father was either Joseph or some unknown male who either seduced or raped the young Mary.

"The world census, the trip to Bethlehem, the star in the East, the astrologers, the flight to Egypt and return, the massacre of the babies, the shepherds in the fields, the kinship to John the Baptist are **all Christian fictions**.

"**The birth and childhood stories in Matthew and Luke were the last part of the gospel tradition to be created. They were not conceived, in all probability, until toward the close of the first century C.E.**" (Funk and the Jesus Seminar, *The Acts of Jesus*, p. 533, emphasis added.)

Because the fellows of the Jesus Seminar do not believe that Jesus Christ was the Son of God, Who was sacrificed for the sins of the world, they adamantly reject the Gospel records of His divine begettal and birth by a virgin. They also reject every record that points to His Messiahship, as demonstrated by their evaluation of the Gospel of Mark: "Mark opens his gospel with the appearance of John the Baptist in the wilderness, the baptism of Jesus by John, and return of Jesus to Galilee where he began preaching. The Seminar colored all or most of these stories red. **The account of Jesus' temptations in the wilderness they colored gray: as reported, these stories are legendary, although they may reflect some actual experience of Jesus as he pondered his mission and prepared to enter public life.**

"The stories that form the turning point of Mark's plot were **all colored black as projections of the convictions of early believers**. Those stories include Peter's confession (Mark 8:27-30), Jesus' predictions of his death (Mark 8:31-33, 9:30-32, 10:32-34), and the transfiguration (Mark 9:2-8).

"**The stories that form the climax of the gospel narrative** [referring to the events before the crucifixion] **appear predominantly in black** [voted as not true] as well" (Ibid., p. 532, emphasis added).

To the fellows of the Jesus Seminar, Jesus was a Jew of dubious birth who rose to prominence as a religious figure in Judea at the beginning of the first century. Although they acknowledge His death by crucifixion, they reject the Gospel accounts of His betrayal, His judgment and His burial as religious myths, concocted in the imaginations of early Christians: "The Fellows believe that the temple incident, Jesus' arrest, and his execution were all historical events. Something Jesus said or did against the temple became the occasion for his arrest. The disciples probably fled when Jesus was arrested. He was turned over to the high priest, who in turn handed him over to Pilate for judgment. Pilate probably condemned Jesus out of hand. **It is not just the content of the trial but the fact of a trial that lacks historical foundation. The Fellows concluded that most of the trial narrative was created** [in the imagination of the storyteller] **on the basis of Psalm 2.**

"Jesus was probably flogged in accordance with Roman practice and then crucified. However, **the narrative depiction of these events has been so heavily influenced by parallel events in the Jewish scriptures** and by prophetic texts, including the Psalms, **that we cannot extract hard information from them. As a consequence, most of the details are colored black** [classified as fiction].

"The assertion that the Romans were innocent of Jesus' death and the Jews responsible is **pure Christian propaganda, in the judgment of the Seminar**.

"**The conspiracy against Jesus and the role of Judas, as well as Judas himself, are probably fictions**. The story of Peter's denial is a fiction. **The two trials are fictions**; Luke has added a third trial before Herod, which is also a fiction. The mocking may be a fiction. Simon of Cyrene is a fiction. **The burial of Jesus is a fiction carried out by a fictional character, Joseph of Arimathea**" (Ibid., p. 532, emphasis added).

The fellows of the Jesus Seminar have labeled nearly every event recorded in the Gospels as fiction. After discrediting the crucifixion accounts, they proceed to pass judgment on the accounts of the resurrection of Jesus Christ. Here is a summary of their conclusions concerning the resurrection of Jesus and His appearances afterwards, as recorded in the Gospels and the writings of Paul: "The Fellows of the Jesus Seminar designated red Paul's claim that Jesus appeared to him, since Paul makes that claim on his own behalf. They colored the assertion pink that Jesus appeared to Simon Peter, since Paul's report in 1 Corinthians is secondhand. **The other appearances listed in 1 Cor. 15:5-8 the Fellows voted gray or black**.

"**The empty tomb stories in all the gospels were colored black. The earlier strata of the gospels contain no appearance stories**. The actual resurrection of Jesus is depicted only in the Gospel of Peter [a Gnostic gospel], and as a fiction that report merited a black designation. **The tale of bribing the guard is likewise a fiction.**

"**The Fellows believe Mary of Magdala to have been among the early witnesses** [not an eyewitness, but a spokeswoman] **to the resurrection, although the stories in Matthew and John about the appearance to her are fictional**. In any case, Mary was considered a leader in the early movement alongside Peter and Paul.

"On the basis of a close analysis of all the resurrection reports, the Seminar decided that the resurrection of Jesus was not perceived initially to depend on what happened to his body. **The body of Jesus probably decayed as do all corpses**. The resurrection of Jesus was not an event that happened on the first Easter Sunday; it was not an event that could have been captured by a video camera.

"The Seminar concluded that it does not seem necessary for Christians to believe the literal veracity of any of the later appearance narratives" (Ibid., p. 533, emphasis added).

Alleged Inconsistencies in the Gospels

The fellows of the Jesus Seminar cast further doubt on the veracity of the Gospel accounts by pointing to differences between the Gospel of John and the Synoptic Gospels of Matthew, Mark and Luke. They view these differences as evidence that the Gospel of John is historically inaccurate: "The first step is to understand the diminished role the Gospel of John plays in the search for the Jesus of history. **The two pictures painted by John and the synoptic gospels cannot both be historically accurate**. In the synoptic gospels, Jesus speaks in brief, pithy one-liners and couplets, and in parables. His witticisms are sometimes embedded in a short dialogue with disciples or opponents. In John, by contrast, Jesus speaks in lengthy discourses or monologues, or in elaborate dialogues prompted by some deed Jesus has performed…or by an ambiguous statement…."

"Such speeches as Jesus makes in Matthew, Mark and Luke are composed of aphorisms and parables strung together like beads on a string. In John, these speeches form coherent lectures on a specific theme, such as 'light,' Jesus as the way, the truth, the life, and the vine and the canes. **The parables, which are so characteristic of Jesus in the synoptic tradition, do not appear in John at all**.

"The ethical teaching of Jesus in the first three gospels is replaced in John by lengthy reflections on Jesus' self-affirmations in the form of 'I AM' sayings.

"**In sum, there is virtually nothing of the synoptic sage in the Fourth Gospel**. That sage has been displaced by Jesus the revealer who has been sent from God to reveal who the Father is."

"**The differences between the two portraits of Jesus show up in a dramatic way in the evaluation, by the Jesus Seminar, of the words attributed to Jesus in the Gospel of John. The Fellows of the Seminar were unable to find a single saying they could with certainty trace back to the historical Jesus**. They did identify one saying that might have originated with Jesus, but this saying (John 4:44) has synoptic parallels. There were no parables to consider. **The words attributed to Jesus in the Fourth Gospel are the creation of the evangelist for the most part, and reflect the developed language of John's Christian community**" (Funk, Hoover, and the Jesus Seminar, *The Search for the Authentic Words of Jesus: The Five Gospels*, p. 10, emphasis added).

The fellows of the Jesus Seminar believe that Jesus was only a wisdom teacher and traveling sage of His time, to Whom many sayings were attributed that were borrowed from earlier scriptures or stories of the day, and were never actually spoken by Him. The few sayings that they acknowledge as the "authentic words of Jesus" give such an incomplete picture that the Christ of the Gospels is virtually obliterated. Here is their conclusion: "In addition to these meager facts, we also have a compendium of teachings consisting of parables, aphorisms, and dialogues, together with a few dubious anecdotes featuring witticisms told about him by his first admirers. **The**

authentic words of Jesus can be isolated, to a greater or lesser degree, from other words borrowed from the old scriptures or common lore and put on his lips and from words created by the evangelists under the poetic license exercised by storytellers the world over. The content of this body of authentic speech material tells a great deal about Jesus, but it does so indirectly.

"Meanwhile, **the scattered facts we can muster do not of themselves produce a Jesus who is the Christ of the Christian faith**. The authors of traditional Christian faith are Peter and Paul" (Ibid., pp. 533-534, emphasis added).

To these scholars, Christianity is of human origin only and is rooted in myths and legends, which were created or borrowed by Jesus' admirers and written in the Gospels. They maintain that to interpret the Gospels in a literal manner does not fulfill the purpose for which they were written, and that their proper place is in the realm of mythology: "The Fellows of the Jesus Seminar are profoundly cognizant that human beings do not live by the bread of facts alone. We live by our stories—by our myths, which is only a fancy word for story—and the fictions are supposed to make sense out of a complex universe of meaning mixed with nonsense. Myths are not true or untrue; as one Fellow puts it, they are either living or dead. Literalism in biblical interpretation in tandem with scientism has helped **strangle the myths of the Christian tradition**. Historical criticism like that practiced by the Jesus Seminar is intended to **release the gospel stories from their literalistic burden**. Exposing them to historical assessment **relocates them in the realm of story and myth, so they can recover their proper function**. When we move them back within that perspective, perhaps new mythmakers and storytellers will once again find voice to celebrate the simple yet enduring story of Jesus of Nazareth" (Ibid., p. 534, emphasis added).

A New Version of the Gospels

After rejecting the entire Gospel of John, as well as most records in the synoptic Gospels, the fellows of the Jesus Seminar have taken upon themselves to produce their own version of the four Gospels together with a spurious gospel of Gnostic origin. Their book *The Search for the Authentic Words of Jesus: The Five Gospels,* presents the Gospels of Matthew, Mark, Luke and John in a new translation, color-coded according to their rating scheme for fact or fiction. They have taken a further ignominious step by placing the Gnostic gospel of Thomas alongside the four Gospels, making a total of five "gospels." The gospel of Thomas, written in Coptic, was discovered in December 1945, along with thirteen other Gnostic codices, in Upper Egypt near the town of Nag Hammadi.

While they admit that the gospel of Thomas is rooted in Gnosticism, the fellows of the Jesus Seminar justify its addition to the four Gospels by claiming that it was one of the earlier Christian writings: "**The Gospel of Thomas reflects the outlook of the gnostic movement** in some respects. Jesus, for example, speaks as the redeemer come from God. He reminds his followers of their forgetfulness and tells them they are in need of enlightenment....

"Thomas is rooted in the Jewish wisdom tradition, such as we find in Psalms and Proverbs. It is a wisdom gospel made up of the teachings of a sage. But it is moving off in the direction of gnostic speculation such as we find in later gnostic documents.

In these respects, **Thomas represents an early stage in Christian gospel writing** and theologizing, quite comparable to what we find in the New Testament, especially in Paul and the Gospel of John" (*The Search for the Authentic Words of Jesus: The Five Gospels*, p. 501, emphasis added).

Those who understand that the books of the New Testament in original Greek are the God-breathed words of God understand that Gnostic writings such as the gospel of Thomas have no place with the four Gospels. The true Gospels of Matthew, Mark, Luke and John were canonized with the other books of the New Testament and have been proclaimed to the world in every generation for nearly 2,000 years. God inspired the apostles to write and canonize them, and He preserved them as part of His Word. He did not bury them in a graveyard in Upper Egypt to hide them from public knowledge. The so-called gospel of Thomas was buried for nearly 1600 years, while the four Gospels have been published around the world as a living witness of Jesus Christ, the Son of God and Savior of the world.

When the apostle John was inspired to write the book of Revelation, the last book of the New Testament that he canonized, he warned of the judgment that awaits those who presume to add to or take away from the words of God: "For I jointly [with the Lord Jesus Christ] testify to everyone who hears the words of the prophecy of this book, *that* **if anyone adds to these things, God shall add to him the plagues that are written in this book** [the entire Bible]. **And if anyone takes away from the words of** *the* **book of this prophecy, God shall take away his part from** *the* **book of life, and from the holy city, and from the things that are written in this book'** " (Rev. 22:18-19).

In taking away from the true Gospels and exalting a spurious gospel, the scholars of the Jesus Seminar have showed open contempt for the Word of God. They have denied the salvation of God through Jesus Christ, which is revealed in the four Gospels. In his epistle to the Romans, the apostle Paul declares that those who reject the salvation of God, and suppress the gospel of Christ, will reap His wrath: "For I am not ashamed of **the gospel of Christ** because it is *the* **power of God unto salvation to everyone who believes**—both to *the* Jew first, and to *the* Greek. For therein *the* righteousness of God is revealed from faith unto faith, according as it is written: 'The just shall live by faith.' Indeed, *the* **wrath of God is revealed from heaven upon all ungodliness and unrighteousness of men who suppress the truth in unrighteousness**" (Rom. 1:16-18).

Suppressing the Gospel of Christ

Robert W. Funk and the fellows of the Jesus Seminar suppress the truth by claiming that the Jesus of the Gospels is a myth. They deny the divinity of Jesus Christ and His role as man's Redeemer and Mediator before God. They view Christianity as an empty faith, built on stories and legends, which has outlived its meaning and usefulness in the modern world of science and technology: "In the global arena, the symbolic world that is ingredient to traditional Christianity no longer occupies a foundational position. As the economic and technological superiority of the West fades, **the symbols that attend the Christian myth will lose whatever appeal they once had**. Meanwhile, in the West, the old symbolic universe is on the decline....Those who cling to the old are having increasing difficulties in assigning meaning to such biblical statements as 'he ascended into heaven.' **Appeals to an endorsing God**, to heaven and hell, **to a divine redeemer, to Christ as the sole mediator between God and humankind**, have begun to lose their bite and more frequently **fall on unhearing ears**.

"Since that symbolic world is crumbling or has crumbled, **the times call for a wholly secular account of the Christian faith, not just for the sake of its appeal to the third world but primarily for the sake of those who inhabit the contemporary, scientifically minded Western world**" (Funk, *Honest to Jesus*, p. 298, emphasis added).

As part of his twenty-one theses, Robert W. Funk proposes a new religion that rejects the sacrifice of Jesus Christ as the means for the atonement of sin: "**We will have to abandon the doctrine of the blood atonement**. The atonement in popular piety is based on **mythology that is no longer credible**—that God is appeased by blood sacrifices. Jesus never expressed the view that God was holding humanity hostage until someone paid the bill. Nor did Amos, Hosea, or other prophets of Israel. In addition, it is the linchpin that holds the divinity of Jesus, his virgin birth, the bodily resurrection, and a sinless life together in a unified but naïve package: God required a perfect sacrifice, so only a divine victim would do" (Ibid., p. 312, emphasis added).

It is clear that Robert W. Funk completely rejects Jesus Christ as divine Redeemer and Savior. He shows his ignorance of the New Testament scriptures by claiming that Jesus is not qualified to be his Redeemer: "A true savior incarnate—*incarnate* literally means embodied—**a true savior embodied must submit to the same limitations imposed on the rest of us** [Jesus did by becoming fully human (John 1:14, Heb. 2:14; 4:15)]. If Jesus of Nazareth is a savior, it is only because he aspired to heaven as all mortals do but was sage enough to reject the temptation and accept the limitations of his finite existence [a total denial of Jesus' divinity (John 1:1; 17:5, 11)]. If he arrived via a miraculous birth, knew himself to be the messiah and son of God, and had foreknowledge that his death would be reversed in a few days, **he is not qualified to function as my redeemer**" (Ibid., p. 308, emphasis added).

Robert W. Funk and the fellows of the Jesus Seminar envision a Christianity that disavows the sacrifice of its Redeemer, the existence of its God, and the inspiration of its Scriptures. As Lloyd Geering, one fellow of the Jesus Seminar wrote, "For most of the post-Christian world, **the Bible will no longer be regarded as the Word of God**, but it will continue to be of value as an historical testimony to Judeo-Christian origins and as an essential resource for the understanding of past western culture. It will take its place alongside other great religious classics from the various cultures of the past. **Jesus will no longer be hailed as the saviour of the world, or as a divine figure**. He will stand among the great pioneering figures of the past, and his sayings and parables will continue to inspire those who take the trouble to search them out.

"**God will no longer be conceived widely as an objective spiritual being—one who personally hears and answers prayers**, and who guides human history from behind the scenes. God language, if used at all, will be treated as symbolic. Spiritual practices may take the form of meditation but will not be understood as conversation with an external personal being. **Life in this world will be acknowledged as the**

only form of human existence. The expectation of conscious personal existence beyond death will gradually be abandoned" (*The World to Come: From Christian Past to Global Future*, p. 87, emphasis added).

The Proposed "Post-Christian" Religious System

The Christianity that Geering envisions will offer no promise of eternal life through Jesus Christ. Reduced to the level of all other religions of the world, it will function only as one choice among countless others for those who seek a belief system to guide their lives: "So what place does conventional Christianity have, in the post-Christian era we are now entering? It is no longer a community-held faith which shapes and motivates society. Instead, in its multiple forms, it is becoming **one set of personal options among numerous others**, including New Age religions and secular ideologies. Together they form **a vast religious supermarket** to which people may go when they are looking for a philosophy or way of life, and in which they are free to choose one tailored to their needs" (Ibid., pp. 86-87, emphasis added).

In this new global religious system that Lloyd Geering envisions, the worship of Mother Earth will replace the worship of God the Father and Jesus Christ: "Some steps towards acknowledging the sacred character of the earth have already been taken. We no longer restrict the concept of 'sanctuary' to the church building or temple but are giving it back to the earth, in bird sanctuaries, fish sanctuaries and so on. The eco-sphere itself is gradually being resanctified. **The loving care of Mother Earth is in many quarters replacing the former sense of obedience to the Heavenly Father**. In her book *The Body of God*, theologian Sallie McFague goes further, suggesting that the combined influence of post-modern science and Christian faith requires the construction of **a new model in which we see the universe as the body of God** [not "new" at all, but the ancient philosophy of pantheism]....we will recreate the appropriate festivals to celebrate the earth's role in our lives. The new religious rituals will be based not only on our relationship to the natural world, they will also celebrate everything we have come to value in human existence..." (Ibid., p. 158, emphasis added).

The value in human existence lies in the fact that each one of us has been made in the image of God, for the ultimate purpose of sharing His glory and immortality. To deny the personal existence of the eternal, all-powerful Being Who created mankind, does not celebrate the value of human life but suppresses the knowledge of man's awesome, God-given potential, and reduces human life to the level of animal life. In his summary of religion in the global era, Geering makes no mention of man's relationship to His Creator, but focuses entirely on man's relationship to the natural world and to the society of his own making: "What then will this new faith, the religion of the future, look like? It is far too early to tell, but some broad outlines can be seen. I suggest that being religious in the global era will be:
- to be devoted to maximizing the future for all living creatures whose destiny is increasingly in our hands;
- to place the needs of the coming global society before those of our own immediate family, tribe or nation;
- to develop a lifestyle consistent with preserving the balance of the planetary eco-system on which all living creatures depend;
- to refrain from all activities which endanger the future of all species;

11

- to set a high value on the total cultural legacy we have received from the past and which enables us to develop our potential to become human;
- to value the importance of the human relationships which bind us together into social groups and which enable us to become fully human;
- to promote the virtues of love, goodwill and peacefulness" (Ibid., p. 159).

Geering's description of the new religion of the global era is filled with idealistic thoughts, but the peace and goodwill that he envisions are not possible in a society that exalts the creation above the Creator, and rejects the knowledge that is revealed in His Word. The apostle Paul condemns this misguided worship of the natural world: "Because that which may be known of God is manifest among them, for God has manifested *it* to them; for the invisible things of Him are perceived from *the* creation of *the* world, being understood by the things that were made—both His eternal power and Godhead—so that **they are without excuse; because when they knew God, they glorified *Him* not as God, neither were thankful**; but they became vain in their own reasonings, and their foolish hearts were darkened. While professing themselves to be *the* wise ones, they became fools and changed the glory of the incorruptible God into *the* likeness of an image of corruptible man, and of birds, and four-footed creatures, and creeping things**. For this cause, God also abandoned them to uncleanness through the lusts of their hearts, to disgrace their own bodies between themselves, **who exchanged the truth of God for the lie; and they worshiped and served the created thing more than the one Who is Creator, Who is blessed into the ages**. Amen" (Rom. 1:19-25).

Rejecting the worship of Jesus Christ and God the Father will not lead to utopia. Instead it will lead to the greatest deception ever to befall mankind. The focus of religion is being shifted from the spiritual realm to the natural world, from the divine to the physical, to prepare the world for the coming of a human messiah who will arise from among the nations. The New Testament reveals that this messiah will be heralded by a great false prophet, who will perform supernatural signs through the power of Satan the devil. These signs and wonders will deceive all nations into accepting the false messiah and worshiping him as God.

Warnings in the New Testament of the Coming Apostate World Religion

The foundation of this worldwide deception was already being laid in the days of the apostles. In writing to the believers at Thessalonica, the apostle Paul warned of the "**mystery of lawlessness**," which was beginning to infiltrate the churches of God and draw believers away from the true faith. Paul's words to the Thessalonians show that Satan was the unseen power behind this insidious movement to corrupt the churches of God. Paul made it clear that this system would continue until the end times, when it would rise to great power. Here is Paul's warning: "Now we beseech you, brethren, concerning the coming of our Lord Jesus Christ and our gathering together to Him, that you not be quickly shaken in mind, nor be troubled—neither by spirit, nor by word, nor by epistle, as if from us, *saying* that the day of Christ is present. **Do not let anyone deceive you by any means because *that day will not* come unless the apostasy** [led by the false prophet (Rev. 13:11-18, 16:13 and 19:20)] **shall come first, and the man of sin** [the antichrist Beast—the coming world dictator (Rev. 13:1-10, 16:13, 19:20)] **shall be revealed—the son of perdition, the one who** opposes and exalts himself above all that is called God, or that is an object of worship; so that he comes into the temple of God and sits down as God, proclaiming that he himself is God.

"Do you not remember that when I was still with you, I told you these things? And now you understand what is holding *him* back **in order for him to be revealed in his own set time. For the mystery of lawlessness is already working**; only *there is* one [Jesus Christ] Who is restraining at the present *time* until it arises out of *the* midst. **And then the lawless one will be revealed (whom the Lord will consume with the breath of His mouth, and will destroy with the brightness of His coming);** *even* **the one whose coming is according to** *the* **inner workings of Satan, with all power and signs and lying wonders, and with all deceivableness of unrighteousness in those who are perishing because they did not receive the love of the truth, so that they might be saved. And for this cause, God will send upon them a powerful deception that will cause them to believe** *the* **lie; so that all may be judged who did not believe the truth, but who took pleasure in unrighteousness"** (II Thes. 2:1-12).

The developing global religious/political system will be used by Satan to deceive the entire world (Rev. 12:9). The underlying philosophy of this religious system is clearly outlined in the *World Scriptures*, which holds the beliefs and writings of all religions of the world to be equal with the teachings of Jesus Christ. The words of Jesus Christ stand in stark contrast to the proclamations of men who claim that there are "various paths to lead to one Supreme God." Jesus Christ declared to His disciples that He is the ONLY WAY to God the Father, the Supreme Sovereign of the universe: **"I am the way, and the truth, and the life; no one comes to the Father except through Me"** (John 14:6).

The Only Way to Eternal Life Is Through Jesus Christ

The scriptures of the New Testament make it clear that there is only one way that leads to eternal life, and that way is through Jesus Christ. In the Sermon on the Mount, Jesus warned His disciples that false prophets would deceive many into following a false way that leads to death: **"Enter in through the narrow gate; for wide** *is* **the gate and broad** *is* **the way that leads to destruction, and many** [the majority] **are those who enter through it; for narrow** *is* **the gate and difficult** *is* **the way that leads to life, and few are those who find it. But beware of false prophets** [whether religious or secular] **who come to you in sheep's clothing; for within** *they* **are ravening wolves.** You shall know them by their fruits" (Matt. 7:13-16).

No religious leader, no prophet, no teacher, no philosopher, can substitute for Jesus Christ, and no so-called "sacred writing" or "religious myths" can replace the God-breathed Word of God. The Old Testament and the New Testament testify, to all who will hear, that salvation through Jesus Christ was planned before the creation of the world. HE ALONE IS "THE WAY, THE TRUTH AND THE LIFE." Jesus came to earth as the only begotten Son of God. Before He came in the flesh, He was the Lord God of the Old Testament. The apostle John makes this truth absolutely clear: **"In** *the* **beginning was the Word, and the Word was with God, and the Word was God.** He was in *the* beginning with God. All things came into being through Him, and not even one *thing* that was created came into being without Him.

13

In Him was life, and the life was the light of men....**And the Word became flesh**, and tabernacled among us (and we ourselves beheld His glory, *the* glory as of *the* **only begotten with *the* Father**), full of grace and truth" (John 1:1-4, 14).

None of the other religions have a Savior comparable to Jesus Christ. They have all been founded by prophets and teachers whose writings are believed to enlighten, but they do not have a Savior Who is the Creator God. Jesus Christ was the only spiritual leader Who was God manifested in the flesh. The apostle Paul fully understood this: "And undeniably, great is the mystery of godliness: '**God was manifested in *the* flesh**, was justified in *the* Spirit, was seen by angels, was proclaimed among *the* Gentiles, was believed on in *the* world, **was received up in glory**' " (I Tim. 3:16). As God in the flesh, Jesus Christ laid down His life to become the Savior of the world. At His resurrection, He was restored to His former glory and ascended to the throne of God the Father. Since that time, He has been fulfilling His work of redemption by purifying each true believer from sin, preparing a people to live forever with Him when He returns in glory. The words of the apostle Paul to Titus describe the work of Jesus Christ as God and Savior: "Looking for the blessed hope, and ***the* appearing of the glory of our Savior and great God, Jesus Christ; Who gave Himself for us, so that He might redeem us from all lawlessness**, and might purify for Himself a unique people, zealous of good works" (Titus 2:13-14).

All prophets or teachers who claim that there is another savior, or another way to eternal life, are frauds. God never sent them. Jesus Christ made it clear that all others who present themselves as "saviors" are thieves and robbers. He alone laid down His life as the perfect sacrifice for the sins of the world. There is no forgiveness or salvation through any other man or by any other way: "Therefore, Jesus again said to them, 'Truly, truly I say to you, I am the door of the sheep. All who ever came before Me are thieves and robbers, but the sheep did not hear them. I am the door. If anyone enters through Me, he shall be saved, and shall go in and out, and shall find pasture. The thief does not come except to steal and kill and destroy. I have come so that they may have life, and may have *it* more abundantly. I am the good Shepherd. The good Shepherd lays down His life for the sheep....I am the good Shepherd, and I know those who *are* Mine, and am known of those who *are* Mine. Just as the Father knows Me, I also know the Father; and I lay down My life for the sheep. And I have other sheep that are not of this fold. I must bring those also, and they shall hear My voice; and there shall be one flock *and* one Shepherd. On account of this, the Father loves Me: because **I lay down My life, that I may receive it back again. No one takes it from Me, but I lay it down of Myself. I have authority to lay it down and authority to receive it back again**. This commandment I received from My Father' " (John 10:7-11, 14-18).

In his epistle to the Hebrews, the apostle Paul makes it clear that, as the Son of God, Jesus Christ is not only greater than any man, but He is also greater than any of the angels. Before He became flesh, He shared the same glory and power as God the Father, but left His glory in order to bring redemption and salvation to mankind. Now He again shares the power and glory of the Father: "God, Who spoke to the fathers at different times in the past and in many ways by the prophets, has spoken to us in these last days by *His* Son, Whom He has appointed heir of all things, by Whom also He made the worlds; **Who, being *the* brightness of *His* glory and *the* exact image of His person, and upholding all things by the word of His own power, when**

He had by Himself purged our sins, sat down at *the* **right hand of the Majesty on high; having been made so much greater than** *any of* **the angels, inasmuch as He has inherited a name exceedingly superior to them.** For to which of the angels did He ever say, 'You are My Son; this day I have begotten You'? And again, 'I will be a Father to Him, and He will be a Son to Me'? And again, when He brought the Firstborn into the world, He said, 'Let all *the* angels of God worship Him' " (Heb. 1:1-6).

Forgiveness of Sin Comes Only Through Jesus Christ

The words of the apostle Peter to the religious leaders of the Jews make it absolutely clear that salvation from sin and the gift of eternal life come only through the name of Jesus Christ. After Peter and John healed a man who had been lame from birth, they were arrested and brought before the chief priests and Pharisees, who demanded to know by what name or what means the lame man had been healed. "Then Peter, filled with *the* Holy Spirit, said to them, 'Rulers of the people and elders of Israel, if we are examined this day as to a good work *done to the* infirm man, by what *power* he has been cured, be it known to you all, and to all the people of Israel, that in the name of Jesus Christ the Nazarean, Whom you crucified, *but* Whom God has raised from *the* dead, by Him this *man* stands before you whole. This is the Stone that was set at naught by you, the builders, which has become the Head of *the* corner. **And there is no salvation in any other, for neither is there another name under heaven which has been given among men, by which we must be saved'** " (Acts 4:8-12).

The only way to receive forgiveness of sin and salvation is through Jesus Christ, the only begotten Son of God. Jesus Christ came for the purpose of bringing repentance and remission of sins to light. The apostles answered the religious authorities after they were arrested a second time the following: "And they brought them in *and* set *them* before the Sanhedrin. And the high priest asked them, saying, 'Did we not order you by a *direct* command not to teach in this name? And look, you have filled Jerusalem with your teaching, with *the* purpose of bringing this man's blood upon us.' But Peter and the apostles answered *and* said, '**We are obligated to obey God rather than men. The God of our fathers raised up Jesus Whom you killed** *by* **hanging** *Him* **on a tree. Him has God exalted by His right hand** *to be* **a Prince and Savior, to give repentance and remission of sins to Israel'** " (Acts 5:27-31).

No other religion has a Savior Who gave up His immortal existence as God and took on human flesh in order to die for the sins of mankind. As the Creator God, He emptied Himself of His power and glory and submitted to the shame and brutality of death by crucifixion: "...Christ Jesus, **Who, although He existed in** *the* **form of God, did not consider it robbery to be equal with God, but emptied Himself,** *and* **was made in** *the* **likeness of men,** *and* **took the form of a servant; and being found in** *the* **manner of man, He humbled Himself,** *and* **became obedient unto death, even** *the* **death of** *the* **cross.** Therefore, God has also highly exalted Him and bestowed upon Him a name which *is* above every name; that at the name of Jesus every knee should bow, of *beings* in heaven and on earth and under the earth, and every tongue should confess that Jesus Christ *is* Lord to *the* glory of God *the* Father" (Phil. 2:5-11).

The Lordship of Jesus Christ and the salvation of God through His name, has no equal in heaven or on earth. The apostle Paul makes this absolutely clear: "In Whom we have redemption through His own blood, *even* the remission of sins; Who is *the* image of the invisible God, *the* firstborn of all creation; because by Him were all things created, the things in heaven and the things on earth, the visible and the invisible, whether *they be* thrones, or lordships, or principalities, or powers: all things were created by Him and for Him. **And He is before all, and by Him all things subsist. And He is the Head of the body, the church; Who is *the* beginning, *the* firstborn from among the dead, so that in all things He Himself might hold the preeminence.** For it pleased *the Father* that in Him all the fullness should dwell, **and, having made peace through the blood of His cross, by Him to reconcile all things to Himself; by Him, whether the things on the earth, or the things in heaven**" (Col. 1:14-20).

Forgiveness of sin and reconciliation with God the Father cannot be granted by any religious leader on earth. That is the work of Jesus Christ Himself, Who alone became the sin offering for the world: "For He [God the Father] made Him Who knew no sin *to be* sin for us, so that we might become *the* righteousness of God in Him" (II Cor. 5:21).

The forgiveness of sins is granted through the sacrifice of Jesus Christ to all who truly repent and confess their sins to God the Father. The apostle John shows the way: "If we confess our own sins [to God the Father through Jesus Christ], He is faithful and righteous, to forgive us our sins, and to cleanse us from all unrighteousness. If we say that we have not sinned, we make Him a liar, and His Word is not in us. My little children, I am writing these things to you so that you may not sin. And *yet*, **if anyone does sin, we have an Advocate with the Father; Jesus Christ *the* Righteous; and He is *the* propitiation for our sins; and not for our sins only, but also for *the sins of* the whole world**" (I John 1:9-10, 2:1-2).

Forgiveness of sin is imparted, by the grace of God, through the blood of Jesus Christ which is able to cover all sins. No good work, acts of penitence, or prayers to so-called saints, can substitute for the sacrifice of Jesus Christ, which alone brings remission of sins. All the religious practices and traditions of men are worthless. These works cannot obtain forgiveness or salvation: "Now you were dead in trespasses and sins, in which you walked in times past according to the course of this world, according to the prince of the power of the air, the spirit that is now working within the children of disobedience; among whom also we all once had our conduct in the lusts of our flesh, doing the things willed by the flesh and by the mind, and were by nature *the* children of wrath, even as the rest *of the world*. **But God, Who is rich in mercy, because of His great love with which He loved us, even when we were dead in *our* trespasses, has made *us* alive together with Christ....For by grace you have been saved through faith, and this *especially* is not of your own selves; *it is* the gift of God, not from works, so that no one may boast.** For we are His workmanship, created in Christ Jesus unto *the* good works that God ordained beforehand in order that we might walk in them" (Eph. 2:1-10).

The whole purpose of Jesus Christ's coming in the flesh was to sacrifice His life for the sins of the world, in order that all who believe in Him may receive forgiveness of sin and the gift of eternal life. The apostle John was inspired to write, "For God so loved the world that He gave His only begotten Son, so that everyone who believes in Him may not perish, but may have everlasting life" (John 3:16).

This third edition has been published to bring the life of the true Jesus Christ of the Gospels into clear focus, and to provide you with a fuller understanding of what God has done for the world and for you personally. The most profound event in the history of the universe and the world was the coming of Jesus Christ, the Creator of all things, to this earth as a human being. God actually came to the earth and became flesh and blood. Jesus Christ's life, death and resurrection have had a massive impact on humanity, even altering the course of history. Whether people have understood or believed this does not take away from the meaning and magnitude of the life of Jesus Christ.

Millions of people in the Western world profess to believe in Jesus Christ, but only a very few truly know Him. This perplexing dilemma has occurred because the real meaning and purpose of Jesus' life has been misunderstood, obscured and darkened by the very ones who teach Christianity. The simple truths of Scripture have been glossed over and misinterpreted, and doctrinal facts have been presented as fallacies. In addition, religious traditions of men have been superimposed upon the Scriptural record of Jesus' life. These traditions have taken away from the actual eyewitness accounts that are preserved in the four Gospels.

Many theologians and scholars have no understanding of the historical facts that were recorded by Matthew, Mark, Luke and John, and have interpreted the Gospel accounts to fit their own traditional beliefs or to reject the true Gospel accounts. As a result, the Gospels as historical documents have been discounted and rejected as unreliable and contradictory. Some erroneously teach that the Gospels were not put into written form for nearly three hundred years after Christ, and therefore have little or no historical value and must be rejected as myth. However, when we examine secular histories of the time of Christ, we find that the opposite is true. Other contemporary histories verify that the Gospels contain accurate historical records (see Appendix A). Moreover, the writings of the apostle Paul show that the teachings of Jesus Christ were written down from the very beginning (Luke 1:1-4, Acts 6:1-4, II Tim. 3:15, Gal. 3:1).

The Gospel of Matthew was the first Gospel to be written and published. There is evidence that Matthew's words were being circulated among the believers in the early months of the New Testament church, with the complete book already available only five years after Jesus Christ's resurrection. Later, but during the lifetimes of the apostles, the other Gospels were compiled and published. Mark's Gospel was written between 38 and 44 AD. Luke wrote his Gospel and the book of Acts before Paul died. In beginning his Gospel account, Luke states that many accounts of the teachings of Jesus Christ had already been written: "Since many have taken in hand to compile a *written* narration of the matters which have been fully believed among us, as they delivered *them* to us, those who from *the* beginning had been eyewitnesses and ministers of the Word, it seemed good to me also, having accurately understood everything from the very first, to write *these things* in an orderly sequence to you, most excellent Theophilus, so that you might know the *absolute* certainty of *the* things in which you have been instructed" (Luke 1:1-4).

In his account of Jesus Christ's birth and the beginning of His ministry, Luke includes some specific historical events. These records, when compared with secular history and the calculations of the Hebrew Calendar, confirm that the Gospels are historically accurate. Three of the Gospel writers were eyewitnesses of Jesus Christ's ministry, and the fourth one, Luke, had read their firsthand accounts, which he used to write his Gospel, under the tutelage of the apostle Paul.

The three synoptic Gospels of Matthew, Mark and Luke vary in the details that are included in their respective accounts, but these variations do not indicate a lack of accuracy or consistency. However, when they are properly understood, these additional details help to clarify the facts. The Gospel of John, which was the last to be written, does not contain the same details that are found in the synoptic Gospels. John was well acquainted with the other three Gospel accounts, but God did not inspire him to follow the same pattern in writing his Gospel. Instead, John based his Gospel on the framework of the Hebrew Calendar. The details that John recorded are not included in the other Gospels. As a result, the Gospel of John adds significantly to our understanding of the events at Jesus' last Passover, and enables us to place His burial and resurrection in their actual historical context.

While the world is searching for the historical Jesus outside the writings of the Bible, the most accurate historical record of the life of Jesus Christ has been preserved in the Gospels. This is the source that God has inspired to be written and preserved for us. The Word of God has withstood the test of time and the determined attacks of disbelievers.

In our time, as never before, the forces of evil are working together in a final attempt to destroy all knowledge of the true Jesus Christ. As the world moves headlong toward globalization in business and commerce, a New World Order in government, and a polytheistic world religion, a full understanding of the life of Jesus Christ is absolutely essential. Our personal salvation depends on understanding and living by the true Jesus Christ, Who is the only Redeemer and Savior of mankind. Without this precious knowledge from the Word of God, we may be deceived into believing the lie that will soon engulf the whole world.

The third edition of *A Harmony of the Gospels in Modern English—The Life of Jesus Christ* has been published to make the Scriptural truth of Jesus' life known. The simple facts contained in the four Gospels, when understood in their Scriptural and historical time setting, reveal the dynamic and awesome meaning and purpose of Jesus' life. As you read and study this book, it is the author's hope that you will find truth more gratifying and rewarding than tradition or myth. Remember that the Gospel accounts were written that you may believe and have eternal life: "But these have been written, so that you may believe that Jesus is the Christ, the Son of God; and that believing, you may have life through His name" (John 20:31).

Fred R. Coulter

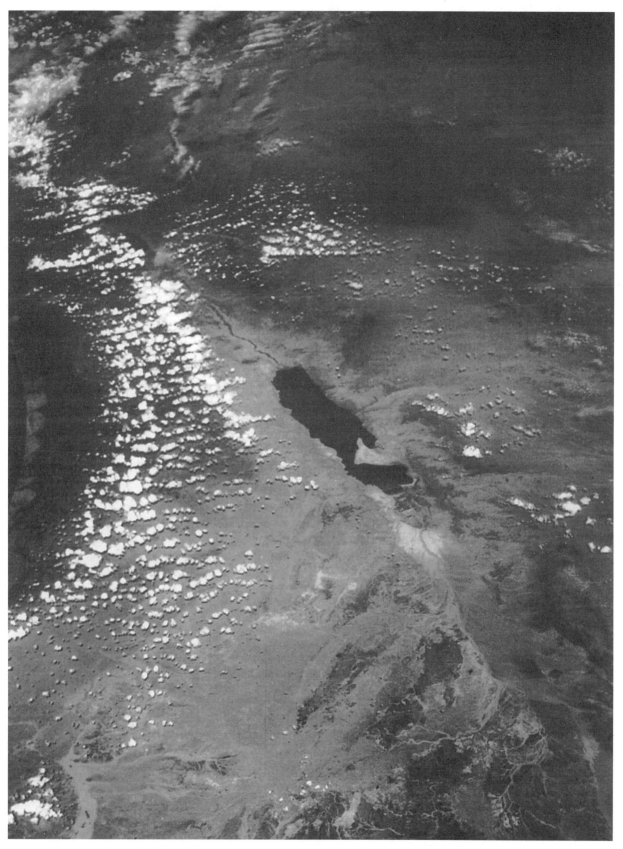

The Holy Land From Apollo 7 (Mediterranean Sea to left - Dead Sea in right center)

Model of Herod's Temple of the First Century AD

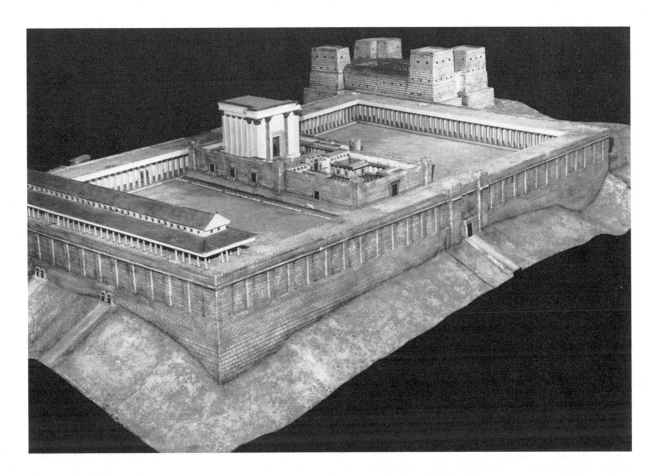

WHEN WAS
JESUS CHRIST BORN?

The date of Jesus Christ's birth has been a topic of controversy for centuries. Various theories place the year of His birth in a range from 6 BC to 1 AD. As to the season of the year, most believe that He was born in the winter. Some claim that He was born in the spring, while others feel that He was born in the fall. Still others are inclined to shrug their shoulders, declaring that they don't know and, it really doesn't matter. While some theologians claim that it is not possible to know when Jesus was born, they readily accept December 25 as the day to celebrate His birth. They reason that the date or season is not as important as remembering the event.

Although an abundance of scriptural and historical evidence proves Jesus was not born on December 25, the majority of professing Christians still observe this date as His birthday. Few realize that this observance is based on ancient pagan tradition that predates Jesus Christ's birth by thousands of years. Age-old customs of pagan origin entered the Christian churches many centuries ago and are now viewed as an essential part of Christian worship. Most churches today encourage their members to freely participate in the popular customs of the Christmas season.

While supposedly honoring the birth of Jesus Christ, the traditional observance of Christmas actually distorts the scriptural story of His birth and ignores the revealed purpose of His coming to earth in the flesh. His birth is, in fact, the chief cornerstone and foundation of true Christianity. The birth of Jesus Christ fulfilled a number of significant prophecies that are recorded in the Old Testament. A proper understanding of the true circumstances of His birth will provide deeper insight into the meaning of His life and the ultimate purpose of His coming.

The scriptural and historical facts concerning the birth of Jesus Christ are readily available to all who are willing to examine them. These combined records clearly reveal the year, season and the approximate day of Jesus Christ's birth.

JESUS WAS BORN DURING
THE REIGN OF HEROD THE GREAT

The Gospel of Matthew records that the birth of Jesus Christ occurred during the reign of Herod the Great. When Herod heard that the prophesied king of the Jews had been born, he feared that the Jews would begin to revolt against his rule. Matthew's account follows: "Now after Jesus had been born in Bethlehem of Judea, in *the* days of Herod the king, behold, Magi from *the* east arrived at Jerusalem, saying, 'Where is the one who has been born King of the Jews? For we have seen His star in the east, and have come to worship Him.' But when Herod the king heard *this*, he was troubled, and all Jerusalem with him" (Matt. 2:1-3).

Intending to slay the infant king, Herod summoned the scribes and chief priests to Jerusalem to inquire where the Messiah would be born, according to the prophecies in the Old Testament. Upon learning that Christ was prophesied to be born in Bethlehem, Herod instructed the Magi to return and inform him after they had found Him. But God intervened, through a dream to Joseph, to prevent Herod from harming the young Jesus:

"And after hearing the king, they departed; and behold, the star that they had seen in the east went in front of them, until it came and stood over *the house* where the little child was. And after seeing the star, they rejoiced *with* exceedingly great joy.

"And when they had come into the house, they found the little child with Mary His mother, and they bowed down and worshiped Him; then they opened their treasures *and* presented their gifts to Him—gold and frankincense and myrrh.

"But being divinely instructed in a dream not to go back to Herod, they returned to their own country by another way. Now after they had departed, behold, an angel of *the* Lord appeared to Joseph in a dream, saying, 'Arise and take the little child and His mother, and escape into Egypt, and remain there until I shall tell you; for Herod is about to seek the little child to destroy Him.' And he arose by night and took the little child and His mother, and went into Egypt, and was there until the death of Herod ..." (Matt. 2:9-15).

Matthew's account of these events indicates that Herod died not long after Jesus was taken to Egypt. After the death of Herod, Joseph brought Jesus and Mary back from Egypt to Nazareth, a city in the district of Galilee: "Now when Herod had died, behold, an angel of *the* Lord appeared to Joseph in Egypt in a dream, saying, 'Arise and take the little child and His mother, and go into *the* land of Israel; for those who were seeking the life of the little child have died.' And he arose *and* took the little child and His mother, and came into *the* land of Israel. But when he heard that Archelaus was reigning over Judea instead of Herod his father, he was afraid to go there; and after being divinely instructed in a dream, he went into the parts of Galilee. And after arriving, he dwelt in a city called Nazareth ..." (Matt. 2:19-23).

This scriptural record offers conclusive evidence that the birth of Jesus Christ occurred a short time before the death of Herod the Great. Through the historical writings of the noted historian Josephus, we can determine precisely when Herod reigned and when he died. Josephus reveals the specific year that Herod was crowned king at Rome: "... And thus did this man receive the kingdom, having obtained it on the hundred and eighty-fourth olympiad, when Caius Domitius Calvinus was consul the second time and Caius Asinius Pollio [the first time]" (Josephus, *Antiquities of the Jews,* 14:14:5).

An olympiad is four years in length and is reckoned from July to July. The 184th olympiad extended from July 1, 44 BC, to June 30, 40 BC. Records of this period show that Calvinus and Pollio were consuls in the year 714 AUC (years from the founding of Rome), which was 40 BC (Finegan, *Handbook of Biblical Chronology*, p. 96). Thus we know that Herod became king in 40 BC. While the olympiad was reckoned from July 1 to June 30, the calendar year for consuls was reckoned from January 1 to December 31. Since the 184th olympiad ended on June 30, 40 BC, and the consuls did not take office until January 1 of that year, we know that Herod was made king sometime during the six-month period from January through June of 40 BC.

Although Herod was crowned at Rome in 40 BC, three years passed before he conquered Jerusalem and began to reign in that city: "When the rigour of winter was over, Herod removed his army, and came near to Jerusalem and pitched his camp hard by the city. Now this was the third year since he had been made king at Rome ..." (Josephus, *Ant.*, 14:15:14).

While Herod launched his attack in the spring, it was not until the summer of that year that he was able to take the city of Jerusalem. Josephus reveals the specific date of this event: "... for it was summer time.... This destruction befell the city of Jerusalem when Marcus Agrippa and Canninius Gallus were consuls of Rome, on the hundred eighty and fifth olympiad, on the third month, on the solemnity of the fast ..." (Ibid., 14:16:2, 4).

The 185th olympiad extended from July 1, 40 BC, to June 30, 36 BC. Agrippa and Gallus became consuls in 717 AUC, which corresponds to 37 BC. The fast of the third month that Josephus refers to was the 23rd of Sivan, according to the Hebrew Calendar, which was June 22 on the Julian Calendar. Herod completed the conquest of the city of Jerusalem in the summer of 37 BC, and began to reign as king in Jerusalem at that time.

Josephus provides additional historical records concerning the reign of Herod that enable us to determine the time of his death: "... he [Herod] died ... having reigned since he had procured Antigonus to be slain, thirty-four years; but since he had been declared king by the Romans, thirty-seven" (Ibid., 17:8:1). Josephus records elsewhere in the same book that Antigonus was killed shortly after Herod had conquered Jerusalem (Ibid., 14:16:4).

In linking Antigonus's death with Herod's conquest of Jerusalem in 37 BC, Josephus confirms that Herod did not reign in Jerusalem until three years after his coronation at Rome. Consequently, there are two methods of reckoning the reign of Herod the Great—the Jewish method, which counts thirty-four years from 37 BC, and the Roman method, which counts thirty-seven years from 40 BC. Since the first year of his reign is included in the count, both methods of reckoning arrive at 4 BC as the end of Herod's reign. This date is conclusively established by the records of history as the year that Herod died.

Josephus' detailed account of Herod's death enables us to further pinpoint the time of the year. In his account, Josephus records that Herod died after an eclipse of the moon but before Passover. The lunar eclipses that occurred during this period of history have been calculated in the book *Solar and Lunar Eclipses of the Ancient near East* by M. Kudler and E. Mickler (published by Neukirchen-Bluyn: Verlas Butson & Bercker Kevelaer, 1971). Here is a listing of the lunar eclipses:

7 BC - No eclipses
6 BC - No eclipses
5 BC - Total eclipse, March 23, 8:30 PM
5 BC - Total eclipse, September 15, 10:30 PM
4 BC - Partial eclipse, March 13, 2:20 AM
3 BC - No eclipses
2 BC - No eclipses

The first lunar eclipse to occur during this period was a total eclipse on March 23 in the year 5 BC. In this year the Passover, Nisan 14, was observed by the Jews on March 22. Because the Scriptural reckoning of days is from sunset to sunset, the Passover day extended from sunset March 21 to sunset March 22. Since the total eclipse that occurred at 8:30 PM on the night of March 23 was after Passover and not before, this was not the eclipse that Josephus refers to in conjunction with Herod's death.

The second total eclipse of the moon during this period took place on September 15, 5 BC, which was a significant day by Scriptural reckoning. According to the Hebrew Calendar, September 15 was the 14th of Tishri (the seventh month). The moon was totally eclipsed at 10:30 PM that night, which was the beginning of the 15th of Tishri, the first day of the Feast of Tabernacles. The twin total eclipses of the moon in 5 BC are so rare that on these dates it only occurs once in 2717 years (*Canon of Lunar Eclipses 1500 B.C.—A. D.* by Bao-Lin and Alan D. Faila).

Josephus' account of this period of Jewish history includes a number of events which point to this eclipse as the one that occurred shortly before the death of Herod. In recounting the final months of Herod's reign, Josephus gives us an accurate time frame for establishing the date of Jesus Christ's birth.

HISTORICAL RECORDS OF HEROD'S DEATH REVEAL THE YEAR OF CHRIST'S BIRTH

Josephus gives us detailed records of some of the events that took place before the death and burial of Herod. These events are listed chronologically in the synchronized Hebrew/Roman calendar on pages 33-36. Events that are not specifically dated by historical records have been given approximate dates based on the evidence that is available in history. This calendar accurately depicts the sequence of events that took place during that time period.

Josephus relates that shortly before his death, Herod sent ambassadors to Rome. As noted on the synchronized Hebrew/Roman calendar, this action is estimated to have occurred during the week ending August 26, 5 BC. Sometime during the next week, a group of zealots stormed the temple and proceeded to chop down the golden idol that Herod had erected over one of its gates. Herod learned that Matthias, the high priest, had incited the zealots to undertake this action in the mistaken belief that Herod was dead. Herod punished Matthias by removing him from the office of high priest and burning him alive, as Josephus relates. In his writings, Josephus shows that these events took place in the fall of the year and were marked by an eclipse of the moon. Josephus' gives this detailed account: "He deprived Matthias of the high priesthood, as in part an occasion of this action, and made Joazar, who was Matthias' wife's brother, high priest in his stead. Now it happened, that during the time of the high priesthood of this Matthias, there was another person made high priest for a single day, that very day which the Jews observe as a fast day [the day of Atonement, the 10th day of Tishri, the seventh month] 'the great day of expiation.' The occasion was this: Matthias the high priest, on the night before the day when the fast was to be celebrated, seemed in a dream to have conversation [sexual relations] with his wife: and because he could not officiate himself on that account, Joseph, the son of Ellemus, his kinsman, assisted him in that sacred office. But Herod deprived this Matthias of the high priesthood, and [later] burnt the other Matthias [on Tishri 14], who had raised the sedition, with his companions, alive. And that very night there was an eclipse of the moon [Tishri 15]" (*Ant.*, 17:6:4).

This eclipse was obviously an autumnal eclipse, as it occurred in Tishri, the seventh month of the Hebrew Calendar, which corresponds to September/October on the Julian Calendar. As documented in the record of lunar eclipses by Kudler and Mickler, only one autumnal eclipse occurred during that period of history. This was the eclipse of September 15, 5 BC, on the evening beginning the Feast of Tabernacles—the 15th day of Tishri.

Josephus records the decline of Herod's health after this autumnal eclipse and the state of insanity that preceded his death. Shortly after the Feast of Tabernacles, Herod's "distemper" increased, and he sought the help of the warm mineral baths at Callirrhoe, which was located beyond the Jordan River. It has been estimated that he went there the week ending November 4. There is no record of the exact length of his stay; but since his funeral procession and burial took place after the winter, he must have stayed there approximately eight or nine weeks. He then went to Jericho, probably arriving by January 13. Josephus describes Herod's deplorable mental state at that time: "... and came again to Jericho, where he grew so choleric, that it brought him to do all things like a madman; and though he was near his death, he contrived the following wicked designs" (Ibid., 17:6:5).

Herod commanded the principal men of his government to come to Jericho, intending to have them killed after his death. It is estimated that these men arrived at Jericho by January 20 to 27. A few days later, Herod received letters from Rome brought by the ambassadors he had sent. Although the news was good and seemed to revive him, he attempted suicide soon afterward. His attempt was not successful, as he was restrained by Achiabus. In his rage he ordered his son Antipater to be killed, and he himself died five days later. Josephus records, "When he had done these things, he died, the fifth day after he had caused Antipater to be slain; having reigned, since he had procured Antigonus to be slain, thirty-four years; but since he had been declared king by the Romans, thirty-seven" (Ibid., 17:8:1).

Herod died thirty-seven years from the time of his coronation at Rome in the spring of 40 BC. Although his reign began near the end of the 184th olympiad (reckoned from July 1 to June 30), it is included as the first year in Josephus' count. Based on the records of Josephus and other historical evidence, Herod's death is estimated to have occurred during the week ending February 17, 4 BC.

After Herod's death, Archelaus succeeded Herod as king. He carried out Herod's wishes for an extended period of mourning and a long funeral before his burial. The time needed for these ceremonies was approximately twenty-five days, not counting Sabbaths. The chronology of these events is laid out step by step on the synchronized Hebrew/Roman calendar on page 36. As illustrated in this calendar, the funeral procession finished its journey with the arrival of Herod's body in Jerusalem during the week ending March 24, 4 BC, at which time Archelaus began his rule in Jerusalem.

The records of Josephus clearly contradict the commonly held theory that the eclipse of March 13, 4 BC, was the eclipse before Herod's death. If Herod had died after March 13, the extended mourning and funeral procession could not possibly have been completed by March 24. As Josephus shows, these extended ceremonies began many weeks before the Passover day and ended with Herod's burial in the middle of the Feast of Unleavened Bread, which followed the Passover. To further substantiate the time of Herod's burial, Josephus records that at that time Archelaus slaughtered 3,000 people who had crowded into the temple area to celebrate the Feast of Unleavened Bread. This slaughter occurred during the week which ended April 14, 4 BC, confirming that Herod's burial took place about two months after his death.

As recorded in the Gospel of Matthew, Jesus was born in Bethlehem of Judea during the reign of Herod the Great. Sometime after His birth, Jesus was taken to Egypt and remained there for a period of time before Herod died. Matthew's record of these events indicates that the birth of Jesus occurred several months before the death of Herod. Since Herod's death occurred very early in 4 BC—approximately mid-February—it is evident that Jesus was born sometime during the preceding year. Thus Herod's death places Christ's birth in the year 5 BC. The Gospel of Luke provides additional evidence that enables us to know the specific season of the year in which Christ was born.

SCRIPTURAL EVIDENCE OF THE
SEASON OF JESUS CHRIST'S BIRTH

In his account of the birth of Jesus Christ, Luke records a major historical event of that time. Luke writes, "Now it happened in those days *that* a decree went out from Caesar Augustus that all the world should be registered. (This registration first occurred when Cyrenius was governor of Syria.) Then all went to be registered, each to his own city" (Luke 2:1-3).

The taxation and census decree by Caesar Augustus was carried out according to the Jewish custom which required that such taxes be collected after the fall harvest (See *Unger's Bible Dictionary*, Chronology, New Testament, pp. 199-200). Luke's record of this taxation reveals that the birth of Jesus took place during the autumn. When we combine Luke's record with Matthew's account of Herod's death, it is evident that Jesus was born in the fall of 5 BC.

Luke gives us additional evidence that Jesus was born during the fall festival season by recording that there were no guest rooms available at the inn when Joseph and Mary arrived in Bethlehem. The scarcity of room was due not only to the taxation but also to the festival days that followed the fall harvest. Many thousands of people were already in the Jerusalem area to observe the fall festival season. Bethlehem was extremely crowded because of its proximity to Jerusalem. Since there was no room at the inn, Joseph and Mary were forced to lodge in a barn. Jesus was born there and was laid in a manger.

In addition, Luke makes it clear that Jesus was not born in the winter by recording that shepherds were tending their flocks in the fields that night (Luke 2:8). The shepherds in that region of Palestine always brought their flocks out of the fields before the onset of winter. The flocks were never left to graze in the pastures during the winter months because the cold weather prevented the grass from growing. There is much discussion in Bible commentaries for those who desire to study these points further.

RECORDS OF JOHN'S MINISTRY CONFIRM
JESUS' BIRTH IN THE FALL OF 5 BC

In his account of the beginning of John the Baptist's ministry, Luke gives another historical reference that helps to verify the date of Jesus Christ's birth: "Now in *the* fifteenth year of the government of Tiberius Caesar ... *the* word of God came unto John, the son of Zacharias, in the wilderness. And he went into all the country around the Jordan, proclaiming *the* baptism of repentance for *the* remission of sins" (Luke 3:1-3).

Luke tells us that John the Baptist began his ministry in the fifteenth year of Tiberius Caesar. A dispute has existed over which year of Tiberius' reign was reckoned by Luke as the fifteenth year because the first two years of Tiberius' reign were a co-rulership with Augustus. Consequently, there are conflicting opinions as to whether the Scriptural record includes Tiberius' co-reign or counts from the beginning of his sole reign.

The dispute is settled when Luke's record is linked with other scriptural and historical records of that time. The reign of Tiberius is firmly established by historical records dating the death of Augustus. Augustus died August 19 in the year that Sextus Apuleius and Sextus Sillus were consuls. The year of the consuls' rule was 767 AUC, which was 14 AD. This date is confirmed by the fact that Augustus died 44 years, lacking 13 days, after the Battle of Actium (*Dio's Roman History*, Loeb ed., Book LVI: 29-30, vol. 7, pp. 65, 69).

Josephus records that the Battle of Actium took place during the 187th olympiad in the seventh year of the reign of Herod (*Ant.*, 15:5:1-2; *Wars*, 1:20:3). The 187th olympiad was the four-year period from July 1, 32 BC, to June 30, 28 BC. The Battle of Actium took place during the second year of the olympiad, which was July 1, 31 BC to June 30, 30 BC. This was the seventh year of Herod's reign by Jewish reckoning, but the tenth year of his reign by Roman reckoning. Counting forward 44 years from the Battle of Actium, which ended in September, 31 BC, we arrive at 14 AD as the year of Augustus' death.

Records of the reign of Augustus reveal that during his final years, "... the consuls caused a law to be passed ... that he [Tiberius] should govern the provinces jointly with Augustus and hold the census with him" (*Seutonius*, Ed. J.C. Rolfe, LCL, vol. 1, p. 323).

Tiberius began his co-rulership with Augustus in 12 AD, two years before the death of Augustus. Counting from this date, we arrive at 26 AD as the fifteenth year of Tiberius and the beginning of John the Baptist's ministry. Other Scriptural and historical records confirm that John the Baptist began his ministry in the spring of 26 AD and that Jesus began His ministry six months later in the fall of 26 AD.

Major supporting evidence is found in the Gospel of John, which records the words of the Jews at the time of the first Passover of Christ's ministry. During this

Passover season, the Jews stated that the temple had been forty-six years in building (John 2:20). We can determine the date of this Passover, and the first year of Christ's ministry, by counting from the year that the building of the temple began.

Josephus records that the building of the temple was begun during the eighteenth year of Herod's reign: "And now Herod, in the eighteenth year of his reign [that is, the eighteenth in Jerusalem, but the twenty-first year from his coronation in Rome] ... undertook a very great work, that is to build of himself the temple of God" (*Ant.*, 15:11:1).

The eighteenth year of Herod's reign in Jerusalem, which was the first year of building the temple, was from the summer of 20 BC to the summer of 19 BC. Counting forward, the forty-sixth year of building was from the summer of 26 AD to the summer of 27 AD. The only Passover that occurred during this period of time was the Passover of 27 AD. Thus, scriptural and historical records place the first Passover of Christ's ministry in the spring of 27 AD. Since His ministry began in the fall of the year, we can date its beginning to the autumn of 26 AD.

THE BIRTH OF JOHN THE BAPTIST
A KEY TO THE DAY OF JESUS CHRIST'S BIRTH

In the first chapter of the Gospel of Luke, we find a detailed account of the circumstances and events that preceded the birth of Jesus Christ. In this account, Luke reveals that the conception of Jesus by the virgin Mary occurred six months after the conception of John by Mary's aunt, Elizabeth, the wife of Zacharias. Zacharias was a priest of God who served at the temple in Jerusalem.

At the beginning of his account, Luke records, "There was in the days of Herod, the king of Judea, a certain priest of *the* course of Abijah, Zacharias by name....And it came to pass *that* in fulfilling his priestly service before God in the order of his course, according to the custom of the priestly service, it fell to him by lot to burn incense when he entered into the temple of the Lord" (Luke 1:5, 8-9).

Zacharias was executing his priestly duties according to the order and course of Abijah. This information is most helpful in establishing the time frame of Luke's account. In ancient Israel, King David divided the duties of the priests into twenty-four working courses, or shifts (I Chron. 24:7-19). Each course or shift was assigned to work one full week, from noon Sabbath to noon Sabbath (Talmud, *Sukkah*). The Old Testament records the exact rotation and time order of the priestly courses, which continued down to New Testament times. Zacharias was of the course of Abijah, which was the eighth course or shift in the series of yearly assignments for the priesthood.

Josephus (noted Jewish historian) was a priest of the first course or shift. Josephus confirms that the priestly courses established by King David were still functioning in New Testament times. He records, "He [King David] divided them also into courses ... and he found [or established] of these priests, twenty-four courses ... and he ordained that one course should minister to God eight days, from sabbath to sabbath ... and this partition hath remained to this day" (*Ant.*, 7:14:7). This record confirms that the courses of priests remained in effect down to the time of

Zacharias and the birth of Jesus Christ. These courses undoubtedly continued until the temple was destroyed in 70 AD.

The Talmud reveals that the first priestly course, or shift, began in the first full week of the first month of the Hebrew Calendar. The second course worked the second week. This rotation continued on a week-by-week basis through all twenty-four courses. Each priestly course served a one-week shift twice each year. In addition, all courses were required to work during the three weeks in the year that coincided with the three festival seasons: Passover, Pentecost, and Tabernacles. Thus all the priests shared equally in the priestly responsibilities for the entire year.

We know that the angel Gabriel delivered the promise of John's birth while Zacharias was serving in his priestly course in the temple. The Gospel of Luke reveals that John was born six months before Jesus (Luke 1:35-36). Our examination of both the scriptural and historical records has established that Jesus was born in the fall of 5 BC. Accordingly, John the Baptist was born in the spring of 5 BC and was conceived six months earlier in the summer of 6 BC. Knowing the year that John was conceived enables us to determine the exact period of time that Zacharias was serving in the temple.

In the year 6 BC, the first day of the first month (the month of Nisan according to the Hebrew Calendar) was a weekly Sabbath. According to calculations synchronizing the Hebrew Calendar and the Julian Calendar, this Sabbath was March 20. Projecting forward, the assignments course by course, or week by week, were: Course 1, the first week; Course 2, the second week; all courses for the Passover and Feast of Unleavened Bread, the third week; Course 3, the fourth week; Course 4, the fifth week; Course 5, the sixth week; Course 6, the seventh week; Course 7, the eighth week; Course 8, the ninth week; and all courses the tenth week, which was the week of Pentecost. (See the synchronized Hebrew/Roman calendar on page 33.)

Because Zacharias was of the course of Abijah, the eighth course, he was assigned the ninth and tenth weeks from the beginning of the year. These weeks of service were counted from noon Sabbath to noon Sabbath. The ninth week was from Iyar 27 through Sivan 5, which corresponds to May 15 through May 22 on the Julian Calendar. The tenth week, Sivan 5 through Sivan 12, or May 22 through May 29, was the week of Pentecost. Sometime during these two weeks, the angel Gabriel appeared to Zacharias in the temple and prophesied the birth of John.

Although the exact time of Gabriel's appearance is not recorded, it is reasonable to conclude that Gabriel delivered this message from God on the day of Pentecost. The announcement that Zacharias's wife Elizabeth would bear a son came during the two weeks in which Zacharias served at the temple, and the day of Pentecost occurred on Sivan 6, in the middle of the two-week period. Since John the Baptist's birth was a major fulfillment of prophecy, it is appropriate that God would send Gabriel on a holy day to announce the promise of his conception to Zacharias. Luke records the angel Gabriel's message to Zacharias as he was in the temple offering incense: "According to the custom of the priestly service, it fell to him by lot to burn incense when he entered into the temple of the Lord. And all the multitude of the people outside were praying at the hour of the *burning of* incense. Then an angel of *the* Lord appeared to him, standing at *the* right side of the altar of incense. And when he saw *the angel*, Zacharias was troubled, and fear fell upon him.

"But the angel said to him, 'Fear not, Zacharias, because your supplication has been heard; and your wife Elizabeth shall bear a son to you, and you shall call his name John. And he shall be a joy and exultation to you; and many shall rejoice at his birth. For he shall be great before the Lord. And he shall never drink wine or strong drink in any form, but he shall be filled with *the* Holy Spirit even from his mother's womb. And many of the children of Israel shall he turn to *the* Lord their God. And he shall go before Him in *the* spirit and power of Elijah, to turn *the* hearts of the fathers to *the* children, and *the* disobedient to *the* wisdom of *the* righteous, to make ready a people prepared for *the* Lord' " (Luke 1:9-17).

Because Zacharias did not believe God's promise, Gabriel pronounced a sign from God. Zacharias would be unable to speak until the child was born and given the name John, which God had chosen (Luke 1:13, 19-20). After completing his service at the temple, Zacharias returned to his house, and John was conceived in the following days: "Now it came to pass *that* when the days of his service were fulfilled, he departed to his house. And after those days, Elizabeth his wife conceived, but hid herself *for* five months ..."(Luke 1:23-24).

The Gospel account indicates that Elizabeth became pregnant shortly after Zacharias returned home. Since he returned on May 29, it is reasonable to assume that she became pregnant between May 30 and June 12 (Sivan 13-26) in the year 6 BC. This estimated time allows a two-week conception period.

Luke was inspired to record that Elizabeth was in the sixth month of her pregnancy when the virgin Mary was miraculously impregnated through the power of the Holy Spirit and conceived Jesus: "Now behold, Elizabeth your kinswoman has also conceived a son in her old age; and this is *the* sixth month for her who *was* called barren" (Luke 1:36). Based on the estimated time of conception, the sixth month of Elizabeth's pregnancy was November/December by Roman reckoning.

Luke gives additional details that indicate Mary became pregnant in the last two weeks of Elizabeth's sixth month. Mary was told by the angel Gabriel that Elizabeth was already in the sixth month of her pregnancy. Mary then visited Elizabeth and stayed with her almost three months (Luke 1:39-40, 56). Soon after Mary left, Elizabeth reached her full term of nine months, and John was born sometime between Adar 19 and Nisan 3, or February 27 and March 11, in 5 BC.

As illustrated by the synchronized Hebrew/Roman calendar on page 34, Mary's probable conception period coincides with the last two weeks of Elizabeth's sixth month. That two-week period was Keslev 17-30, or November 28-December 11. Projecting forward nine months from the estimated time of Mary's conception, we arrive at the two-week period during which Christ was probably born. This two-week time period was Elul 24-Tishri 8, or August 27-September 9. As the synchronized Hebrew/Roman calendar shows on page 35, the Feast of Trumpets was the middle day of this two-week period.

Many passages in the Bible show that the Feast of Trumpets pictures the second coming of Jesus Christ. The Day of the Lord and the angelic trumpets in the book of Revelation clearly project this symbolism and meaning. Is it not reasonable to conclude that God also chose the Feast of Trumpets as the day of Jesus Christ's birth? The apostle Paul reveals that the prophesied birth of Jesus was fulfilled at a set time. Paul wrote, "But when the time for the fulfillment came, God sent forth His own Son, born of a woman ..." (Gal. 4:4). While the Gospels do not reveal the specific day, the birth of Jesus Christ on the Feast of Trumpets would be in harmony with God's great plan as portrayed through His annual holy days.

Although the Scriptures do not record the exact date of His birth, the biblical and historical evidence makes it abundantly clear that Jesus Christ was not born in the middle of winter, or any time during winter or spring. All the evidence clearly points to the two-week period around the Feast of Trumpets, in the fall of 5 BC, as the time of the birth of Jesus Christ. Professing Christians today need to open their eyes to this truth and forsake their misguided belief that Jesus was born on December 25. The observance of Christmas neither honors Jesus Christ nor commemorates His birth. In fact, the traditional festivities that are observed each year at Christmas time are a perpetuation of ancient pagan customs that no true Christian should practice (Deut. 12:29-32, Jer. 10:1-8). These traditions, like other religious traditions of this world, are neither pleasing nor acceptable to God (Mark 7:6-9), and those who practice them dishonor God the Father and Jesus Christ.

Winter in the Holy Land, Jerusalem after a snowstorm in January

The Birth of Jesus
The Calculated Hebrew Calendar
with the Julian Calendar

This synchronized calculated Hebrew/Julian calendar illustrates the time period from March 6 BC to April 4 BC. The sequence of scriptural, historical and astronomical events depicted in this calendar reveals the actual year, season, and the most likely day of Jesus Christ's birth. *(See Appendix A for "A Synchronized Chart of Historical and Scriptural Records That Establish the Year of Christ's Birth," pp. 348-352.)* **Note:** The columns read downward—left column first.

6 B.C.

NISAN

MARCH					APRIL	
S	M	T	W	T	F	SAB
						20
						1
21	22	23	24	25	26	27
2	*3*	*4*	*5*	*6*	*7*	*8*
28	29	30	31	1	2	3
9	*10*	*11*	*12*	*13*	*14*	*15*
4	5	6	7	8	9	10
16	*17*	*18*	*19*	*20*	*21*	*22*
11	12	13	14	15	16	17
23	*24*	*25*	*26*	*27*	*28*	*29*
18						
30						

1st Course begins - noon Sabbath.

1st Course works - 2nd Course begins noon Sabbath.

2nd Course works - All courses begin at Passover.

All work - 3rd Course begins noon Sabbath.

3rd Course works - 4th Course begins noon Sabbath.

14th - Passover, 15th-21st - Feast of Unleavened Bread.

6 B.C.

TAMMUZ

JUNE					JULY	
S	M	T	W	T	F	SAB
				17	18	19
				1	*2*	*3*
20	21	22	23	24	25	26
4	*5*	*6*	*7*	*8*	*9*	*10*
27	28	29	30	1	2	3
11	*12*	*13*	*14*	*15*	*16*	*17*
4	5	6	7	8	9	10
18	*19*	*20*	*21*	*22*	*23*	*24*
11	12	13	14	15		
25	*26*	*27*	*28*	*29*		

End of 1st month of Elizabeth's pregnancy.

6 B.C.

IYAR

APRIL					MAY	
S	M	T	W	T	F	SAB
	19	20	21	22	23	24
	1	*2*	*3*	*4*	*5*	*6*
25	26	27	28	29	30	1
7	*8*	*9*	*10*	*11*	*12*	*13*
2	3	4	5	6	7	8
14	*15*	*16*	*17*	*18*	*19*	*20*
9	10	11	12	13	14	15
21	*22*	*23*	*24*	*25*	*26*	*27*
16	17					
28	*29*					

4th Course works - 5th Course begins noon Sabbath.

5th Course works - 6th Course begins noon Sabbath.

6th Course works - 7th Course begins noon Sabbath.

7th Course works - 8th Course begins noon Sabbath.

8th Course works.

6 B.C.

AB

JULY					AUGUST	
S	M	T	W	T	F	SAB
					16	17
					1	*2*
18	19	20	21	22	23	24
3	*4*	*5*	*6*	*7*	*8*	*9*
25	26	27	28	29	30	31
10	*11*	*12*	*13*	*14*	*15*	*16*
1	2	3	4	5	6	7
17	*18*	*19*	*20*	*21*	*22*	*23*
8	9	10	11	12	13	14
24	*25*	*26*	*27*	*28*	*29*	*30*

End of 2nd month of Elizabeth's pregnancy.

6 B.C.

SIVAN

MAY					JUNE	
S	M	T	W	T	F	SAB
		18	19	20	21	22
		1	*2*	*3*	*4*	*5*
23	24	25	26	27	28	29
6	*7*	*8*	*9*	*10*	*11*	*12*
30	31	1	2	3	4	5
13	*14*	*15*	*16*	*17*	*18*	*19*
6	7	8	9	10	11	12
20	*21*	*22*	*23*	*24*	*25*	*26*
13	14	15	16			
27	*28*	*29*	*30*			

8th Course works - All courses begin at noon Sabbath.

9th Course begins noon Sabbath.
Zacharias leaves.

Elizabeth's probable two-week conception period ends.

6th - Day of Pentecost (probably day that Gabriel appeared to Zacharias).

6 B.C.

ELUL

AUGUST		SEPTEMBER				
S	M	T	W	T	F	SAB
15	16	17	18	19	20	21
1	*2*	*3*	*4*	*5*	*6*	*7*
22	23	24	25	26	27	28
8	*9*	*10*	*11*	*12*	*13*	*14*
29	30	31	1	2	3	4
15	*16*	*17*	*18*	*19*	*20*	*21*
5	6	7	8	9	10	11
22	*23*	*24*	*25*	*26*	*27*	*28*
12						
29						

End of 3rd month of Elizabeth's pregnancy.

33

6 B.C.

TISHRI

SEPTEMBER			OCTOBER			
S	M	T	W	T	F	SAB
		13	14	15	16	17	18
		1	*2*	*3*	*4*	*5*	*6*
19	20	21	22	23	24	25
7	*8*	*9*	*10*	*11*	*12*	*13*
26	27	28	29	30	1	2
14	**15*	*16*	*17*	*18*	*19*	*20*
3	4	5	6	7	8	9
21	*22*	*23*	*24*	*25*	*26*	*27*
10	11	12
28	*29*	*30*

1st of Tishri - Feast of Trumpets.

10th of Tishri - Day of Atonement.

End of 4th month of Elizabeth's pregnancy.
**15th-21st - Feast of Tabernacles.
22nd - Last Great Day.*

6 B.C.

HESHVAN

OCTOBER			NOVEMBER			
S	M	T	W	T	F	SAB
			13	14	15	16
			1	*2*	*3*	*4*
17	18	19	20	21	22	23
5	*6*	*7*	*8*	*9*	*10*	*11*
24	25	26	27	28	29	30
12	*13*	*14*	*15*	*16*	*17*	*18*
31	1	2	3	4	5	6
19	*20*	*21*	*22*	*23*	*24*	*25*
7	8	9	10	11
26	*27*	*28*	*29*	*30*

End of 5th month of Elizabeth's pregnancy.

6 B.C.

KISLEV

NOVEMBER			DECEMBER			
S	M	T	W	T	F	SAB
					12	13
					1	*2*
14	15	16	17	18	19	20
3	*4*	*5*	*6*	*7*	*8*	*9*
21	22	23	24	25	26	27
10	*11*	*12*	*13*	*14*	*15*	*16*
28	29	30	1	2	3	4
17	*18*	*19*	*20*	*21*	*22*	*23*
5	6	7	8	9	10	11
24	*25*	*26*	*27*	*28*	*29*	*30*

The angel Gabriel is sent to the virgin Mary. The power of the Holy Spirit overshadows her and she is impregnated. Then Mary visits Elizabeth.

End of 6th month of Elizabeth's pregnancy.

6 B.C. / 5 B.C.

TEBETH

DECEMBER			JANUARY			
S	M	T	W	T	F	SAB
12	13	14	15	16	17	18
1	*2*	*3*	*4*	*5*	*6*	*7*
19	20	21	22	23	24	25
8	*9*	*10*	*11*	*12*	*13*	*14*
26	27	28	29	30	31	1
15	*16*	*17*	*18*	*19*	*20*	*21*
2	3	4	5	6	7	8
22	*23*	*24*	*25*	*26*	*27*	*28*
9
29

End of 1st month of Mary's pregnancy.

End of 7th month of Elizabeth's pregnancy.

5 B.C.

SHEBAT

JANUARY			FEBRUARY			
S	M	T	W	T	F	SAB
	10	11	12	13	14	15
	1	*2*	*3*	*4*	*5*	*6*
16	17	18	19	20	21	22
7	*8*	*9*	*10*	*11*	*12*	*13*
23	24	25	26	27	28	29
14	*15*	*16*	*17*	*18*	*19*	*20*
30	31	1	2	3	4	5
21	*22*	*23*	*24*	*25*	*26*	*27*
6	7	8
28	*29*	*30*

End of 2nd month of Mary's pregnancy.
End of 8th month of Elizabeth's pregnancy.

5 B.C.

ADAR

FEBRUARY			MARCH			
S	M	T	W	T	F	SAB
			9	10	11	12
			1	*2*	*3*	*4*
13	14	15	16	17	18	19
5	*6*	*7*	*8*	*9*	*10*	*11*
20	21	22	23	24	25	26
12	*13*	*14*	*15*	*16*	*17*	*18*
27	28	29	1	2	3	4
19	*20*	*21*	*22*	*23*	*24*	*25*
5	6	7	8
26	*27*	*28*	*29*

End of 3rd month of Mary's pregnancy.
End of 9th month of Elizabeth's pregnancy.
John the Baptist born.

5 B.C.

NISAN

MARCH			APRIL			
S	M	T	W	T	F	SAB
					9	10	11
					1	*2*	*3*
12	13	14	15	16	17	18
4	*5*	*6*	*7*	*8*	*9*	*10*
19	20	21	22	㉓	24	25
11	*12*	*13*	**14*	*15*	*16*	*17*
26	27	28	29	30	31	1
18	*19*	*20*	*21*	*22*	*23*	*24*
2	3	4	5	6	7
25	*26*	*27*	*28*	*29*	*30*

㉓ Total eclipse on March 23 at 8:30 PM.
**14th - Passover,
15th-21st - Feast of Unleavened Bread.*
End of 4th month of Mary's pregnancy.

5 B.C.

IYAR

APRIL			MAY			
S	M	T	W	T	F	SAB
						8
						1
9	10	11	12	13	14	15
2	*3*	*4*	*5*	*6*	*7*	*8*
16	17	18	19	20	21	22
9	*10*	*11*	*12*	*13*	**14*	*15*
23	24	25	26	27	28	29
16	*17*	*18*	*19*	*20*	*21*	*22*
30	1	2	3	4	5	6
23	*24*	*25*	*26*	*27*	*28*	*29*

End of 5th month of Mary's pregnancy.

34

5 B.C.

SIVAN

MAY						JUNE
S	M	T	W	T	F	SAB
7	8	9	10	11	12	13
1	*2*	*3*	*4*	*5*	*6*	*7*
14	15	16	17	18	19	20
*8	*9*	*10*	*11*	*12*	*13*	*14*
21	22	23	24	25	26	27
15	*16*	*17*	*18*	*19*	*20*	*21*
28	29	30	31	1	2	3
22	*23*	*24*	*25*	*26*	*27*	*28*
4	5					
29	*30*					

*Day of Pentecost.

End of 6th month of Mary's pregnancy.

5 B.C.

TISHRI

SEPTEMBER		OCTOBER				
S	M	T	W	T	F	SAB

Feast of Trumpets, Tishri 1 ➤ 2
*1

3	4	5	6	7	8	9
2	*3*	*4*	*5*	*6*	*7*	***8*
10	11	12	13	14	**⑮**	16
9	*10*	*11*	*12*	*13*	*14*	*15*
17	18	19	20	21	22	23
16	*17*	*18*	*19*	*20*	*21*	*22*
24	25	26	27	28	29	30
23	*24*	*25*	*26*	*27*	*28*	*29*
1						
30						

Probable two-week period of Jesus' birth-Tishri 1 middle day..

**Probable day of Jesus' circumcision-Sabbath Tishri 8.

⑮Total eclipse on September 15, at 10:30 PM.

1st - Feast of Trumpets.
10th - Day of Atonement.
15th-21st - Feast of Tabernacles
22nd - Last Great Day.

5 B.C.

TAMMUZ

JUNE					JULY	
S	M	T	W	T	F	SAB
		6	7	8	9	10
		1	*2*	*3*	*4*	*5*
11	12	13	14	15	16	17
6	*7*	*8*	*9*	*10*	*11*	*12*
18	19	20	21	22	23	24
13	*14*	*15*	*16*	*17*	*18*	*19*
25	26	27	28	29	30	1
20	*21*	*22*	*23*	*24*	*25*	*26*
2	3	4				
27	*28*	*29*				

End of 7th month of Mary's pregnancy.

5 B.C.

HESHVAN

OCTOBER						
S	M	T	W	T	F	SAB
	2	3	4	5	6	7
	1	*2*	*3*	*4*	*5*	*6*
8	9	10	11	12	13	14
7	*8*	*9*	*10*	*11*	*12*	*13*
15	16	17	18	19	20	21
14	*15*	*16*	*17*	*18*	*19*	*20*
22	23	24	25	26	27	28
21	*22*	*23*	*24*	*25*	*26*	*27*
29	30	31				
28	*29*	*30*				

Wise men arrive and meet with Herod.

Probable two-week period for the presentation and blessing of Jesus at the temple. Wise men find Jesus and present their gifts. Joseph, Mary and Jesus escape into Egypt.

Herod orders the slaughter of all male children two years and younger.

5 B.C.

AB

JULY			AUGUST			
S	M	T	W	T	F	SAB
		5	6	7	8	
		1	*2*	*3*	*4*	
9	10	11	12	13	14	15
5	*6*	*7*	*8*	*9*	*10*	*11*
16	17	18	19	20	21	22
12	*13*	*14*	*15*	*16*	*17*	*18*
23	24	25	26	27	28	29
19	*20*	*21*	*22*	*23*	*24*	*25*
30	31	1	2	3		
26	*27*	*28*	*29*	*30*		

End of 8th month of Mary's pregnancy.

5 B.C.

KISLEV

NOVEMBER						
S	M	T	W	T	F	SAB
				1	2	3	4
				1	*2*	*3*	*4*
5	6	7	8	9	10	11
5	*6*	*7*	*8*	*9*	*10*	*11*
12	13	14	15	16	17	18
12	*13*	*14*	*15*	*16*	*17*	*18*
19	20	21	22	23	24	25
19	*20*	*21*	*22*	*23*	*24*	*25*
26	27	28	29	30		
26	*27*	*28*	*29*	*30*		

Herod goes beyond Jordan.

5 B.C.

ELUL

AUGUST		SEPTEMBER				
S	M	T	W	T	F	SAB
					4	5
					1	*2*
6	7	8	9	10	11	12
3	*4*	*5*	*6*	*7*	*8*	*9*
13	14	15	16	17	18	19
10	*11*	*12*	*13*	*14*	*15*	*16*
20	21	22	23	24	25	26
17	*18*	*19*	*20*	*21*	*22*	*23*
27	28	29	30	31	1	
24	*25*	*26*	*27*	*28*	*29*	

End of 9th month of Mary's pregnancy;

5 B.C.

TEBETH

DECEMBER						
S	M	T	W	T	F	SAB
					1	2
					1	*2*
3	4	5	6	7	8	9
3	*4*	*5*	*6*	*7*	*8*	*9*
10	11	12	13	14	15	16
10	*11*	*12*	*13*	*14*	*15*	*16*
17	18	19	20	21	22	23
17	*18*	*19*	*20*	*21*	*22*	*23*
24	25	26	27	28	29	
24	*25*	*26*	*27*	*28*	*29*	

Herod still beyond Jordan.

5 B.C. / 4 B.C.

SHEBAT

DECEMBER   JANUARY
S M T W T F SAB
                  30
                  1

31 1 2 3 4 5 6
2 3 4 5 6 7 8

7 8 9 10 11 12 13
9 10 11 12 13 14 15

14 15 16 17 18 19 20
16 17 18 19 20 21 22

21 22 23 24 25 26 27
23 24 25 26 27 28 29

28
30

Herod orders principal men to come to Jericho.

4 B.C.

ADAR II

FEBRUARY   MARCH
S M T W T F SAB
            28 1 2 3
                1 2 3 4

4 5 6 7 8 9 10
5 6 7 8 9 10 11

11 12 13 14 15 16 17
12 13 14 15 16 17 18

18 19 20 21 22 23 24
19 20 21 22 23 24 25

25 26 27 28
26 27 28 29

Funeral procession proceeds slowly from Jericho toward Jerusalem.

Herod's body arrives at Herodium in Bethlehem via Jerusalem.

Archelaus begins reign in Jerusalem.

4 B.C.

ADAR I

JANUARY   FEBRUARY
S M T W T F SAB
      29 30 31 1 2 3
         1 2 3 4 5 6

4 5 6 7 8 9 10
7 8 9 10 11 12 13

11 12 13 14 15 16 17
14 15 16 17 18 19 20

18 19 20 21 22 23 24
21 22 23 24 25 26 27

25 26 27
28 29 30

Herod locks up principal men in Hyppodrome.

Letters come from Rome. Herod attempts suicide. Antipater is killed.

Herod dies. Principal men released from Hyppodrome.

Herod's funeral preparations and 7 days of mourning in Jericho.

Archelaus becomes king. Herod's funeral procession begins.

4 B.C.

NISAN

MARCH   APRIL
S M T W T F SAB
            29 30 31
                1 2 3

1 2 3 4 5 6 7
4 5 6 7 8 9 10

8 9 10 11 12 13 14
*11 12 13 *14 15 16 17*

15 16 17 18 19 20 21
18 19 20 21 22 23 24

22 23 24 25 26 27
25 26 27 28 29 30

Revolt by Jews over the lack of mourning for Mathias, the high priest who was burned to death by Herod on September 15, 5 BC.

Revolt grows as thousands of Jews arrive for Passover and the Feast of Unleavened Bread.

Archelaus orders the slaughter of 3,000 in the middle of the Feast of Unleavened Bread. Herod's burial takes place.

*14th - Passover,
15th-21st - Feast of Unleavened Bread.*

Outskirts of Bethlehem

PART I

FROM JESUS' PRE-EXISTENCE AS GOD TO THE FIRST PASSOVER OF HIS MINISTRY IN 27 AD

1. JESUS CHRIST'S PRE-EXISTENCE AS CREATOR GOD OF ALL THINGS AND THE LORD GOD OF ISRAEL

JOHN 1

1. In *the* beginning [a] was the Word, and the Word was with God, and the Word was God.
2. He was in *the* beginning with God.
3. All things came into being through Him, and not even one *thing* that was created came into being without Him.
4. In Him was life, and the life was the light of men.
5. And the light shines in the darkness, but the darkness does not comprehend it.

a - Gen. 1:1

2. LUKE'S PREFACE AND DECLARATION

LUKE 1

1. Since many have taken in hand to compile a *written* narration of the matters which have been fully believed among us,
2. As they delivered *them* to us, those who from *the* beginning had been eyewitnesses and ministers of the Word,
3. It seemed good to me also, having accurately understood everything from the very first, to write *these things* in an orderly sequence to you, most excellent Theophilus,
4. So that you might know the *absolute* certainty of *the* things in which you have been instructed.

3. THE CONCEPTION OF JOHN THE BAPTIST

LUKE 1

5. There was in the days of Herod, the king of Judea, a certain priest of *the* course of Abijah, [a] Zacharias by name; and his wife *was* of the daughters of Aaron, and her name *was* Elizabeth.
6. Now they were both righteous before God, walking blamelessly in all the commandments and ordinances of the Lord.
7. But they did not have a child, as Elizabeth was barren; and both were *well* advanced in age.
8. And it came to pass *that* in fulfilling his priestly service before God in the order of his course,
9. According to the custom of the priestly service, it fell to him by lot to burn incense when he entered into the temple of the Lord.
10. And all the multitude of the people outside were praying at the hour of the *burning of* incense.
11. Then an angel of *the* Lord appeared to him, standing at *the* right side of the altar of incense.
12. And when he saw *the angel*, Zacharias was troubled, and fear fell upon him.

a - I Chron. 24:10

13. But the angel said to him, "Fear not, Zacharias, because your supplication has been heard; and your wife Elizabeth shall bear a son to you, and you shall call his name John.

14. And he shall be a joy and exultation to you; and many shall rejoice at his birth.

15. For he shall be great before the Lord. And he shall never drink wine or strong drink in any form, [b] but he shall be filled with *the* Holy Spirit even from his mother's womb.

16. And many of the children of Israel shall he turn to *the* Lord their God.

17. And he shall go before Him in *the* spirit and power of Elijah, to turn *the* hearts of the fathers to *the* children, and *the* disobedient to *the* wisdom of *the* righteous, to make ready a people prepared for *the* Lord." [c]

18. Then Zacharias said to the angel, "By what *means* shall I know this? For I am an old man, and my wife *is* advanced in years."

19. And the angel answered *and* said to him, "I am Gabriel, who stands in the presence of God; and I was sent to speak to you, and to announce this good news to you.

20. But behold, you shall be silent and unable to speak until the day in which these things shall take place, because you did not believe my words, which shall be fulfilled in their time."

21. Now the people were expecting Zacharias, and they were wondering *why* he was taking such a long time in the temple.

22. But when he came out, he was not able to speak to them. Then they perceived that he had seen a vision in the temple; for he was making signs to them, but he remained mute.

23. Now it came to pass *that* when the days of his service were fulfilled, he departed to his house.

24. And after those days, Elizabeth his wife conceived, but hid herself *for* five months, saying,

25. "The Lord has intervened for me in this, at *the* time in which He looked upon *me* to take away my reproach among men."

b - Num. 6:1-21; Judg. 13:4-5; I Sam. 1:11   c - Mal. 3:1; 4:5-6

An-Karem, Traditional Birth Place of John the Baptist

4. THE ANGEL GABRIEL ANNOUNCES THE MIRACULOUS CONCEPTION OF JESUS CHRIST TO THE VIRGIN MARY

LUKE 1

26. And in the sixth month *of her pregnancy*, the angel Gabriel was sent by God to a city of Galilee, named Nazareth,

27. To a virgin betrothed to a man whose name *was* Joseph, of *the* lineage of David; and the name of the virgin *was* Mary.

28. And after coming to her, the angel said, "Hail, you who are highly favored! The Lord *is* with you; blessed *are* you among women."

29. But when she saw *him*, she was *greatly* perplexed at his message, and was considering what kind of salutation this might be.

30. Then the angel said to her, "Do not be afraid, Mary, because you have found grace with God;

31. And behold, you shall conceive in *your* womb and give birth to a son; and you shall call His name Jesus. [a]

32. He shall be great, and shall be called *the* Son of *the* Highest; and *the* Lord God shall give Him the throne of David, His forefather; [b]

33. And He shall reign over the house of Jacob into the ages, and of His kingdom there shall be no end." [c]

34. But Mary said to the angel, "How shall this be, since I have not had sexual relations with a man?"

35. And the angel answered *and* said to her, "*The* Holy Spirit shall come upon you, and *the* power of *the* Highest shall overshadow you; and for this reason, the Holy One being begotten in you shall be called *the* Son of God.

36. Now behold, Elizabeth your kinswoman has also conceived a son in her old age; and this is *the* sixth month for her who *was* called barren.

37. For with God nothing shall be impossible."

38. And Mary said, "Behold the handmaid of *the* Lord; may it be *done* to me according to your word." And the angel departed from her.

a - Isa. 7:14   b - II Sam. 7:12-17   c - Isa. 9:6-7; Psa. 132:11; Jer. 23:5-6

5. AFTER THE HOLY CONCEPTION OF JESUS CHRIST, THE VIRGIN MARY LEAVES TO VISIT HER AUNT ELIZABETH, WHO IS SIX MONTHS PREGNANT WITH JOHN THE BAPTIST

LUKE 1

39. And Mary rose up in those days *and* went with haste into the hill country, to a city of Judah,

40. And entered the house of Zacharias and greeted Elizabeth.

41. Now it came to pass *that* when Elizabeth heard Mary's greeting, the babe leaped in her womb; and Elizabeth was filled with *the* Holy Spirit,

42. And she cried out with a loud voice and said, "Blessed *are* you among women, and blessed *is* the fruit of your womb.

43. But why is this *happening* to me, that the mother of my Lord should come to me?

44. For behold, as soon as the sound of your greeting reached my ears, the babe in my womb leaped in exultation.

45. And blessed *is* she who has believed, for there shall be a fulfillment of the things spoken to her from *the* Lord."

46. Then Mary said, "My soul magnifies the Lord,

47. And my spirit has exulted in God my Savior;

48. For He has looked upon the humble estate of His handmaid; for behold, from this time forward all generations shall count me blessed, [a]

a - I Sam. 1:11; Psa. 128:6

49. Because the Mighty One has done great things to me, and holy *is* His name; [b]
50. And His mercy *is* toward those who fear Him, from generation to generation. [c]
51. He has worked strength with His arm; He has scattered *the* haughty in *the* imagination of their hearts. [d]
52. He has put down rulers from thrones, and has exalted *the* lowly. [e]
53. He has filled *the* hungry with good things, and *the* rich He has sent away empty. [f]
54. He has helped His servant Israel, in remembering *His* mercy, [g]
55. Exactly as He spoke to our fathers, to Abraham and to his seed forever."
56. And Mary dwelt with her about three months, and returned to her house.

b - Psa. 99:3; 111:9 c - Ex. 20:6; Psa. 103:17 d - 1 Sam. 2:4; Psa. 89:10
e - Psa. 113:7; Job 5:11; 12:19; I Sam. 2:7 f - I Sam. 2:5; Psa. 107:9 g - Gen. 17:7; Isa. 41:8-9

6. THE VIRGIN MARY IS THREE MONTHS PREGNANT – AN ANGEL TELLS JOSEPH TO ACCEPT MARY AS HIS WIFE

MATTHEW 1

18. And the birth of Jesus Christ was as follows: Now His mother Mary had been betrothed to Joseph; *but* before they came together, she was found to be with child of *the* Holy Spirit.
19. And Joseph her husband, being a righteous *man*, and not willing to expose her publicly, was planning to divorce her secretly.
20. But as he pondered these things, behold, an angel of *the* Lord appeared to him in a dream, saying, "Joseph, son of David, do not be afraid to take Mary to *be* your wife, because that which has been begotten in her is of *the* Holy Spirit.
21. And she shall give birth to a son, and you shall call His name Jesus; for He shall save His people from their sins."
22. Now all this came to pass, that it might be fulfilled which was spoken by the Lord through the prophet, saying,
23. "Behold, the virgin shall be with child and shall give birth to a son, and they shall call His name Emmanuel"; which is, being interpreted, "God with us." [a]
24. And when Joseph was awakened from his sleep, he did as the angel of *the* Lord had commanded, and took his wife to *wed;*
25. But he did not have sexual relations *with* her until *after* she had given birth to her son, the firstborn; and he called His name Jesus.

a - Isa. 7:14

7. THE BIRTH AND PROPHECIES OF JOHN THE BAPTIST

LUKE 1

57. Now Elizabeth's time was fulfilled that she should give birth, and she bore a son.
58. And her neighbors and kinfolk heard that *the* Lord had magnified His mercy toward her, and they rejoiced with her.
59. And it came to pass on the eighth day [a] *that* they came to circumcise the little child; and they were calling him Zacharias, after the name of his father.
60. Then his mother answered *and* said, "No! But he shall be named John."
61. And they said to her, "*There* is no one among your kinfolk who is called by this name."
62. Then they made signs to his father *as to* what he desired him to be named.
63. And after signaling for a writing tablet, he wrote, saying, "John is his name." And they were all amazed.
64. Then his mouth was immediately opened, and his tongue *was loosed*; and he spoke, praising God.
65. And fear came upon all those who dwelt around them; and in the entire hill country of Judea, all these things were being talked about.

a - Gen 17:10-14; Lev. 12:3

66. And all who heard *these things* laid *them* up in their hearts, saying, "What then will this little child be?" And *the* hand of *the* Lord was with him.

67. And Zacharias his father was filled with *the* Holy Spirit, and prophesied, saying,

68. "Blessed be *the* Lord, the God of Israel, because He has visited and has worked redemption for His people, [b]

69. And has raised up a horn of salvation for us in the house of His servant David; [c]

70. Exactly as He spoke by *the* mouth of His holy prophets since the world began;

71. Salvation from our enemies and from *the* hand of all those who hate us; [d]

72. To fulfill *the promise of* mercy *made* to our fathers, and to remember His holy covenant, [e]

73. *The* oath that He swore to Abraham our father; to grant us *that,*

74. Being saved from *the* hand of our enemies, we might serve Him without fear,

75. *Walking* in holiness and righteousness before Him all the days of our lives.

76. And you, little child, shall be called *the* prophet of *the* Highest; for you shall go before *the* face of *the* Lord, to prepare His ways; [f]

77. To give *the* knowledge of salvation to His people by *the* remission of their sins,

78. Through *the* deep inner compassions of our God; in which *the* dayspring from on high has visited us,

79. To shine upon those who are sitting in darkness and in *the* shadow of death, to direct our feet into *the* way of peace." [g]

80. And the little child grew and was strengthened in spirit; and he was in the deserts until *the* day of his appearing to Israel.

b - Psa. 72:18; 111:9   c - I Sam. 2:10; Psa. 18:2   d - Psa. 18:3; 106:10
e - Gen. 17:7; Lev. 26:42; Psa. 105:8   f - Mal. 3:1; Isa. 40:3   g - Isa. 8:22; 9:2

8. THE BIRTH OF JESUS CHRIST
LUKE 2

1. Now it happened in those days *that* a decree went out from Caesar Augustus that all the world should be registered.

2. (This registration first occurred when Cyrenius was governor of Syria.)

3. Then all went to be registered, each to his own city.

4. And Joseph also went up from Galilee, out of *the* city *of* Nazareth, into Judea, to *the* city of David which is called Bethlehem, because he was from *the* house and lineage of David

5. To register himself along with Mary, who was betrothed to him as wife, *and* was great with child.

6. And it came to pass *that* during the *time* they were there, the days were fulfilled for her to give birth.

7. And she gave birth to her son, the firstborn, and wrapped Him in swaddling clothes, and laid Him in a manger, because there was no place for them in the inn.

8. Now *there* were shepherds in the same country, who were dwelling in the fields and keeping watch over their flock by night;

9. And suddenly an angel of *the* Lord stood by them, and *the* glory of *the* Lord shined round about them; and they were seized *with* great fear.

10. But the angel said to them, "Do not be afraid; for behold, I am announcing to you glad tidings *of* great joy, which shall be to all people;

11. For today, in *the* city of David, a Savior was born to you, Who is Christ *the* Lord.

12. Now this *is* the sign for you: you shall find a babe wrapped in swaddling clothes, lying in a manger."

13. And suddenly there was with the angel a multitude of *the* heavenly host praising God, and saying,

14. "Glory to God in *the* highest, and peace on earth among men *of* goodwill."

15. And it came to pass, as the angels were departing from them into heaven, that the shepherds said to one another, "Let us go now as far as Bethlehem, and let us see this thing that has taken place, which the Lord has made known to us."

16. And they made haste, *and* came and found both Mary and Joseph, and the babe lying in the manger.

17. Now after seeing *Him*, they made known everywhere the proclamation that they had been told concerning this little child.

18. And all those who heard were filled with wonder by the things that were spoken to them by the shepherds.

19. But Mary stored up all these sayings, pondering *them* in her heart.

20. And the shepherds returned, glorifying and praising God for all *the* things that they had heard and seen, as it was said to them.

9. JESUS' CIRCUMCISION AND PRESENTATION AT THE TEMPLE

LUKE 2

21. Now when eight days were fulfilled for circumcising the little child, [a] His name was called Jesus, which *He* was named by the angel before He was conceived in the womb.

22. And when the days were fulfilled for their purification according to the law of Moses, they brought Him to Jerusalem to present *Him* to the Lord;

23. As it is written in *the* law of *the* Lord that every male opening the womb shall be called holy to the Lord; [b]

24. And to offer a sacrifice according to that which is said in *the* law of *the* Lord: a pair of turtledoves or two young pigeons.

a - Gen. 17:12; Lev. 12:3   b - Ex. 13:2

10. THE BLESSING AND PROPHECY OF SIMEON

LUKE 2

25. And behold, there was a man in Jerusalem whose name *was* Simeon; and this man *was* righteous and reverent, waiting for *the* consolation of Israel; and *the* Holy Spirit was upon him.

26. Now it had been divinely communicated to him by the Holy Spirit that he would not see death before he had seen the Christ of *the* Lord.

27. And he came in the Spirit into the temple; and when the parents brought in the little child Jesus, to do for Him according to the custom of the law,

28. He also received Him into his arms, and blessed God, and said,

29. "Now You may let your servant depart in peace, O Master, according to Your word;

30. For my eyes have seen Your salvation, [a]

31. Which You have prepared before *the* face of all peoples;

32. A light for *the* revelation of *the* Gentiles and *the* glory of Your people Israel." [b]

33. And Joseph and His mother wondered at the things that were being spoken concerning Him.

34. Then Simeon blessed them, and said to Mary, His mother, "Behold, this *child* is set for *the* fall and rising up of many in Israel, and for a sign that shall be spoken against,

35. (And you also, a sword shall go through your own soul) in order that *the* imaginations of many hearts may be revealed."

a - Isa. 52:10   b - Isa. 42:6; 49:6

11. THE LEGAL GENEALOGY OF JESUS CHRIST THROUGH JOSEPH'S LINEAGE*

MATTHEW 1

1. *The* book of *the* genealogy of Jesus Christ, *the* son of David, *the* son of Abraham:

2. Abraham begat Isaac; and Isaac begat Jacob; and Jacob begat Judah and his brethren;

3. And Judah begat Phares and Zara of Thamar; and Phares begat Esrom; and Esrom begat Aram;

4. And Aram begat Aminadab; and Aminadab begat Naasson; and Naasson begat Salmon;

5. And Salmon begat Boaz of Rachab; and Boaz begat Obed of Ruth; and Obed begat Jesse;

6. And Jesse begat David the king; and David the king begat Solomon of the one *who had been wife* of Uriah;

7. And Solomon begat Roboam; and Roboam begat Abia; and Abia begat Asa;

8. And Asa begat Josaphat; and Josaphat begat Joram; and Joram begat Ozias;

9. And Ozias begat Joatham; and Joatham begat Achaz; and Achaz begat Ezekias;

10. And Ezekias begat Manasses; and Manasses begat Amon; and Amon begat Josias;

11. And Josias begat Jechonias and his brethren at *the time* of the carrying away to Babylon.

12. And after the captivity in Babylon, Jechonias begat Salathiel; and Salathiel begat Zorobabel;

13. And Zorobabel begat Abiud; and Abiud begat Eliakim; and Eliakim begat Azor;

14. And Azor begat Sadoc; and Sadoc begat Achim; and Achim begat Eliud;

15. And Eliud begat Eleazar; and Eleazar begat Matthan; and Matthan begat Jacob;

16. And Jacob begat Joseph the husband of Mary, from whom was born Jesus, Who is called *the* Christ.

17. So then, all the generations from Abraham to David *were* fourteen generations; and from David until the carrying away to Babylon, fourteen generations; and from the carrying away to Babylon to the Christ, fourteen generations.

* Chron. 1:34; 2:1-15; 3:1-19

12. THE PHYSICAL GENEALOGY OF JESUS CHRIST THROUGH MARY'S LINEAGE*

LUKE 3

23. And Jesus Himself began *to be* about thirty years *old*, being, as was supposed, *the* son of Joseph, *the son-in-law* of Eli,

24. *The son* of Matthat, *the son* of Levi, *the son* of Melchi, *the son* of Janna, *the son* of Joseph,

25. *The son* of Mattathias, *the son* of Amos, *the son* of Naoum, *the son* of Esli, *the son* of Naggai,

26. *The son* of Maath, *the son* of Mattathias, *the son* of Semei, *the son* of Joseph, *the son* of Juda,

27. *The son* of Joannes, *the son* of Rhesa, *the son* of Zorobabel, *the son* of Salathiel, *the son* of Neri,

28. *The son* of Melchi, *the son* of Addi, *the son* of Cosam, *the son* of Elmodam, *the son* of Er,

29. *The son* of Joses, *the son* of Eliezer, *the son* of Joreim, *the son* of Matthat, *the son* of Levi,

30. *The son* of Simeon, *the son* of Juda, *the son* of Joseph, *the son* of Jonan, *the son* of Eliakim,

31. *The son* of Meleas, *the son* of Menna, *the son* of Mattatha, *the son* of Nathan, *the son* of David,

32. *The son* of Jesse, *the son* of Obed, *the son* of Boaz, *the son* of Salmon, *the son* of Naasson,

33. *The son* of Aminadab, *the son* of Aram, *the son* of Esrom, *the son* of Phares, *the son* of Juda,

34. *The son* of Jacob, *the son* of Isaac, *the son* of Abraham, *the son* of Terah, *the son* of Nachor,

35. *The son* of Saruch, *the son* of Ragau, *the son* of Phalek, *the son* of Eber, *the son* of Sala,

36. *The son* of Cainan, *the son* of Arphaxad, *the son* of Shem, *the son* of Noe, *the son* of Lamech,

37. *The son* of Mathusalah, *the son* of Enoch, *the son* of Jared, *the son* of Mahalelel, *the son* of Cainan,

38. *The son* of Enos, *the son* of Seth, *the son* of Adam, *the son* of God.

* I Chron. 1:1-4, 24-28; 2:1-15; 3:17; Ruth 4:18-22

It is the general consensus of opinion among most scholars that the two apparently differing genealogies in Matthew 1 and Luke 3 are very easily reconciled. The one given in Matthew is the legal genealogy. The one in Luke is the bloodline from the physical inheritance through Mary his mother. Therefore it should read as follows: "Now Jesus Himself began to be about thirty years old, being as was supposed, the son of Joseph, who was the son-in-law of Eli ..." The physical genealogy to Mary comes from David through David's son, Nathan, not Solomon (Luke 3:31).

13. THE BLESSING OF ANNA
LUKE 2

36. Now there was Anna, a prophetess, *the* daughter of Phanuel, of *the* tribe of Asher; she was of a great age, having lived with a husband seven years from her virginity;
37. And she *was* a widow of about eighty-four years, who did not depart from the temple, serving day and night with fastings and supplications.
38. And at the same time she came up, giving praise to the Lord; and *she* spoke concerning Him to all those in Jerusalem who were waiting for redemption.

14. THE VISIT OF THE WISE MEN FROM THE EAST
MATTHEW 2

1. Now after Jesus had been born in Bethlehem of Judea, in *the* days of Herod the king, behold, Magi from *the* east arrived at Jerusalem,
2. Saying, "Where is the one who has been born King of the Jews? For we have seen His star in the east, [a] and have come to worship Him."
3. But when Herod the king heard *this*, he was troubled, and all Jerusalem with him.
4. And after gathering together all the chief priests and scribes of the people, he inquired of them where the Christ should be born.
5. Then they said to him, "In Bethlehem of Judea, for thus it has been written by the prophet:
6. 'And you, Bethlehem, land of Judea, in no way are you least among the princes of Judea; for out of you shall come forth a Prince, Who shall shepherd My people Israel.' " [b]
7. Then Herod secretly called *for* the Magi *and* ascertained from them the *exact* time of the appearing of *the* star.
8. And he sent them to Bethlehem, saying, "Go and search diligently for the little child; and when you have found *Him*, bring word back to me, so that I also may go and worship Him."
9. And after hearing the king, they departed; and behold, the star that they had seen in the east went in front of them, until it came and stood over *the house* where the little child was.
10. And after seeing the star, they rejoiced *with* exceedingly great joy.

a - Num. 24:17   b - Mic. 5:2

15. AFTER OFFERING GIFTS TO JESUS,
THE WISE MEN RETURN A DIFFERENT WAY
MATTHEW 2

11. And when they had come into the house, they found the little child with Mary His mother, and they bowed down and worshiped Him; then they opened their treasures *and* presented their gifts to Him—gold and frankincense and myrrh.
12. But being divinely instructed in a dream not to go back to Herod, they returned to their own country by another way.

16. THE ESCAPE INTO EGYPT
MATTHEW 2

13. Now after they had departed, behold, an angel of *the* Lord appeared to Joseph in a dream, saying, "Arise and take the little child and His mother, and escape into Egypt, and remain there until I shall tell you; for Herod is about to seek the little child to destroy Him."
14. And he arose by night and took the little child and His mother, and went into Egypt,
15. And was there until the death of Herod; that it might be fulfilled which was spoken by the Lord through the prophet, saying, "Out of Egypt I have called My Son." [a]

a - Hos. 11:1

17. THE SLAUGHTER OF CHILDREN BY HEROD
MATTHEW 2

16. Then Herod, seeing that he had been mocked by the Magi, was filled with rage; and he sent *and* put to death all the boys who *were* in Bethlehem and in the area all around, from two years old and under, according to the time that he had ascertained from the Magi.
17. Then was fulfilled that which was spoken by Jeremiah the prophet, saying,
18. "A voice was heard in Rama, lamentation and weeping and great mourning, Rachel weeping *for* her children; and she would not be comforted, because they were not." [a]

a - Jer. 31:15

18. JOSEPH AND FAMILY LEAVE EGYPT AND RETURN TO NAZARETH
MATTHEW 2

19. Now when Herod had died, behold, an angel of *the* Lord appeared to Joseph in Egypt in a dream,
20. Saying, "Arise and take the little child and His mother, and go into *the* land of Israel; for those who were seeking the life of the little child have died."
21. And he arose *and* took the little child and His mother, and came into *the* land of Israel.
22. But when he heard that Archelaus was reigning over Judea instead of Herod his father, he was afraid to go there; and after being divinely instructed in a dream, he went into the parts of Galilee.
23. And after arriving, he dwelt in a city called Nazareth; that it might be fulfilled which was spoken by the prophets, "He shall be called a Nazarean."

Nazareth Today

LUKE 2

39. Now when they had completed all things according to the law of *the* Lord, they returned to Galilee, to their *own* city, Nazareth.

45

19. THE CHILDHOOD AND GROWTH OF JESUS CHRIST
LUKE 2

40. And the little child grew and became strong in spirit, being filled with wisdom; and *the* grace of God was upon Him.

41. Now His parents went to Jerusalem every year at the feast of the Passover. [a]

42. And when He was twelve years *old*, they went up to Jerusalem according to the custom of the feast.

43. But when they departed after completing the days, the child Jesus remained behind in Jerusalem, and Joseph and His mother did not know *it*;

44. But supposing Him to be in the company, they went a day's journey, and looked for Him among the relatives and among the acquaintances.

45. And when they did not find Him, they returned to Jerusalem, seeking Him.

46. Now it came to pass *that* after three days they found Him in the temple, sitting in *the* midst of the teachers, both hearing them and questioning them.

47. And all those who were listening to Him were amazed at *His* understanding and His answers.

48. But when they saw Him, they were astonished; and His mother said to Him, "Son, why have you dealt with us in this manner? Look, Your father and I have been *very* distressed *while* searching for You."

49. And He said to them, "Why *is it* that you were looking for Me? Don't you realize that I must be about My Father's *business*?"

50. But they did not understand the words that He spoke to them.

51. Then He went down with them and came to Nazareth, and He was subject to them. But His mother kept all these things in her heart.

52. And Jesus increased in wisdom and stature, and in favor with God and men.

a - Ex. 12:3-14; 23:14-17; Deut. 16:1-8

20. THE MINISTRY OF JOHN THE BAPTIST
AS A MESSENGER TO PREPARE THE WAY FOR THE LORD

JOHN 1	LUKE 3	MATTHEW 3	MARK 1
6. There was a man sent by God, whose name *was* John.	1. Now in *the* fifteenth year of the government of Tiberius Caesar, when Pontius Pilate was governor of Judea, and Herod was tetrarch of Galilee, and Philip his brother was tetrarch of Iturea and *the* region of Trachonitis, and Lysanias was tetrarch of Abilene,	1. Now in those days John the Baptist came preaching in the wilderness of Judea,	1. The beginning of the gospel of Jesus Christ, *the* Son of God;
7. He came for a witness, that he might testify concerning the light, so that through him all might believe.		2. And saying, "Repent, for the kingdom of heaven is at hand."	2. As it is written in the prophets: "Behold, I send My messenger before Your face, who shall prepare Your way before You. [a]
8. He was not the light, but *came* that he might testify concerning the light.		3. For this is he who was spoken of by Isaiah the prophet, saying, *The* voice of one crying in the wilderness, 'Prepare the way of *the* Lord, make straight His paths.' "	3. *The* voice of one crying in the wilderness, 'Prepare the way of *the* Lord, make straight His paths.' " [b]
9. The true light was that which enlightens everyone who comes into the world.		4. Now John himself wore a garment of camel's hair, and a leather belt around his waist; and his food was locusts and wild honey.	a - Mal. 3:1 b - Isa. 40:3
10. He was in the world, and the world came into being through Him, but the world did not know Him.			

JOHN 1

11. He came to His own, and His own did not receive Him;
12. But as many as received Him, to them He gave authority to become *the* children of God, *even* to those who believe in His name;
13. Who were not begotten by bloodlines, nor by *the* will of *the* flesh, nor by *the* will of man, but *by the will* of God.
14. And the Word became flesh, and tabernacled among us (and we ourselves beheld His glory, *the* glory as of *the* only begotten with *the* Father), full of grace and truth.
15. John testified concerning Him, and proclaimed, saying, "This was He of Whom I said, 'He Who comes after me has precedence over me because He was before me.' "
16. And of His fullness we have all received, and grace upon grace.
17. For the law was given through Moses, *but* the grace and the truth came through Jesus Christ.
18. No one has seen God at any time; the only begotten Son, Who is in the bosom of the Father, He has declared *Him.*

LUKE 3

2. In *the time of the* priesthood of Annas and Caiaphas, *the* word of God came unto John, the son of Zacharias, in the wilderness.
3. And he went into all the country around the Jordan, proclaiming *the* baptism of repentance for *the* remission of sins;
4. As it is written in *the* book of *the* words of the prophet Isaiah, saying, "*The* voice of one crying in the wilderness, 'Prepare the way of *the* Lord; make straight His paths.'
5. Every valley shall be filled, and every mountain and hill shall be made low; and the crooked *places* shall be made into straight *paths,* and the rough *places* into smooth ways;
6. And all flesh shall see the salvation of God." [a]

a - Isa. 40:3-5

The Jordan River East of Bethel

Orchards in Galilee

A Harmony of the Gospels in Modern English—The Life of Jesus Christ

---

21. JOHN'S RECORD – HE WAS NOT THE CHRIST

JOHN 1

19. And this is the testimony of John, when the Jews sent priests and Levites from Jerusalem to ask him, "Who are you?"

20. Then he *freely* admitted, and did not deny, but declared, "I am not the Christ."

21. And they asked him, "Then who *are you*? Are you Elijah?" And he said, "I am not." *Then they asked,* "Are you the Prophet?" And he answered, "No."

22. Therefore, they said to him, "Who are you? What do you say about yourself so that we may give an answer to those who sent us?"

23. He said, "I *am* a voice crying in the wilderness, 'Make straight the way of *the* Lord,' as Isaiah the prophet said." [a]

24. Now those who had been sent belonged to *the sect* of the Pharisees,

25. And they asked him, saying to him, "Why then are you baptizing, if you are not the Christ, nor Elijah, nor the Prophet?"

26. John answered them, saying, "I baptize with water, but there is one *Who* stands among you Whom you do not know.

27. He it is Who comes after me, *but* Who has precedence over me; of Whom I am not worthy to loose the thong of His sandal."

a - Isa. 40:3

---

22. JOHN'S BAPTISM TO REPENTANCE, AND WARNING TO THOSE WHO WANTED TO BE BAPTIZED WITHOUT REPENTING

MATTHEW 3	MARK 1	LUKE 3
5. Then went out to him *those from* Jerusalem, and all Judea, and all the country around the Jordan,	4. John came baptizing in the wilderness, and preaching *the* baptism of repentance for *the* remission of sins.	7. For this reason, he said to the multitudes who were coming out to be baptized by him, "*You* offspring of vipers, who has forewarned you to flee from the coming wrath?
6. And were being baptized by him in the Jordan, confessing their sins.	5. And all *those* of the country of Judea went out, and those of Jerusalem, and were all baptized by him in the Jordan River, confessing their sins.	8. Therefore, bring forth fruits worthy of repentance; and do not begin to say to yourselves, 'We have Abraham *for our* father,' because I tell you that God has the power to raise up children to Abraham from these stones.
7. But after seeing many of the Pharisees and Sadducees coming to his baptism, he said to them, "*You* brood of vipers, who has forewarned you to flee from the coming wrath?	6. Now John was clothed with camel's hair and *wore* a leather belt around his waist, and he ate locusts and wild honey.	9. But the axe is already being laid to the roots of the trees. Therefore, every tree *that* is not producing good fruit is cut down and is cast into *the* fire."
8. Therefore, produce fruits worthy of repentance;	7. And he preached, saying, "The one Who is coming after me *is* mightier than I, of Whom I am not worthy to stoop down to loose the thong of His sandals.	10. And the multitudes asked him, saying, "What then shall we do?"
9. And do not think to say within yourselves, 'We have Abraham *for our* father'; for I tell you that God is able from these stones to raise up children to Abraham.	8. I have indeed baptized you with water, but He shall baptize you with *the* Holy Spirit."	
10. But already the axe is striking at the roots of the trees; therefore, every tree that is not producing good fruit is cut down and thrown into *the* fire.		

MATTHEW 3

11. I indeed baptize you with water unto repentance; but the one Who *is* coming after me is mightier than I, of Whom I am not fit to carry His sandals; He shall baptize you with *the* Holy Spirit, and with fire;

12. Whose winnowing shovel *is* in His hand, and He will thoroughly purge His floor, and will gather His wheat into the granary; but the chaff He will burn up with unquenchable fire."

The "Nahr Et Leddon" - One of Four Sources of Jordan

LUKE 3

11. And he answered *and* said to them, "The one who has two coats, let him give to the one who has none; and the one who has food, let him do the same."

12. Now the tax collectors also came to be baptized, and they said to him, "Master, what shall we do?"

13. And he said to them, "Exact nothing beyond that which is appointed to you."

14. Then those who were soldiers also asked him, saying, "And we, what shall we do?" And he said to them, "Do not oppress or falsely accuse anyone, and be satisfied with your wages."

15. But as the people were *filled* with expectation, and they were all reasoning in their hearts about John, whether or not he might be the Christ,

16. John answered all *of them*, saying, "I indeed baptize you with water; but He is coming Who *is* mightier than I, of Whom I am not fit to loose the thong of His sandals. He shall baptize you with *the* Holy Spirit, and with fire;

17. Whose fan *is* in His hand, and He will thoroughly purge His floor, and will gather the wheat into His granary; but the chaff He will burn with unquenchable fire."

18. And *with* many other exhortations he preached the gospel to the people.

Jordan River

49

THE FOUR PASSOVER SEASONS

THE BASIC FRAMEWORK FOR JESUS CHRIST'S THREE-AND-ONE-HALF-YEAR MINISTRY

By recording Jesus' observance of the Passover and the feasts of God, the Gospel writers enable us to know the exact timing of His ministry. During the lifetime of Jesus Christ, all the feasts of God in the Hebrew Calendar were calculated by the same method that is in use today. This method was used by the priests and Levites as early as the sixth century BC for proclaiming the holy days of God. Therefore, it is possible to know the exact dates of the feasts and holy days during the lifetime of Jesus Christ. In this book, when the dates in the Hebrew Calendar are used, the corresponding dates in the Julian Calendar are also given.

In the Gospel accounts, we find more references to the Passover than to any other feast. The four Passover seasons that are recorded by the Gospel writers give us the basic framework for Jesus Christ's three-and-one-half-year ministry, which culminated in His death in 30 AD. He died on the Passover day, Nisan 14, which corresponds to April 5 on the Julian Calendar.

Jesus Christ always observed the Passover on Nisan 14. The first Passover of His ministry took place in 27 AD. In that year, Nisan 14 fell on Wednesday, April 9. Since the days of the Hebrew Calendar are reckoned from sunset to sunset, Nisan 14 began when the sun set on Tuesday, April 8. The observance of this Passover is recorded in John 2:13 and 23.

The second Passover of Jesus' ministry is not recorded in the Gospel accounts. However, we do find a reference to the Feast of Unleavened Bread which followed that Passover. The Gospel of Luke directly refers to the last day of this feast, which was an annual Sabbath: "Now it came to pass on *the* second Sabbath of *the* first rank *that* He was walking through the grain fields; and His disciples were plucking the ears and were eating, after rubbing *them* in their hands" (Luke 6:1).

As the account shows, the disciples were plucking the ears of grain before the kernels had matured and become hard, indicating that the time setting was the spring of the year. The Greek text provides additional information to verify that this event occurred during the spring festival season, which included the Passover and the Feast of Unleavened Bread. In the Greek text, the term δευτεροπροτος was used by Luke. This term, which is translated "the second Sabbath after the first," literally means "the second-first Sabbath," or "the second Sabbath of the first rank or order." The term δευτερσπροτος, specifically refers to annual Sabbaths, which always take precedence over the weekly Sabbath. Luke's use of this term reveals that Jesus and the disciples were going through the grain fields on the second annual Sabbath of that year, the last day of the Feast of Unleavened Bread, which occurred on Nisan 21, or Monday, April 5, in 28 AD. Luke's reference to this holy day is the only Gospel record of the second Passover/Unleavened Bread season during Jesus' ministry.

The third Passover season of Jesus' ministry is recorded in the Gospel of John. The reference that we find in John 6:4 relates to events that took place shortly before the Passover, which occurred on Nisan 14, or Saturday, April 16, 29 AD.

The fourth Passover of Jesus' ministry, which was His last Passover, occurred on Nisan 14, or Wednesday, April 5, 30 AD. All the Gospel writers recorded the events of the fourth and last Passover in great detail.

When we compare the four Gospel accounts, we find that Matthew and Mark recorded only the last Passover. Luke recorded the second Passover season as well as the fourth and last Passover. John recorded the first and third Passovers in addition to the last Passover, omitting only the second Passover from his Gospel. John, who wrote the last of the Gospel accounts, recorded the Passover seasons not found in the other accounts. He did not need to include the second Passover/Unleavened Bread season because Luke had recorded it in his account.

Together, the Gospel accounts give us the four Passover seasons that form the framework for the ministry of Jesus Christ.

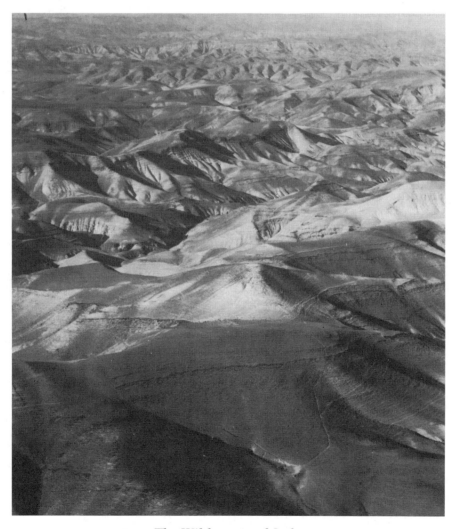

The Wilderness of Judea

23. CHRIST'S BAPTISM AT 30 YEARS OF AGE BY JOHN THE BAPTIST IN THE JORDAN RIVER AT BETHABARA NEAR THE SEA OF GALILEE

MATTHEW 3	MARK 1	LUKE 3	JOHN 1

MATTHEW 3

13. Then Jesus came from Galilee to the Jordan to John, to be baptized by him.

14. But John tried to prevent Him, saying, "I have need to be baptized by You, and You come to me?"

15. Then Jesus answered and said to him, "You must permit *it* at this time; for in this manner it is fitting for us to fulfill all righteousness." Then he permitted Him *to be baptized*.

16. And after He was baptized, Jesus came up immediately out of the water; and behold, the heavens were opened to him, and he saw the Spirit of God descending as a dove, and coming upon Him.

17. And lo, a voice from heaven said, "This is My Son, the Beloved, in Whom I have *great* delight." [a]

MARK 1

9. And it came to pass in those days *that* Jesus came from Nazareth of Galilee, and was baptized by John in the Jordan.

10. And immediately, as He was coming up out of the water, he saw the heavens open, and the Spirit descending upon Him like a dove.

11. And a voice came from heaven, *saying*, "You are My Son, the Beloved, in Whom I have *great* delight." [a]

a – Psa. 2:7; Isa. 42:1

LUKE 3

21. Now it came to pass after all the people were baptized, and Jesus was baptized and was praying, *that* the heaven was opened,

22. And the Holy Spirit descended upon Him in a bodily form like a dove; and there came a voice from heaven, saying, "You are My beloved Son; in You I am well pleased." [a]

JOHN 1

28. These things took place in Bethabara across the Jordan, where John was baptizing.

29. On the next day, John sees Jesus coming to him, and he says, "Behold the Lamb of God, Who takes away the sin of the world.

30. He is the one concerning Whom I said, 'After me comes a man Who has precedence over me, because He was before me.'

31. And I did not know Him; but that He might be manifested to Israel, therefore I came baptizing with water."

32. And John testified, saying, "I myself beheld the Spirit descending as a dove out of heaven, and it remained upon Him.

33. And I did not know Him *before*; but He Who sent me to baptize with water said to me, 'Upon Whom you shall see the Spirit descending, and remaining on Him, He is the one Who baptizes with *the* Holy Spirit.'

34. And I have seen, and have borne witness that this is the Son of God."

Headwaters of Jordan

24. JOHN THE BAPTIST SHOWS JESUS TO ANDREW AND PETER

JOHN 1

35. On the next day, John was again standing *there*, and two of his disciples *with him*.
36. And as he gazed upon Jesus walking, he said, "Behold the Lamb of God!" [a]
37. And the two disciples heard him say *this*, and they followed Jesus.
38. Now when Jesus turned and saw them following, He said to them,
39. "What are you seeking?" And they said to Him, "Rabbi (which is to say, being interpreted, "Teacher"), where do You dwell?"
40. He said to them, "Come and see." They went and saw where He was dwelling, and they remained with Him that day. Now it was about *the* tenth hour.
41. Andrew, the brother of Simon Peter, was one of the two who heard *this* from John and followed Him.
42. First, he found his own brother Simon and said to him, "We have found the Messiah" (which is, being interpreted, "the Christ").

a - Isa. 53:7, 11; Ex. 12:3

25. PHILIP AND NATHANAEL FIND JESUS CHRIST

JOHN 1

43. And he led him to Jesus. And when He saw him, Jesus said, "You are Simon, the son of Jona. You shall be called Cephas" (which is, *being* interpreted, "a stone").
44. On the next day, Jesus desired to go into Galilee; and He found Philip and said to him, "Follow Me."
45. Now Philip was from Bethsaida, the city of Andrew and Peter.
46. Philip found Nathanael and said to him, "We have found *Him* of Whom Moses wrote in the Law, and *also* the prophets, Jesus, the son of Joseph; He *is* from Nazareth."
47. And Nathanael said to him, "Can any good thing come out of Nazareth?" Philip said to him, "Come and see."
48. Jesus saw Nathanael coming to Him, and said concerning him, "Behold, truly an Israelite in whom *there* is no guile."
49. Nathanael said to Him, "How did you know me?" Jesus answered and said to him, "Before Philip called you, *when you* were under the fig tree, I saw you."
50. Nathanael answered and said to Him, "Rabbi, You are the Son of God; You are the King of Israel." [a]
51. Jesus answered and said to him, "Because I told you, 'I saw you under the fig tree,' do you believe? Greater things than these shall you see."
52. And He said to him, "Truly, truly I say to you, hereafter you shall see heaven open, and the angels of God descending to and ascending from the Son of man."

a - Psa. 2:6

26. JESUS CHRIST'S FIRST RECORDED MIRACLE: TURNING WATER INTO WINE

JOHN 2

1. Now on the third day, there was a marriage in Cana of Galilee; and the mother of Jesus was there.
2. And Jesus and His disciples were also invited to the marriage *feast*.
3. And *when* there was a shortage of wine, Jesus' mother said to Him, "They have no wine."
4. Jesus said to her, "Woman, what *do* you *desire to have* Me *do*? My time has not yet come."
5. *Then* His mother said to the servants, "Whatever He says to you, do."
6. Now there were six water vessels of stone standing there, in accordance with the *traditional* purification of the Jews, each one *having* a capacity of two or three firkins.
7. Jesus said to them, "Fill the water vessels with water." And they filled them to *the* brim.

JOHN 2

8. Then He said to them, "Now draw *some* out and bring *it* to the master of the feast." And they brought *it to him*.

9. Now when the master of the feast tasted the water that had become wine, not knowing from where it had come (but the servants who had drawn the water knew), the master of the feast called the bridegroom,

10. And said to him, "Every man serves the good wine first; and when the *guests* have drunk freely, then *he serves* the inferior *wine. But* you have kept the good wine until now."

11. This beginning of the miracles *that* Jesus did *took place* in Cana of Galilee, and revealed His glory; and His disciples believed in Him.

12. After this He went down to Capernaum, He and His mother and His brothers and His disciples; and they remained there not many days.

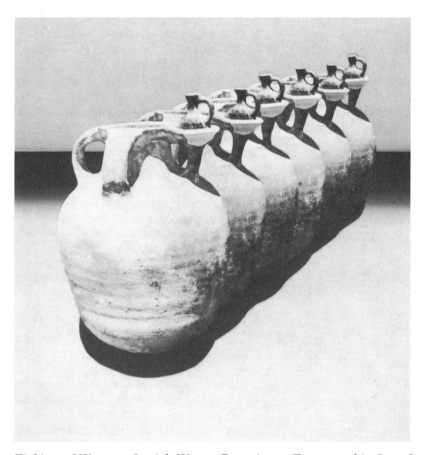

Firkins of Water – Jewish Water Containers Excavated in Israel

27. JESUS CHRIST'S IS TEMPTED FOR FORTY DAYS
AND NIGHTS BY SATAN THE DEVIL

MATTHEW 4

1. Then Jesus was led up into the wilderness by the Spirit in order to be tempted by the devil.

2. And when He had fasted *for* forty days and forty nights, afterwards He was famished.

3. And when the tempter came to Him, he said, "If You are the Son of God, command that these stones become bread."

4. But He answered *and* said, "It is written, 'Man shall not live by bread alone, but by every word that proceeds out of *the* mouth of God.' " [a]

5. Then the devil took Him to the holy city and set Him upon the edge of the temple,

6. And said to Him, "If You are the Son of God, cast Yourself down; for it is written, 'He shall give His angels charge concerning You, and they shall bear You up in *their* hands, lest You strike Your foot against a stone.' " [b]

7. Jesus said to him, "Again, it is written, 'You shall not tempt *the* Lord your God.' "

8. After that, the devil took Him to an exceedingly high mountain, and showed Him all the kingdoms of the world and their glory,

9. And said to Him, "All these things will I give You, if You will fall down and worship me."

10. Then Jesus said to him, "Begone, Satan! For it is written, 'You shall worship the Lord your God, and Him alone shall you serve.' " [c]

11. Then the devil left Him; and behold, angels came and ministered to Him.

MARK 1

12. And soon after, the Spirit compelled Him to go out into the wilderness;

13. And He was there in the wilderness *for* forty days, tempted by Satan, and was with the wild animals; and *afterwards* angels ministered to Him.

"Command These Stones"

"... To Become Food"
– American Stock Photo

Pinnacle of Tower of David

LUKE 4

1. And Jesus, filled with *the* Holy Spirit, returned from the Jordan, and was led by the Spirit into the wilderness

2. *For* forty days to be tempted by the devil. And He ate nothing in those days; and after they had come to an end, He hungered.

3. Then the devil said to Him, "If You are *the* Son of God, command that this stone become bread."

4. But Jesus answered him, saying, "It is written, 'Man shall not live by bread alone, but by every word of God.' " [a]

5. Then the devil led Him up into a high mountain *and* showed Him all the kingdoms of the world in a moment of time.

6. And the devil said to Him, "I will give You all this authority, and the glory of them *all*; for it has been delivered to me, and I give it to whomever I desire.

7. Therefore, if You will worship me in *my* presence, all things shall be Yours."

8. But Jesus answered *and* said to him, "Get behind Me, Satan; for it is written, 'You shall worship *the* Lord your God, and Him only shall you serve.' " [c]

9. Then he led Him to Jerusalem and set Him upon the edge of the temple, and said to Him, "If You are the Son of God, cast Yourself down from here;

10. For it is written, 'He shall give His angels charge concerning You to keep You;

11. And in *their* hands they shall bear You up, lest You strike Your foot against a stone.' " [b]

a - Deut. 8:3 b - Psa. 91:11-12 c - Deut. 6:13; 10:20

Dead Sea

LUKE 4

12. But Jesus answered *and* said to him, "It is *clearly* stated, 'You shall not tempt *the* Lord your God.' " [d]
13. Now when the devil had completed every temptation, he departed from Him for a time.

d - Deut. 6:16

Temple Mount and Dome of the Rock with the Mosque of Omar

PART II

FROM PASSOVER 27 AD
TO PASSOVER 28 AD

28. AFTER THE TEMPTATION, JESUS FIRST SHOWS HIMSELF
AT THE TEMPLE IN POWER AND ZEAL—
THIS IS FIRST PASSOVER AND FEAST OF UNLEAVENED BREAD
DURING CHRIST'S MINISTRY

JOHN 2

13. Now the Passover of the Jews was near, and Jesus went up to Jerusalem.

14. And He found in the temple those who were selling oxen and sheep and doves, and the money exchangers sitting *there*;

15. And after making a scourge of cords, He drove them all out of the temple, *with* both the sheep and the oxen; and He poured out the coins of the money exchangers, and overturned the tables.

16. And to those who were selling the doves, He said, "Take these things out of here! Do not make My Father's house a house of merchandise."

17. Then His disciples remembered that it was written, "The zeal of Your house has eaten Me up." [a]

18. As a result, the Jews answered and said to Him, "What sign do You show to us, seeing that You do these things?"

19. Jesus answered and said to them, "Destroy this temple, and in three days I will raise it up."

20. Then the Jews said, "This temple was forty-six years in building, and You will raise it up in three days?"

21. But He spoke concerning the temple of His body.

22. Therefore, when He was raised from *the* dead, His disciples remembered that He had said this to them; and they believed the Scriptures, and the word that Jesus had spoken.

23. Now when He was in Jerusalem at the Passover, during the feast, many believed on His name, as they observed the miracles that He was doing.

24. But Jesus did not entrust Himself to them, because He knew all *men*;

25. And He did not need anyone to testify concerning man, for He Himself knew what was in man.

a - Psa. 69:9

29. NICODEMUS COMES TO JESUS AT NIGHT—
THE PHARISEES KNEW JESUS CAME FROM GOD

JOHN 3

1. Now there was a man of the Pharisees, Nicodemus by name, a ruler of the Jews.

2. He came to Jesus by night and said to Him, "Rabbi, we know that You are a teacher *Who* has come from God; because no one is able to do the miracles that You are doing unless God is with him."

3. Jesus answered and said to him, "Truly, truly I say to you, unless anyone is born again,* he cannot see the kingdom of God."

4. Nicodemus said to Him, "How can a man who is old be born? Can he enter his mother's womb a second time and be born?"

* *anew*

The Court of the Gentiles—South Side of the Temple

JOHN 3

5. Jesus answered, "Truly, truly I say to you, unless anyone has been born of water and of Spirit, [a] he cannot enter the kingdom of God.

6. That which has been born of the flesh is flesh; and that which has been born of the Spirit is spirit.

7. Do not be amazed that I said to you, 'It is necessary for you to be born again.'*

8. The wind blows where it wills, and you hear its sound, but you do not know *the place* from which it comes and *the place* to which it goes; so *also* is everyone who has been born of the Spirit."

9. Nicodemus answered and said to Him, "How can these things be?"

10. Jesus answered and said to him, "You are a teacher of Israel, and you do not know these things?

11. Truly, truly I say to you, We speak that which We know, and We testify of that which We have seen; but you do not receive Our testimony.

12. If I have told you earthly things, and you do not believe, how will you believe if I tell you heavenly things?

13. (And no one has ascended into heaven, except He Who came down from heaven, *even* the Son of man, Who is in heaven.)"

a - *To be "born of water" refers to one's natural fleshly birth. To be "born of Spirit" refers to the resurrection from the dead to eternal life as a glorified spirit being, and not to an emotional "conversion experience."*

30. A PROPHECY OF HIS OWN DEATH AND CRUCIFIXION

JOHN 3

14. "And even as Moses lifted up the serpent in the wilderness, in the same way it is ordained that the Son of man be lifted up, [a]

15. So that everyone who believes in Him may not perish, but may have everlasting life."

a - Num. 21:8-9

31. GOD GAVE HIS ONLY BEGOTTEN SON TO SAVE THE WORLD

JOHN 3

16. "For God so loved the world that He gave His only begotten Son, so that everyone who believes** in Him may not perish, but may have everlasting life.

17. For God sent not His Son into the world that He might judge the world, but that the world might be saved through Him.

18. The one who believes in Him is not judged, but the one who does not believe has already been judged because he has not believed in the name of the only begotten Son of God.

19. And this is the judgment: that the light has come into the world, but men loved darkness rather than the light because their works were evil.

20. For everyone who practices evil hates the light, and does not come to the light, so that his works may not be exposed;

21. But the one who practices the truth comes to the light, so that his works may be manifested, that they have been accomplished by *the power of* God."

32. JESUS BEGINS BAPTIZING

JOHN 3

22. After these things, Jesus and His disciples came into the land of Judea; and there He stayed with them and was baptizing.

* *anew*

**The Greek present tense participle ο πιστευων *pisteuon means, "everyone who continually believes in Him." Such belief is a continuous deep, life-long, inner conviction of faith accompanied by loving obedience to God the Father and Jesus Christ, rather than a mere mental or verbal acknowledgement of Jesus Christ.*

33. JOHN IS STILL BAPTIZING AT THE SAME TIME

JOHN 3

23. And John was also baptizing in Aenon, near Salim because there was much water there; and the *people* were coming and were being baptized,

34. JOHN NOT YET PUT IN PRISON

JOHN 3

24. For John had not yet been cast into prison.

35. JOHN THE BAPTIST'S MINISTRY TO DECREASE, AND JESUS' MINISTRY TO INCREASE—JOHN EXPLAINS WHO AND WHAT HE IS, AND WHO AND WHAT CHRIST IS

JOHN 3

25. Then there arose a question *between* the disciples of John and *some of the* Jews about purification.
26. And they came to John and said to him, "Rabbi, He Who was with you beyond Jordan, to Whom you have borne witness, behold, He is baptizing, and all are coming to Him."
27. John answered and said, "No one is able to receive anything unless it has been given to him from heaven.
28. You yourselves bear witness to me that I said, 'I am not the Christ,' but that I am sent before Him.
29. The one who has the bride is *the* bridegroom; but the friend of the bridegroom, who stands by and hears him, rejoices greatly because of the voice of the bridegroom; *in this* then, my joy has been fulfilled.
30. It is ordained that He increase, and that I decrease.
31. He Who comes from above is above all. The one who is of the earth is earthy, and speaks of the earth. He Who comes from heaven is above all;
32. And what He has seen and heard, this *is what* He testifies; but no one receives His testimony.
33. The one who has received His testimony has set his seal that God is true;
34. For He Whom God has sent speaks the words of God; and God gives not the Spirit by measure *unto Him.*"

36. MUST BELIEVE AND HAVE COMPLETE TRUST AND FAITH IN JESUS CHRIST

JOHN 3

35. "The Father loves the Son and has given all things into His hand.
36. The one who believes in the Son has everlasting life; but the one who does not obey the Son shall not see life, for the wrath of God remains on him."

37. JESUS CHRIST'S DISCIPLES DO THE BAPTIZING

JOHN 4

1. Therefore, when the Lord knew that the Pharisees had heard that Jesus was making and baptizing more disciples than John,
2. (Although Jesus Himself was not baptizing, but His disciples,)
3. He left Judea and departed again into Galilee.
4. Now it was necessary for Him to pass through Samaria.

38. JESUS CHRIST AND THE WOMAN OF SAMARIA AT THE WELL
JOHN 4

5. And He came to a city of Samaria called Sychar, near the land that Jacob had given to his son Joseph. [a]

6. And Jacob's fountain was there; Jesus, therefore, being wearied from the journey, sat there by the fountain. *It* was about *the* sixth hour.

7. A woman came out of Samaria to draw water. Jesus said to her, "Give me *some water* to drink."

8. For His disciples had gone away into the city, so that they might buy provisions.

9. Therefore, the Samaritan woman said to Him, "How *is it that* You, being a Jew, ask me, a Samaritan woman, *to give You water* to drink? For Jews do not associate with Samaritans."

10. Jesus answered and said to her, "If you had known the gift of God, and Who it is that said to you, 'Give Me *some water* to drink,' you would have asked Him, and He would have given you living water."

11. The woman said to Him, "Sir, You have nothing with *which* to draw *water*, and the well is deep; how then do You have the living water?

12. Are You greater than our father Jacob, who gave us the well, and drank from it, and his sons, and his cattle?"

13. Jesus answered and said to her, "Everyone who drinks of this water will thirst again;

14. But whoever drinks of the water that I will give him shall never thirst; rather, the water that I will give him shall become a fountain of water within him, springing up into everlasting life."

15. The woman said to Him, "Sir, give me this water, so that I will not thirst or *need to* come here to draw *water*."

16. Jesus said to her, "Go, call your husband and come *back* here."

17. The woman answered and said, "I do not have a husband." Jesus said to her, "You have spoken well in saying, 'I do not have a husband';

18. For you have had five husbands, and the one whom you now have is not your husband. This you have spoken truly."

19. The woman said to Him, "Sir, I perceive that You are a prophet.

20. Our fathers worshiped in this mountain, but you say that the place where it is obligatory to worship is in Jerusalem."

21. Jesus said to her, "Woman, believe Me, the hour is coming when you shall neither in this mountain nor in Jerusalem worship the Father.

22. You do not know what you worship. We know what we worship, for salvation is of the Jews.

23. But the hour is coming, and now is, when the true worshipers shall worship the Father in spirit and in truth; for the Father is indeed seeking those who worship Him in this manner.

24. God *is* Spirit, and those who worship Him must worship in spirit and in truth."

25. The woman said to Him, "I know that Messiah is coming, Who is called Christ; when He comes, He will tell us all things."

26. Jesus said to her, "I Who speak to you am *He*."

27. Now at this *time* His disciples came, and they were amazed that He was speaking with a woman; however, no one said, "What are You seeking?" or, "Why are You talking with her?"

28. Then the woman left her waterpot and went away into the city, and said to the men,

29. "Come *and* see a man who told me everything that I have done. Can it be that He is the Christ?"

30. Then they went out of the city and came to Him.

31. But in the meantime, the disciples were urging Him, saying, "Rabbi, eat."

32. And He said to them, "I have meat to eat that you are not aware of."

33. Then the disciples said to one another, "Did anyone bring Him *something* to eat?"

34. Jesus said to them, "My meat is to do the will of Him Who sent Me, and to finish His work.

a - Josh. 24:32

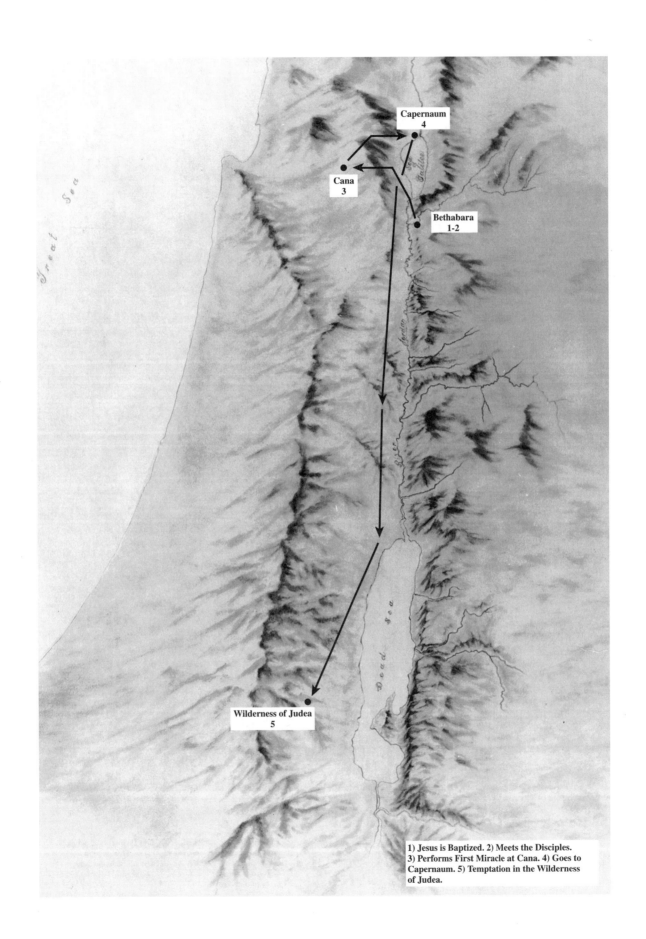

Capernaum
4

Cana
3

Bethabara
1-2

Wilderness of Judea
5

1) Jesus is Baptized. 2) Meets the Disciples.
3) Performs First Miracle at Cana. 4) Goes to
Capernaum. 5) Temptation in the Wilderness
of Judea.

63

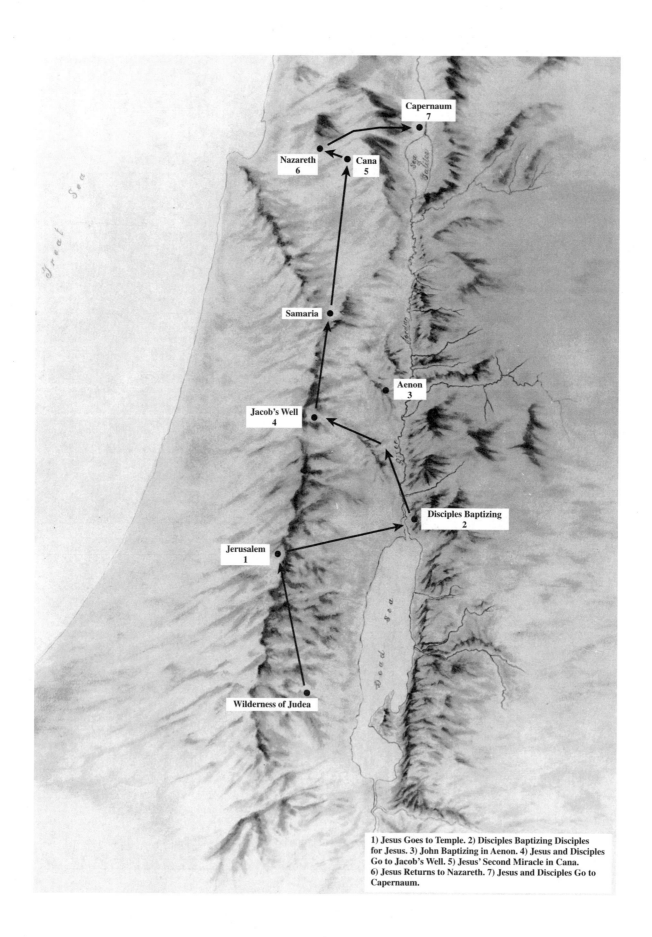

Capernaum
7

Nazareth
6

Cana
5

Samaria

Aenon
3

Jacob's Well
4

Disciples Baptizing
2

Jerusalem
1

Wilderness of Judea

1) Jesus Goes to Temple. 2) Disciples Baptizing Disciples for Jesus. 3) John Baptizing in Aenon. 4) Jesus and Disciples Go to Jacob's Well. 5) Jesus' Second Miracle in Cana. 6) Jesus Returns to Nazareth. 7) Jesus and Disciples Go to Capernaum.

JOHN 4

35. "Do not say that there are yet four months, and *then* the harvest comes. I say to you, look around. Lift up your eyes and see the fields, for they are already white to harvest.

36. And the one who reaps receives a reward, and gathers fruit unto eternal life; so that the one who is sowing and the one who is reaping may both rejoice together.

37. For in this the saying is true, that one sows and another reaps.

38. I sent you to reap that in which you have not labored; others have labored, and you have entered into their labor."

39. Now many of the Samaritans from that city believed on Him because of the word of the woman, who testified, "He told me everything that I have done."

40. Therefore, when the Samaritans came to Him, they asked Him to remain with them; and He remained there two days.

41. And many more believed because of His word;

42. And they said to the woman, "We no longer believe because of your word, for we have heard *Him* ourselves, and we know that this is truly the Christ, the Savior of the world."

39. JOHN IS CAST INTO PRISON

LUKE 3

19. But Herod the tetrarch, after being reproved by him for *marrying* Herodias, the wife of Philip his brother, and for all *the* evils that Herod had done,

20. Added this to all that: he locked up John in prison.

40. JESUS RETURNS INTO GALILEE

JOHN 4

43. And after two days, He departed from there and went into Galilee;

44. For Jesus Himself testified that a prophet has no honor in his own country.

45. Therefore, when He came into Galilee, the Galileans received Him, having seen all *the* things that He did in Jerusalem during the feast, for they also had gone to the feast.

46. Then Jesus came again to Cana of Galilee, where He had made the water *become* wine. And there was a certain royal official in Capernaum whose son was sick.

47. When he heard that Jesus had come out of Judea into Galilee, *he* went to Him and asked Him if He would come down and heal his son; for he was about to die.

48. Therefore, Jesus said to him, "Unless you see signs and wonders, you will not believe at all."

49. The royal official said to Him, "Sir, come down before my little child dies."

50. Jesus said to him, "Go; your son shall live." And the man believed the word that Jesus said to him and went away.

51. Now as he was going down *to his house*, his servants met him and reported, saying, "Your child is alive *and well*."

52. Then he inquired of them at what hour he began to improve. And they said to him, "Yesterday, *at the* seventh hour, the fever left him."

53. Therefore, the father knew that *it was* at the hour that Jesus said to him, "Your son shall live." And he himself believed and his whole household.

54. This *was* the second miracle *that* Jesus did after again coming out of Judea into Galilee.

JESUS BEGINS PREACHING IN GALILEE AFTER JOHN THE BAPTIST IS PUT IN PRISON

The first six months of Jesus' ministry was used for private teaching. During that time He was baptized, made initial contact with His disciples, performed His first miracle—changing the water into the wine at the wedding feast—then He was tempted of the Devil for forty days and nights. After that, He presented Himself at the temple in Jerusalem. Jesus began His public preaching and ministry at the temple in Jerusalem during the Passover and the Feast of Unleavened Bread in 27 AD.

Following the Feast of Unleavened Bread, Jesus and His disciples spent several weeks baptizing in Judaea (John 3:22). At the same time John the Baptist was still baptizing at Aenon, because he had not yet been put in prison. After John's imprisonment, Jesus returned through Samaria into Galilee, just before the Feast of Pentecost, and began preaching.

The Account written in the book of John correlates the events and fills in the details not contained in the summary account recorded in the book of Mark. Together John and Mark give the complete picture.

41. AFTER JOHN IS PUT IN PRISON, JESUS COMES INTO GALILEE PREACHING IN POWER AND ANNOUNCING THE KINGDOM OF GOD

MARK 1	MATTHEW 4	LUKE 4
14. Now after the imprisonment of John, Jesus came into Galilee, proclaiming the gospel of the kingdom of God, 15. And saying, "The time has been fulfilled, and the kingdom of God is near at hand; repent, and believe in the gospel."	12. Now when Jesus had heard that John was put in prison, He went into Galilee.	14. Then Jesus returned in the power of the Spirit to Galilee; and word about Him went out into the entire country around. 15. And He taught in their synagogues, *and* was glorified by all.

42. JESUS PREACHES IN NAZARETH ON THE SABBATH DAY

LUKE 4

16. And He came to Nazareth, where He had been brought up; and according to His custom, He went into the synagogue on the Sabbath day* and stood up to read. [a]
17. And there was given Him *the* book of the prophet Isaiah; and when He had unrolled the scroll, He found the place where it was written,

a - Lev. 23:10-21; Deut. 16:9-10

The words "on the Sabbath day" are translated from the Greek words εν τη ημερα των σαββατων. A literal translation would be, "Now on the day of the sabbaths"; or, "Now on the day of the weeks." The use of the Greek των σαββατων, meaning "Sabbaths" or "weeks," indicates that this verse is referring to the day of Pentecost. Because this day is observed after counting a period of seven full weeks, it was known in New Testament times as "the day of the weeks." The day of Pentecost does not fall on the weekly Sabbath but is an annual Sabbath.

LUKE 4

18. "*The* Spirit of *the* Lord *is* upon Me; for this reason, He has anointed Me to preach the gospel to *the* poor; He has sent Me to heal those who are brokenhearted, to proclaim pardon to *the* captives and recovery of sight to *the* blind, to send forth in deliverance those who have been crushed,

19. To proclaim *the* acceptable year of *the* Lord." [b]

20. And after rolling up the scroll *and* delivering *it* to the attendant, He sat down; and the eyes of everyone in the synagogue were fixed on Him.

21. Then He began to say to them, "Today, this scripture is being fulfilled in your ears."

22. And all bore witness to Him and were amazed at the words of grace that were coming out of His mouth; and they said, "Is not this the son of Joseph?"

23. And He said to them, "Surely, you will say this parable to Me: 'Physician, heal Yourself! Whatever we have heard being done in Capernaum, do also here in Your *own* country.' "

24. But He said, "Truly I say to you, no prophet is acceptable in his *own* country.

25. For in truth, I say to you, many widows were in Israel in the days of Elijah, when the heavens were shut up for three years and six months, and there was great famine upon all the land;

26. And Elijah was not sent to any of them, but only to a widow in Sarepta, *a city* of Sidonia.

27. There were also many lepers in Israel in the time of Elisha the prophet; and none of them were cleansed, but only Naaman the Syrian." [c]

28. Now all in the synagogue who heard these things were filled with indignation.

29. And they rose up *and* cast Him out of *the* city, and led Him to the edge of the mountain on which their city was built, in order to throw Him down headlong;

30. But He passed *safely* through their midst *and* departed.

b - Isa. 58:6; 61:1-2   c - I Kings 17:8-9; 18:1-2; II Kings 5:1, 14

43. JESUS GOES TO CAPERNAUM

LUKE 4

31. Then He went down to Capernaum, a city of Galilee, and taught them on the Sabbath days.

32. And they were astonished at His teaching, for His word was with authority.

Hill Country of Galilee

MATTHEW 4

13. And after leaving Nazareth, He came and dwelt in Capernaum, which *is* on the seaside, on the borders of Zabulon and Nephthalim;

14. That it might be fulfilled which was spoken by the prophet Isaiah, saying,

15. "*The* land of Zabulon and the land of Nephthalim, *by the* way of *the* sea, beyond the Jordan, Galilee of the Gentiles;

16. The people who were sitting in darkness have seen a great light; and to those who were sitting in *the* realm and shadow of death, light has sprung up." [a]

17. From that time Jesus began to preach and to say, "Repent, for the kingdom of heaven is at hand."

a - Isa. 9:1–2

44. JESUS CALLS THE DISCIPLES TO FOLLOW HIM—
THEY GO ON FIRST PREACHING TOUR OF GALILEE

MARK 1

16. And *as* He was walking by the Sea of Galilee, He saw Simon and his brother Andrew casting a large net into the sea, for they were fishermen.
17. And Jesus said to them, "Follow Me, and I will make you to become fishers of men."
18. And they immediately left their nets *and* followed Him.
19. And after moving on a little way from there, He saw James, the *son* of Zebedee, and his brother John; and they *were* in the ship, mending the nets.
20. And He called them at once; and leaving their father Zebedee in the ship with the hired servants, they followed Him.

MATTHEW 4

18. And as Jesus was walking by the Sea of Galilee, He saw two brothers, Simon who is called Peter, and Andrew his brother, casting a large net into the sea; for they were fishermen.
19. And He said to them, "Follow Me, and I will make you fishers of men."
20. Then they immediately left their nets *and* followed Him.
21. And after leaving there, He saw two other brothers, James the *son* of Zebedee, and John his brother, in the ship with Zebedee their father, mending their nets; and He called them.
22. And they immediately left the ship and their father *and* followed Him.

LUKE 5

1. Now it came to pass that while the multitude was pressing on Him to hear the Word of God, He stood by the Lake of Gennesaret;
2. And He saw two ships standing by the *shore of the* lake, but the fishermen had left them and were washing *their* nets.
3. And after going into one of the ships, which was Simon's, He asked him to put out from the shore a little; and He sat down *and* taught the multitudes from the ship.
4. Now when He had finished speaking, He said to Simon, "Put out into the deep, and let your nets down for a haul."
5. Then Simon answered *and* said, "Master, we have labored through the entire night, *and* we have taken nothing; but at Your word, I will let the net down."
6. And when they did this, they enclosed a great school of fish; and their net was breaking.
7. Then they signaled to their partners, those in the other ship, that they should come *and* help them; and they came and filled both the ships, so that they began to sink.
8. And when he saw *this*, Simon Peter fell at Jesus' knees, saying, "Depart from me, for I am a sinful man, Lord."
9. For great astonishment came upon him and all those with him, on account of the *miraculous* haul of fish that they had taken;

"I Will Make You Fishers of Men"

Ruins of Marketplace in Gerasa

LUKE 5

10. And in like manner also *upon* James and John, *the* sons of Zebedee, who were partners with Simon. Then Jesus said to Simon, "Fear not; from this time forth you shall be catching men."

11. And after bringing the ships to land, they forsook everything and followed Him.

45. JESUS CAST OUT A DEMON AFTER TEACHING IN THE SYNAGOGUE ON THE SABBATH AND HIS FAME SPREADS FAR AND WIDE

MARK 1

21. Then they went into Capernaum; and on the Sabbath day He immediately went into the synagogue *and* taught *the people*.

22. And they were astonished at His doctrine; for He was teaching them as *one* having authority, and not as the scribes.

23. Now in their synagogue there was a man with an unclean spirit; and it cried out,

24. Saying, "Ah! What have we to do with You, Jesus, *the* Nazarene? Have You come to destroy us? I know Who You are—the Holy *One* of God!" [a]

25. But Jesus rebuked it, saying, "Be silent, and come out of him."

26. And after throwing him into convulsions and crying out with a loud voice, the spirit came out of him.

27. Then all were astonished, so that they questioned among themselves, saying, "What is this? What new teaching is this, that with authority He commands even the unclean spirits, and they obey Him?"

28. And His fame swiftly spread into all the country around Galilee.*

LUKE 4

33. Now a man who had an unclean spirit was in the synagogue; and he cried out with a loud voice,

34. Saying, "Ah! What have we to do with You, Jesus *the* Nazarean? Have You come to destroy us? I know Who You are, the Holy *One* of God." [a]

35. And Jesus rebuked him, saying, "Be silent, and come out of him." And after throwing him into the midst, the demon came out of him *and* did not hurt him in any way.

36. Then astonishment came upon everyone, and they spoke to one another, saying, "What message *is* this, that with authority and power He commands the unclean spirits, and they come out?"

37. And news of His *powerful deeds* spread through every place in the surrounding country.*

a - Psa. 16:10; Dan. 9:24

Jesus' Galilean ministry began on a Sabbath, which probably was the Feast of Pentecost. From that time his fame spread far and wide, which must have taken many months. The chronology would certainly indicate that it took most of the next year. He preached throughout Galilee, and people were coming from as far away as Syria, Decapolis, Jerusalem, Judea, and beyond the Jordan River. Jesus preached throughout all the synagogues in Galilee. Covering all the synagogues in all of Galilee required a great deal of time. This section gives a summary of what Jesus did during this time.

46. JESUS HEALS PETER'S MOTHER-IN-LAW

MARK 1

29. And as soon as they had gone out of the synagogue, they came into the house of Simon and Andrew, with James and John.
30. And Simon's mother-in-law was lying sick with a fever. And they spoke to Him at once about her.
31. And He came to *her*, and took her by the hand and raised her up. And immediately the fever left her, and she served them.

LUKE 4

38. Now after going out of the synagogue, He went into Simon's house. And Simon's mother-in-law was sick with a great fever; and they asked Him *to intervene* for her.
39. Then He stood over her and rebuked the fever, and it left her. And immediately she arose and served them.

MATTHEW 8

14. And after coming into Peter's house, Jesus saw Peter's mother-in-law lying *sick* with a fever;
15. Then He touched her hand, and the fever left her; and she arose and served them.

47. AFTER THE SABBATH, IN THE EVENING, JESUS HEALS MANY

MARK 1

32. Now in *the* evening, when the sun had gone down, they brought to Him all who were diseased, and those who were possessed by demons;
33. And the entire city was gathered together at the door.
34. Then He healed many who were sick with various diseases, and He cast out many demons; but He did not allow the demons to speak because they knew Him.

LUKE 4

40. Now as the sun was going down, all those who had sick *persons* with various diseases brought them to Him; and He laid His hands on each one of them *and* healed them.
41. And demons went out from many, crying out and saying, "You are the Christ, the Son of God." But He rebuked them *and* did not allow them to speak, because they knew *that* He was the Christ.

MATTHEW 8

16. Now when evening had come, they brought to Him many possessed with demons, and He cast out the spirits by *His* word, and healed all who were sick;
17. So that it might be fulfilled which was spoken by Isaiah the prophet, saying, "*He* Himself took our infirmities and bore our diseases."

48. JESUS RISES EARLY IN THE MORNING TO PRAY

MARK 1

35. And at *the time* of the morning watch, while it was still night, He rose up; and going out, *He* departed into a desert place, and was praying there.
36. And Simon, and those who were with him, went out after Him.
37. And after finding Him, they said to Him, "Everyone is looking for You."
38. But He said to them, "Let us go to the towns in the neighboring countryside, so that I may also preach there; because I have come for this *purpose*."

A Desert Place

49. JESUS PREACHES THROUGHOUT GALILEE

MARK 1

39. And He preached in all their synagogues in Galilee, and cast out demons.

LUKE 4

42. Now when day came, He departed and went into a desert place; but the multitudes searched for Him, and came to Him and were detaining Him, that He might not leave them.

43. Then He said to them, "It is necessary for me to preach the gospel *of* the kingdom of God to the other cities; for this *is* the reason that I have been sent."

44. And He went *about* preaching in the synagogues of Galilee.

MATTHEW 4

23. And Jesus went throughout all Galilee, teaching in their synagogues, and preaching the gospel of the kingdom, and healing every disease and every bodily ailment among the people.

24. Then His fame went out into all Syria; and they brought to Him all who were sick, oppressed by various diseases and torments, and possessed by demons, and lunatics, and paralytics; and He healed them.

25. And great multitudes followed Him from Galilee, and Decapolis, and Jerusalem, and Judea, and beyond the Jordan.

Synagogue Ruins in Capernaum

71

Gilead Looking Toward Jordan Valley

Fishermen in Boat on Sea of Galilee

THE SERMON ON THE MOUNT

The Sermon on the Mount was delivered at the beginning of Jesus Christ's ministry. After choosing twelve of His disciples to be witnesses of all the words that He spoke, Jesus taught them the basic spiritual principles that are recorded in Matthew 5-7 and Luke 6. These teachings, now known as the Sermon on the Mount, were the beginning words of the New Covenant. Unlike the Old Covenant, which offered the physical blessings of health and prosperity, the New Covenant opened the way to the spiritual blessings of eternal life with everlasting power and glory.

Throughout the Bible, there is a contrast between the physical and the spiritual. The words of the apostle Paul show that the physical comes first, then the spiritual (I Cor. 15:45-47). Adam, the first man on earth, came from the earth and was physical. The second Adam, Jesus Christ, came from heaven and is spiritual. In like manner, the Old Covenant, which was physical, was established before the New Covenant, which is spiritual. On the day of Pentecost, God established the Old Covenant with the children of Israel by proclaiming the Ten Commandments from the top of Mount Sinai. The event was so terrifying to the people that they pleaded with Moses not to have God speak to them any longer: "And all the people saw the thunderings, and the lightnings, and the noise of the trumpet, and the mountain smoking: and when the people saw it, they removed and stood afar off. And they said unto Moses, 'Speak thou with us, and we will hear: but let not God speak with us, lest we die' " (Ex. 20:18-19, *KJV*).

Because the children of Israel were afraid to hear God speak, Moses stood between God and the people to bring them all the words of God. Moses went up to the top of Mount Sinai to meet with God. At that time, God gave him the statutes, judgments and other laws to deliver to the children of Israel. As the intermediary who delivered the law to the people, Moses was considered a lawgiver, although he did not originate any of the laws or commandments himself (Ex. 20-23).

When Moses came down from meeting with God, he read all the words of God in the hearing of the people. With one voice, the people agreed to obey all that God had commanded. Then the covenant was ratified with a blood sacrifice: "And Moses came and told the people all the words of the LORD, and all the judgments: and all the people answered with one voice, and said, 'All the words which the LORD hath said will we do.' And Moses wrote all the words of the LORD, and rose up early in the morning, and builded an altar under the hill, and twelve pillars, according to the twelve tribes of Israel. And he sent young men of the children of Israel, which offered burnt offerings, and sacrificed peace offerings of oxen unto the LORD. And Moses took half of the blood, and put *it* in basins; and half of the blood he sprinkled on the altar. And he took the book of the covenant, and read in the audience of the people: and they said, 'All that the Lord hath said will we do, and be obedient.' And Moses took the blood, and sprinkled *it* on the people, and said, '**Behold the blood of the covenant, which the LORD hath made with you concerning all these words**' " Ex. 24:3-8, *KJV*).

The covenant that God made with the children of Israel at Mount Sinai contained blessings and cursings. God promised to bless the children of Israel if they would obey His commands and laws; but if they disobeyed, they would reap curses in return for their sins and transgressions. In this manner, God established the Old Covenant with the twelve tribes of Israel: **"See, I have set before thee this day life and good, and death and evil; in that I command thee this day to love the LORD thy God, to walk in His ways, and to keep His commandments and His statutes and His judgments, that thou mayest live and multiply: and the LORD thy God shall bless thee in the land whither thou goest to possess it.**

"But if thine heart turn away, so that thou wilt not hear, but shalt be drawn away, and worship other gods, and serve them; I denounce unto you this day, that ye shall surely perish, *and that* ye shall not prolong *your* days upon the land, whither thou passest over Jordan to go to possess it. **I call heaven and earth to record this day against you,** *that* **I have set before you life and death, blessing and cursing**: therefore choose life, that both thou and thy seed may live: that thou mayest love the LORD thy God, *and* that thou mayest obey His voice, and that thou mayest cleave unto Him: for He *is* thy life, and the length of thy days: that thou mayest dwell in the land which the LORD sware unto thy fathers, to Abraham, to Isaac, and to Jacob, to give them" (Deut. 30:15-20, *KJV*).

Moses' office as mediator and lawgiver was a physical type of the coming spiritual Lawgiver, Jesus Christ. When the children of Israel were about to enter the Promised Land, God gave Moses this prophecy of the coming Messiah: "And the LORD said unto me, 'They have well *spoken that* which they have spoken [that they did not want God to speak to them, but Moses]. I will raise them up a Prophet from among their brethren, like unto thee, and will put My words in His mouth; and He shall speak unto them all that I shall command Him. And it shall come to pass, *that* whosoever will not hearken unto My words which He shall speak in My name, I will require *it* of him' " (Deut. 18:17-19, *KJV*).

Jesus Christ the Spiritual Lawgiver

This prophecy of the coming Messiah reveals that every person who rejects the words of Jesus Christ will be held accountable by God in the judgment day. During His ministry, Jesus confirmed that He was that Prophet and that His words are the standard by which all will be judged: "But if anyone hears My words and does not believe, I do not judge him; for I did not come to judge the world, but to save the world. **The one who rejects Me and does not receive My words has one who judges him; the word which I have spoken, that shall judge him in the last day. For I have not spoken from Myself; but the Father, Who sent Me, gave Me commandment Himself, what I should say and what I should speak**" (John 12:47-49).

The spiritual office of Jesus Christ far overshadows the physical office of Moses. Jesus Christ was God manifested in the flesh. He was the Lord God of the Old Testament Who had established the Old Covenant with the children of Israel. He came to earth to deliver them from the curses that the covenant had imposed for their sins, and to redeem all mankind from the death penalty for their transgressions of God's holy and righteous laws (Rom. 7:14; 3:9-19). His death ended the Old Covenant with the administration of death, and established the New Covenant, which offers the gift of eternal life.

Unlike the Old Covenant, which required obedience to the letter of the law, the New Covenant is based on obedience from the heart—fulfilling the laws of God not only in the letter, but also in their complete spiritual intent. For this reason, Jesus Christ came as the spiritual Lawgiver to amplify and magnify the commandments and laws of God, as prophesied by Isaiah: "The LORD is well pleased for His righteousness' sake; He will magnify the law, and make *it* honourable [or glorious]" (Isa. 42:21, *KJV*).

As the spiritual Lawgiver, Jesus Christ revealed the full meaning of the laws of God. He received a commission from God the Father to preach the gospel and proclaim the spiritual meaning of the commandments of God, in order to bring the knowledge of salvation to the world. After John the Baptist was put in prison, Jesus Christ began His ministry. He commanded the people to repent of their sins and believe the gospel: "The beginning of the gospel of Jesus Christ, *the* Son of God....And saying, 'The time has been fulfilled, and the kingdom of God is near at hand; repent, and believe in the gospel' " (Mark 1:1, 15).

Throughout His ministry, Jesus taught repentance from sin, which is clearly defined in the New Testament as the transgression of the laws of God (I John 3:4). God inspired the words of Jesus Christ to be recorded in the Gospels and canonized by the apostles with the other books of the New Testament. Through the ages, from Jesus' time until now, God has divinely preserved these Scriptures for the world.

The four Gospel accounts of the life and ministry of Jesus Christ reveal that God now requires obedience to His commandments not only in the letter of the law but in the spirit of the law. But in spite of Jesus' teachings, which magnify the laws and commandments of God, most professing Christians have been taught that Jesus Christ came to abolish the laws of God. Jesus emphatically denounced this teaching in the Sermon on the Mount: "**Do not think that I have come to abolish the Law or the Prophets; I did not come to abolish, but to fulfill. For truly I say to you, until the heaven and the earth shall pass away, one jot or one tittle shall in no way pass from the Law until everything has been fulfilled**" (Matt. 5:17-18).

How Did Jesus Christ Fulfill the Law?

When Jesus Christ fulfilled the law, He did not abolish it. Jesus' own words in the Gospel of Matthew make this fact very clear. Then in what way did He fulfill the law?

In order to recognize how He fulfilled the law, we must understand the meaning of the word, "fulfill." The English word, "fulfill," is translated from the Greek verb, πληροω *pleeroo,* which means: "to make full, to fill full, to fulfill....in Mt. 5:17 depending on how one prefers to interpret the context, πληροω *pleeroo* is understood here either as *fulfill* = do, carry out, or *bring to full expression* = show forth in its true spiritual meaning, or as fill up = complete" (Arndt and Gingrich, *A Greek-English Lexicon of the New Testament*).

As the spiritual Lawgiver, Jesus Christ fulfilled the Law of God by bringing it to its full expression, revealing its complete spiritual meaning and intent. He "filled the law to the full" by teaching obedience in the spirit of the law. To fulfill the Law of God by amplifying its meaning and application is the exact opposite of abolishing the law. If Jesus had come to abolish the laws of God, He would not have magnified and expanded their meaning, making them even more binding. If the laws of God were not binding today, there could be no sin, because "sin is lawlessness" (I John 3:4). And if there were no sinners, there would be no need of a Savior. But the Scriptures of both the Old Testament and the New Testament testify that Jesus Christ came to save mankind from sin. Instead of abolishing or "doing away with the law," Jesus came to take upon Himself the penalty for our sins and transgressions of the laws of God, and to show us the way to eternal life through spiritual obedience from the heart. That is how He magnified the laws and commandments of God and made them honorable.

The Spiritual Meaning of the Commandments Revealed in the Sermon on the Mount

As the spiritual Lawgiver, Jesus Christ taught His disciples the spiritual meaning and application of every one of God's laws and commandments. Let us examine how He magnified the Sixth Commandment in the Sermon on the Mount: "You have heard that it was said to those *in* ancient *times*, 'You shall not commit murder; but whoever commits murder shall be subject to judgment.' But I say to you, everyone who is angry with his brother without cause shall be subject to judgment. Now *you have heard it said*, 'Whoever shall say to his brother, "Raca," shall be subject to *the judgment of* the council.' But *I say to you*, whoever shall say, '*You* fool,' shall be subject to the fire of Gehenna" (Matt. 5:21-22).

Jesus made it clear that murder begins in the heart and is rooted in hatred and anger. The spiritual amplification of the Sixth Commandment, as taught by Jesus Christ, extends far beyond the letter of the law, which judges only physical acts of violence. Under the New Covenant, this commandment must be obeyed in the thoughts and intents of the heart. Obedience is no longer restricted to the letter of the law and the actual committing of murder. By the new spiritual standard for obedience, hatred in one's heart is judged as murder. This spiritual standard also applies to hatred for an enemy: **"You have heard that it was said, 'You shall love your neighbor and hate your enemy.' But I say to you** [as the spiritual Lawgiver], **love your enemies, bless those who curse you, do good to those who hate you, and pray for those who despitefully use you and persecute you, so that you yourselves may be *the* children of your Father Who *is* in heaven;** for He causes His sun to rise on *the* evil and *on the* good, and sends rain on *the* just and *on the* unjust. For if you love those who love you, what reward do you have? Do not the tax collectors practice the same *thing?* And if you salute your brethren only, what have you done *that is* extraordinary? Do not the tax collectors practice the same *thing?* Therefore, you shall be perfect, even as your Father Who *is* in heaven is perfect" (Matt. 5:43-48).

When Jesus was dying on the cross, He set the perfect example of loving His enemies and praying for those who despitefully used Him. Notice Jesus' prayer for them as He suffered agony and ignominy at their hands: "Then Jesus said, 'Father, forgive them, for they do not know what they are doing' " (Luke 23:34).

In the Sermon on the Mount, Jesus also taught the spiritual meaning and application of the Seventh Commandment: "Thou shalt not commit adultery." Notice how Jesus magnified this commandment: "You have heard that it was said to those *in* ancient *times*, 'You shall not commit adultery.' **But I say to you** [as the spiritual Lawgiver], **everyone who looks upon a woman to lust after her has already committed adultery with her in his heart**" (Matt. 5:27-28).

Jesus made the Seventh Commandment far more binding than the letter of the law. From the time that Jesus Christ taught the spiritual meaning of this commandment, every individual has been held accountable for his or her thoughts of adultery, whether or not the physical act was committed. Jesus Christ magnified the Seventh Commandment by revealing its full spiritual meaning and application. An examination of the following teachings in the Sermon on the Mount, as recorded in Matthew 5-7, will show that Jesus revealed the full spiritual meaning of all the laws and commandments of God.

Applying the Spirit of the Law
Does Not Nullify the Letter

More than thirty years after Jesus delivered the Sermon on the Mount, the apostle James wrote an epistle in which he expounded on the spiritual meaning of the commandments of God. In his epistle, James shows that Jesus' teachings concerning the spirit of the law did not eliminate the need to obey the letter of the law. James explains that Jesus' command to "love your neighbor as yourself" requires us to live in obedience to the commandments of God. James specifically refers to the Sixth and Seventh Commandments, and makes it very clear that to break any of God's commandments is sin: "**If you are truly keeping** *the* **Royal Law according to the scripture**, 'You shall love your neighbor as yourself,' you are doing well. But if you have respect of persons, **you are practicing sin, being convicted by the law as transgressors; for** *if* **anyone keeps the whole law, but sins in one** *aspect*, **he becomes guilty of all**. For He Who said, 'You shall not commit adultery,' also said, 'You shall not commit murder.' Now if you do not commit adultery, but you commit murder, you have become a transgressor of *the* law. In this manner speak and in this manner behave: as those who are about to be judged by *the* law of freedom" (James 2:8-12).

When we study the writings of the apostles in the New Testament, there is no question that they taught the full, spiritual meaning of the laws and commandments of God, exactly as Jesus did. Never at any time did they write or teach that Jesus Christ came to abolish the laws of God. The words of James leave no doubt whatsoever. He wrote, "Whoever shall keep the whole law, but sin in one aspect, becomes guilty of all." There is nothing in the apostle James' statement which remotely hints that the laws of God were abolished when Jesus died on the cross. In writing these words many years after the death and resurrection of Jesus Christ, James confirms that Jesus did not "do away with" the laws of God. James makes it explicitly clear that Christians are obligated to keep the commandments of God.

The apostle John, who outlived all the other apostles, also taught obedience to the laws and commandments of God. In the last decade of the first century, John wrote his Gospel, three epistles, and the book of Revelation. In his first epistle, he wrote most emphatically that obedience to the commandments of God is the standard that separates the true followers of Jesus Christ from those who merely profess His name. Notice: "**And by this** *standard* **we know that we know Him: if we keep His commandments. The one who says, 'I know Him,' and does not keep His commandments, is a liar, and the truth is not in him.** On the other hand, *if* anyone is keeping His word, truly in this one the love of God is being perfected [*made complete*]. By this *means* we know that we are in Him. Anyone who claims to dwell in Him is obligating himself also to walk even as He Himself walked" (I John 2:3-6).

John makes it very clear that those who truly believe in Jesus Christ will be walking as Jesus walked. They will be keeping the commandments of God, as Jesus did, and as He taught others to do (John 15:10, Matt. 19:17-19). Anyone who professes to believe in Jesus Christ but does not keep the commandments of God is a liar, according to the New Testament scriptures. For a minister or teacher to claim that the laws and commandments of God have been abolished is a blatant denial of the true teachings of Jesus Christ and His apostles, which are preserved in the New Testament. True Christians need to be on guard against such "workers of lawlessness," who preach against the laws of God and condemn commandment keeping.

As the apostle John shows, those who keep God's commandments are not under condemnation but can approach God with confidence, knowing that He will hear and answer their prayers: "Beloved, if our hearts do not condemn us, *then* we have confidence toward God. And whatever we may ask we receive from Him **because we keep His commandments and practice those things that are pleasing in His sight**" (I John 3:21-22).

The New Testament does not support the widely accepted teaching that commandment keeping is contrary to faith. Rather, the words of John show that keeping the commandments of God is a sign of true faith and the love that God imparts through the indwelling of His Spirit: "And this is His commandment: that we **believe on the name of His Son Jesus Christ**, and that we **love one another** [fulfilling the Royal Law by keeping God's commandments], exactly as He gave commandment to us. And **the one who keeps His commandments is dwelling in Him, and He in him; and by this we know that He is dwelling in us: by the Spirit which He has given to us**" (verses 23-24).

Mainstream Christianity ignores these inspired New Testament scriptures and teaches that loving God and one another eliminates the need to keep God's commandments. Again John exposes the error in this theology. John points out that obedience to God's commandments is the very standard by which love for God and His children is measured: "**By this** *standard* **we know that we love the children of God: when we love God and keep His commandments. For this is the love of God: that we keep His commandments; and His commandments are not burdensome**" (I John 5:2-3).

The Scriptural truth is this: If we love Jesus Christ and God the Father, we will be motivated to keep the commandments of God. We will desire to keep His commandments in the spirit of the law as an outward manifestation of our love for Him. Those who profess to love God, but refuse to keep His commandments, do not understand the love of God. They are being led by their own human emotions and not by the love that God imparts to His children through the gift of the Holy Spirit. Emotional feelings cannot be substituted for keeping the commandments of God. Those who claim to love God, but are practicing lawlessness, are deceiving themselves.

Jesus Christ specifically instructs those who love Him to keep His commandments: **"If you love Me, keep the commandments—namely, My commandments….The one who has My commandments and is keeping them, that is the one who loves Me; and the one who loves Me shall be loved by My Father, and I will love him and will manifest Myself to him….If anyone loves Me, he will keep My word; and My Father will love him, and We will come to him and make Our abode with him. The one who does not love Me does not keep My words; and the word that you hear is not Mine, but the Father's, Who sent Me"** (John 14:15, 21-24).

Jesus Christ left no room for doubt or misinterpretation. If you love Him, you will keep His commandments. If you do not keep His words, you do not love Him. Unless you are keeping His commandments, any profession of faith and love toward Jesus Christ and God the Father is empty and vain.

Jesus Christ set the perfect example of true godly love by keeping all the commandments of God in the full spirit of the law. Before His death, He delivered a new command to His disciples—that they follow His example by practicing the same love that He had manifested during His life with them on earth: "A new commandment I give to you: that you love one another in the same way that I have loved you, that *is how* you are to love one another. By this shall everyone know that you are My disciples—if you love one another….**As the Father has loved Me, I also have loved you; live in My love. If you keep My commandments, you shall live in My love; just as I have kept My Father's commandments and live in His love**. These things I have spoken to you, in order that My joy may dwell in you, and *that* your joy may be full. **This is My commandment, that you love one another, as I have loved you"** (John 13:34-35; 15:9-12).

Jesus Christ taught His followers to obey all the commandments of God in the full spirit of the law, as He did. Jesus magnified the laws of God by revealing their full spiritual meaning. Jesus Christ, as the spiritual Lawgiver, made the laws and commandments of God far more binding by setting a higher, spiritual standard of obedience for Christians under the New Covenant.

Jesus Brought the Physical Rituals of the Law to Completion

The second meaning of the Greek word πληροω *pleeroo,* translated, "to fulfill," in Matthew 5:17, is, "to complete," or, "bring to completion." Jesus Christ came to bring the animal sacrifices and other temple rituals and laws for the Aaronic priesthood to completion. Through His death, He ended the Old Covenant, which had imposed the physical requirements of these laws. In its place, He established the New Covenant, replacing the old requirements of the law with a higher spiritual application.

The laws concerning the animal sacrifices were brought to completion through the superior sacrifice of Jesus Christ. The sacrifice of Himself as the Lamb of God, "Who takes away the sin of the world," superseded and replaced all the animal sacrifices and other physical rituals and ceremonies that were performed at the temple of God in Jerusalem. The apostle Paul confirms the completion of the animal sacrifices and the temple rituals through the one perfect sacrifice of Jesus Christ: "For this reason, when He comes into the world, He says, 'Sacrifice and offering You did not desire, but You have prepared a body for Me. You did not delight in burnt offerings and *sacrifices* for sin. Then said I, "Lo, I come (*as* it is written of Me in *the* scroll of *the* book) to do Your will, O God." ' In the saying above, *He said*, '**Sacrifice and offering and burnt offerings and** *sacrifices* **for sin (which are offered according to the law) You did not desire nor delight in**'; then He said, '**Lo, I come to do Your will, O God.**' He takes away the first *covenant* in order that He may establish the second *covenant*; by Whose will we are sanctified through the offering of the body of Jesus Christ once for all. **Now every high priest** [of the order of Aaron] **stands ministering day by day, offering the same sacrifices repeatedly, which are never able to remove sins; but He, after offering one sacrifice for sins for ever, sat down at** *the* **right hand of God**" (Heb. 10:5-12).

The spiritual priesthood of Jesus Christ was effective immediately after He ascended to heaven and sat down at the right hand of God. Although His death had completed the animal sacrifices and temple rituals which were required under the Old Covenant, the priesthood continued to carry out these functions until the temple was destroyed. With the destruction of the temple in 70 AD, the priesthood of Aaron and the Levites came to an end. There was no need for a physical priesthood on earth because Jesus Christ was serving as High Priest in heaven above, making intercession for sin before God the Father. The spiritual priesthood of Jesus Christ superseded the priesthood of Aaron. The New Covenant has a greater High Priest—the resurrected Jesus Christ—to make intercession for the people of God and to propitiate their sins before God the Father.

In the same way, the spiritual temple in heaven has superseded the physical temple that was on earth. Under the New Covenant, true believers now have direct access through prayer to the throne of God the Father in heaven above. Jesus Christ sits at the right hand of God the Father, where He carries out His spiritual work as High Priest: " '**This** *is* **the covenant that I will establish with them after those days, says** *the* **Lord: I will give My laws into their hearts, and I will inscribe them in their minds** [far from abolishing His laws]; **and their sins and lawlessness I will not remember ever again.**' **Now where remission of these** *is***, it is** **no longer** *necessary to offer* **sacrifices for sin.** Therefore, brethren, having confidence to enter into the *true* holiest by the blood of Jesus, by a new and living way, which He consecrated for us through the veil (that is, His flesh), and *having* a great High Priest over the house of God, let us approach *God* with a true heart, with full conviction of faith, our hearts having been purified from a wicked conscience, and our bodies having been washed with pure water" (Heb. 10:16-22).

True worshipers of God need no priesthood to intercede for them in an earthly temple because they have direct access to the throne of God the Father in His heavenly temple, where Jesus Christ intercedes as High Priest. In addition, each one who receives the Holy Spirit in his or her mind as a begettal from God the Father becomes part of the temple of God. As the apostle Paul shows, God is now building a spiritual temple within fleshly human beings through the indwelling of His Spirit: "**Don't you understand that you are God's temple and** *that* **the Spirit of God is dwelling in**

you? If anyone defiles the temple of God, God shall destroy him because **the temple of God is holy, which temple you are**" (I Cor. 3:16-17).

Isaiah prophesied of the spiritual temple that God is building: "For thus saith the high and lofty One [God the Father] that inhabiteth eternity, whose name is Holy; I dwell in the high and holy *place* [the holy of holies in heaven], with him also *that is* of a contrite and humble spirit, to revive the spirit of the humble, and revive the heart of the contrite ones" (Isa. 57:15, *KJV*).

This spiritual temple is composed of all true believers, both Jews and Gentiles: "For through Him we both have *direct* access by one Spirit to the Father. So then, you are no longer aliens and foreigners; but *you are* **fellow citizens with the saints, and** *are* **of the household of God. You are being built up on the foundation of the apostles and prophets. Jesus Christ Himself being** *the* **chief Cornerstone in Whom all the building, being conjointly fitted together, is increasing into a holy temple in** *the* **Lord; in Whom you also are being built together for a habitation of God in** *the* **Spirit**" (Eph. 2:18-22).

The need for the earthly temple in Jerusalem was fulfilled and brought to completion by the sacrifice of Jesus Christ, which ended the Old Covenant and the need for a physical priesthood. Under the New Covenant, the spiritual temple of God in heaven, where Jesus Christ is High Priest, has superseded the physical temple of God on earth. Through the intercession of Jesus Christ, each believer becomes a temple for God's Holy Spirit, and the collective body of believers is built up as a holy temple in the Lord.

Jesus Brought the Circumcision of the Flesh to Completion

When Jesus brought the Old Covenant to an end, the requirement for circumcision of the flesh was superseded by spiritual circumcision of the heart. The apostle Paul makes this very clear: "For he is not a Jew who *is one* outwardly, neither *is* that circumcision which *is* external in *the* flesh; rather, he *is* a Jew who *is one* inwardly, and circumcision *is* of *the* heart, in *the* spirit *and* not in *the* letter; whose praise *is* not from men but from God" (Rom. 2:28-29).

Under the New Covenant, God does not require physical circumcision. Rather, the spiritual circumcision of the heart has superseded the circumcision of the flesh. Spiritual circumcision brings conversion of the mind and heart, which physical circumcision in the flesh could never accomplish. To be circumcised in the heart, a person must repent of his or her sins and be baptized by full immersion in water. The act of baptism is a type of circumcision because the sins of the flesh are removed. Then, through the laying on of hands, the believer receives the Holy Spirit, converting the heart and mind. The apostle Paul describes the spiritual circumcision that takes place at baptism: "For in Him [Jesus Christ] dwells all the fullness of the Godhead bodily; and you are complete in Him, Who is the Head of all principality and power; in Whom **you have also been circumcised with** *the* **circumcision not made by hands, in putting off the body of the sins of the flesh by the circumcision of Christ; having been buried with Him in baptism**, by which you have also been raised with *Him* through the inner working of God, Who raised Him from the dead. For you, who were *once* dead in *your* sins and in the uncircumcision of your flesh, He has *now* made alive with Him, having forgiven you all trespasses" (Col. 2:9-13).

Paul understood very clearly that the Gentile believers did not need to be circumcised in the flesh because they had received spiritual circumcision through faith in Jesus Christ. The spiritual circumcision of the heart has superseded the physical circumcision of the flesh. Likewise, all the animal sacrifices that were required for sin were superseded by Jesus Christ's sacrifice once for all time. The physical priesthood of Aaron was replaced by the spiritual priesthood of Jesus Christ. The temple of God in heaven has superseded the physical temple on earth, which was only a copy of the heavenly one. When Jesus Christ brought the physical rituals of the Old Covenant to completion, He did not abolish the law. Rather, the physical foretypes of the Old Covenant were superseded by the spiritual fulfillment of the New Covenant.

Other Laws That Have Been Transferred to the New Covenant

Under the Old Covenant, God gave authority to the priests and Levites, who served at the altar, to collect tithes and offerings from the children of Israel. Under the New Covenant, there is no priesthood of men but only one High Priest, Jesus Christ, Who is "a high priest forever after the order of Melchisedec." The apostle Paul explains that Melchisedec was Priest of God at Jerusalem in the days of Abraham, long before the Old Covenant was established. In describing how Abraham paid tithes to Melchisedec, Paul reveals that He was the one Who later came to earth as Jesus Christ: "For on one hand, those from among the sons of Levi who receive the priesthood are commanded by the law to collect tithes from the people—that is, *from* their brethren—even though they are *all* descended from Abraham; but on the other hand, He [Jesus Christ, Who was Melchisedec of the Old Testament] Who was not descended from them received tithes from Abraham, and blessed him who had the promises. Now it is beyond all doubt *that* the inferior *one* is blessed by the superior *one*.

"And in the first case, men who die receive tithes; but in the other case, *He received tithes* of *Whom it is* witnessed that He lives *forever*. And in one sense, Levi, who receives tithes, also gave tithes through Abraham; for he was still in his forefather's loins when Melchisedec met him. Therefore, if perfection was indeed *possible* through the Levitical priesthood—for *the* law *that* the people had received *was based* on it—what further need *was there for* another priest to arise according to the order of Melchisedec, and not to be named after the order of Aaron? For since the priesthood has changed, it is obligatory *that* a change of *the* law [for the priesthood and the receiving of tithes and offerings] also take place; because the one of Whom these things are said belongs to another tribe, from which no one was appointed to serve at the altar" (Heb. 7:5-13).

As Paul shows, the entire Levitical priesthood has been superseded by one immortal High Priest, Jesus Christ, who is of the order of Melchisedec. There is no longer a priesthood on earth ministering at the altar in the temple of God at Jerusalem. However, there is still a need to teach the true worship of God, and to preach and publish the Word of God as a witness to the world. Those who repent and believe the gospel must be taught the way of eternal life that Jesus Christ committed to His disciples. It is for this reason that Jesus Christ sent them forth as apostles to the world, and it is for this reason that He raised up His church. Within the church, He has provided a ministry that is able to teach the Word of God and to preach the gospel to the world. Moreover, He has provided a way to support the work of preaching the gospel and teaching the brethren of Jesus Christ. Instead of the priests and Levites at the temple collecting tithes and offerings, the authority to receive tithes and offerings has been transferred to the ministry of Jesus Christ by the command of the Lord. The apostle Paul makes this very clear: "Don't you know that those who are laboring *in* the sacred things of the temple live *of the things* of the temple, *and* those who are ministering at the altar are partakers with the altar? **In the same way also, the Lord did command that those who preach the gospel are to live of the gospel**" (I Cor. 9:13-14).

The command of God under the Old Covenant concerning the tithes and offerings that the children of Israel were to give to the priests and Levites was brought to completion. Instead of abolishing the laws of tithes and offerings, Jesus Christ transferred the authority to receive tithes and offerings to the ministers of the gospel, who are under His authority as the High Priest and Mediator of the New Covenant.

How Did Jesus Christ Fulfill the Prophets?

Jesus also said that He had come to fulfill the prophets. How did Jesus fulfill the prophets? During His life in the flesh, all the Old Testament prophecies concerning His first coming were fulfilled. These prophecies included His miraculous conception and birth from the virgin Mary, the flight to Egypt to escape Herod, the return to Galilee and dwelling in Nazareth, the announcing of His ministry by John the Baptist, the healings and mighty works during His ministry, the preaching of the gospel throughout the land of Judea and Galilee, the persecution and suffering that followed, His death by crucifixion, the place of His burial, and the time of the resurrection. Most of the prophecies that were fulfilled concern His suffering and death on the Passover day. (See the section *Twenty-eight Prophecies Fulfilled On the Crucifixion Day* on pages 268-273.)

Although nearly two thousand years have passed since these prophecies were completed, all the prophecies about His second coming have yet to be fulfilled. There are a great number of prophecies in both the Old Testament and the New Testament that are awaiting fulfillment. Every prophecy in the Word of God will be fulfilled in its set time as determined by God the Father. Jesus Christ did not abolish or set aside a single prophecy or even a single word of the Old Testament scriptures. Remember what Jesus said concerning the Scriptures: "For truly I say to you, **until the heaven and the earth shall pass away, one jot or one tittle shall in no way pass from the Law until everything has been fulfilled**" (Matt. 5:18).

Jesus gave an absolute guarantee that all the prophecies of Scripture will be fulfilled in their time: "Now learn this parable from the fig tree: When its branches have already become tender, and it puts forth its leaves, you know that summer *is* near. In like manner also, when you see all these things [the events prophesied for the end time taking place], know that it [the second return of Jesus Christ] is near, even at *the* doors. **Truly I say to you, this [end time] generation shall in no wise pass away until all these things have taken place. The heaven and the earth shall pass away, but My words shall never pass away.** But concerning that day, and the hour, no one knows, not even the angels of heaven, but My Father only" (Matt. 24:32-36).

According to the words of Jesus Christ, all the prophecies that are recorded in Scripture will be fulfilled at the time that God has ordained. Jesus did not come to abolish the words of the prophets, but to fulfill them. As He came in the flesh to fulfill the prophecies of a Savior, so He will return in glory to fulfill the prophecies of the coming King Who will bring the government of God to earth.

The Commandments of God Are To Be Taught and Practiced Under the New Covenant

In the Sermon on the Mount, Jesus made it absolutely clear that the commandments of God are in force under the New Covenant: "**Therefore, whoever shall break one of these least commandments, and shall teach men so, shall be called least in the kingdom of** [from] **heaven; but whoever shall practice and teach** *them***, this one shall be called great in the kingdom of heaven**" (Matt. 5:19).

Which commandments of God are rejected and considered the least by mainstream Christianity today? The two that are considered the least are the Fourth Commandment and the Second Commandment. As strange as it may seem, many of those who reject these commandments will profess to keep the other commandments and claim that they are doing the will of God. But as the apostle James shows, breaking even one of the commandments of God is sin, and brings the same condemnation as breaking them all.

Let us examine the two commandments that are considered the least by mainstream Christianity, beginning with the Fourth Commandment: "**Remember the sabbath day, to keep it holy**. Six days shalt thou labor, and do all thy work: but the seventh day *is* the sabbath of the LORD thy God: *in it* thou shalt not do any work, thou, nor thy son, nor thy daughter, thy manservant, nor thy maidservant, nor thy cattle, nor thy stranger that *is* within thy gates: **for** *in* **six days the LORD made heaven and earth, the sea, and all that in them** *is***, and rested the seventh day: wherefore the LORD blessed the sabbath day, and hallowed it**" (Ex. 20:8-11, *KJV*).

Nowhere in the entire Bible do we find a single scripture that changes the day of rest and worship from the seventh day of the week to Sunday, the first day of the week. Several scriptures are often used by Sunday keepers to support their belief that Christians should worship on the first day of the week. However, when those scriptures are correctly understood and interpreted, it is clear that Jesus Christ did not change the Sabbath from the seventh day of the week to the first day of the week.

Jesus said, "The Sabbath was made **for man**…" (Mark 2:27). Contrary to the teachings of mainstream theologians, God did not command Sabbath keeping for the Jews only. In the beginning, God created the Sabbath day, hallowing the seventh day as the weekly day of worship, when there was not a single Jew on earth. The only humans at that time were Adam and Eve, the progenitors of all mankind. It was for all humanity that God blessed and sanctified the seventh day, making it holy: "Thus the heavens and the earth were finished, and all the host of them. And on the seventh day God ended His work which He had made; and He rested on the seventh day from all His work which He had made. And God blessed the seventh day, and sanctified it:

because that in it He had rested from all His work which God created and made" (Gen. 2:1-3, *KJV*).

The seventh day was sanctified at the creation of the world. God established that day as a time for rest and worship from the beginning. He sanctified it, and blessed it, and rested on it, setting the example for mankind. Down through the ages, the record of this act of God has been preserved in the book of Genesis, one of the books of the Law. Remember what Jesus Christ declared concerning the Law: "For truly I say to you, **until the heaven and the earth shall pass away, one jot or one tittle shall in no way pass from the Law until everything has been fulfilled**" (Matt. 5:18).

Since God created time, and time is measured by the movement of the earth in relationship to the heavens, time will exist as long as the heavens and the earth exist. As long as the heavens and the earth exist, the seventh-day Sabbath will not pass from the Law. Consequently, the Fourth Commandment is still in force and remains binding on all mankind.

Contrary to what mainstream Christianity may teach or what people may practice, Sunday has never been and will never be the Lord's day. The seventh day of the week, called Saturday today, is the Lord's Sabbath day. Jesus Christ emphatically declared that He is Lord of the Sabbath day: "And He said to them, 'The Sabbath was made for man, *and* not man for the Sabbath; therefore, the Son of man is Lord even of the Sabbath' " (Mark 2:27-28). **Jesus Himself declared that He is Lord of the Sabbath—the seventh day of the week. Therefore, the Sabbath day is the Lord's day—not Sunday.**

Some have misconstrued Jesus' declaration that He is Lord of the Sabbath as signifying that He was abolishing the Sabbath by His authority. This interpretation of Jesus' words is completely unfounded. Among the scholars who understand the true meaning of these scriptures are the writers of *The Anchor Bible Dictionary*. Notice what they have written about these critical verses: "At times Jesus is interpreted to have abrogated or suspended the sabbath commandment on the basis of the controversies brought about by sabbath healings and other acts. Careful analysis of the respective passages does not seem to give credence to this interpretation. The action of plucking the ears of grain on the sabbath by the disciples is particularly important in this matter. Jesus makes a foundational pronouncement at that time in a chiastically structured statement of antithetic parallelism: 'The sabbath was made for man and not man for the sabbath' (Mark 2:27). The disciples' act of plucking the grain infringed against the rabbinic *halakhah* of minute causistry in which it was forbidden to reap, thresh, winnow, and grind on the sabbath (*Sabb.* 7.2). Here again rabbinic sabbath *halakhah* is rejected, as in other sabbath conflicts. Jesus reforms the sabbath and restores its rightful place as designed in creation, where sabbath is made for all mankind and not specifically for Israel, as claimed by normative Judaism (*cf. Jub.* 2:19-20, see D.3). The subsequent logion, 'The Son of Man is Lord even of the sabbath' (Mark 2:28; Matt. 12:8; Luke 6:5), indicates that man-made Sabbath *halakhah* does not rule the sabbath, but that the Son of Man as Lord determines the true meaning of the sabbath. The sabbath activities of Jesus are neither hurtful provocations nor mere protests against rabbinic legal restrictions, but are part of Jesus' essential proclamation of the inbreaking of the kingdom of God in which man is taught the original meaning of the sabbath as the recurring weekly proleptic 'day of the Lord' in which God manifests his healing and saving rulership over man" (vol. 5, pp. 854-55).

As these scholars show, the Gospel accounts do not support the widespread belief that Jesus abolished the Sabbath day. Rather, as the Lord of the Sabbath, He taught the true meaning of the Sabbath day and set the example for its proper observance. His apostles continued to keep the Sabbath and to teach the early believers to keep it, as Paul's epistle to the Hebrews clearly demonstrates. The apostle Paul wrote this epistle in 61 AD, more than thirty years after the beginning of the New Testament church. In his epistle, Paul makes it absolutely clear that the seventh-day Sabbath had not been abolished. At that time, there were false ministers who were teaching that Sunday, the first day of the week, had replaced the Sabbath. To counter these false teachings, Paul gave the brethren a sober warning that to reject the Sabbath and neglect to rest and worship God was sin, just as it was for the children of Israel in the wilderness:

"For He spoke in a certain place about the seventh *day* in this manner: '**And God rested on the seventh day from all His works**'; and again concerning this: 'If they shall enter into My rest—' consequently, since it remains *for* some to enter into it, and those who had previously heard the gospel did not enter in because of disobedience, again He marks out a certain day, 'Today,' saying in David after so long a time (exactly as it has been quoted *above*), 'Today, if you will hear *His* voice, harden not your hearts.' For if Joshua had given them rest, He would not have spoken *long* afterwards of another day. **There remains, therefore, Sabbath keeping for the people of God**" (Heb. 4:4-9). Paul did not write, "There remains Sabbath keeping for the Jews." He clearly declared, "There remains Sabbath keeping for the people of God." The people of God include the Gentiles as well as the Jews (I Pet. 2:10 and Eph. 2:11-19).

Many ministers and theologians have applied the opposite meaning to Hebrews 4:9. They have completely misinterpreted the King James translation of this verse, which reads, "There remaineth therefore a rest to the people of God." They teach that Christians are no longer required to observe the Sabbath because Jesus Christ has given them "rest" by "fulfilling the law" for them and thereby releasing them from commandment keeping. Such reasoning is completely false. Jesus did not fulfill the commandments of God in order to release us from the obligation to keep them, but to set the example for us (I Pet. 2:21-22, I John 3:4).

When we understand the meaning of the Greek text, there is no question that the New Testament upholds the authority of the Fourth Commandment for Christians today. The Greek word that is used in Hebrews 4:9 is σαββατισμος, *sabbatismos,* which means "Sabbath rest, Sabbath observance" (Arndt and Gingrich, *A Greek-English Lexicon of the New Testament*). This definition of the Greek word, *sabbatismos,* is confirmed by other historical works: "The words 'sabbath rest' translate the GK noun *sabbatismos,* a unique word in the NT. This term appears also in Plutarch (*Superset. 3 [Moralia 166a]*) for sabbath observance, and in four postcanonical Christian writings which are not dependent on Heb. 4:9" (*The Anchor Bible Dictionary*, vol. 5, p. 856).

The Greek word, σαββατισμος, *sabbatismos,* is a noun. The verb form of the word is σαββατιςω, *sabbatizo,* which means, "to keep the Sabbath" (Arndt and Gingrich, *A Greek-English Lexicon of the New Testament*). The meaning of *sabbatizo* is confirmed by its use in the Septuagint, a Greek translation of the Old Testament which dates from the third century BC. It is called the Septuagint, meaning "Seventy," because the first five books were translated by seventy scholars who were Greek-speaking Jews in Alexandria, Egypt. The Septuagint was used by the Jews in synagogues throughout the Roman Empire, and by the Greek-speaking Jewish and Gentile converts in the early New Testament churches.

The apostle Paul quotes exclusively from the Septuagint in his epistle to the Hebrews. When Paul used the Greek word σαββατισμος, *sabbatismos,* in Hebrews 4:9, he knew that the meaning of this word was well known to the Greek-speaking believers of that day. The verb form σαββατιςω, *sabbatizo,* was used in the Septuagint, which was as familiar to the believers of New Testament times as the King James Bible is to Christians today.

A Greek-English Lexicon of the Septuagint defines σαββατιςω, *sabbatizo* as "to keep sabbath, to rest" (Lust, Eynikel, Hauspie). The use of the verb *sabbatizo* in Leviticus 23:32 in the Septuagint leaves no room to mistake its meaning. Here is the English translation of this verse in the Septuagint: "It [the Day of Atonement] shall be a holy sabbath [literally, "a Sabbath of Sabbaths"] to you; and ye shall humble your souls, from the ninth day of the month: from evening to evening **shall ye keep your sabbaths**" (Brenton, *The Septuagint With Apocrypha*).

The clause "shall ye keep your sabbaths" is translated from the Greek words σαββατιετε τα σαββατα, *sabbatieite ta sabbata,* which literally mean, "You shall **sabbathize** the Sabbaths." The Greek verb σαββατιετε, *sabbatieite,* which means "ye shall keep," is the second person plural form of the verb σαββατιςω, *sabbatizo.* Since the verb *sabbatizo* means "to keep the Sabbath," this verb applies not only to the weekly Sabbath and the annual Sabbaths of God, but also to God's command for the seventh-year rest from farming the land. Throughout the Septuagint, the verb σαββατιςω, *sabbatizo* is used in relation to Sabbath keeping and Sabbath rest only.

In accord with this definition, the KJV translates σαββατιετε, *sabbatieite* in Leviticus 23:32 as "shall ye celebrate your sabbath." There is no question that this form of the Greek verb *sabbatizo* is specifically referring to Sabbath observance. This meaning applies equally to the noun form σαββατισμος, *sabbatismos,* which we find in Paul's epistle to the Hebrews. The fact that Paul uses the Septuagint translation in this epistle confirms that the meaning of the word σαββατισμος, *sabbatismos* in Hebrews 4:9 is in complete accord with the meaning of *sabbatieite* in Leviticus 23:32. Paul is clearly upholding the observance of the Sabbath, the seventh day of the week.

The use of the Greek word *sabbatismos* in Hebrews 4:9 clearly shows that the teaching that the Fourth Commandment has been abolished is a false interpretation and doctrine. As the context of this verse shows, the observance of the seventh day as a day of rest and worship is as binding for the people of God today as it was for Israel of old. In addition to the weekly Sabbath, the annual holy days that God commanded, which are also called Sabbaths, are included in the Fourth Commandment. In the same manner as true believers are commanded to keep the seventh-day Sabbath, they are also commanded to observe the annual holy days of God. The early New Testament churches kept the holy days of God, as determined by the calculated Hebrew Calendar. The apostle Paul kept the holy days and commanded Gentile converts to keep them (I Cor. 5:7-8). None of the apostles or the early converts to Christianity observed the pagan holidays that are now called Christmas and Easter. These holidays, which originated in sun worship, were later adopted into Christianity through the influence of the Roman church. They became false substitutes for the annual holy days that are commanded by God, just as Sunday has become a false substitute for the weekly Sabbath. (If the reader desires to know more about the Sabbath and the holy days of God, please write to the publisher at the address in the front of the book.)

The Second Commandment: As the Roman church succeeded in subverting the observance of the Fourth Commandment by Christians, so it succeeded in subverting the observance of the Second Commandment, which prohibits the use of idols and images in worship. There is no ambiguity in the wording of this command of God: **"Thou shalt not make unto thee any graven image, or any likeness *of any thing* that *is* in heaven above, or that *is* in the earth beneath, or that *is* in the water under the earth: thou shalt not bow down thyself to them, nor serve them: for I the LORD thy God *am* a jealous God, visiting the iniquity of the fathers upon the children unto the third and fourth *generation* of them that hate Me; and showing mercy unto thousands of them that love Me, and keep My commandments"** (Ex. 20:4-6, *KJV*).

Because this commandment is so clear in its condemnation of idols and images, the Roman church has removed it from their listing of the Ten Commandments in all their catechisms. In order to make up for the missing commandment, they have split the Tenth Commandment into two commandments. Although they have officially removed the Second Commandment from their catechisms, because they cannot justify their unlawful use of idols and images, the full text of the Second Commandment remains in their approved Bibles as a testimony against their idolatry.

The Second Commandment makes it absolutely clear that God abhors the use of idols and images of any kind by His people. Yet the churches of professing Christianity are filled with idols, images and pictures. But no church, however great it may be in the world, can justify the use of idols and images in its worship when God has strictly forbidden this practice. God the Father and Jesus Christ cannot be worshiped through idols or images. Nor will God tolerate the use of images to worship and venerate other persons or beings. The worship of Mary and the veneration of the apostles and other saints has no place in true Christianity. All such worship is strictly forbidden by the Second Commandment. It is blatant idolatry to venerate any person or being in addition to or in place of God. The apostle Paul warned the believers of his day that those who take part in idolatry will suffer the judgment of God, as did the Israelites of old who committed this sin. Paul wrote to the believers at Corinth, who were being tempted to return to their former idolatry, as Israel had returned to the idolatry of Egypt: **"Neither be idolaters**, as *were* some of them; as it is written, 'The people sat down to eat and to drink, and rose up to play.' Neither should we commit sexual immorality, as some of them committed, and twenty-three thousand were destroyed in one day. Neither should we tempt Christ, as some of them also tempted *Him*, and were killed by serpents....**Therefore, my beloved, flee from idolatry"** (I Cor. 10:7-9, 14).

Paul's warning to the Corinthians makes it clear that the Second Commandment is still in force. It is even more binding under the New Covenant than it was under the Old, because Jesus has magnified it by His example and His teaching. The worship of God in spirit and in truth requires loving God with the whole heart and mind. The true worship of God the Father and His Son Jesus Christ leaves no room in the heart and mind to worship others. As the Scriptures show, idolatry begins in the mind and heart. Notice the words of God in the book of Ezekiel: "Then came certain of the elders of Israel unto me, and sat before me. And the word of the LORD came unto me, saying, '**Son of man, these men have set up their idols in their heart**, and put the stumblingblock of their iniquity before their face: should I be inquired of at all by them? Therefore speak unto them, and say unto them, "Thus saith the Lord GOD; **every man of the house of Israel that setteth up his idols in his heart, and putteth the stumblingblock of his iniquity before his face, and cometh to the prophet; I the LORD will answer him that cometh according to the multitude of his idols; that I may take the house of Israel in their own heart, because they are all estranged from me through their idols**."

" 'Therefore say unto the house of Israel, "Thus saith the Lord GOD; **repent, and turn** *yourselves* **from your idols; and turn away your faces from all your abominations**. For every one of the house of Israel, or of the stranger that sojourneth in Israel, which **separateth himself from Me, and setteth up his idols in his heart**, and putteth the stumblingblock of his iniquity before his face, and cometh to a prophet to inquire of him concerning Me; I the LORD will answer him by Myself: and I will set My face against that man, and will make him a sign and a proverb, and I will cut him off from the midst of My people; and ye shall know that *I am* the LORD" ' " (Ezek. 14:1-8, *KJV*).

Like Israel of old, the believers in the New Testament churches were drawn away from the true worship of God and led into idol worship. Images of pagan deities were introduced into the churches and palmed off as representations of Jesus' mother and His apostles. More and more images were added, each said to represent a chosen saint of God. But the apostle Paul reveals the true origin of these idols: "What then am I saying? That an idol is anything, or that which is sacrificed to an idol is anything? But **that which the Gentiles sacrifice, they sacrifice to demons, and not to God; and I do not wish you to have fellowship with demons. You cannot drink** *the* **cup of** *the* **Lord, and** *the* **cup of demons. You cannot partake of** *the* **table of** *the* **Lord, and** *the* **table of demons**" (I Cor. 10:19-21).

The apostle John understood the pagan origin of the images that were brought into the early churches, drawing many believers into a false worship. Toward the close of the first century, John wrote three different epistles to admonish the believers to remain faithful to the true worship of God. At the end of his first epistle, he commanded, "Little children, **keep yourselves from idols**" (I John 5:21).

There is no question that, in the Old Testament and the New Testament, any worship of idols and images is condemned. Those who teach and practice the use of idols and images to worship God are in direct defiance of the Second Commandment and will be rejected by Him. God the Father and Jesus Christ will not share Their glory and honor with an idol. Any attempt to worship God through the use of an idol, or physical object of any kind, including rosaries or prayer beads, is worshiping in vain. True worship requires loving God with the whole heart and mind, in spirit and in truth, leaving no room for reverence or devotion to images created by the imaginations and hands of men.

The Spirit and Intent of the Law and the Prophets

The purpose of the Law and the Prophets, and all the writings of the Old Testament, was to teach the people to love and worship God, and Him alone. Jesus Christ revealed the spirit and intent of the Law and the Prophets when He was asked which commandment was the greatest: "And one of them, a doctor of the law, questioned *Him*, tempting Him, and saying, 'Master, which commandment *is the* great commandment in the law?' And Jesus said to him, ' **"You shall love *the* Lord your God with all your heart, and with all your soul, and with all your mind." This is *the* first and greatest commandment; and *the* second *one is* like it: "You shall love your neighbor as yourself." On these two commandments hang all the Law and the Prophets"** ' "(Matt. 22:35-40).

Under the New Covenant, true worship and love toward God is made possible through the indwelling of the Holy Spirit, which enables the believer to reverence God and obey Him from the heart. Through faith in Jesus Christ and the indwelling of the Holy Spirit, the believer learns to obey every command of God in the full spirit and intent of the law, as magnified by Jesus Christ. This is the manner in which every true believer will be keeping the laws and commandments of God, because he or she loves God the Father and Jesus Christ with all the heart, mind, soul and strength. This righteousness, which is based on faith and love, far exceeds the righteousness of the scribes and Pharisees. Jesus said, "For I say to you, unless your righteousness shall exceed *the righteousness* of the scribes and Pharisees, there is no way *that* you shall enter into the kingdom of heaven" (Matt. 5:20).

The righteousness that exceeds the righteousness of the scribes and Pharisees is the righteousness of Jesus Christ, Who obeyed all of His Father's commandments in the full spirit and intent of the law. Through faith, His righteousness is imputed to each believer who loves God and keeps His commandments. This imputed righteousness is a gift that the believer receives through the abundance of the Father's grace. It is called "the righteousness of faith" because only through faith in Jesus Christ is it possible to partake of this righteousness.

The Righteousness of Faith of the True Believer

When a believer is justified from past sins through faith in the sacrifice of Jesus Christ, and is baptized by full immersion in water, he or she receives the gift of the Holy Spirit as a begettal from God the Father. Then the Father imputes to the believer the very righteousness of Jesus Christ, that "so also might the grace *of God* reign through righteousness unto eternal life through Jesus Christ our Lord" (Rom. 5:21).

The righteousness of Jesus Christ, which is imputed to the believer by God the Father, far exceeds the righteousness required by the letter of the law. His spiritual obedience was so perfect, pure and wholehearted that He always did the things that pleased God the Father. This perfect righteousness was accomplished through the power of the Holy Spirit, which Jesus received without measure from the Father.

By His personal example and His teachings, Jesus magnified the laws and commandments of God and revealed the fullness of their intent and meaning. He showed that the spirit of the law does not nullify the letter of the law but requires a fuller, spiritual obedience. This spiritual obedience is beyond the capacity of the natural mind and human will and can only be accomplished through Jesus Christ. The Scriptures reveal that when the believer is begotten with the Holy Spirit of God the Father, he or she begins to receive the very mind of Christ. With Christ's mind, the believer is strengthened to live by every word of God in the full spirit of the law. The apostle Paul describes this spiritual transformation in the mind as "Christ in you, the hope of glory" (Col. 1:27). Each believer begins to have the laws and commandments of God written upon his or her mind: "But He, after offering one sacrifice for sins for ever, sat down at *the* right hand of God. Since that time, He is waiting until His enemies are placed *as* a footstool for His feet. For by one offering He has obtained eternal perfection *for* those who are sanctified. And the Holy Spirit also bears witness to us; for after He had previously said, '**This *is* the covenant that I will establish with them after those days,' says *the* Lord: 'I will give My laws into their hearts, and I will inscribe them in their minds; and their sins and lawlessness I will not remember ever again'** " (Heb. 10:12-17).

Under the New Covenant, the laws and commandments of God are inscribed in the mind of each believer through the gift of the Holy Spirit, which gives the believer the power to bring forth the fruits of righteousness unto eternal life.

Rejecting the Commandments of God Is Lawlessness

In the Sermon on the Mount, Jesus left no doubt that the commandments of God are to be taught and practiced not only in the letter of the law but in the spirit of the law. Anyone who teaches that Jesus Christ abolished the laws and commandments of God is a liar. As He was completing the Sermon on the Mount, Jesus warned of false prophets who would teach that obedience to the commandments and laws of God is no longer required: "But beware of false prophets who come to you in sheep's clothing, for within *they* are ravening wolves....Therefore, you shall assuredly know them by their fruits. **Not everyone who says to Me, 'Lord, Lord,' shall enter into the kingdom of heaven; but the one who is doing the will of My Father, Who *is* in heaven. Many will say to Me in that day, 'Lord, Lord, did we not prophesy through Your name? And *did we not* cast out demons through Your name? And *did we not* perform many works of power through Your name?' And then I will confess to them, 'I never knew you. Depart from Me, you who work lawlessness'** " (Matt. 7:15, 20-23).

These prophets and teachers are not of God in spite of the fact that they use Jesus' name, and call Him their Lord, and even do wonderful works in His name. They present themselves as His ministers and preachers of truth, but in reality they are serving the god of this world, Satan the devil, who rejected the commandments of God from the beginning. Everyone who teaches disobedience to the laws and commandments of God is following in the steps of Satan, who was the first lawbreaker. That is why Jesus told the Pharisees that their father was the devil. While professing to teach and practice the laws and commandments of God, they were teaching and practicing their own religious laws and traditions in place of the commandments of God.

During His ministry, Jesus condemned the religious leaders of Judaism for their traditions, which they held in higher esteem than the laws and commandments of God. He made it clear that in observing their own human traditions, they were rejecting the commandments of God: "…The Pharisees and the scribes questioned Him, *saying*, 'Why don't Your disciples walk according to the tradition of the elders, but eat bread with unwashed hands?' And He answered *and* said to them, 'Well did Isaiah prophesy concerning you hypocrites, as it is written, **"This people honors me with their lips, but their hearts are far away from Me." But in vain do they worship Me, teaching *for* doctrine the commandments of men. For leaving the commandment of God, you hold fast the tradition of men,** *such as* **the washing of pots and cups; and you practice many other things like** *this*.'

"Then He said to them, '**Full well do you reject the commandment of God, so that you may observe your** *own* **tradition.** For Moses said, "Honor your father and your mother"; and, "The one who speaks evil of father or mother, let him be put to death." But you say, "If a man shall say to *his* father or mother, 'Whatever benefit you might receive from me *is* corban' (that is, *set aside as* a gift to God), he is not obligated to help his parents." **And you excuse him from doing anything for his father or his mother, nullifying the authority of the Word of God by your tradition which you have passed down; and you practice many** *traditions* **such as this**' " (Mark 7:5-13).

Most of the world's professing Christians have committed the same mistake as the Pharisaic Jews. Many church denominations teach that divine revelation is contained in church tradition as well as in Holy Scripture. In the majority of churches, the religious leaders elevate their traditions to a higher status than the Word of God. It is evident that they have done so with the Fourth Commandment. They have exalted their unscriptural tradition of Sunday-keeping above the Sabbath commandment of God. In rejecting His commandment to keep the Sabbath day holy, they have become lawbreakers in His eyes. According to Jesus' teaching, they are workers of lawlessness. Likewise, those churches that use any form of idols—including statues, pictures, relics, icons or other symbolic objects—are rejecting the Second Commandment for the sake of their tradition. Because they are breaking the commandment of God, they are guilty of practicing lawlessness.

In his first epistle, the apostle John clearly defines lawlessness: "Whosoever committeth sin transgresseth also the law, for sin is the transgression of the law" (I John 3:4, *KJV*). Although this is a correct translation, it does not convey the literal meaning of the Greek text. Here is a more precise translation of John's words: **"Everyone who practices sin is also practicing lawlessness, for sin is lawlessness"**.

To practice lawlessness is to live in a state of sin, committing sin as a habitual way of life. In other words, lawlessness is the habitual breaking of God's laws and commandments, which is sin. Religious leaders who teach and practice lawlessness appear to be righteous, because they use the names of God and Jesus Christ and often quote Scripture. However, they are not true servants of God because they reject His laws and commandments.

The apostle Jude, the brother of Jesus Christ, witnessed the rise of lawlessness among the churches of his day. Jude delivered an urgent plea to the believers to reject ungodly teachers of lawlessness, who were turning the grace of God into license to sin by preaching a false gospel of faith without obedience, and by replacing the commandments of God with traditions that originated in ancient paganism. Jude wrote: "Beloved, when personally exerting all *my* diligence to write to you concerning the common salvation, I was compelled to write to you, exhorting *you* to **fervently fight for the faith, which once for all *time* has been delivered to the saints. For certain men have stealthily crept in**; those who long ago have been written about, condemning *them* to this judgment. *They are* ungodly men, who are perverting the grace of our God, *turning it* into licentiousness, and are personally denying the only Lord God and our Lord Jesus Christ**" (Jude 3-4).

The apostle Peter also warned of false teachers who would reject the way of obedience to God's commandments, as taught and practiced by Jesus Christ: "But there were also false prophets among the people, as indeed **there will be false teachers among you, who will stealthily introduce destructive heresies, personally denying *the* Lord who bought them** [by rejecting His teachings]**, and bringing swift destruction upon themselves. And many people will follow** *as authoritative* [exalting church tradition] **their destructive ways;** *and* **because of them, the way of the truth will be blasphemed**" (II Pet. 2:1-2).

Those Who Reject the Commandments of God Are Judging the Law and the Lawgiver

Those who teach that the commandments of God have been abolished have presumptuously passed judgment on the laws of God and declared them to be null and void: "In fact, the whole law of Moses has been rendered inoperative. The New Testament message is clear for all who have 'ears to hear.' **The whole of the law of Moses has been rendered inoperative by the death of the Lord Jesus. The law, in its entirety, no longer has any immediate and forensic authority or jurisdiction whatsoever over anyone**....Christ is the complete end and fulfillment of all of the laws' 613 commandments, ending their jurisdiction over us completely" (Tardo, *Sunday Facts & Sabbath Fiction*, p. 26-27).

By nullifying the laws of God in this manner, the religious teachers of this world are denying the authority of God as Lawgiver. The apostle James condemns this ungodly attitude, which presumes to judge the laws that God has established for all mankind: "Brethren, do not talk against one another. The one who talks against a brother, and judges his brother, **is speaking against *the* law, and is judging the law. But if you judge *the* law, you are not a doer of *the* law; rather, *you are* a judge. *But* there is *only* one Lawgiver, Who has power to save and to destroy**. Who are you that you presume to judge another?" (James 4:11-12).

Those who judge the laws of God are, in fact, usurping the authority of God, Who is the only Lawgiver. To judge the laws and commandments of God and reject Him as Lawgiver is the epitome of lawlessness. This spirit of judging God and His laws is the spirit and attitude of Satan the devil, and the foundation of all religions that are based on the traditions and commandments of men. This form of religion is rooted in human self-righteousness, not in the righteousness that Jesus Christ taught and practiced.

The book of Job holds a lasting lesson for all who exalt their own righteousness above the righteousness of God. The ancient patriarch Job viewed himself as righteous because he continually offered sacrifices to God. However, he began to exalt himself and trust in his own righteousness, rather than trusting in God. He bragged and boasted of his own righteousness so much that God brought a series of grievous trials upon Job. After losing his children and all his possessions, he was smitten with boils from his head to his toes. When his trial was more than he could bear, three friends came to visit him, but they did not give him any comfort. His friends began to accuse him of evildoing and urged him to repent in order to escape further punishment from God. The more they condemned him, the more Job defended his own righteousness. He began to condemn God and accuse Him of being unjust and unrighteous in His acts. When he expressed a desire to plead his cause before God Himself, God responded by answering him in person: "Then answered the LORD unto Job out of the whirlwind, and said, 'Gird up thy loins now like a man: I will demand of thee, and declare thou unto Me. **Wilt thou also disannul My judgment? wilt thou condemn Me, that thou mayest be righteous?**' " (Job 40:6-8, *KJV*.)

These words of God also apply to the self-righteous attitude that the workers of lawlessness have toward God's laws and commandments. They disannul God's judgment by claiming that His holy, righteous and spiritual laws are evil and harsh, and that keeping them is a curse. In doing this, they are condemning God and going about to establish their own righteousness. Because they use the Scriptures and retain some of the commandments of God in their self-righteous religion, they appear to teach the way to salvation. But their self-righteous traditions and false grace will not bring salvation. As Job learned, God, and God alone, is Savior. He powerfully declared to Job that his own righteousness could never save him: "**Hast thou an arm like God? or canst thou thunder with a voice like Him? Deck thyself now** *with* **majesty and excellency; and array thyself with glory and beauty**. Cast abroad the rage of thy wrath: and behold everyone *that is* proud, and abase him. Look on every one *that is* proud, *and* bring him low; and tread down the wicked in their place. Hide them in the dust together; *and* bind their faces in secret. **Then will I also confess unto thee that thine own right hand can save thee**" (verses 9-14, *KJV*).

After hearing these words of God, Job abhorred himself for his sin of self-righteousness and repented to God "in dust and ashes" (Job 42:6). That is what professing Christians of this world need to do. They need to forsake the self-righteous traditions of men that they have been practicing and submit to the righteousness of God the Father and Jesus Christ.

The leaders of Christianity today need to remember the words of warning that Jesus spoke to the scribes and Pharisees during His ministry. Like these self-righteous leaders of the Jews, the leaders of the Christian churches have adopted traditions and dogmas that conflict with the commandments of God. A close examination of the history of Christianity will show that the traditional doctrines and practices of the churches of this world are not the teachings of Jesus Christ. True Christianity, as originally taught by Jesus Christ and His apostles, was subverted from within by false teachers of lawlessness. The teachings of these "ungodly men" that Jude and Peter wrote about were passed down in the writings of the "early church fathers" and were accepted by the Roman church as authoritative traditions. Through the centuries the Roman church grew in power, using its influence to stamp out every remaining vestige of the true teachings of Jesus Christ. After a power struggle between the bishop of Rome and the bishop of Constantinople, the church split into the Roman Catholic and the Eastern Orthodox churches.

As the influence of the Orthodox church dominated the East, so the teachings of the Roman Catholic Church molded the thinking of the entire Western world. The authority of Catholic doctrine and tradition was not seriously challenged until the time of Martin Luther. When Martin Luther rejected the corruption and lawlessness of the Roman Catholic Church, he appeared to be seeking the truth of God. He labored diligently to translate the Scriptures into the German language so that the common people could read and learn from the Word of God. But the religion that developed as a result of Martin Luther's teachings, known as Lutheranism, did not restore the true teachings of Jesus Christ. The reformation that Martin Luther initiated was never completed, because he rejected the Second and Fourth Commandments. As a result, the new religion that he founded began to promote another form of lawlessness.

Luther taught that a person who had been saved through the grace of God could not lose salvation, regardless of the degree or intensity of the sins that might be committed. This perverse teaching is clearly expressed in a letter written by Luther: "Be a sinner, and let your sins be strong, but let your faith in Christ be stronger, and rejoice in Christ who is the victor over sin, death, and the world. We will commit sins while we are here, for this life is not a place where righteousness can exist….**No sin can separate us from Him, even if we were to kill or commit adultery a thousand times each day**" (Martin Luther, Saemmtliche Schriften, Letter 99, 1 August 1521, translated by Erika Flores in *The Wittenberg Project, The Wartburg Segment*, as published in *Grace and Knowledge*, Issue 8, September 2000, Article "Ecclesiasticus: The Wisdom of Ben-Sirach," p. 27).

The words of Martin Luther reveal the depth of lawlessness to which many religious leaders have descended. This teaching is the epitome of the perverted "grace" that Jude condemned, which rejects the commandments of God and grants license to commit sin with no limitations whatsoever. Luther's teaching concerning murder and adultery is diametrically opposed to the teachings of Jesus Christ, Who magnified and greatly expanded the application of the Sixth and Seventh Commandments.

The promoters of lawlessness have succeeded in deceiving the vast majority of professing Christians into accepting a false grace. As the New Testament shows, this distorted view of grace does not lead to salvation. In the Judgment Day, the teachers of lawlessness, who have been honored as religious leaders and have even done noteworthy deeds in the name of Jesus Christ, will be rejected: "Many will say to Me in that day, 'Lord, Lord, did we not prophesy through Your name? And *did we not* cast out demons through Your name? And *did we not* perform many works of power through Your name?' And then I will confess to them, 'I never knew you. **Depart from Me, you who work lawlessness**' " (Matt. 7:22-23).

95

The workers of lawlessness will depart into the lake of fire to suffer the judgment of eternal death, from which there is no resurrection: "But *the* cowardly, and unbelieving, and abominable, and **murderers, and fornicators, and sorcerers, and idolaters, and all liars, shall have their part in the lake that burns with fire and brimstone; which is *the* second death**" (Rev. 21:8).

During His ministry, Jesus declared that those who refuse to hear His teachings would be judged by the words He had spoken: "Then Jesus called out and said, 'The one who believes in Me does not believe in Me, but in Him Who sent Me. And the one who sees Me sees Him Who sent Me. I have come *as* a light into the world so that everyone who believes in Me may not remain in darkness. **But if anyone hears My words and does not believe, I do not judge him; for I did not come to judge the world, but to save the world. The one who rejects Me and does not receive My words has one who judges him; the word which I have spoken, that shall judge him in the last day. For I have not spoken from Myself; but the Father, Who sent Me, gave Me commandment Himself, what I should say and what I should speak.** And I know that His commandment is eternal life. Therefore, whatever I speak, I speak exactly as the Father has told Me" (John 12:44-50).

The teachings of Jesus Christ, as recorded in the Sermon on the Mount, carry the full authority of God the Father: "**Now it came to pass *that* when Jesus had finished these words, the multitudes were amazed at His teaching; for He taught them as one Who had authority, and not as the scribes**" (Matt. 7:28-29). In the Sermon on the Mount, Jesus taught the full intent and application of the laws and commandments of God, which is the spiritual standard for the New Covenant. This is the standard by which every true believer is now being judged, and by which all mankind will ultimately be judged.

Mountains in Judea

50. JESUS, THROUGHOUT THE SERMON ON THE MOUNT, GIVES THE FULL SPIRITUAL MEANING AND AMPLIFICATION OF GOD'S LAW

MATTHEW 5

1. But seeing the multitudes, He went up into the mountain; and when He sat down, His disciples came to Him.

2. And He opened His mouth *and* taught them, saying,

3. "Blessed *are* the poor in spirit, for theirs is the kingdom of heaven.

4. Blessed *are* those who mourn, for they shall be comforted. [a]

5. Blessed *are* the meek, for they shall inherit the earth. [b]

6. Blessed *are* those who hunger and thirst after righteousness, for they shall be filled. [c]

7. Blessed *are* the merciful, for they shall find mercy. [d]

8. Blessed *are* the pure in heart, for they shall see God. [e]

9. Blessed *are* the peacemakers, for they shall be called *the* sons of God.

10. Blessed *are* those who have been persecuted for the sake of righteousness, for theirs is the kingdom of heaven.

11. Blessed are you when they shall reproach you, and shall persecute you, and shall falsely say every wicked thing against you, for My sake.

12. Rejoice and be filled with joy, for great *is* your reward in heaven; for in this same manner they persecuted the prophets who *were* before you.

LUKE 6

20. And He lifted up His eyes upon His disciples *and* said, "Blessed *are you,* the poor, for yours is the kingdom of God.

21. Blessed *are* those who hunger now, for you shall be filled. Blessed *are* those who weep now, for you shall laugh. [a]

22. Blessed are you when men shall hate you, and when they shall cut you off, and shall reproach *you,* and cast out your name as wicked, for the Son of man's sake.

23. Rejoice in that day and leap for joy; for behold, great *is* your reward in heaven; for their fathers did these same things to the prophets.

24. But woe to you, the rich, for you are receiving your consolation!

25. Woe to you who have been filled, for you shall hunger! Woe to you who laugh now, for you shall mourn and weep!

26. Woe to you when all men shall speak well of you! For their fathers did these same things to the false prophets.

a - Isa. 61:2-3   b - Psa. 37:11; Isa. 29:19   c - Psa. 63:1-4, 84:1-2
d - Psa. 18:25; Prov. 11:17   e - Psa. 24:3-5

51. TRUE CHRISTIANS ARE TO BE THE SALT OF THE EARTH AND THE LIGHT OF THE WORLD

MATTHEW 5

13. You are the salt of the earth; but if the salt has become tasteless, with what shall it be salted? For it no longer has any strength, but *is* to be thrown out and to be trampled upon by men.

14. You are the light of the world. A city that is set on a mountain cannot be hid.

15. Neither do they light a lamp and put it under a bushelbasket, but on the lampstand; and it shines for all who *are* in the house.

16. In the same way also, you are to let your light shine before men, so that they may see your good works, and may glorify your Father Who *is* in heaven.

52. JESUS CAME TO MAGNIFY AND FINISH GIVING THE LAW—
HE PREACHED OBEDIENCE TO THE LAWS OF GOD

MATTHEW 5

17. Do not think that I have come to abolish the Law or the Prophets; I did not come to abolish, but to fulfill.

18. For truly I say to you, until the heaven and the earth shall pass away, one jot or one tittle shall in no way pass from the Law until everything has been fulfilled.

19. Therefore, whoever shall break one of these least commandments, and shall teach men so, shall be called least in the kingdom of heaven; but whoever shall practice and teach *them*, this one shall be called great in the kingdom of heaven.

20. For I say to you, unless your righteousness shall exceed *the righteousness* of the scribes and Pharisees, there is no way *that* you shall enter into the kingdom of heaven.

53. EXAMPLES OF THE SPIRITUAL APPLICATION OF THE LAW

MATTHEW 5

21. You have heard that it was said to those *in* ancient *times*, 'You shall not commit murder; but whoever commits murder shall be subject to judgment.' [a]

22. But I say to you, everyone who is angry with his brother without cause shall be subject to judgment. Now *you have heard it said,* 'Whoever shall say to his brother, "Raca," shall be subject to *the judgment of* the council.' But *I say to you*, whoever shall say, '*You* fool,' shall be subject to the fire of Gehenna.

23. For this reason, if you bring your gift to the altar, and there remember that your brother has something against you,

24. Leave your gift there before the altar, and go *your* way; first be reconciled with your brother, and then come and offer your gift.

25. Agree with your adversary quickly, while you are in the way with him; lest your adversary deliver you to the judge, and the judge deliver you to the officer, and you be cast into prison.

26. Truly I say to you, there is no way that you shall come out of there until you have paid the *very* last coin.

a - Ex. 20:13; Deut 5:17

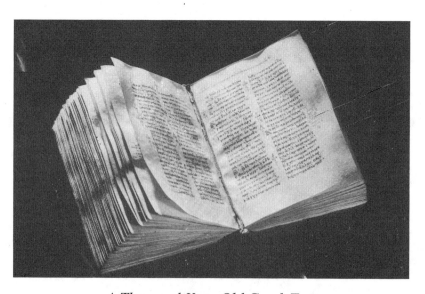

A Thousand-Year-Old Greek Text

54. LUST IS SPIRITUAL ADULTERY

MATTHEW 5

27. "You have heard that it was said to those *in* ancient *times*, 'You shall not commit adultery.' [a]

28. But I say to you, everyone who looks upon a woman to lust after her has already committed adultery with her in his heart.

29. So then, if your right eye shall cause you to offend, pluck it out and cast it from you; for it is better for you that one of your members should perish than *that* your whole body be cast into Gehenna.

30. And if your right hand shall cause you to offend, cut it off and cast *it* from you; for it is better for you that one of your members should perish than *that* your whole body be cast into Gehenna."

a - Ex. 20:14; Deut. 5:18

55. DIVORCE AND REMARRIAGE CAN BE ADULTERY

MATTHEW 5

31. "It was also said *in ancient times*, 'Whoever shall divorce his wife, let him give her a writing of divorcement.' [a]

32. But I say to you, whoever shall divorce his wife, except for the cause of sexual immorality, causes her to commit adultery; and whoever shall marry her who has been divorced is committing adultery."

a - Deut. 24:1

56. CHRISTIANS ARE NOT TO VOW OR SWEAR

MATTHEW 5

33. "Again, you have heard that it was said to those *in* ancient *times*, 'You shall not forswear yourself, but you shall perform your oaths to the Lord.' [a]

34. But I say to you, do not swear at all, neither by heaven, for it is God's throne; [b]

35. Nor by the earth, for it is the footstool of His feet; nor by Jerusalem, because it is *the* city of the great King.

36. Neither shall you swear by your head, because you do not have the power to make one hair white or black.

37. But let your word be *good, your* 'Yes' *be* yes *and your* 'No' *be* no; for anything that *is* added to these is from the evil one."

a - Ex. 20:7; Lev. 19:12; Deut. 5:11   b - Isa. 66:1

57. CHRISTIANS MUST HAVE AN ATTITUDE OF GOING ABOVE AND BEYOND

MATTHEW 5	LUKE 6
38. "You have heard that it was said, '*An* eye for *an* eye, and *a* tooth for *a* tooth'; [a]	29. "If anyone strikes you on the cheek, offer the other *cheek* also; and if anyone takes your cloak, do not forbid your coat also.
39. But I say to you, do not resist evil; rather, *if* anyone shall strike you on the right cheek, turn to him the other also.	30. Give to everyone who asks you; and if anyone takes what *is* yours, do not ask *for it* back.
40. And *if* anyone shall sue you before the law and take your garment, give him *your* coat also.	31. And exactly as you would have men do to you, you do the same to them also."
41. And *if* anyone shall compel you to go one mile, go with him two.	
42. Give to the one who asks of you; and do not turn away from the one who wishes to borrow from you."	

a - Ex. 21:24-25

99

58. LOVE YOUR ENEMIES AND BECOME PREFECT, AS IS THE FATHER IN HEAVEN

MATTHEW 5

43. "You have heard that it was said, 'You shall love your neighbor and hate your enemy.' [a]
44. But I say to you, love your enemies, bless those who curse you, do good to those who hate you, and pray for those who despitefully use you and persecute you,
45. So that you yourselves may be *the* children of your Father Who *is* in heaven; for He causes His sun to rise on *the* evil and *on the* good, and sends rain on *the* just and *on the* unjust.
46. For if you love those who love you, what reward do you have? Do not the tax collectors practice the same *thing?*
47. And if you salute your brethren only, what have you done *that is* extraordinary? Do not the tax collectors practice the same *thing?*
48. Therefore, you shall be perfect, even as your Father Who *is* in heaven is perfect."

a - Lev. 19:17-18

LUKE 6

27. "But I say to you who hear, love your enemies, *and* do good to those who hate you.
28. Bless those who curse you, and pray for those who despitefully use you.
32. But if you love *only* those who love you, what praise is it to you? For even sinners love those who love them.
33. And if you do good *only* to those who are doing good to you, what praise is it to you? For even sinners do the same.
34. And if you lend *to those* from whom you hope to receive, what praise is it to you? For even sinners lend to sinners, that they may receive as much again.
35. But love your enemies, and do good, and lend, hoping for nothing again; and your reward shall be great, and you shall be *the* children of the Highest; for He is good to the unthankful and *the* wicked.
36. Therefore, you also be compassionate, *even* as your Father is compassionate."

59. HOW TO DO YOUR WORKS

MATTHEW 6

1. "Beware *that* you do not bestow your alms in the sight of men in order to be seen by them; otherwise you have no reward with your Father Who *is* in heaven.
2. Therefore, when you give *your* alms, do not sound the trumpet before you, as the hypocrites do in the synagogues and in the streets, so that they may have glory from men. Truly I say to you, they have their reward.
3. But *when* you give your alms, do not let your left hand know what your right hand is doing,
4. So that your alms may be in secret; and your Father Who sees in secret shall Himself reward you openly."

60. HOW TO PRAY

MATTHEW 6

5. "And when you pray, you shall not be as the hypocrites, for they love to pray standing in the synagogues and on the corners of the streets, in order *that* they may be seen by men. Truly I say to you, they have their reward.
6. But you, when you pray, enter into a private room; and after shutting the door, pray to your Father Who *is* in secret; and your Father Who sees in secret shall reward you openly.
7. And when you pray, do not use vain repetitions, as the heathen *do*; for they think that by multiplying their words they shall be heard.
8. Now then, do not be like them; for your Father knows what things you have need of before you ask Him."

61. PRAYER GUIDE AND OUTLINE
MATTHEW 6

9. "Therefore, you are to pray after this manner: 'Our Father Who *is* in heaven, hallowed be Your name;
10. Your kingdom come; Your will be done on earth, as *it is* in heaven;
11. Give us this day our daily bread;
12. And forgive us our debts, as we also forgive our debtors;
13. And lead us not into temptation, but rescue us from the evil one. For Yours is the kingdom and the power and the glory forever. Amen.'
14. For if you forgive men their trespasses, your heavenly Father will also forgive you.
15. But if you do not forgive men their trespasses, neither will your Father forgive your trespasses."

62. HOW TO FAST
MATTHEW 6

16. "And when you fast, do not be as the hypocrites, dejected in countenance; for they disfigure their faces in order that they may appear to men to fast. Truly I say to you, they have their reward.
17. But *when* you fast, anoint your head and wash your face,
18. So that you may not appear to men to fast, but to your Father Who *is* in secret; and your Father Who sees in secret shall reward you openly."

63. HOW TO USE YOUR MONEY
MATTHEW 6

19. "Do not store up treasures for yourselves on earth, where moth and rust spoil, and where thieves break through and steal;
20. But store up treasures for yourselves in heaven, where neither moth nor rust spoils, and where thieves do not break through nor steal.
21. For where your treasure is, there will your heart be also."

64. THE EYE IS THE LIGHT OF THE BODY
MATTHEW 6

22. "The light of the body is the eye. Therefore, if your eye be sound, your whole body shall be *full of* light.
23. But if your eye be evil, your whole body shall be *full of* darkness. Therefore, if the light that *is* in you be darkness, how great *is* that darkness!"

65. NO ONE IS CAPABLE OF SERVING TWO MASTERS
MATTHEW 6

24. "No one is able to serve two masters; for either he will hate the one and love the other, or he will hold to *the* one and despise the other. You cannot serve God and mammon."

66. ATTITUDE TOWARD GOD AND MATERIAL GOODS—SEEK THE KINGDOM OF GOD AND HIS CHARACTER QUALITIES FIRST—AND YOUR NEEDS WILL BE SUPPLIED

MATTHEW 6

25. "Because of this I say to you, do not be anxious about your life *as to* what you shall eat and what you shall drink; nor about your body *as to* what you shall wear. Is not life more than food, and the body *more* than clothing?

26. Observe the birds of heaven: they do not sow, neither do they reap, nor do they gather into granaries; and your heavenly Father feeds them. Are you not much better than they?

27. But who among you, by taking careful thought, is able to add one cubit to his stature?

28. And why are you anxious about clothing? Observe the lilies of the field, how they grow: they do not labor, nor do they spin;

29. But I say to you, not even Solomon in all his glory was arrayed as one of these.

30. Now if God so arrays the grass of the field, which today is and tomorrow is cast into the oven, *shall* He not much rather clothe you, O *you* of little faith?

31. Therefore, do not be anxious, saying, 'What shall we eat?' or 'What shall we drink?' or 'With what shall we be clothed?'

32. For the nations seek after all these things. And your heavenly Father knows that you have need of all these things.

33. But *as for* you, seek first the kingdom of God and His righteousness, and all these things shall be added to you.

34. Therefore, do not be anxious about tomorrow; for tomorrow shall take care of the *things* of itself. Sufficient for the day *is* the evil of that *day*."

67. THE PRINCIPLE OF PROPER JUDGMENT

MATTHEW 7

1. "Do not condemn *others*, so that you yourself will not be condemned;

2. For with what judgment you judge, you shall be judged; and with what measure you mete out, it shall be measured again to you.

3. Now why do you look at the sliver that *is* in your brother's eye, but you do not perceive the beam in your *own* eye?

4. Or how will you say to your brother, 'Allow *me* to remove the sliver from your eye'; and behold, the beam *is* in your *own* eye?

5. *You* hypocrite, first cast out the beam from your *own* eye, and then you shall see clearly to remove the sliver from your brother's eye."

Mount Tabor Today

LUKE 6

37. "And do not judge *others*, so that you yourself will not be judged in any way. Do not condemn *others*, so that you will not be condemned in any way. Forgive, and you shall be forgiven.

38. Give, and it shall be given to you. Good measure, pressed down and shaken together and running over, shall they give into your bosom. For with the same measure that you mete *out*, it shall be measured again to you."

39. Then He spoke a parable to them, *saying*, "Is a blind *man* able to lead a blind *man*? Will not both fall into the ditch?

40. A disciple is not above his teacher; but everyone who is perfected shall be like his teacher.

41. And why do you look at the sliver that *is* in your brother's eye, but you do not perceive the beam that *is* in your own eye?

42. Or how can you say to your brother, 'Brother, allow me to cast out the sliver that *is* in your eye,' *but* you do not see the beam that *is* in your own eye? Hypocrite! First cast out the beam from your *own* eye, and then shall you see clearly to cast out the sliver that *is* in your brother's eye."

68. GOD'S HOLY TRUTH NOT TO BE TREATED LIGHTLY
MATTHEW 7

6. "Do not give that which *is* holy to the dogs, nor cast your pearls before the swine, lest they trample them under their feet, and turn around and tear you in pieces."

69. ASK, SEEK, AND KNOCK, AND YOU WILL RECEIVE
MATTHEW 7

7. "Ask, and it shall be given to you. Seek, and you shall find. Knock, and it shall be opened to you.
8. For everyone who asks receives, and the one who seeks finds, and to the one who knocks it shall be opened.
9. Or what man is there of you who, if his son shall ask *for* bread, will give him a stone?
10. And if he shall ask *for* a fish, will give him a serpent?
11. Therefore, if you, being evil, know *how* to give good gifts to your children, how much more shall your Father Who *is* in heaven give good things to those who ask Him?
12. Therefore, everything that you would have men do to you, so also do to them; for this is the Law and the Prophets."

70. YOU MUST ENTER THROUGH THE NARROW GATE
MATTHEW 7

13. "Enter in through the narrow gate; for wide *is* the gate and broad *is* the way that leads to destruction, and many are those who enter through it;
14. For narrow *is* the gate and difficult *is* the way that leads to life, and few are those who find it."

71. BE ON GUARD AGAINST FALSE PROPHETS—
KNOW THEM BY THEIR FRUITS

MATTHEW 7

15. "But beware of false prophets who come to you in sheep's clothing, for within *they* are ravening wolves.
16. You shall know them by their fruits. They do not gather grapes from thorns, or figs from thistles, do they?
17. In the same way, every good tree produces good fruit, but a corrupt tree produces evil fruit.
18. A good tree cannot produce evil fruit, nor can a corrupt tree produce good fruit.
19. Every tree *that is* not producing good fruit is cut down and is cast into the fire.
20. Therefore, you shall assuredly know them by their fruits."

LUKE 6

43. "For there is not a good tree that is producing corrupt fruit; nor *is there* a corrupt tree that is producing good fruit.
44. For every tree is known by its own fruit; for they do not gather figs from thorns, nor do they gather a bunch of grapes from a bramble.
45. The good man out of the good treasure of his heart brings forth that which *is* good; and the wicked man out of the wicked treasure of his heart brings forth that which *is* wicked; for out of the abundance of the heart his mouth speaks."

72. OBEDIENCE IS REQUIRED—PROFESSION OF THE LORD'S NAME NOT ENOUGH TO OBTAIN ETERAL LIFE

MATTHEW 7

21. "Not everyone who says to Me, 'Lord, Lord,' shall enter into the kingdom of heaven; but the one who is doing the will of My Father, Who *is* in heaven.
22. Many will say to Me in that day, 'Lord, Lord, did we not prophesy through Your name? And *did we not* cast out demons through Your name? And *did we not* perform many works of power through Your name?'
23. And then I will confess to them, 'I never knew you. Depart from Me, you who work lawlessness.'
24. Therefore, everyone who hears these words of Mine and practices them, I will compare him to a wise man, who built his house upon the rock;
25. And the rain came down, and the floods came, and the winds blew, and beat upon that house; but it did not fall, for it was founded upon the rock.
26. And everyone who hears these words of Mine and does not practice them shall be compared to a foolish man, who built his house upon the sand;
27. And the rain came down, and the floods came, and the winds blew, and beat upon that house; and it fell, and great was the fall of it."
28. Now it came to pass *that* when Jesus had finished these words, the multitudes were amazed at His teaching;
29. For He taught them as one Who had authority, and not as the scribes.

MATTHEW 8

1. When He came down from the mountain, great multitudes followed Him.

LUKE 6

46. "And why do you call Me, 'Lord, Lord,' but *you* do not practice what I say?
47. Everyone who comes to Me and hears My words and practices them, I will show you what he is like:
48. He is like a man building a house, who dug deep and laid *the* foundation on the rock; and a flood came, and the torrent beat against that house, but could not shake it, because it was founded on the rock.
49. But the one who has heard *My words* and has not practiced *them* is like a man who built a house on *top of* the ground, without a foundation; and *when* the torrent beat against it, it fell at once, and the ruin of that house was great."

LUKE 7

1. And when He had finished all His sayings in the ears of the people, He went into Capernaum.

A Tree Is Known By Its Fruits

73. JESUS TOUCHES A LEPER, HEALING AND CLEANSING HIM

MARK 1

40. And a leper came to Him, beseeching Him and kneeling down to Him, and saying to Him, "If You will, You have the power to cleanse me."

41. Then Jesus, being moved with compassion, stretched out *His* hand *and* touched him, and said to him, "I will. Be cleansed."

42. And as soon as He had spoken, the leprosy immediately departed from him, and he was cleansed.

43. Now after strictly commanding him, He sent him away at once,

44. And said to him, "See *that* you do not say anything to anyone; but go *and* show yourself to the priest, and offer for your cleansing what Moses commanded, for a testimony to them." [a]

45. But after leaving, he began to proclaim *it* extensively and to spread the matter abroad, so that He was no longer able to enter *the* city openly, but stayed outside *the city* in desert places; and they came to Him from every region.

LUKE 5

12. Now it came to pass that as He was in one of the cities, a man full of leprosy saw Jesus *and* immediately fell on *his* face, beseeching Him *and* saying, "Lord, if You will, You have *the* power to cleanse me."

13. And after stretching out *His* hand, He touched him, saying, "I will. Be cleansed!" And the leprosy instantly left him.

14. Then He charged him to tell no one, and *said*, "Go *and* show yourself to the priest, and bring an offering for your cleansing as Moses commanded, for a witness to them." [a]

15. But reports of His *miracles* were spread abroad even more; and great multitudes came to hear *Him* and to be healed by Him of their infirmities.

MATTHEW 8

2. And behold, a leper came and worshiped Him, saying, "Lord, if You will, You have the power to cleanse me."

3. Then Jesus stretched out *His* hand *and* touched him, saying, "I will. Be cleansed." And immediately *he* was cleansed *from* his leprosy.

4. And Jesus said to him, "See *that* you tell no one; but go *and* show yourself to the priest, and offer the gift that Moses commanded, for a witness to them." [a]

Lepers in Kidron Valley
East of Jerusalem
- Matson Photo Services

a - Lev. 13:49; 14:1-32

74. JESUS WITHDRAWS TO PRAY

LUKE 5

16. Then He withdrew into the wilderness and prayed.

75. JESUS RETURNS TO CAPERNAUM

MARK 2

1. And after *some* days, He again entered into Capernaum, and it was reported that He was in *the* house.

2. And immediately many gathered together, so that there was no longer any room, not even at the door; and He preached the Word to them.

76. JESUS HEALS A PARALYTIC ON THE SABBATH, AND THE PHARISEES ARE CRITICAL OF HIM

MARK 2

3. Then they came to Him, bringing a paraplegic borne by four *men*.
4. And since they were not able to come near to Him because of the crowd, they uncovered the roof where He was; and after breaking *it* open, they let down the stretcher on which the paraplegic was lying.
5. Now when Jesus saw their faith, He said to the paraplegic, "Child, your sins have been forgiven you."
6. But some of the scribes were sitting there and reasoning in their hearts,
7. "Why does this *man* speak such blasphemies? Who has the power to forgive sins, except one, *and that is* God?"
8. And Jesus immediately knew in His spirit what they were reasoning within themselves, *and* said to them, "Why are you reasoning these things in your hearts?
9. Which is easier, to say to the paraplegic, '*Your* sins have been forgiven you'? or to say, 'Arise, and take up your stretcher and walk'?
10. But in order that you may understand that the Son of man has authority on the earth to forgive sins," He said to the paraplegic,
11. "I say to you, arise and pick up your stretcher, and go to your house."
12. And immediately he arose and, after picking up his stretcher, went out in the presence of them all; so that they were all amazed and glorified God, saying, "We have never seen the like!"

LUKE 5

17. Now it came to pass that on one of the days when He was teaching, Pharisees and teachers of the law were sitting there who had come out of every village from Galilee and from Judea, including *the villages* around Jerusalem. And *the* power of *the* Lord was *there* for healing the *sick*.
18. And behold, men *came*, carrying on a stretcher a man who was paralyzed; and they sought to bring him in and place *him* before Him.
19. But when they could not find a way to bring him in because of the multitude, they went up on the rooftop and lowered him with the stretcher through the tiles into the midst, *directly* in front of Jesus.
20. And seeing their faith, He said to him, "Man, your sins have been forgiven you."
21. Then the scribes and the Pharisees began to reason, saying, "Who is this Who speaks blasphemies? Who has the power to forgive sins, except God alone?"
22. But Jesus, perceiving their thoughts, answered *and* said to them, "Why do you reason in your hearts?
23. Which is easier, to say, 'Your sins have been forgiven you'? or to say, 'Arise and walk'?
24. But that you may know that the Son of man has authority on the earth to forgive sins," He said to the one who was paralyzed, "I say to you, arise and take up your stretcher, and go to your house."
25. And he immediately stood up in front of them; *and* after taking up *the stretcher* on which he had been lying, he went to his house, glorifying God.

MATTHEW 9

2. And behold, they brought to Him a paralytic lying on a stretcher. Then Jesus, seeing their faith, said to the paralytic, "Be of good courage, child; your sins have been forgiven you."
3. And immediately some of the scribes said within themselves, "This *man* blasphemes."
4. But Jesus, perceiving their thoughts, said, "Why are you thinking evil in your hearts?
5. For which is easier to say, '*Your* sins have been forgiven you,' or to say, 'Arise and walk'?
6. But *I speak these words so* that you may understand that the Son of man has authority on earth to forgive sins." Then He said to the paralytic, "Arise, take up your bed, and go to your house."
7. And he arose and went away to his house.
8. Now when the multitudes saw *it*, they were amazed and glorified God, Who had given such authority to men.

Village of Rephaim

LUKE 5

26. And amazement seized everyone, and they glorified God, and were filled with fear, saying, "We have seen strange things today."

77. MATTHEW IS CALLED BY JESUS

MARK 2	LUKE 5	MATTHEW 9
13. Then He went by the sea again; and all the multitude came to him, and He taught them. 14. Now as He was passing by, He saw Levi, the *son* of Alpheus, sitting at the tax office; and He said to him, "Follow Me." And he arose and followed Him.	27. Now after these things, He went out and saw a tax collector named Levi sitting at the tax office, and said to him, "Follow Me." 28. Then he arose, leaving everything, *and* followed Him.	9. And passing from there, Jesus saw a man named Matthew sitting at the tax office, and said to him, "Follow Me." And he arose *and* followed Him.

78. MATTHEW HAS A FEAST FOR JESUS

MARK 2	LUKE 5	MATTHEW 9
15. And it came to pass that, when He sat down to eat in his house, many tax collectors and sinners sat down with Jesus and His disciples; for there were many, and they followed Him.	29. And Levi made a great feast for Him in his house, and there were a large number of tax collectors and others who sat down with them.	10. Then it came to pass, when Jesus sat down *to eat* in the house, that behold, many tax collectors and sinners came and sat down with Him and His disciples.

79. THE SCRIBES AND PHARISEES ACCUSE JESUS AND HIS DISCIPLES

MARK 2	LUKE 5	MATTHEW 9
16. But when the scribes and the Pharisees saw Him eating with tax collectors and sinners, *they* said to His disciples, "Why *is it* that He eats and drinks with tax collectors and sinners?" 17. And after hearing *this*, Jesus said to them, "Those who are strong do not need a physician, but those who are sick. I did not come to call *the* righteous, but sinners to repentance."	30. But the scribes and the Pharisees complained to His disciples, saying, "Why do you eat and drink with tax collectors and sinners?" 31. Then Jesus answered *and* said to them, "Those who are in *good* health do not need a physician, but those who are sick. 32. I did not come to call *the* righteous, but sinners to repentance."	11. And after seeing *this*, the Pharisees said to His disciples, "Why does your Master eat with tax collectors and sinners?" 12. But when Jesus heard *it*, He said to them, "Those who are strong do not have need of a physician, but those who are sick. 13. Now go and learn what this means: 'I desire mercy and not sacrifice.' For I did not come to call *the* righteous, but sinners to repentance."

80. THE PHARISEES ASK WHY JESUS' DISCIPLES DID NOT FAST

MARK 2	**LUKE 5**	**MATTHEW 9**
18. Now the disciples of John and the *disciples* of the Pharisees were fasting; and they came and said to Him, "Why do the disciples of John and the *disciples* of the Pharisees fast, but Your disciples do not fast?" 19. And Jesus said to them, "Can the children of the bridal chamber fast while the bridegroom is with them? As long as they have the bridegroom with them, they are not able to fast. 20. But the days will come when the bridegroom shall be taken away from them; and then shall they fast in those days."	33. Then they said to Him, "Why do the disciples of John fast often and make supplications, and those of the Pharisees do the same, but Your *disciples* are eating and drinking?" 34. And He said to them, "Can you make the children of the bride chamber fast, while the bridegroom is with them? 35. But the time will come when the bridegroom shall be taken from them, and in those days they shall fast."	14. Then the disciples of John came to Him, saying, "Why do we and the Pharisees fast often, but Your disciples do not fast?" 15. And Jesus said to them, "Are the children of the bridechamber able to mourn while the bridegroom is with them? But the days will come when the bridegroom shall be taken away from them, and then they shall fast."

Wall of Jerusalem

81. THE PARABLE OF THE WINESKINS

MARK 2	**LUKE 5**	**MATTHEW 9**
21. "And no one sews a piece of new cloth onto an old garment; otherwise the new *piece* filling up *the hole* tears away from the old, and a worse hole is made. 22. And no one puts new wine into old wineskins; otherwise the new wine bursts the *old* wineskins, and the wine spills out, and the wineskins are destroyed; but new wine must be put into new wineskins."	36. Then He also spoke a parable to them: "No one puts a piece of new cloth on an old garment, or the new *cloth* will make a tear; for *the* piece that *is* from the new *cloth* is not compatible with the old *piece*. 37. And no one puts new wine into old skins, or the new wine will burst the skins and will spill out, and the skins will be destroyed; 38. But new wine must be put into new skins, and both will be preserved together. 39. And no one after drinking *the* old *wine* immediately desires *the* new; for he says, 'The old is better.' "	16. "Now no one sews a new piece of cloth onto an old garment; for that which is put in to fill up *the hole* takes away from the garment, and a worse tear develops. 17. Neither do they put new wine into old wineskins; otherwise the wineskins will burst, and the wine will spill out, and the wineskins will be destroyed; but they put new wine into new wineskins, and both are preserved together."

The Gate Beautiful—Entrance to Women's Court Looking Toward the Temple

PART III

FROM PASSOVER 28 AD
TO PASSOVER 29 AD

82. THE SECOND PASSOVER SEASON—
JESUS SHOWS THAT HE IS THE LORD AND MASTER

LUKE 6	MARK 2	MATTHEW 12

LUKE 6

1. Now it came to pass on *the* second Sabbath of *the* first rank* *that* He was walking through the grain fields; and His disciples were plucking the ears and were eating, after rubbing *them* in their hands.
2. But some of the Pharisees said to them, "Why are you doing that which is not lawful to do on the Sabbaths?"
3. And Jesus answered *and* said to them, "Have you not read even this, that which David did when he himself hungered, and those who were with him?
4. How he went into the house of God and took the loaves of showbread, and he ate *of them*, and also gave *some* to those with him, which it is not lawful to eat except *for* the priests only?" [a]
5. And He said to them, "The Son of man is Lord even of the Sabbath."

MARK 2

23. Now it came to pass that He went through the grain fields on the Sabbath; and as His disciples made *their* way *through the fields*, they were picking *and eating* the grain.
24. Then the Pharisees said to Him, "Look *at them*! Why are they doing that which is not lawful on the Sabbath?"
25. And He said to them, "Have you never read what David did when he was hungry and in need *of food*, he and those with him?
26. How in *the days of* Abiathar the high priest, he entered into the house of God and he ate the showbread, which it is not lawful to eat except for the priests, and he also gave *it* to those who were with him?" [a]
27. And He said to them, "The Sabbath was made for man, *and* not man for the Sabbath;
28. Therefore, the Son of man is Lord even of the Sabbath."

a - Lev. 24:9; I Sam. 21:1-6   b - Num. 28:9-10
c - Hos. 6:6; Jer. 7:22-23; Psa. 51:16-19

MATTHEW 12

1. At that time Jesus went through the grain fields on the Sabbath day; and His disciples were hungry, and they began to pluck the heads of grain and to eat *them*.
2. But after seeing *this*, the Pharisees said to Him, "Behold, Your disciples are doing what is not lawful to do on *the* Sabbath."
3. But He said to them, "Have you not read what David did when he himself and those with him were hungry?
4. How he went into the house of God and he ate the loaves of showbread, which it was not lawful for him to eat, nor for those who were with him, but for the priests only? [a]
5. Or have you not read in the law that on the Sabbaths the priests in the temple profane the Sabbath and are guiltless? [b]
6. But I say to you, there is *one* here Who is greater than the temple.
7. Now if you had known what this *means*, 'I desire mercy and not sacrifice,' you would not have condemned the guiltless. [c]
8. For the Son of man is Lord even of the Sabbath day."

---

*The Greek phrase εν σαββατο δευτεροπροτος, *used here by Luke, is literally translated "on the second-first Sabbath," or "on the second Sabbath of the first rank or order." The Sabbaths of the first order or rank are annual Sabbaths, which take precedence over the weekly Sabbath. Luke is clearly recording that Jesus and the disciples were going through the grain fields on the second annual Sabbath, which was the last day of the Feast of Unleavened Bread.*

83. THE HEALING OF THE MAN WITH A WITHERED HAND
IN A SYNAGOGUE ON THE SABBATH

LUKE 6	MARK 3	MATTHEW 12
6. Now it also came to pass on another Sabbath *that* He went into the synagogue and taught; and a man was there whose right hand was withered. 7. And the scribes and the Pharisees were watching Him, whether He would heal on the Sabbath, so that they might find an accusation against Him. 8. But He knew their thoughts, and said to the man who had the withered hand, "Arise and stand in the midst." And he arose *and* stood *in their midst*. 9. Then Jesus said to them, "I will ask you *one thing*: is it lawful to do good or to do evil on the Sabbaths? to save life or to destroy *it*?" 10. And after looking around on them all, He said to the man, "Stretch out your hand." And he did so, and his hand was restored *as* sound as the other.	1. And again He went into the synagogue, and a man who had a withered hand was there. 2. And they were watching Him *to see* if He would heal him on the Sabbath, in order that they might accuse Him. 3. Then He said to the man who had the withered hand, "Stand up *here* in the center." 4. And He said to them, "Is it lawful to do good on the Sabbaths, or to do evil? To save life, or to kill?" But they were silent. 5. And after looking around at them with anger, being grieved at the hardness of their hearts, He said to the man, "Stretch out your hand." And he stretched *it* out, and his hand was restored *as* sound as the other.	9. And after leaving there, He went into their synagogue. 10. And, behold, a man was there who had a withered hand. And they asked Him, saying, "Is it lawful to heal on the Sabbaths?" so that they might accuse Him. 11. But He said to them, "What man is there among you who, if he has one sheep that falls into a pit on the Sabbath, will not lay hold of it and lift *it out*? 12. And how much better is a man than a sheep? So then, it is lawful to do good on the Sabbaths." 13. And He said to the man, "Stretch out your hand." And he stretched it out, and it was restored *as* sound as the other.

Jericho from Top of a Mountain Road

84. THE PHARISEES PLOT TO KILL CHRIST

LUKE 6	MARK 3	MATTHEW 12
11. But they were filled with rage, and consulted with one another *as to* what they should do with Jesus.	6. Then the Pharisees left *and* immediately took counsel with the Herodians against Him *as to* how they might destroy Him.	14. Then the Pharisees went out *of the synagogue* and held a council against Him *to discuss* how they might destroy Him.

85. JESUS ESCAPES FROM THE PHARISEES
AND HEALS THE MULTITUDES

MARK 3

7. But Jesus withdrew to the sea with His disciples; and a great multitude from Galilee followed Him, and from Judea,
8. And from Jerusalem, and from Idumea and beyond the Jordan; and those around Tyre and Sidon, a great multitude, when they heard what great things He was doing, came to Him.
9. Then He told His disciples to have a small ship wait for Him on account of the multitude, in order that they might not press upon Him.
10. For He had healed so many that they *began* to crowd around Him, as many as had plagues, in order that they might touch Him;
11. And when the unclean spirits saw Him, they fell down before Him and cried aloud, saying, "You are the Son of God."
12. But He sharply rebuked them so that they would not make Him known.

MATTHEW 12

15. But when Jesus knew of it, He withdrew from there; and great multitudes followed Him, and He healed all of them.
16. And He strictly commanded them not to make Him known publicly;
17. So that it might be fulfilled which was spoken by Isaiah the prophet, saying,
18. "Behold My Servant, Whom I have chosen; My Beloved, in Whom My soul has found delight. I will put My Spirit upon Him, and He shall declare judgment to the Gentiles.
19. He shall not strive nor cry out, neither shall anyone hear His voice in the streets.
20. A bruised reed shall He not break, and smoking flax shall He not quench, until He brings forth the judgment unto victory.
21. And *the* Gentiles shall hope in His name." [a]
22. Then was brought to Him one who was possessed by a demon, blind and dumb; and He healed him, so that the one *who had been* blind and dumb both spoke and saw.
23. And the multitudes were all amazed, and said, "Is this the Son of David?"

a - Isa. 42:1-4

86. JESUS PRAYS ALL NIGHT, SELECTS 12 DISCIPLES
AND ORDAINS THEM TO BE THE 12 APOSTLES

MARK 3

13. Then He went up into the mountain and called to *Him* those whom He desired, and they came to Him.
14. And He ordained twelve, that they might be with Him, and that He might send them to preach,
15. And to have authority to heal diseases and to cast out demons.
16. Then He *chose* Simon and added to *him the* name Peter;
17. And *He chose* James, the *son* of Zebedee, and John, the brother of James; and He added to them *the* name Boanerges, which means "sons of thunder."
18. And *He chose* Andrew, and Philip, and Bartholomew, and Matthew, and Thomas. And *He chose* James, the *son* of Alpheus; and Thaddeus; and Simon, the Cananean;
19. And Judas Iscariot, who also betrayed Him. And they went into a house.

LUKE 6

12. Now it came to pass in those days *that* He went up into the mountain to pray, and He spent the *entire* night in prayer to God.
13. And when it was day, He called His disciples to *Him* and chose from them twelve, whom He also named apostles:
14. Simon, whom He also named Peter, and his brother Andrew; James and John; Philip and Bartholomew;
15. Matthew and Thomas; James, the *son* of Alpheus, and Simon who *was* called Zealot;
16. Judas, *brother* of James; and Judas Iscariot, who also became *the* betrayer.

87. JESUS COMES DOWN FROM THE MOUNTAIN WITH HIS DISCIPLES AND HEALS A MULTITUDE

LUKE 6

17. And after descending with them, He stood on a level place with a crowd of His disciples; and a great multitude of people from all Judea and Jerusalem, and *from* the seacoast of Tyre and Sidon, came to hear Him and to be healed of their diseases;
18. And those who were tormented by unclean spirits *also came*; and they were healed.
19. And all the crowd sought to touch Him, for power went out from Him and healed all.

Mountain Scene Near Galilee

88. JESUS HEALS THE CENTURION'S SERVANT

LUKE 7

2. Now a certain centurion's servant, who was cherished by him, was ill and about to die.
3. And after hearing about Jesus, he sent *the* elders of the Jews to beseech Him to come and heal his servant.
4. And after coming to Jesus, they besought Him earnestly, saying that he was worthy to whom He should grant this.
5. "For he loves our nation," *they said*, "and he built the synagogue for us."
6. Then Jesus went with them; but when He was not far from the house, the centurion sent friends to Him, saying to Him, "Lord, do not trouble *Yourself*, for I am not worthy that You should come under my roof;
7. Therefore, neither did I count myself worthy to come to You; but say *the* word, and my servant shall be healed.
8. For I also am a man appointed under authority, having soldiers under myself, and I say to this *one*, 'Go,' and he goes; and to another, 'Come,' and he comes; and to my servant, 'Do this,' and he does *it*."
9. And when He heard these things, Jesus was amazed at him; and turning to the multitude following Him, He said, "I tell you, not even in Israel have I found such great faith."
10. And when those who had been sent returned to the house, *they* found the sick servant in good health.

MATTHEW 8

5. Now when Jesus had entered Capernaum, a centurion came to Him, beseeching Him,
6. And saying, "Lord, my servant is lying in the house paralyzed *and* grievously tormented."
7. And Jesus said to him, "I will come and heal him."
8. But the centurion answered *and* said, "Lord, I am not worthy that You should come under *the* roof *of* my *house*; but speak the word only, and my servant shall be healed.
9. For I also am a man under authority, having soldiers under me; and I say to this *one*, 'Go,' and he goes; and to another *one*, 'Come,' and he comes; and to my servant, 'Do this,' and he does *it*."
10. Now when Jesus heard these *words*, He was amazed; and He said to those who were following, "Truly I say to you, nowhere in Israel have I found such great faith.
11. But I say to you, many shall come from *the* east and *the* west, and shall sit down with Abraham and Isaac and Jacob in the kingdom of heaven. [a]
12. But the children of the kingdom shall be cast into outer darkness; there shall be weeping and gnashing of teeth."
13. Then Jesus said to the centurion, "Go, and as you have believed, *so* be it *done* to you." And his servant was healed in that hour.

a - Isa. 49:12; 43:5-6

89. THEN JESUS COMES TO A HOUSE AT CAPERNAUM

MARK 3

20. Then a multitude gathered together again, so that they were not able even to eat bread.
21. And after hearing *of it*, those who were contrary to Him went to restrain Him; for they said, "He is out of His mind!"

90. THE SCRIBES AND PHARISEES ACCUSE JESUS CHRIST OF DOING THE WORK OF GOD THROUGH THE POWER OF SATAN

MARK 3

22. Then the scribes who had come down from Jerusalem said, "He has Beelzebub; and by the *power of the* prince of the demons He is casting out demons."
23. And after calling them to *Him*, He spoke to them in parables, *saying*, "How can Satan cast out Satan?
24. For if a kingdom is divided against itself, that kingdom is not able to stand;
25. And if a house is divided against itself, that house is not able to stand.
26, And if Satan has risen up against himself and has been divided, he does not have the power to stand, but has an end.
27. There is no way that anyone who enters a strong man's house is able to plunder his goods, unless he first binds the strong man; and then he can plunder his house."

MATTHEW 12

24. But when the Pharisees heard *this*, they said, "This *man* does not cast out demons except by Beelzebub, prince of the demons."
25. But Jesus, knowing their thoughts, said to them, "Every kingdom divided against itself is brought to desolation, and every city or house divided against itself shall not stand.
26. And if Satan casts out Satan, he is divided against himself. How then shall his kingdom stand?
27. And if I by Beelzebub cast out demons, by whom do your sons cast *them* out? On account of this, they shall be your judges.
28. But if I by *the* Spirit of God cast out demons, then the kingdom of God has come upon you.
29. Or how is anyone able to enter into the house of a strong *man* and plunder his goods, if he does not first bind the strong man? And then he will plunder his house.
30. The one who is not with Me is against Me, and the one who does not gather with Me scatters."

91. JESUS WARNS THEM OF THE UNPARDONABLE SIN

MARK 3

28. "Truly I say to you, all sins and every blasphemy that they may blaspheme shall be forgiven to the children of men;
29. But whoever shall commit blasphemy against the Holy Spirit shall not be forgiven, *even* into eternity, but is subject to eternal judgment."
30. *He spoke these things* because they said, "He has an unclean spirit."

MATTHEW 12

31. "Because of this, I say to you, every sin and blasphemy shall be forgiven to men except the blasphemy against the *Holy* Spirit; *that* shall not be forgiven to men.
32. And whoever speaks a word against the Son of man, it shall be forgiven him; but whoever speaks against the Holy Spirit, it shall not be forgiven him, neither in this age nor in the coming *age*.
33. Either make the tree good and the fruit good, or make the tree corrupt and its fruit corrupt; for a tree is known by its fruit."

Palestinian Viper

MATTHEW 12

34. "Offspring of vipers, how are you able to speak good things, being evil? For out of the abundance of the heart the mouth speaks.

35. The good man out of the good treasure of his heart brings out good things; and the wicked man out of the wicked treasure brings out wicked things.

36. But I say to you, for every idle word that men may speak, they shall be held accountable in *the* day of judgment.

37. For by your words you shall be justified, and by your words you shall be condemned."

92. THE SCRIBES AND PHARISEES SEEK A SIGN
MATTHEW 12

38. Then some of the scribes and Pharisees answered, saying, "Master, we desire to see a sign from You."

39. And He answered *and* said to them, "A wicked and adulterous generation seeks after a sign, but no sign shall be given to it except the sign of Jonah the prophet."

93. THE SIGN OF JONAH TO BE THE ONLY SIGN GIVEN
MATTHEW 12

40. "For just as Jonah was in the belly of the whale three days and three nights, in like manner the Son of man shall be in the heart of the earth three days and three nights. [a]

41. *The* men of Nineveh [b] shall stand up in the judgment with this generation and shall condemn it, because they repented at the proclamation of Jonah; and behold, a greater than Jonah *is* here.

42. *The* queen of *the* south [c] shall rise up in the judgment with this generation and shall condemn it, because she came from the ends of the earth to hear the wisdom of Solomon; and behold, a greater than Solomon *is* here."

a - Jonah 1:17; 2:1   b - Jonah 3:5-10   c - I Kings 10:1-13; II Chron. 9:1-12

94. THAT WICKED GENERATION LIKENED TO WICKED SPIRITS
MATTHEW 12

43. "But when the unclean spirit has departed from a man, it goes through dry places seeking rest, but finds none.

44. Then it says, 'I will return to my house, from which I came out.' And after coming, it finds *it* unoccupied, swept and set in order.

45. Then it goes and takes with it seven other spirits more wicked than itself, and they enter in and dwell there; and the last *state* of that man is worse than the first. Likewise shall it also be with this wicked generation."

95. JESUS' MOTHER AND BROTHERS COME TO SEE HIM—
JESUS EXPLAINS WHO ARE HIS SPIRITUAL MOTHERS AND BROTHERS

MARK 3

31. Then *His* brothers and His mother came and were standing outside; *and* they sent to Him, calling Him.
32. And the multitude sat around Him; and they said to Him, "Behold, Your mother and Your brothers *are* outside; *and* they are seeking You."
33. But He answered them, saying, "Who is My mother and *who are* My brothers?"
34. And He looked around at those who were sitting in a circle around Him, *and* said, "Behold My mother and My brothers;
35. For whoever shall do the will of God, that one is My brother, and My sister, and mother."

MATTHEW 12

46. But while He was still speaking to the multitudes, behold, *His* mother and His brothers were standing outside, seeking to speak with Him.
47. Then one said to Him, "Behold, Your mother and Your brothers are standing outside, seeking to speak with You."
48. But He answered *and* said to him, "Who is My mother? And who are My brothers?"
49. And stretching out His hand to His disciples, He said, "Behold, My mother and My brothers.
50. For whoever shall do the will of My Father, Who is in heaven, that one is My brother and sister and mother."

LUKE 8

19. Then *His* mother and His brothers came to Him, but were not able to get to Him because of the multitude.
20. And it was told Him, saying, "Your mother and Your brothers are standing outside, desiring to see You."
21. But He answered *and* said to them, "My mother and My brothers are those who are hearing the Word of God and are doing it."

96. THE ONLY SON OF A WIDOW IS RAISED
FROM THE DEAD BY JESUS

LUKE 7

11. Now it came to pass on the next *day that* He went into a city called Nain; and many of His disciples went with Him, and a great multitude.
12. And as He drew near to the gate of the city, behold, *one* who had died was being carried out, an only son to his mother, and she was a widow; and a considerable crowd from the city *was* with her.
13. And when the Lord saw her, He was moved with compassion for her and said to her, "Do not weep."
14. And He came up to the bier *and* touched *it*, and those who were bearing *it* stopped. Then He said, "Young man, I say to you, arise!"
15. And the dead man sat up and began to speak, and He gave him to his mother.

97. THE PEOPLE ACKNOWLEDGE JESUS TO BE A GREAT PROPHET

LUKE 7

16. Then fear seized everyone, and they glorified God, saying, "A great prophet has risen up among us," and, "God has visited His people."
17. And this report about Him went out into all Judea and all the country around.
18. Then John's disciples brought word to him about all these things.

98. JOHN THE BAPTIST IN PRISON HEARS OF JESUS' MIRACLE

LUKE 7

19. And after calling two certain disciples, John sent *them* to Jesus, saying, "Are You He Who was to come, or are we to look for another?"
20. And when the men came to Him, *they* said, "John the Baptist has sent us to You, saying, 'Are You He Who was to come, or are we to look for another?' "
21. Now in the same hour, He healed many of diseases and scourges and evil spirits, and He granted sight to many *who were* blind.
22. And Jesus answered *and* said to them, "When you have gone, relate to John the things you have seen and heard: that *the* blind receive sight, *the* lame walk, *the* lepers are cleansed, *the* deaf hear, *the* dead are raised, *and* the gospel is preached to *the* poor. [a]
23. And blessed is everyone who shall not be offended in Me."

MATTHEW 11

2. Now John, having heard in prison *of* the works of Christ, sent two of his disciples,
3. Saying to Him, "Are You the one Who is coming, or are we to look for another?"
4. Jesus answered and said to them, "Go and report to John what you hear and see:
5. *The* blind receive sight, and *the* lame walk; *the* lepers are cleansed, and *the* deaf hear; *the* dead are raised, and *the* poor are evangelized. [a]
6. And blessed is everyone who shall not be offended in Me."

a - Isa. 35:3-6; 61:1-2; 29:18-19

99. JESUS EXPLAINS JOHN WAS A MESSENGER TO PREPARE THE WAY FOR HIM

LUKE 7

24. Now after the messengers of John had left, He began to speak to the multitudes concerning John: "What did you go out into the wilderness to gaze at? A reed shaken by *the* wind?
25. But what did you go out to see? A man dressed in soft clothing? Behold, those who *dress* in splendid clothing and live in luxury are in the palaces.
26. But what did you go out to see? A prophet? Yes, I tell you, and *one* more excellent than a prophet.
27. This is he concerning whom it is written, 'Behold, I send My messenger before Your face, who shall prepare Your way before You.' [a]
28. For I tell you, among *those* who have been born of women there is not a greater prophet than John the Baptist; but the one who *is* least in the kingdom of God is greater than he."
29. Now all the people and the tax collectors who heard this justified God *because* they had been baptized *with* the baptism of John.
30. But the Pharisees and the doctors of the law had set aside the counsel of God concerning themselves, *and* had not been baptized by him.

MATTHEW 11

7. And as they were leaving, Jesus said to the multitudes concerning John, "What did you go out into the wilderness to see? A reed shaken by *the* wind?
8. But what did you go out to see? A man clothed in soft garments? Behold, those who wear soft *clothing* are in kings' houses.
9. But what did you go out to see? A prophet? Yes, I tell you, and *one* more excellent than a prophet.
10. For this is *he* of whom it is written, 'Behold, I send My messenger before Your face, who shall prepare Your way before You.' [a]
11. Truly I say to you, there has not arisen among *those* born of women *anyone* greater than John the Baptist. But the one who *is* least in the kingdom of heaven is greater than he.
12. For from the days of John the Baptist until now, the kingdom of heaven is taken with a *great* struggle, and *the* zealous *ones* lay hold on it.
13. For all the prophets and the law prophesied until John.
14. And if you are willing to receive *it*, he is Elijah who was to come. [b]
15. The one who has ears to hear, let him hear."

a - Mal. 3:1   b - Mal. 4:5

117

100. JESUS EXPOSES THAT GENERATION'S ATTITUDE

LUKE 7	MATTHEW 11

LUKE 7

31. And the Lord said, "To what then shall I compare the men of this generation? And what are they like?

32. They are like little children sitting and calling to one another in the marketplace, and saying, 'We have piped to you, but you did not dance; we have mourned to you, but you did not weep.'

33. For John the Baptist came neither eating bread nor drinking wine, and you said, 'He has a demon.'

34. The Son of man has come eating and drinking, and you say, 'Behold, a gluttonous man and a winebibber, a friend of tax collectors and sinners';

35. But wisdom is justified by all her children.'"

MATTHEW 11

16. "But to what shall I compare this generation? It is exactly like little children sitting in *the* markets and calling to their companions,

17. And saying, 'We have piped to you, and you did not dance; we have mourned to you, and you did not wail.'

18. For John came neither eating nor drinking, and they say, 'He has a demon.'

19. The Son of man came eating and drinking, and they say, 'Behold, a man who is a glutton and a winebibber, a friend of tax collectors and sinners.' But wisdom is justified by her children."

101. JESUS CORRECTS THESE CITIES FOR THEIR LACK OF REPENTANCE

MATTHEW 11

20. Then He began to castigate the cities in which most of His miracles had taken place, because they did not repent:

21. "Woe to you, Chorazin! Woe to you, Bethsaida! For if the miracles that have taken place in you had taken place in Tyre and Sidon, they would have repented long ago in sackcloth and ashes.

22. But I tell you, it shall be more tolerable for Tyre and Sidon in *the* day of judgment than for you.

23. And you, Capernaum, who have been exalted to heaven, shall be cast down to the grave. For if the miracles that have taken place in you had taken place in Sodom, it would have remained until this day. [a]

24. But I tell you, it shall be more tolerable for *the* land of Sodom in *the* day of judgment than for you."

a - Gen. 19:24-25

102. JESUS IS THANKFUL THAT THE FATHER HAS REVEALED THE KINGDOM OF GOD TO SPIRITUAL BABES

MATTHEW 11

25. At that time Jesus answered and said, "I praise You, O Father, Lord of heaven and earth, that You have hidden these things from the wise and intelligent, and have revealed them to babes.

26. Yes, Father, for it was well pleasing in Your sight *to do* this.

27. All things were delivered to Me by My Father; and no one knows the Son except the Father; neither does anyone know the Father except the Son, and the one to whom the Son personally chooses to reveal *Him.*

28. Come to Me, all you who labor and are *overly* burdened, and I will give you rest.

29. Take My yoke upon you, and learn from Me; for I am meek and lowly in heart; and you shall find rest for your souls. [a]

30. For My yoke *is* easy, and My burden is light."

a - Jer. 6:16

103. A WOMAN WASHES JESUS' FEET WITH HER TEARS AND HER HAIR, SHOWING AN ATTITUDE OF LOVE AND REPENTANCE

LUKE 7

36. Now one of the Pharisees invited Him to eat with him. And after going into the Pharisee's house, He sat down *at the table*.

37. And behold, a woman in the city who was a sinner, when she knew that He was sitting in the Pharisee's house, took an alabaster flask of ointment;

38. And she stood weeping behind Him, *and knelt* at His feet, *and* began to wash His feet with *her* tears and to wipe *them* with the hairs of her head*;* and she was ardently kissing His feet and anointing *them* with the ointment.

39. But when he saw *this*, the Pharisee who had invited Him spoke within himself, saying, "This *man*, if He were a prophet, would have known who and what the woman *is* who is touching Him because she is a sinner."

40. Then Jesus answered *and* said to him, "Simon, I have something to say to you." And he said, "Teacher, say *on*."

41. "There were two debtors of a certain creditor; one owed five hundred silver coins, and the other fifty.

42. But when they did not have *anything with which* to pay *him*, he forgave *them* both. Tell *Me* then, which of them will love him most?"

43. And Simon answered *and* said, "I suppose *the one* whom he forgave the most." And He said to him, "You have judged rightly."

44. And after turning to the woman, He said to Simon, "Do you see this woman? I came into your house, and you did not provide *any* water *to wash* My feet; but she has washed My feet with *her* tears and wiped *them* with the hairs of her head.

45. You did not give Me a kiss; but she, from the *time* I came in, has not ceased to ardently kiss My feet.

46. You did not anoint My head with oil; but she has anointed My feet with ointment.

47. For this cause, I tell you, her many sins have been forgiven because she loved much. But to whom little is forgiven, he loves little."

48. And He said to her, "Your sins have been forgiven."

49. Then those who were sitting with *Him* began to say within themselves, "Who is this, Who even forgives sins?"

50. But He said to the woman, "Your faith has saved you. Go in peace."

Pool of Siloam

104. AT THE FALL FESTIVAL SEASON IN JERUSALEM, JESUS HEALS A MAN OF A 38-YEAR INFIRMITY ON THE SABBATH

JOHN 5

1. After these things *there* was a feast* of the Jews, [a] and Jesus went up to Jerusalem.

2. And there is in Jerusalem at the sheep gate a pool, called Bethesda in Hebrew, which has five porches.

3. And in these *porches* were lying a great multitude of those who were sick, blind, lame *and* withered. They were waiting for the stirring of the water.

4. For from time to time, an angel descended into the pool and agitated the water; and the first one to enter after the agitation of the water was made well from whatever disease he had.

5. Now a certain man was there who had been *suffering with* an infirmity for thirty-eight years.

6. Jesus saw him lying *there*, and, knowing that he had been there a long time, said to him, "Do you desire to be made whole?"

7. And the infirm *man* answered Him, "Sir, I do not have anyone to put me in the pool after the water has been agitated. But while I am going, another *one* steps down before me."

8. Jesus said to him, "Arise, take up your bedroll and walk."

9. And immediately the man was made whole; and he took up his bedroll and walked. Now that day was a Sabbath.

10. For this reason, the Jews said to the man who had been healed, "It is *the* Sabbath *day*. It is not lawful for you to take up your bedroll."

11. He answered them, "The one Who made me whole said to me, 'Take up your bedroll and walk.' "

12. Then they asked him, "Who is the one Who said to you, 'Take up your bedroll and walk'? "

13. But the man who had been healed did not know Who it was, for Jesus had moved away, *and* a crowd was in the place.

14. After these things, Jesus found him in the temple and said to him, "Behold, you have been made whole. Sin no more, so that something worse does not happen to you."

15. The man went away and told the Jews that it was Jesus Who had made him whole.

16. And for this cause, the Jews persecuted Jesus and sought to kill Him, because He had done these things on a Sabbath.

a - Lev. 23:23-44

---

*This Feast has been a topic of varying discussion by many students and scholars. Most have supposed that this Feast was a Passover. But a further examination of the substance and topics of this feast actually shows that it was a fall festival season. The topics are the resurrections and the judgments. The first resurrection, the resurrection to eternal life, occurs at the second coming of Christ. The resurrection to judgment and/or damnation occurs after the Millennium, as pictured by the Last Great Day. We find both of these events recorded in the twentieth chapter of Revelation. This festival season could only be the fall festival season. The Feast of Trumpets, the Day of Atonement, the Feast of Tabernacles and the Last Great Day comprise the entire fall festival season. All of these feasts are known as judgment feasts. Another contextual verification is the pattern of John's writings. Chapters 2 and 3 record the Passover. Chapter 4 has an allusion to Pentecost. Chapter 5 shows the fall festival season. Chapter 6 shows the Passover. Chapters 7-10:21 show the Feast of Tabernacles and the Last Great Day. The last part of Chapter 10 records the events surrounding the Feast of Dedication in the winter. Then the rest of the Book of John is devoted to the final Passover, and the resurrection, and the events occurring directly afterwards. Following this pattern we see that John wrote in this following sequence: Passover, fall festival season, Passover, fall festival season, Passover. This internal evidence clearly indicates that this Feast in John 5 could be nothing other than a fall festival.

105. JESUS WORKS, THE FATHER WORKS; AND HAS GIVEN ALL JUDGMENT AND THE POWER OF RESURRECTION TO JESUS

JOHN 5

17. But Jesus answered them, "My Father is working until now, and I work."

18. So then, on account of this *saying*, the Jews sought all the more to kill Him, not only because He had loosed the Sabbath,* but also *because* He had called God His own Father, making Himself equal with God.

19. Therefore, Jesus answered and said to them, "Truly, truly I say to you, the Son has no power to do anything of Himself, but only what He sees the Father do. For whatever He does, these things the Son also does in the same manner.

20. For the Father loves the Son, and shows Him everything that He Himself is doing. And He will show Him greater works than these, so that you may be filled with wonder.

21. For even as the Father raises the dead and gives life, in the same way also, the Son gives life to whom He will.

22. For the Father judges no one, but has committed all judgment to the Son

23. So that all may honor the Son, even as they honor the Father. The one who does not honor the Son does not honor the Father Who sent Him.

24. Truly, truly I say to you, the one who hears My word, and believes Him Who sent Me, has everlasting life and does not come into judgment; for he has passed from death into life.

25. Truly, truly I say to you, *the* hour is coming, and now is, when the dead shall hear the voice of the Son of God; and those who hear shall live.

26. For even as the Father has life in Himself, so also has He given to the Son to have life in Himself;

27. And has also given Him authority to execute judgment because He is *the* Son of man.

28. Do not wonder at this, for *the* hour is coming in which all who are in the graves shall hear His voice

29. And shall come forth: those who have practiced good unto a resurrection of life, and those who have practiced evil unto a resurrection of judgment.

30. I have no power to do anything of Myself; but as I hear, I judge; and My judgment is just because I do not seek My own will but the will of the Father, Who sent Me.

31. If I bear witness of Myself, My testimony is not true.

32. There is another who bears witness of Me, and I know that the testimony that he witnesses concerning Me is true.

33. You have sent to John, and he has borne witness to the truth.

34. Now I do not receive witness from man, but I say these things so that you may be saved.

35. He was a burning and shining light, and you were willing for a time to rejoice in his light.

36. But I have a greater witness than John's; for the works that the Father gave Me to complete, the *very* works that I am doing, themselves bear witness of Me, that the Father has sent Me.

37. And the Father Himself, Who sent Me, has borne witness of Me. You have neither heard His voice nor seen His form at any time.

38. And you do not have His word dwelling in you, for you do not believe Him Whom He has sent."

The Greek verb λυω, luoo, is properly translated into the English word, "loosed." Luoo means "to loose," as in loosing a law or regulation. In this case, Jesus loosed a law of Judaism that the Jews had added to the commandment of God. In loosing this law of Judaism, He did not break the Sabbath or transgress against the Fourth Commandment, which prohibits working on the Sabbath. Jesus Christ did not abrogate the seventh day as the Sabbath. Rather, He "loosed" the Sabbath from a traditional law of Judaism, which prohibited a person from carrying his bedroll on the Sabbath day.

106. YOU MUST BELIEVE MOSES AND THE SCRIPTURES TO BELIEVE JESUS AND HIS MESSAGE

JOHN 5

39. "You search the Scriptures, for in them you think that you have eternal life; and they are the ones that testify of Me.

40. But you are unwilling to come to Me, that you may have life.

41. I do not receive glory from men;

42. But I have known you, that you do not have the love of God in yourselves.

43. I have come in My Father's name, and you do not receive Me; *but* if another comes in his own name, you will receive him.

44. How are you able to believe, you who receive glory from one another, and do not seek the glory that *comes* from the only God?

45. Do not think that I will accuse you to the Father. There is *one* who accuses you, *even* Moses, in whom you have hope.

46. But if you believed Moses, you would have believed Me; for he wrote about Me.

47. And if you do not believe his writings, how shall you believe My words?"

107. JESUS TEACHES IN EVERY CITY AND VILLAGE

LUKE 8

1. Now it came to pass afterwards that He traveled through *all the land*, city by city and village by village, preaching and proclaiming the gospel *of* the kingdom of God; and the twelve *were* with Him,

2. And certain women who had been healed of evil spirits and infirmities: Mary who is called Magdalene, from whom seven demons had gone out;

3. And Joanna, wife of Chuza, a steward of Herod; and Susanna, and many others who were ministering to Him from their own substance.

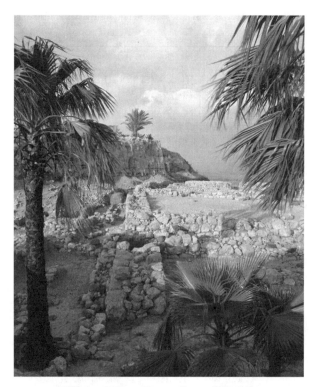

Village Ruins Near Sea of Galilee

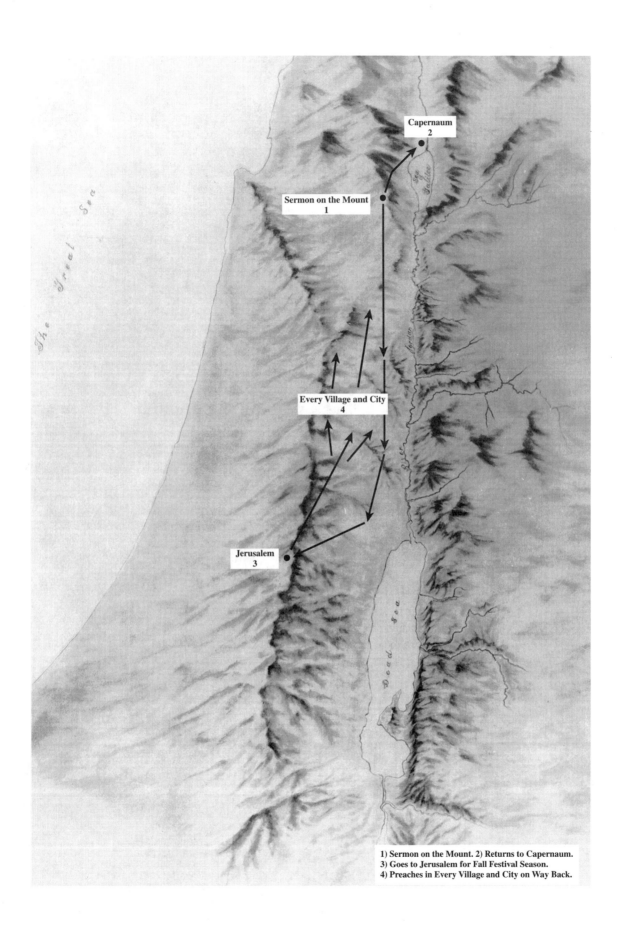

Capernaum
2

Sermon on the Mount
1

Every Village and City
4

Jerusalem
3

1) Sermon on the Mount. 2) Returns to Capernaum.
3) Goes to Jerusalem for Fall Festival Season.
4) Preaches in Every Village and City on Way Back.

123

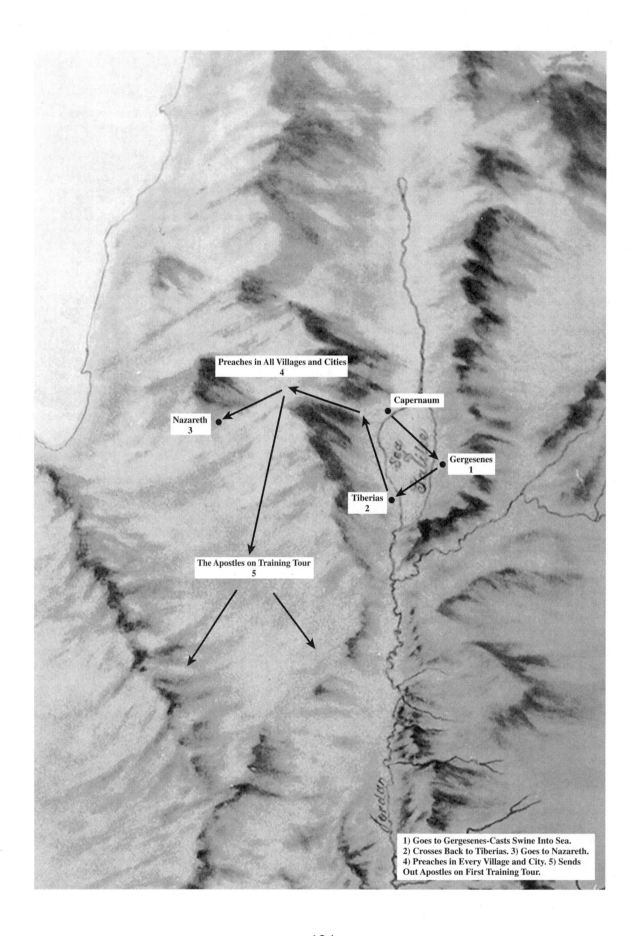

Preaches in All Villages and Cities
4

Nazareth
3

Capernaum

Gergesenes
1

Tiberias
2

The Apostles on Training Tour
5

1) Goes to Gergesenes-Casts Swine Into Sea.
2) Crosses Back to Tiberias. 3) Goes to Nazareth.
4) Preaches in Every Village and City. 5) Sends
Out Apostles on First Training Tour.

108. THE PARABLE OF THE SOWER

MATTHEW 13

1. Now in that same day, Jesus departed from the house and sat down by the sea.

2. And so great *a* multitude gathered around Him that He went into a ship and sat down, and all the multitude stood on the shore.

3. And He spoke many things to them in parables, saying, "Behold, the sower went out to sow.

4. And as he was sowing, some *of the seed* fell by the way; and the birds came and devoured them.

5. And some fell upon the rocky places, where they did not have much soil; and immediately they sprang up because the soil was not deep enough;

6. But after *the* sun rose, they were scorched; and because they did not have roots, they dried up.

7. And some *of the seed* fell among the thorns, and the thorns grew up and choked them.

8. And some fell upon the good ground, and yielded fruit—some a hundredfold, and some sixtyfold, and some thirtyfold.

9. The one who has ears to hear, let him hear."

MARK 4

1. Then He again began to teach by the sea. And a great multitude gathered together to Him, so that He went aboard the ship and sat in *it on* the sea; and the whole multitude was on the land by the sea.

2. And He taught them many things in parables, and said to them in His teaching,

3. "Listen well *to this*! Behold, the sower went out to sow.

4. And it happened *that* as he was sowing, one *seed* fell by the way; and the birds of heaven came and devoured it.

5. And another *seed* fell on a rocky place, where it did not have much soil; and it quickly sprang up, because it did not have depth of soil;

6. But after *the* sun rose, it was scorched; and because it did not have root, it withered away.

7. And another *seed* fell among the thorns, and the thorns grew up and choked it, and it did not yield *any* fruit.

8. And others fell into the good ground and yielded fruit, growing up and increasing; and one brought forth thirtyfold, and one sixtyfold, and one a hundredfold."

9. Then He said to them, "The one who has ears to hear, let him hear."

LUKE 8

4. And *as* a great multitude *was* assembling, and those who were coming to Him from every city, He spoke a parable:

5. "The sower went out to sow his seed; and as he sowed, some *seed* fell by the road; and it was trampled upon, and the birds of heaven devoured it.

6. And other *seed* fell upon the rock; and after it had sprung up it withered because it did not have *any* moisture.

7. And other *seed* fell among the thorns; and after springing up together, the thorns choked it.

8. And other *seed* fell upon the good ground, and after springing up produced fruit a hundredfold." *And* when He had said these things, He cried aloud, saying, "The one who has ears to hear, let him hear."

Fertile Valley Near Nazareth

125

109. THE PARABLES WERE GIVEN SO THE MULTITUDE WOULD NOT UNDERSTAND

MATTHEW 13

10. And His disciples came to Him and asked, "Why do You speak to them in parables?"

11. And He answered *and* said to them, "Because it has been given to you to know the mysteries of the kingdom of heaven, but to them it has not been given.

12. For whoever has *understanding*, to him more shall be given, and he shall have an abundance; but whoever does not have *understanding*, even what he has shall be taken away from him.

13. For this *reason* I speak to them in parables, because seeing, they see not; and hearing, they hear not; neither do they understand.

14. And in them is fulfilled the prophecy of Isaiah, which says, 'In hearing you shall hear, and in no way understand; and *in* seeing you shall see, and in no way perceive;

15. For the heart of this people has grown fat, and their ears are dull of hearing, and their eyes they have closed; lest they should see with their eyes, and should hear with their ears, and should understand with their hearts, and should be converted, and I should heal them.'

16. But blessed *are* your eyes, because they see; and your ears, because they hear.

17. For truly I say to you, many prophets and righteous *men* have desired to see what you see, and have not seen; and to hear what you hear, and have not heard." [a]

MARK 4

10. Now when He was alone, those who were around Him with the twelve asked Him *about* the parable.

11. And He said to them, "To you *it* has been given to know the mystery of the kingdom of God; but to those who are without, all things are done in parables;

12. So that *in* seeing they may see, and not perceive; and *in* hearing they may hear, and not understand; lest they should be converted, and *their* sins should be forgiven them." [a]

a - Isa. 6:9-10

LUKE 8

9. Then His disciples asked Him, saying, "What might this parable be?"

10. And He said, "To you it has been given to know the mysteries of the kingdom of God; but to the rest *it is given* in parables, so that *in* seeing they may not see, and *in* hearing they may not understand." [a]

Typical Outdoor Market

126

110. JESUS' EXPLANATION OF THE PARABLE
OF THE SOWER TO HIS DISCIPLES

MATTHEW 13	MARK 4	LUKE 8

MATTHEW 13

18. "Therefore, hear the parable of the sower:

19. When anyone hears the Word of the kingdom and does not understand *it*, the wicked one comes and snatches away that which was sown in his heart. This is the one who was sown by the way.

20. Now the one who was sown upon the rocky places is the one who hears the Word and immediately receives it with joy;

21. But *because* he has no root in himself, *he* does not endure; for when tribulation or persecution arises because of the Word, he is quickly offended.

22. And the one who was sown among the thorns is the one who hears the Word, but the cares of this life and the deceitfulness of riches choke the Word, and it becomes unfruitful.

23. But the one who was sown on good ground, this is the one who hears the Word and understands, who indeed brings forth fruit and produces—one a hundredfold, another sixtyfold *and* another thirtyfold."

MARK 4

13. And He said to them, "Don't you understand this parable? Then how will you know all the *other* parables?

14. The sower sows the Word.

15. Now the ones by the way, where the Word was sown, these are the ones who hear, but Satan comes at once and takes away the Word that was sown in their hearts.

16. And the ones which were in like manner sown upon the rocky places, these are *the ones* who when they hear the Word, immediately receive it with joy;

17. But *because* they have no root in themselves, they do not endure; when tribulation or persecution arises because of the Word, they are quickly offended.

18. And those which were sown among the thorns, these are the ones who hear the Word,

19. But the cares of this life, and the deceitfulness of riches, and the lusts of other things *that* come into *their lives* choke the Word, and it becomes unfruitful.

20. Now those which were sown upon the good ground, these are *the ones* who hear the Word and receive *it*, and bring forth fruit, one thirtyfold, and one sixtyfold, and one a hundredfold."

LUKE 8

11. "Now this is the parable: The seed is the Word of God;

12. And those *that fell* by the road are the ones who hear, but the devil comes and takes away the Word from their heart, lest they should believe *and* be saved.

13. And those *that fell* upon the rock *are* the ones who, when they hear, receive the Word with joy; but these do not have any root, who believe *only* for a while, and in time of trial fall away.

14. And those that fell into the thorns are the ones who have heard, but are choked *while* pursuing *the* cares and riches and pleasures of life, and do not bring *any fruit* to maturity.

15. And those that *fell* on the good ground are the ones who, in a right and good heart, hear the Word *and* keep *it*, and bring forth fruit with endurance."

*Rocky Places
Did Not Produce*

*"Some Will Produce A
Hundred Times"*

111. ALL SECRETS SHALL BE REVEALED, AND NOTHING SHALL BE HIDDEN

MARK 4

21. And He said to them, "Is a lamp *lit* to be put under a bushelbasket or under a bed? *Is it* not rather *lit* to be put on a lampstand?
22. For there is nothing hidden that shall not be made manifest; nor has any secret thing taken place, but that it should come to light.
23. If anyone has ears to hear, let him hear."

LUKE 8

16. "Now no one after lighting a lamp covers it with a vessel, or puts *it* under a couch, but puts *it* on a lampstand, so that those who are entering may see the light.
17. For *there* is nothing hidden that shall not be made manifest, nor *any* secret that shall not be known and come to light."

112. YOU ARE RESPONSIBLE FOR WHAT YOU HEAR

MARK 4

24. And He said to them, "Take heed *to* what you hear: *for* with whatever measure you use, it shall be measured back to you; and to those who hear, *it* shall be added.
25. For whoever has, to him shall *more* be given; but the one who does not have, even that which he has shall be taken from him."

LUKE 8

18. "Therefore, take heed how you hear. For whoever has, to him shall be given; but whoever does not have, even what he seems to have shall be taken from him."

113. THE PARABLE OF THE TARES

MATTHEW 13

24. And He put another parable before them, saying, "The kingdom of heaven is compared to a man who was sowing good seed in his field;
25. But while men were sleeping, his enemy came and sowed tares among the wheat, and went away.
26. Now when the blades sprouted and produced fruit, then the tares also appeared.
27. And the servants came to the master of the house *and* said to him, 'Sir, did you not sow good seed in your field? Then where did these tares come from?'
28. And he said to them, 'A man *who is* an enemy has done this.' Then the servants said to him, 'Do you want us to go out and gather them?'
29. But he said, 'No, lest while you are gathering the tares, you *also* uproot the wheat with them.
30. Allow both to grow together until the harvest; and at the time of the harvest, I will say to the reapers, "Gather the tares first, and bind them into bundles to burn them; but gather the wheat into my granary." ' "

114. A PARABLE OF HOW GOD FULFILLS HIS PURPOSE COMPARED TO A HARVEST

MARK 4

26. Then He said, "The kingdom of God is likened to this: *It is* as if a man should cast seed upon the earth,
27. And should sleep and rise night and day, and the seed should sprout and grow, *but* he does not know how.
28. For the earth brings forth fruit of itself, first a blade, then a head, then full grain in the head.
29. And when the grain is mature, immediately he puts in the sickle, for the harvest has come." [a]

a - Joel 3:13; Rev. 14:15

115. THE PARABLE OF THE GRAIN OF MUSTARD SEED

MATTHEW 13

31. Another parable He presented to them, saying, "The kingdom of heaven is compared to a *tiny* mustard seed which a man took and sowed in his field;
32. Which indeed is very small among all the seeds; but after it is grown, it is greater than all the herbs, and becomes a tree, so that the birds of heaven come and roost in its branches." [a]

a - Dan. 4:12

MARK 4

30. And He said, "To what *then* shall we liken the kingdom of God? Or with what parable shall we compare it?
31. *It is* like a *tiny* mustard seed, which, when it has been sown upon the earth, is less than all the seeds that *are* upon the earth;
32. But when it has been sown, it grows up and becomes greater than all the herbs, and produces great branches, so that the birds of heaven are able to roost under the shadow of it." [a]

116. THE KINGDOM OF GOD COMPARED TO LEAVEN
MATTHEW 13

33. Another parable He spoke to them: "The kingdom of heaven is compared to leaven which a woman took and hid in three measures of flour until all was leavened."

117. THE PURPOSE OF PARABLES
MATTHEW 13

34. Jesus spoke all these things to the multitudes in parables, and without a parable He did not speak to them;
35. So that it might be fulfilled which was spoken by the prophet, saying, "I will open My mouth in parables; I will utter things hidden from *the* foundation of *the* world." [a]

a - Psa. 78:2; 49:4

118. THE EXPLANATION OF THE PARABLES TO HIS DISCIPLES

MATTHEW 13

36. And after dismissing the multitude, Jesus went into the house. Then His disciples came to Him, saying, "Explain to us the parable of the tares of the field."
37. And He answered *and* said to them, "The one Who sows the good seed is the Son of man;
38. And the field is the world; and the good seed, these are the children of the kingdom; but the tares are the children of the wicked *one*.
39. Now the enemy who sowed them is the devil; and the harvest is *the* end of the age, and the reapers are the angels.
40. Therefore, as the tares are gathered and consumed in the fire, so shall it be in the end of this age.
41. The Son of man shall send forth His angels, and they shall gather out of His kingdom all the offenders and those who are practicing lawlessness;

MARK 4

33. And with many such parables He spoke the Word to them, as they were able to hear;
34. For without a parable He did not speak to them; but He explained all things to His disciples privately.

Nazareth

129

MATTHEW 13

42. And they shall cast them into the furnace of fire; there shall be weeping and gnashing of teeth.
43. Then shall the righteous shine forth as the sun in the kingdom of their Father. The one who has ears to hear, let him hear." [a]

a - Dan. 12:3

Pearl of Great Price

119. THE KINGDOM OF GOD COMPARED TO HIDDEN TREASURE

MATTHEW 13

44. "Again, the kingdom of heaven is compared to treasure hidden in a field; which when a man finds, he conceals, and for the joy of *finding* it, goes and sells everything that he has, and buys that field."

120. THE KINGDOM OF GOD COMPARED TO THE PEARL OF GREAT PRICE

MATTHEW 13

45. "Again, the kingdom of heaven is compared to a merchant seeking beautiful pearls;
46. Who, after finding one very precious pearl, went and sold everything that he had, and bought it."

121. THE KINGDOM OF GOD COMPARED TO A FISHERMAN'S NET

MATTHEW 13

47. "Again, the kingdom of heaven is compared to a dragnet cast into the sea, gathering in every kind *of fish;*
48. Which after it was filled was drawn up on shore; and they sat down and collected the good into vessels, and the unfit they threw away.
49. This is the way it will be in the end of the age: the angels shall go out, and shall separate the wicked from among the righteous,
50. And shall cast them into the furnace of fire; there shall be wailing and gnashing of teeth."

122. HIS DISCIPLES UNDERSTOOD THE PARABLES

MATTHEW 13

51. Jesus said to them, "Have you understood all these things?" They said to Him, "Yes, Lord."
52. Then He said to them, "Therefore, every scribe who has been instructed in the kingdom of heaven is like a man *who is* a householder, who brings forth out of his treasure *things* new and old."
53. And it came to pass *that* when Jesus had finished these parables, He departed from there.

123. YOU MUST FOLLOW JESUS IN SPITE OF ALL PERSONAL CIRCUMSTANCES

MATTHEW 8

18. But when Jesus saw great multitudes around Him, He commanded *His disciples* to depart to the other side.

19. And a certain scribe came to *Him* and said, "Master, I will follow You wherever You may go."

20. Then Jesus said to him, "Foxes have holes, and birds of heaven *have* nests; but the Son of man has no place to lay His head."

21. And another of His disciples said to Him, "Lord, allow me first to go and bury my father."

22. But Jesus said to him, "Follow Me, and leave the dead to bury their own dead."

124. JESUS REBUKES A STORM

MARK 4

35. Now on the same day, when evening came, He said to them, "Let us go over to the other side."

36. And after dismissing the multitude, they took Him with *them*, as He was *already* in the ship; and there were many other small ships with Him also.

37. And a violent windstorm came up, and the waves were crashing into the ship so forcefully that it was rapidly filling up.

38. Now He was at the stern sleeping on a cushion. And they aroused Him, and said to Him, "Master, don't You care that we are perishing?"

39. And after being awakened, He rebuked the wind and said to the sea, "Silence! Be still." And the wind died, and there was a great calm.

40. And He said to them, "Why are you so fearful? Why do you not have faith?"

41. But they were afraid, and said to one another in great fear, "Who then is this, that even the wind and the sea obey Him?"

LUKE 8

22. Now it came to pass on one of those days that He and His disciples went into a ship; and He said to them, "Let us go over to the other side of the lake." And they put off *from the shore*.

23. And as they sailed, He fell asleep; and a windstorm came down on the lake, and they were being filled *with water*, and were in danger.

24. Then they came to *Him and* awoke Him, saying, "Master, Master, we are perishing!" And He arose *and* rebuked the wind and the raging of the water; and they ceased, and there was a calm.

25. And He said to them, "Where is your faith?" But they were afraid, *and* wondered, saying to one another, "Who then is this that He commands even the winds and the water, and they obey Him?"

MATTHEW 8

23. And when He entered into the ship, His disciples followed Him.

24. Now a great tempest suddenly arose in the sea, so great that the ship was being covered by the waves; but He was sleeping.

25. And His disciples came to *Him* and awoke Him, saying, "Lord, save us! We are perishing."

26. And He said to them, "Why are you afraid, O *you* of little faith?" Then He arose *and* rebuked the winds and the sea, and there was a great calm.

27. But the men were amazed, saying, "What kind *of man* is this, that even the winds and the sea obey Him?"

Violent Storm
- H. Armstrong Roberts

125. JESUS CASTS THE LEGION OF DEMONS OUT OF A MAN AND THEY GO INTO A HERD OF SWINE

LUKE 8

26. Then they sailed down to the country of the Gadarenes, which is across from Galilee.
27. And when He went out on the land, *there* met Him a certain man from the city who had *been possessed by* demons for a long time; and he was not wearing *any* clothes, and did not dwell in a house, but in the tombs.
28. Now when he saw Jesus, he cried out and fell down in front of Him, and said with a loud voice, "What do You have to do with me, Jesus, Son of God the Most High? I beseech You, do not torment me."
29. For He had commanded the unclean spirit to come out of the man. For many times it had seized him, and *each time* he was restrained, being bound with chains and fetters; but *after* breaking the bonds, he was driven by the demon into the desert.
30. And Jesus asked it, saying, "What is your name?" And it said, "Legion," because many demons had entered into him.
31. Then it begged Him that He would not command them to go away into the abyss.
32. Now there was a herd of many swine feeding there on the mountain, and they begged Him that He would allow them to enter into the *swine*; and He gave them permission.
33. And the demons went out of the man *and* entered into the swine, and the *whole* herd rushed *headlong* down the steep *slope* into the lake and were drowned.

MARK 5

1. And they came to the other side of the sea, to the country of the Gadarenes.
2. And as soon as He had left the ship, *there* met Him from out of the tombs a man with an unclean spirit,
3. Who had his dwelling among the tombs; and no one had the power to restrain him even with chains;
4. For he had often been bound with fetters and chains, but the chains had been torn to pieces by him, and the fetters had been shattered; and no one had the strength to subdue him.
5. And continually, night and day, in the mountains and in the tombs, he was screaming and cutting himself with stones.
6. But when He saw Jesus from afar, he ran and worshiped Him.
7. And crying *out* with a loud voice, he said, "What have I to do with You, Jesus, Son of God the Most High? I adjure You by God, do not torment me."
8. For He was saying to it, "Unclean spirit, come out of the man."
9. And He asked it, "What *is* your name?" And it answered, "My name *is* Legion, because we are many."
10. And it begged Him again and again that He would not send them out of the country.
11. Now near the mountain, there was a large herd of swine feeding;
12. And all the demons pleaded with Him, saying, "Send us to the swine, so that we may enter into them."

MATTHEW 8

28. And when He had come to the other side into the country of the Gergesenes, *there* met Him two who were possessed by demons coming out of the tombs, so violent that no one was able to pass by that way.
29. And they cried out at once, saying, "What do You have to do with us, Jesus, *the* Son of God? Have You come here to torment us before *the* time?"
30. Now there was far off from them a herd of many swine feeding;
31. And the demons pleaded with Him, saying, "If You cast us out, allow us to go into the herd of swine."
32. And He said to them, "Go!" And after coming out, they went into the herd of swine; and the entire herd of swine suddenly rushed down the steep *slope* into the sea and died in the waters.
33. But those who were tending *them* fled, and after going into the city reported everything, and what had happened to those *who had been* possessed by demons.
34. And the entire city immediately went out to meet Jesus; and when they saw Him, they besought Him to depart from their borders.

*Mountain Slope
Runs into Sea*

LUKE 8

34. Now when those who were feeding *the swine* saw what had taken place, they fled; and they went *and* reported *it* to the city and to the country.

35. And those *who heard* went out to see what had taken place; and they came to Jesus, and found the man from whom the demons had gone out, clothed and of a sound mind, seated at Jesus' feet. And they were afraid.

36. And those who had seen *it* related to them how the one who had been possessed by demons was healed.

37. Then all the multitude of the Gadarenes from the country around asked Him to depart from them; for they were filled with great fear. And He went into the ship to return.

38. And the man from whom the demons had gone out begged to be *taken* with Him. But Jesus sent him away, saying,

39. "Return to your own house and declare all that God has done for you." And he went throughout the whole city, proclaiming all that Jesus had done for him.

MARK 5

13. Then Jesus immediately permitted them *to go*. And the unclean spirits went out *of the man and* entered into the swine; and the herd stampeded down the steep *slope* into the sea (now they were about two thousand), and they *all* drowned in the sea.

14. And those who were feeding the swine fled *in fear* and reported *it* in the city and in the country. Then they went out to see what it was that had been done.

15. And they came to Jesus and saw the man who had been possessed by demons, the one who had the Legion, sitting and clothed and of a sound mind; and they were afraid.

16. Then those who had seen *it* reported to them what had happened to the one who had been possessed by demons, and *the things* concerning the swine.

17. And they began to urge Him to depart from their borders.

18. Now when He boarded the ship, the one who had been possessed by demons begged Him that he might be with Him.

19. But Jesus did not permit him, rather he said to him, "Go to your house and to your own, and tell them how much the Lord has done for you, and *how He* has pitied you."

20. Then he departed and began to proclaim in Decapolis how much Jesus had done for him; and all were amazed.

Demon Possession
- Wide World Photos

Fishermen and Boat on Sea of Galilee
- Matson Photo Service

South of Sea of Galilee

Beth Gerah South End of Sea of Galilee

133

126. JESUS RETURNS TO THE OTHER SIDE OF THE SEA, AND MULTITUDES ARE WAITING FOR HIM

LUKE 8	MARK 5	MATTHEW 9
40. Now it came to pass *that* when Jesus returned, the multitude gladly received Him; for they had all been looking for Him.	21. Now when Jesus had again crossed to the other side *of the sea* by ship, a great multitude was gathered to Him; and He was by the sea.	1. And after going into the ship, He passed over and came to His own city.

127. JAIRUS REQUESTS HEALING FOR HIS DAUGHTER

LUKE 8	MARK 5	MATTHEW 9
41. And behold, a man came whose name *was* Jairus, and he was a ruler of the synagogue; and after falling at Jesus' feet, he begged Him to come to his house, 42. Because his only daughter, about twelve years *old*, was dying. And as He went, the multitudes were thronging Him.	22. And behold, one of the rulers of the synagogue came, Jairus by name; and when he saw Him, he fell at His feet; 23. And he earnestly besought Him, saying, "My little daughter is at the point of death. *I beg* You to come *and* lay *Your* hands on her, so that she may be healed; and she shall live." 24. And He departed with him; and a great multitude followed Him, pressing around Him.	18. While He was saying these things to them, behold, a ruler came and worshiped Him, saying, "My daughter has just died, but come and lay Your hands on her, and she shall live." 19. Then Jesus and His disciples arose and followed him.

128. A WOMAN IS HEALED OF A HEMORRHAGE SHE HAD FOR TWELVE YEARS

LUKE 8	MARK 5	MATTHEW 9
43. And a woman who had been *afflicted* with a flow of blood for twelve years, *and* had spent *her* whole living on physicians, *but* could not be cured by anyone, 44. Came behind *Him and* touched the border of His garment; and immediately the flow of her blood stopped. 45. And Jesus said, "Who touched Me?" And as everyone began to deny *it*, Peter and those with Him said, "Master, the multitudes are thronging and pressing You, and You ask, 'Who touched Me?'"	25. Then a certain woman who had been *afflicted with* an issue of blood *for* twelve years, 26. And had suffered greatly under *the hand of* many physicians, and had spent all that she had, and was not benefited in any way but rather was getting worse, 27. When she heard about Jesus, came in the multitude behind *Him and* touched His garment; 28. For she said, "If I can only touch His garments, I shall be cured." 29. And at once the fountain of her blood was dried up,	20. And behold, a woman who had been *afflicted* with a flow of blood *for* twelve years, after coming behind *Him*, touched the hem of His garment. 21. For she said within herself, "If only I shall touch His garment, I shall be healed." 22. But Jesus turned; and seeing the woman, He said to her, "Be of good courage, daughter; your faith has made you whole." And from that hour the woman was healed.

LUKE 8

46. But Jesus said, "Someone touched Me, because I know *that* power went out from Me."
47. Then the woman, seeing that her *act* was not concealed, came trembling; and after falling down in front of Him before all the people, she declared for what cause she had touched Him, and how she had immediately been healed.
48. And He said to her, "Be of good courage, daughter; your faith has healed you. Go in peace."

MARK 5

and she knew in *her* body that she was healed from the scourge.
30. Now Jesus knew immediately within Himself *that* power had gone out of Him; *and* turning in the crowd, He said, "Who touched My garments?"
31. But His disciples said to Him, "You see the crowd pressing around You, and You ask, 'Who touched Me?'"
32. Then He looked around to see who had done this.
33. And the woman, frightened and trembling, knowing what had been done in her, came and fell down before Him, and told Him all the truth.
34. Then He said to her, "Daughter, your faith has cured you. Go in peace, and be whole from your scourge."

City of Tiberius

Stone from Synagogue

129. JAIRUS' DAUGHTER DIES AND IS RAISED TO LIFE AGAIN

LUKE 8

49. While He was yet speaking, one came from the ruler of the synagogue's *house*, saying to him, "Your daughter has died. Do not trouble the Master."
50. But hearing *this*, Jesus answered him, saying, "Do not be afraid. Only believe, and she shall be restored."
51. And when He went into the house, He did not allow anyone to go in *with Him* except Peter and James and John, and the father and the mother of the child.
52. And they were all weeping and bewailing her. But He said, "Do not weep. She is not dead, but is sleeping."

MARK 5

35. *While* He was still speaking, they came from the ruler of the synagogue's *house*, saying, "Your daughter is dead. Why bother the Teacher any longer?"
36. But when Jesus heard the words that were spoken, He said to the ruler of the synagogue, "Do not be afraid. Only believe."
37. And He did not allow anyone to accompany Him except Peter and James and John, the brother of James.
38. Now when He came to the house of the ruler of the synagogue, He saw a tumult, and *people* weeping and wailing loudly.

MATTHEW 9

23. Now when Jesus came into the ruler's house, and saw the flute players and the multitude making an uproar,
24. He said to them, "Back away! For the damsel is not dead, but is sleeping." And they laughed at Him.
25. But when the multitude had been put out, He went in *and* took hold of her hand, and the damsel arose.
26. And this report went out into all that land.

LUKE 8

53. Then they laughed at Him, knowing that she was dead.

54. But after putting everyone outside, He took hold of her hand and called out, saying, "Child, arise."

55. And her spirit returned, and she immediately arose; and He directed *that something* to eat should be given to her.

56. And her parents were amazed, but He charged them not to tell anyone what had happened.

MARK 5

39. And when He had entered, He said to them, "Why are you making a tumult and weeping? The child is not dead, but is *only* sleeping."

40. And they laughed at Him *in disbelief*. But after He had put *them* all out, He took with *Him* the father and the mother of the child, and those with Him, and went into *the room* where the child was lying.

41. And taking the child by the hand, He said to her, "Talitha, cumi"; which is, being interpreted, "Little girl, I say to you, arise!"

42. And immediately the little girl arose and walked, for she was twelve years *old*. And they were filled with great amazement.

43. Then He strictly charged them that no one should know this, and He told *them* to give her *something* to eat.

Two Synagogue Scenes of Jesus' Times

130. JESUS HEALS TWO BLIND MEN

MATTHEW 9

27. Now as Jesus was traveling from there, two blind *men* followed, crying and saying, "Have pity on us, Son of David!"

28. And after coming into the house, the blind *men* came to Him; and Jesus said to them, "Do you believe that I have the power to do this?" They said to Him, "Yes, Lord."

29. Then He touched their eyes, saying, "According to your faith be it to you."

30. And their eyes were opened. And He sternly warned them, saying, "See that you do not let anyone know *it*."

31. But they went out *and* made Him known in all that land.

131. JESUS HEALS DUMB MAN POSSESSED BY A DEMON

MATTHEW 9

32. And as they were leaving, behold, they brought to Him a dumb man, possessed by a demon;

33. And when the demon had been cast out, the *one who had been* dumb spoke. And the multitudes wondered, saying, "Never has the like been seen in Israel."

34. But the Pharisees said, "By the prince of the demons He casts out demons."

35. Then Jesus went around to all the cities and the villages, teaching in their synagogues, and preaching the gospel of the kingdom, and healing every disease and every bodily weakness among the people.

132. JESUS IS MOVED WITH COMPASSION FOR THE PEOPLE
MATTHEW 9

36. And seeing the multitudes, He was moved with compassion for them, because they were wearied and scattered abroad, as sheep who did not have a shepherd. [a]
37. Then He said to His disciples, "The harvest *is* truly great, but the workmen *are* few;
38. Therefore, beseech the Lord of the harvest, that He may send out workmen into His harvest."

a - Num. 27:17; Isa. 53:6

133. A PROPHET HAS NO HONOR AND RESPECT IN HIS OWN COUNTRY

MARK 6

1. And He left there and came into His *own* country, and His disciples followed Him.
2. Now when the Sabbath day came, He began to teach in the synagogue; and many *of those* who heard Him were astonished, saying, "From where did this *man* get these things? And what *is* this wisdom that has been given to Him, that by His hands many miracles are done also?
3. Is this not the carpenter, the son of Mary, and the brother of James and Joses and Judas and Simon? And are not His sisters here with us?" And they were offended in Him.
4. But Jesus said to them, "A prophet is not without honor except in his *own* country, and among *his own* kinsmen, and in his *own* house."
5. And He was not able to do any works of power there, except that He laid *His* hands on a few sick people *and* healed *them.*
6. And He was amazed by their unbelief. Then He went about the villages in a circuit, teaching *the people.*

MATTHEW 13

54. And after coming into His *own* country, He taught them in their synagogue, so that they were amazed and said, "From where did this *man receive* this wisdom and *these* works of power?
55. Is this not the carpenter's son? *Is* not His mother called Mary, and His brothers James and Joses and Simon and Judas?
56. And His sisters, are they not all with us? From where then did this *man receive* all these things?"
57. And they were offended in Him. Then Jesus said to them, "A prophet is not without honor, except in his *own* country and in his *own* house."
58. And He did not do many works of power there because of their unbelief.

134. JESUS AUTHORIZES THE TWELVE APOSTLES TO HEAL AND PREACH, AND SENDS THEM ON THEIR FIRST TRAINING TOUR

MATTHEW 10

1. And when He had called His twelve disciples, He gave them authority over unclean spirits, to cast them out, and to heal every disease and every kind of sickness.
2. Now the names of the twelve apostles are these: first, Simon who is called Peter, and his brother Andrew; James, the *son* of Zebedee, and his brother John;

MARK 6

7. And He called the twelve to *Him* and began to send them out, two by two; and He gave them authority over unclean spirits.
8. And He commanded them not to take anything for *the* journey except a staff—no bag of provisions, nor bread, nor money in the belt;
9. But *to* be shod with sandals; and not to put on two coats.

LUKE 9

1. Then He called His twelve disciples together *and* gave them power and authority over all the demons, and to heal diseases;
2. And He sent them to proclaim the kingdom of God, and to heal those who were sick.
3. And He said to them, "Take nothing for the journey—neither staffs, nor provision bag, nor bread, nor money, nor two coats apiece.

MATTHEW 10	MARK 6	LUKE 9
3. Philip and Bartholomew; Thomas and Matthew, the *former* tax collector; James, the *son* of Alpheus; and Lebbeus, who was surnamed Thaddeus;	10. Then He said to them, "Wherever you *go, and* come into a house, remain there until you leave that *city*.	4. And whatever house you may enter, lodge there and go forth from there.

3. Philip and Bartholomew; Thomas and Matthew, the *former* tax collector; James, the *son* of Alpheus; and Lebbeus, who was surnamed Thaddeus;
4. Simon, the Cananean; and Judas Iscariot, who also betrayed Him.

10. Then He said to them, "Wherever you *go, and* come into a house, remain there until you leave that *city*.
11. But as many as will not receive you, nor hear you, when you depart from there, shake off the dust that *is* under your feet as a witness against them. Truly I say to you, it shall be more tolerable for Sodom and Gomorrah in *the* day of judgment than for that city."
12. And they went out and proclaimed that *all* should repent.
13. And they cast out many demons; and *they* anointed with oil many sick people, and healed *them*.

4. And whatever house you may enter, lodge there and go forth from there.
5. But whoever will not receive you, *as* you are departing from that city, shake off even the dust from your feet for a testimony against them."
6. Then they went out *and* passed through the villages, preaching the gospel and healing everywhere.

Desert Area of Sodom and Gomorrah

Dead Sea Near Sodom and Gomorrah

Desolate Region South of Sodom and Gomorrah

135. COMMISSION TO THE 12 APOSTLES: GO TO THE LOST SHEEP OF THE HOUSE OF ISRAEL

MATTHEW 10

5. These twelve Jesus sent out after commanding them, saying, "Do not go into *the* way of the Gentiles, and do not enter into a city of the Samaritans;
6. But go instead to the lost sheep of *the* house of Israel.
7. And *as you are* going, proclaim, saying, 'The kingdom of heaven is at hand.'
8. Heal *the* sick. Cleanse *the* lepers. Raise *the* dead. Cast out demons. Freely you have received; freely give.
9. Do not provide gold, nor silver, nor money in your belts,
10. Nor a provision bag for *the* way, nor two coats, nor shoes, nor a staff; for the workman is worthy of his food.
11. And whatever city or village you enter, inquire who in it is worthy, and there remain until you leave.
12. When you come into the house, salute it;
13. And if the house is indeed worthy, let your peace be upon it. But if it *is* not worthy, let your peace return to you.
14. And whoever shall not receive you, nor hear your words, when you leave *that* house or that city, shake off the dust from your feet.
15. Truly I say to you, it shall be more tolerable for *the* land of Sodom and Gomorrha in *the* day of judgment than for that city."

136. BE WISE AS SERPENTS, HARMLESS AS DOVES
MATTHEW 10

16. "Behold, I am sending you forth as sheep in *the* midst of wolves. Therefore, be wise as serpents and harmless as doves.
17. But beware of men; for they will deliver you up to councils, and they will scourge you in their synagogues;"

137. WHEN YOU ARE DELIVERED UP FOR A WITNESS, THE HOLY SPIRIT WILL INSPIRE YOU
MATTHEW 10

18. "And you shall also be brought before governors and kings for My sake, for a witness to them and to the Gentiles.
19. Now when they deliver you up, do not be anxious *about* how or what you should speak; for in that hour it shall be given to you what you shall speak.
20. For it is not you who speak, but the Spirit of your Father that speaks in you.
21. Then brother will deliver up brother to death; and *the* father, the child; and children will rise up against *their* parents and *have* them put to death.
22. And you shall be hated by all for My name's sake; but the one who endures to *the* end, that one shall be saved.
23. But when they persecute you in this city, escape into another; for truly I say to you, in no way shall you have completed *witnessing* to the cities of Israel until the Son of man has come.
24. A disciple is not above his teacher, nor a servant above his master.
25. It is sufficient for the disciple that he become as his teacher, and the servant as his master. If they have called the master of the house Beelzebub, how much more *shall they call* those of his household?
26. Therefore, do not fear them because there is nothing covered that shall not be uncovered, and *nothing* hidden that shall not be known.
27. What I tell you in the darkness, speak in the light; and what you hear in the ear, proclaim upon the housetops."

138. FEAR GOD, NOT MEN
MATTHEW 10

28. "Do not be afraid of those who kill the body, but do not have power to destroy the life; rather, fear Him Who has the power to destroy both life and body in Gehenna.
29. Are not two sparrows sold for a coin? And *yet* not one of them shall fall to the ground without your Father *taking account of it*.
30. But even the hairs of your head are all numbered.
31. Therefore, do not be afraid; you are better than many sparrows.
32. Now then, whoever shall confess Me before men, that one will I also confess before My Father Who *is* in heaven.
33. But whoever shall deny Me before men, that one will I also deny before My Father, Who *is* in heaven."

139. JESUS CAME NOT TO BRING PEACE, BUT A SWORD
MATTHEW 10

34. "Do not think that I have come to bring peace on the earth; I did not come to bring peace, but a sword.
35. For I have come to set a man at variance against his father, and a daughter against her mother, and a daughter-in-law against her mother-in-law.
36. And a man's enemies *shall be those of* his own household."

140. YOU MUST LOVE JESUS MORE THAN YOUR OWN FAMILY
MATTHEW 10

37. "The one who loves father or mother more than Me is not worthy of Me; and the one who loves son or daughter more than Me is not worthy of Me.
38. And the one who does not take up his cross and follow Me is not worthy of Me."

141. YOU MOST LOSE YOUR LIFE IN JESUS
MATTHEW 10

39. "The one who has found his life shall lose it; and the one who has lost his life for My sake shall find it."

142. THE BLESSING OF RECEIVING JESUS CHRIST
MATTHEW 10

40. "The one who receives you receives Me, and the one who receives Me receives Him Who sent Me.
41. The one who receives a prophet in *the* name of a prophet shall receive *the* reward of a prophet; and the one who receives a righteous *man* in *the* name of a righteous *man* shall receive the reward of a righteous *man*.
42. And *if* anyone shall in *the* name of a disciple give to one of these little ones to drink a cup of cold *water* only, truly I say to you, he shall in no way lose his reward."

MATTHEW 11

1. And it came to pass *that*, when Jesus had finished commanding His twelve disciples, He left there to teach and to preach in their cities.

143. HEROD THINKS JESUS IS JOHN THE BAPTIST RISEN FROM THE DEAD

MATTHEW 14	MARK 6	LUKE 9
1. At that time Herod the tetrach heard of the fame of Jesus, 2. And said to his servants, "This is John the Baptist; he has risen from the dead, and that is why these powerful deeds are at work in him."	14. Then King Herod heard *of Jesus*, because His name had become widely known; and he said, "John the Baptist has risen from *the* dead, and because of this these miracles are being worked by him."	7. Now Herod the tetrarch heard of all the things *that* were being done by Him; and he was perplexed because it was said by some that John had been raised from *the* dead,

MARK 6	LUKE 9
15. Others said, "It is Elijah." And others said, "It is a prophet, or one like the prophets."	8. And by some that Elijah had appeared, and by others that one of the ancient prophets had arisen.
16. But after hearing *these reports,* Herod said, "It is John, whom I beheaded. He has risen from *the* dead."	9. And Herod said, "I beheaded John, but Who is this about Whom I hear such things?" And he desired to see Him.

144. HOW JOHN THE BAPTIST WAS BEHEADED

MATTHEW 14

3. For Herod had arrested John, bound him and put *him* in prison, for the sake of Herodias, the wife of his brother Philip;

4. Because John had said to him, "It is not lawful for you to have her *as your wife.*"

5. And he desired to put him to death; *but he* feared the multitude because they held him to be a prophet.

6. Now when they were celebrating Herod's birthday, the daughter of Herodias danced before *them*; and it pleased Herod.

7. Therefore, he promised with an oath to give her whatever she might ask.

8. Then, being urged by her mother, she said, "Give me, here on a platter, the head of John the Baptist."

9. And the king was grieved; but because of the oaths and those who were sitting with him, he commanded *that it* be given.

10. And he sent *and* beheaded John in the prison.

11. And his head was brought on a platter and given to the damsel, and she brought *it* to her mother.

MARK 6

17. For Herod himself had sent and arrested John and had him bound in prison, because of Herodias, the wife of Philip his brother, whom he had married.

18. For John had said to Herod, "It is not lawful for you to have your brother's wife." [a]

19. And Herodias held it against him, and desired to kill him, but was not able;

20. Because Herod feared John, realizing *that* he *was* a righteous and holy man, and kept him safe. And after hearing him, *he* did many things; and *he* listened to him gladly.

21. But an opportune day came when Herod prepared a banquet on his birthday for his principal men, and for the chief captains and the important *men* of Galilee.

22. And the daughter of Herodias herself came in and danced, and *it* pleased Herod and those sitting with *him at the banquet; and* the king said to the young woman, "Ask me whatever you desire, and I will give *it* to you."

23. Then he swore to her, "Whatever you ask of me I will give to you, *up* to half of my kingdom."

24. And after going out, she said to her mother, "What shall I ask?" And she said, "The head of John the Baptist."

25. Then she immediately returned to the king with haste and said, "I desire that you give me at once the head of John the Baptist on a platter."

26. Now although the king was personally very sorrowful, because of the oaths and those who were sitting with *him*, he would not reject *her request.*

27. Then without delay, the king sent a guardsman *and* ordered his head to be brought.

28. And he went *and* beheaded him in the prison, and brought his head on a platter, and gave it to the young woman; and the young woman gave it to her mother.

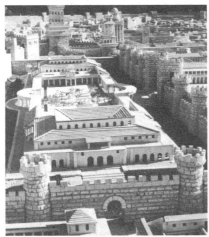

Herod's Palace—Model City Jerusalem

a - Lev. 18:16; 20:21

THE LENGTH OF JOHN THE BAPTIST'S MINISTRY

John the Baptist's ministry can be divided into two parts. The first part was his active ministry. The second part was his inactive ministry, which took place during the time he was in prison. He began preaching and baptizing in the spring of 26 AD, close to the Passover, when he was about thirty years old. After John's second Passover, which was the first Passover during Jesus' ministry in 27 AD, (John 2:13-25), he was still baptizing (John 3:23-24). Shortly thereafter he was arrested and imprisoned. This occurred before Jesus came into Galilee preaching the kingdom of God and repentance (Mark 1:14-15). The first part of John's ministry apparently lasted about 13 or 14 months.

Sometime after John's third Passover (the second during Jesus' ministry—see the explanation of Luke 6:1 in the section showing the Passover framework), which was in 28 AD, while in prison, he sent two of his disciples to ask Jesus if He were really the Messiah. (See Luke 7:19-23, Matt. 11:2-6.)

According to the chronology, sometime before the Passover in 29 AD (which would have been the fourth during John's ministry—the third during Jesus' ministry), John was beheaded by Herod. After John's disciples buried him, they came and told Jesus (Matt. 14:1-12). John's inactive ministry, while in prison apparently lasted just under two years. In summary, this makes the total length of John's ministry, active and inactive, approximately three years.

145. JOHN THE BAPTIST WAS BURIED BY HIS DISCIPLES

MATTHEW 14

12. Then his disciples came, and took the body, and buried it; and they went and told Jesus.

MARK 6

29. Now when his disciples heard of *it*, they came and took up his body, and laid it in the tomb.

Ancient Jewish Graveyard Restored

PART IV

FROM PASSOVER 29 AD
TO PASSOVER 30 AD

146. FEEDING OF 5,000 BEFORE THE THIRD PASSOVER

JOHN 6	MARK 6	LUKE 9	MATTHEW 14

JOHN 6

1. After these things, Jesus crossed over the Sea of Galilee (*or Sea* of Tiberias);
2. And a great multitude followed Him, because they had seen the miracles that He worked upon those who were sick.
3. Then Jesus went up into a mountain and sat there with His disciples.
4. Now the Passover, a feast of the Jews, was near. [a]
5. And when Jesus lifted up *His* eyes and saw a great multitude coming toward Him, He said to Philip, "How shall we buy enough loaves to feed *all* these?"
6. But He said this to test him, because He knew what He was about to do.
7. Philip answered Him, "Two hundred silver coins would not be sufficient to buy enough loaves for each of them to receive a little."
8. *Then* one of His disciples, Andrew, the brother of Simon Peter, said to Him,
9. "Here is a little boy who has five barley loaves and two small fish; but what are these for so many *people*?"

a - Lev. 23:5

MARK 6

30. Then the apostles gathered together with Jesus, and they related to Him everything, both what they had done and what they had taught.
31. And He said to them, "All of you come away into a desert place, and rest a while." For there were so many people coming and going that they did not have an opportunity even to eat.
32. Then they departed alone by ship to a place in *the* wilderness.
33. But the multitudes saw them leaving, and many recognized Him; and they all ran together there from all the cities, and went ahead of them; and they came together to Him.
34. And when Jesus arrived, He saw a great multitude; and He was moved with compassion toward them because they were like sheep without a shepherd. Then He began to teach them many things.

LUKE 9

10. Now when they returned, the apostles related to Him everything they had done. Then He took them *and* withdrew privately into a desert place of a city called Bethsaida.
11. And when the multitudes knew *it*, they followed Him; and He received them *and* spoke to them about the kingdom of God, and He healed those who had need of healing.
12. But when the day began to decline, the twelve came to Him and said, "Dismiss the multitude, so that they may go into the villages and the country round about, and may find lodging and provisions; for we are here in a desert place."
13. Then He said to them, "You give them *something* to eat." But they said, "There is nothing more than five loaves and two fish with us, unless we go *and* buy food for all the people."
14. For there were about five thousand men. Then He said to His disciples, "Make them sit in companies by fifties."

MATTHEW 14

13. Now after hearing *this*, Jesus departed from there by ship into a wilderness place apart. But when the multitudes heard *that He had left*, they followed Him on foot from the cities.
14. And after going out, Jesus saw a great multitude; and He was moved with compassion toward them, and healed their sick.
15. Now when evening was approaching, His disciples came to Him, saying, "*This* place is a wilderness, and the time *to eat* has already passed; dismiss the multitude so that they may go into the villages and buy food for themselves."
16. But Jesus said to them, "They do not need to go away. You give them *something* to eat."
17. But they said to Him, "We do not have *anything* here except five loaves and two fish."
18. And He said to them, "Bring them here to Me."

JOHN 6

10. Then Jesus said, "Have the men sit down." Now there was much grass in the place; therefore the men sat down, about five thousand in number.

11. And Jesus took the loaves; and when He had given thanks, He distributed *them* to the disciples, and the disciples to those who were sitting; and in like manner the small fish, as much as they desired.

12. And when they were filled, He said to His disciples, "Gather together the fragments that are left over, so that nothing may be lost."

13. Then they gathered *them* together, filling twelve baskets with fragments from the five barley loaves, which were left over by those who had eaten.

Spring of En-Gedi

MARK 6

35. Now because *it* was already a late hour, His disciples came to Him, saying, "This place is a wilderness, and the time *is* already late.

36. Dismiss them so that they may go into the country round about and buy food for themselves in the villages; for they have nothing to eat."

37. But He answered and said to them, "You give them *something* to eat." And they said to Him, "Shall we go *and* buy two hundred silver coins' worth of bread, and give *it* to them to eat?"

38. Then He said to them, "How many loaves do you have? Go and see." And when they knew, they said, "Five *loaves*, and two fish."

39. And He ordered them to make everyone sit down by companies on the green grass.

40. Then they sat down in ranks, by hundreds and by fifties.

41. And after taking the five loaves and the two fish, He looked up into heaven and blessed *them*; and He broke the loaves and gave *them* to His disciples, so that they might set *them* before the *people*. And the two fish He divided among *them* all.

42. And *they* all ate and were satisfied.

LUKE 9

15. And they did so, and made everyone sit down.

16. Then He took the five loaves and the two fish; *and* looking up into heaven, He blessed them and broke *them*, and gave *them* to the disciples to set before the multitude.

17. And they ate, and everyone was satisfied; and that which was left by them was taken up, twelve baskets *full*.

MATTHEW 14

19. And He commanded the multitude to sit on the grass. Then He took the five loaves and the two fish; *and* looking up into heaven, He blessed *them*; and He broke the loaves, and gave *them* to His disciples, and the disciples to the multitude.

20. And they all ate and were filled; and they took up twelve baskets full of the fragments that were left.

21. Now those who ate were about five thousand men, besides women and children.

Sea of Galilee

MARK 6

43. Then they took up twelve baskets full of fragments *of bread* and of fish.
44. And those who ate of the loaves were about five thousand men.

Loaves of Bread

147. JESUS GOES UP INTO A MOUNTAIN TO PRAY

JOHN 6

14. Now when the men saw the miracle that Jesus had done, they said, "Of a truth, this is the Prophet Who was to come into the world." [a]
15. Because Jesus perceived that they were about to come and seize Him, so that they might make Him king, He withdrew again to a mountain by Himself alone.
16. Now when evening came, His disciples went down to the sea;
17. And they went into a ship *and* were crossing the sea to Capernaum; for it had already become dark, and Jesus had not come to them.

a - Deut. 18:15

MARK 6

45. Then He commanded His disciples to get into the ship at once and go ahead *of Him* to the other side to Bethsaida, while He dismissed the multitude.
46. And after He had sent them away, He departed to the mountain to pray.

MATTHEW 14

22. And immediately Jesus compelled His disciples to enter the ship and go before Him to the other side, while He dismissed the multitude.
23. And after dismissing the multitude, He went up into the mountain apart to pray; and when evening came, He was there alone.

Mount Tabor

Sea of Galilee

148. JESUS WALKS ON THE WATER

JOHN 6	MARK 6	MATTHEW 14

JOHN 6

18. But the sea was tossing because a strong wind was blowing.

19. And after rowing about twenty-five or thirty furlongs, they saw Jesus walking on the sea and approaching the ship; and they were afraid.

20. But He said to them, "I am *He*. Do not be afraid."

21. Then they willingly received Him into the ship; and immediately the ship was at the land to which they were going.

MARK 6

47. Now when evening arrived, the ship was in the middle of the sea, and He *was* alone on the land.

48. And He saw them laboring in their rowing, because the wind was contrary to them. And about *the* fourth watch of the night, He came to them, walking on the sea, and would have passed by them.

49. But when they saw Him walking on the sea, they thought *it* was an apparition; and they cried out,

50. Because they all saw Him and were alarmed. And immediately He spoke to them, and said to them, "Be of good courage; *it* is I. Do not fear."

MATTHEW 14

24. But the ship was now in *the* middle of the sea, being tossed by the waves, because the wind was contrary.

25. Now in *the* fourth watch of the night, Jesus went to them, walking on the sea.

26. And when the disciples saw Him walking on the sea, they were troubled and said, "It is an apparition!" And they cried out in fear.

27. But immediately Jesus spoke to them, saying, "Be of good courage; *it* is I. Do not be afraid."

149. PETER WALKS ON THE WATER TO JESUS
MATTHEW 14

28. Then Peter answered Him *and* said, "Lord, if it is You, bid me to come to You upon the waters."

29. And He said, "Come." And after climbing down from the ship, Peter walked upon the waters to go to Jesus.

30. But when he saw *how* strong the wind *was*, he became afraid; and *as he* was beginning to sink, he cried out, saying, "Lord, save me!"

31. And immediately Jesus stretched out His hand and took hold of him, and said to him, "O *you* of little faith, why did you doubt?"

150. THE STORM CEASES WHEN JESUS COMES INTO THE BOAT

MATTHEW 14	MARK 6

MATTHEW 14

32. Now when they went into the ship, the wind ceased.

33. And those in the ship came and worshiped Him, saying, "You are truly the Son of God."

MARK 6

51. Then He went up to them into the ship, and the wind ceased. And they were amazed in themselves far beyond measure, and wondered.

52. For they did not understand *the miracle* of the loaves, because their hearts were hardened.

146

151. THE SICK ARE HEALED IN GENNESARET
BY TOUCHING JESUS' CLOTHES

MATTHEW 14	MARK 6
34. And after passing over *the sea*, they came to the land of Gennesaret.	53. And after crossing over *the sea*, they came to the land of Gennesaret and drew to shore.
35. And when the men of that place recognized Him, they sent to all the country around; and they brought to Him all those who were sick.	54. And when they came out of the ship, those *who dwelt there* immediately recognized Him.
36. And *they* besought Him that they might only touch the hem of His garment; and as many as touched *it* were healed.	55. Then they ran through all the country around, *and* began to carry those who were sick on stretchers, *taking them* wherever they heard that He was.
	56. And wherever He entered into villages or cities or fields, they laid in the marketplaces those who were sick; and they besought Him that they might only touch the border of His garment; and all those who touched Him were healed.

152. THE LESSON FOR THE THIRD PASSOVER:
JESUS IS THE BREAD OF LIFE

JOHN 6

22. On the next day, the multitude standing *on* the other side of the sea, who had observed that no other small ship was there besides the one into which the disciples had entered, and that Jesus had not gone into the small ship with His disciples, but that His disciples had departed alone;

23. (But other small ships had come from Tiberias near the place where they had eaten the bread, after the Lord had given thanks;)

24. Accordingly, when the multitude saw that Jesus was not there, nor His disciples, they also went in the ships and came to Capernaum, looking for Jesus.

25. And after finding Him *on* the other side of the sea, they said to Him, "Rabbi, when did You come here?"

26. Jesus answered them and said, "Truly, truly I say to you, you do not seek Me because you saw *the* miracles, but because you ate the bread and were satisfied.

27. Do not labor *for* the food that perishes, but *for* the food that endures unto eternal life, which the Son of man shall give to you; for Him has God the Father sealed."

28. Therefore, they said to Him, "What shall we do, in order that we ourselves may do the works of God?"

29. Jesus answered and said to them, "This is the work of God: that you believe in Him Whom He has sent."

30. Therefore, they said to Him, "What sign will You perform, that we may see *it* and believe You? What work will You do?

31. Our fathers ate manna in the wilderness, as it is written: 'He gave them bread to eat *that came down* from heaven.' " [a]

32. Then Jesus said to them, "Truly, truly I say to you, Moses did not give you the bread from heaven; but My Father gives you the true bread from heaven.

33. For the bread of God is He Who comes down from heaven and gives life to the world."

34. Therefore, they said to Him, "Lord, give this bread to us always."

35. Jesus said to them, "I am the bread of life; the one who comes to Me shall never hunger; and the one who believes in Me shall never thirst at any time."

a - Ex. 16:4; Psa. 78:24

153. JESUS CAME TO DO THE FATHER'S WILL

JOHN 6

36. "But *as* I said to you, you also have seen Me, yet you do not believe.

37. All whom the Father gives Me shall come to Me, and the one who comes to Me I will in no wise cast out.

38. For I did not come down from heaven to do My own will, but the will of Him Who sent Me.

39. And this is the will of the Father, Who sent Me: that *of* all whom He has given Me, I should not lose any, but should raise them up in the last day.

40. And this is the will of Him Who sent Me: that everyone who sees the Son, and believes in Him, may have eternal life; and I will raise him up at the last day."

154. THE JEWS DID NOT BELIEVE JESUS IS THE TRUE BREAD FROM HEAVEN

JOHN 6

41. Then the Jews were complaining against Him, because He said, "I am the bread that came down from heaven."

42. And they were saying, "Is this not Jesus, the son of Joseph, whose father and mother we know? Why then does He say, 'I came down from heaven'?"

43. For this reason, Jesus answered them and said, "Do not be complaining among one another."

155. A PERSON CAN COME TO JESUS ONLY AS THE FATHER DRAWS HIM

JOHN 6

44. "No one can come to Me unless the Father, Who sent Me, draws him; and I will raise him up at the last day.

45. It is written in the prophets, 'And they shall all be taught by God.' Therefore, everyone who has heard from the Father, and has learned, comes to Me. [a]

46. No one has seen the Father except He Who is from God; He has seen the Father.

47. Truly, truly I say to you, the one who believes in Me has eternal life."

a - Isa. 54:13

156. JESUS IS THE LIVING BREAD FROM HEAVEN— A TRUE CHRISTIAN MUST SYMBOLICALLY EAT HIS FLESH AND DRINK HIS BLOOD BY PARTAKING OF THE PASSOVER

JOHN 6

48. "I am the bread of life.

49. Your fathers ate manna in the desert, but they died.

50. This is the bread which comes down from heaven so that anyone may eat of it and not die.

51. I am the living bread, which came down from heaven; if anyone eats of this bread, he shall live forever; and the bread that I will give is even My flesh, which I will give for the life of the world."

52. Because of this, the Jews were arguing with one another, saying, "How is He able to give us *His* flesh to eat?"

53. Therefore, Jesus said to them, "Truly, truly I say to you, unless you eat the flesh of the Son of man, and drink His blood, you do not have life in yourselves.

54. The one who eats My flesh and drinks My blood has eternal life, and I will raise him up in the last day;

JOHN 6

55. For My flesh is truly food, and My blood is truly drink.

56. The one who eats My flesh and drinks My blood is dwelling in Me, and I in him.

57. As the living Father has sent Me, and I live by the Father; so also the one who eats Me shall live by Me.

58. This is the bread which came down from heaven; not as your fathers ate manna, and died. The one who eats this bread shall live forever."

59. These things He said in *the* synagogue as He was teaching in Capernaum.

157. MANY DISCIPLES LEAVE, AND FOLLOW HIM NO MORE

JOHN 6

60. Therefore, after hearing *these words*, many of His disciples said, "This is a hard saying. Who is able to hear *it*?"

61. But Jesus, knowing that His disciples were complaining about this, said to them, "Does this offend you?

62. What if you shall see the Son of man ascending up where He was before?

63. It is the Spirit that gives life; the flesh profits nothing. The words that I speak to you, *they* are spirit and *they* are life.

64. But there are some of you who do not believe." For Jesus knew from *the* beginning who were the ones that did not believe, and who would betray Him.

65. And He said, "For this reason, I have said to you, no one can come to Me unless it has been given to him from My Father."

66. From that *time*, many of His disciples went back and walked no more with Him.

67. Therefore, Jesus said to the twelve, "Are you also desiring to go away?"

68. Then Simon Peter answered Him, "Lord, to whom shall we go? You have the words of eternal life;

69. And we have believed and have known that You are the Christ, the Son of the living God."

70. Jesus answered them, "Did I not choose you twelve, and one of you is *the* devil?"

71. Now He spoke of Judas Iscariot, Simon's *son*; for he was about to betray Him, being one of the twelve.

JOHN 7

1. After these things, Jesus was sojourning in Galilee, for He did not desire to travel in Judea because the Jews were seeking to kill Him.

Ancient Village Near Capernaum

158. MAN'S VAIN TRADITIONS ARE NOT ACCEPTABLE TO GOD—PHYSICAL RITUAL WILL NEVER SPIRITUALLY CLEANSE ONE'S EVIL HEART AND MIND

MARK 7

1. Then the Pharisees and some of the scribes from Jerusalem came together to Him.
2. And when they saw some of His disciples eating with defiled hands (that is, unwashed *hands*), they found fault.
3. For the Pharisees and all the Jews, holding fast to the tradition of the elders, do not eat unless they wash their hands thoroughly.
4. Even *when coming* from the market, they do not eat unless they *first* wash themselves. And there are many other things that they have received to observe, *such as the* washing of cups and pots and brass utensils and tables.
5. For this reason, the Pharisees and the scribes questioned Him, *saying,* "Why don't Your disciples walk according to the tradition of the elders, but eat bread with unwashed hands?"
6. And He answered *and* said to them, "Well did Isaiah prophesy concerning you hypocrites, as it is written, 'This people honors Me with their lips, but their hearts are far away from Me.'
7. But in vain do they worship Me, teaching *for* doctrine the commandments of men. [b]
8. For leaving the commandment of God, you hold fast the tradition of men, *such as* the washing of pots and cups; and you practice many other things like *this.*"
9. Then He said to them, "Full well do you reject the commandment of God, so that you may observe your *own* tradition.
10. For Moses said, 'Honor your father and your mother'; and, 'The one who speaks evil of father or mother, let him be put to death.' [a]
11. But you say, 'If a man shall say to *his* father or mother, "Whatever benefit you might receive from me *is* corban" (that is, *set aside as* a gift to God), he is not obligated to help his parents.'
12. And you excuse him from doing anything for his father or his mother,
13. Nullifying the authority of the Word of God by your tradition which you have passed down; and you practice many *traditions* such as this."

MATTHEW 15

1. Then the scribes and Pharisees from Jerusalem came to Jesus, saying,
2. "Why do Your disciples transgress the tradition of the elders? For they do not wash their hands when they eat bread."
3. But He answered *and* said to them, "Why do you also transgress the commandment of God for the sake of your tradition?
4. For God commanded, saying, 'Honor your father and your mother'; and, 'The one who speaks evil of father or mother, let him die the death.' [a]
5. But you say, 'Whoever shall say to father or mother, "Whatever benefit you might receive from me *is being given as* a gift *to the temple,*" *he* is not at all *obligated to* honor his father or his mother.'
6. And you have made void the commandment of God for the sake of your tradition.
7. Hypocrites! Isaiah has prophesied well concerning you, saying,
8. 'This people draw near to Me with their mouths, and with their lips they honor Me; but their hearts are far away from Me.'
9. But they worship Me in vain, teaching *for* doctrine *the* commandments of men." [b]

Ruins of Tyre

Sidon

a - Ex. 20:12; 21:17; Lev. 20:9 b - Isa. 29:13-14

159. UNWASHED HANDS DO NOT DEFILE ONE SPIRITUALLY

MARK 7

14. And after calling all the multitude to *Him*, He said to them, "Hear Me, all of you, and understand.
15. There is nothing that enters into a man from outside which is able to defile him; but the things that come out from *within* him, those are the things which defile a man.
16. If anyone has ears to hear, let him hear."

MATTHEW 15

10. And after calling the multitude to *Him*, He said to them, "Hear, and understand.
11. That which goes into the mouth does not defile the man; but that which comes out of his mouth, this defiles the man."

160. KEY LESSON: EVIL ORIGINATES IN THE HEART AND MIND— NOT FROM UNWASHED HANDS

MARK 7

17. Now when He went into a house away from the multitude, His disciples asked Him concerning the parable.
18. And He said to them, "Are you likewise without understanding? Don't you perceive that anything that enters into a man from outside is not able to defile him?
19. For it does not enter into his heart, but into the belly, and *then* passes out into the sewer, purging all food."
20. And He said, "That which springs forth from *within* a man, that defiles the man.
21. For from within, out of the hearts of men, go forth evil thoughts, adulteries, fornications, murders,
22. Thefts, covetousness, wickednesses, guile, licentiousness, an evil eye, blasphemy, pride, foolishness;
23. All these evils go forth from within, and *these* defile a man."

MATTHEW 15

12. Then His disciples came to Him and said, "Do You realize that the Pharisees were offended when they heard this saying?"
13. But He answered *and* said, "Every plant that My heavenly Father has not planted shall be rooted up.
14. Leave them alone. They are blind leaders of *the* blind. And if *the* blind lead *the* blind, both shall fall into the pit."
15. Then Peter answered *and* said to Him, "Explain this parable to us."
16. But Jesus said to him, "Are you also still without understanding?
17. Do you not perceive that everything that enters the mouth goes into the belly, and is expelled into *the* sewer?
18. But the things that go forth from the mouth come out of the heart, and these defile the man.
19. For out of the heart proceed evil thoughts, murders, adulteries, fornications, thefts, false witnessing *and* blasphemies.
20. These are the things that defile the man; but to eat with unwashed hands does not defile the man."

Typical Marketplace

161. JESUS TRAVELS TO AREA NEAR TYRE AND SIDON AND HEALS THE DAUGHTER OF A CANAANITE WOMAN

MARK 7	MATTHEW 15

MARK 7

24. Then He rose up from there and went into the district of Tyre and Sidon; and when He came into the house, He desired *that* no one should know, but He could not be concealed.

25. For after hearing about Him, a woman who had a little daughter *with* an unclean spirit came and fell at His feet.

26. Now the woman was a Greek, Syrophenician by race, and *she* requested *of* Him that He cast the demon out of her daughter.

27. But Jesus said to her, "Allow the children to be satisfied first; for it is not fitting to take the children's bread and cast *it* to the dogs."

28. But she answered and said to Him, "Yes, Lord, but even the dogs under the table eat of the children's crumbs."

29. Then He said to her, "Because of this saying, go; the demon has gone out of your daughter."

30. And when she came to her house, she found the demon gone and her daughter lying on the bed.

MATTHEW 15

21. Then Jesus left there and withdrew into the area of Tyre and Sidon;

22. And, behold, a Canaanite woman who came from those borders cried to Him, saying, "Have mercy on me, Lord, Son of David; my daughter is grievously possessed by a demon."

23. But He did not answer her a word. And His disciples came *and* requested of Him, saying, "Send her away, for she is crying out behind us."

24. But He answered *and* said, "I have not been sent except to the lost sheep of the house of Israel."

25. Then she came and worshiped Him, saying, "Lord, help me!"

26. But He answered *and* said, "It is not proper to take the children's bread and throw *it* to the dogs."

27. And she said, "Yes, Lord, but even the dogs eat of the crumbs that fall from their master's table."

28. Then Jesus answered *and* said to her, "O woman, great *is* your faith! As you have desired, so be it to you." And her daughter was healed from that hour.

162. JESUS RETURNS TO GALILEE THROUGH DECAPOLIS AND HEALS A DEAF MAN

MARK 7

31. And after departing from the district of Tyre and Sidon, *and passing* through *the* middle of the borders of Decapolis, He again came to the Sea of Galilee.

32. Then they brought to Him a deaf man who spoke with difficulty, and they requested *of* Him that He lay *His* hands on him.

33. And after taking him apart from the multitude, He put His fingers into his ears; and *then* He spit *on His finger* and touched his tongue;

34. And after looking up to heaven, He groaned, and said to him, "Ephphatha"; that is, "Be opened!"

35. And immediately his ears were opened, and the band of his tongue was loosed, and he spoke plainly.

36. Then He commanded them not to tell anyone. But although He had ordered them *to keep quiet*, they proclaimed *it* more and more.

37. For they were astonished above measure, saying, "He has done all things well; He makes both the deaf to hear and the dumb to speak."

163. JESUS HEALS MANY IN GALILEE
MATTHEW 15

29. Now after leaving there, Jesus came toward the Sea of Galilee; and He went up into the mountain and sat there.
30. Then great multitudes came to Him, having with them *the* lame, *the* blind, *the* dumb, *the* maimed, and many others; and they laid them at the feet of Jesus, and He healed them;
31. So that the multitudes were amazed, when they saw the dumb speaking, *the* maimed *made* whole, *the* lame walking, and *the* blind seeing; and they glorified the God of Israel.

164. JESUS FEEDS THE 4,000

MATTHEW 15

32. And after calling His disciples to *Him,* Jesus said, "I am moved with compassion toward the multitude because they have been with Me for three days, and they have nothing to eat; and I will not send them away fasting, lest they faint along the way."
33. Then His disciples said to Him, "Where in this wilderness can we find enough loaves *of bread* to satisfy so great a multitude?"
34. And Jesus said to them, "How many loaves do you have?" And they said, "Seven, and a few small fish."
35. Then He commanded the multitude to sit on the ground;
36. And He took the seven loaves and the fish, and gave thanks, and broke *them,* and gave *them* to His disciples, and the disciples to the multitude.
37. And they all ate and were satisfied; and they took up seven baskets full of fragments that were left.
38. Now those who ate were four thousand men, besides women and children.

MARK 8

1. In those days *the* multitude *of people* was very great, and they had nothing to eat. *And* when Jesus had called His disciples to *Him,* He said to them,
2. "I am moved with compassion for the multitude because they have continued with Me three days already and have nothing to eat;
3. And if I send them to their homes fasting, they will faint on the way; for some of them have come from far away."
4. Then His disciples answered Him, "How could anyone be able to satisfy *all* these with bread in a desert?"
5. And He asked them, "How many loaves do you have?" And they said, "Seven."
6. Then He commanded the multitude to sit on the ground; and He took the seven loaves; and after giving thanks, He broke *the loaves* and gave *them* to His disciples so that they might set *them* before *the* people. And they set *the loaves* before the multitude.
7. They also had a few small fish; and after blessing *them,* He commanded *His disciples* to set these before *them* also.
8. And they *all* ate and were satisfied. Then they took up over seven baskets of fragments *that were* left.
9. Now those who had eaten were about four thousand; and He sent them away.

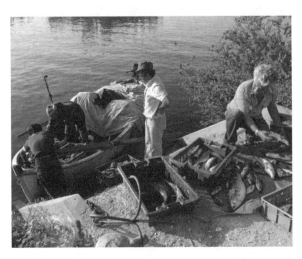

Common Fish from Sea of Galilee

165. THE PHARISEES DEMAND A SIGN

MATTHEW 15

39. And after dismissing the multitude, He went into the ship and came to the area of Magdala.

MATTHEW 16

1. Then the Pharisees and Sadducees came to *Him*, tempting *Him and* asking Him to show them a sign from heaven.
2. But He answered *and* said to them, "When evening has come, you say, '*It will be* fair weather, for the sky is red.'
3. And in the morning, *you say*, 'Today *it will* storm, for the sky is red and lowering.' Hypocrites! You know *how* to discern the face of the sky, but you cannot *discern* the signs of the times.
4. A wicked and adulterous generation seeks after a sign, but no sign shall be given to it except the sign of Jonah the prophet." [a] Then He left them and went away.

a - Jonah 1:17

MARK 8

10. And immediately *afterwards*, He went aboard the ship with His disciples, *and they* came to the district of Dalmanutha.
11. And the Pharisees came out and began to dispute with Him, tempting Him *and* seeking from Him a sign from heaven.
12. But after sighing deeply in His spirit, He said, "Why does this generation seek a sign? Truly I say to you, there shall no sign be given to this generation."
13. Then He left them; *and* after going aboard the ship again, He departed for the other side.

166. THE LEAVEN OF THE PHARISEES IS THEIR DOCTRINE

MATTHEW 16

5. Now when His disciples came to the other side, they had forgotten to take bread.
6. And Jesus said to them, "Watch out, and be on guard against the leaven of the Pharisees and Sadducees."
7. Then they reasoned among themselves, saying, "*It is* because we did not take bread."
8. But when Jesus knew *this*, He said to them, "O *you* of little faith, why are you reasoning among yourselves that *it is* because you did not bring bread?
9. Do you still not understand? *Do you* not remember the five loaves of the five thousand, and how many baskets you took *up*?
10. Nor the seven loaves of the four thousand, and how many baskets you took *up*?
11. How is it that you do not understand that I was not speaking of bread *when I told* you to beware of the leaven of the Pharisees and Sadducees?"
12. Then they understood that He did not say to beware of the leaven of bread, but of the doctrine of the Pharisees and Sadducees.

MARK 8

14. But they had forgotten to take bread; and they did not have *any* with them, except one loaf in the ship.
15. Then He charged them, saying, "Watch out! Be on guard against the leaven of the Pharisees and the leaven of Herod."
16. And they were reasoning with one another, saying, "*It is* because we do not have *any* bread."
17. But Jesus knew *it and* said to them, "Why do you reason *that I said this* because you do not have *any* bread? Do you still not perceive or understand? Are your hearts still hardened?
18. Don't you see with your eyes? Don't you hear with your ears? And don't you remember? [a]
19. When I broke the five loaves for the five thousand, how many baskets full of fragments did you take up?" They said to Him, "Twelve."
20. "And when *I broke* the seven *loaves* for the four thousand, how many baskets full of fragments did you take up?" And they said, "Seven."
21. Then He said to them, "Why is it that you *still* don't understand?"

a - Isa. 6:9-10; Jer. 5:21; Ezek. 12:2

167. JESUS HEALS A BLIND MAN AT BATHSAIDA

MARK 8

22. And He came to Bethsaida, and they brought to Him a blind man and besought Him that He might touch him.

23. Then He took hold of the blind man's hand *and* led him out of the village, and He spit on his eyes *and* laid His hands on him, *and* then He asked him if he saw anything.

24. And when he looked up, he said, "I see men as trees walking."

25. Then He again laid *His* hands on his eyes and made him look up. And he was restored, and he saw everything clearly.

26. And He sent him to his house, saying, "You must not enter the village, nor tell *it* to anyone in the village."

168. JESUS' CHURCH BUILT UPON HIMSELF.
HE REVEALS THAT HE IS THE CHRIST, THE ROCK*

MATTHEW 16	MARK 8	LUKE 9
13. Now after coming into the parts of Caesarea Philippi, Jesus questioned His disciples, saying, "Whom do men declare Me, the Son of man, to be?"	27. Then Jesus and His disciples went into the villages of Caesarea Philippi. And along the way He was questioning His disciples, saying to them, "Whom do men say that I am?"	18. Now it came to pass as He was praying alone, and the twelve disciples were with Him, *that* He questioned them, saying, "Whom do the multitudes declare Me to be?"

A Massive Cliff—"PETRA"

*See footnote on page 156.

MATTHEW 16

14. And they said, "Some *say* John the Baptist; and others, Elijah; and others, Jeremiah, or one of the prophets."

15. He said to them, "But you, whom do you declare Me to be?"

16. Then Simon Peter answered *and* said, "You are the Christ, the Son of the living God."

17. And Jesus answered *and* said to him, "Blessed are you, Simon Bar-Jona, for flesh and blood did not reveal *it* to you, but My Father, Who *is* in heaven.

18. And I say also to you, that you are Peter; but upon this Rock* I will build My church, and *the* gates of the grave shall not prevail against it. [a]

a - Psa. 37:1-4, 26-37

MARK 8

28. And they answered, "John the Baptist; and others, Elijah. And some *say*, one of the prophets."

29. And He said to them, "But you, Whom do you say that I am?" And Peter answered and said to Him, "You are the Christ."

30. Then He strictly charged them that they should tell no one about Him.

LUKE 9

19. And they answered *and* said, "*Some say* John the Baptist; and others, Elijah; and others, that some prophet from ancient times has risen *from the dead.*"

20. Then He said to them, "But Whom do you declare Me to be?" And Peter answered *and* said, "The Christ of God."

21. And He charged them, strictly forbidding *them* to tell this to anyone,

Water Flowing From Cliff to Stones

*The geographic location of Caesarea Philippi was a fitting place for Jesus Christ to reveal that He was the Messiah and that He would build His Church upon Himself. Just prior to entering Caesarea Philippi, there was a huge cliff which dominated the scene. At the base of this cliff, during the time of Jesus, a major spring gushed out from under the cliff; it was one of the sources of the Jordan River. Pure water is symbolic of God's Holy Spirit (John 7:37-39). In Revelation 22:1, pure crystal-clear waters of life, portraying God's Holy Spirit of eternal life, are flowing from the throne of God and the Lamb. The spiritual and symbolic lessons Jesus was teaching in this setting are obvious. Jesus Christ was the Massive Cliff through whom the Holy Spirit would flow to His Church. In the river were small stones, to which the water flowed. Christians are called lively stones (I Peter 2:5). Jesus was clearly teaching the disciples that God's Holy Spirit would flow out from God the Father through Jesus to them. This was the perfect setting to graphically illustrate a lasting lesson to Peter and the rest of the apostles. In fact, Jesus was telling the apostles and disciples that He would build His Church on Himself, and definitely not on Peter, as traditionally thought and claimed by many. The key to this understanding is in the Greek words that Jesus used. Jesus said to Peter, "You are Peter" (Greek Petros). The meaning of this word was given definition by Jesus Himself. In John 1:42, the interpretation of Peter, also Cephas, is "a stone." This is what Jesus was emphasizing here. Peter was a stone. Next Jesus said of Himself, "But upon this Rock I will build my Church." The Greek clearly conveys the meaning. The Greek word translated "Rock" is Petra, which means "massive cliff." Christ Himself is that Rock, the Massive Cliff, exactly like the one dominating the scene as they came into Caesarea Philippi. Peter was a pebble or a stone in comparison. Jesus built His Church on Himself. He never would build it on any man! Other scriptures verify this truth. Jesus Christ is called the Rock, Petra (I Cor. 10:4; Eph. 2:20). Even Peter later wrote about Jesus as the chief corner, or the main foundational undergirding of the Church Jesus said He would build, in I Peter 2:4-6. Jesus Christ is called the Head of the Church; no man can be the Head (Eph. 1:22; Col. 1:18). Peter himself, shortly after the resurrection of Jesus Christ, said that the stone which the builders set at nought had become the head of the corner (Acts 4:11). This shows that Peter knew he was not the head stone, or the head of the Church of God. I Corinthians 3:11 shows that all who are Christians must be built on the foundation of Jesus Christ, and not on Peter. Through the clear and direct words of Jesus Christ Himself, we know that He has built His Church on Himself, not on any stone of a man or a man's successor.

169. JESUS DELEGATES BINDING AND LOOSING AUTHORITY TO HIS APOSTLES

MATTHEW 16

19. And I will give to you the keys of the kingdom of heaven; and whatever you may bind on the earth will have already been bound in heaven; and whatever you may loose on the earth will have already been loosed in heaven." [a]

20. Then He charged His disciples not to tell anyone that He was Jesus the Christ.

a - Isa. 22:22; Rev. 3:7-8

170. JESUS TEACHES HE MUST BE CRUCIFIED, AND BE RESURRECTED AFTER THREE DAYS

MATTHEW 16	MARK 8	LUKE 9
21. From that time Jesus began to explain to His disciples that it was necessary for Him to go to Jerusalem, and to suffer many things from the elders and chief priests and scribes, and to be killed, and to be raised the third day.	31. And He began to teach them that it was necessary for the Son of man to suffer many things, and to be rejected by the elders and chief priests and scribes, and to be killed, but after three days to rise *from the dead*.	22. Saying, "It is necessary for the Son of man to suffer many things, and to be rejected by the elders and chief priests and scribes, and to be killed, and to be raised the third day."

171. JESUS REBUKES PETER FOR A SATANIC ATTITUDE

MATTHEW 16	MARK 8
22. But after taking *Him* aside, Peter personally began to rebuke Him, saying, *"God will be* favorable to you, Lord. In no way shall this *happen* to You." 23. Then He turned and said to Peter, "Get behind Me, Satan! You are an offense to Me, because your thoughts are not *in accord* with the things of God, but the things of men."	32. And He spoke these words openly. Then Peter took *Him* aside *and* began to rebuke Him. 33. But He turned and looked at His disciples, *and then* rebuked Peter, saying, "Get behind Me, Satan, because your thoughts are not of the things of God, but of the things of men."

172. YOU MUST LOSE YOUR LIFE IN JESUS CHRIST, AND TAKE UP YOUR CROSS AND FOLLOW HIM

MATTHEW 16	MARK 8	LUKE 9
24. And Jesus said to His disciples, "If anyone desires to come after Me, let him deny himself, and let him take up his cross and follow Me. 25. For whoever desires to save his life shall lose it; but whoever will lose his life for My sake shall find it.	34. And when He had called the multitude to *Him* with His disciples, He said to them, "Whoever desires to come after Me, let him deny himself, and let him take up his cross and follow Me.	23. Then He said to all, "If anyone desires to come after Me, let him deny himself, and let him take up his cross daily, and let him follow Me; 24. For whoever desires to save his life shall lose it; but whoever will lose his life for My sake shall save it.

MATTHEW 16	**MARK 8**	**LUKE 9**
26. For what does it profit a man if he gains the whole world, but loses his life? Or what shall a man give in exchange for his life?	35. For whoever desires to save his life shall lose it; but whoever will lose his life for My sake and for the gospel's, he shall save it.	25. For what is a man profited by gaining the whole world, if he himself is lost or destroyed?
27. For the Son of man shall come in the glory of His Father with His angels; and then He shall render to everyone according to his doings. [a]	36. For what shall it profit a man, if he shall gain the whole world and lose his life?	26. For whoever shall be ashamed of Me and My words, of him shall the Son of man be ashamed when He comes in His own glory, and *in the glory* of the Father and of the holy angels. [a]
	37. Or what shall a man give in exchange for his life?	
	38. For whoever shall be ashamed of Me and My words in this adulterous and sinful generation, of him shall the Son of man be ashamed when He comes in the glory of His Father with the holy angels." [a]	

a - Isa. 40:9-11; Prov. 24:12; Mal. 3:2; Zech. 14:4-5

Possible Mount of Transfiguration

173. THE VISION OF THE TRANSFIGURATION OF JESUS IN HIS COMING GLORY*

MATTHEW 16

28. "Truly I say to you, there are some of those standing here who shall not taste of death until they have seen the Son of man coming in His kingdom."

MATTHEW 17

1. And after six days, Jesus took with *Him* Peter and James and his brother John, and brought them up into a high mountain by themselves.
2. And He was transfigured before them; and His face shined as the sun, and His garments became white as the light.

MARK 9

1. And He said to them, "Truly I say to you, there are some of those standing here who shall not taste of death until they have seen the kingdom of God come with power."
2. And after six days, Jesus took with *Him* Peter and James and John, leading them alone up into a high mountain by themselves. And He was transfigured in their presence;
3. And His garments became exceedingly white, like glistening snow, such a white as no bleacher of cloth on earth is able to make.
4. Then appeared to them Elijah with Moses, and they were talking with Jesus.

LUKE 9

27. "But I tell you in truth, there are some of those standing here who shall not taste of death until they have seen the kingdom of God."
28. Now it came to pass about eight days after these words, that He took Peter and John and James and went up into the mountain to pray.
29. And it came to pass *that* as He prayed, the appearance of His face was changed, and His clothing *became* radiantly white.
30. And suddenly two men *appeared*, talking with Him; they were Moses and Elijah,

---

The time, the place, and the awesome meaning of this transfiguration were truly significant, and carried a deep and moving lesson for the apostles. Here again, the pattern and parallel between the Old Covenant and the New Covenant is clearly evident. When the Lord God of the Old Testament, who was the one Who became Jesus Christ, confirmed the Old Covenant with ancient Israel, Moses was called and chosen to be the prophet between God and the people (Ex. 19:7-8). Moses desired to see the glory of the Lord God. He was granted this request by being allowed to see the back part of God in His glorified form (Ex. 33:18-23). He was the first human ever allowed to see the Lord God in his glorified form. Moses was thus established as a unique prophet of God.

When the Lord God, the one Who became Jesus Christ, was about ready to establish the New Covenant and the New Testament Church, He also gave this same stamp of approval to the leading apostles: Peter, James, and John. This is the reason Jesus took the three of them with Him up into the mountain (probably Mount Hermon) and was transfigured in a vision before them. They saw the glory of God in this vision. They also saw, in vision, what Moses and Elijah will look like in glory after the resurrection, in the kingdom of God. Keep in mind that Elijah was the second greatest prophet of God, after Moses. Elijah also was spoken to by God at Mount Sinai, and later was carried away through the sky by a flaming, glorious chariot of God to a place of retirement.

This event then takes on a dynamic and powerful meaning for the apostles. With this transfiguration vision, they had proof that the same one Who dealt with and led Moses and the children of Israel was going to lead them with His Holy Spirit. It was a tremendous event, which would always burn in their minds to inspire them to portray the hope of glory for all true Christians. It was a prophetic vision showing what it will be like to be born again by the power of God through the resurrection.

The meaning of this event is profound! But add to this the very day and season when this event took place. The natural flow of events and the chronology show that this took place some time just before the Feast of Tabernacles. The holy day which pictures the return of Jesus Christ in all His power and glory is the Feast of Trumpets. This feast occurs on the first day of the seventh month, the first of Tishri. The Jews had a custom that they were not to construct or build any of the tabernacles or booths for the Feast of Tabernacles until the day after the Feast of Trumpets. Remember, Peter said, "Let us make here three tabernacles." This verse gives a very strong indication that this event probably occurred on or immediately following the Feast of Trumpets. Though the Bible does not tell us directly that this was the first of Tishri, it seems logical that God would use the Feast of Trumpets, which shows a future fulfillment, to portray, in vision, this momentous event. It is a reasonable conclusion that God would inspire an event of such magnitude and significance to occur on that holy day, the Feast of Trumpets, because that is the very meaning of the feast day.

MATTHEW 17

3. Then behold, there appeared to them Moses and Elijah talking with Him.

4. And Peter answered *and* said to Jesus, "Lord, it is good for us to be here. If You desire, let us make three tabernacles here: one for You, and one for Moses, and one for Elijah."

5. While he was speaking, a bright cloud suddenly overshadowed them; and behold, a voice out of the cloud said, "This is My Son, the Beloved, in Whom I delight. Listen to Him!" [a]

6. And when the disciples heard it, they fell on their faces in extreme terror.

7. But Jesus came *and* touched them, and said, "Arise, and do not be terrified."

8. And when they looked up, they saw no one except Jesus alone.

9. Now as they were descending from the mountain, Jesus commanded them, saying, "Tell the vision to no one until the Son of man has risen from *the* dead."

MARK 9

5. And Peter responded *by* saying to Jesus, "Master, it is good for us to be here. Now let us make three tabernacles; one for You, and one for Moses, and one for Elijah."

6. For he did not know what he should say because they were terrified.

7. Then a cloud came *and* overshadowed them; and there came a voice out of the cloud, saying, "This is My Son, the Beloved. Listen to Him!" [a]

8. And suddenly, when they looked around, they no longer saw anyone but Jesus alone with themselves.

9. Now as they were descending from the mountain, He charged them not to tell anyone what they had seen until the Son of man had risen from *the* dead.

10. And they kept that saying among themselves, questioning what was *the meaning of* rising from *the* dead.

a - Deut. 18:15; Psa. 2:7

LUKE 9

31. Who appeared in glory *and* spoke of His departure, which He was about to accomplish in Jerusalem.

32. But Peter and those with him were heavy with sleep; and when they were fully awake, they saw His glory, and the two men who were standing with Him.

33. And it came to pass *that*, as these were departing from Him, Peter said to Jesus, "Master, it is good for us to be here; now let us make three tabernacles, one for You, and one for Moses, and one for Elijah"—not realizing what he was saying.

34. But as he was saying these things, a cloud came and overshadowed them, and they feared as those *three* entered into the cloud.

35. Then a voice came out of the cloud, saying, "This is My Son, the Beloved. Listen to Him!" [a]

36. And as the voice ended, Jesus was found alone. And they kept silent, and told no one in those days of anything that they had seen.

View of Jordan River from Mountain

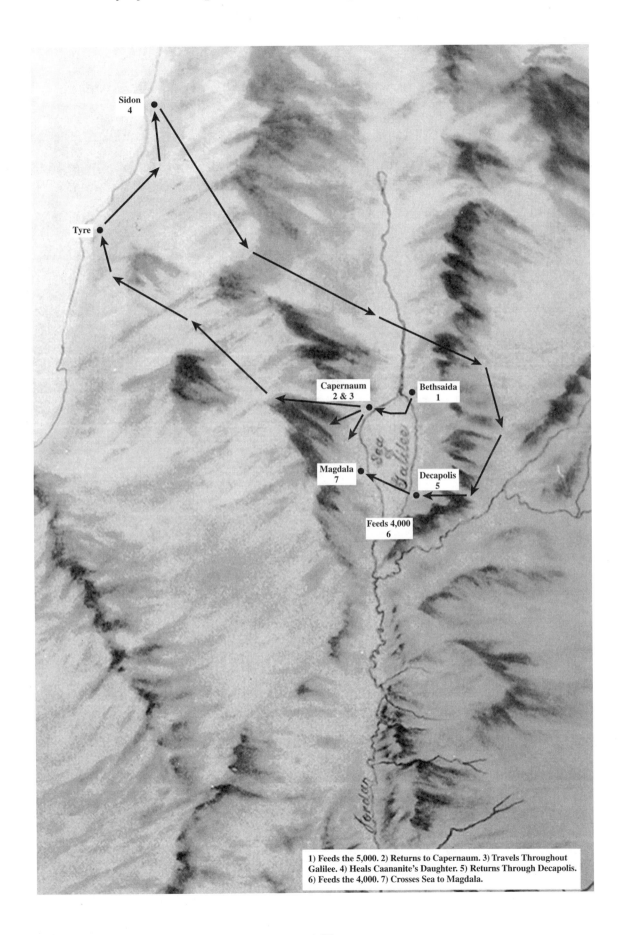

1) Feeds the 5,000. 2) Returns to Capernaum. 3) Travels Throughout Galilee. 4) Heals Caananite's Daughter. 5) Returns Through Decapolis. 6) Feeds the 4,000. 7) Crosses Sea to Magdala.

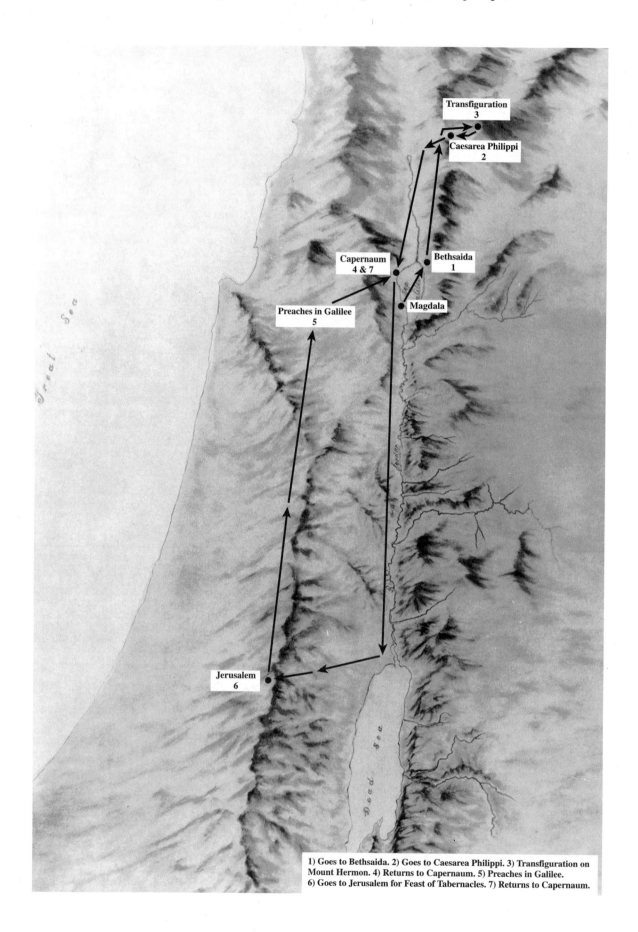

1) Goes to Bethsaida. 2) Goes to Caesarea Philippi. 3) Transfiguration on Mount Hermon. 4) Returns to Capernaum. 5) Preaches in Galilee. 6) Goes to Jerusalem for Feast of Tabernacles. 7) Returns to Capernaum.

174. JOHN THE BAPTIST WAS A TYPE OF ELIJAH

MATTHEW 17

10. Then His disciples asked Him, saying, "Why then do the scribes say that Elijah must come first?"
11. And Jesus answered *and* said to them, "Elijah shall indeed come first and restore all things. [a]
12. But I tell you that Elijah has already come, and they did not recognize him; but they did to him whatever they desired. In like manner also, the Son of man is about to suffer from them."
13. Then the disciples understood that He was speaking to them about John the Baptist.

MARK 9

11. Then they asked Him, saying, "Why do the scribes say that Elijah must come first?"
12. And He answered them and said, "Truly, Elijah comes first and restores all things; [a] and it is *also* written of the Son of man, how He must suffer many things and be treated with contempt.
13. But I tell you that Elijah has already come, and they have done to him what they desired, as it is written of him."

Spring in Galilee

a - Mal. 4:5

175. JESUS CASTS OUT A DEAF AND DUMB SPIRIT FROM A BOY

MARK 9

14. And after returning to the disciples, He saw a great multitude around them, and the scribes disputing with them.
15. And all the people who saw Him ran to *Him* at once in great amazement and saluted Him.
16. And He asked the scribes, "What are you disputing with them?"
17. Then one from the multitude said, "Master, I brought my son who has a dumb spirit to You;
18. For wherever it seizes him it dashes him down; and he foams and gnashes his teeth, and is withering away. And I spoke to Your disciples, in order that they might cast it out, but they did not have *the* power."

MATTHEW 17

14. And when they had come to the multitude, a man came to Him, kneeling down to Him,
15. And saying, "Lord, have mercy on my son, for he is insane and suffers miserably; for he often falls into the fire, and often into the water.
16. And I brought him to Your disciples, but they were not able to heal him."
17. Then Jesus answered *and* said, "O faithless and perverse generation, how long shall I be with you? How long shall I bear with you *in your unbelief*? Bring him here to Me."
18. And Jesus rebuked the demon, and it departed from him; and the boy was healed from that hour.

LUKE 9

37. Now it came to pass *that* on the next day, when they had come down from the mountain, a great multitude met Him.
38. And a man in the crowd immediately cried out, saying, "Master, I beseech You, look upon my son, because he is my only child;
39. And a spirit takes him, and he suddenly cries out; and it throws him into convulsions with foaming, and *then* departs from him with difficulty, leaving him bruised.
40. And I besought Your disciples, that they might cast it out; but they were not able."
41. Then Jesus answered *and* said, "O faithless and perverted generation, how long shall I be with you, and bear with you? Bring your son here."

MARK 9

19. And He answered him, saying, "O faithless generation! How long shall I be with you? How long shall I bear with you? Bring him to Me."

20. Then they brought him to Him. But when the spirit saw Him, *it* immediately threw him into convulsions; and he fell down on the ground *and* began rolling about *and* foaming *at the mouth.*

21. And He asked his father, "How long a time has this *demon* been with him?" And he said, "From childhood.

22. For it often throws him both into the fire and into the water, that it might destroy him. But if You have the power *to do* anything, have compassion on us *and* help us."

23. And Jesus said to him, "If you can believe, all things are possible to the one who believes."

24. And the father of the little child cried out at once, saying with tears, "Lord, I believe. Help my unbelief."

25. Then Jesus, seeing that the multitude was running together, rebuked the unclean spirit, saying to it, "You deaf and dumb spirit, I command you *to* come out of him, and you are not allowed to go into him any more!"

26. And after crying out and throwing him into severe convulsions, it came out; and he became as dead, so much so that many said, "He is dead."

27. But Jesus took him by the hand *and* lifted him up, and he arose.

Field in Galilee

Ruins of Samaria

Sea of Galilee

LUKE 9

42. And as he was approaching, the demon flung him down and threw *him* into convulsions. But Jesus rebuked the unclean spirit, and healed the child, and gave him back to his father.

176. LESSON: FAITH TO ACCOMPLISH MIRACLES COMES ONLY THROUGH PRAYER AND FASTING

MARK 9

28. And when He came into a house, His disciples asked Him apart, "Why were we not able to cast it out?"
29. Then He said to them, "This kind cannot *be made to* go out by anything except prayer and fasting."

MATTHEW 17

19. Then the disciples came to Jesus privately *and* said, "Why were we not able to cast it out?"
20. And Jesus said to them, "Because of your unbelief. For truly I say to you, if you have faith as a *tiny* mustard seed, you shall say to this mountain, 'Remove from here,' and it shall remove; and nothing shall be impossible to you.
21. But this kind does not go out except by prayer and fasting."

Nazareth

177. JESUS TEACHES HIS DISCIPLES ABOUT HIS DEATH AND RESURRECTION

MARK 9

30. And after leaving there, they went through Galilee; but He desired that no one know *it*,
31. Because He was teaching His disciples; and He said to them, "The Son of man is delivered into *the* hands of men, and they shall kill Him; but He shall arise on the third day after He has been killed."
32. Now they did not understand the saying, but they were afraid to ask Him *about it*.

MATTHEW 17

22. And while they were dwelling in Galilee, Jesus said to them, "The Son of man is about to be betrayed into *the* hands of men,
23. And they shall kill Him; but the third day He shall be raised up." And they were exceedingly sorrowful.

LUKE 9

43. And all were astonished at the majesty of God. And *while* everyone was wondering about all *the things* that Jesus had done, He said to His disciples.
44. "Let these words sink deep into your ears, for the Son of man is about to be delivered into *the* hands of men."
45. But they did not understand this saying; for it was concealed from them, so that they would not perceive it. And they were afraid to ask Him about this saying.

178. THE GREAT FEAST OF TABERNACLES IN JERUSALEM— JESUS COMMANDS HIS FAMILY TO GO UP TO THE FEAST

JOHN 7

2. Now the Jews' feast of tabernacles was near. [a]
3. For this reason, His brothers said to Him, "Leave this place and go into Judea, so that Your disciples may see the works that You are doing;
4. Because no one does anything in secret, but seeks to be *seen* in public. If You do these things, reveal Yourself to the world."
5. For neither did His brothers believe in Him.
6. Therefore, Jesus said to them, "My time has not yet come, but your time is always ready.
7. The world cannot hate you; but it hates Me because I testify concerning it, that its works are evil."

a - Lev. 23:33-44

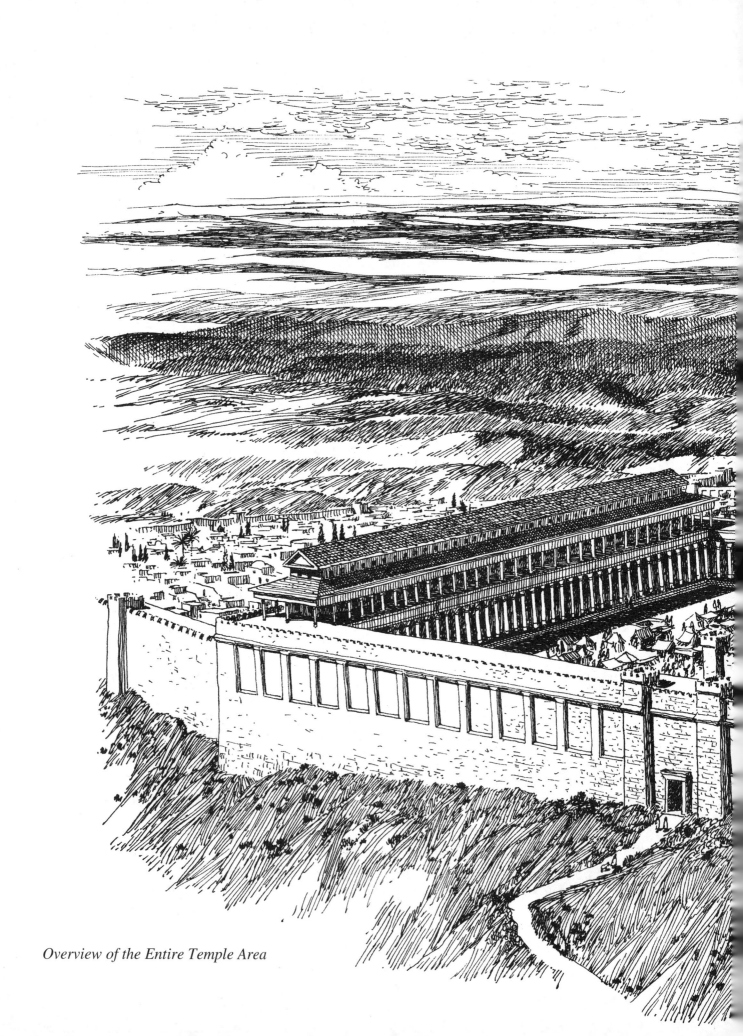

Overview of the Entire Temple Area

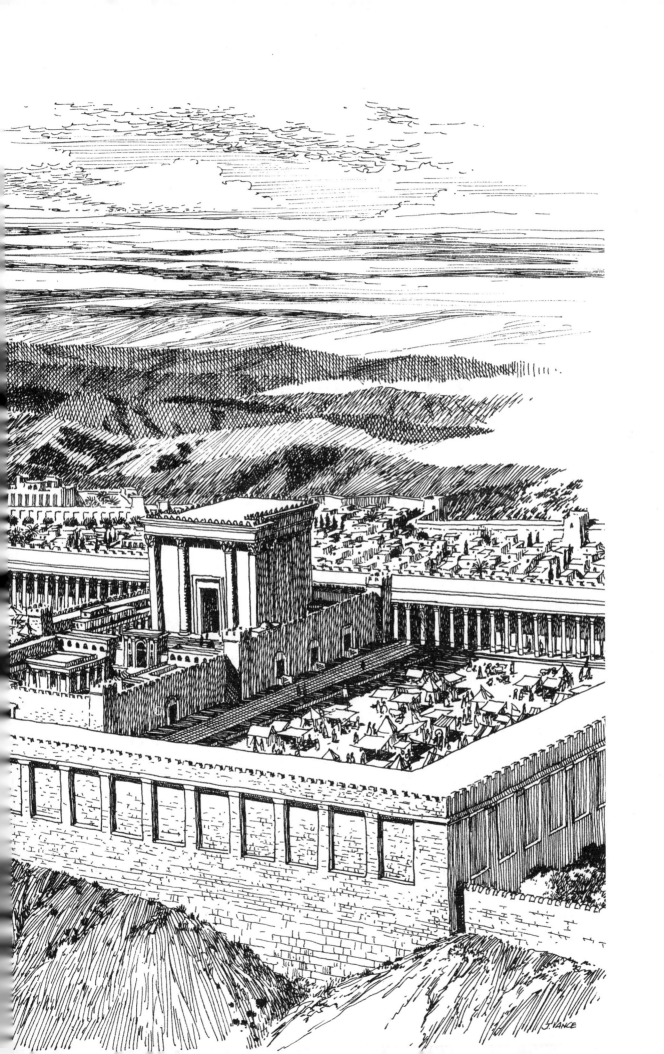

JOHN 7

8. "You go up to this feast. I am not going up to this feast now, for My time has not yet been fulfilled."

179. JESUS GOES TO THE FEAST SECRETLY
JOHN 7

9. And after saying these things to them, He remained in Galilee.
10. But after His brothers had gone up, then Jesus also went up to the feast, not openly, but as it were in secret.

180. THE JEWS LOOK FOR JESUS AT THE FEAST
JOHN 7

11. As a result, the Jews were seeking Him at the feast, and said, "Where is He?"
12. Now there was much debating about Him among the people. Some said, "He is a good man." But others said, "No, but He is deceiving the people."
13. However, no one spoke publicly about Him for fear of the Jews.

181. IN THE MIDDLE OF THE FEAST, JESUS SHOWS HIMSELF OPENLY AND TEACHES IN THE TEMPLE
JOHN 7

14. But then, about the middle of the feast, Jesus went up into the temple and was teaching.
15. And the Jews were amazed, saying, "How does this man know letters, having never been schooled?"
16. Jesus answered them and said, "My doctrine is not Mine, but His Who sent Me.
17. If anyone desires to do His will, he shall know of the doctrine, whether it is from God, or *whether* I speak from My own self.
18. The one who speaks of himself is seeking his own glory; but He Who seeks the glory of Him Who sent Him is true, and there is no unrighteousness in Him.
19. Did not Moses give you the law, and not one of you is practicing the law? Why do you seek to kill Me?"
20. The people answered and said, "You have a demon. Who is seeking to kill You?"
21. Jesus answered and said to them, "I did one work, and you were all amazed.
22. Now then, Moses gave you circumcision—not that it was from Moses, but from the fathers—and on *the* Sabbath you circumcise a man.
23. If a man receives circumcision on *the* Sabbath, so that the law of Moses may not be broken, why are you angry with Me because I made a man entirely whole on *the* Sabbath?
24. Judge not according to appearance, but judge righteous judgment."
25. Then some of those from Jerusalem said, "Is not this the one Whom they seek to kill?
26. But look, He is speaking publicly, and they are saying nothing to Him. Can it be that the authorities have recognized that this man truly is the Christ?
27. Now this man, we know where He comes from. But the Christ, whenever He may appear, no one knows where He comes from."
28. Then Jesus spoke out, teaching in the temple and saying, "You know Me, and you also know where I come from; yet I have not come of Myself; but He Who sent Me is true, Whom you do not know.
29. But I know Him because I am from Him, and He sent Me."

JOHN 7

30. Because of this *saying*, they were looking *for a way* to take Him; but no one laid a hand on Him because His time had not yet come.
31. Then many of the people believed in Him, saying, "When the Christ comes, will He do more miracles than those that this *man* has done?"
32. The Pharisees heard the crowds debating these things about Him, and the Pharisees and the chief priests sent officers to arrest Him.

182. LATER THE JEWS WOULD SEEK JESUS
JOHN 7

33. Then Jesus said to them, "I am with you yet a little while, and *then* I go to Him Who sent Me.
34. You shall seek Me, but shall not find *Me*; and where I am *going*, you are not able to come."
35. Therefore, the Jews said among themselves, "Where is He about to go, that we shall not find Him? Is He about to go to the Diaspora among the Greeks, and teach the Greeks?
36. What is this saying that He said, 'You shall seek Me, but shall not find *Me*'; and, 'Where I am *going*, you are not able to come'?"

183. ON THE LAST GREAT DAY IN THE EVENING AS THE DAY BEGINS, JESUS TEACHES ABOUT THE HOLY SPIRIT
JOHN 7

37. Now in the last day, the great *day* of the feast, Jesus stood and called out, saying, "If anyone thirsts, let him come to Me and drink.
38. The one who believes in Me, as the scripture has said, out of his belly shall flow rivers of living water." [a]
39. But this He spoke concerning the Spirit, which those who believed in Him would soon receive; for *the* Holy Spirit was not yet *given* because Jesus was not yet glorified.

a - Prov. 18:4; Rev. 22:1

184. A DISPUTE ABOUT JESUS BEING THE CHRIST
JOHN 7

40. Now after hearing these words, many of the people said, "This is truly the Prophet."
41. Others said, "This is the Christ." But others said, "Does the Christ then come out of Galilee?
42. Does not the scripture say that the Christ comes from the seed of David, and from Bethlehem, the town where David was?" [a]
43. Therefore, a division arose among the people because of Him.
44. Now some of them desired to take Him, but no one laid hands on Him.
45. As a result, *when* the officers came to the chief priests and the Pharisees, they said to them, "Why did you not bring Him?"
46. The officers answered, "Never has a man spoken like this man."
47. Then the Pharisees answered them, "Are you also being deceived?
48. Has even one of the rulers or of the Pharisees believed in Him?
49. But these people who do not know the law are accursed."
50. *Then* Nicodemus (being one of them, the one who came to Him by night) said to them,
51. "Does our law judge any man without first hearing from him in person, and knowing what he does?"
52. They answered and said to him, "Are you also from Galilee? Search and see, for no prophet has *ever* come out of Galilee."
53. And each one went to his house.

a - II Sam. 7:12-16; Isa. 11:1; Mic. 5:2

185. JESUS TEACHES AT THE TEMPLE ON THE
DAY PORTION OF THE LAST GREAT DAY

JOHN 8

1. But Jesus went to the Mount of Olives.
2. And at dawn He came again into the temple, and all the people came to Him; and He sat down and taught them.

186. A WOMAN CAUGHT IN AN ACT OF ADULTRY
IS AN EXAMPLE OF JUDGMENT

JOHN 8

3. Then the scribes and the Pharisees brought to Him a woman who had been taken in adultery; and after setting her in *the* center,
4. They said to Him, "Teacher, this woman was caught in the very act of committing adultery.
5. And in the law, Moses commanded us that those who commit such *a sin* should be stoned. [a] Therefore, what do You say?"
6. Now they said this to tempt Him, so that they might have *cause* to accuse Him. But Jesus stooped down *and* wrote on the ground with *His* finger.
7. And as they continued to ask Him, He lifted Himself up *and* said to them, "Let the sinless one among you cast the first stone at her."
8. And again He stooped down *and* wrote on the ground.
9. But after hearing *this*, they were convicted *each* by *his own* conscience, and went out one by one, beginning with the older ones until the last. And Jesus was left alone, with the woman standing in *the* center.

a - Lev. 20:10; Deut. 22:22-24

187. JESUS LETS THE WOMAN GO WITH A WARNING TO SIN NO MORE

JOHN 8

10. And when Jesus lifted Himself up and saw no one but the woman, He said to her, "Woman, where are your accusers? Did anyone condemn you?"
11. And she said, "No one, Lord." And Jesus said to her, "Neither do I condemn you. Go, and sin no more."

188. PHARISEES LAUNCH A VERBAL ATTACK AGAINST JESUS

JOHN 8

12. Then Jesus spoke to them again, saying, "I am the light of the world; the one who follows Me shall never walk in darkness, but shall have the light of life."
13, Therefore, the Pharisees said to Him, "You are testifying about Yourself; Your testimony is not true."
14. Jesus answered and said to them, "Even if I testify about Myself, My testimony is true, because I know where I have come from and where I am going. But you do not know where I come from and where I go.
15. You judge according to the flesh; I judge no one.
16. Yet if I do judge, My judgment is true, for I am not alone; but I and the Father Who sent Me.
17. And it is written in your law that the testimony of two men is true. [a]
18. I am *one* Who bears witness of Myself, and the Father, Who sent Me bears witness of Me."
19. Then they said to Him, "Where is Your Father?" Jesus answered, "You know neither Me nor My Father. If you had known Me, you would also have known My Father."
20. Jesus spoke these words in the treasury *while* teaching in the temple; but no one arrested Him because His time had not yet come.

a - Deut. 17:6; 19:15

189. PHARISEES ARE OF THIS WORLD AND
CANNOT UNDERSTAND JESUS' WORDS

JOHN 8

21. Then Jesus said to them again, "I am going away; and you shall seek Me, but you shall die in your sin. Where I am going, you are not able to come."
22. Therefore, the Jews said, "Will He kill Himself? *Is* that *why* He says, 'Where I am going, you are not able to come'?"
23. And He said to them, "You are from beneath; I am from above. You are of this world; I am not of this world.
24. That is why I said to you that you shall die in your sins; for if you do not believe that I AM, you shall die in your sins."
25. Then they said to Him, "Who are You?" And Jesus said to them, "The one that I said to you from the beginning.
26. I have many things to say and to judge concerning you; but He Who sent Me is true, and what I have heard from Him, these things I speak to the world."
27. *But* they did not know that He was speaking to them of the Father.
28. Then Jesus said to them, "When you have lifted up the Son of man, then you yourselves shall know that I AM, and *that* I do nothing of Myself. But as the Father taught Me, these things I speak.
29. And He Who sent Me is with Me. The Father has not left Me alone because I always do the things that please Him."

190. OBEYING THE TRUTH MAKES YOU FREE FROM SIN

JOHN 8

30. As He spoke these things, many believed in Him.
31. Therefore, Jesus said to the Jews who had believed in Him, "If you continue in My word, you are truly My disciples.
32. And you shall know the truth, and the truth shall set you free."
33. They answered Him, "We are Abraham's seed, and have never been in bondage to anyone. What do You mean by saying, 'You shall become free'?"
34. Jesus answered them, "Truly, truly I say to you, everyone who practices sin is a servant of sin.
35. And the servant does not live in the house forever; *but* the Son lives forever.
36. Therefore, if the Son shall set you free, you shall truly be free."

191. PHARISEES ARE OF THEIR SPIRITUAL FATHER, THE DEVIL

JOHN 8

37. "I know that you are Abraham's seed; but you are seeking to kill Me, because My words do not enter into your *minds.*
38. I speak the things that I have seen from My Father, and you do the things that you have seen from your father."
39. They answered and said to Him, "Our father is Abraham." Jesus said to them, "If you were Abraham's children, you would do the works of Abraham. [a]
40. But now you seek to kill Me, a man who has spoken the truth to you, which I have heard from God; Abraham did not do this.
41. You are doing the works of your father." Then they said to Him, "We have not been born of fornication. We have one Father, *and that is* God."
42. Therefore, Jesus said to them, "If God were your Father, you would love Me, because I proceeded forth and came from God. For I have not come of Myself, but He sent Me.
43. Why don't you understand My speech? Because you cannot *bear* to hear My words."

a - Gen. 12:1-4; 17:1-8; 26:5

JOHN 8

44. "You are of *your* father the devil, and the lusts of your father you desire to practice. He was a murderer from *the* beginning, and has not stood in the truth because there is no truth in him. Whenever he speaks a lie, he is speaking from his own *self*; for he is a liar, and the father of it.

45. And because I speak the truth, you do not believe Me.

46. Which *one* of you can convict Me of sin? But if I speak *the* truth, why don't you believe Me?

47. The one who is of God hears the words of God. For this reason you do not hear, because you are not of God."

48. Then the Jews answered and said to Him, "Are we not right in saying that You are a Samaritan and have a demon?"

49. Jesus answered, "I do not have a demon. But I honor My Father, and you dishonor Me.

50. Yet I do not seek My own glory; there is one Who seeks and judges.

51. Truly, truly I say to you, if anyone keeps My words, he shall not see death forever."

52. Then the Jews said to Him, "Now we know that You have a demon. Abraham and the prophets died; yet You say, 'If anyone keeps My words, he shall not taste of death forever.'

53. Are You greater than our father Abraham who died? And the prophets, *who* died? Whom do You make Yourself *to be?*"

54. Jesus answered, "If I glorify Myself, My glory is nothing. It is My Father Who glorifies Me, *of* Whom you say that He is your God.

55. Yet you have not known Him; but I know Him. And if I say that I do not know Him, I shall be a liar, like you. But I know Him, and I keep His Word.

56. Abraham your father was overjoyed to see My day; and he saw *it*, and rejoiced."

57. Then the Jews said to Him, "You are not even fifty years *old*, and You have seen Abraham?"

58. Jesus said to them, "Truly, truly I say to you, before Abraham was born, I AM."

192. JESUS ESCAPES FROM BEING STONED

JOHN 8

59. Then they picked up stones to throw at Him. But Jesus concealed Himself and went out of the temple, passing through the midst of them, and in this manner departed.

193. JESUS HEALS A MAN WHO WAS BORN BLIND

JOHN 9

1. Now *as Jesus was* passing by, He saw a man who was blind from birth.

2. And His disciples asked Him, saying, "Rabbi, who sinned, this man or his parents, that he was born blind?"

3. Jesus answered, "Neither did this man sin, nor his parents; rather, *this blindness came* so that the works of God might be manifested in him.

4. I must work the works of Him Who sent Me while it is still day. When *the* night comes, no one is able to work.

5. As long as I am in the world, I am *the* light of the world."

6. After saying these things, He spat on *the* ground, and made clay of the spittle, and applied the clay to the eyes of the blind man.

7. And He said to him, "Go *and* wash in the pool of Siloam" (which is, by interpretation, "Sent"). Then he went and washed, and came *from there* seeing.

8. Therefore, the neighbors and those who had seen him before, *and knew* that he was blind, said, "Isn't he the one who was sitting and begging?"

9. Some said, "It is he." But others said, "He is like him." He said, "I am *the one*."

10. Then they said to him, "How were your eyes opened?"

JOHN 9

11. He answered and said, "A man called Jesus made clay, and applied *it* to my eyes, and said to me, 'Go to the pool of Siloam and wash'; and after I went and washed, I received sight."

12. Then they said to him, "Where is He?" He said, "I do not know."

13. They brought him who *was* once blind to the Pharisees.

14. Now it was *the* Sabbath when Jesus made the clay and opened his eyes.

15. Therefore, the Pharisees in turn also asked him how he had received sight. And he said to them, "He put clay on my eyes, and I washed; and *now* I see."

16. Then some of the Pharisees said, "This man is not from God because He does not keep the Sabbath." * Others said, "How can a man who is a sinner do such miracles?" And there was a division among them.

17. They said to the blind man again, "What do you say about Him since He opened your eyes?" And he said, "He is a prophet."

18. However, the Jews did not believe *this* about him, that he was blind and had received sight, until they called the parents of the one who had received sight.

19. And they asked them, saying, "Is this your son, who you say was born blind? How then does he now see?"

20. His parents answered them and said, "We know that this is our son, and that he was born blind.

21. But how he now sees, we do not know; or who opened his eyes, we do not know. He is of age; ask him. He will speak for himself."

22. His parents said these things because they were afraid of the Jews; for the Jews had already agreed among themselves that if anyone confessed Him *to be the* Christ, he would be put out of the synagogue.

23. For this reason, his parents said, "He is of age; ask him."

24. Therefore, they called a second time *for* the man who had been born blind, and said to him, "Give glory to God. We know that this man is a sinner."

25. Then he answered and said, "Whether He is a sinner, I do not know. One *thing* I do know, that I was blind, *and* now I see."

26. And they said to him again, "What did He do to you? How did He open your eyes?"

27. He answered them, "I have already told you, and you did not listen. Why do you want to hear *it* again? Do you desire to become His disciples, too?"

28. Then they railed at him and said, "You are His disciple, but we are Moses' disciples.

29. We know that God spoke to Moses. As for this man, we do not know where He has come from."

30. The man answered and said to them, "This is truly an amazing thing, that you do not know where He has come from, yet He has opened my eyes.

31. Now we know that God does not hear sinners. But if anyone is God-fearing and is doing His will, He hears him.

32. From the beginning of the world it has never been heard of that anyone has opened *the* eyes of *one* who was born blind.

33. If this *man* were not from God, He could do nothing."

34. They answered and said to him, "You were born wholly in sin, and you are teaching us?" And they cast him out.

35. Jesus heard that they had cast him out; and when He found him, He said to him, "Do you believe in the Son of God?"

36. He answered and said, "Who is He, Lord, that I may believe in Him?"

The Pharisees were judging Jesus' action of making the clay on the Sabbath as a sin. Because in their view He was laboring, they condemned Jesus and claimed that He did not keep the Sabbath. But Jesus Christ is Lord of the Sabbath day and never broke the command to refrain from servile work on the Sabbath. The records of the New Testament make it explicitly clear that Jesus never sinned by breaking any of the Ten Commandments, including the Fourth Commandment, which sanctifies the Sabbath day.

JOHN 9

37. And Jesus said to him, "You have seen Him, and He is the one Who is even now speaking to you."
38. Then he said, "Lord, I believe." And he worshiped Him.
39. And Jesus said, "For judgment I have come into this world so that those who do not see might see, and those who see might become blind."
40. And those of the Pharisees who were with Him heard these things; and they said to Him, "Are we also blind?"
41. Jesus said to them, "If you were blind, you would not have sin. But now you say, 'We see.' Therefore, your sin remains."

194. JESUS IS THE ONLY TRUE SHEPHERD

JOHN 10

1. "Truly, truly I say to you, the one who does not enter the sheepfold through the door, but climbs up some other way, that one is a thief and a robber.
2. But the one who enters through the door is the shepherd of the sheep.
3. To him the doorkeeper opens, and the sheep hear his voice; and he calls his own sheep by name and leads them out.
4. When he brings the sheep out, he goes before them; and the sheep follow him because they know his voice.
5. But they will never follow a stranger for they will flee from him because they do not know the voice of strangers."
6. Jesus spoke this parable to them, but they did not understand what He was saying to them.
7. Therefore, Jesus again said to them, "Truly, truly I say to you, I am the door of the sheep.
8. All who ever came before Me are thieves and robbers, but the sheep did not hear them.
9. I am the door. If anyone enters through Me, he shall be saved, and shall go in and out, and shall find pasture.
10. The thief does not come except to steal and kill and destroy. I have come so that they may have life, and may have *it* more abundantly.
11. I am the good Shepherd. The good Shepherd lays down His life for the sheep.
12. But the one who is a hireling, and who is not *the* shepherd, whose own the sheep are not, sees the wolf coming and leaves the sheep, and flees. And the wolf seizes the sheep and scatters them.
13. Now the hireling flees because he is a hireling and has no concern for the sheep.
14. I am the good Shepherd, and I know those who *are* Mine, and am known of those who *are* Mine.
15. Just as the Father knows Me, I also know the Father; and I lay down My life for the sheep.
16. And I have other sheep that are not of this fold. I must bring those also, and they shall hear My voice; and there shall be one flock *and* one Shepherd. [a]
17. On account of this, the Father loves Me: because I lay down My life, that I may receive it back again.
18. No one takes it from Me, but I lay it down of Myself. I have authority to lay it down and authority to receive it back again. This commandment I received from My Father."
19. Therefore, there was a division again among the Jews because of these words.
20. And many of them said, "He has a demon and is crazy. Why do you listen to Him?"
21. Others said, "These sayings are not *those* of one who is possessed by a demon. Does a demon have the power to open *the* eyes of *the* blind?"

a - Matt. 10:6; II Kings 17:23; Ezek. 34:23-24; 37:24

His Sheep Hear His Voice

195. BACK IN CAPERNAUM: JESUS PAYS TAXES
WITH A COIN FROM A FISH
MATTHEW 17

24. Now after coming to Capernaum, those who received the tribute money came to Peter and said, "Does not your Master pay tribute?"

25. And he said, "Yes." And when he came into the house, Jesus, anticipating his *question*, said, "What do you think, Simon? From whom do the kings of the earth receive custom or tribute? From their own children, or from strangers?"

26. Peter said to Him, "From strangers." Jesus said to him, "Then the children are indeed free.

27. Nevertheless, so that we may not offend them, go to the sea and cast a hook, and take the first fish that comes up; and when you have opened its mouth, you shall find a coin. Take that, and give *it* to them for Me and you."

196. A DISPUTE AMONG THE DISCIPLES: WHO WOULD BE THE GREATEST?

MATTHEW 18

1. At that time the disciples came to Jesus, saying, "Who then is *the* greatest in the kingdom of heaven?"
2. And after calling a little child to *Him,* Jesus set him in their midst,
3. And said, "Truly I say to you, unless you are converted and become as little children, there is no way that you shall enter into the kingdom of heaven.
4. Therefore, whoever shall humble himself as this little child, he is the greatest in the kingdom of heaven.
5. And whoever shall receive one such little child in My name receives Me.

MARK 9

33. Then He came to Capernaum; and when He was in the house, He asked them, "What were you discussing among yourselves on the way *here?*"
34. But they were silent because, while on the way, they had discussed who *would be* the greatest.
35. And after sitting down, He called the twelve and said to them, "If anyone desires to be first, he shall be last of all and servant of all."
36. Then He took a little child and set it in their midst; and after taking it in *His* arms, He said to them,
37. "Whoever shall receive one of such little children in My name receives Me; and whoever shall receive Me does not receive Me *only,* but Him Who sent Me."

LUKE 9

46. Then an argument arose among them *which was* this: who would be *the* greatest among them.
47. And when Jesus perceived the thoughts of their hearts, He took hold of a little child *and* set it by Him,
48. And said to them, "Whoever shall receive this little child in My name receives Me; and whoever shall receive Me receives Him Who sent Me. For the one who is least among you all shall be great."

Hills of Galilee

197. A MAN NOT FOLLOWING JESUS HEALS IN HIS NAME, AND JESUS ALLOWS IT

MARK 9

38. Then John answered Him, saying, "Master, we saw someone who does not follow us casting out demons in Your name, and we forbad him because he does not follow us."
39. But Jesus said, "Do not forbid him; for no one who does a work of power in My name can easily speak evil of Me.
40. And the one who is not against you is for you.
41. For whoever shall give you a cup of water to drink in My name, because you are Christ's, truly I say to you, he shall in no way lose his reward.

LUKE 9

49. Then John answered *and* said, "Master, we saw someone casting out demons in Your name, and we forbad him because he does not follow with us."
50. But Jesus said to him, "Do not forbid *him,* because everyone who is not against us is for us."

198. A WARNING AGAINST OFFENDING THE
LITTLE ONES IN JESUS CHRIST

MATTHEW 18

6. "But whoever shall cause one of these little ones who believe in Me to offend, it would be better for him that a millstone be hung around his neck and he be sunk in the depths of the sea.

7. Woe to the world because of offenses! For it is necessary that offenses come, yet woe to that man by whom the offense comes!

8. And if your hand or your foot causes you to offend, cut it off and cast *it* from you; for it is better for you to enter into life lame or maimed than to have two hands or two feet *and* be cast into the eternal fire.

9. And if your eye causes you to offend, pluck it out and throw *it* away; for it is better for you to enter into life one-eyed than to have two eyes *and* be cast into the fire of Gehenna.

10. Take heed *that* you do not despise one of these little ones; for I tell you that their angels in heaven continually look upon the face of My Father, Who is in heaven.

11. For the Son of man has come to save those who are lost.

12. What do you think? If a man has a hundred sheep and one of them has gone astray, *does he* not leave the ninety-nine on the mountains and search for the one that went astray?

13. And if he finds it, truly I say to you, he rejoices over it more than over the ninety-nine that did not go astray.

14. Likewise, it is not *the* will of your Father Who *is* in heaven that one of these little ones should perish."

MARK 9

42. "But whoever shall cause one of the little ones who believe in Me to offend, it would be better for him that a millstone be put around his neck and he be cast into the sea.

43. And if your hand shall cause you to offend, cut it off; it is better for you to enter into life maimed than to go with two hands into the unquenchable fire of Gehenna,

44. Where their worm does not die, and the fire is not quenched.

45. And if your foot shall cause you to offend, cut it off; it is better for you to enter into life lame than to be cast with two feet into the unquenchable fire of Gehenna,

46. Where their worm does not die, and the fire is not quenched.

47. And if your eye shall cause you to offend, thrust it out; it is better for you to enter into the kingdom of God with one eye than to be cast with two eyes into the fire of Gehenna,

48. Where their worm does not die, and the fire is not quenched. [a]

49. For everyone shall be salted with fire, and every sacrifice shall be salted with salt. [b]

50. The salt *is* good, but if the salt becomes tasteless, how will you season it? Have salt in yourselves, and be at peace with one another."

a - Isa. 66:24   b - Lev. 2:13; Ezek. 43:24

199. WHAT TO DO WHEN A BROTHER SINS AGAINST A BROTHER
MATTHEW 18

15. *So* then, if your brother sins against you, go and show him his fault between you and him alone. If he is willing to hear you, you have gained your brother.

16. But if he will not listen, take with you one or two others, so that in *the* mouth of two or three witnesses every word may be established. [a]

17. And if he fails to listen to them, tell *it* to the church. But if he also fails to listen to the church, let him be to you as the heathen and the tax collector.

a - Deut. 19:15

A Millstone—The Size Turned By a Donkey

200. JESUS GIVES AUTHORITY TO BIND AND LOOSE TO SETTLE DISPUTES
MATTHEW 18

18. "Truly I say to you, whatever you shall bind on the earth will have already been bound in heaven; and whatever you shall loose on the earth will have already been loosed in heaven.
19. Again I say to you, that if two of you on earth shall agree concerning any matter that they wish to request, it shall be done for them by My Father, Who *is* in heaven.
20. For where two or three are gathered together in My name, I am there in *the* midst of them."

201. THE LESSON OF FORGIVENESS:
FORGIVE UNTIL 70 x 7 (SYMBOLIC OF NO LIMITATION)
MATTHEW 18

21. Then Peter came to Him *and* said, "Lord, how often shall my brother sin against me and I forgive him? Until seven times?"
22. Jesus said to him, "I do not say to you until seven times, but until seventy times seven."

202. THE PARABLE OF THE UNFORGIVING SERVANT
MATTHEW 18

23. "Therefore, the kingdom of heaven is compared to a man, a *certain* king, who would take account with his servants.
24. And after he began to reckon, there was brought to him one debtor who owed *him* ten thousand talents.
25. But since he did not have *anything* to pay, his lord commanded him to be sold, and his wife and children, and all that he had, and payment to be made.
26. Because of this, the servant fell down *and* worshiped him, saying, 'Lord, have patience with me, and I will pay you all.'
27. And being moved with compassion, the lord of that servant released him, and forgave him the debt.

MATTHEW 18

28. Then that servant went out *and* found one of his fellow servants, who owed him a hundred silver coins; and after seizing him, he choked *him*, saying, 'Pay me what you owe.'

29. As a result, his fellow servant fell down at his feet and pleaded with him, saying, 'Have patience with me, and I will pay you everything.'

30. But he would not *listen*; instead, he went and cast him into prison, until he should pay the amount that he owed.

31. Now when his fellow servants saw the things *that* had taken place, they were greatly distressed; and they went to their lord *and* related all that had taken place.

32. Then his lord called him *and* said to him, '*You* wicked servant, I forgave you all that debt, because you implored me.

33. Were you not also obligated to have compassion on your fellow servant, even as I had compassion on you?'

34. And in anger, his lord delivered him up to the tormentors, until he should pay all that he owed to him.

35. Likewise shall My heavenly Father also do to you, if each *of* you does not forgive his brother's offenses from the heart."

203. JESUS LEAVES GALILEE AND GOES THROUGH SAMARIA TO JUDEA

LUKE 9

51. Now it came to pass, when the days were being fulfilled that He should be received up, that He steadfastly set His face to go to Jerusalem.

52. And He sent messengers before His face. And as they went, they came to a village of Samaritans to prepare for Him;

53. But they did not receive Him, because His face was *as if He were* going to Jerusalem.

54. And seeing *this*, His disciples James and John said, "Lord, will You have us call fire to come down from heaven and consume them, as Elijah did?"

55. But He turned *and* rebuked them, and said, "You do not understand of what spirit you are.

56. For the Son of man did not come to destroy men's lives, but to save *them*." And they went to another village.

MATTHEW 19

1. And it came to pass *that* when Jesus had finished these sayings, He departed from Galilee and came to the borders of Judea beyond the Jordan.

2. And great multitudes followed Him, and He healed them there.

MARK 10

1. And He rose up from there and came into the borders of Judea, by the other side of the Jordan. And the multitudes again came together to Him; and as had been His custom, He again taught them.

Put Your Hand to the Plow and Don't Look Back

204. LET THE DEAD BURY THE DEAD—
PUT YOUR HAND TO THE PLOW AND DON'T LOOK BACK

LUKE 9

57. Now it came to pass *that* as they were going along the road, someone said to Him, "I will follow You wherever You may go, Lord."
58. But Jesus said to him, "The foxes have holes, and the birds of heaven *have* nests; but the Son of man does not have *any* place to lay *His* head."
59. Then He said to another, "Follow Me." And he said, "Lord, allow me first to go and bury my father."
60. But Jesus said to him, "Let the dead bury their own dead, but you go and preach the kingdom of God."
61. And another also said, "I will follow You, Lord, but allow me first to bid farewell to those who are at my house."
62. But Jesus said to him, "No one who sets his hand to *the* plow, and looks back at the things behind, is fit for the kingdom of God."

205. JESUS APPOINTS SEVENTY MORE TO PREPARE THE WAY
THROUGH EVERY VILLAGE AND CITY

LUKE 10

1. Now after these things, the Lord appointed seventy others and sent them two by two before His face, into every city and place where He Himself was about to come.
2. And so He said to them, "The harvest *is* indeed great, but the workmen *are* few. Therefore, beseech the Lord of the harvest that He may send out workmen into His harvest.
3. Go forth! Behold, I am sending you out as lambs in *the* midst of wolves.
4. Carry no purse, nor provision bag, nor sandals, and do not salute anyone on the way.
5. But whatever house you may enter, first say, 'Peace *be* to this house.'
6. And if indeed a son of peace be there, your peace shall rest upon it; but if, on the other hand, *it be* not so, *your peace* shall return to you.
7. And lodge in the same house, eating and drinking that which *is supplied* by them; for the workman is worthy of his hire. Do not move from house to house.
8. And whatever city you may enter, and they receive you, eat the things set before you,
9. And heal the sick in it, and say to them, 'The kingdom of God has drawn near to you.'
10. But whatever city you may enter, and they do not receive you, go into the streets *and* say,
11. 'Even the dust of your city, which clings to us, we wipe off against you; yet know this, that the kingdom of God has drawn near to you.'
12. For I tell you, it shall be more tolerable for Sodom in that day than for that city. [a]
13. Woe to you, Chorazin! Woe to you, Bethsaida! For if the mighty works which have been taking place in you had taken place in Tyre and Sidon, they would have repented long ago, sitting in sackcloth and ashes.
14. But it will be more tolerable for Tyre and Sidon in the judgment than for you.
15. And you, Capernaum, who have been lifted up to heaven, shall be brought down to *the* grave.
16. The one who hears you hears Me; and the one who rejects you rejects Me; and the one who rejects Me rejects Him Who sent Me."

a - Gen. 19:24

206. THE SEVENTY RETURN JOYOUSLY BECAUSE THE DEMONS ARE SUBJECT TO THEM THROUGH JESUS' NAME

LUKE 10

17. Then the seventy returned with joy, saying, "Lord, even the demons are subject to us through Your name."
18. And He said to them, "I beheld Satan fall as lightning from heaven.
19. Behold, I give you authority to tread upon serpents and scorpions, and upon all the power of the enemy, and nothing shall injure you in any way.
20. Yet do not rejoice in this, that the spirits are subject to you; but rejoice that your names are written in heaven."

207. THE DISCIPLES ARE BLESSED FOR HEARING AND SEEING GOD'S WAY

LUKE 10

21. In the same hour Jesus rejoiced in the Spirit, and said, "I praise You, O Father, Lord of heaven and earth, that You did hide these things from *the* wise and intelligent, and did reveal them to babes. Yes, Father, for it was well pleasing in Your sight *to do* so."
22. Then He turned to the disciples *and* said, "All things were delivered to Me by My Father; and no one knows Who the Son is, except the Father; and Who the Father is, except the Son, and the one to whom the Son personally chooses to reveal *Him*."
23. And He turned to His disciples *and* said privately, "Blessed *are* the eyes that have seen the things that you see.
24. For I tell you, many prophets and kings have desired to see the things that you see, and have not seen *them*; and to hear the things that you hear, and have not heard *them*."

208. THE PARABLE OF THE GOOD SAMARITAN

LUKE 10

25. Now a certain doctor of the law suddenly stood up, tempting Him and saying, "Master, what shall I do to inherit eternal life?"
26. And He said to him, "What is written in the law? How do you read *it?*"
27. Then he answered *and* said, "You shall love *the* Lord your God with all your heart, and with all your soul, and with all your strength, and with all your mind; and your neighbor as yourself." [a]
28. And He said to him, "You have answered correctly. Do this, and you shall live."
29. But he, desiring to justify himself, said to Jesus, "And who is my neighbor?"
30. And taking *it* up, Jesus said, "A certain man was going down from Jerusalem to Jericho, and was encircled by thieves; *and* after they had stripped him *of his goods* and inflicted *him with* wounds, they went away, leaving *him* half dead.
31. Now by coincidence, a certain priest went down that road; and when he saw him, he passed by on the opposite side.
32. And in like manner also, a Levite, when he was at the place, came and saw *him*, and passed by on the opposite side.
33. But a certain Samaritan, *as* he was journeying, came to him; and when he saw him, he was moved with compassion.
34. And he went *to him* and bound up his wounds, pouring on oil and wine; then he put him on his own beast *and* brought him to an inn, and took care of him.
35. And when he left on the next day, he took out two silver coins *and* gave *them* to the innkeeper, and said to him, 'Take care of him, and whatever you may expend above *this*, I will repay you when I come back.'

a - Deut. 6:5; Lev. 19:18

LUKE 10

36. Therefore, which of these three seems to you to have been a neighbor of him who fell among the thieves?"

37. And he said, "The one who showed compassion toward him." Then Jesus said to him, "You go and do likewise."

209. MARTHA FRETS AT MARY

LUKE 10

38. Now it came to pass as they were going that He came into a certain village; and a certain woman named Martha received Him into her house.

39. And she had a sister called Mary, who sat down at Jesus' feet and was listening to His message.

40. But Martha was distracted because of much serving; and she came *to Jesus and* said, "Lord, is it of no concern to You that my sister has left me to serve alone? Now then, speak to her, so that she will help me."

41. Then Jesus answered *and* said to her, "Martha, Martha, you are full of care and troubled about many things;

42. But there is one need *above all else*; and Mary has chosen the good part, which shall not be taken from her."

210. JESUS TEACHES THE DISCIPLES HOW TO PRAY

LUKE 11

1. Now it came to pass *that* as He was praying in a certain place, when He finished, one of His disciples said to Him, "Lord, teach us how to pray, as John also taught his disciples."

2. And He said to them, "When you pray, say, 'Our Father Who *is* in heaven, hallowed be Your name; Your kingdom come; Your will be done, as in heaven, *so* also upon the earth.

3. Give us our bread *as* needed day by day;

4. And forgive us our sins, as we ourselves also forgive everyone who is indebted to us; and lead us not into temptation, but rescue us from the evil one.' "

211. THE FATHER GIVES THE HOLY SPIRIT
TO THOSE WHO ASK HIM

LUKE 11

5. Then He said to them, "Who among you has a friend that he shall go to at midnight, and say to him, 'Friend, lend me three loaves;

6. For a friend of mine has come to me on a journey, and I do not have anything to set before him';

7. And from within he shall answer, saying, 'Do not disturb me. The door has already been shut, and my children are in bed with me. I cannot get up to give to you.'

8. I say to you, even if he will not rise to give to him on account of being his friend, yet because of his importunity he will rise and give him as much as he needs.

9. And I say to you, ask, and it shall be given to you; seek, and you shall find; knock, and it shall be opened to you.

10. For everyone who asks receives; and the one who seeks finds; and to the one who knocks, it shall be opened.

11. But which of you who *is* a father, *if* a son shall ask for bread, will give him a stone? Or if *he shall ask for* a fish, will give him a serpent instead of a fish?

12. Or if he shall ask *for* an egg, will give him a scorpion?

13. Therefore if you, being evil, know *how* to give good gifts to your children, how much more shall your Father Who *is* in heaven give *the* Holy Spirit to those who ask Him?"

212. JESUS IS ACCUSED OF CASTING OUT DEMONS THROUGH THE POWER OF BEELZEBUB

LUKE 11

14. Now He was casting out a demon, and it was dumb; but it came to pass *that* when the demon had gone out, the *one who had been* dumb spoke. And the multitudes were amazed.
15. But some of them said, "He is casting out demons by *the power of* Beelzebub, prince of the demons."
16. And others, tempting Him, were seeking a sign from heaven.
17. But He, knowing their thoughts, said to them, "Every kingdom divided against itself is brought to desolation; and a house *divided* against a house falls.
18. And if Satan also is divided against himself, how shall his kingdom stand? *Consider now*, because you are saying *that* I cast out demons by Beelzebub.
19. And if I by Beelzebub cast out demons, by whom do your sons cast them out? Because of this, they shall be your judges.
20. But if I by *the* finger of God cast out demons, then the kingdom of God has come upon you.
21. When a strong *man* who is armed guards his own dwelling, his goods are safe.
22. But when a stronger man than he comes upon *him*, he overcomes him, *and* takes away his armor in which he trusted, and divides his spoil.
23. The one who is not with Me is against Me, and the one who does not gather with Me scatters."

213. DEMON REPOSSESSION SEVEN TIMES WORSE

LUKE 11

24. "When the unclean spirit has gone out of a man, it goes through waterless places, seeking rest; and *when it does* not find *any*, it says, 'I will return to the house from which I came out.'
25. And when it comes, it finds *it* swept and adorned.
26. Then it goes and takes seven other spirits more wicked than itself, and they enter in *and* dwell there; and the last *state* of that man is worse than the first."

214. A BLESSING FOR THOSE WHO HEAR AND KEEP GOD'S WORD

LUKE 11

27. And it came to pass *that* as He spoke these things, a certain woman lifted up *her* voice from the multitude *and* said to Him, "Blessed *is* the womb that bore You, and *the* breasts that You sucked."
28. And He said, "Yes, rather, blessed *are* those who hear the Word of God and keep it."

215. THE SIGN OF JONAH WOULD BE THE ONLY SIGN GIVEN

LUKE 11

29. Now when the multitudes had crowded around even more, He began to say, "This is an evil generation, seeking after a sign; but no sign shall be given to it except the sign of Jonah the prophet. [a]
30. For as Jonah was a sign to the Ninevites, in the same way also shall the Son of man be *a sign* to this generation.
31. *The* queen of *the* south shall rise up in the judgment with the men of this generation, and shall condemn them, for she came from the ends of the earth to hear the wisdom of Solomon; and behold, a greater than Solomon *is* here. [b]
32. *The* men of Nineveh shall stand up in the judgment with this generation, and shall condemn it, because they repented at Jonah's proclamation; and behold, a greater than Jonah *is* here." [c]

a - Jonah 1:17   b - I Kings 10:1-13; II Chron. 9:1-12   c - Jonah 3:5-10

216. YOU MUST LET YOUR LIGHT SHINE

LUKE 11

33. "Now no one who lights a lamp sets it in a secret *place* or under a bushelbasket, but on a lampstand, so that those who are entering may see the light.
34. The light of the body is the eye. Therefore, when your eye is without guile, your whole body is light; but when *your eye* is evil, your body also *is* dark.
35. Therefore, beware *that* the light that *is* in you is not darkness.
36. Now then, if your whole body *is* light, not having any part dark, it shall be full of light, as when a lamp shining brightly gives you light."

217. A WARNING TO THE PHARISEES BECAUSE OF THEIR SINS

LUKE 11

37. Now while He was speaking, a certain Pharisee asked Him to dine with him; and He went in *and* sat down.
38. But the Pharisee, seeing *this*, wondered why He had not first washed before dinner.
39. Then the Lord said to him, "Now, you Pharisees cleanse the outside of the cup and the dish, but inside you are full of greediness and wickedness.
40. Fools, *did* not He Who made the outside also make the inside?
41. Rather, give alms *from* the things that are within; and behold, all things are clean to you.
42. But woe to you, Pharisees! For you pay tithes [a] of mint and rue and every herb, but you pass over the judgment and the love of God. [b] It is obligatory *for you* to do these things, and not to set aside those *lesser things*.
43. Woe to you, Pharisees! For you love the chief seat in the synagogues and the salutations in the marketplaces.
44. Woe to you, scribes and Pharisees, hypocrites! For you are as unseen tombs, and men who walk over *them* do not know *it*."

a - Num. 18:8, 21-24   b - II Chron. 19:5-7; Deut. 16:18-20

218. A WARNING TO THE LAWYERS BECAUSE OF THEIR SINS

LUKE 11

45. And one of the doctors of the law answered *and* said to Him, "Teacher, *by* saying these things You are also insulting us."
46. And He said, "Woe to you also, doctors of the law! For you weigh men down *with* burdens heavy to bear, but you yourselves do not touch the burdens with one of your fingers.
47. Woe to you! For you build the tombs of the prophets, whom your fathers killed.
48. Therefore, you are bearing witness and consenting to the works of your fathers; for they indeed killed them, and you build their tombs.
49. Because of this, the wisdom of God also said, 'I will send prophets and apostles to them; and *some* of them they shall kill, and *others they shall* drive out
50. So that the blood of all the prophets, poured out from *the* foundation of *the* world, may be required of this generation
51. From the blood of Abel [a] to the blood of Zacharias, [b] who perished between the altar and the house *of God*.' Yes, I tell you, it shall be required of this generation.
52. Woe to you, doctors of the law! For you have taken away the key of knowledge; you yourselves did not enter, and you prevented those who were entering."

a - Gen. 4:8   b - II Chron. 24:20-22

219. THE PHARISEES AND SCRIBES SEEK TO MAKE
AN ACCUSATION AGAINST JESUS

LUKE 11

53. And as He was saying these things to them, the scribes and the Pharisees began vehemently to press and provoke Him to speak about many things,
54. While they kept a close watch on Him, seeking to catch something out of His mouth so that they might accuse Him.

220. THE HYPOCRISY OF THE PHARISEES TO BE
EXPOSED AND JUDGED

LUKE 12

1. During this *time*, an innumerable multitude was gathering, *crowding* so *close* together that they were stepping on one another. First of all He began to speak to His disciples, *saying*, "Guard yourselves from the leaven of the Pharisees, which is hypocrisy;
2. For there is nothing covered that shall not be uncovered, nor hidden that shall not be known.
3. Therefore, whatever you have spoken in the darkness shall be heard in the light; and what you have spoken in the ear in closed rooms shall be proclaimed on the housetops." [a]

a - Isa. 58:1

221. DON'T FEAR ANYONE WHO CAN KILL YOU,
BUT FEAR GOD WHO CAN TAKE AWAY YOUR LIFE FOREVER

LUKE 12

4. "But I tell you, My friends, you should not be afraid of those who kill the body, and after that are not able to do anything more.
5. But I will show you Whom you should fear. Fear Him Who, after He has killed, has authority to cast into the *fire of* Gehenna. Yes, I tell you, fear Him!
6. Are not five sparrows sold for two coins? And not one of them is forgotten before God.
7. But even the hairs of your head have all been numbered. Therefore, do not be afraid; you are of greater value than many sparrows."

222. THE UNPARDONABLE SIN IS BLASPHEMY
AGAINST THE HOLY SPIRIT

LUKE 12

8. "And I tell you, everyone who shall confess Me before men shall the Son of man also confess before the angels of God;
9. But the one who has denied Me before men shall be denied before the angels of God.
10. And everyone who shall say a word against the Son of man, it shall be forgiven him; but the one who has blasphemed against the Holy Spirit shall not be forgiven."

223. THE HOLY SPIRIT WILL TEACH YOU DURING TIME OF PERSECUTION

LUKE 12

11. "But when they bring you before the synagogues and the rulers and the authorities, do not be anxious *about* how or what you should reply in defense, or what you should say;
12. For the Holy Spirit shall teach you in that same hour what needs to be said."

224. LIFE IS MORE THAN PHYSICAL POSSESSIONS ALONE

LUKE 12

13. Then one from the multitude said to Him, "Master, tell my brother to divide the inheritance with me."
14. But He said to him, "Man, who has appointed Me a judge or a divider over you?"
15. And He said to them, "Watch out, and keep yourselves from covetousness, for no one's life is in the abundance of the things that he possesses."
16. Then He spoke a parable to them, saying, "The ground of a certain rich man brought forth abundantly.
17. And he was reasoning within himself, saying, 'What shall I do, for I have nowhere to lay up my fruit?'
18. And he said, 'I will do this: I will tear down my granaries and build greater *ones*, and there will I lay up all my produce and my good things.
19. Then I will say to my soul, "Soul, you have many good things laid up for many years; take your rest, eat, drink, *and* be merry." '
20. But God said to him, 'Fool, this night your soul shall be required of you; and to whom will you leave what you have prepared for yourself?'
21. So *shall it be to* the one who lays up treasure for himself, and is not rich toward God."

225. SEEK THE KINGDOM OF GOD FIRST, AND YOU WILL HAVE SUFFICIENT

LUKE 12

22. And He said to His disciples, "Because of this, I tell you, do not be anxious about your life, what you shall eat; nor about your body, what you shall put on.
23. The life is more than food, and the body *is more* than clothing.
24. Consider the ravens; for they do not sow, nor reap; neither have they a storehouse or granary; but God feeds them. *Of* how much greater value are you than the birds?
25. And which one of you, *by* taking *careful* thought, has the power to add one cubit to his stature?
26. Therefore, if you do not have the power *to do* even *the* least, why are you anxious about the rest?
27. Consider the lilies, how they grow; they do not labor, nor do they spin; but I tell you, not even Solomon in all his glory was adorned like one of these.
28. But if God so adorns the grass that today is in the field, and tomorrow is cast into an oven, how much more *shall He clothe* you, O *you* of little faith?
29. Then do not be seeking what you shall eat or what you shall drink, and do not be anxious.
30. For all the nations of the world seek after these things; and your Father knows that you have need of these things.
31. But seek the kingdom of God, and all these things shall be added to you.
32. Do not be afraid, little flock, for your Father delights in giving you the kingdom."

226. WHERE YOUR HEART IS, THERE WILL YOUR TREASURE BE ALSO

LUKE 12

33. "Sell your possessions, and give alms. Make for yourselves purses *that* do not grow old, an unfailing treasure in heaven, where no thief can come near, and no moth can destroy.
34. For where your treasure is, there will your heart be also."

227. ALWAYS BE READY AND WATCHING FOR CHRIST'S RETURN

LUKE 12

35. "Let your loins be girded about and *your* lamps burning,
36. And you yourselves be like men who are waiting for their lord, whenever he shall return from the wedding feast; so that when he comes and knocks, they may immediately open to him.
37. Blessed *are* those servants whom the lord, when he comes, shall find watching. Truly I say to you, he will gird himself, and will make them sit down, and will come *and* serve them.
38. And if he comes in the second watch, or comes in the third watch, and finds *them watching*, blessed are those servants.
39. But know this, that if the master of the house had known in what hour the thief would come, he would have watched, and would not have allowed his house to be broken into.
40. Now you, therefore, be ready; for the Son of man is coming in an hour *that* you do not think."
41. Then Peter said to Him, "Lord, are You speaking this parable to us *only*, or also to all?"
42. And the Lord said, "Who then is the wise and faithful steward, whom the lord shall put in charge of his household, to give *to each one* the portion of food in season?
43. Blessed *is* that servant whom the lord, when he comes, shall find so doing.
44. Of a truth, I tell you, he will set him over all his possessions.
45. But if that servant shall say in his heart, 'My lord delays *his* coming,' and shall begin to beat the menservants and maidservants, and to be gluttonous and become drunk,
46. The lord of that servant will come in a day that he does not expect, and in an hour that he does not know, and will cut him asunder, and will appoint his portion with the unbelievers.
47. And that servant who knew the will of his lord, but did not prepare, nor did according to his will, shall be beaten with many *stripes*;
48. But the one who did not know, and did *things* worthy of stripes, shall be beaten with few. For to whomever much has been given, from him shall much be required; and to whom much has been committed, from him they will demand the more."

228. JESUS DID NOT COME TO BRING PEACE, BUT DIVISION

LUKE 12

49. "I came to cast fire into the earth, and what will I, if it already be kindled?
50. For I have a baptism to be baptized *with*, and how burdened I am until it be accomplished!
51. Do you think that I came to bring peace on the earth? No, I tell you, but rather division;
52. Because from this time forward there shall be five in one house divided, three against two and two against three.
53. Father shall be divided against son, and son against father; mother against daughter, and daughter against mother; mother-in-law against her daughter-in-law, and daughter-in-law against her mother-in-law." [a]

a - Mic. 7:6

229. THE MULTITUDES CAN DISCERN THE WEATHER, BUT NOT THE TIMES

LUKE 12

54. Then He also said to the multitudes, "When you see a cloud rising up from *the* west, immediately you say, 'A rainstorm is coming.' And so it happens.
55. And when a south wind *is* blowing, you say, 'It will be hot.' And it happens.
56. Hypocrites! You know *how* to discern the appearance of the earth and the sky; how then do you not discern this time?
57. And why even among yourselves do you not judge what *is* right?"

230. AGREE WITH YOUR ADVERSARY

LUKE 12

58. "For as you are going with your adversary before *the* magistrate, be diligent to settle with him *while you are* on the way; lest he drag you off to the judge, and the judge deliver you to the officer, and the officer cast you into prison.
59. I tell you, *there is* no way *that* you shall come out of there until you have paid the very last coin."

231. YOU MUST REPENT OF YOUR SINS, OR PERISH

LUKE 13

1. Now at the same time, *there* were present some who were telling Him about the Galileans, whose blood Pilate had mingled with their sacrifices.
2. And Jesus answered *and* said to them, "Do you suppose that these Galileans were sinners above all Galileans, because they suffered such things?
3. No, I tell you; but if you do not repent, you shall all likewise perish.
4. Or those eighteen on whom the tower in Siloam fell, and killed them, do you suppose that these were debtors above all men who dwelt in Jerusalem?
5. No, I tell you; but if you do not repent, you shall all likewise perish."

232. THE PARABLE OF THE UNFRUITFUL FIG TREE

LUKE 13

6. And He spoke this parable: "A certain *man* had planted a fig tree in his vineyard; and he came seeking fruit on it, but he did not find *any*.
7. Then he said to the vinedresser, 'Look *here*! *For* three years I have come seeking fruit on this fig tree and have not found *any*. Cut it down. Why should it *continue* to waste *space in* the ground?'
8. But he answered *and* said to him, 'Sir, let it alone this year also, until I dig about it and put *in* manure,
9. And *see* if in fact it will bear fruit; but if not, after that you shall cut it down.' "

Synagogue Ruins in Capernaum

A Back Yard in Jericho

233. JESUS HEALS A WOMAN OF AN 18-YEAR INFIRMITY ON A SABBATH
LUKE 13

10. Now He was teaching in one of the synagogues on *one of* the Sabbaths;
11. And lo, there was a woman who had *been afflicted with* a spirit of infirmity *for* eighteen years, and she was bent over and unable to straighten herself up.
12. And when He saw her, Jesus called *her* to *Him* and said to her, "Woman, you have been loosed from your infirmity."
13. Then He laid *His* hands on her; and immediately she was made straight, and she glorified God.
14. But the ruler of the synagogue answered with indignation because Jesus had healed on the Sabbath, *and* said to the people, "There are six days in which *men* are obligated to work; therefore, during those *days* come and be healed, but not on the Sabbath day."
15. Therefore, the Lord answered him and said, "Hypocrite! Does not each one of you on the Sabbath loose his ox or his ass from the manger and lead *it* away to drink?
16. And is it not *just as* necessary *for* this woman, being a daughter of Abraham, whom Satan has bound, lo, eighteen years, to be loosed from this bond on the Sabbath day?"
17. And after He said these things, all those who opposed Him were ashamed; and all the people rejoiced at all the glorious things that were being done by Him.

234. THE PARABLES OF THE MUSTARD SEED AND HIDDEN LEAVEN
LUKE 13

18. Then He said, "What is the kingdom of God like? And to what shall I compare it?
19. It is like a *tiny* mustard seed, which a man took and cast into his garden; and it grew and developed into a great tree, and the birds of heaven roosted in its branches."
20. And again He said, "To what shall I compare the kingdom of God?
21. It is like leaven, which a woman took and hid in three measures of flour until all was leavened."

235. JESUS WENT CITY BY CITY AND VILLAGE BY VILLAGE ON HIS WAY TO JERUSALEM
LUKE 13

22. Now He was going through *the* cities and villages teaching, *while* making progress toward Jerusalem.

236. ENTER IN THROUGH THE NARROW GATE
OR YOU WILL BE REJECTED BY GOD

LUKE 13

23. And one said to Him, "Lord, *are* those who are being saved few?" Then He said to them,

24. "Strive with *your* whole being to enter in through the narrow gate; for many, I say to you, will seek to enter in, but shall not be able.

25. Once the Master of the house has risen up and has shut the door, and you begin to stand outside the door and knock, saying, 'Lord, Lord, open to us'; then shall He answer *and* say to you, 'I do not know you *or* where you are from.'

26. And you shall begin to say, 'We ate and drank in Your presence, and You have taught in our streets.'

27. And He shall say, 'I tell you, I do not know you *or* where you are from. Depart from Me, all *you* workers of unrighteousness.' [a]

28. There shall be weeping and gnashing of teeth when you see Abraham and Isaac and Jacob and all the prophets in the kingdom of God, but you yourselves are cast out.

29. Then they shall come from *the* east and *the* west, and from *the* north and *the* south, and shall sit down in the kingdom of God. [b]

30. And behold, there are *the* last who shall be first, and *the* first who shall be last."

a - Psa. 6:8   b - Psa. 107:3

237. JESUS PROPHESIES HE WILL DIE LATER IN JERUSALEM

LUKE 13

31. On the same day certain Pharisees came to Him, saying, "Go out and depart from this place because Herod desires to kill You."

32. And He said to them, "Go *and* say to that fox, 'Behold, I cast out demons and complete healings today and tomorrow, and the third *day* I shall be perfected;

33. But it is necessary for Me to proceed today and tomorrow and the following *day*; because it is not possible *for* a prophet to perish outside of Jerusalem.'

34. Jerusalem, Jerusalem, you who kill the prophets and stone those who have been sent to you; how often would I have gathered your children, as a hen *gathers* her brood under *her* wings, but you refused!

35. Behold, your house is left to you desolate. And truly I say to you, you shall not see Me at all until *the time* comes that you say, 'Blessed *is* He Who comes in *the* name of *the* Lord.' "

238. IN JERUSALEM AT THE FEAST OF DEDICATION,
JESUS ESCAPES ANOTHER STONING

JOHN 10

22. Now it was winter, and the feast of dedication was taking place at Jerusalem.

23. And Jesus was walking in the temple in Solomon's porch.

24. Then the Jews encircled Him and said to Him, "How long are You going to hold us in suspense? If You are the Christ, tell us plainly."

25. Jesus answered them, "I have told you, but you do not believe. The works that I am doing in My Father's name, these bear witness of Me.

26. But you do not believe because you are not of My sheep, as I said to you.

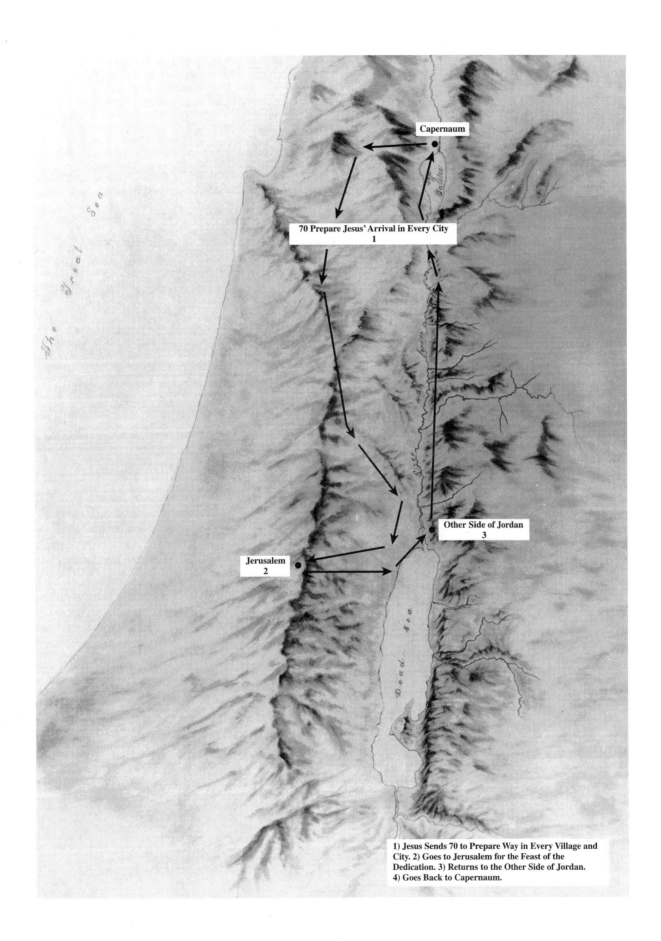

Capernaum

70 Prepare Jesus' Arrival in Every City
1

Other Side of Jordan
3

Jerusalem
2

1) Jesus Sends 70 to Prepare Way in Every Village and
City. 2) Goes to Jerusalem for the Feast of the
Dedication. 3) Returns to the Other Side of Jordan.
4) Goes Back to Capernaum.

191

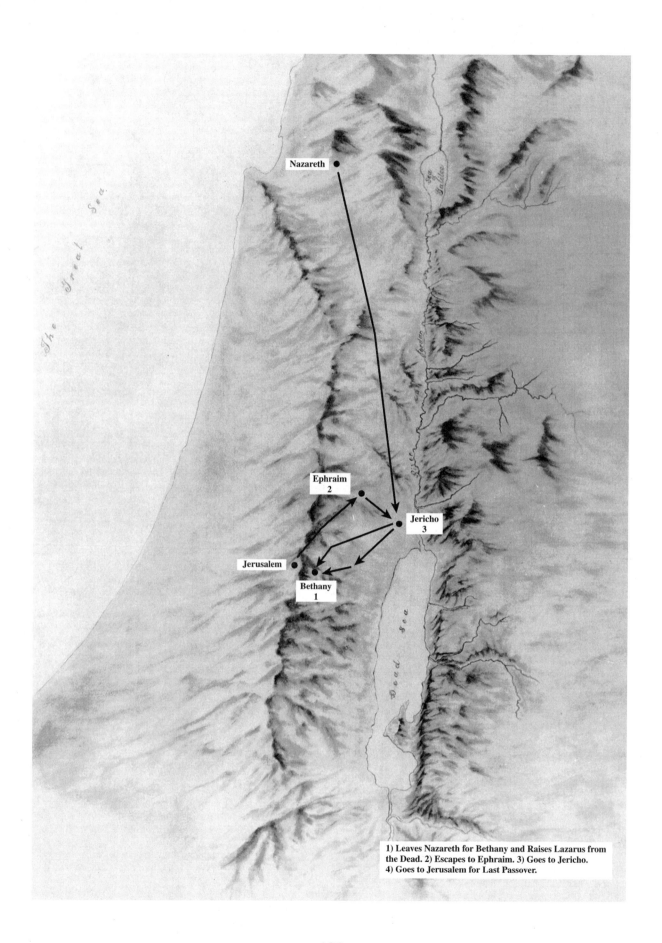

Nazareth

Ephraim
2

Jericho
3

Jerusalem

Bethany
1

Sea of Galilee

Dead Sea

The Great Sea

1) Leaves Nazareth for Bethany and Raises Lazarus from the Dead. 2) Escapes to Ephraim. 3) Goes to Jericho. 4) Goes to Jerusalem for Last Passover.

192

JOHN 10

27. My sheep hear My voice, and I know them, and they follow Me.

28. And I give them eternal life, and they shall never perish; and no one shall take them out of My hand.

29. My Father, Who has given *them* to Me, is greater than all; and no one has the power to seize *them* from My Father's hand.

30. I and the Father are one."

31. Then the Jews again picked up stones so that they might stone Him.

32. Jesus answered them, "Many good works I have showed you from My Father. For which of them are you about to stone Me?"

33. The Jews answered Him, saying, "We will not stone You for a good work, but for blasphemy, and because You, being a man, are making Yourself God." [a]

34. Jesus answered them, "Is it not written in your law, 'I said, "You are gods" '?

35. If He called them gods, to whom the Word of God came (and the Scriptures cannot be broken),

36. *Why* do you say *of Him* Whom the Father has sanctified and sent into the world, 'You are blaspheming,' because I said, 'I am *the* Son of God'?

37. If I do not do the works of My Father, do not believe Me.

38. But if I do, even if you do not believe Me, believe the works; so that you may perceive and may believe that the Father *is* in Me, and I in Him."

39. Then they again sought to take Him; but He escaped out of their hands,

a - Psa. 82:6

239. JESUS LEAVES JERUSALEM AND RETURNS AGAIN TO THE AREA BEYOND JORDAN

JOHN 10

40. And departed again beyond Jordan to the place where John was first baptizing; and He remained there.

41. And many came to Him and said, "John did not do even one miracle, but everything that John said concerning this *man* is true."

42. And many believed in Him there.

240. JESUS HEALS A MAN OF DROPSY AT A PHARISEE'S HOUSE ON A SABBATH

LUKE 14

1. Now it came to pass, when He went into a house of one of the rulers of the Pharisees on *the* Sabbath to eat bread, that they were watching Him.

2. And behold, there was a certain man *who had* dropsy *standing* in front of Him.

3. Then Jesus answered *and* spoke to the doctors of the law and to *the* Pharisees, saying, "Is it lawful to heal on the Sabbath?"

4. But they were silent. And after taking hold *of him*, He healed him and *then* let *him* go.

5. And He answered *and* said to them, "Who among you shall have an ass or an ox fall into a pit, and will not immediately pull it out on the Sabbath day?"

6. But again, they were not able to answer Him concerning these things.

241. THOSE WHO EXALT THEMSELVES SHALL BE ABASED

LUKE 14

7. Then, observing how those who were invited were choosing out the chief places, He spoke a parable to them, saying,

LUKE 14

8. "When you are invited by anyone to a wedding feast, do not sit in the chief place, lest someone more honorable than you has been invited by him.

9. For the one who invited you and him shall come to you and say, 'Give place to this one,' and then shall you begin with shame to take the last place.

10. But when you are invited, go and sit down in the last place, so that when the one who invited you comes, he may say to you, 'Friend, come up higher.' Then shall you have honor in the presence of those who are sitting *at the table* with you.

11. For everyone who exalts himself shall be humbled, and the one who humbles himself shall be exalted."

242. PARABLE OF GOD'S GREAT SUPPER
LUKE 14

12. And He also said to him who had invited Him, "When you make a dinner or supper, do not call your friends, nor your brethren, nor your relatives, nor rich neighbors, lest they also invite you in return, and a recompense be made to you.

13. But when you make a feast, call *the* poor, *the* crippled, *the* lame, *and the* blind;

14. And you shall be blessed, for they do not have *the means* to repay you. But you shall be recompensed at the resurrection of the just."

15. Then one of those who sat *at the table* with *Him*, after hearing these things, said to Him, "Blessed *is* the one who shall eat bread in the kingdom of God."

16. But He said to him, "A certain man made a great supper, and invited many.

17. And he sent his servants at supper time to say to those who had been invited, 'Come, for everything is now ready.'

18. But everyone with one *consent* began to excuse himself. The first said to him, 'I have bought a field, and I need to go out to see it; I beg you to have me excused.'

19. And another said, 'I have bought five pairs of oxen, and I am going to try them out; I beg you to have me excused.'

20. And another said, 'I have married a wife, and because of this I am unable to come.'

21. And that servant came and reported these things to his lord. Then the master of the house was angry; *and* he said to his servant, 'Go out quickly into the streets and lanes of the city, and bring in here the poor, *the* crippled, *the* lame and *the* blind.'

22. And the servant said, 'Sir, it has been done as you commanded, and there is still room.'

23. Then the lord said to the servant, 'Go out into the highways and hedges, and compel *them* to come in, so that my house may be filled.

24. For I tell you, not one of those men who were invited shall taste of my supper.' "

243. EVERYONE WHO WANTS TO BE A CHRISTIAN MUST COUNT THE COST OF FOLLOWING JESUS CHRIST
LUKE 14

25. And great multitudes were going with Him; and He turned *and* said to them,

26. "If anyone comes to Me and does not hate his father, and mother, and wife, and children, and brothers and sisters, and, in addition, his own life also, he cannot be My disciple.

27. And whoever does not carry his cross and come after Me cannot be My disciple;

LUKE 14

28. For which one of you, desiring to build a tower, does not first sit down and count the cost, whether he has *sufficient* for *its* completion;
29. Lest perhaps, after he has laid its foundation and is not able to finish, all who see *it* begin to mock him,
30. Saying, 'This man began to build, and was not able to finish'?
31. Or what king, when he goes out to engage another king in war, does not first sit down *and* take counsel, whether he will be able with ten thousand to meet him who is coming against him with twenty thousand?
32. But if not, while his *enemy* is still far off, he sends ambassadors and desires the *terms* for peace.
33. In the same way also, each one of you who does not forsake all that he possesses cannot be My disciple.
34. Salt *is* good; but if the salt becomes tasteless, with what shall it be seasoned?
35. It is fit neither for the land, nor for the manure; *but* they cast it out. The one who has ears to hear, let him hear."

244. THE PARABLE OF THE LOST SHEEP THAT IS FOUND

LUKE 15

1. Now all the tax collectors and the sinners were drawing near to hear Him;
2. And the Pharisees and the scribes criticized *Him*, saying, "This *man* welcomes sinners and eats with them."
3. Then He spoke this parable to them, saying,
4. "Which man of you who has a hundred sheep, and has lost one of them, does not leave the ninety-nine in the wilderness and go after the one that is lost, *searching* until he finds it?
5. And when he finds *it*, he lays *it* on his shoulders, rejoicing;
6. And after coming to his house, he calls together *his* friends and neighbors, saying to them, 'Rejoice with me, for I have found my sheep that was lost.'
7. I tell you that likewise, *there* shall be joy in heaven over one sinner who repents, *more* than over ninety-nine righteous ones who have no need of repentance.

245. THE PARABLE OF A LOST COIN THAT IS FOUND

LUKE 15

8. Or what woman who has ten coins, if she should lose one, does not light a lamp and sweep the house, and search diligently until she finds *it*?
9. And after finding *it*, she calls together *her* friends and neighbors, saying, 'Rejoice with me, for I have found the coin that I lost.'
10. I tell you *that* in like manner, there is joy before the angels of God over one sinner who repents."

246. THE PARABLE OF THE PRODIGAL SON

LUKE 15

11. Then He said, "A certain man had two sons;
12. And the younger of them said to *his* father, 'Father, give me that portion of the property which falls to me.' And he divided to them *his* living.
13. And not many days after, the younger son gathered everything together *and* departed into a distant country. And there he wasted *all* his substance, living *in* debauchery.
14. But after he had spent everything, there arose a severe famine throughout that country, and he began to be in need.

LUKE 15

15. Then he went and hired himself out to one of the citizens of that country, and he sent him into his fields to feed swine.

16. And he was longing to fill his stomach with the husks that the swine were eating, but no one gave *anything* to him.

17. And when he came to himself, he said, 'How many of my father's hired servants have *an* abundance of bread, and I am dying of hunger?

18. I will arise and go to my father, and I will say to him, "Father, I have sinned against heaven and before you;

19. And I am no longer worthy to be called your son; make me as one of your hired servants." '

20. And he arose *and* went to his father. But while he was still a long way off, his father saw him and was moved with compassion, and ran *and* embraced him, and ardently kissed him.

21. And his son said to him, 'Father, I have sinned against heaven and before you, and I am no longer worthy to be called your son.'

22. But the father said to his servant, 'Bring out a robe, the best robe, and clothe him, and give *him* a ring for his hand and sandals for *his* feet;

23. And bring the fattened calf and kill *it*, and let us eat and be merry.

24. For this my son was dead, but is alive again; and he was lost, but is found.' And they began to be merry.

25. But his elder son was in a field; and when he was coming *back, and* approached the house, he heard music and dancing.

26. And after calling one of the servants nearby, he inquired what these things might be.

27. And he said to him, 'Your brother has come *home*, and your father has killed the fattened calf because he has received him safe and well.'

28. Then he was angry and would not go in. As a result, his father came out and pleaded with him.

29. But he answered *and* said to *his* father, 'Behold, I have served you so many years, and never did I transgress your commandment; yet you never gave me a kid, so that I might make merry with my friends;

30. But when this son of yours came, who has devoured your living with harlots, you killed the fattened calf for him.'

31. Then he said to him, 'Son, you are always with me, and all that *is* mine is yours.

32. But it was fitting to make merry and rejoice because your brother was dead, and is alive again; and was lost, but is found.' "

247. THE PARABLE OF THE UNJUST STEWARD
LUKE 16

1. And He also said to His disciples, "There was a certain rich man who had a steward, and he was accused of wasting his *master's* goods.

2. And after calling him, he said to him, 'What *is* this I hear concerning you? Render an account of your stewardship, for you can no longer be steward.'

3. Now the steward said within himself, 'What shall I do, for my lord is taking away the stewardship from me? I am not able to dig; I am ashamed to beg.

4. I know what I will do, that, when I have been removed *from* the stewardship, they may receive me into their houses.'

5. And after calling each one of his lord's debtors to *him*, he said to the first, 'How much do you owe my lord?'

LUKE 16

6. And he said, 'A hundred baths of oil.' And he said to him, 'Take your bill, and sit down immediately *and* write fifty.'
7. Then to another he said, 'And how much do you owe?' And he said, 'A hundred measures of wheat.' And he said to him, 'Take your bill and write eighty.'
8. And the lord praised the unrighteous steward, because he had acted prudently. For the children of this world are more prudent in their own generation than the children of light.
9. And I tell you, make friends for yourselves by means of the mammon of unrighteousness; so that, when you fail, they may receive you into the everlasting dwellings."

248. ONE MUST BE FAITHFUL IN THE LITTLE THINGS
TO BE TRUSTED WITH THE TRUE RICHES OF GOD'S GLORY

LUKE 16

10. "The one who *is* faithful in *the things that are* least is also faithful in much; and the one who *is* unrighteous in *the things that are* least is also unrighteous in much.
11. Therefore, if you have not been faithful in the unrighteous mammon, who will entrust to you the true *riches*?
12. And if you have not been faithful in that which *is* another's, who will give to you your own?"

249. NO ONE IS CAPABLE OF SERVING TWO MASTERS

LUKE 16

13. "No servant is able to serve two masters; for either he will hate the one, and he will love the other; or he will hold to *the* one and will despise the other. You cannot serve God and mammon."
14. Now the Pharisees who were also covetous, heard all these things; and they ridiculed Him.
15. And He said to them, "You are those who justify themselves before men, but God knows your hearts; for that which is highly esteemed among men is an abomination before God.
16. The Law and the Prophets *were* until John; from that time the kingdom of God is preached, and everyone zealously strives to enter it.
17. But it is easier *for* heaven and earth to pass away than *for* one tittle of the law to fail.
18. Everyone who divorces his wife and marries another commits adultery; and everyone who marries a woman who is divorced from her husband commits adultery."

250. THE PARABLE OF LAZARUS AND THE RICH MAN

LUKE 16

19. "Now there was a certain rich man, and he was clothed in purple and fine linen, and daily indulged himself in luxury.
20. And there was a certain poor man named Lazarus, who was laid at his porch, full of sores.
21. And he longed to be nourished with the crumbs that fell from the rich man's table; and the dogs even came and licked his sores.
22. Now it came to pass *that* the poor man died, and he was carried away by the angels into Abraham's bosom. And the rich man also died and was buried.
23. And in the grave he lifted up his eyes and was in torment, *for* he saw Abraham afar off, and Lazarus in his bosom.

LUKE 16

24. And he cried out *and* said, 'Father Abraham, have compassion on me and send Lazarus, so that he may dip the tip of his finger in water and cool my tongue; for I am suffering because of this flame.'
25. Then Abraham said, 'Child, remember that in your lifetime you received good things to the full, and likewise Lazarus evil things. But now he is comforted, and you are suffering.
26. And besides all these things, between us and you a great chasm has been fixed; so that those who desire to pass from here to you are not able, nor can those from there pass to us.'
27. And he said, 'I beseech you then, father, that you would send him to my father's house,
28. For I have five brothers; so that he may earnestly testify to them, in order that they also may not come to this place of torment.'
29. Abraham said to him, 'They have Moses and the prophets. Let them hear them.'
30. But he said, 'No, Father Abraham, but if one from *the* dead would go to them, they would repent.'
31. And he said to him, 'If they will not hear Moses and the prophets, they would not be persuaded even if one rose from *the* dead.' "

251. A WARNING AGAINST OFFENDING
LITTLE ONES IN JESUS
LUKE 17

1. Then He said to the disciples, "It is impossible that no offenses will come, but woe *to the one* by whom they come!
2. It is better for him that a millstone be put around his neck and he be cast into the sea, than that he should cause one of these little ones to offend."

252. FORGIVE YOUR BROTHER'S TRESPASSES
SEVEN TIMES A DAY
LUKE 17

3. "Watch yourselves; and if your brother commits a sin against you, rebuke him; and if he repents, forgive him.
4. And if he sins against you seven times in a day, and seven times in a day returns to you, saying, 'I repent,' you shall forgive him."

253. INCREASE YOUR FAITH
BY GOING ABOVE AND BEYOND
LUKE 17

5. Then the apostles said to the Lord, "Increase our faith."
6. But the Lord said, "If you had faith as a *tiny* mustard seed, you might say to this sycamine tree, 'Be rooted up, and be planted in the sea,' and it would obey you.
7. But which of you having a servant plowing or shepherding will immediately say *to him when* he comes in from the field, 'Come and sit down *and eat*'?
8. Rather, will he not say to him, 'Prepare what I may eat, and gird yourself, *and* serve me while I eat and drink; and afterwards you may eat and drink'?
9. Is he thankful to that servant because he did the things that were commanded him? I think not.
10. Likewise you also, when you have done all *the* things that are commanded you, say, 'We are unprofitable servants, because we have done that which we were obligated to do.' "

254. JESUS ON HIS WAY BACK TO JERUSALEM PASSES THROUGH GALILEE AND SAMARIA

LUKE 17

11. Now it came to pass that as He was going up to Jerusalem, He passed through *the* middle of Samaria and Galilee.

255. JESUS HEALS TEN LEPERS, BUT ONLY ONE GLORIFIES GOD AND THANKS JESUS

LUKE 17

12. And as He went into a certain village, He was met *by* ten leprous men, who stood at a distance.
13. And they lifted up *their* voices, saying, "Jesus, Master, have mercy on us!"
14. And when He saw *them*, He said to them, "Go show yourselves to the priests." [a] And it came to pass *that* while they were going, they were cleansed.
15. Then one of them, seeing that he was healed, turned back, glorifying God with a loud voice;
16. And he fell on *his* face at His feet, giving thanks to Him; and he was a Samaritan.
17. And answering, Jesus said, "Were not ten cleansed? But where *are* the *other* nine?
18. Are not *any* found returning to give glory to God except this stranger?"
19. Then He said to him, "Arise *and* go. Your faith has healed you."

a - Lev. 14:1-32

256. THE KINGDOM OF GOD COMES NOT THROUGH OBSERVATION

LUKE 17

20. Now when the Pharisees demanded *of Him* when the kingdom of God would come, He answered them and said, "The kingdom of God does not come with observation;
21. Neither shall they say, 'Behold, *it is* here!' Or, 'Behold, *it is* there!' For behold, the kingdom of God is *standing* in the midst of you."

257. SOME OF THE SIGNS OF JESUS' RETURN

LUKE 17

22. Then He said to the disciples, "*The* days will come when you shall desire to see one of the days of the Son of man, and shall not see *it*.
23. And they shall say to you, 'Look here,' or, 'Look there.' Do not go, neither follow *them*.

258. JESUS WILL RETURN SHINING AS A GREAT LIGHT

LUKE 17

24. "For as the light of day, whose light shines from *one end* under heaven to the *other end* under heaven, so also shall the Son of man be in His day.
25. But first it is necessary *for* Him to suffer many things and to be rejected by this generation."

259. THE END TIMES WILL BE THE SAME
AS IN THE DAYS OF NOAH

LUKE 17

26. "Now as it was in the days of Noah, so also shall it be in the days of the Son of man. [a]
27. They were eating, they were drinking, they were marrying, they were being given in marriage, until the day *that* Noah went into the ark, and the Flood came and destroyed *them* all."

a - Gen. 6:5-13

260. THE END TIMES WILL ALSO BE THE SAME
AS THE DAYS OF LOT IN SODOM

LUKE 17

28. "And it was the same way in the days of Lot: they were eating, they were drinking, they were buying, they were selling, they were planting, they were building;
29. But on the day *that* Lot went out from Sodom, [a] it rained fire and sulphur from heaven and destroyed *them* all.
30. This *is* how it shall be in the day *that* the Son of man is revealed.
31. In that day, let not the one who is on the housetop, and his goods in the house, come down to take them away; and likewise, let not the one who is in the field return to the things behind.
32. Remember Lot's wife. [b]
33. Whoever shall seek to save his life shall lose it; and whoever shall lose *his life* shall preserve it."

a - Gen. 18:20-24; 19:24-25   b - Gen. 19:26

261. TWO TOGETHER: ONE IS TAKEN, ONE IS LEFT

LUKE 17

34. "I tell you, in that night there shall be two in one bed; one shall be taken, and the other shall be left.
35. Two *women* shall be grinding together; one shall be taken, and the other shall be left.
36. Two men shall be in the field; one shall be taken, and the other shall be left."
37. And they answered, saying to Him, "Where, Lord?" And He said to them, "Where the body *is*, there will the eagles be gathered together."

262. THE PARABLE OF THE UNJUST JUDGE

LUKE 18

1. And He also spoke a parable to them to show that it is necessary to pray always, and not to give up,
2. Saying, "There was in a certain city a certain judge who neither feared God nor respected man.
3. And there was a widow in that city; and she kept coming to him, saying, 'Avenge me of my adversary.'
4. Now for a time he would not; but afterwards he said within himself, 'Although I do not fear God and do not respect man,
5. Yet because this widow is causing me trouble, I will avenge her, lest she wear me out by *her* continual coming.' "
6. Then the Lord said, "Hear what the unrighteous judge says.
7. And shall not God execute vengeance for His elect, who cry out to Him day and night, and patiently watch over them?
8. I tell you that He will execute vengeance for them speedily. Nevertheless, when the Son of man comes, shall He find the *true* faith on the earth?"

263. THE PARABLE OF A SINFUL PUBLICAN
AND A SELF-RIGHTEOUS PHARISEE

LUKE 18

9. And to some who trusted in themselves that they were righteous, and despised others, He also spoke this parable:

10. "Two men went up into the temple to pray; the one *was* a Pharisee and the other a tax collector.

11. The Pharisee stood and prayed with himself in this manner: 'God, I thank You that I am not like other men—extortioners, unrighteous, adulterers—or even as this tax collector.

12. I fast twice in the week, *and* I give a tithe *of* everything that I gain.'

13. And the tax collector, standing afar off, would not even lift up his eyes to heaven, but beat himself on *the* chest, saying, 'God, be merciful to me, a sinner.'

14. I tell you, this man went down to his house justified, rather than the other. For everyone who exalts himself shall be humbled; and the one who humbles himself shall be exalted."

Judean Hills

264. THE RAISING OF LAZARUS FROM THE DEAD

JOHN 11

1. Now there was a certain *man* who was sick, Lazarus of Bethany, *which was* the town of Mary and her sister Martha.

2. And it was Mary who *later* anointed the Lord with ointment and wiped His feet with her hair, whose brother Lazarus was sick.

3. Therefore, the sisters sent to Him, saying, "Lord, take notice: the one whom You love is sick."

4. But after hearing *this*, Jesus said, "This sickness is not unto death, but for the glory of God, so that the Son of God may be glorified by it."

5. Now Jesus loved Martha and her sister and Lazarus.

6. But when He heard that he was sick, He deliberately remained in the same place two days.

7. And after this, He said to the disciples, "Let us go into Judea again."

8. The disciples said to Him, "Master, the Jews were just seeking to stone You, and You are going there again?"

9. Jesus answered, "Are there not twelve hours in the day? If anyone walks in the day, he does not stumble because he sees the light of the world.

10. But if anyone walks in the night, he stumbles because the light is not in him."

11. These things He said; and after that He said to them, "Our friend Lazarus has fallen asleep, but I am going so that I may awaken him."

12. Then His disciples said, "Lord, if he has fallen asleep, he will get well."

13. Now Jesus had spoken of his death, but they thought that He was speaking of the rest of sleep.

JOHN 11

14. For this reason, Jesus then said to them plainly, "Lazarus has died.

15. And I am glad for your sakes that I was not there, in order that you may believe. But let us go to him."

16. Then Thomas, called Didymus, said to his fellow disciples, "Let us go also, so that we may die with Him."

17. And so, when Jesus came, He found *that* he had already been lying in the tomb *for* four days.

18. Now Bethany was near Jerusalem, about fifteen furlongs away,

19. And many of the Jews had come to *join* those around Martha and Mary, so that they might console them concerning their brother.

20. And when Martha heard that Jesus was coming, she *went and* met Him. But Mary was sitting in the house.

21. And Martha said to Jesus, "Lord, if You had been here, my brother would not have died.

22. But even now I know that whatever You ask of God, God will give You."

23. Jesus said to her, "Your brother shall rise again."

24. Martha said to Him, "I know that he will rise again in the resurrection at the last day."

25. Jesus said to her, "I am the resurrection and the life. He who believes in Me, though he die, shall live *again*;

26. And everyone who lives and believes in Me shall not die forever. Do you believe this? "

27. She said to Him, "Yes, Lord; I believe that You are the Christ, the Son of God, Who was to come into the world."

28. And after saying these things, she went away and secretly called her sister Mary, saying, "The Teacher has come and is calling *for* you."

29. When she heard *this*, she rose up quickly and came to Him.

30. Now Jesus had not yet come into the town, but was in the place where Martha had met Him.

31. Therefore, when the Jews who were with Mary in the house, consoling her, saw that she had quickly risen up and gone out, they followed her, saying, "She is going to the tomb to weep there."

32. Then Mary, when she came where Jesus was *and* saw Him, fell at His feet, saying to Him, "Lord, if You had been here, my brother would not have died."

33. As a result, when Jesus saw her weeping, and the Jews who came with her weeping, He groaned in spirit and was Himself inwardly moved.

34. And He said, "Where have you laid him?" They said to Him, "Lord, come and see."

35. Jesus wept.

36. Then the Jews said, "See how much He loved him!"

37. But some of them said, "Could not this man, Who had the power to open the eyes of the blind, also have caused this one not to die?"

38. Because of this, Jesus again groaned within Himself *as* He came to the tomb. Now it was a cave, and a stone was laid over the opening.

39. Jesus said, "Take away the stone." Martha, the sister of him who had died, said to Him, "Lord, he already stinks, for it has been four days."

40. Jesus said to her, "Did I not say to you that if you will believe, you shall see the glory of God?"

41. Then they removed the stone *from the tomb* where the dead man had been laid. And Jesus lifted *His* eyes upward and said, "Father, I thank You that You have heard Me.

42. And I know that You hear Me always; but because of the people who stand around I say *this*, so that they may believe that You did send Me."

43. And after He had spoken these things, He cried with a loud voice, "Lazarus, come forth."

44. And he who had been dead came forth, his feet and hands bound with grave clothes, and his face bound up with a napkin. Jesus said to them, "Loose him and let *him* go."

45. Then many of the Jews who had come to *console* Mary, and had seen what Jesus did, believed in Him.

265. THE PHARISEES AND PRIESTS PLOT JESUS' DEATH

JOHN 11

46. But some of them went to the Pharisees and told them what Jesus had done.

47. Then the chief priests and the Pharisees gathered a council and said, "What shall we do? For this man does many miracles.

48. If we allow Him to continue in this manner, all will believe in Him, and the Romans will come and take away from us both this place and the nation."

49. But a certain one of them, Caiaphas, being high priest that year, said to them, "You have no understanding,

50. Nor consider that it is better for us that one man die for the people, than that the whole nation should perish."

51. Now he did not say this of himself, but being high priest that year, he prophesied that Jesus would die for the nation;

52. And not for the nation only, but also that He might gather together into one the children of God who were scattered abroad.

53, Therefore, from that day they took counsel together, so that they might kill Him.

266. JESUS ESCAPES TO THE CITY OF EPHRAIM

JOHN 11

54. For this reason, Jesus no longer walked publicly among the Jews, but went away from there into the country near the desert to a city called Ephraim; and He stayed there with His disciples.

267. THE PHARISEES QUESTION JESUS ABOUT DIVORCE

MATTHEW 19	MARK 10

3. Then the Pharisees came to Him and tempted Him, saying to Him, "Is it lawful for a man to divorce his wife for any cause?"

4. But He answered them, saying, "Have you not read that He Who made *them* from *the* beginning made them male and female, [a]

5. And said, 'For this cause shall a man leave his father and mother, and shall be joined to his wife; and the two shall become one flesh'? [b]

6. So then, they are no longer two, but one flesh. Therefore, what God has joined together, let not man separate."

7. They said to Him, "Why then did Moses command to give a certificate of divorce, and to put her away?" [c]

8. He said to them, "Because of your hardheartedness, Moses allowed you to divorce your wives; but from the beginning it was not so.

9. And I say to you, whoever shall divorce his wife, except *it be* for sexual immorality, and shall marry another, is committing adultery; and the one who marries her who has been divorced is committing adultery."

a - Gen. 1:26-27   b - Gen. 2:24
c - Deut. 24:1

2. Then the Pharisees came to *Him and*, tempting Him, asked Him, "Is it lawful for a husband to divorce his wife?"

3. But He answered *and* said to them, "What did Moses command you?"

4. And they said, "Moses allowed a bill of divorcement to be written to divorce." [c]

5. Then Jesus answered *and* said to them, "He wrote this commandment for you because of your hardheartedness.

6. But from *the* beginning of creation God made them male and female. [a]

7. For this cause shall a man leave his father and mother, and shall be joined to his wife;

8. And the two shall become one flesh. So then, they are no longer two, but one flesh.

9. Therefore, what God has joined together, let not man separate."

10. And when He was in the house again, His disciples asked Him concerning the same thing.

11. And He said to them, "Whoever shall put away his wife, and marry another, commits adultery against her.

12. And if a woman shall divorce her husband, and be married to another, she commits adultery."

268. THE CLASSIFICATION OF IMPOTENT MEN
MATTHEW 19

10. His disciples said to Him, "If that is the case of a man with a wife, it is better not to marry."

11. But He said to them, "Not everyone can receive this word, but *only those* to whom it has been given.

12. For there are eunuchs who were born that way from *their* mother's womb, and there are eunuchs who were made eunuchs by men, and there are eunuchs who have made themselves eunuchs for the sake of the kingdom of heaven. The one who is able to receive *it*, let him receive *it*."

269. WHEN BLESSING THE CHILDREN AND INFANTS, JESUS TEACHES THE PROPER ATTITUDE NECESSARY FOR ENTERING INTO THE KINGDOM OF GOD

MATTHEW 19	MARK 10	LUKE 18

13. Then little children were brought to Him, so that He might lay *His* hands on them and pray *for them*; but the disciples rebuked *those who brought* them.

14. But Jesus said, "Let the little children come to Me, and do not forbid them; for of such is the kingdom of heaven."

15. And after laying *His* hands on them, He departed from there.

13. Then they brought little children to Him so that He might touch them. But the disciples rebuked those who brought them.

14. And after seeing *it*, Jesus was indignant, and said to them, "Allow the little children to come to Me, and do not forbid them; for of such is the kingdom of God.

15. Truly I say to you, whoever shall not receive the kingdom of God like a little child shall in no way enter into it."

16. And He took them up in *His* arms, laid *His* hands on them *and* blessed them.

15. Then they brought to Him infants also, so that He might touch them; but when the disciples saw *it*, they rebuked them.

16. But Jesus called them to *Him and* said, "Permit the little children to come to Me, and do not forbid them; for of such is the kingdom of God.

17. Truly I say to you, whoever shall not receive the kingdom of God like a little child shall in no way enter into it."

Lush Gardens Surround Old Fortress Tower

View of Jordan River Valley

204

270. A RICH MAN REFUSES TO FOLLOW JESUS
BECAUSE HE LOVES HIS WEALTH MORE

MATTHEW 19

16. Now at that time, one came to Him *and* said, "Good Master, what good *thing* shall I do, that I may have eternal life?"
17. And He said to him, "Why do you call Me good? No one *is* good except one—God. But if you desire to enter into life, keep the commandments."
18. Then he said to Him, "Which?" And Jesus said, " 'You shall not commit murder'; 'You shall not commit adultery'; 'You shall not steal'; 'You shall not bear false witness';
19. 'Honor your father and your mother'; [a] and, 'You shall love your neighbor as yourself.' " [b]
20. The young man said to Him, "I have kept all these things from my youth. What do I yet lack?"
21. Jesus said to him, "If you desire to be perfect, go *and* sell your property, and give to *the* poor, and you shall have treasure in heaven; and come *and* follow Me."
22. But after hearing this word, the young man went away grieving, because he had many possessions.

MARK 10

17. And as He went out to *the* road, one came running up and knelt down before Him, *and* asked Him, "Good Master, what shall I do that I may inherit eternal life?"
18. But Jesus answered him, "Why do you call Me good? No one *is* good except one; *that is* God.
19. You know the commandments: 'You shall not commit adultery'; 'You shall not commit murder'; 'You shall not steal'; 'You shall not bear false witness'; 'You shall not defraud'; 'Honor your father and mother.' " [a]
20. And he answered and said to Him, "Master, I have kept all these from my youth."
21. And Jesus, *as He* was looking upon him, loved him, and said to him, "*There is* one thing *that* you are lacking. Go and sell everything that you have, and give to the poor, and you shall have treasure in heaven; and come, take up the cross and follow Me."
22. But he was *very* sad upon *hearing* these words, *and* he went away grieving, because he had many possessions.

LUKE 18

18. And a certain ruler asked Him, saying, "Good Master, what shall I do to inherit eternal life?"
19. Then Jesus said to him, "Why do you call Me good? No one *is* good except one—God.
20. You know the commandments: 'You shall not commit adultery. You shall not commit murder. You shall not steal. You shall not bear false witness. Honor your father and your mother.' " [a]
21. And he said, "I have kept all these *commandments* from my youth."
22. And after hearing these things, Jesus said to him, "You still lack one thing; sell everything that you have, and distribute to *the* poor, and you shall have treasure in heaven; and come *and* follow Me."
23. But when he heard these things, he became very sorrowful; for he was quite rich.

a - Ex. 20:12-17; Deut. 5:16-21   b - Lev. 19:18

271. A KEY LESSON: DON'T SET YOUR HEART ON MATERIAL RICHES

MATTHEW 19

23. Then Jesus said to His disciples, "Truly I say to you, it *is extremely* difficult for a rich man to enter into the kingdom of heaven.
24. And again I say to you, it is easier for a camel to pass through *the* eye of a needle than *for* a rich man to enter into the kingdom of God."

MARK 10

23. And after looking around, Jesus said to His disciples, "How difficult it is for those who have riches to enter into the kingdom of God!"
24. But the disciples were astonished at His words. And again Jesus answered *and* said to them, "Children, how difficult it is *for* those

LUKE 18

24. Now when Jesus saw him become so sorrowful, He said, "How difficult *it is for* those who have riches to enter into the kingdom of God!
25. For it is easier *for* a camel to go through an eye of a needle than *for* a rich man to enter into the kingdom of God."

MATTHEW 19

25. But after hearing this, the disciples were greatly astonished *and* said, "Who then is able to be saved?"
26. But Jesus looked at them and said, "With men this is impossible; but with God all things are possible." ᵃ

Solid Gold Bars

MARK 10

who trust in riches to enter into the kingdom of God!
25. It is easier *for* a camel to pass through the eye of a needle than *for* a rich man to enter into the kingdom of God."
26. And they were astonished beyond measure, saying among themselves, "Who then is able to be saved?"
27. But Jesus looked at them *and* said, "With men *it is* impossible, but not with God; for all things are possible with God." ᵃ

a - Gen. 18:14; Jer. 32:17; Zech. 8:6

LUKE 18

26. And those who heard *this* said, "Who then is able to be saved?"
27. But He said, "The things *that are* impossible with men are possible with God." ᵃ

Don't Set Your Heart On Wealth

272. THE BLESSING FOR LEAVING EVERYTHING AND FOLLOWING JESUS

MATTHEW 19

27. Then Peter answered *and* said to Him, "Behold, we have left everything and have followed You. What then shall be for us?"
28. And Jesus said to them, "Truly I say to you who have followed Me: in the regeneration when the Son of man shall sit upon *the* throne of His glory, you also shall sit on twelve thrones, judging the twelve tribes of Israel.
29. And everyone who has left houses, or brothers, or sisters, or father, or mother, or wife, or children, or lands, for My name's sake, shall receive a hundredfold, and shall inherit eternal life.
30. But many *of the* first shall be last, and *the* last first."

MARK 10

28. Then Peter began to say to Him, "Behold, we have left everything and have followed You."
29. And Jesus answered *and* said, "Truly I say to you, there is not one who has left house, or brothers, or sisters, or father, or mother, or wife, or children, or lands, for My sake and for the gospel's,
30. Who shall not receive a hundredfold now in this time: houses, and brothers, and sisters, and mothers, and children, and lands, with persecutions; and in the age that is coming, eternal life.
31. But many *of the* first shall be last, and the last *shall be* first."

LUKE 18

28. Then Peter said, "Behold, we have left everything and have followed You."
29. And He said to them, "Truly I say to you, there is no one who has left house, or parents, or brothers, or wife, or children, for the sake of the kingdom of God,
30. Who shall not receive manifold more in this time, and in the age that is coming—eternal life."

273. THE PARABLE OF THE WORKERS IN THE VINEYARD
MATTHEW 20

1. "The kingdom of heaven shall be compared to a man, a master of a house, who went out early in *the* morning to hire workmen for his vineyard.
2. And after agreeing with the workmen on a silver coin *for* the day's *wage*, he sent them into his vineyard.
3. And when he went out about the third hour, he saw others standing idle in the market-place;
4. And he said to them, 'Go also into the vineyard, and whatever is right I will give you.'
5. And they went. Again, after going out about *the* sixth hour and *the* ninth hour, he did like-wise.
6. And about the eleventh hour, he went out *and* found others standing idle, and said to them, 'Why have you been standing here idle all the day?'
7. They said to him, 'Because no one has hired us.' He said to them, 'Go also into my vine-yard, and whatever is right you shall receive.'
8. And when evening came, the lord of the vineyard said to his steward, 'Call the workmen and pay them *their* hire, beginning from the last unto the first.'
9. And when those who *were hired* about the eleventh hour came, they each received a silver coin.
10. But when the first ones came, they thought that they would receive more; but each of them also received a silver coin.
11. And after receiving *it*, they complained against the master of the house,
12. Saying, 'These *who came* last have worked one hour, and you have made them equal to us, who have carried the burden and the heat of the day.'
13. But he answered *and* said to them, 'Friend, I am not doing you wrong. Did you not agree with me on a silver coin *for the day*?
14. Take *what* is yours and go, for I also desire to give to the last *ones* exactly as I gave to you.
15. And is it not lawful for me to do what I will with that which *is* my own? Is your eye evil because I am good?'
16. So the last shall be first, and the first *shall be* last; for many are called, but few *are* cho-sen."

274. JESUS REVEALS HOW HE WILL DIE

MATTHEW 20	MARK 10	LUKE 18
17. And while they were going up to Jerusalem, Jesus took the twelve disciples aside in the way and said to them, 18. "Behold, we are going up to Jerusalem, and the Son of man shall be betrayed to the chief priests and scribes, and they shall condemn Him to death; 19. And they shall deliver Him up to the Gentiles to mock *Him*, and to scourge *Him*, and to crucify *Him*; but He shall rise again the third day."	32. And they were on the road going up to Jerusalem, and Jesus went in front of them; and they were amazed *at this*; and *as they* followed *Him*, they were afraid. Then He again took the twelve *and* began to tell them the things that were about to happen to Him: 33. "Behold, we are going up to Jerusalem, and the Son of man shall be delivered up to the chief priests and the scribes; and they shall con-demn Him to death, and shall deliver Him up to the Gentiles;	31. And after taking the twelve *aside* to *Himself*, He said to them, "Behold, we are going up to Jerusalem, and all things that have been written about the Son of man by the prophets shall be fulfilled. 32. For He shall be deliv-ered up to the Gentiles, and shall be mocked and in-sulted and spit upon. 33. And after scourging *Him*, they shall kill Him; but on the third day, He shall rise again."

MARK 10	**LUKE 18**
34. And they shall mock Him, and shall scourge Him, and shall spit on Him, and shall kill Him; and on the third day He shall rise again."	34. But they understood none of these things, and this saying was hidden from them, and they did not comprehend what was said.

275. JAMES AND JOHN ASK TO SIT AT JESUS' RIGHT HAND AND LEFT HAND IN THE KINGDOM OF GOD

MATTHEW 20	**MARK 10**
20. Then the mother of the sons of Zebedee came to Him with her sons, worshiping Him and asking a certain thing from Him.	35. Then James and John, the sons of Zebedee, came to Him, saying, "Master, we desire that whatever we ask, You would do for us."
21. And He said to her, "What do you desire?" She said to Him, "Grant that these my two sons may sit one at Your right hand and one at *Your* left *hand* in Your kingdom."	36. And He said to them, "What do you desire to have Me do for you?"
22. But Jesus answered *and* said, "You do not know what you are asking. Are you able to drink the cup that I am about to drink, and to be baptized *with* the baptism that I am baptized *with*?" They said to Him, "We are able."	37. And they said to Him, "Grant to us that we may sit one at Your right hand and one at Your left hand in Your glory."
23. And He said to them, "You shall indeed drink of My cup, and shall be baptized *with* the baptism that I am baptized *with*; but to sit at My right hand and at My left *hand* is not Mine to give, but *shall be given to those* for whom it has been prepared by My Father."	38. But Jesus said to them, "You do not know what you are asking. Are you able to drink the cup that I drink, and to be baptized *with* the baptism that I am baptized *with*?"
24. And after hearing *this*, the ten were indignant against the two brothers.	39. And they said to Him, "We are able." Then Jesus said to them, "You shall indeed drink the cup that I drink; and you shall be baptized *with* the baptism that I am baptized *with*.
	40. But to sit at My right hand and at My left hand is not Mine to give, but *to those* for whom it has been prepared."
	41. And when the ten heard *this*, they began to show indignation toward James and John.

276. JESUS TEACHES THE LESSON THAT THE GREATEST OF ALL SHALL SERVE ALL

MATTHEW 20	**MARK 10**
25. But Jesus called them to *Him and* said, "You know that the rulers of the nations exercise lordship over them, and the great ones exercise authority over them.	42. Then Jesus called them to *Him and* said to them, "You know that those who are counted worthy to rule over the Gentiles exercise lordship over them; and their great ones exercise authority over them.
26. However, it shall not be this way among you; but whoever would become great among you, let him be your servant;	43. But it shall not be this way among you; rather, whoever desires to become great among you shall be your servant;
27. And whoever would be first among you, let him be your slave;	44. And whoever desires to be first among you shall be *the* bondslave of all.
28. Just as the Son of man did not come to be served, but to serve, and to give His life *as* a ransom for many."	45. For even the Son of man came not to be served, but to serve, and to give His life *as* a ransom for many."

277. JESUS HEALS A BLIND MAN AS HE COMES TO JERICHO

LUKE 18

35. Now it came to pass *that* as He drew near to Jericho, *there was* a certain blind *man* who sat begging beside the road.

36. And hearing a multitude passing by *him*, he asked what this might be.

37. And they told him, "Jesus the Nazarean is passing by."

38. Then he called out, saying, "Jesus, Son of David, have mercy on me."

39. And those who were going in front rebuked him, so that he would be silent; but he cried out all the more, "Son of David, have mercy on me."

40. Then Jesus stopped *and* commanded him to be brought to Him. And when he came near, He asked him,

41. Saying, "What do you desire to have Me do for you?" And he said, "Lord, that I may receive sight."

42. Then Jesus said to him, "Receive sight. Your faith has healed you."

43. And immediately he received sight; and he followed Him, glorifying God. Now after seeing *this*, all the people gave praise to God.

278. JESUS AT ZACCHEUS' HOUSE IN JERICHO

LUKE 19

1. Then *Jesus* entered Jericho and was passing through.

2. And behold, a man named Zaccheus *was there*. Now he was a chief tax collector, and he was rich.

3. And he was seeking to see Jesus, Who He was; but he was not able because of the multitude, for he was a man of small stature.

4. But after running ahead, in front *of the multitude*, he climbed up into a sycamore *tree* so that he might see Him; for He was about to pass that *way*.

5. And when He came to the place, Jesus looked up *and* saw him, and said to him, "Zaccheus, make haste to come down, for today it is necessary for Me to stay at your house."

6. And he came down in haste and received Him joyfully.

7. But after seeing *this*, everyone began to criticize, saying, "He has gone in to lodge with a sinful man."

8. Then Zaccheus stood *and* said to the Lord, "Behold, the half of my possessions, Lord, I give to the poor; and if I have taken anything from anyone by false accusation, I return fourfold." [a]

9. And Jesus said to him, "Today, salvation has come to this house, inasmuch as he also is a son of Abraham.

10. For the Son of man has come to seek and to save that which is lost."

a - Ex. 22:1

279. JESUS HEALS BLIND MEN AS HE LEAVES JERICHO

MATTHEW 20	**MARK 10**
29. And as they were going out of Jericho, a great multitude followed Him.	46. Then they came to Jericho. And as He and His disciples were going up from Jericho with a large multitude, Bartimeus the blind *man*, the son of Timeus, was sitting beside the road begging.
30. And behold, two blind *men* sitting beside the road, when they heard that Jesus was passing by, cried out, saying, "Have mercy on us, Lord, Son of David."	47. And after hearing that it was Jesus the Nazarene, he began to cry out, saying, "Jesus, Son of David, have mercy on me!"
31. Then the multitude rebuked them, so that they would be silent. But they cried out *all* the more, saying, "Have mercy on us, Lord, Son of David."	48. Then many began to rebuke him, so that he would be silent; but he cried out all the more, "Son of David, have mercy on me!"

MATTHEW 20

32. And Jesus stopped and called them, and said, "What do you desire *that* I do for you?"
33. They said to Him, "Lord, that our eyes may be opened."
34. And being moved with compassion, Jesus touched their eyes; and immediately their eyes received sight, and they followed Him.

MARK 10

49. And Jesus stood still and asked for him to be called. And they called the blind *man*, saying to him, "Be of good courage; rise up, *for* He is calling you."
50. And after casting aside his *beggar's* cloak, he arose and came to Jesus.
51. Then Jesus answered him and said, "What do you desire to have Me do for you?" And the blind *man* said to Him, "Master, that I may receive sight."
52. And Jesus said to him "Go your way, *for* your faith has healed you." Then he immediately received sight, and *he* followed Jesus in the way.

280. THE PARABLE OF THE POUNDS

LUKE 19

11. Now as they were listening to these things, He went on to speak a parable, because He was near Jerusalem, and they thought that the kingdom of God was going to appear immediately.
12. Therefore, He said, "A certain nobleman set out to a distant country to receive a kingdom for himself, and to return.
13. And after calling ten of his servants, he gave to them ten pounds, and said to them, 'Trade until I come *back.*'
14. But his citizens hated him and sent an ambassador after him, saying, 'We are not willing to have this man reign over us.'
15. And it came to pass that when he returned after receiving the kingdom, he directed that those servants to whom he had given the money be called to him, in order that he might know what each one had gained by trading.
16. And the first one came up, saying, 'Lord, your pound has produced ten pounds.'
17. Then he said to him, 'Well *done*, good servant; because you were faithful in a very little, you shall have authority over ten cities.'
18. And the second one came, saying, 'Lord, your pound has made five pounds.'
19. Then he also said to this one, 'And you be over five cities.'
20. But another came, saying, 'Lord, behold your pound, which I kept laid up in a handkerchief.
21. For I was afraid of you, because you are a harsh man. You take up what you did not lay down, and you reap what you did not sow.'
22. Then he said to him, 'Out of your *own* mouth I will judge you, *you* wicked servant! You knew that I am a harsh man, taking up what I did not lay down and reaping what I did not sow.
23. Then why didn't you deposit my money in the bank, so that at my coming I might have received it with interest?'
24. And he said to those who were standing by, 'Take the pound from him, and give *it* to the one who has ten pounds.'
25. (And they said to him, 'Lord, he has ten pounds.')
26. For I tell you that to everyone who has, *more* shall be given; but the one who does not have, even what he has shall be taken from him.
27. Moreover, bring my enemies, those who were not willing *for* me to reign over them, and slay *them* here before me.' "
28. And after saying these things, He went on ahead, going up to Jerusalem.

281. JESUS' LAST PASSOVER APPROACHES
JOHN 11

55. Now the Passover [a] of the Jews was near, and many went up out of the country to Jerusalem before the Passover, so that they might purify themselves.

56. Then they were watching for Jesus, and were saying to one another *while* standing in the temple, "What do you think, that He will not come to the feast at all?"

57. For both the chief priests and the Pharisees had given a command that if anyone knew where He was, he should reveal *it*, so that they might seize Him.

a - Ex. 12:4-14; Lev. 23:5

Mount of Olives

PART V

THE EVENTS BEFORE
JESUS' LAST PASSOVER, 30 AD

SIX DAYS BEFORE JESUS' LAST PASSOVER

The Gospel of Luke records that Jesus was teaching in the temple in the days leading up to His arrest and crucifixion: "Now He was teaching day by day in the temple; and the chief priests and the scribes and the chief of the people were seeking to destroy Him" (Luke 19:47).

In the final days before His crucifixion, a series of confrontations took place at the temple between Jesus and the scribes, Pharisees, Sadducees and chief priests. The Gospel accounts give four chronological keys that enable us to understand the events of those days. It is clear that the Gospel writers followed the Hebrew Calendar, which reckons each day from sunset to sunset, or evening to evening, when they were inspired to record their accounts of these days leading up to Jesus' crucifixion. They wrote of the events as they occurred each day, making particular note of the mornings and evenings. By recording each day as it ended at evening, or sunset, the Gospel writers enable us to understand the exact time frame of these events.

The Gospel of John records that six days before His last Passover, Jesus came to Lazarus' house in Bethany (John 12:1). Counting backward six days from the beginning of Nisan 14, we come to the beginning of Nisan 8, which was Wednesday evening, March 29. We know that the time was in the evening, because the account tells us that Jesus ate supper (verse 2). The word "supper" is translated from the Greek word το δειπονον, *to deiponon*, which means "the chief or evening meal, supper" (Berry, *Greek-English New Testament Lexicon*). After Jesus ate supper, Lazarus' sister Mary anointed His feet with ointment (verses 3-4). In the morning of Nisan 8, which was Thursday, March 30, Jesus made His triumphal entry into Jerusalem (verse 12). His triumphal entry could not have been on a Sabbath, as some claim, because the disciples were breaking off boughs from palm trees to spread in the way before Him. If the disciples had done this on the weekly Sabbath, the scribes and Pharisees would have vigorously protested, claiming that His disciples were breaking the Sabbath.

Those who teach that Jesus was resurrected on a Sunday also claim that His triumphal entry into Jerusalem took place on a Sunday. They call this day Palm Sunday. But according to the chronology that is recorded in the Gospel accounts, the day that Jesus made His triumphal entry was Thursday, Nisan 8, or March 30, 30 AD. This is the first key of understanding. (*See the synchronized Hebrew/Julian calendar on pp. 216-217.*)

The Gospel of Mark adds further details about the events that took place on Nisan 8. Mark records that after Jesus made His triumphal entry into Jerusalem, He went into the temple and looked around. Shortly afterward, He and His disciples went back to Bethany (Mark 11:11). This completes the events of Nisan 8, which ended at sunset.

Mark continues with the events of the next morning, which was Friday, Nisan 9, or March 31. This was the preparation day for the weekly Sabbath. Mark shows that on the morning of Nisan 9, as He was on the way to the temple, Jesus cursed the fig tree (verses 13-14). Later, He went into the temple area and cast out the money exchangers, overturning their tables and driving out the animals. It is evident that Jesus was cleansing the temple, removing the money exchangers with their greed and corruption, in preparation for the Sabbath. After Jesus had cleansed the temple, He taught the people. At evening, Jesus left the temple and Jerusalem and went back to Bethany for the night (Mark 11:19, Matt. 21:17).

The next morning, which was the weekly Sabbath, Nisan 10, or Saturday, April 1, the disciples saw that the fig tree that Jesus had cursed was withered (Mark 11:20). Only Mark records that the cursing and shriveling of the fig tree took place over a two-day period. Matthew records these events as if they had occurred on the same day. If Mark had not made it clear that a second day was involved, it would not be possible to accurately determine the chronology of the events leading up to Jesus' last Passover. This critical two-day period is the second key in understanding the timing of the events that took place before Jesus' last Passover.

The Gospel of John records other events that occurred on Nisan 10, or April 1, 30 AD. Certain Hellenist Jews who had heard about Jesus asked Philip where they could find Him. Philip went to Andrew, and together they came and told Jesus (John 12:20-22). While Jesus was teaching the people, a voice spoke from heaven: " 'Now My soul is troubled, and what shall I say? Father, save Me from this hour? But for this *very* purpose I have come to this hour. Father, glorify Your name.' Then a voice came from heaven, *saying*, 'I have both glorified *it* and will glorify *it* again.' Then the people standing *there*, who heard *it*, said, 'It thundered.' Others said, 'An angel spoke to Him.' Jesus answered and said, 'This voice did not come because of Me, but because of you' " (John 12:27-30).

After this, Jesus left the temple and hid Himself, apparently for the rest of the Sabbath. This completes the events of the Sabbath, Nisan 10, or Saturday, April 1, 30 AD. The third key to understanding is that on Nisan 10, Jesus was selected as God the Father's Passover Lamb, Who would be sacrificed for the sins of the world.

Jesus and His disciples returned to Jerusalem the next morning, Sunday, Nisan 11, or April 2. On this day, His final confrontations with the scribes, Pharisees, Sadducees and chief priests took place. These lasted for most of the day, until late afternoon (Mark 11:27-13:1). Then Jesus and His disciples left the temple, and He instructed them privately (Mark 13:1-3, Matt. 24:1-3). Jesus finished instructing them just before sunset on Nisan 11. Then He declared to His disciples that He would be crucified on the Passover, which would take place after two days (Mark 14:1, Matt. 26:2).

The fourth and final key in understanding the six-day chronology before the Passover is that the two-day period recorded in Mark 14:1 and Matthew 26:2 is counted from the end of Nisan 11. The two days yet remaining before the Passover were Monday, Nisan 12, and Tuesday, Nisan 13. Nisan 12 began at sunset, April 2, and ended at sunset, April 3, and Nisan 13 began at sunset, April 3, and ended at sunset,

April 4. After those two days came the Passover day, Nisan 14, which began at sunset, April 4, and ended at sunset, April 5.

Please study the chart on pages 216-217, which shows the chronological sequence of the events leading up to Jesus' last Passover as they occurred day by day.

Merchant Riding Donkey—Old Jerusalem

282. SIX DAYS BEFORE HIS LAST PASSOVER, JESUS COMES TO BETHANY

JOHN 12

1. Now six days before the Passover, Jesus came to Bethany, where Lazarus was who had died, *and* whom He had raised from *the* dead.
2. There they made a supper *for* Him, and Martha served; and Lazarus was one of those who sat with Him.
3. Mary then took a pound of pure spikenard ointment worth a great price *and* anointed * Jesus' feet, wiping His feet with her hair. And the house was filled with the aroma of the ointment.
4. As a result, one of His disciples, Judas Iscariot, Simon's *son*, who was about to betray Him, said,
5. "Why was this ointment not sold for three hundred silver coins, and given to *the* poor?"
6. Now he said this, not because he cared for the poor, but because he was a thief, and had the bag, and carried what was put in *it*.
7. Then Jesus said, "Let her alone; she has been keeping it toward the day of My burial.
8. For you have the poor with you always, but you do not always have Me."
9. Then a great crowd of the Jews found out that He was there. And they came, not only because of Jesus, but also that they might see Lazarus, whom He had raised from *the* dead.
10. But the chief priests took counsel in order that they might kill Lazarus also;
11. Because by reason of him, many of the Jews were leaving *them* and believing in Jesus.

LUKE 19

47. Now He was teaching day by day in the temple; and the chief priests and the scribes and the chief of the people were seeking to destroy Him.

Model City

In the Gospels there are three accounts given about the anointings of Jesus before his crucifixion. The two accounts in Matthew 26 and Mark 14 are parallel accounts of the same anointing. Both describe how a woman anointed Jesus' head two days before the Passover. In John 12, Mary of Bethany anointed His feet. This occurred six days before the Passover. It is very obvious that these are two separate occasions. The reaction of Judas Iscariot and some of the other disciples was, of course, the same.

Six Days Before
Hebrew Calendar Nisan

HEBREW DAYS OF WEEK

	1ST DAY – NISAN 4	2ND DAY – NISAN 5	3RD DAY – NISAN 6	4TH DAY – NISAN 7
	Sunrise — Sunset	Sunrise — Sunset	Sunrise — Sunset	Sunrise — Sunset
Roman Days of Week	Sunday – March 26	Monday – March 27	Tuesday – March 28	Wednesday

HEBREW DAYS OF WEEK

	1ST DAY – NISAN 11	2ND DAY – NISAN 12	3RD DAY – NISAN 13	4TH DAY – NISAN 14
	Third Day Before The Passover	Second Day Before The Passover	First Day Before The Passover	PASSOVER DAY
	At The Temple Jesus Has The Great Confrontation Mk 11:27 - Mk 13:2 Mat 21:23 - Mat 24:2 Lk 20:1 - Lk 21:4		Disciples Prepare For Passover Mat 26:17-19 Mk 14:12-16 Lk 22:7-13	A Preparation Day For The Holy Day
	Olivet Instruction To Jesus' Disciples Mk 13:3-37 Mat 24:3 – Mat 26:2 Lk 21:7-38			
	After Instruction Near Evening Jesus Tells His Disciples The Passover Is After Two Days Mat 26:2 Mk 14:1	The First Day After Instruction	The Second Day After Instruction	Passover Started Approximately 7 - 7:30 PM Sunset, About 6 PM
	Sunrise — Sunset	Sunrise — Sunset	Sunrise — Sunset	Sunrise — Sunset
Roman Days of Week	Sunday – April 2	Monday – April 3	Tuesday – April 4	Wednesday

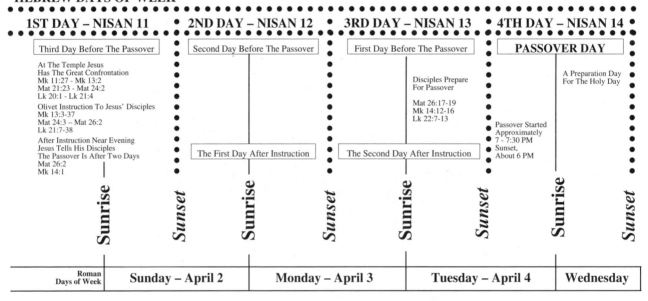

The Key to Jesus' Activities: Luke 19:47
Luke 21:37-38

In the Daytime He Taught at The Temple.
At Night He Went Out and
Stayed at the Mount of Olives.
Then to Bethany Mark 11:11

Jesus' Last Passover
Roman Calendar March/April AD 30

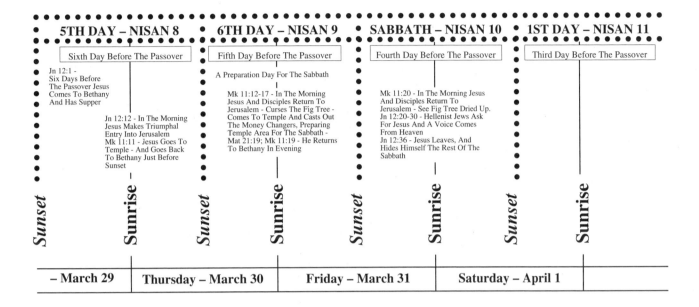

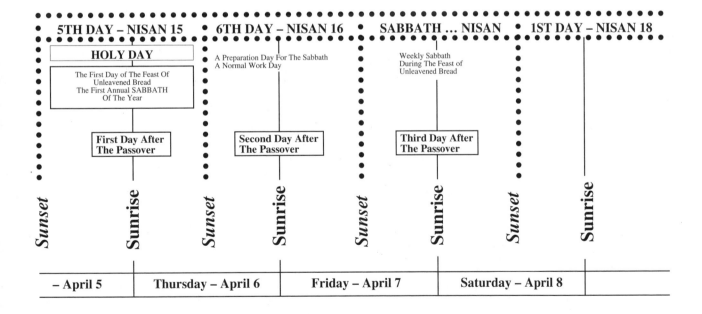

217

THE DAY PORTION – NISAN 8 – THURSDAY, MARCH 30 – 30 AD
282. JESUS' TRIUMPHAL ENTRY INTO JERUSALEM

JOHN 12	MARK 11	LUKE 19	MATTHEW 21

JOHN 12

12. On the next day, a great crowd *of people* who had come for the feast, when they heard that Jesus was coming into Jerusalem,

13. Took branches from palm trees and went out to meet Him, and were shouting, "Hosanna! Blessed *is* He Who comes in *the* name of *the* Lord, the King of Israel."

14. Now after finding a young ass, Jesus sat upon it, exactly as it is written:

15. "Fear not, daughter of Sion. Behold, your King comes, sitting on a colt of an ass." [a]

16. And His disciples did not understand these things at the beginning; but when Jesus was glorified, then they remembered that these things were written about Him, and that they had done these things to Him.

17. Then the group that was with Him when He called Lazarus out of the tomb, and raised him from *the* dead, testified of *what they had seen.*

18. Because of this, the people also met Him, for they had heard of this miracle that He had done.

19. Then the Pharisees said among themselves, "Do you see that we are not gaining in any way? Look! The world has gone after Him."

MARK 11

1. And when they came to Bethphage and Bethany, *which were* near to Jerusalem, toward the Mount of Olives, He sent two of His disciples;

2. And He said to them, "Go into the village ahead of you, and as soon as you enter it you will find a colt tied, upon which no man has sat. After loosing it, lead *it to Me.*

3. And if anyone says to you, 'Why are you doing this?' say, 'The Lord has need of it'; and he will send it here immediately."

4. And they went *to the village* and found the colt tied outside, at the door *of a house* by the crossroad; and they loosed it.

5. Then some of those who were standing there said to them, "Why are you loosing the colt?"

6. And they answered them as Jesus had commanded. Then they allowed them *to take it.*

7. And they led the colt to Jesus; and they laid their garments upon it, and He sat on it.

8. Then many spread their garments in the road, and others cut down branches from the trees, and scattered *them* in the road.

LUKE 19

29. Now it came to pass *that* as He approached Bethphage and Bethany, toward the mountain called *the Mount* of Olives, He sent two of His disciples,

30. Saying, "Go into the village across from *you.* Upon entering it, you shall find a colt tied, on which no one has ever yet sat; loose it, and bring *it* to Me.

31. And if anyone asks you why you are loosing *it,* this is what you shall say to him: 'Because the Lord has need of it.' "

32. And those who had been sent went *and* found *it* exactly as He had said to them.

33. And as they were loosing the colt, the owners of it said to them, "Why are you loosing the colt?"

34. Then they said, "The Lord has need of it."

35. And they led it to Jesus; and after laying their garments on the colt, they put Jesus on *it.*

36. Now as He went *along,* they spread their garments in the road.

37. And as He drew near *to the city,* already *being* at the descent of the Mount of Olives, all the multitude of the disciples began to rejoice *and* to praise

a - Zech. 9:9

MATTHEW 21

1. Now as they were approaching Jerusalem, they came to Bethphage, near the Mount of Olives; and Jesus sent two disciples,

2. Saying to them, "Go into the village, the one ahead of you, and immediately you shall find an ass tied, and a colt with her. Loose *them* and bring *them* to Me.

3. And if anyone says anything to you, tell *him,* 'The Lord has need of them.' And he will send them at once."

4. But this all took place so that it might be fulfilled which was spoken by the prophet, saying,

5. "Say to the daughter of Sion, 'Behold, your King comes to you, meek and mounted on an ass, and *on* a colt *the* foal of an ass.' " [a]

6. And the disciples left, and did as Jesus had ordered them;

7. They brought the ass and the colt, and put their garments upon them; and He sat on them.

8. And a great number *of the* multitude spread their garments on the road; and others were cutting down branches from the trees and spreading *them* on the road.

MARK 11	LUKE 19	MATTHEW 21
9. And those who went before and those who followed *behind* were crying out, saying, "Hosanna! Blessed *is* He Who comes in the name of *the* Lord. [a] 10. Blessed *is* the kingdom of our father David, coming in *the* name of *the* Lord. Hosanna in the highest!"	God with a loud voice for all *the* works of power that they had seen, 38. Saying, "Blessed *be* the King, Who comes in *the* name of *the* Lord. Peace in heaven and glory in *the* highest!" [a] 39. And some of the Pharisees in the multitude said to Him, "Master, rebuke Your disciples." 40. But He answered *and* said to them, "I tell you that if these were silent, the stones would cry out."	9. And the multitudes, those who were going before and those who were following behind, were shouting, saying, "Hosanna to the Son of David! Blessed is He Who comes in *the* name of *the* Lord. Hosanna in the highest!" [a] 10. Now when He entered Jerusalem, the entire city was moved, saying, "Who is this?" 11. And the multitudes said, "This is Jesus the prophet, the one Who *is* from Nazareth of Galilee."

a - Psa. 118:26

284. JESUS WEEPS OVER THE CITY OF JERUSALEM

LUKE 19

41. And when He came near *and* saw the city, He wept over it,
42. Saying, "If you had known, even you, at least in this your day, the things for your peace; but now they are hidden from your eyes.
43. For *the* days shall come upon you that your enemies shall cast a rampart about you, and shall enclose you around and keep you in on every side,
44. And shall level you to the ground, and your children within you; and they shall not leave in you a stone upon a stone, because you did not know the season of your visitation."

285. JESUS GOES INTO THE TEMPLE
AND RETURNS THAT EVENING TO BETHANY

MARK 11

11. And Jesus entered Jerusalem and went into the temple; and *because* the hour was already late, after looking around at everything *there*, He went out to Bethany with the twelve.

286. JESUS TEACHES DAILY IN THE TEMPLE

LUKE 19

47. Now He was teaching day by day in the temple; and the chief priests and the scribes and the chief of the people were seeking to destroy Him,
48. But could not find what they might do; for all the people were listening *intently*, hanging on His *every word*.

219

NISAN 9 – FRIDAY, MARCH 31 – 30 AD
287. THE NEXT MORNING JESUS CURSES THE FIG TREE, CASTS OUT THE MONEY CHANGERS, AND RETURNS TO BETHANY FOR THE NIGHT

MARK 11

12. And in the morning, after they left Bethany, He became hungry.
13. Then, seeing a fig tree afar off that had leaves, He went *to it to see* if He might possibly find something on it. But after coming to it, He found nothing except leaves because it was not yet *the* season for figs.
14. And Jesus responded *by* saying to it, "Let no one eat fruit from you any more forever!" And His disciples heard *it.*
15. Then they came into Jerusalem; and after entering the temple, Jesus began to cast out those who were buying and selling in the temple; and He overthrew the tables of the money exchangers and the seats of those who were selling doves.
16. Moreover, He did not allow anyone to carry a vessel through the temple.
17. And He taught, saying to them, "Is it not written, 'My house shall be called a house of prayer for all nations'? But you have made it a den of robbers." [a]
18. Now the chief priests and the scribes heard *this,* and they sought how they might destroy Him; for they feared Him, because all the multitudes marveled at His teaching.
19. And when evening came, He went out of the city.

MATTHEW 21

12. And Jesus went into the temple of God and cast out all those who were buying and selling in the temple; and He overthrew the tables of the money exchangers, and the seats of those who were selling doves.
13. Then He said to them, "It is written, 'My house shall be called a house of prayer'; but you have made it a den of thieves." [a]
14. And *the* blind and *the* lame came to Him in the temple, and He healed them.
15. But when the chief priests and the scribes saw the wonderful things that He did, and the children shouting in the temple and saying, "Hosanna to the Son of David," they were indignant,
16. And said to Him, "Do You hear what they are saying?" Then Jesus said to them, "Yes! Have you never read, 'Out of *the* mouths of little children and infants You have perfected praise'?" [b]
17. And leaving them, He went out of the city to Bethany and spent the night there.
18. Now early in the morning, *as He was* coming back into the city, He hungered;

LUKE 19

45. Then He went into the temple *and* began to cast out those who were selling and those who were buying in it,
46. Saying to them, "It is written, 'My house is a house of prayer'; but you have made it a den of robbers." [a]

Bethany

Fig Tree Before Cursing

a - Isa. 56:7; Jer. 7:11   b - Psa. 8:2

SABBATH, NISAN 10 – SATURDAY, APRIL 1 – 30 AD

288. THEY GO UP TO JERUSALEM THE NEXT MORNING

MARK 11

20. And in the morning, as they passed by, they saw the fig tree dried up from *the* roots.
21. Then Peter remembered *and* said to Him, "Look, Master! The fig tree that You cursed has dried up."
22. And Jesus answered and said to them, "Have faith *from* God.
23. For truly I say to you, whoever shall say to this mountain, 'Be taken away and be cast into the sea,' and shall not doubt in his heart, but shall believe that what he said will take place, he shall have whatever he shall say.
24. For this reason I say to you, all *the* things that you ask *when* you are praying, believe that you will receive *them*, and *they* shall be *given* to you.
25. But when you stand praying, if you have anything against anyone, forgive, so that your Father Who *is* in heaven may forgive you your offenses.
26. For if you do not forgive, neither will your Father Who *is* in heaven forgive you your offenses."

MATTHEW 21

19. And seeing a fig tree by the road, He came *up* to it, but found nothing on it except leaves only. And He said to it, "Let there never again be fruit from you forever." And immediately the fig tree dried up.
20. And after seeing *it*, the disciples were amazed, saying, "How quickly the fig tree has dried up!"
21. Then Jesus answered *and* said to them, "Truly I say to you, if you have faith and do not doubt, not only shall you do the *miracle* of the fig tree, but even if you shall say to this mountain, 'Be removed and be cast into the sea,' it shall come to pass.
22. And everything that you shall ask in prayer, believing, you shall receive."

Fig Tree After Cursing

289. CERTAIN HELLENIST JEWS WANT TO SEE JESUS

JOHN 12

20. Now there were certain Greeks among those who had come up to worship at the feast.
21. And these came to Philip, who was from Bethsaida of Galilee; and they asked him, saying, "Sir, we desire to see Jesus."
22. Philip came and told Andrew, and Andrew and Philip in turn told Jesus.
23. But Jesus answered them, saying, "The time has come for the Son of man to be glorified.
24. Truly, truly I say to you, unless a grain of wheat falls into the ground and dies, it remains alone; but if it dies, it bears much fruit.
25. The one who loves his life shall lose it, and the one who hates his life in this world shall keep it unto eternal life.
26. If anyone will serve Me, let him follow Me; and where I am, there shall My servant be also. And if anyone serves Me, him shall the Father honor.
27. Now My soul is troubled, [a] and what shall I say? Father, save Me from this hour? But for this *very* purpose I have come to this hour.

a - Psa. 42:6

The Temple and Burnt Offering Altar

SABBATH, NISAN 10 – SATURDAY, APRIL 1 – 30 AD
290. A VOICE THUNDERS FROM HEAVEN

JOHN 12

28. "Father, glorify Your name." Then a voice came from heaven, *saying*, "I have both glorified *it* and will glorify *it* again."
29. Then the people standing *there*, who heard *it*, said, "It thundered." Others said, "An angel spoke to Him."
30. Jesus answered and said, "This voice did not come because of Me, but because of you.
31. Now is *the* judgment of this world. Now shall the prince of this world be cast out.
32. And if I be lifted up from the earth, I will draw all to Myself."
33. But He said this to signify by what death He was about to die.
34. The people answered Him, "We have heard out of the law that the Christ lives forever, and why do You say that the Son of man must be lifted up? Who is this Son of man?"
35. Then Jesus said to them, "Yet a little while the light is with you. Walk while you have the light, so that *the* darkness will not overtake you. For the one who walks in darkness does not know where he is going.
36. While you have the light, believe in the light, so that you may become *the* children of light…"

291. JESUS LEAVES THE CITY AGAIN AND
HIDES HIMSELF FOR THE REMAINDER OF THE SABBATH

JOHN 12

36. …Jesus spoke these things and *then* departed from them *and* was *in* hiding.

292. ISAIAH QUOTED – THE PEOPLE DO NOT
UNDERSTAND WHO AND WHAT CHRIST IS

JOHN 12

37. Although He had done so many miracles in their presence, they did not believe in Him,
38. So that the word of Isaiah the prophet might be fulfilled who said, "Lord, who has believed our report? And to whom has the arm of *the* Lord been revealed?" [a]
39. For this *very* reason they could not believe because again Isaiah said,
40. "He has blinded their eyes and hardened their hearts so that they would not see with *their* eyes and understand with *their* hearts, and be converted, and I would heal them." [b]
41. Isaiah said these things when he saw His glory and spoke concerning Him.

a - Isa. 53:1   b - Isa. 6:9-10

Jerusalem and Temple Area   - Matson Photo Service

NISAN 11 – SUNDAY, APRIL 2 – 30 AD

293. THE NEXT DAY, THE DAY AFTER THE WEEKLY SABBATH, THE PRIEST AND PHARISEES CHALLENGE JESUS' AUTHORITY

MARK 11	MATTHEW 21	LUKE 20

27. Then they came again to Jerusalem. And as He was walking in the temple, the chief priests and the scribes and the elders came to Him;
28. And they said to Him, "By what authority are You doing these things? And who gave You this authority, that You do these things?"
29. Then Jesus answered and said to them, "I also will ask you one thing, and *if* you answer Me, I will also tell you by what authority I do these things.
30. The baptism of John, was it from heaven or from men? Answer Me."
31. And they reasoned among themselves, saying, "If we say, 'From heaven,' He will say, 'Why then did you not believe him?'
32. But if we say, 'From men' " —they feared the people, because everyone held that John was indeed a prophet.
33. And they answered Jesus by saying, "We do not know." Then Jesus answered *and* said to them, "Neither will I tell you by what authority I do these things."

23. Now when He entered the temple *and* was teaching, the chief priests and the elders of the people came up to Him, saying, "By what authority do You do these things? And who gave You this authority?"
24. And Jesus answered *and* said to them, "I will also ask you one thing, which if you tell Me, I will also tell you by what authority I do these things.
25. The baptism of John, where did it come from? From heaven, or from men?" Then they reasoned among themselves, saying, "If we say, 'From heaven,' He will say to us, 'Why then did you not believe him?'
26. But if we say, 'From men,' we fear the multitude; for everyone holds John as a prophet."
27. And they answered Jesus *and* said, "We do not know." He said to them also, "Neither will I tell you by what authority I do these things.

1. Now it came to pass on one of those days, as He was teaching the people in the temple and proclaiming the gospel, *that* the chief priests and the scribes came up with the elders,
2. And spoke to Him, saying, "Tell us by what authority You do these things, and who gave You this authority?"
3. And He answered *and* said to them, "I also will ask you one thing, and you tell Me:
4. The baptism of John, was it from heaven or from men?"
5. And they reasoned among themselves, saying, "If we say, 'From heaven,' He will say, 'Why then did you not believe him?'
6. But if we say, 'From men,' all the people will stone us, for they are persuaded *that* John was a prophet."
7. And they replied *that* they did not know where *it was* from.
8. Then Jesus said to them, "Neither do I tell you by what authority I do these things."

294. THE PARABLE OF THE TWO SONS

MATTHEW 21

28. "But what do you think? A man had two sons, and he came to the first one and said, 'Son, go work in my vineyard today.'
29. And he answered *and* said, 'I will not'; but afterwards he repented *and* went.
30. Then he came to the second *son and* said the same thing. And he answered *and* said, 'Sir, I will *go*'; but he did not go.
31. Which of the two did the will of the father?" They said to Him, "The first *one*." Jesus said to them, "I tell you truly, the tax collectors and *the* harlots are going into the kingdom of God before you.
32. For John came to you in *the* way of righteousness, and you did not believe him; but the tax collectors and *the* harlots believed him. Yet you, after seeing *this*, did not afterwards repent and believe him."

NISAN 11 – SUNDAY, APRIL 2 – 30 AD
295. THE PARABLE OF THE VINEYARD

MARK 12	MATTHEW 21	LUKE 20

MARK 12

1. And He began to speak to them in parables: "A man planted a vineyard, and put a fence around *it*, and dug a winevat, and built a tower, and leased it out to husbandmen, and *then* left the country. [a]

2. And at the *harvest* season he sent a servant to the husbandmen, so that he might receive the fruit of the vineyard from the husbandmen.

3. But they took him *and* beat *him*, and sent *him* away empty.

4. And in turn, he sent another servant to them; but they stoned him and wounded him on the head, and after insulting *him* sent *him* away.

5. And in turn, he sent still another *servant*, and they killed him; and *he sent* many others, *and* some were beaten and others were killed.

6. Now then, he had yet one son, his own beloved. And so, last of *all* he sent him to them also, saying, 'They will have respect for my son.'

7. But those husbandmen said among themselves, 'This is the heir. Come, let us kill him, and the inheritance shall be ours.'

8. And after seizing him, they killed *him* and cast *him* out of the vineyard.

9. Therefore, what will the lord of the vineyard do? He will come and destroy the husbandmen and will give the vineyard to others.

10. Have you not read even this scripture: '*The* Stone that the builders rejected, this has become *the* head of *the* corner;

11. This was from *the* Lord, and it is wonderful in our eyes'?" [b]

MATTHEW 21

33. "Hear another parable: There was a certain man, a master of a house, who planted a vineyard, and put a fence around it, and dug a winepress in it, and built a tower, and *then* leased it to husbandmen and left the country. [a]

34. Now when the season of the fruits was drawing near, he sent his servants to the husbandmen to receive his fruits.

35. But the husbandmen took his servants and beat one, and killed another, and stoned another.

36. Again he sent other servants, more than the first *time*; and they did the same thing to them.

37. Then at last he sent his son to them, saying, 'They will have respect for my son.'

38. But when the husbandmen saw the son, they said among themselves, 'This is the heir; come, let us murder him and gain possession of his inheritance.'

39. Then they took him, *and* cast *him* out of the vineyard, and murdered *him*.

40. Therefore, when the lord of the vineyard shall come, what will he do to those husbandmen?"

41. They said to Him, "Evil *men*! He will utterly destroy them, and he will lease his vineyard to other husbandmen, who will render to him the fruits in their seasons."

42. Jesus said to them, "Have you never read in the Scriptures, '*The* Stone that the builders rejected, this has become *the* head of *the* corner. This was from *the* Lord, and it is wonderful in our eyes'? [b]

LUKE 20

9. And He began to speak this parable to the people: "A certain man planted a vineyard, and leased it out to husbandmen, and left the country for a long time. [a]

10. And in *the harvest* season he sent a servant to the husbandmen, so that they might give him *some* of the fruit from the vineyard; but the husbandmen beat him *and* sent *him* away empty.

11. And after that he sent another servant; but they also beat him and scorned *him and* sent *him* away empty.

12. And after that he sent a third *servant;* but they also wounded him *and* cast *him* out.

13. Then the lord of the vineyard said, 'What shall I do? I will send my beloved son; perhaps when they see him, they will respect *him*.'

14. But when they saw him, the husbandmen reasoned among themselves, saying, 'This is the heir. Come, let us kill him, so that the inheritance may be ours.'

15. And they cast him outside the vineyard *and* killed *him*. Therefore, what will the lord of the vineyard do to them?

16. He will come and destroy these husbandmen, and will give the vineyard to others." Now after hearing *this*, they said, "May *it* never be!"

17. But He looked at them *and* said, "What then is this that is written: '*The* Stone that the builders rejected, this one has become the head of *the* corner? [b]

a - Isa. 5:1-17   b - Psa. 118:22-23; Isa. 28:16

NISAN 11 – SUNDAY, APRIL 2 – 30

MATTHEW 21

43. "Because of this, I say to you, the kingdom of God shall be taken from you, and it shall be given to a nation *that* produces the fruits of it.
44. And the one who falls on this Stone shall be broken; but on whomever it shall fall, it will grind him to powder." [a]

LUKE 20

18. "Everyone who falls on that Stone shall be broken; but on whomever it shall fall, it will grind him to powder.' " [a]

a - Isa. 8:14-15; Dan. 2:44

296. THE PRIESTS AND SCRIBES SEEK TO ARREST HIM

MARK 12

12. Then they sought to arrest Him, but they feared the multitude; for they knew that He had spoken the parable against them. And they left Him and went their way.

MATTHEW 21

45. Now after hearing His parables, the chief priests and the Pharisees knew that He was speaking about them.
46. And they sought to arrest Him, but they were afraid of the multitudes, because they held Him as a prophet.

LUKE 20

19. And the chief priests and the scribes sought to lay hands on Him in that hour, because they knew that He had spoken this parable against them; but they feared the people.

297. MANY LEADERS SECRETLY BELIEVE IN JESUS

JOHN 12

42. But even so, many among the rulers believed in Him; but because of the Pharisees they did not confess *Him,* so that they would not be put out of the synagogue;
43. For they loved the glory of men more than the glory of God.

298. TO BELIEVE IN JESUS IS TO BELIEVE IN THE FATHER

JOHN 12

44. Then Jesus called out and said, "The one who believes in Me does not believe in Me, but in Him Who sent Me.
45. And the one who sees Me sees Him Who sent Me.
46. I have come *as* a light into the world so that everyone who believes in Me may not remain in darkness.
47. But if anyone hears My words and does not believe, I do not judge him; for I did not come to judge the world, but to save the world.
48. The one who rejects Me and does not receive My words has one who judges him; the word which I have spoken, that shall judge him in the last day.

NISAN 11 – SUNDAY, APRIL 2 – 30 AD

JOHN 12

49. For I have not spoken from Myself; but the Father, Who sent Me, gave Me commandment Himself, what I should say and what I should speak.
50. And I know that His commandment is eternal life. Therefore, whatever I speak, I speak exactly as the Father has told Me."

299. THE PARABLE OF THE WEDDING AND THE WEDDING FEAST

MATTHEW 22

1. And again Jesus answered and spoke to them in parables, saying,
2. "The kingdom of heaven is compared to a man *who was* a king, who made a wedding feast for his son,
3. And sent his servants to call those who had been invited to the wedding feast; but they refused to come.
4. Afterwards he sent out other servants, saying, 'Say to those who have been invited, "Behold, I have prepared my dinner; my oxen and the fatted beasts are killed, and all things *are* ready. Come to the wedding feast." '
5. But they paid no attention and went away, one to his farm, and another to his business.
6. And the rest, after seizing his servants, insulted and killed *them.*
7. Now when the king heard *it*, he became angry; and he sent his armies *and* destroyed those murderers, and burned up their city.
8. Then he said to his servants, 'The wedding feast indeed is ready, but those who were invited were not worthy;
9. Therefore, go into the well-traveled highways, and invite all that you find to the wedding feast.'
10. And after going out into the highways, those servants brought together everyone that they found, both good and evil; and the wedding feast was filled with guests.
11. And when the king came in to see the guests, *he* noticed a man there who was not dressed in *proper* attire for *the* wedding feast;
12. And he said to him, 'Friend, how did you enter here without a garment *fit* for *the* wedding feast?' But he had no answer.
13. Then the king said to the servants, 'Bind his hands and feet, *and* take him away, and cast *him* into the outer darkness.' There shall be weeping and gnashing of teeth.
14. For many are called, but few *are* chosen."

300. SPIES ARE SENT TO ENTANGLE HIM

MARK 12	MATTHEW 22	LUKE 20
13. But they sent to Him some of the Pharisees and the Herodians, in order to entrap Him in His words. 14. And after coming to Him, they said, "Master, we know that You are true, and *that* You court no man's favor; because You do not look on *the* appearance of men, but You teach the way of God in truth. Is it lawful to give tribute to Caesar or not? 15. Should we give *it*, or should we not give *it*?" But perceiving their hypocrisy, He said to them, "Why do you tempt Me? Bring Me a silver coin, so that I may look *at it*."	15. Then the Pharisees went and took counsel *as to* how they might entrap Him in *His* speech. 16. And they sent their disciples *along* with the Herodians to Him, saying, "Master, we know that You are true, and *that You* teach the way of God in truth, and *that* You are not concerned about *pleasing* anyone; for You do not respect *the* persons of men. 17. Therefore, tell us, what do You think? Is it lawful to give tribute to Caesar, or not?" 18. But Jesus, knowing their wickedness, said, "Why do you tempt Me, *you* hypocrites?	20. And they kept *Him* under surveillance, *and* sent out secret agents who pretended that they were righteous, so that they might catch Him in His words, in order to deliver Him up to the power and authority of the governor. 21. And they questioned Him, saying, "Master, we realize that You speak and teach rightly, and do not accept *any man's* person, but teach the way of God in truth. 22. Is it lawful for us to give tribute to Caesar, or not?" 23. But perceiving their craftiness, He said to them, "Why do you tempt Me?

NISAN 11 – SUNDAY, APRIL 2 – 30 AD

301. RENDER TO CAESAR THE THINGS OF CAESAR, AND TO GOD THE THINGS OF GOD

MARK 12	MATTHEW 22	LUKE 20
16. Then they brought *it.* And He said to them, "Whose image and super-scription *is on* this *coin*?" And they said to Him, "Caesar's." 17. And Jesus answered and said to them, "Render the things of Caesar to Caesar, and the things of God to God." And they were amazed at Him.	19. "Show Me the tribute coin." And they brought to Him a silver coin. 20. And He said to them, "Whose image and inscription *is on* this?" 21. They said to Him, "Caesar's." And He said to them, "Render then the things of Caesar to Caesar, and the things of God to God." 22. And when they heard *this,* they were amazed; and *they* left Him *and* went *their* way.	24. "Show Me a silver coin. Whose image and inscription does it have?" And they answered *and* said, "Caesar's." 25. Then He said to them, "Render therefore the things of Caesar to Caesar, and the things of God to God." 26. And they were not able to catch Him in His speech in the presence of the people. But being filled with amazement by His answer, they were silent.

Front   *Back*

Roman Brass Coin
Caesar Augustus ~ 27 BC to 14 AD
– courtesy of Leon Ritchie

Front   *Back*

Roman Brass Coin
Titus ~ 79 AD to 81 AD
– courtesy of Leon Ritchie

302. THE QUESTION CONCERNING MARRIAGE IN THE RESURRECTION

MARK 12	MATTHEW 22	LUKE 20
18. Then the Sadducees, who say there is no resurrection, came to Him, and they questioned Him, saying, 19. "Master, Moses wrote for us that if the brother of anyone should die and leave behind a wife, but leave no children, then his brother should take his wife and raise up seed for his brother. [a]	23. On that same day, *the* Sadducees, who say there is no resurrection, came to Him and questioned Him, 24. Saying, "Master, Moses said, 'If anyone dies without having children, his brother shall marry his wife and shall raise up seed to his brother.' [a] 25. Now there were with us seven brothers; and the first one, being married, died with no seed; and he left his wife to his brother.	27. Then some of the Sadducees, who do not believe there is a resurrection, came *and* questioned Him, 28. Saying, "Master, Moses wrote to us that if anyone's brother who had a wife should die, and he should die childless, his brother should take his *dead* brother's wife and raise up seed for his brother. [a]

a - Deut. 25:5-6

NISAN 11 – SUNDAY, APRIL 2 – 30 AD

MARK 12	MATTHEW 22	LUKE 20

MARK 12

20. *Now* there were seven brothers; the first took a wife and died, leaving no seed;

21. And the second took her and died, and neither did he leave seed; and the third likewise.

22. And the seven had her and left no seed. Last of all the woman died also.

23. Now then, in the resurrection, when they shall arise, to which of them shall she be wife? For all seven had her as wife."

24. Then Jesus answered them and said, "In *asking* this, do you not err, not knowing the Scriptures nor the power of God?

25. For when they rise from *the* dead, they neither marry nor are given in marriage, but are as the angels who *are* in heaven.

26. But concerning the dead, that they do rise, have you not read in the book of Moses about the burning bush, how God spoke to him, saying, 'I *am* the God of Abraham, and the God of Isaac, and the God of Jacob'?

27. He is not the God of *the* dead, but *the* God of *the* living. Therefore, you err greatly."

MATTHEW 22

26. And likewise the second also, and the third, unto *the* seventh.

27. And last of all the woman died also.

28. Therefore, in the resurrection, whose wife of the seven shall she be, for all had her?"

29. Then Jesus answered *and* said to them, "You do err, not knowing the Scriptures, nor the power of God.

30. For in the resurrection they neither marry nor are given in marriage, but they are as *the* angels of God in heaven.

31. Now concerning the resurrection of the dead, have you not read that which was spoken to you by God, saying,

32. 'I am the God of Abraham, and the God of Isaac, and the God of Jacob'? God is not *the* God of *the* dead, but of *the* living."

33. And when the multitudes heard *this*, they were amazed at His teaching.

LUKE 20

29. Therefore, there were seven brothers; and the first one, after taking a wife, died childless;

30. And the second one took the woman, and he died childless;

31. And the third one took her, and likewise the *rest of the* seven, and died, and did not leave children;

32. And last of all, the woman died also.

33. Therefore, in the resurrection, of which of them shall she be wife? For all seven had her as wife."

34. And Jesus answered *and* said to them, "The children of this age marry and are given in marriage;

35. But those who are accounted worthy to obtain that age, and the resurrection from *the* dead, neither marry nor are given in marriage;

36. And neither can they die any more, for they are equal to *the* angels, and are *the* children of God, being children of the resurrection.

37. But that the dead are raised, even Moses showed *by his words* at the *burning* bush, when he called *the* Lord the God of Abraham, and the God of Isaac, and the God of Jacob;

38. For He is not *the* God of *the* dead, but of *the* living; for all live unto Him."

39. And some of the scribes answered *and* said, "Master, You have spoken well."

40. And *after that* they did not dare to ask Him any more *questions*.

Wailing Wall

NISAN 11 – SUNDAY, APRIL 2 – 30 AD

303. THE TWO GREAT COMMANDMENTS: LOVE GOD AND LOVE YOUR NEIGHBOR

MARK 12	MATTHEW 22

28. And one of the scribes who had come up *to Him*, after hearing them reasoning together *and* perceiving that He answered them well, asked Him, "Which is *the* first commandment of all?"

29. Then Jesus answered him, "*The* first of all the commandments *is*, 'Hear, O Israel: *the* Lord our God is one Lord.

30. And you shall love *the* Lord your God with all your heart, and with all your soul, and with all your mind, and with all your strength.' This *is the* first commandment. [a]

31. And *the* second *is* like this: 'You shall love your neighbor as yourself.' [b] There is no other commandment greater than these."

32. Then the scribe said to Him, "Right, Master. You have spoken according to truth that God is one, and there is not another besides Him;

33. And to love Him with all the heart, and with all the understanding, and with all the soul, and with all the strength, and to love *one's* neighbor as oneself, is more than all burnt offerings and sacrifices." [c]

34. And Jesus, seeing that he answered with understanding, said to him, "You are not far from the kingdom of God." And no one dared to question Him any more.

34. But after the Pharisees heard that He had silenced the Sadducees, they came together *before Him*.

35. And one of them, a doctor of the law, questioned *Him*, tempting Him, and saying,

36. "Master, which commandment *is the* great commandment in the Law?"

37. And Jesus said to him, " 'You shall love *the* Lord your God with all your heart, and with all your soul, and with all your mind.' [a]

38. This is *the* first and greatest commandment;

39. And *the* second *one is* like it: 'You shall love your neighbor as yourself.' [b]

40. On these two commandments hang all the Law and the Prophets."

Monument of Nycanus
Jerusalem Model City

a - Deut. 6:4-6; 10:12-13   b - Lev. 19:18   c - I Sam. 15:22; Psa. 41:16-17

304. HOW IS CHRIST THE SON OF DAVID?

MARK 12	MATTHEW 22	LUKE 20

35. And *while* teaching in the temple, Jesus answered *and* said, "How can the scribes say that the Christ is *the* Son of David?

36. For David himself said by the Holy Spirit, 'The Lord said to my Lord, "Sit at My right hand, until I make Your enemies a footstool for Your feet." ' [a]

41. While the Pharisees were assembled together, Jesus questioned them,

42. Saying, "What do you think concerning the Christ? Whose son is He?" They said to Him, "*The Son* of David."

43. He said to them, "How then does David in spirit call Him Lord, saying,

44. 'The LORD said to my Lord, "Sit at My right hand, until I make Your enemies a footstool for Your feet" '? [a]

41. Then He said to them, "Why do they say *that* the Christ is *the* Son of David?

42. Even David himself says in *the* book of Psalms, 'The Lord said to my Lord, "Sit at My right hand

43. Until I make Your enemies a footstool for Your feet." ' [a]

44. Therefore, *since* David calls Him Lord, how is He his Son?"

a - Psa. 110:1

230

NISAN 11 – SUNDAY, APRIL 2 – 30 AD

MARK 12	MATTHEW 22
37. Now then, *if* David himself called Him Lord, how can He be his Son?" And the whole multitude listened to Him eagerly.	45. Therefore, if David calls Him Lord, how is He his Son?" 46. And no one was able to answer Him a word, neither dared anyone from that day to question Him any more.

305. A WARNING AGAINST THE SCRIBES AND PHARISEES

MARK 12	LUKE 20
38. And He said to them in His teaching, "Beware of the scribes, who take pleasure in walking around in robes, and in salutations in the marketplaces, 39. And in *the* chief seats in the synagogues and *the* chief places in the feasts; 40. Who devour the houses of widows, and for a pretext make long prayers. These shall receive *the* greater condemnation."	45. And as all the people were listening, He said to His disciples, 46. "Beware of the scribes, who like to walk in robes, and love salutations in the marketplaces, and *the* chief seats in the synagogues, and *the* chief places at the suppers; 47. Who devour the houses of widows, and as a pretext pray at great length. These shall receive the greater judgment."

MATTHEW 23

1. Then Jesus spoke to the multitudes and to His disciples,
2. Saying, "The scribes and the Pharisees have sat down on Moses' seat *as judges*;
3. Therefore, every judgment that they tell you to observe, observe and do. But do not do according to their works; for they say and do not.
4. For they bind heavy burdens and hard to bear, and lay *them* on the shoulders of men; but they will not move them with *one of* their own fingers.
5. And they do all their works to be seen by men. They make broad their phylacteries and enlarge the borders of their garments;
6. And they love the first place at the suppers, and the chief seats in the synagogues,
7. And the salutations in the marketplaces, and to be called by men, 'Rabbi, Rabbi.'
8. But you are not to be called Rabbi; for one is your Master, the Christ, and all of you are brethren.
9. Also, do not call *anyone* on the earth your Father; for one is your Father, Who *is* in heaven.
10. Neither be called Master; for one is your Master, the Christ.
11. But the greatest among you shall be your servant.
12. And whoever will exalt himself shall be humbled; and whoever will humble himself shall be exalted.
13. But woe to you, scribes and Pharisees, hypocrites! For you devour widows' houses, and as a pretext you offer prayers of great length. Because of this, you shall receive *the* greater judgment.
14. Woe to you, scribes and Pharisees, hypocrites! For you shut up the kingdom of heaven before men; for neither do you yourselves enter, nor do you allow those who are entering to enter.

NISAN 11 – SUNDAY, APRIL 2 – 30 AD
MATTHEW 23

15. Woe to you, scribes and Pharisees, hypocrites! For you travel the sea and the land to make one proselyte, and when he has become one, you make him twofold more a son of Gehenna than yourselves.

16. Woe to you, blind guides, who say, 'Whoever shall swear by the temple, it is not binding; but whoever shall swear by the gold of the temple, he is obligated *to fulfill* his oath.'

17. *You* fools and blind! For which is greater, the gold, or the temple which sanctifies the gold?

18. And *you say*, 'Whoever shall swear by the altar, it is not binding; but whoever shall swear by the gift that *is* upon it, he is obligated *to fulfill* his oath.'

19. *You* fools and blind! For which is greater, the gift, or the altar which sanctifies the gift?

20. Therefore, the one who swears by the altar swears by it, and by all things that *are* upon it.

21. And the one who swears by the temple swears by it, and by Him Who dwells in it.

22. And the one who swears by heaven swears by the throne of God, and by Him Who sits upon it.

23. Woe to you, scribes and Pharisees, hypocrites! For you pay tithes [a] of mint and anise and cummin, but you have abandoned the more important *matters* of the law—judgment, and mercy and faith. These *you* were obligated to do, and not to leave the others undone.

24. Blind guides, who filter out a gnat, but swallow a camel!

25. Woe to you, scribes and Pharisees, hypocrites! For you cleanse the outside of the cup and the dish, but within you are full of extortion and excess.

26. Blind Pharisees! First cleanse the inside of the cup and the dish, so that the outside may also become clean.

27. Woe to you, scribes and Pharisees, hypocrites! For you are like whited sepulchers, which indeed appear beautiful *on the* outside, but within are full of the bones of the dead, and of all uncleanness.

28. Likewise, you also outwardly appear to men *to be* righteous, but within you are full of hypocrisy and lawlessness.

29. Woe to you, scribes and Pharisees, hypocrites! For you build the sepulchers of the prophets, and adorn the tombs of the righteous;

30. And you say, 'If we had been in the days of our fathers, we would not have been partakers with them in the blood of the prophets.'

31. So then, you are testifying against yourselves, that you are the sons of those who killed the prophets;

32. And *as for* you, you are filling up the measure of your fathers.

33. *You* serpents, *you* offspring of vipers, how shall you escape the judgment of Gehenna?

34. Because of this, behold, I send to you prophets and wise *men* and scribes; and *some* of them you shall kill and crucify, and *some* of them you shall scourge in your synagogues, and *some of them you* shall persecute from city to city;

35. So that upon you may come all *the* righteous blood poured out upon the earth, from the blood of Abel [b] the righteous, unto the blood of Zacharias [c] son of Barachias, whom you murdered between the temple and the altar.

36. Truly I say to you, all these things shall come upon this generation.

37. Jerusalem, Jerusalem, *you* who kill the prophets and stone those who have been sent to you, how often would I have gathered your children together, even as a hen gathers her brood under *her* wings, but you refused!

38. Behold, your house is left to you desolate. [d]

39. For I say to you, you shall not see Me at all from this time forward, until you shall say, 'Blessed *is* He Who comes in *the* name of *the* Lord.' " [e]

a - Lev. 27:30; Num. 18:21-26   b - Gen. 4:8
c - II Chron. 24:20-21   d - Jer. 22:5   e - Psa. 118:26

NISAN 11 – SUNDAY, APRIL 2 – 30 AD

306. A WIDOW'S MITE IS MORE THAN LARGE DONATIONS BY THE RICH

MARK 12

41. And after sitting down opposite the *temple* treasury, He observed how the people were casting money into the treasury; and many rich ones were putting *in* much.
42. And one poor widow came *and* dropped *in* two tiny coins, which is equal to one copper coin.
43. Then He called His disciples to *Him* and said to them, "Truly I say to you, this poor widow has put *in* more than all of those who are casting *money* into the treasury.
44. For everyone *else* contributed out of their abundance; but she out of her destitution put *in* as much as she had, *giving* all her living."

LUKE 21

1. When He looked up, He saw the rich men tossing their offerings into the treasury.
2. Then He also saw a certain poor widow drop in two small coins.
3. And He said, "Of a truth, I tell you, this poor widow has put in more than all *of them*;
4. For all these have from their abundance cast into the offerings to God; but she, out of her poverty, did put *in* all the livelihood that she had."

Temple Coins - Widow's Mite
- courtesy of Leon Ritchie

307. JESUS AND HIS DISCIPLES LEAVE THE TEMPLE AREA

MATTHEW 24

1. And after going out, Jesus departed from the temple; and His disciples came to *Him* to point out the buildings of the temple.
2. But Jesus said to them, "Do you not see all these things? Truly I say to you, there shall not be left here even a stone upon a stone that shall not be thrown down."

MARK 13

1. And as He was going out of the temple, one of His disciples said to Him, "Master, see how splendid *the* stones and buildings *are*!"
2. Then Jesus answered and said to him, "Do you see these great buildings? There shall not be left *a* stone upon *a* stone that shall not be thrown down."

LUKE 21

5. And while some were speaking about the temple, how it was adorned with beautiful stones and consecrated gifts, He said,
6. "*As for* these things that you now see, *the* days will come in which *there* shall not be left *one* stone upon another that shall not be thrown down."

NISAN 11 – SUNDAY, APRIL 2 – 30 AD
308. ON THE MOUNT OF OLIVES JESUS PROPHESIES TO HIS DISCIPLES ABOUT THE EVENTS LEADING UP TO:
1. THE SIGN OF HIS SECOND COMING
2. THE COMPLETION OF THE AGE

MATTHEW 24

3. And as He was sitting on the Mount of Olives, His disciples came to Him alone, saying, "Tell us, when shall these things be? And what *shall be* the sign of Your coming, and of the completion of the age?"
4. Then Jesus answered *and* said to them, "Be on guard, so that no one deceives you.
5. For many shall come in My name, saying, 'I am the Christ'; and they shall deceive many.
6. And you shall hear of wars and rumors of wars. See *that* you do not let *these things* disturb you. For it is necessary *that* all *these* things take place, but the end is not yet.
7. For nation shall rise against nation, and kingdom against kingdom; and there shall be famines and pestilences and earthquakes in *different* places.
8. Now all these *things are* the beginning of sorrows.
9. Then shall they deliver you up to affliction, and shall kill you; and you shall be hated by all nations for My name's sake.
10. And then shall many be led into sin, and shall betray one another, and shall hate one another;
11. And many false prophets shall arise, and shall deceive many;

MARK 13

3. And as He was sitting on the Mount of Olives across from the temple, Peter and James and John and Andrew *came* privately *and* asked Him,
4. "Tell us, when shall these things be? And what *shall be* the sign when all these things are about to be accomplished?"
5. And Jesus *in* answering them began to say, "Be on guard lest anyone deceive you.
6. For many shall come in My name, saying, 'I am *the Christ'*; and they shall deceive many.
7. But when you hear of wars and rumors of wars, do not be troubled; for it is necessary for *these things* to come to pass, but the end *is* not yet.
8. For nation shall rise up against nation, and kingdom against kingdom; and there shall be earthquakes in different places, and there shall be famines and disasters. These things *are* the beginning of sorrows.
9. But keep yourselves on guard, for they shall deliver you up to councils and synagogues. You shall be beaten, and you shall be brought before governors and kings for My sake, for a witness against them.

LUKE 21

7. And they asked Him, saying, "Master, when shall these things be? And what *shall be* the sign that these things are about to take place?"
8. And He said, "Beware *that* you be not deceived; for many shall come in My name, saying, 'I am *Christ'*; and, 'The time has drawn near.' Therefore, do not go after them.
9. And when you hear of wars and revolutions, do not be terrified; for it is necessary *that* these things take place first, but the end *will* not *come* immediately."
10. Then He said to them, "Nation shall rise up against nation, and kingdom against kingdom;
11. There shall also be great earthquakes in different places, and famines and pestilences; and there shall be fearful sights and great signs from heaven.
12. But before all these things, they shall lay their hands on you and shall persecute *you*, delivering *you* up to synagogues and prisons, *and* bringing *you* before kings and governors, for My name's sake.

NISAN 11 – SUNDAY, APRIL 2 – 30 AD

MATTHEW 24	MARK 13	LUKE 21

MATTHEW 24

12. And because lawlessness shall be multiplied, the love of many shall grow cold.
13. But the one who endures to *the* end, that one shall be saved.
14. And this gospel of the kingdom shall be proclaimed in all the world for a witness to all nations; and then shall the end come.
15. Therefore, when you see the abomination of desolation, which was spoken of by Daniel the prophet, [a] standing in the holy place (the one who reads, let him understand),
16. Then let those who are in Judea flee into the mountains.
17. Let the one *who is* on the housetop not come down to take anything out of his house;
18. And let the one *who is* in the field not go back to take his garments.
19. But woe to those *women* who are expecting a child, and to those who are nursing infants in those days!
20. And pray that your flight be not in *the* winter, nor on *the* Sabbath;
21. For then shall there be great tribulation, such as has not been from *the* beginning of *the* world until this time, nor ever shall be *again*. [b]
22. And if those days were not limited, there would no flesh be saved; but for the elect's sake those days shall be limited.
23. Then if anyone says to you, 'Behold, here *is* the Christ,' or, '*He is* there,' do not believe *it*.

MARK 13

10. And the gospel must first be published among all nations.
11. But whenever they lead you away *and* deliver *you* up, do not be anxious beforehand nor meditate *on what you should say*; but whatever shall be given to you in that hour, that speak. For you are not the ones who are speaking, but the Holy Spirit.
12. Then shall brother betray brother to death, and *the* father *the* child. And children shall rise up against *their* parents and shall put them to death.
13. And you shall be hated by all *men* for My name's sake; but the one who endures to *the* end, that one shall be saved.
14. Now when you see the abomination of desolation, which was spoken of by Daniel the prophet, [a] standing where it should not *stand* (let the one who reads understand), then let those *who are* in Judea flee into the mountains.
15. And let the one who is on the housetop not come down into the house, nor go in to take anything out of his house;

Earthquakes

LUKE 21

13. But it shall turn to you for a testimony.
14. Settle therefore in your hearts not to premeditate what you shall answer.
15. For I will give you a mouth and wisdom that all those who are opposing you shall not be able to reply to nor resist.
16. But you shall be delivered up even by parents and brothers and relatives and friends, and they shall put *some* of you to death;
17. And you shall be hated by all because of My name.
18. But not a hair of your head shall by any means perish.
19. By your patient endurance you *shall* gain your lives.
20. But when you see Jerusalem being surrounded by armies, then know that her desolation has drawn near. [a]
21. Then let those who are in Judea flee to the mountains, and let those within her go out, and let not those in the countries come into her;
22. For these are *the* days of vengeance, so that all things that have been written may be accomplished.
23. But woe to those who are with child and those who are giving suck in those days! For there shall be great distress upon the land and wrath upon this people. [b]

NISAN 11 – SUNDAY, APRIL 2 – 30 AD

MATTHEW 24	MARK 13	LUKE 21
24. For there shall arise false Christs and false prophets, and they shall present great signs and wonders, in order to deceive, if possible, even the elect. 25. Behold, I have foretold *it* to you. 26. Therefore, if they say to you, 'Come and see! He is in the wilderness'; do not go forth. 'Come and see! *He is* in the secret chambers'; do not believe *it*. 27. For as the light of day, which comes forth from *the* east and shines as far as *the* west, so also shall the coming of the Son of man be. 28. For wherever the carcass may be, there will the eagles be gathered together. 29. But immediately after the tribulation of those days, the sun shall be darkened, and the moon shall not give her light, and the stars shall fall from heaven, and the powers of the heavens shall be shaken. [c] 30. And then shall appear the sign of the Son of man in heaven; and then shall all the tribes of the earth mourn, and they shall see the Son of man coming upon the clouds of heaven with power and great glory. [d] 31. And He shall send His angels with a great sound of a trumpet; and they shall gather together His elect from the four winds, from one end of heaven to *the* other.	16. And let the one who is in the field not return to the things *he left* behind to take his garment. 17. But woe to those who are with child and to those who are nursing infants in those days! 18. And pray that your flight may not be in winter; 19. For *in* those days shall be *great* tribulation, such as has not been the like from *the* beginning of *the* creation that God created until this time, nor ever shall be *again*; [b] 20. And unless *the* Lord had limited the days, no flesh would be saved; but for the sake of the elect, whom He has chosen, He has limited the days. 21. And then if anyone says to you, 'Look, here *is* the Christ'; or, 'Look, there *is* the Christ'; do not believe *it*. 22. For there shall arise false Christs and false prophets, and they shall give signs and wonders, in order to deceive, if possible, even the elect. 23. But you, watch out *for them*! Behold, I have foretold all *these* things to you. 24. Now in those days, after that tribulation, the sun shall be darkened, and the moon shall not give its light; [c] 25. And the stars of heaven shall fall, and the powers that *are* in heaven shall be shaken; 26. And then they shall see the Son of man coming in *the* clouds with great power and glory. [d]	24. And they shall fall by *the* edge of *the* sword, and shall be led away captive into all nations; and Jerusalem shall be trodden down by *the* Gentiles, until *the* times of *the* Gentiles be fulfilled. 25. And there shall be signs in *the* sun and moon and stars, and on the earth distress and anxiety among *the* nations, *the* seas roaring with rolling surges; [c] 26. Men dying of heart attacks from fear and dread of the things that are coming on the whole world; for the powers of heaven shall be shaken. 27. And then shall they see the Son of man coming in a cloud with great power and glory. [d]  *"The Stars Shall Fall From Heaven"* - Wide World Photos

a - Dan. 9:27; 11:31; 12:11   b - Dan. 12:1
c - Joel 2:30-31; Amos 8:9   d - Dan. 7:13

NISAN 11 – SUNDAY, APRIL 2 – 30 AD

MATTHEW 24

32. Now learn this parable from the fig tree: When its branches have already become tender, and it puts forth its leaves, you know that summer *is* near.
33. In like manner also, when you see all these things, know that it is near, even at *the* doors.
34. Truly I say to you, this generation shall in no wise pass away until all these things have taken place.
35. The heaven and the earth shall pass away, but My words shall never pass away.
36. But concerning that day, and the hour, no one knows, not even the angels of heaven, but My Father only.
37. Now as *it was in* the days of Noah, [a] so shall *it* also be *at* the coming of the Son of man.
38. For as in the days that *were* before the Flood, they were eating and drinking, marrying and giving in marriage, until the day that Noah entered the ark;
39. And they were not aware until the Flood came and took *them* all away; so shall *it* also be *at* the coming of the Son of man.
40. Then two shall be in the field; one shall be taken, and one shall be left;
41. Two *women shall be* grinding at the mill; one shall be taken, and one shall be left.
42. Watch, therefore, because you do not know in what hour your Lord is coming.

MARK 13

27. And then He shall send His angels, and shall gather together His elect from the four winds, *and* from *the* extremity of earth to *the* extremity of heaven.
28. But learn the parable of the fig tree: When its branches become tender, and it puts forth leaves, you know that summer is near.
29. In the same way also, when you see these things coming to pass, know that it is near, *even* at *the* doors.
30. Truly I say to you, this generation shall in no way pass away until all these things have taken place.
31. The heaven and the earth shall pass away, but My words shall never pass away.
32. But concerning that day and the hour, no one knows, not even the angels in heaven, nor the Son, but the Father *only*.
33. Take heed, be watching and praying. For you do not know when the time is *coming*.
34. *It is* like a man journeying to a far country, leaving his house and giving authority to his servants, and to each one his work, and commanding the doorkeeper to watch.
35. Be watching, therefore, for you do not know when the master of the house is coming: at evening, or at midnight, or at *the* cock's crowing, or *in the* morning;
36. Lest he come suddenly and find you sleeping.
37. And what I say to you, I say to all: Watch!"

LUKE 21

28. But when these things begin to take place, look up, and lift up your heads, because your redemption is drawing near."
29. Then He spoke a parable to them: "Observe the fig tree, and all the trees.
30. When they have already begun to bud, *and* you look *at them,* you yourselves know that summer is near.
31. In the same way also, when you see these things coming to pass, know that the kingdom of God is near.
32. Truly I say to you, *there is* no way that this generation shall pass away until all *these things* have taken place.
33. Heaven and earth shall pass away, but My words shall never pass away.
34. Watch yourselves, lest your hearts be preoccupied with high living and drinking and *the* cares of *this* life, and that day come upon you suddenly.
35. For as a snare it shall come upon all those who dwell on the face of the earth.
36. Watch therefore, *and* pray at all times that you may be accounted worthy to escape all these things that shall come to pass, and to stand before the Son of man."

a - Gen. 6:11-13; 7:7, 21-24

NISAN 11 – SUNDAY, APRIL 2 – 30 AD

MATTHEW 24

43. But know this, that if the master of the house had known in what watch the thief would come, he would have been watching, and would not have allowed his house to be broken into.

44. Therefore, you also be ready. For the Son of man is coming at a time that you do not think.

45. Who then is the faithful and wise servant whom his lord has set over his household, to give them food in due season?

46. Blessed *is* that servant, whom his lord when he comes shall find so doing.

47. Truly I say to you, he will set him over all his property.

48. But if that evil servant shall say in his heart, 'My lord delays *his* coming,'

49. And shall begin to beat *his* fellow servants, and to eat and drink with the drunken,

50. The lord of that servant will come in a day that he does not expect, and in an hour that he does not know.

51. And he shall cut him asunder and shall appoint his portion with the hypocrites. There shall be weeping and gnashing of teeth."

Famine   – DPA Bild

War   – Wide World Photos

Utter Destruction   – H. Armstrong Roberts

309. JESUS LEAVES THE CITY EACH NIGHT
LUKE 21

37. And during *the* day He was in the temple teaching, and at night He went out and lodged on the mountain called *the Mount* of Olives.

38. And all the people came to Him in the temple early in the morning to hear Him.

NISAN 11 – SUNDAY, APRIL 2 – 30 AD

310. THE PARABLE OF THE TEN VIRGINS

MATTHEW 25

1. "Then shall the kingdom of heaven be compared *to* ten virgins, who took their lamps *and* went out to meet the bridegroom.
2. And five of them were wise, and five *were* foolish.
3. The ones who were foolish took their lamps, *but* they did not take oil with them;
4. But the wise took oil in their vessels *along* with their lamps.
5. Now when the bridegroom was gone a long time, they all became drowsy and slept.
6. But in *the* middle of *the* night there was a cry: 'Look, the bridegroom is coming! Go out to meet him.'
7. Then all those virgins arose and trimmed their lamps.
8. And the foolish said to the wise, 'Give us *some* of your oil, because our lamps are going out.'
9. But the wise answered, saying, '*No,* lest *there* not *be* enough for us and *for* you. But instead, go to those who sell, and buy for yourselves.'
10. And while they went to buy, the bridegroom came; and those who were ready went in with him to the wedding feast, and the door was shut.
11. And afterwards the other virgins also came, saying, 'Lord, Lord, open to us.'
12. But He answered *and* said, 'Truly I say to you, I do not know you.'
13. Watch, therefore, for you do not know the day nor the hour in which the Son of man is coming.

Oil Lamp
– courtesy of Timothy Schmidt

311. THE PARABLE OF THE TALENTS

MATTHEW 25

14. For *the kingdom of heaven is* like a man leaving the country, who called his own servants and delivered to them his property.
15. Now to one he gave five talents, and to another two, and to another one; he *gave* to each one according to his own ability, and immediately left the country.
16. Then the one who had received five talents went and traded with them, and made an additional five talents.
17. In the same way also, the one who had *received* two *talents* also gained two others.
18. But the one who had received the single *talent* went and dug in the earth, and hid his lord's money.
19. Now after a long time, the lord of those servants came to take account with them.
20. Then the one who had received five talents came to *him and* brought an additional five talents, saying, 'Lord, you delivered five talents to me; see, I have gained five other talents besides them.'
21. And his lord said to him, 'Well *done*, good and faithful servant! *Because* you were faithful over a few things, I will set you over many things. Enter into the joy of your lord.'

NISAN 11 – SUNDAY, APRIL 2 – 30 AD

MATTHEW 25

22. "And the one who had received two talents also came to him *and* said, 'Lord, you delivered to me two talents; see, I have gained two other talents besides them.'
23. His lord said to him, 'Well *done,* good and faithful servant! *Because* you were faithful over a few things, I will set you over many things. Enter into the joy of your lord.'
24. Then the one who had received the single talent also came to *him and* said, 'Lord, I knew that you are a hard man, reaping where you did not sow, and gathering where you did not scatter.
25. And *because* I was afraid, I went and hid your talent in the earth. *Now* look, you have your own.'
26. His lord answered *and* said to him, '*You* wicked and lazy servant! You knew that I reap where I did not sow, and gather what I did not scatter.
27. Because *you knew* this, you were duty-bound to take my talent to the money exchangers, *so that* when I came, I could have received my own with interest.
28. Therefore, take the talent from him, and give *it* to the one who has ten talents.
29. For to everyone who has, *more* shall be given, and *he* shall have abundance; on the other hand, *as for* the one who does not have, even that which he has shall be taken from him.
30. And cast the worthless servant into the outer darkness.' There shall be weeping and gnashing of teeth."

312. THE JUDGMENT OF THE NATIONS

MATTHEW 25

31. "Now when the Son of man shall come in His glory, and all the holy angels with Him, then shall He sit upon *the* throne of His glory; [a]
32. And He shall gather before Him all the nations; and He shall separate them one from another, as a shepherd separates the sheep from the goats.
33. And He shall set the sheep at His right hand, but the goats at *His* left.
34. Then shall the King say to those at His right hand, 'Come, you who are blessed of My Father, inherit the kingdom prepared for you from *the* foundation of *the* world.
35. For I was hungry, and you gave Me *something* to eat; I was thirsty, and you gave Me *something* to drink; I was a stranger, and you took Me in;
36. *I was* naked, and you clothed Me; I was sick, and you visited Me; I was in prison, and you came to Me.'
37. Then shall the righteous answer Him, saying, 'Lord, when did we see You hungry, and fed *You*? or thirsty, and gave *You* a drink?
38. And when did we see You a stranger, and took *You in*? or naked, and clothed *You*?
39. And when did we see You sick, or in prison, and came to You?'
40. And answering, the King shall say to them, 'Truly I say to you, inasmuch as you have done *it* to one of the least *of* these My brethren, you have done *it* to Me.'
41. Then shall He also say to those on *the* left, 'Depart from Me, *you* cursed ones, into the eternal fire, which has been prepared for the devil and his angels.
42. For I was hungry, and you did not give Me *anything* to eat; I was thirsty, and you did not give Me *anything* to drink;
43. I was a stranger, and you did not take Me in; *I was* naked, and you did not clothe Me; *I was* sick, and in prison, and you did not *come to* visit Me.'
44. Then they also shall answer Him, saying, 'Lord, when did we see You hungry, or thirsty, or a stranger, or naked, or sick, or in prison, and we did not minister to You?'
45. Then shall He answer them, saying, 'Truly I say to you, inasmuch as you did not do *it* to one of the least *of* these, neither did you do *it* to Me.'
46. And they shall go away into eternal punishment, but the righteous into eternal life." [b]

a - Zech. 14:4-5; Micah 4:1-4; Rev. 19:11; 20:4-6 b - Dan. 12:2

NISAN 11 – SUNDAY, APRIL 2 – 30 AD
313. AFTER TWO DAYS THE PASSOVER COMES

MATTHEW 26	MARK 14	LUKE 22
1. Now it came to pass *that* when Jesus had finished all these sayings, He said to His disciples, 2. "You know that after two days the Passover takes place, and the Son of man is delivered up to be crucified." 3. Then the chief priests and the scribes and the elders of the people assembled together in the court of the high priest, who was called Caiaphas; 4. And *they* took counsel together for the purpose of seizing Jesus by treachery, and killing *Him*. 5. But they said, "Not during the feast, so that there will not be a riot among the people."	1. Now after two days was the Passover and the *feast of* unleavened bread, and the chief priests and the scribes were seeking how they might stealthily lay hold of Him *and* kill *Him.* 2. But they said, "Not during the feast, lest there be a riot among the people."	1. Now the feast of unleavened *bread,* which *is* called Passover, was approaching; 2. And the chief priests and the scribes were speculating as to how they might put Him to death, for they feared the people.

Huge Stones of the Antonio Fortress

314. IN BETHANY, JESUS IS ANOINTED FOR HIS BURIAL

MATTHEW 26	MARK 14
6. Now when Jesus was in Bethany, in Simon the leper's house, 7. A woman came to Him with an alabaster flask of ointment, very precious, and poured *it* on His head as He sat down *to eat.* 8. But when His disciples saw *it, they* became indignant *and* said, "What reason *is there* for this waste? 9. For this ointment could have been sold for much, and *the money* given to *the* poor." 10. But Jesus knew *this* and said to them, "Why do you cause trouble for this woman? For she has performed a good work toward Me. 11. For you have the poor with you always, but you do not always have Me. 12. What this *woman did* in pouring this ointment on My body, she did for My burial.	3. Now He was in Bethany, in the house of Simon the leper; *and* as He was sitting *to eat,* a woman came carrying an alabaster flask of ointment of pure spikenard *worth* a great price; and after breaking the alabaster flask, she poured *it* on His head. 4. But some were indignant within themselves and said, "Why has this ointment been wasted? 5. For it was possible *for* this to be sold for over three hundred silver coins, and to give to the poor." And they were criticizing her. 6. But Jesus said, "Let her alone; why are you causing her trouble? She has performed a good work toward Me. 7. For you have the poor with you always, and you are able to do good for them whenever you desire; but you do not always have Me.

241

NISAN 11 – SUNDAY, APRIL 2 – 30 AD

MATTHEW 26

13. Truly I say to you, wherever this gospel shall be preached in the whole world, what this *woman* has done shall also be spoken of for a memorial of her."

MARK 14

8. She did what she could *for Me*. She came to anoint My body beforehand for the burial.
9. Truly I say to you, wherever this gospel shall be preached in all the world, what this *woman* has done shall also be spoken of for a memorial of her."

NISAN 12 – MONDAY, APRIL 3 – 30 AD

315. JUDAS BETRAYS JESUS TO THE CHIEF PRIESTS FOR 30 PIECES OF SILVER

LUKE 22

3. Then Satan entered into Judas, who was surnamed Iscariot, being of the number of the twelve.
4. And he went away, *and* spoke with the chief priests and the captains about a way by which he might betray Him to them.
5. And they rejoiced, and agreed to give him money. [a]
6. And he promised, and sought *an* opportunity to betray Him to them away from *the* multitude.

MARK 14

10. Then Judas Iscariot, one of the twelve, went to the chief priests in order that he might deliver Him up to them.
11. And after hearing *this*, they were delighted and promised to give him money. [a] And he sought how he might conveniently betray Him.

a - Zech. 11:12

MATTHEW 26

14. Then one of the twelve, who was called Judas Iscariot, went to the chief priests,
15. *And* said, "What are you willing to give me, and I will deliver Him up to you?" And they offered him thirty pieces of silver. [a]
16. And from that time he sought an opportunity to betray Him.

"Thirty Pieces of Silver"—Actual Temple Coins of the First Century, During the Reign of Tiberius

NISAN 13 – TUESDAY, APRIL 4 – 30
316. THE DISCIPLES PREPARE FOR THE PASSOVER

MATTHEW 26	MARK 14	LUKE 22	JOHN 13
17. Now on the first of the unleaveneds*, the disciples came to Jesus, saying to Him, "Where do You desire *that* we prepare for You to eat the Passover?" 18. And He said, "Go into the city to such a man, and say to him, 'The Teacher says, "My time is near; I will keep the Passover with My disciples at your *house.*"'"	12. And on the first day of the unleaveneds,* when they were killing the Passover *lambs*, His disciples said to Him, "Where do You desire that we go and prepare, so that You may eat the Passover?" 13. And He sent two of His disciples, and said to them, "Go into the city, and you shall meet a man carrying a pitcher of water; follow him.	7. Then came the day of the unleaveneds* in which it was obligatory to kill the Passover *lambs.* 8. And He sent Peter and John, saying, "Go *and* prepare the Passover for us that we may eat." 9. But they said to Him, "Where do You desire *that* we prepare *it?*" 10. And He said to them, "Watch, *and* when you come into the city, you will meet a man carrying a pitcher of water; follow him into the house that he enters;	1. Now before the feast of the Passover, knowing that His time had come to depart from this world to the Father, Jesus, having loved His own who *were* in the world, loved them to *the* end.

This phrase has caused some confusion. It is certain that this phrase does not refer to the first day of the Feast of Unleavened Bread, because the Feast of Unleavened Bread begins after, not before, the Passover. As recorded in the Gospels, "the first of the unleaveneds" was the day that the lambs were killed. Those who obeyed God's ordinances in Exodus 12 and kept the domestic Passover killed their lambs at the beginning of the 14th of Nisan. Those who followed the traditions of Judaism killed the lambs at the temple on the afternoon of the 14th. The Gospel writers were clearly referring to the 14th, and not to the 15th, as "the first of the unleaveneds." In New Testament times, this term was commonly used for the 14th day of the first month.

"In the first century, it was commonly known that 'the day of the unleaveneds' in Luke 22:7 was the 14th Passover day. G. Amadon, in an article entitled, 'The Crucifixion Calendar,' pointed out the error of those translators who translated this verse to read 'the first day of the festival.' [The following words are cited from this article.] 'But on what authority should the Hebrew translators, as Salkinson and Delitzch, introduce the word chag [a Hebrew word for "feast"], into these texts when the corresponding Greek has no word for "feast," and speaks only of the "first of the unleavened bread"—a common expression for the Jewish 14th with practically all first century writers'" (Journal of Biblical Literature, vol. LXIII, 1944, pp. 188-189, emphasis added).

When we understand the duties that were required to be performed on the Passover day, it becomes clear why that day was called "the first of the unleaveneds" (a literal translation from the Greek). According to Jewish law, all leaven in all residences and properties owned by Jews was to be searched out on Nisan 13. The unleavened bread for the Passover was to be made and ready by 3 p.m. on Nisan 13. The leaven was then gathered and burned by 10 a.m. in the morning on Nisan 14. No one was to eat leaven in any form after 11 a.m. These required practices clearly show why Nisan 14 was referred to as "the first of the unleaveneds": because on that day leaven was removed and burned. Hence, Nisan 14 was the first unleavened day of the year.

NISAN 13 – TUESDAY, APRIL 4 – 30 AD

MATTHEW 26	MARK 14	LUKE 22

MATTHEW 26

19. Then the disciples did as Jesus had directed them, and prepared the Passover.

MARK 14

14. "And whatever house he shall enter, say to the master of the house *that* the Teacher says, 'Where is the guest chamber, where I may eat the Passover with My disciples?'

15. And he shall show you a large upper room, furnished *and* ready. There prepare for us."

16. And His disciples went away: and *when* they came into the city, they found *it* exactly as He had said to them; and they prepared the Passover.

LUKE 22

11. "And you shall say to the master of the house, 'The Teacher says to you, "Where is the guest chamber, where I may eat the Passover with My disciples?"'

12. And he shall show you a large upper room furnished; there prepare."

13. Then they went *and* found *everything* exactly as He had said to them; and they prepared the Passover.

Road to Jerusalem

PART VI

JESUS' LAST PASSOVER
AND CRUCIFIXION

THE DAY GOD DIED!

The greatest event since the creation of the world was about to take place. Jesus Christ, Who was God manifested in the flesh (I Tim. 3:16), was going to die! He would give His life as the supreme sacrifice for the sins of all mankind. John the Baptist understood this when he said of Jesus: "Behold the Lamb of God, Who takes away the sin of the world" (John 1:29). This momentous event had been planned before the creation of the world: "…the Lamb, slain from *the* foundation of *the* world" (Rev. 13:8).

When and how did sin enter the world? Why was it necessary for Jesus Christ to lay down His life for the sins of mankind? How can His one sacrifice purge all sin?

The sin of Adam and Eve was not the first transgression against God. The original sin was committed by Lucifer and the angels who followed him. *Lucifer* (Latin, "Light Bringer" or "Shining One") was the first created being to commit sin; therefore he is the author of sin. He boasted that he would become like the Most High and sit on God's throne (Isa. 14:14-15; Ezek. 28:12-18). One third of the angels followed him in his rebellion (Rev. 12:3-4). At that time, Lucifer became Satan the devil, the adversary of God, and the rebelling angels who followed him became known as demons.

When Satan and the demons attempted to seize the throne of God, they were cast back down to the earth (Luke 10:18). That war left the earth in ruin and parts of the heavens in shambles. Everything that Lucifer and his angels had established on earth before the rebellion was destroyed, and the earth was covered with a flood (Gen. 1:2). Then God, the one Who became Jesus Christ, recreated the surface of the earth and filled it with life.

On the sixth day of creation, God made man in His own image and likeness, male and female (Gen. 1:26-27). God gave Adam and Eve free moral agency. He set before them the way of eternal life, as symbolized by the Tree of Life. He also set before them the Tree of the Knowledge of Good and Evil, which represented the way that seemed right to them, under the sway of Satan the devil. But God commanded them not to eat of the fruit of that tree, and warned them that if they ate of it they would surely die.

Under the influence of Satan the devil, Adam and Eve chose to disobey God by eating the fruit from the Tree of the Knowledge of Good and Evil. Through their disobedience sin and death passed to all mankind (Rom. 5:12). As a result, nearly all of humanity has followed the dictates of human nature under Satan's sway, cut off from God. Although God has set limits on Satan, God has not yet removed Satan and his evil influence. In His own time, God will ultimately bring mankind out from subjection to sin and Satan. Through His plan of redemption, initiated by His Son's perfect sacrifice, God has made it possible for all mankind to be delivered from sin and the penalty of death.

God as Lawgiver and Creator has decreed that the wages of sin for all human beings is death (Rom. 6:23). Sin is the transgression of God's holy, spiritual laws and commandments (I John 3:4). All have sinned and have come short of the glory of God, so all face death unless they accept the way of salvation that God has provided (Rom. 3:23). The death that is decreed for sin is the second death in the lake of fire. From that death there is no resurrection (Rev. 20:13-15; 21:8).

After Adam and Eve sinned, God pronounced His judgment upon them. Within His sentence, we find the first prophecy of the death of the Messiah: "And I will put enmity between thee [the serpent – Satan the devil] and the woman [a type of Israel, and later, the Church of God], and between thy seed [the followers of Satan] and her Seed [Jesus Christ, the coming Messiah]; *it* [the Seed] shall bruise thy head [Satan], and thou [Satan] shalt bruise His heel [the crucifixion of Christ]" (Gen. 3:15, *KJV*).

This prophecy was spoken by God Himself, the one Who was to become Jesus Christ. As the Lord God of the Old Testament, He prophesied His own death to atone for the sins of Adam and Eve and all their descendants to come. This prophecy was spoken more than 4,000 years before His beating, scourging and crucifixion on the Passover day, Nisan 14, April 5, 30 AD.

The Promised Seed of the Covenant With Abraham

The promise of a Seed who would conquer sin and banish Satan was confirmed by the covenant that God made with Abraham. The words of the covenant were a prophecy of His own future birth as the fleshly Seed of Abraham. Let us examine the account in the book of Genesis: "And, behold, the word of the LORD *came* unto him [Abraham], saying, 'This [his steward Eliezer] shall not be thine heir; but *he* that shall come forth out of thine own bowels shall be thine heir' " (Gen. 15:4, *KJV*).

The birth of Isaac, the son of Abraham and Sarah, was only the beginning of the fulfillment of this promise to Abraham. The promise was not only for Isaac but also for his future descendant, the coming Messiah. The birth of Jesus Christ was the ultimate fulfillment of the promise, the Seed to Whom the promises were given: "Now to Abraham and to his Seed were the promises spoken. He does not say, 'and to *your* seeds,' as of many; but as of one, 'and to your Seed,' which is Christ" (Gal. 3:16). Jesus Christ is the promised Seed and true Heir of the promises God made to Abraham.

The account in Genesis 15 reveals that evening had come when God began to give the promises to Abraham. On that night, God took Abraham outside and showed him the stars of heaven. Then He gave Abraham another promise: "And He brought *him* forth abroad, and said, 'Look now toward heaven, and tell the stars, if thou be able to number *them*': and He said unto him, 'So shall thy seed be' " (Gen. 15:5, *KJV*). The New Testament shows that these words of God do not refer to Abraham's physical descendants but to those who would become the children of Abraham through faith in Jesus Christ. The apostle Paul wrote: "Because of this, *you should* understand that those who *are* of faith are the *true* sons of Abraham" (Gal. 3:7).

The true children of Abraham are not counted by their physical lineage. They are a spiritual nation, composed of individuals of every race and every bloodline who follow in the faith of Abraham (verses 8, 14). At the return of Jesus Christ, they will be resurrected to eternal life as glorified spirit beings and will shine as the stars forever (Dan. 12:3, Matt. 13:43, I Cor. 15:40-44).

Next, God promised to give to Abraham and his physical seed the land of the Canaanites: "And He said unto him, '*I am* the LORD that brought thee out of Ur of the Chaldees, to give thee this land to inherit it' " (Gen. 15:7, *KJV*). This promise was for his physical descendants, the children of Israel. Many generations would pass before the promised Seed, Jesus Christ, would come to prepare a spiritual people for a spiritual kingdom—the sons of God in the Kingdom of God. Abraham received the promises with complete faith that God would fulfill them: "And he believed in the LORD; and He counted it to him for righteousness" (verse 6, *KJV*).

The Covenant Confirmed by a Maledictory Oath

When God established His covenant with Abraham, He confirmed it with a maledictory oath, which was a pledge and prophecy of His own future death. On the morning after giving Abraham the promises, God spoke to him and instructed him to prepare a special sacrifice to seal the covenant: "And He said unto him, 'Take Me an heifer of three years old, and a she goat of three years old, and a ram of three years old, and a turtledove, and a young pigeon.' And he took unto him all these, and divided *them* in the midst [cut them down the middle], and laid each piece one against [opposite one] another: but the birds divided he not. And when the fowls came down upon the carcasses, Abram drove *them* away" (verses 9-11, *KJV*). The bloody carcasses of the sacrificial animals were laid on the ground to represent the symbolic death of the one Who would confirm the covenant. By passing between the parts, He would pledge His own life to fulfill the covenant.

By the time that Abraham had finished preparing the covenant sacrifice, it was late in the day: "And when the sun was going down, a deep sleep fell upon Abram; and, lo, an horror of great darkness fell upon him" (verse 12, *KJV*). While Abraham lay sleeping, God appeared to him in a vision and promised that his physical descendants would inherit the land. However, this would not happen until they had lived in another land for four generations: "And He said unto Abram, 'Know of a surety that thy seed shall be a stranger in a land *that is* not theirs, and shall serve them; and they shall afflict *them* four hundred years; and also that nation, whom they shall serve, will *I* judge: and afterward shall they come out with great substance. And *thou* shalt go to thy fathers in peace; thou shalt be buried in a good old age. But in the fourth generation they shall come hither again: for the iniquity of the Amorites *is* not yet full' " (verses 13-16, *KJV*).

After prophesying these events, God bound Himself to fulfill them by passing between the sacrificial animals to seal the covenant: "And it came to pass, that, **when the sun went down** [beginning the next day], and it was dark, behold a smoking furnace, and a burning lamp that passed between those pieces. In the same day the LORD made a covenant with Abram…" (verses 17-18, *KJV*).

After the sun had gone down, God passed through the middle of the sacrificial animals, revealing His presence by the smoking furnace and flaming torch. When God passed between the parts, He walked a death walk, pledging His future death. Apparently, the smoking furnace wholly consumed the sacrificial animals. That is how God ratified His unilateral covenant with Abraham.

The full account in Genesis 15 reveals that the making of the covenant took place during two consecutive days. When God first spoke to Abraham, it was night because the stars could be seen (verse 5). In the morning, God gave Abraham instructions for preparing the covenant sacrifice. Abraham prepared the sacrifice that same day. We know that he completed the preparations while the sun was still high because the birds of prey were flying about and attempting to land on the sacrifice (verse 11). The next verse records the end of the day: "And when the sun was going down, a deep sleep fell upon Abram" (verse 12). After the sun had gone down, God appeared to Abraham and ratified the covenant (verse 18).

There is great significance in the fact that the covenant was established over a two-day period, with the promises being given on the first night and the covenant being ratified on the second night. The timing of these events has an exact parallel in the chronology of the Passover and the Exodus, which were the first acts in the fulfillment of God's promises for the physical seed—the descendants of Abraham through Isaac and Jacob.

Israel's First Passover and the Exodus from Egypt

Exodus 12 records that the children of Israel kept the Passover on the 14th day of the first month, or Abib (this month was later known as Nisan). The Passover lamb, a type of the coming Messiah, was killed immediately after sunset at the beginning of the 14th. The people took some of the blood and put it on the side posts and lintel of the doors of their houses so that God would pass over their houses and spare their firstborn. Then they roasted the lamb with fire and ate it with bitter herbs.

At midnight on the 14th, God executed His final judgment on the Egyptians and their gods by killing all the firstborn of men and beasts. When God saw the blood of the Passover lambs on the houses of the children of Israel, He passed over them, sparing their firstborn.

At sunrise, as the day portion of Nisan 14 began, the children of Israel left their houses to assemble at Rameses for the Exodus. As they journeyed to Rameses, they completely spoiled the Egyptians, fulfilling God's promise to Abraham that his descendants would depart from the land of their servitude with great substance. God commanded the children of Israel to observe this day, the 14th day of the first month, as the feast of the Passover for all generations to come, in commemoration of His final judgment against the Egyptians and their gods and His sparing of the firstborn of Israel (Ex. 12:3-14, 21-28, Lev. 23:5).

After the children of Israel had assembled in Rameses, the Exodus from Egypt began. The people departed from Rameses as the 14th day was ending at sunset and the 15th day was beginning. The timing of this event fulfilled another promise that God had made to Abraham: "Now the sojourning of the children of Israel, who dwelt in Egypt, *was* **four hundred and thirty years**. And it came to pass at the end of the **four hundred and thirty years, EVEN THE SELFSAME DAY it came to pass, that all the hosts of the LORD went out from the land of Egypt.** *It is* **a night to be much observed unto the LORD for bringing them out from the land of Egypt**..." (Ex. 12:40-42, *KJV*).

The phrase "**the selfsame day**" refers to **a specific day exactly four hundred and thirty years before the Exodus**. What day was this? The Scriptures reveal that it was the "selfsame day" that God established His covenant with Abraham. On that day, God promised that He would bring his descendants out of bondage with great substance. On that "selfsame day," the 15th day of the first month, God fulfilled His promise. Therefore, God established the 15th day of the first month as a holy day to commemorate the beginning of the Exodus (Ex. 12:37-42; 13:3-10; Lev. 23:6-8).

The Foundation of the Christian Passover in the Covenant with Abraham

Four hundred and thirty years after establishing His covenant with Abraham, God brought the children of Israel out of Egypt. After bringing them out, He established a covenant with them now called the Old Covenant. In his epistle to the Galatians, the apostle Paul confirms that the Old Covenant was established four hundred and thirty years after God's covenant with Abraham: "Now this I say, *that the* covenant ratified beforehand by God to Christ [Abraham's true Heir] cannot be annulled by the law [the physical requirements of the Old Covenant], which was *given* four hundred and thirty years later, so as to make the promise of no effect" (Gal. 3:17).

The Old Covenant with the children of Israel did not fulfill God's promise to Abraham of a spiritual seed that would shine as the stars forever. This promise did not begin to be fulfilled until the coming of the New Covenant, the covenant of everlasting life, which was established nearly 2,000 years later. As God manifested in the flesh, Jesus Christ, the promised Seed of Abraham, instituted the New Covenant on the Passover night, the 14th day of the first month, named Nisan. The Passover that initiated the New Covenant was not a supper of lamb and bitter herbs, as was the Passover of the children of Israel under the Old Covenant. When Jesus instituted the new Christian Passover, He changed the symbols of the Passover to represent His own body and blood, which He sacrificed as the true Passover Lamb of God to ratify the New Covenant. Although He changed the symbols, He did not change the day, or the time of day, on which the Passover was to be observed.

The Christian Passover, as instituted by Jesus Christ, is to be observed on the night of Nisan 14. The new ceremony consists of three parts: 1) footwashing (John 13:2-17); 2) partaking of the broken unleavened bread, symbolizing Jesus' broken body (Matt. 26:26, Mark 14:22, Luke 22:19, I Cor. 11:23-24); and 3) partaking of the wine, symbolizing the blood of Jesus shed for the remission of sins so that all who accept His sacrifice may enter the New Covenant (Matt. 26:27-29, Mark 14:23-25, Luke 22:17-20, I Cor. 11:25-26).

Why Did God Have to Die?

As we have learned, God ratified His promises to Abraham with a maledictory oath. By passing between the parts of the covenant sacrifice, He pledged that He would give His own life to fulfill the promises. The bloody slaughter of these sacrificial animals symbolized the brutal suffering and crucifixion of Jesus Christ, which occurred in 30 AD on the Passover day—Nisan 14. The deep sleep and horror of great darkness that Abraham experienced was symbolic of Jesus Christ's burial in the tomb as Nisan 14 was ending at sunset. Thus, 2,000 years later, on the very same day that God ratified His covenant with Abraham, His lifeless body was in the tomb. He had carried out His pledge that He would die in order to fulfill the promises.

Before we can comprehend the death of God manifested in the flesh, we need to understand a fundamental truth about God. The Scriptures reveal that the Godhead is composed of more than one divine Being. In the first chapter of Genesis, the Hebrew name *Elohim* is used to describe God. In the Hebrew language, the suffix *im* added to a word makes it plural. Thus *Elohim* is a plural noun, meaning that there is more than one Being in the Godhead. When God created Adam and Eve, God said, "Let **Us** make man in **Our** image, after **Our** likeness…" (Gen. 1:26, *KJV*).

John begins his Gospel by revealing this fundamental truth: "**In** *the* **beginning was the Word, and the Word was with God, and the Word was God. He was in** *the* **beginning with God**. All things came into being through Him, and not even one *thing* that was created came into being without Him. In Him was life, and the life was the light of men….**He was in the world, and the world came into being through Him, but the world did not know Him**….**And the Word became flesh, and tabernacled** [temporarily dwelt] **among us** (and we ourselves beheld His glory, *the* glory as of *the* only begotten with the Father), full of grace and truth" (John 1:1-4, 10, 14).

Jesus Himself testified that He was with the Father in glory before the world existed. In His final prayer to God the Father before He was arrested, tried and crucified, He said, "I have glorified You on the earth. I have finished the work that You gave Me to do. And now, **Father, glorify Me with Your own self, with the glory that I had with You before the world existed**" (John 17:4-5).

The Scriptures of the Old Testament and the New Testament consistently reveal that from the beginning there were two Beings Who existed together as God, or Elohim. The one of Elohim Who created all things was the one Who became Jesus Christ, the Messiah and the Savior of the world. The other one of Elohim became the Father. We find a prophecy of this in the book of Psalms: "I [the one of Elohim Who became the Son, Jesus Christ] will declare the decree: the LORD [the one of Elohim Who became the Father] hath said unto Me, *Thou* **art My Son; this day have I begotten Thee** [the day He was begotten in the womb of the virgin Mary]" (Psa. 2:7, *KJV*).

The one of Elohim Who became Jesus Christ, the Son of God and Savior of the world, had to divest himself of His power and glory as God. He had to become a pinpoint of life in order to be begotten by the Father in the womb of the virgin Mary. The apostle Paul reveals how this was accomplished: "Let this mind be in you, which *was* also in Christ Jesus; Who, although He existed [Greek υπαρχων, *huparchoon*, to exist or pre-exist] in *the* form of God, did not consider it robbery to be equal with God, but emptied Himself [of His power and glory], *and* was made in *the* likeness [Greek ομοιωμα *homoioma*, the same existence] of men, *and* took the form of a servant [Greek δουλος *doulos*, a slave]; and being found in *the* manner of man, He humbled Himself, *and* became obedient unto death, even *the* death of *the* cross" (Phil. 2:5-8).

These inspired words of Paul confirm that before Jesus Christ became human He was, in fact, Jehovah Elohim, the Lord God of the Old Testament. Existing as God, He was composed of ever-living Spirit. In this existence, it was impossible for Him to die. The only way for God to die was to become fully human—to be "manifested in the flesh." The God Who had created man in His image and likeness took on the same flesh and nature as man in order to redeem man from sin.

Jesus Christ voluntarily became a man in order to give His life as an offering for the sin of the world. The Father gave Him authority to lay down His life and to receive it back, as Jesus Himself testified: "Just as the Father knows Me, I also know the Father; and **I lay down My life for the sheep**. And I have other sheep that are not of this fold. I must bring those also, and they shall hear My voice; and there shall be one flock *and* one Shepherd. **On account of this, the Father loves Me: because I lay down My life, that I may receive it back again. No one takes it from Me, but I lay it down of Myself. I have authority to lay it down and authority to receive it back again. This commandment I received from My Father**" (John 10:15-18).

Jesus Christ came to do the will of the Father and to give His life as the sacrifice for sin. In his epistle to the Hebrews, Paul quotes the words of the prophecy of Psalm 40:6-8: "For this reason, when He comes into the world, He says, 'Sacrifice and offering You did not desire, but You have prepared a body for Me [Christ's human body of flesh]. You did not delight in burnt offerings and *sacrifices* for sin. Then said I, "**Lo, I come** (*as* it is written of Me in *the* scroll of *the* book) **to do Your will, O God**" ' " (Heb. 10:5-7).

It was the purpose of the two Beings Who were Elohim that one of Them would be made fully human in order to die, so that through His sacrifice, all mankind might be granted grace unto salvation. Paul makes this absolutely clear: "But we see Jesus, **Who *was* made a little lower than *the* angels**, crowned with glory and honor on account of suffering the death, in order that **by *the* grace of God He Himself might taste [partake of] death for everyone**; because it was fitting for Him, for Whom all things *were created*, and by Whom all things *exist*, in bringing many sons unto glory, to make the Author of their salvation perfect through sufferings" (Heb. 2:9-10).

The Scriptures reveal that Jesus Christ was a mortal human being. He was not an angelic being that appeared to be a man. Paul states very clearly that He shared the same flesh and blood as all human beings: "**Therefore, since the children are partakers of flesh and blood, in like manner He also took part in the same**, in order that through death He might annul him who has the power of death—that is, the devil; and *that* He might deliver those who were subject to bondage all through their lives by *their* fear of death.

"For surely, He is not taking upon Himself to help *the* angels; but He is taking upon Himself to help *the* seed of Abraham. For this reason, it was obligatory for *Him* to be made like *His* brethren in everything [sharing the same flesh and nature], that He might be a merciful and faithful High Priest *in* things pertaining to God, in order to make propitiation for the sins of the people. For because He Himself has suffered, having been tempted *in like manner*, He is able to help those who are being tempted" (Heb. 2:14-18).

What a magnificent expression of God's love! The Creator of all mankind temporarily gave up His eternal existence as God and lowered Himself to the level of mortal man so that He could suffer and die for every human being! By the grace and love of God, through the power of the Holy Spirit, He willingly took upon Himself the death penalty that He had pronounced upon Adam and Eve and their descendants.

Jesus Christ voluntarily chose to lay down His life to reconcile mankind to God so that all who accept His sacrifice may have the opportunity to receive salvation and eternal life. Jesus endured all His suffering in the flesh so that He might become the Author of eternal salvation, "Who, in the days of His flesh, offered up both prayers and supplications with strong crying and tears to Him Who was able to save Him from death, and was heard because *He* feared *God*. Although He was a Son, *yet* He learned obedience from the things that He suffered; and having been perfected, He became *the* Author of eternal salvation to all those who obey Him" (Heb. 5:7-9).

It took the death of the Creator God, manifested in the flesh, to become the perfect sacrifice for the forgiveness of human sin. No other sacrifice could bring forgiveness of sin to mankind. All the animal sacrifices and the shedding of their blood could never bring full forgiveness for human sin before God. The apostle Paul makes this truth very clear: "For the law, having *only* a shadow of the good things that are coming *and* not the image of those things, with the same sacrifices which they offer continually year by year, is never able to make perfect those who come *to worship*. Otherwise, would they not have ceased to be offered? For once those who worship had been purified, *they would* no longer be conscious of sin. On the contrary, in *offering* these *sacrifices* year by year, *there is* a remembrance of sins; **because *it is* impossible *for the* blood of bulls and goats to take away sins**" (Heb. 10:1-4).

***Man Cannot Save Himself*:** No other fleshly human being could have sacrificed his life to redeem mankind. If it were possible for a man to live perfectly in the letter of the law and never sin, his perfect human life, if sacrificed for sin, would not be sufficient to redeem even one human life. Redemption from sin and death requires greater obedience than the letter of the law. This is the whole lesson of Job's trials and suffering. Although he was perfect in the letter of the law, His own righteousness could not save him: "Moreover the LORD answered Job, and said, 'Shall he that contendeth with the Almighty instruct *Him*? he that reproveth *God*, let him answer it.'
"Then Job answered the LORD, and said, 'Behold, I am vile [all human beings have a sinful nature, regardless of perfect behavior in the letter of the law]; what shall I answer Thee? I will lay mine hand upon my mouth. Once have I spoken; but I will not answer: yea, twice; but I will proceed no further.' Then answered the LORD unto Job out of the whirlwind, and said, 'Gird up thy loins now like a man: I will demand of thee, and declare thou unto Me. Wilt thou also disannul My judgment? wilt thou condemn Me, that thou mayest be righteous?

" 'Hast thou an arm like God? or canst thou thunder with a voice like Him? Deck thyself now *with* majesty and excellency; and array thyself with glory and beauty. Cast abroad the rage of thy wrath: and behold every one *that is* proud, and abase him. Look on every one *that is* proud, *and* bring him low; and tread down the wicked in their place. Hide them in the dust together; *and* bind their

faces in secret. Then will *I* also confess unto thee that thine own right hand can save thee' " (Job 40:1-14, *KJV*). As God told Job, it is impossible for any man to save himself—much less all of humanity.

***Angels Cannot Save Mankind*:** God created angels to be ministering spirits. Angels are in a completely different category than human beings or God. While God created them out of spirit, they do not have the potential to enter into the God Family, as do human beings who will be transformed to spirit at the resurrection. Neither are they like the one of Elohim Who became the Son, as Paul wrote: "God, Who spoke to the fathers at different times in the past and in many ways by the prophets, has spoken to us in these last days by *His* Son, Whom He has appointed heir of all things, by Whom also He made the worlds; Who, being *the* brightness of *His* glory and *the* exact image of His person, and upholding all things by the word of His own power, when He had by Himself purged our sins, sat down at *the* right hand of the Majesty on high; **having been made so much greater than *any of* the angels, inasmuch as He has inherited a name exceedingly superior to them**.

"For to which of the angels did He ever say, 'You are My Son; this day have I begotten You'? And again, 'I will be a Father to Him, and He will be a Son to Me'? And again, when He brought the Firstborn into the world, He said, 'Let all *the* angels of God worship Him.' Now on one hand, of the angels He says, 'Who makes His angels spirits, and His ministers a flame of fire'….But unto which of the angels did He ever say, 'Sit at My right hand, until I make Your enemies a footstool for Your feet'? **Are they not all ministering spirits, sent forth to minister to those who are about to inherit salvation**?" (Heb. 1:1-7, 13-14) It was not possible for the sacrifice of angels to pay for the sins of all mankind.

***Only God Can Save Man*:** The only Being whose life could purchase redemption from sin for all humanity is the Creator God. If the one Who had created man died, complete and total payment for human sin could be made, and reconciliation with God would be possible for all humanity. God's mercy could then be extended to all who repent and accept the death of Jesus Christ, God manifested in the flesh, as payment for their sins. This is why God had to die!

The one of Elohim Who created the heavens and the earth became Jesus Christ—God manifested in the flesh. He was divinely begotten by God the Father and born of the virgin Mary, His physical mother. He was the same as any ordinary human being, except that He had the Holy Spirit from conception. Only the death of God could reconcile man and God. Thus Jesus had to be God in the flesh—human as well as divine.

While He lived in the flesh, Jesus Christ was subject to every type of temptation that a human being can experience, but He never yielded to a single temptation of the flesh or of Satan. Jesus Christ never sinned. His obedience was perfect in the full spirit of the law. By living a sinless life, He was qualified to become not only the Savior and Redeemer of mankind but also the High Priest and Mediator between God and man: "Having therefore a great High Priest, *Who* has passed into the heavens, Jesus the Son of God, we should hold fast the confession *of our faith*. **For we do not have a high priest who cannot empathize with our weaknesses, but *one* Who** was tempted in all things according to *the* likeness of *our own temptations*,

yet *He was* without sin. Therefore, we should come with boldness to the throne of grace, so that we may receive mercy and find grace to help in time of need" (Heb. 4:14-16).

Jesus' life in the flesh was able to purchase redemption from sin for all humanity because:

1) He was the Creator of all human beings.
2) He was divinely begotten by God the Father.
3) He was God manifested in the flesh.
4) He was the only human to live His entire life according to the will of God.
5) He was the only human never to sin.
6) He was the only human never to yield to a single temptation of the flesh or of Satan the devil.
7) He was the only human not to come under the death penalty for sin.

Only the precious blood of the Lamb of God could atone for all human sin. The death of God in the flesh was complete and perfect as a sacrifice and an atonement because His life in the flesh encompassed the full scope of human experience. On the human level, He suffered every type of temptation possible. He suffered the vilest of human indignities and excruciating tortures, enduring a violent beating, scourging, and crucifixion, and the shame of public death. He suffered rejection by His own people and injustice at the hands of religious and civil authorities. He was the victim of political expediency and religious hypocrisy. He overcame all, gaining total victory over Satan the devil and the pulls of the flesh through His perfect love and obedience to God the Father. The sacrifice of His perfect life opened the way for all mankind to receive salvation through faith in Jesus Christ: "For God so loved the world that He gave His only begotten Son, so that everyone who believes in Him may not perish, but may have everlasting life. For God sent not His Son into the world that He might judge the world, but that the world might be saved through Him" (John 3:16-17).

God the Father accepted the death of Jesus Christ once for all time as full payment for human sin. But before the sacrifice of Jesus Christ can be applied to an individual, he or she must first repent of sin, accept Jesus Christ as personal Savior and be baptized by full immersion in water. At baptism, he or she is conjoined into Christ's death by symbolic burial in a watery grave. Each one who is raised out of that baptismal burial is to walk in newness of life, learning to love God the Father and Jesus Christ with all the heart and to keep Their commandments in the full spirit of the law. This is the way of life that Jesus established for those who enter the New Covenant through faith in His sacrifice for sin.

All who enter the New Covenant are commanded to observe the Passover year by year as a renewal of the covenant of everlasting life. By partaking of the Passover as Jesus taught, they acknowledge that they have accepted the body and blood of Jesus Christ as full payment for their sins and have dedicated their lives to live by Him (John 6:57). When they partake of the broken unleavened bread, they acknowledge that they are healed of their diseases by the broken body of Jesus Christ: "…by Whose stripes you were healed" (I Pet. 2:24). When they partake of the wine, they acknowledge that they trust in His shed blood "for the remission of sins" (Matt. 26:28).

All true Christians have been bought with a great price. They belong to Jesus Christ, Who paid with His own blood to release them from the power of Satan and the bondage of sin, and to reconcile them to God the Father. "Christ our Passover was sacrificed for us" (I Cor. 5:7). This is the meaning of the DAY JESUS THE CHRIST DIED FOR THE SINS OF THE WHOLE WORLD!

Darkness Covered the Land the Day God Died

- Harold M. Lambert

Jesus' Last Passover - Nisan 14
From Sunset - Tuesday, April 4 to Sunset - Wednesday, April 5, AD 30

HEBREW TIME	The Place For The Passover Already Prepared Earlier	ROMAN TIME
12th Hour	**SUNSET - NISAN 13 ENDS**	6 P.M.
	NISAN 14 BEGINS	
1st Hour		7 P.M.
2nd Hour	1. Passover Begins 2. During Supper Jesus Institutes New Testament Passover With Footwashing 3. Judas Dips The Sop And Leaves To Betray Jesus 4. Breaking And Eating Unleavened Bread As Broken Body Of Jesus 5. Drinking Of Wine As Blood Of Jesus For Forgiveness of Sin 6. Contention - Which Disciple Would Be Greatest 7. Jesus Prophesies That Peter Will Deny Him Three Times 8. Final Message To Disciple 9. Final Instruction Take A Sword 10. Sing A Hymn And Leave Toward Mount Of Olives	8 P.M.
3rd Hour		9 P.M.
4th Hour	1. On The Way To Gethsemane Jesus Tells Disciples He Is The True Vine. 2. Final Words Of Encouragement 3. Tells Disciples All Would Be Scattered	10 P.M.
5th Hour	1. Prays The Lord's Prayer The Third Hour - John 17 2. Jesus Takes Peter, James And John With Him And Prays For Three Hours But The Disciples Sleep 3. Jesus Prays So Hard That His Sweat Appears Like Great Drops Of Blood	11 P.M.
6th Hour	**MIDNIGHT** **April 4 Ends** / **April 5 Begins**	12 Midnight
7th Hour	1. Judas Comes With Crowd Of Soldiers And Betrays Jesus With A Kiss 2. Peter Cuts Off An Ear Of The High Priest's Servant - Jesus Heals Him 3. All Is Done To Fulfill Prophesy - Disciples Escape - Mark Escapes Naked	1 A.M.
8th Hour	1. Jesus Led Away To Annas The Priest First 2. Peter Follows At A Distance And Goes Into The Courtyard 3. Annas Questions Jesus And Beats Him And Sends Him To Caiaphas	2 A.M.
9th Hour		3 A.M.
10th Hour	1. The Chief Priests And Sanhedrin Question Jesus - Hear False Witnesses - Condemn Jesus 2. Peter Denies Jesus Twice - Cock Crows Once 3. About An Hour Later Peter Denies Jesus The Third Time The Cock Crows Again - Jesus Looks Right At Peter	4 A.M.
11th Hour	1. At Daybreak - The Whole Sanhedrin Condemns Jesus To Death And Sends Him To Pilate 2. Jesus Accused Before Pilate - He Questions Jesus And Finds He is From Galilee, Then Sends Him To Herod. Herod Sends Him Back To Pilate	5 A.M.
12th Hour	**SUNRISE**	6 A.M.

HEBREW TIME	SUNRISE	ROMAN TIME
12th Hour —		— 6 A.M.
	1. Judas Repents And Hangs Himself 2. Priests Decide To Buy Potter's Field With Thirty Pieces Of Silver	
1st Hour —		— 7 A.M.
	1. Pilate Finds Jesus Innocent - Wants To Release Him - Priests and Multitudes Yell Crucify Him And Release Barabbas 2. Pilate Washes Hands In Innocency - Releases Barabbas - Jesus Beaten And Scourged 3. Pilate Has Second Thoughts About Crucifying Jesus But It Is Too Late	
2nd Hour —		— 8 A.M.
	1. Jesus Led Away To Be Crucified - Simon Carries His Cross 2. Jesus Crucified With Two Malefactors - Accusation And Title Put On The Cross - Jesus Asks God To Forgive Them	
3rd Hour —		— 9 A.M.
4th Hour —		— 10 A.M.
	1. The People, Priests And Two Thieves Vilify And Mock Jesus	
5th Hour —		— 11 A.M.
6th Hour —		— 12 Noon
7th Hour —		— 1 P.M.
	1. Darkness Covers All The Land From The Sixth Hour Until The Ninth Hour 2. Jesus Makes John Responsible For Mary His Mother	
8th Hour —		— 2 P.M.
9th Hour —		— 3 P.M.
	1. At The Ninth Hour Jesus Is Forsaken - Offered Vinegar 2. A Spear Is Thrust Into His Side - Jesus Dies - The Veil In Temple Is Torn In Two	
10th Hour —	1. The Jews Want Jesus' Body Off The Cross Before The Holy Day Begins At Sunset	— 4 P.M.
	1. Joseph Of Arimathea Gets The Body Of Jesus Just Before Sunset 2. Nicodemus Helps Joseph Wrap Jesus' Body In Linen With Aromatics 3. Tomb Sealed Just Before Sunset 4. Many Of The Women Watch Until The End	
11th Hour —		— 5 P.M.
12th Hour —	**SUNSET NISAN 14 ENDS**	— 6 P.M.

NISAN 15 BEGINS

257

Genesis 15 Covenant Sacrifice and the Death of Jesus Christ

Sunset	13th	Genesis 15	Death of Christ	13th	Sunset
		Between the Two Evenings - *Ben ha arbayim*			
Night of 14th Passover Night		**Vs 4-5 Words of the covenant** Spiritual seed as the stars of heaven (Dan. 12:1-3, Mat. 13:43 1 John 3:1-3, Rev. 1:10) Midnight	New Covenant Passover instituted with footwashing, bread and wine Words of the New Covenant (John 13-17) Midnight		Night of 14th Passover Night
			Jesus Betrayed and Arrested Taken to Annas - Caiaphas		
Sunrise		*Boqer* - Morning (Dawn)	*Boqer* - Morning (Dawn)		Sunrise
14th Day Passover Day	Time Frame Same as Christ	**Vs 9-10 COVENANT SACRIFICE PREPARED** 3-year-old heifer 3-year-old she goat 3-year-old ram Turtledove and pigeon The death of Jesus Christ portrayed **MALEDICTORY OATH** Unilateral oath of the death of God The burial of Jesus Christ portrayed Vs 12 Going down of sun Great darkness - type of burial of Christ	TRIAL BEFORE PILATE BEATEN, SCOURGED JESUS LED AWAY - CARRIES OWN CROSS CRUCIFIED AT THIRD HOUR (9 AM) SEVEN SAYINGS OF JESUS **GREAT DARKNESS - SIXTH TO NINTH HOUR** **CHRIST DIES AT NINTH HOUR (3 PM)** Jesus' Body Wrapped in Linen and Put in Tomb Tomb Sealed at Sunset		14th Day Passover Day
Sunset	14th	*Ba arev* - SUNSET	*Ba erev* - SUNSET	14th	Sunset
Night of 15th 1st Day Fst Unlvnd Brd		**Between the Two Evenings - *Ben ha arbayim***			Night of 15th 1st Day Fst Unlvnd Brd
		Vs 13-16 COVENANT TO BRING ISRAEL OUT OF EGYPT Vs 17 After sundown - dark - type of tomb **God walked between the animal sacrifices** Vs 18 Oath to give the land to Abraham's seed Exodus 12:40-41, Israel begins Exodus from Egypt the night of the 15th	**CHRIST'S FIRST NIGHT IN TOMB**		
Sunrise		*Boqer* - Morning (Dawn)	*Boqer* - Morning (Dawn)		Sunrise
15th Day 1st Day Fst Unlvnd Brd			**CHRIST'S FIRST DAY IN TOMB** The scribes and Pharisees receive guards to secure tomb, then they seal it (Matt. 27:62-66)		15th Day 1st Day Fst Unlvnd Brd
Sunset	15th	*Ba erev* - SUNSET	*Ba erev* - SUNSET	15th	Sunset
	16th			16th	

THE AGONY OF THE CRUCIFIXION

At His last Passover meal with the apostles, Jesus said, "Behold, even *now* the hand of him who is betraying Me *is* with Me at the table" (Luke 22:21). Although Jesus knew that Judas would betray Him, He washed Judas' feet along with the other apostles' (John 13:2-5, 11). Then Judas left. As Jesus administered the symbols of His body and His blood to the eleven apostles who were with Him, He knew that the time of His betrayal was near. When He departed with the apostles to the Mount of Olives, walking into the darkness of that dread night, Jesus began to feel the melancholy oppressiveness of the sins of the whole world weighing on Him, and His mind was filled with thoughts of the suffering and agony that lay ahead. Though His apostles were with Him, an overwhelming feeling of isolation penetrated every cell of His being. He could not share His sorrow with them because they did not understand what the rest of that Passover night and day would bring. He had spoken to them in the days leading up to the Passover, forewarning them of His betrayal and death, but they did not grasp the meaning of His words. They did not know that His life was about to end with a gruesome death on the cross as the TRUE PASSOVER SACRIFICE OF GOD—THE SIN OFFERING FOR THE WORLD.

The time had come! His rendezvous with destiny drew closer and closer to its ultimate climax! The Lord God of the Old Testament, Who had come to earth in the flesh, was about to die the agonizing death that He and the prophets had foretold. This was the reason He had come into the world. He had come in the flesh in order to die—to give His body to be beaten, scourged and crucified, and to offer His blood for the sins of mankind. But no human being desires to die a slow death in great pain and agony. As Jesus anticipated His suffering, His flesh cried out to be spared. Only the love of God, which had sustained Him and brought Him to this day, could give Him the strength to endure the suffering that was appointed to Him.

He had manifested the love of God during His days in the flesh, setting a perfect example for His disciples. Now the love of God would be manifested by His death. As they were walking to the Mount of Olives, He charged His apostles, "LOVE ONE ANOTHER, AS I HAVE LOVED YOU." He spoke from the depths of His innermost being, desiring to indelibly etch His words into their minds: "If you keep My commandments, you shall live in My love; just as I have kept My Father's commandments and live in His love.

"These things I have spoken to you, in order that My joy may dwell in you, and *that* your joy may be full. **This is My commandment: that you love one another, as I have loved you**. No one has greater love than this: that one lay down his life for his friends" (John 15:10-13).

Jesus was about to manifest the greatest love of all by laying down His life for them, as well as for the whole world. But the apostles did not know this yet, nor did they know that some of them would also lose their lives for His name's sake in the days ahead. Jesus warned the disciples that the world would hate them and persecute them, just as the world had hated and persecuted Him: "If the world hates you, you know that it hated Me before *it hated* you. If you were of the world, the world would love its own. However, because you are not of the world, but I have personally chosen you out of the world, the world hates you for this. Remember the word that I spoke to you: a servant is not greater than his master. If they persecuted Me, they will persecute you also. If they kept My word, they will keep your *word* also. But they will do all these things to you for My name's sake, because they do not know Him Who sent Me.

"If I had not come and spoken to them, they would not have had sin; but now they have nothing to cover their sin. **The one who hates Me hates My Father also**. If I had not done among them the works that no other man has done, they would not have had sin; but now they have both seen and hated both Me and My Father. But this has happened so that the saying might be fulfilled which is written in their law, 'They hated Me without *a* cause.' But when the Comforter has come, which I will send to you from the Father, *even* the Spirit of the truth, which proceeds from the Father, that one shall bear witness of Me. Then you also shall bear witness, because you have been with Me from *the* beginning. I have spoken these things to you so that you will not be offended" (John 15:18-16:1).

Jesus continued to warn them, telling them that they, too, would be killed for preaching the truth of God: "They shall cast you out of the synagogues; furthermore, **the time is coming that everyone who kills you will think that he is rendering service to God**. And they shall do these things to you because they do not know the Father, nor Me. But **I have told you these things so that when the time comes, you may remember** that I said *them* to you. However, I did not say these things to you at *the* beginning because I was with you....These things I have spoken to you, so that in Me you may have peace. **In the world you shall have tribulation. But be courageous! I have overcome the world**" (John 16:2-4; 33).

When they arrived at the Mount of Olives, Jesus told His apostles, "My soul is deeply grieved, even to death. Stay here and watch with Me" (Matt. 26:38). Then, taking Peter, James and John, He went into the Garden of Gethsemane. "And when He arrived at the place, He said to them, 'Pray *that you* do not enter into temptation.' And He withdrew from them about a stone's throw; and falling to *His* knees, He prayed, saying, 'Father, if You are willing to take away this cup from Me—; NEVERTHELESS, NOT MY WILL, BUT YOUR *WILL* BE DONE' " (Luke 22:40-42).

Jesus Knew That He Could Not Escape Death

Even as He prayed to the Father, Jesus knew that the prophecies of His suffering and death must be fulfilled. As the Lord God of the Old Testament, He had given the first prophecy of His suffering to Adam and Eve in the presence of Satan, who would instigate His death (Gen. 3:15, *KJV*).

Jesus knew that He was the Lamb of God "slain from *the* foundation of *the* world" (Rev. 13:8). He knew from the beginning that He was destined to die on this Passover day—Nisan 14, April 5, 30 AD. As the Lord God of the Old Testament, He had entered into covenant with Abraham by passing between the parts of the sacrificial animals to represent His own death (Gen. 15:5-18). At the beginning of the 14th, during the dark hours of the night, He had delivered the promises of the covenant, foreshadowing the time when, as Jesus Christ, He would deliver the promises of the New Covenant. On the day portion of the 14th, the animals for the covenant sacrifice were slaughtered and their bodies were split asunder, allowing their blood to spill on the ground. During those same hours, the body of Jesus Christ would be beaten and broken open, and His blood would be poured out unto death. In the late afternoon of the 14th, the slaughtered animals lay still on the ground, and Abraham watched and waited. In like manner, Jesus' body would remain on the cross as the end of the 14th drew near, while his followers watched and waited (Luke 23:49). Although Jesus died at the "ninth hour," or approximately 3 PM, His body was not placed in the tomb until the 14th was ready to end at sunset.

At the exact time that Jesus would be buried, nearly 2000 years before, Abraham experienced a foretype of His death and burial: "And when the sun was going down, **a deep sleep fell upon Abram; and, lo, an horror of great darkness fell upon him**" (Gen. 15:12, *KJV*). Abraham remained in this symbolic burial after the sun had gone down. When the darkness of night had come, the Lord God passed between the parts of the sacrifice: "And it came to pass, that, when the sun went down, and it was dark, behold a smoking furnace, and a burning lamp that passed between those pieces" (verse 17, *KJV*).

By this maledictory oath, God Himself confirmed that He would fulfill the covenant through His own death and burial. This event, which took place during "the horror of great darkness," also had a fulfillment in Jesus Christ. The only sign that Jesus gave of His Messiahship was the length of time that He would be "in the heart of the earth" (Matt. 12:40). As He lay in the darkness of the tomb for three days and three nights, He was confirming that He was the Messiah Who would fulfill the promises of the New Covenant.

Jesus Knew That the Words of the Prophets Would All Be Fulfilled

As the covenant sacrifice had foreshadowed and the prophets had foretold, the suffering and death that were appointed to Jesus would surely come to pass. Every detail would be fulfilled, exactly as recorded in Scripture. When Judas left His presence on that Passover night, Jesus knew that Judas was on his way to the authorities to betray Him, as it was written: "Yea, mine own familiar friend, in whom I trusted, which did eat of my bread, hath lifted up *his* heel against me" (Psa. 41:9, *KJV*). Jesus also knew that the elders and the chief priests would pay Judas thirty pieces of silver to betray Him: "And I said unto them, 'If ye think good, give me my price; and if not, forbear.' So **they weighed for my price thirty *pieces* of silver**" (Zech. 11:12, *KJV*). Thirty pieces of silver was the price of a dead slave (Ex. 21:32).

Jesus also remembered the prophecy of Isaiah that He would be led as a lamb to the slaughter: "**He is despised and rejected of men**; a man of sorrows, and acquainted with grief: and we hid as it were *our* faces from him; he was despised, and we esteemed him not. Surely he hath borne our griefs, and carried our sorrows: yet we did esteem him stricken, smitten of God, and afflicted.

"**But he *was* wounded for our transgressions, *he was* bruised for our iniquities: the chastisement of our peace *was* upon him; and with his stripes we are healed**. All we like sheep have gone astray; we have turned every one to his own way; and **the LORD hath laid on him the iniquity of us all. He was oppressed, and he was afflicted, yet he opened not his mouth: he is brought as a lamb to the**

slaughter, and as a sheep before her shearers is dumb, so he openeth not his mouth....for he was cut off out of the land of the living: for the transgression of my people was he stricken....Yet it pleased the LORD to bruise him; he hath put *him* to grief: when thou shalt make his soul an offering for sin....he shall see of the travail of his soul, *and* shall be satisfied: by his knowledge shall my righteous servant justify many; for he shall bear their iniquities....because he hath poured out his soul unto death: and he was numbered with the transgressors; and he bare the sin of many, and made intercession for the transgressors" (Isa. 53:3-12, *KJV*).

Jesus was fully aware that He would be mocked, beaten and spit upon, and would suffer a terrible scourging. The whip that would inflict His scourging would have tips of nails and glass and would literally rip the flesh off His body. After forty lashes, He would be near death. He knew that this torturous ordeal would leave Him so horribly disfigured that He would be almost unrecognizable. Isaiah prophesied all of these things: "**I gave my back to the smiters, and my cheeks to them that plucked off the hair**: I hid not my face from shame and spitting....As many were astonied at thee; **his visage was so marred more than any man, and his form more than the sons of men**" (Isa. 50:6; 52:14, *KJV*).

Jesus knew that the prophecy of David in Psalm 22 was about to be fulfilled. He would cry out these very words while He was hanging on the cross: "**My God, my God, why hast thou forsaken me?** *why art thou so* far from helping me, *and from* the words of my roaring? O my God, I cry in the daytime, but thou hearest not; and in the night season, and am not silent....But *I am* a worm, and no man; **a reproach of men, and despised of the people**. All they that see me laugh me to scorn: they shoot out the lip, they shake the head, *saying*, 'He trusted on the LORD *that* he would deliver him: let him deliver him, seeing he delighted in him" (Psa. 22:1-2, 6-8, *KJV*).

Even during the mocking and jeering of the people, priests and Pharisees, He would trust God the Father, as He had from His earliest days in the flesh: "But thou *art* he that took me out of the womb: thou didst make me hope *when I was* upon my mother's breasts. I was cast upon thee from the womb: thou *art* my God from my mother's belly. Be not far from me; for trouble *is* near; for *there is* none to help. Many bulls [the demons] have compassed me: strong *bulls* of Bashan [Satan and his chief demons] have beset me round. They gaped upon me *with* their mouths, *as* a ravening and a roaring lion" (verses 9-13, *KJV*).

The next prophecies of David reveal the excruciating agony that He would suffer during His crucifixion as His physical life drained away: "I am poured out like water, and all my bones are out of joint [from the jolt of the cross falling into its hole]: my heart is like wax; it is melted in the midst of my bowels [from loss of blood]. My strength is dried up like a potsherd; and my tongue cleaveth to my jaws; and thou hast brought me into the dust of death.

"For dogs [the soldiers] have compassed me: the assembly of the wicked [the priests and Pharisees] have inclosed me: **they pierced my hands and my feet** [nailing Him to the cross]. **I may tell** [count] **all my bones** [because the flesh had been ripped open]: they look *and* stare upon me [in astonishment because He was so disfigured]. **They part my garments among them, and cast lots upon my vesture**" (verses 14-18, *KJV*).

In the midst of this agonizing ordeal, Jesus would pray to God the Father for strength to endure: "But be not thou far from me, O LORD: **O my strength, haste thee to help me**. Deliver my soul from the sword; my darling from the power of the dog. Save me from the lion's mouth: **for thou hast heard me**....For he hath not despised nor abhorred the affliction of the afflicted [Jesus Christ]; **neither hath he hid his face from him; but when he cried unto him, he heard**" (verses 19-24, *KJV*). These prophetic words of David show that God the Father would not truly forsake His Son at any time during His suffering and crucifixion but would be with Him as He bore the sins of all mankind.

In Psalm 69, God inspired David to write more of the thoughts that Jesus would have while on the cross. Although He had done no wrong, He would be hated and condemned to die by crucifixion, which was the lot of criminals. His death would bring great disrepute upon His disciples, and He would be rejected by His own physical brothers and sisters: "**They that hate me without a cause are more than the hairs of mine head**: they that would destroy me, *being* mine enemies wrongfully, are mighty....Let not them that wait on thee, O Lord GOD of hosts, be ashamed for my sake: **let not those that seek thee be confounded for my sake**, O God of Israel. Because **for thy sake I have borne reproach; shame hath covered my face**. I am become a stranger unto my brethren, and an alien unto my mother's children" (Psa. 69:4-8, *KJV*).

Jesus would suffer all the shame and agony of the crucifixion because of His profound love and zeal for God the Father: "**For the zeal of thine house hath eaten me up; and the reproaches of them that reproached thee are fallen upon me**....Hear me, O LORD; for thy lovingkindness *is* good: turn unto me according to the multitude of thy tender mercies. And hide not thy face from thy servant; for I am in trouble: hear me speedily. Draw nigh unto my soul, *and* redeem it: deliver me because of mine enemies. **Thou hast known my reproach, and my shame, and my dishonour** [being executed like a criminal]: mine adversaries *are* all before thee. **Reproach hath broken my heart; and I am full of heaviness: and I looked *for some* to take pity, but *there was* none; and for comforters, but I found none**. They gave me also gall for my meat; and **in my thirst they gave me vinegar to drink**" (verses 9, 16-21, *KJV*).

Jesus knew that He would have to bear this shameful and agonizing ordeal to the end. He knew that His suffering would become so unbearable that He would feel as if the Father had abandoned Him. He knew that a spear would be thrust into the side of His body, as the prophet Zechariah was inspired to write: "...and **they shall look upon me whom they have pierced**, and they shall mourn for him, as one mourneth for *his* only *son*, and shall be in bitterness for him, as one that is in bitterness for *his* firstborn" (Zech. 12:10, *KJV*).

Knowing that every one of these prophecies must be fulfilled, Jesus was in great anguish as He prayed to the Father. The thought of suffering such a hideous and merciless death was nearly overwhelming. Luke records, "Then an angel from heaven appeared to Him, strengthening Him. **And being in AGONY** [in His mind and spirit, knowing that all eternity hinged on this day], **He prayed more earnestly. And His sweat became as great drops of blood falling down to the ground**" (Luke 22:43-44).

Jesus Looked Forward to the Kingdom of God

Throughout His suffering, Jesus would keep His mind on His coming resurrection and the Kingdom of God. He knew that He would be raised from the dead by the power of God the Father and would give praise and glory to Him at the future resurrection of the saints, when His kingdom would be established over all the earth: "My praise *shall be* of thee in the great congregation: I will pay my vows before them that fear him [the resurrected saints]. The meek shall eat and be satisfied: they shall praise the LORD that seek him: your heart shall live for ever. All the ends of the world shall remember and turn unto the LORD [because of Jesus Christ's sacrifice for sin]: and all the kindreds of the nations shall worship before thee [at His return]. For the kingdom *is* the LORD'S: and he *is* the governor [Ruler] among the nations.

"All *they that be* fat upon earth shall eat and worship: all they that go down to the dust shall bow before him: and none can keep alive his own soul. A seed shall serve him; it shall be accounted to the LORD for a generation. They shall come, and shall declare his righteousness unto a people that shall be born, that he hath done *this* [through the crucifixion and resurrection of Jesus Christ]" (Psa. 22:25-31, *KJV*).

In the final words of His prayer, Jesus asked God the Father to restore Him to the glory that He had with the Father before the world existed. He also prayed for His disciples and for those who would become His disciples through the preaching of the gospel, that they all might be one with Him and the Father: "Jesus spoke these words, and lifted up His eyes to heaven and said, 'Father, **the hour has come**; glorify Your own Son, so that Your Son may also glorify You; since You have given Him authority over all flesh, in order that He may give eternal life to all whom You have given Him. For this is eternal life, that they may know You, the only true God, and Jesus Christ, Whom You did send. **I have glorified You on the earth. I have finished the work that You gave Me to do.**

"And now, **Father, glorify Me with Your own self, with the glory that I had with You before the world existed**. I have manifested Your name to the men whom You have given Me out of the world. They were Yours, and You have given them to Me, and they have kept Your Word. Now they have known that all things that You have given Me are from You. For I have given them the words that You gave to Me; and they have received *them* and truly have known that I came from You; and they have believed that You did send Me.

"I am praying for them; I am not praying for the world, but for those whom You have given Me, for they are Yours. All Mine are Yours, and all Yours *are* Mine; and I have been glorified in them. **And I am no longer in the world, but these are in the world, and I am coming to You. Holy Father, keep them in Your name, those whom You have given Me, so that they may be one, even as We *are one*.** When I was with them in the world, I kept them in Your name. I protected those whom You have given Me, and not one of them has perished except the son of perdition, in order that the Scriptures might be fulfilled.

"But now I am coming to You; and these things I am speaking *while yet* in the world, that they may have My joy fulfilled in them. **I have given them Your words,**

and the world has hated them because they are not of the world, just as I am not of the world. I do not pray that You would take them out of the world, but that You would **keep them from the evil one**. They are not of the world, just as I am not of the world. **Sanctify them in Your truth; Your Word is the truth.**

"Even as You did send Me into the world, I also have sent them into the world. **And for their sakes I sanctify Myself, so that they also may be sanctified in *Your* truth.** I do not pray for these only, but also for those who shall believe in Me through their word; that **they all may be one, even as You, Father, *are* in Me, and I in You; that they also may be one in Us**, in order that the world may believe that You did send Me.

"And I have given them the glory that You gave *to* Me, in order that they may be one, in the same way *that* We are one: I in them, and You in Me, that they may be perfected into one; and that the world may know that You did send Me, and have loved them as You have loved Me. Father, I desire that those whom You have given Me may also be with Me where I am, so that they may behold My glory, which You have given Me; because **You did love Me before *the* foundation of *the* world**. Righteous Father, the world has not known You; but I have known You, and these have known that You did send Me. **And I have made known Your name to them, and will make *it* known** [through His death and resurrection]; **so that the love with which You have loved Me may be in them, and I in them**" (John 17:1-26).

When Jesus finished this prayer, He arose and returned to His disciples. "After saying these things, Jesus went out with His disciples *to a place* beyond the winter stream of Kidron, where *there* was a garden into which He and His disciples entered. And Judas, who was betraying Him, also knew of the place because Jesus had often gathered there with His disciples" (John 18:1-2).

The time had come for Jesus to be betrayed into the hands of sinners, and to give His life for their sins and for the sins of the world. It was the death of God manifested in the flesh—THE CREATOR GOD! **His death and only His death could pay for the sins of all mankind.** Because of God's profound love for mankind, He personally and willingly took upon Himself the penalty for sin, which is death. Though He was made in the likeness of sinful flesh (Rom. 8:2-3), He never sinned. Thus He could offer Himself as the perfect sacrifice for sin.

He would experience a cruel death not only at the hands of wicked and treacherous men, **but at the hands of Satan the devil, the author of sin and the enemy of God and man!** Could God manifested in the flesh conquer sin and overcome Satan by enduring the suffering and shame of the cross?

In fact, there was no question about whether He would be able to endure the pain and agony of the beating, scourging and crucifixion. Why? What was Jesus' mindset? In the book of Hebrews, the apostle Paul wrote of Jesus' attitude: "... **Who for the joy that lay ahead of Him endured *the* cross, *although* He despised *the* shame**, and has sat down at *the* right hand of the throne of God" (Heb. 12:2).

The very fact that Jesus was to die in this manner was the ultimate purpose of His coming in the flesh. He was to taste death for every person because He alone was the

Savior of mankind: "But we see Jesus, Who *was* made a little lower than *the* angels, crowned with glory and honor **on account of suffering the death, in order that by *the* grace of God He Himself might taste death for everyone**; because it was fitting for Him, for Whom all things *were created*, and by Whom all things *exist*, in bringing many sons unto glory, to make the Author of their salvation perfect through sufferings. For both He Who is sanctifying and those who are sanctified *are* all of one; for which cause He is not ashamed to call them brethren, saying, 'I will declare Your name to My brethren; in *the* midst of *the* church I will sing praise to You.' And again, 'I will be trusting in Him.' And again, 'Behold, I and the children whom God has given Me' " (Heb. 2:9-13).

This is what Jesus must have been thinking as He finished His prayer. Now the moment had arrived! The time of His betrayal was at hand. Judas was coming. Jesus was ready.

The Ordeal Begins

His fervent prayers in the Garden of Gethsemane had brought Jesus strength from the Father (Luke 22:43). Determined to do His Father's will, Jesus said to His apostles, "Behold, the hour has drawn near, and the Son of man is betrayed into *the* hands of sinners. Arise! Let us be going. Look, the one who is betraying Me is approaching" (Matt. 26:45-46).

Then Jesus stepped forward to meet Judas, who was now possessed of Satan. The prophecy of His arrest was being fulfilled: "And immediately, while He was speaking, Judas, being one of the twelve, came up with a great multitude with swords and clubs, from the chief priests and the scribes and the elders. Now the one who was betraying Him had given them a sign, saying, '**Whomever I shall kiss, He is *the one*. Arrest Him** and take Him securely away.' And as soon as he came up to Him, he said, 'Master, Master,' and kissed Him earnestly . Then they laid their hands on Him and arrested Him" (Mark 14:43-46).

Jesus was arrested like a common criminal, exactly as the Scriptures had prophesied: "At that point Jesus said to the crowd, 'Have you come out to take Me with swords and clubs, as against a robber? I sat day after day with you, teaching in the temple, and you did not arrest Me. **But all this has happened so that the Scriptures of the prophets might be fulfilled**.' Then all the disciples forsook Him and fled [fulfilling the prophecy in Zechariah 13:7]" (Matt. 26:55-56).

As the chain of agonizing events unfolded—the false accusations and unjust trials, the cruel beatings, the humiliating mocking and spitting, the brutal scourging and a slow death by crucifixion—Jesus Christ remained steadfast in His love and loyalty to God the Father. But the disciples and women who looked upon Jesus' mutilated and bloodied body did not understand what they were witnessing. They stood afar off, watching His crucifixion in stunned bewilderment and disbelief that this could be happening to Jesus Christ, Whom they believed to be the Son of God. How could the promised Savior be nailed to the cross in naked shame, dying before their very eyes? They had hoped that He would save them from the Roman oppression and establish the Kingdom of God. Now there would be no salvation, not at that time or ever, so they thought, as they witnessed Jesus drawing His last breath on the cross. They did not realize until after the resurrection that **the outpouring of Jesus' blood was the beginning of the salvation of the world.**

The Son of God had died to atone for the sins of the world! As the God Who had created man, His death paid the penalty for the sins of every human being, opening the way for all mankind to receive the gift of eternal life. This was the beginning of the New Covenant, sealed with the body and the blood of Jesus Christ, which would bring salvation to all the world.

Hebrew Scroll

TWENTY-EIGHT PROPHECIES FULFILLED ON THE CRUCIFIXION DAY

On that Passover day, the day of the crucifixion, all the words of the prophets concerning the suffering of the Christ, or the Anointed One, were fulfilled. Their fulfillment in every detail stands today as a lasting testimony to the Messiahship of Jesus Christ.

The first prophecy, the oldest of all, had been given by the Lord Himself at the time of Adam and Eve's first sin:

1) The serpent would bruise the seed of the woman.

Prophesied: "And I will put enmity between thee and the woman, and between thy seed and her seed; *it* shall bruise thy head, and *thou* shalt bruise his heel" (Gen. 3:15, *KJV*).

Fulfilled: " 'Now is *the* judgment of this world. Now shall the prince of this world be cast out. And if I be lifted up from the earth, I will draw all to Myself.' But He said this to signify by what death He was about to die" (John 12:31-33).

2) The Messiah would be cut off, but not for Himself, as prophesied by Daniel.

Prophesied: "And after threescore and two weeks shall Messiah be cut off, but not for himself..." (Dan. 9:26, *KJV*).

Fulfilled: " 'Nor consider that it is better for us that one man die for the people, than that the whole nation should perish.' Now he did not say this of himself, but being high priest that year, prophesied that Jesus would die for the nation; and not for the nation only, but also that He might gather together into one the children of God who were scattered abroad" (John 11:50-52).

3) The betrayal of Jesus by Judas was foretold by David.

Prophesied: "Yea, mine own familiar friend, in whom I trusted, which did eat of my bread, hath lifted up *his* heel against me" (Psa. 41:9, *KJV*).

Fulfilled: "Then Judas Iscariot, one of the twelve, went to the chief priests in order that he might deliver Him up to them. And after hearing *this*, they were delighted and promised to give him money. And he sought how he might conveniently betray Him" (Mark 14:10-11).

4) Jesus Christ would be forsaken by His disciples, as prophesied by Zechariah.

Prophesied: "Awake, O sword, against my shepherd, and against the man *that is* my fellow, saith the LORD of hosts: smite the shepherd [Jesus], and the sheep shall be scattered..." (Zech. 13:7, *KJV*).

Fulfilled: "Then they all forsook Him and fled" (Mark 14:50).

5) The price of His betrayal was also foretold by Zechariah.

Prophesied: "And I said unto them, If ye think good, give *me* my price; and if not, forbear. So they weighed for my price thirty *pieces* of silver" (Zech. 11:12, *KJV*).

Fulfilled: "*And* said, 'What are you willing to give me, and I will deliver Him up to you?' And they offered him thirty pieces of silver" (Matt. 26:15).

6) Zechariah also foretold what would be done with the betrayal money.

Prophesied: "And the LORD said unto me, Cast it unto the potter: a goodly price that I was prised at of them. And I took the *thirty* pieces of silver, and cast them to the potter in the house of the LORD" (Zech. 11:13, *KJV*).

Fulfilled: "Now when Judas, who had betrayed Him, saw that He was condemned, he changed his mind *and* returned the thirty pieces of silver to the chief priests and the elders, saying, 'I have sinned and have betrayed innocent blood.' But they said, 'What *is that* to us? You see *to it* yourself.' And after throwing down the pieces of silver in the temple, he went out and hanged himself. But the chief priests took the pieces of silver *and* said, 'It is not lawful to put them into the treasury, since it is *the* price of blood.' And after taking counsel, they bought a potter's field with the *pieces of silver*, for a burial ground for strangers" (Matt. 27:3-7).

7) Isaiah prophesied that Jesus Christ would be sacrificed as the Passover Lamb of God.

Prophesied: "He is brought as a lamb to the slaughter..." (Isa. 53:7, *KJV*).

Fulfilled: "For Christ our Passover was sacrificed for us" (I Cor. 5:7). "Knowing that you were not redeemed by corruptible things … but by *the* precious blood of Christ, as of a lamb without blemish and without spot; Who truly was foreknown before *the* foundation of *the* world, but was manifested in *these* last times for your sakes" (I Pet. 1:18-20).

8) Isaiah also prophesied the scourging and mocking that He would suffer.

Prophesied: "I gave my back to the smiters [scourgers], and my cheeks to them that plucked off the hair: I hid not my face from shame and spitting" (Isa. 50:6, *KJV*).

Fulfilled: "Then he released Barabbas to them; but after scourging Jesus, he delivered *Him* up so that He might be crucified. Then the governor's soldiers, after taking Jesus with *them* into the Praetorium, gathered the entire band against Him; and they stripped Him *and* put a scarlet cloak around Him. And after platting a crown of thorns, they put *it* on His head; and a rod in His right hand; and bowing *on* their knees before Him, they mocked Him, and *kept on* saying, 'Hail, king of the Jews!' Then, after spitting on Him, they took the rod and struck *Him* on the head" (Matt. 27:26-30).

9) Both Isaiah and David prophesied that Jesus' body would be mutilated.

Prophesied: "As many were astonied at thee; his visage was so marred more than any man, and his form more than the sons of men" (Isa. 52:14, *KJV*). "I may tell [count] all my bones: *they* look *and* stare upon me" (Psa. 22:17, *KJV*).

Fulfilled: "But after scourging Jesus, he delivered *Him* up so that He might be crucified" (Matt. 27:26). "Then Pilate therefore took Jesus and scourged *Him*" (John 19:1).

10) David prophesied the shame and dishonor that Jesus would suffer, being condemned as a criminal.

Prophesied: "The reproaches of them that reproached thee are fallen upon me....*Thou* hast known my reproach, and my shame, and my dishonour: mine adversaries *are* all before thee. Reproach hath broken my heart; and I am full of heaviness: and I looked *for some* to take pity, but *there was* none; and for comforters, but I found none" (Psa. 69:9, 19-20, *KJV*).

Fulfilled: "At that point Jesus said to the crowd, 'Have you come out to take Me with swords and clubs, as against a robber?' " (Matt. 26:55) "They answered *and* said, 'He is deserving of death!' " (Matt. 26:66).

11) David also foretold that false witnesses would testify against Christ.

Prophesied: "False witnesses did rise up; they laid to my charge *things* that I knew not" (Psa. 35:11, *KJV*).

Fulfilled: "And the chief priests and the whole Sandhedrin were trying to find testimony against Jesus, to put Him to death; but they did not find *any*. For many bore false witness against Him, but their testimonies did not agree. And some rose up and bore false witness against Him, saying..." (Mark 14:55-57).

12) Isaiah prophesied that Jesus would not make an effort to defend Himself at the trial.

Prophesied: "He was oppressed, and *he* was afflicted, yet he opened not his mouth: he is brought as a lamb to the slaughter, and as a sheep before her shearers is dumb, so he openeth not his mouth" (Isa. 53:7, *KJV*).

Fulfilled: "Then Pilate said to Him, 'Don't You hear how many things they testify against You?' And He did not answer even one word to him, so that the governor was greatly amazed" (Matt. 27:13-14).

13) Isaiah also foretold Jesus Christ's crucifixion as the sin offering for the world.

Prophesied: "Surely *he* hath borne our griefs, and carried our sorrows: yet *we* did esteem him stricken, smitten of God, and afflicted. But *he was* wounded for our transgressions, *he was* bruised for our iniquities: the chastisement of our peace *was* upon him; and with his stripes we are healed. All we like sheep have gone astray; we have turned every one to his own way; and the LORD hath laid on him the iniquity of us all....Yet it pleased the LORD to bruise him; he hath put *him* to grief: when thou shalt make his soul an offering for sin, he shall see *his* seed, he shall prolong *his* days, and the pleasure of the LORD shall prosper in his hand. He shall see of the travail of his soul, and shall be satisfied: by his knowledge shall my righteous servant justify many; for *he* shall bear their iniquities" (Isa. 53:4-6, 10-11, *KJV*).

Fulfilled: "Therefore, he then delivered Him up to them so that He might be crucified. Now they took Jesus and led *Him* away; and He went out bearing His own cross to the place called 'A Skull,' which is called in Hebrew, 'Golgotha'; where they crucified Him, and with Him two others, one on this side and *one* on the other side, and Jesus in the middle. Now Pilate also wrote a title and put it on the cross. And it was written, 'Jesus the Nazarean, the King of the Jews' " (John 19:16-19).

14) As Isaiah had prophesied, He was numbered among lawbreakers.

Prophesied: "He was numbered with the transgressors…" (Isa. 53:12, *KJV*).

Fulfilled: "And also two other malefactors were led away with Him to be put to death. And when they came to the place called 'Skull,' there they crucified Him and the malefactors, one on *the* right and one on *the* left" (Luke 23:32-33).

15) David prophesied that His hands and His feet would be pierced.

Prophesied: "For dogs have compassed me: the assembly of the wicked have inclosed me: they pierced my hands and my feet" (Psa. 22:16, *KJV*).

Fulfilled: "And they crucified Him" (Mark 15:25). "Then the other disciples said to him, 'We have seen the Lord!' But he said to them, 'If I do not see the nail marks in His hands, and put my finger into the nail marks, and put my hand into His side, I will not believe at all!' Now after eight days, His disciples were within, and Thomas with them. After the doors were shut, Jesus came and stood in the midst, and said, 'Peace to you.' Then He said to Thomas, 'Bring forth your finger, and see My hands; and bring *forth* your hand, and put *it* into My side; and be not unbelieving, but believing' " (John 20:25-27).

16) The parting of His garments was also prophesied by David.

Prophesied: "They part my garments among them, and cast lots upon my vesture" (Psa. 22:18, *KJV*).

Fulfilled: "Then they said to one another, 'Let us not tear it, but let us cast lots for it *to determine* whose it shall be'; that the Scripture might be fulfilled, which says, 'They divided My garments among them, and they cast lots for My vesture.' Therefore the soldiers did these things" (John 19:24).

17) In another psalm, David prophesied that they would give Him vinegar to drink.

Prophesied: "They gave me also gall for my meat; and in my thirst they gave me vinegar to drink" (Psa. 69:21, *KJV*).

Fulfilled: "They gave Him vinegar mingled with gall to drink; but after tasting *it*, He would not drink" (Matt. 27:34).

18) David also prophesied that many would be watching Jesus during the crucifixion.

Prophesied: "*They* look *and* stare upon me" (Psa. 22:17, *KJV*).

Fulfilled: "And the guards sat down there to guard Him" (Matt. 27:36). "And all the people who were gathered together to this sight, after seeing the things that took place, beat their breasts *and* returned" (Luke 23:48).

19) Among those watching would be Jesus' family and friends, who would stand at a distance.

Prophesied: "My friends stand aloof from my sore [wounds]; and my kinsmen stand afar off" (Psa. 38:11, *KJV*).

Fulfilled: "Now all those who knew Him stood afar off observing these things, *the* women also who followed Him from Galilee" (Luke 23:49).

20) Some of His observers would shake their heads at Him.

Prophesied: "*I* became also a reproach unto them: *when* they looked upon me they shaked their heads" (Psa. 109:25, *KJV*).

Fulfilled: "But those who were passing by railed at Him, shaking their heads and saying, "You who *would* destroy the temple and build *it* in three days, save Yourself! If You are the Son of God, come down from the cross!" (Matt. 27:39-40)

21) Even the words of His reproachers were prophesied by David.

Prophesied: "He trusted on the LORD *that* he would deliver him: let him deliver him, seeing he delighted in him" (Psa. 22:8, *KJV*).

Fulfilled: " 'He trusted in God; let Him deliver Him now, if He will *have* Him; for He said, "I am the Son of God." ' And the two robbers who were also crucified with Him reproached Him with the same *words*" (Matt. 27:43-44).

22) Isaiah prophesied that Jesus would make intercession for sinners. This intercession began even during His crucifixion.

Prophesied: "*He* bare the sin of many, and made intercession for the transgressors" (Isa. 53:12, *KJV*).

Fulfilled: "Then Jesus said, 'Father, forgive them, for they do not understand what they are doing.' And they divided His garments, and cast lots" (Luke 23:34).

23) David prophesied the thoughts of Jesus at the height of His suffering.

Prophesied: "My God, my God, why hast thou forsaken me? *why art thou so* far from helping me, *and from* the words of my roaring?" (Psa. 22:1, *KJV.*)

Fulfilled: "And about the ninth hour, Jesus cried out with a loud voice, saying, 'Eli, Eli, lama sabachthani?' That is, 'My God, My God, why have You forsaken Me?' " (Matt. 27:46)

24) Zechariah prophesied that His body would be pierced with a spear.

Prophesied: "And they shall look upon me whom they have pierced..." (Zech. 12:10, *KJV*).

Fulfilled: "But one of the soldiers had pierced His side with a spear, and immediately water and blood had come out....And again another scripture says, 'They shall look upon Him Whom they pierced' " (John 19:34, 37).

25) David prophesied that Jesus would commit His spirit to God.

Prophesied: "Into thine hand I commit my spirit..." (Psa. 31:5, *KJV*).

Fulfilled: "And after crying out with a loud voice, Jesus said, 'Father, into Your hands I commit My spirit.' And when He had said these things, He expired" (Luke 23:46).

26) David also prophesied Jesus' last words.

Prophesied: "… that he hath done *this*" (Psa. 22:31, *KJV*). The Hebrew literally reads, "For it is finished."

Fulfilled: "Therefore, when Jesus had received the vinegar, He said, 'It is finished.' And after bowing His head, He yielded up *His* spirit" (John 19:30).

27) As no bone of the Passover lamb was to be broken (Ex. 12:46), not a bone of His would be broken.

Prophesied: "He keepeth all his bones: not one of them is broken" (Psa. 34:20, *KJV*).

Fulfilled: "Then the soldiers came and broke the legs of the first *one*, and *the legs* of the other who was crucified with Him. But when they came to Jesus *and* saw that He was already dead, they did not break His legs....For these things took place so that the Scripture might be fulfilled, 'Not a bone of Him shall be broken' " (John 19:32-33, 36).

28) His burial in the tomb of a rich man was foretold by Isaiah.

Prophesied: "He was taken from prison and from judgment: and who shall declare his generation? for he was cut off out of the land of the living: for the transgression of my people was he stricken. And he made his grave with the wicked [criminals], and with the rich in his death; because he had done no violence, neither *was any* deceit in his mouth" (Isa. 53:8-9, *KJV*).

Fulfilled: "And when evening was coming on, a rich man of Arimathea came, named Joseph, who was himself a disciple of Jesus. After going to Pilate, he begged *to have* the body of Jesus. [Jesus would otherwise have been buried among the criminals] Then Pilate commanded the body to be given over *to him*. And after taking the body, Joseph wrapped it in clean linen cloth, and placed it in his new tomb which he had hewn in the rock; and after rolling a great stone to the door of the tomb, he went away" (Matt. 27:57-60).

All these prophecies were fulfilled by the suffering, death and burial of Jesus Christ on the Passover day. In the next chapter, we will learn the significance of the timing of Jesus' death and of the miraculous events which occurred on that Passover day, Nisan 14, April 5, 30 AD.

PASSOVER DAY NISAN 14 – TUESDAY EVENING, APRIL 4 – 30 AD
APPROXIMATELY 7 – 7:30 PM
317. JESUS' LAST PASSOVER BEGINS AT EVENING

MATTHEW 26	MARK 14	LUKE 22
20. And after evening had come, He sat down with the twelve.	17. Now after evening had come, He came with the twelve.	14. Now when the hour had come, He sat *down,* and the twelve apostles with Him. 15. And He said to them, "With *earnest* desire I have desired to eat this Passover with you before I suffer. 16. For I tell you that I will not eat of it again until it be fulfilled in the kingdom of God."

318. JESUS INSTITUTES THE NEW COVENANT PASSOVER:
1) FOOTWASHING 2) EATING THE UNLEAVENED BREAD
3) DRINKING THE WINE

FIRST PART OF THE NEW COVENANT PASSOVER: THE FOOTWASHING

JOHN 13

2. And during supper (the devil having already put into the heart of Judas Iscariot, Simon's *son,* that he should betray Him),
3. Jesus, knowing that the Father had given all things into *His* hands, and that He had come from God and was going to God,
4. Rose from supper and laid aside *His* garments; and after taking a towel, He secured it around Himself.
5. Next, He poured water into a washing basin and began to wash the disciples' feet, and to wipe *them* with the towel which He had secured.
6. Then He came to Simon Peter; and he said to Him, "Lord, are You going to wash my feet?"
7. Jesus answered and said to him, "What I am doing you do not understand now, but you shall know after these things."
8. Peter said to Him, "You shall not wash my feet, not ever." Jesus answered him, "If I do not wash you, you have no part with Me."
9. Simon Peter said to Him, "Lord, not my feet only, but also *my* hands and *my* head."
10. Jesus said to him, "The one who has been washed does not need to wash *anything other* than the feet, but is completely clean; and you are clean, but not all."
11. For He knew the one who was betraying Him; this was the reason He said, "Not all of you are clean."
12. Therefore, when He had washed their feet, and had taken His garments, *and* had sat down again, He said to them, "Do you know what I have done to you?
13. You call Me the Teacher and the Lord, and you speak rightly, because I am.
14. Therefore, if I, the Lord and the Teacher, have washed your feet, you also are duty-bound to wash one another's feet;
15. For I have given you an example, *to show* that you also should do exactly as I have done to you.
16. Truly, truly I tell you, a servant is not greater than his lord, nor a messenger greater than he who sent him.
17. If you know these things, blessed are you if you do them.

PASSOVER DAY NISAN 14 – TUESDAY NIGHT, APRIL 4 – 30 AD
319. JUDAS DIPS THE SOP, AND LEAVES TO BETRAY JESUS

MATTHEW 26	MARK 14	LUKE 22	JOHN 13

21. And as they were eating, He said, "Truly I say to you, one of you shall betray Me." [a]
22. And being sorely grieved, each of them began to say to Him, "Am I *the one*, Lord?"
23. But He answered and said, "He who dipped *his* hand with Me in the dish, he shall betray Me.
24. The Son of man indeed goes, as it has been written concerning Him, but woe to that man by whom the Son of man is betrayed! It would be better for him if that man had not been born."
25. Then Judas, who was betraying Him, answered and said, "Am I *the one*, Master?" He said to him, "You have said *it*."

18. And as they sat and were eating, Jesus said, "Truly I say to you, one of you shall betray[a] Me, *even* he who is eating with Me."
19. And they began to be extremely sad, and said to Him one by one, "*Is it* I?" And another, "*Is it* I?"
20. But He answered *and* said to them, "The one who is dipping *a morsel* into the dish with Me, *he is* the one of *you* twelve.
21. The Son of man indeed goes, just as it has been written of Him; but woe to that man by whom the Son of man is betrayed! It would be better for that man if he had not been born."

21. "Behold, even *now* the hand of him who is betraying Me *is* with Me at the table;
22. And the Son of man indeed goes, according as it has been appointed, but woe to that man by whom He is betrayed!"
23. Then they began to question this among themselves, which of them it might be who was about to do this.

18. "I am not speaking of you all; *for* I know whom I have chosen, in order that the scripture might be fulfilled: 'He who eats bread with Me has lifted up his heel against Me.' [a]
19. I am telling you at this time, before it happens, so that when it does happen, you may believe that I AM.
20. Truly, truly I tell you, the one who receives whomever I send is receiving Me; and the one who receives Me is receiving Him Who sent Me."
21. *As He* was saying these things, Jesus was troubled in spirit, and testified, saying, "Truly, truly I tell you, one of you shall betray Me."
22. Then the disciples looked at one another, wondering of whom He was speaking.
23. Now one of His disciples, the one whom Jesus loved, was leaning on Jesus' chest.
24. And so, Simon Peter motioned to him to ask who was the one of whom He was speaking.
25. Then he leaned back on Jesus' chest *and* asked Him, "Lord, who is it?"
26. Jesus answered, "It is the one to whom I shall give a sop after I have dipped *it*."

a - Psa. 41:9

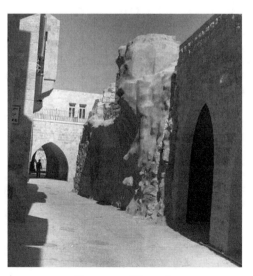

Street to Temple

PASSOVER DAY NISAN 14 – TUESDAY NIGHT, APRIL 4 – 30 AD

City of David—Model City Jerusalem

JOHN 13

And when He had dipped the sop, He gave *it* to Judas Iscariot, Simon's *son*.

27. And after the sop, Satan entered into him. Then Jesus said to him, "What you do, do quickly."

28. But not one of those sitting at the table knew why He said *this* to him;

29. For some thought, since Judas had the bag, that Jesus was telling him, "Buy the things that we need for the feast"; or that he should give something to the poor.

30. So then, after receiving the sop, he immediately went out; and it was night.

31. When he was gone, Jesus said, "Now has the Son of man been glorified, and God has been glorified in Him.

32. If God has been glorified in Him, God shall also glorify Him in Himself, and shall immediately glorify Him.

320. SECOND PART: EATING THE UNLEAVENED BREAD

MATTHEW 26	MARK 14	LUKE 22	I CORINTHIANS 11
26. And as they were eating, Jesus took the bread and blessed *it*; *then He* broke *it* and gave *it* to the disciples, and said, "Take, eat; this is My body."	22. And as they were eating, Jesus took bread; *and* after blessing *it*, He broke *it* and gave *it* to them, and said, "Take, eat; this is My body."	19. And He took bread; *and* after giving thanks, He broke *it* and gave *it* to them, saying, "This is My body, which is given for you. This do in the remembrance of Me."	23. For I received from the Lord that which I also delivered to you, that the Lord Jesus in the night in which He was betrayed took bread; 24. And after giving thanks, He broke *it* and said, "Take, eat; this is My body, which *is* being broken for you. This do in the remembrance of Me."

PASSOVER DAY – TUESDAY NIGHT, APRIL 4 – 30 AD
321. THIRD PART: DRINKING THE WINE

MATTHEW 26	MARK 14	LUKE 22	I CORINTHIANS 11
27. And He took the cup; and after giving thanks, He gave *it* to them, saying, "All of you drink of it; 28. For this is My blood, the *blood* of the New Covenant, which is poured out for many for *the* remission of sins. [a] 29. But I say to you, from this time forward I will not drink at all of this fruit of the vine, until that day when I drink *it* anew with you in the kingdom of My Father."	23. And He took the cup; *and* after giving thanks, He gave *it* to them; and they all drank of it. 24. And He said to them, "This is My blood, the blood of the New Covenant, which is poured out for many. [a] 25. Truly I say to you, I will not drink again at all of the fruit of the vine until that day when I drink it new in the kingdom of God."	17. And He took a cup; *and* after giving thanks, He said, "Take this, and divide *it* among yourselves. 18. For I say to you, I will not drink at all of the fruit of the vine until the kingdom of God has come." 20. In like manner also, *He took* the cup after supper, saying, "This cup *is* the New Covenant in My blood, which is poured out for you. [a]	25. In like manner, *He* also *took* the cup after He had supped, saying, "This is *the* cup *of* the New Covenant in My blood. [a] This do, as often as you drink *it*, in the remembrance of Me." 26. For as often as you eat this bread and drink this cup, you *solemnly* proclaim the death of the Lord until He comes. 27. For this reason, *if* anyone shall eat this bread or shall drink the cup of the Lord unworthily, he shall be guilty of the body and *the* blood of the Lord. 28. But let a man examine himself, and let him eat of the bread and drink of the cup accordingly 29. Because the one who eats and drinks unworthily is eating and drinking judgment to himself, not discerning the body of the Lord.

a - Ex. 24:8; Lev. 4:18-20; Isa. 53: 8-11; Jer. 31:31

322. CONTENTION AMONG THE DISCIPLES
AS TO WHO WOULD BE THE GREATEST

LUKE 22

24. And there was also an argument among them, *even* this: which of them should be considered *the* greatest.
25. And He said to them, "The kings of the nations lord over them, and those who exercise authority over them are called benefactors.
26. But *it shall* not be this way *among* you; rather, let the one who is greatest among you be as the younger, and the one who is leading as the one who is serving.
27. For who *is* greater, the one who is sitting *at the table*, or the one who is serving? *Is* not the one who sits *at the table*? But I am among you as one who is serving.
28. Now you are the ones who have continued with Me in My temptations.

PASSOVER DAY NISAN 14 – TUESDAY NIGHT, APRIL 4 – 30 AD

LUKE 22

29. "And I appoint to you, as My Father has appointed to Me, a kingdom;
30. So that you may eat and drink at My table in My kingdom, and may sit on thrones judging the twelve tribes of Israel."

323. A NEW COMMANDMENT— LOVE EACH OTHER AS JESUS LOVED HIS DISCIPLES

JOHN 13

33. "Little children, I am with you yet a little while. You shall seek Me; but as I told the Jews, 'Where I am going, you cannot come,' I am now telling you also.
34. A new commandment I give to you: that you love one another in the same way that I have loved you, that *is how* you are to love one another.
35. By this shall everyone know that you are My disciples—if you love one another."

324. JESUS PROPHESIES THAT PETER WILL DENY HIM THREE TIMES

MATTHEW 26	MARK 14	LUKE 22	JOHN 13
31. Then Jesus said to them, "All of you shall be offended in Me during this night; for it is written, 'I will smite the Shepherd, and the sheep of the flock shall be scattered abroad.' [a] 32. But after I have been raised, I will go before you into Galilee." 33. Then Peter answered *and* said to Him, "Even if all shall be offended in You, I will never be offended." 34. Jesus said to him, "Truly I say to you, during this *very* night, before *the* cock crows, you yourself shall deny Me three times." 35. Peter said to Him, "Even if I were required to die with You, in no way would I ever deny You." All the disciples also spoke in like manner.	27. Then Jesus said to them, "All of you shall be offended in Me in this night; for it is written, 'I will smite the Shepherd, and the sheep shall be scattered.' [a] 28. But after I have risen, I will go before you into Galilee." 29. Then Peter said to Him, "Even if all shall be offended, yet I *shall* not." 30. And Jesus said to him, "Truly I say to you, today, in this *very* night, before *the* cock crows twice, you shall deny Me three times." 31. But he spoke more adamantly, "If it were necessary for me to die with You, I would not deny You in any way." And they all spoke in the same manner also.	31. Then the Lord said, "Simon, Simon, listen *well*. Satan has demanded to have you, to sift *you* as wheat. 32. But I have prayed for you, that your faith may not fail; and when you are converted, strengthen your brethren." 33. And he said to Him, "Lord, I am ready to go with You both to prison and to death." 34. But He said, "I tell you, Peter, *the* cock shall in no wise crow today before you have denied knowing Me three times."	36. Simon Peter said to Him, "Lord, where are You going?" Jesus answered him, "Where I am going, you cannot follow Me now; but you shall follow Me afterwards." 37. Peter said to Him, "Why can't I follow You now? I will lay down my life for You." 38. Jesus answered him, "You will lay down your life for Me? Truly, truly I tell you, *the* cock shall not crow until you have denied Me three times."

a - Zech. 13:7

"Before the Cock Crows..."
Bob Taylor Photography

PASSOVER DAY NISAN 14 – TUESDAY NIGHT, APRIL 4 – 30 AD
325. THE BEGINNING OF THE FINAL MESSAGE TO HIS DISCIPLES
JOHN 14

1. "Let not your heart be troubled. You believe in God; believe also in Me.

2. In My Father's house are many dwelling places; if it were otherwise, I would have told you. I am going to prepare a place for you.

3. And if I go and prepare a place for you, I will come again and receive you to Myself; so that where I am, you may be also.

4. And where I am going you know, and the way you know."

5. Thomas said to Him, "Lord, we do not know where You are going; how then can we know the way?"

6. Jesus said to him, "I am the way, and the truth, and the life; no one comes to the Father except through Me.

7. If you had known Me, you would have known My Father also. But from this time forward, you know Him and have seen Him."

8. Philip said to Him, "Lord, show us the Father, and that will be sufficient for us."

9. Jesus said to him, "Have I been with you so long a time, and you have not known Me, Philip? The one who has seen Me has seen the Father; why then do you say, 'Show us the Father'?

10. Don't you believe that I am in the Father, and the Father is in Me? The words that I speak to you, I do not speak from My own self; but the Father Himself, Who dwells in Me, does the works.

11. Believe Me that I am in the Father and the Father is in Me; but if not, believe Me because of the works themselves.

12. Truly, truly I say to you, the one who believes in Me shall also do the works that I do; and greater works than these shall he do because I am going to the Father.

13. And whatever you shall ask in My name, this will I do that the Father may be glorified in the Son.

14. If you ask anything in My name, I will do *it*.

15. If you love Me, keep the commandments—namely, My commandments.

16. And I will ask the Father, and He shall give you another Comforter, that it may be with you throughout the age:

17. *Even* the Spirit of the truth, which the world cannot receive because it perceives it not, nor knows it; but you know it because it dwells with you, and shall be within you.

18. I will not leave you orphans; I will come to you. *(See Appendix C, p. 358)*

19. Yet a little while and the world shall see Me no longer; but you shall see Me. Because I live, you shall live also.

20. In that day, you shall know that I am in My Father, and you *are* in Me, and I am in you.

21. The one who has My commandments and is keeping them, that is the one who loves Me; and the one who loves Me shall be loved by My Father, and I will love him and will manifest Myself to him."

22. Judas (not Iscariot) said to him, "Lord, what has happened that You are about to manifest Yourself to us, and not to the world?"

23. Jesus answered and said to him, "If anyone loves Me, he will keep My word; and My Father will love him, and We will come to him and make Our abode with him.

24. The one who does not love Me does not keep My words; and the word that you hear is not Mine, but the Father's, Who sent Me.

25. I have spoken these things to you while I am yet present with you.

26. But *when* the Comforter *comes, even* the Holy Spirit, which the Father will send in My name, that one shall teach you all things, and shall bring to your remembrance everything that I have told you. *(See Appendix C, p. 358)*

27. Peace I leave with you; My peace I give to you; not as the world gives do I give *it* to you. Let not your heart be troubled, nor let it fear.

**PASSOVER DAY NISAN 14 – TUESDAY NIGHT, APRIL 4 – 30 AD
APPROXIMATELY 9 PM**

JOHN 14

28. You have heard Me say to you that I am going away, and *that* I will come to you *again*. If you loved Me, you would have rejoiced that I said, 'I am going to the Father' because My Father is greater than I.

29. And now I have told you before it happens, so that when it comes to pass, you may believe.

30. I will not speak with you much longer because the ruler of this world is coming; but he does not have a single thing in Me.

31. Yet *he comes* so that the world may know that I love the Father, and that I do exactly as the Father has commanded Me. Arise, let us go out."

326. SOME FINAL INSTRUCTIONS TO THE DISCIPLES

LUKE 22

35. And He said to them, "When I sent you without purse and provision bag and sandals, did you lack anything?" And they said, "Nothing."

36. Then He said to them, "Now, however, let the one who has a purse take *it, and* likewise *his* provision bag; and let the one who does not have a sword sell his garment and buy *one*.

37. For I say to you, that which has been written must yet be accomplished in Me: 'And He was reckoned with *the* lawless' [a]; for the things concerning Me have a fulfillment."

a - Isa. 53:12

327. TAKE TWO SWORDS

LUKE 22

38. And they said, "Lord, see, here *are* two swords." And He said to them, "It is enough."

328. THEY SING A HYMN AND LEAVE

MATTHEW 26

30. And after singing a hymn, they went out to the Mount of Olives.

MARK 14

26. And after singing a hymn, they went out to the Mount of Olives.

**329. JESUS CHRIST IS THE TRUE VINE—
LAST COMMANDS TO HIS DISCIPLES**

JOHN 15

1. "I am the true vine, and My Father is the husbandman.

2. He takes away every branch in Me *that* does not bear fruit; but He cleanses each one that bears fruit, in order that it may bear more fruit.

3. You are already clean through the word that I have spoken to you.

4. Dwell in Me, and I in you. As a branch cannot bear fruit of itself, but only if it remains in the vine, neither *can* you *bear fruit* unless you are dwelling in Me.

5. I am the vine, *and* you *are* the branches. The one who is dwelling in Me, and I in him, bears much fruit; because apart from Me you can do nothing.

6. If anyone does not dwell in Me, he is cast out as a branch, and is dried up; and men gather them and cast *them* into a fire, and they are burned.

PASSOVER DAY NISAN 14 – TUESDAY NIGHT, APRIL 4 – 30 AD
JOHN 15

7. If you dwell in Me, and My words dwell in you, you shall ask whatever you desire, and it shall come to pass for you.

8. In this is My Father glorified, that you bear much fruit; so shall you be My disciples.

9. As the Father has loved Me, I also have loved you; live in My love.

10. If you keep My commandments, you shall live in My love; just as I have kept My Father's commandments and live in His love.

11. These things I have spoken to you, in order that My joy may dwell in you, and *that* your joy may be full.

12. This is My commandment: that you love one another, as I have loved you.

13. No one has greater love than this: that one lay down his life for his friends.

14. You are My friends, if you do whatever I command you.

15. No longer do I call you servants, because the servant does not know what his master is doing. But I have called you friends because I have made known to you all *the* things that I have heard from My Father.

16. You yourselves did not choose Me, but I have personally chosen you, and ordained you, that you should go *forth* and bear fruit, and that your fruit should remain; so that whatever you shall ask the Father in My name, He may give you.

17. These things I command you, that you love one another.

18. If the world hates you, you know that it hated Me before *it hated* you.

19. If you were of the world, the world would love its own. However, because you are not of the world, but I have personally chosen you out of the world, the world hates you for this.

20. Remember the word that I spoke to you: a servant is not greater than his master. If they persecuted Me, they will persecute you also. If they kept My word, they will keep your *word* also.

21. But they will do all these things to you for My name's sake, because they do not know Him Who sent Me.

22. If I had not come and spoken to them, they would not have had sin; but now they have nothing to cover their sin.

23. The one who hates Me hates My Father also.

24. If I had not done among them the works that no other man has done, they would not have had sin; but now they have both seen and hated both Me and My Father.

25. But this has happened so that the saying might be fulfilled which is written in their law, 'They hated Me without *a* cause.' [a]

26. But when the Comforter has come, which I will send to you from the Father, *even* the Spirit of the truth, which proceeds from the Father, that one shall bear witness of Me. *(See Appendix C, p. 355)*

27. Then you also shall bear witness, because you have been with Me from *the* beginning."

a - Psa. 35:19; 69:4

330. FINAL WORDS OF ENCOURAGEMENT
JOHN 16

1. "I have spoken these things to you so that you will not be offended.

2. They shall cast you out of the synagogues; furthermore, the time is coming that everyone who kills you will think that he is rendering service to God.

3. And they shall do these things to you because they do not know the Father, nor Me.

4. But I have told you these things so that when the time comes, you may remember that I said *them* to you. However, I did not say these things to you at *the* beginning because I was with you.

5. But now I am going to Him Who sent Me; and none of you asks Me, 'Where are You going?'

6. But because I have spoken these things to you, grief has filled your hearts.

PASSOVER DAY NISAN 14 – TUESDAY NIGHT, APRIL 4 – 30 AD
JOHN 16

7. But I am telling you the truth. It is profitable for you that I go away because if I do not go away, the Comforter will not come to you. However, if I go, I will send it to you.

8. And when that one has come, it will convict the world concerning sin, and righteousness, and judgment: *(See Appendix C, p. 355)*

9. Concerning sin, because they do not believe in Me;

10. Concerning righteousness, because I am going to the Father and you no longer will see Me;

11. And concerning judgment, because the ruler of this world has been judged.

12. I have yet many things to tell you, but you are not able to bear them now.

13. However, when that one has come, *even* the Spirit of the truth, it will lead you into all truth because it shall not speak from itself, but whatever it shall hear, it shall speak. And it shall disclose to you the things to come.

14. That one shall glorify Me because it shall disclose to you *the things that* it receives from Me. *(See Appendix C, p. 355)*

15. Everything that the Father has is Mine; for this reason, I said that it shall receive from Me and shall disclose *these things* to you.

16. A little *while*, and you shall not see Me; and again a little *while*, and you shall see Me, because I am going to the Father."

17. Then *some* of His disciples said to one another, "What is this that He is saying to us, 'A little *while*, and you shall not see Me; and again a little *while*, and you shall see Me,' and, 'because I am going to the Father'? "

18. Therefore they said, "What is this that He is saying, the 'little *while*'? We do not understand what He is saying."

19. Then Jesus, knowing that they desired to ask Him, said to them, "*Why* are you inquiring among one another about this that I said, 'A little *while*, and you shall not see Me; and again a little *while*, and you shall see Me'?

20. Truly, truly I tell you, you shall weep and lament, but the world shall rejoice; and you shall be grieved, but your grief shall be turned into joy.

21. A woman when she is giving birth has grief because her time *of travail* has come; but after she gives birth to the child, she no longer remembers the anguish because of the joy that a child has been born into the world.

22. And likewise, you indeed have grief now; but I will see you again, and your heart shall rejoice, and no one shall take your joy from you. [a]

23. And in that day you shall ask Me nothing. Truly, truly I tell you, whatever you shall ask the Father in My name, He will give you.

24. Until this day, you have asked nothing in My name. Ask, and you shall receive, that your joy may be full.

25. These things I have spoken to you in allegories; but the time is coming when I will no longer speak to you in allegories, but I will plainly disclose to you *the things* of the Father.

26. In that day, you shall ask in My name; and I do not tell you that I will beseech the Father for you,

27. For the Father Himself loves you, because you have loved Me, and have believed that I came forth from God.

28. I came forth from the Father and have come into the world; again, I am leaving the world and am going to the Father."

29. *Then* His disciples said to Him, "Behold, now You are speaking plainly and are not speaking *in* an allegory.

30. Now we know that You understand all things, and do not need to have someone ask You. By this we believe that You came forth from God."

31. Jesus answered them, "Do you now believe?

a - Isa. 66:14

PASSOVER DAY NISAN 14 – TUESDAY NIGHT, APRIL 4 – 30 AD
331. ALL WILL BE SCATTERED.
JESUS HAS OVERCOME THE WORLD
JOHN 16

32. Listen, the time is coming, and has already come, that you shall be scattered each to his own, and you shall leave Me alone; and *yet* I am not alone because the Father is with Me.
33. These things I have spoken to you, so that in Me you may have peace. In the world you shall have tribulation. But be courageous! I have overcome the world."

332. JESUS COMES TO GETHSEMANE TO PRAY

MATTHEW 26	MARK 14	LUKE 22
36. Then Jesus came with them to a place called Gethsemane; and He said to His disciples, "Sit here, while I go onward and pray."	32. Then they came to a place that was *called* Gethsemane; and He said to His disciples, "Sit here while I pray."	39. Then He left *the house and* went, as He was accustomed, to the Mount of Olives; and His disciples also followed Him.

333. JESUS TAKES PETER, JAMES AND JOHN WITH HIM

MATTHEW 26	MARK 14	LUKE 22
37. And He took with *Him* Peter and the two sons of Zebedee, *and* He began to be very melancholy and deeply depressed. 38. Then He said to them, "My soul is deeply grieved, [a] even to death. Stay here and watch with Me."	33. And He took Peter and James and John with Him; and He began to be deeply troubled and heavy-hearted. 34. And He said to them, "My soul is filled with anguish, even to death; [a] remain here and watch."	40. And when He arrived at the place, He said to them, "Pray *that you* do not enter into temptation."

a - Psa. 42:5-6

Garden at Gethsemane

PASSOVER DAY NISAN 14 – TUESDAY NIGHT, APRIL 4 – 30 AD
APPROXIMATELY 9:30 PM - 12:30 AM
334. JESUS PRAYS FOR THREE HOURS

MATTHEW 26	MARK 14	LUKE 22
39. And after going forward a little, He fell on His face, praying, and saying, "My Father, if it be possible, let this cup pass from Me; nevertheless, not as I will, but as You *will*." 40. Then He came to His disciples and found them sleeping. And *He* said to Peter, "What! Were you not able to watch with Me one hour? 41. Watch and pray, so that you do not enter into temptation; the spirit indeed *is* willing, but the flesh is weak." 42. The second time He went again *and* prayed, saying, "My Father, if this cup cannot pass from Me unless I drink it, Your will be done." 43. Now when He came to them, He found them asleep again, because their eyes were heavy. 44. And leaving them, He went again and prayed the third time, saying the same thing.	35. Then He went forward a little, dropped to the ground, and prayed that, if it were possible, the hour might pass from Him. 36. And He said, "Abba, Father, all things *are* possible with You. Remove this cup from Me! Yet not what I will, but what You *will*." 37. Then He came and found them sleeping. And He said to Peter, "Simon, are you sleeping? Were you not able to watch one hour? 38. Watch and pray, so that you do not enter into temptation. The spirit truly *is* willing, but the flesh *is* weak." 39. And again He went away and prayed, saying the same thing. 40. And when He returned, He again found them sleeping, for their eyes were heavy; and they did not know what to answer Him.	41. And He withdrew from them about a stone's throw; and falling to *His* knees, He prayed, 42. Saying, "Father, if You are willing to take away this cup from Me—; nevertheless, not My will, but Your *will* be done." 43. Then an angel from heaven appeared to Him, strengthening Him. 44. And being in agony, He prayed more earnestly. And His sweat became as great drops of blood falling down to the ground. 45. And after rising up from prayer, He came to *His* disciples *and* found them sleeping for grief. 46. Then He said to them, "Why are you sleeping? Arise and pray, so that you do not enter into temptation."

335. THE LORD'S PRAYER
JOHN 17

1. Jesus spoke these words, and lifted up His eyes to heaven and said, "Father, the hour has come; glorify Your own Son, so that Your Son may also glorify You;
2. Since You have given Him authority over all flesh, in order that He may give eternal life to all whom You have given Him.
3. For this is eternal life, that they may know You, the only true God, and Jesus Christ, Whom You did send.
4. I have glorified You on the earth. I have finished the work that You gave Me to do.
5. And now, Father, glorify Me with Your own self, with the glory that I had with You before the world existed.
6. I have manifested Your name to the men whom You have given Me out of the world. They were Yours, and You have given them to Me, and they have kept Your Word.
7. Now they have known that all things that You have given Me are from You.
8. For I have given them the words that You gave to Me; and they have received *them* and truly have known that I came from You; and they have believed that You did send Me.

PASSOVER DAY NISAN 14 – WEDNESDAY MORNING, APRIL 5 – 30 AD
JOHN 17

9. I am praying for them; I am not praying for the world, but for those whom You have given Me, for they are Yours.

10. All Mine are Yours, and all Yours *are* Mine; and I have been glorified in them.

11. And I am no longer in the world, but these are in the world, and I am coming to You. Holy Father, keep them in Your name, those whom You have given Me, so that they may be one, even as We *are one.*

12. When I was with them in the world, I kept them in Your name. I protected those whom You have given Me, and not one of them has perished except the son of perdition, in order that the Scriptures might be fulfilled. [a]

13. But now I am coming to You; and these things I am speaking *while yet* in the world, that they may have My joy fulfilled in them.

14. I have given them Your words, and the world has hated them because they are not of the world, just as I am not of the world.

15. I do not pray that You would take them out of the world, but that You would keep them from the evil one.

16. They are not of the world, just as I am not of the world.

17. Sanctify them in Your truth; Your Word is the truth.

18. Even as You did send Me into the world, I also have sent them into the world.

19. And for their sakes I sanctify Myself, so that they also may be sanctified in *Your* truth.

20. I do not pray for these only, but also for those who shall believe in Me through their word;

21. That they all may be one, even as You, Father, *are* in Me, and I in You; that they also may be one in Us, in order that the world may believe that You did send Me.

22. And I have given them the glory that You gave *to* Me, in order that they may be one, in the same way *that* We are one:

23. I in them, and You in Me, that they may be perfected into one; and that the world may know that You did send Me, and have loved them as You have loved Me.

24. Father, I desire that those whom You have given Me may also be with Me where I am, so that they may behold My glory, which You have given Me; because You did love Me before *the* foundation of *the* world.

25. Righteous Father, the world has not known You; but I have known You, and these have known that You did send Me.

26. And I have made known Your name to them, and will make *it* known; so that the love with which You have loved Me may be in them, and I in them."

a - Psa. 41:9; 109:8

336. THE TIME OF THE BETRAYAL
APPROXIMATELY 12:20 AM

MATTHEW 26	MARK 14
45. Then He came to His disciples and said to them, "Sleep on now, and take your rest. Behold, the hour has drawn near, and the Son of man is betrayed into *the* hands of sinners.	41. And He came the third time, and said to them, "Sleep on now, and take your rest. It is enough. The hour has come. Behold, the Son of man is betrayed into the hands of sinners.
46. Arise! Let us be going. Look, the one who is betraying Me is approaching."	42. Arise! Let us be going. Look, the one who is betraying Me is approaching."

PASSOVER DAY NISAN 14 – WEDNESDAY MORNING, APRIL 5 – 30 AD

337. JUDAS BETRAYS JESUS WITH A KISS

MATTHEW 26	MARK 14	LUKE 22	JOHN 18

47. And while He was yet speaking, Judas, one of the twelve, suddenly appeared, and with him a great crowd with swords and clubs, from the chief priests and elders of the people.
48. Now the one who was betraying Him gave them a sign, saying, "Whomever I shall kiss, He is *the One*. Arrest Him!"
49. And as soon as he came to Jesus, he said, "Hail, Rabbi," and earnestly kissed Him.

43. And immediately, while He was speaking, Judas, being one of the twelve, came up with a great multitude with swords and clubs, from the chief priests and the scribes and the elders.
44. Now the one who was betraying Him had given them a sign, saying, "Whomever I shall kiss, He is *the one*. Arrest Him and take Him securely away."
45. And as soon as he came up to Him, he said, "Master, Master," and kissed Him earnestly.

47. And while He was still speaking, a crowd suddenly *appeared*, with the one who was called Judas, one of the twelve, going in front of them; and he came near to Jesus to kiss Him.
48. But Jesus said to him, "Judas, are you betraying the Son of man with a kiss?"

1. After saying these things, Jesus went out with His disciples *to a place* beyond the winter stream of Kidron, where *there* was a garden into which He and His disciples entered.
2. And Judas, who was betraying Him, also knew of the place because Jesus had often gathered there with His disciples.
3. Then Judas, after receiving a band and officers from the chief priests and Pharisees, came there with torches and lamps and weapons.
4. Jesus, therefore, knowing all *the* things that were coming upon Him, went forward *and* said to them, "Whom are you seeking?"
5. They answered Him, "Jesus the Nazarean." Jesus said to them, "I AM." And Judas, who was betraying Him, was also standing with them.
6. But when He said to them, "I AM," they went backward and fell to *the* ground.
7. Then He asked them again, "Whom are you seeking?" And they said, "Jesus the Nazarean."
8. Jesus answered, "I told you that I AM. Therefore, if you are seeking Me, allow these to go their way";

Ancient Olive Tree in the Garden of Gethsemane

PASSOVER DAY NISAN 14 – WEDNESDAY MORNING, APRIL 5 – 30 AD

JOHN 18

9. So that the saying might be fulfilled which He had said, "Of those whom You have given Me, not one of them have I lost."

338. PETER CUTS OFF AN EAR OF THE HIGH PRIEST'S SERVANT— JESUS HEALS HIM

MATTHEW 26	MARK 14	LUKE 22	JOHN 18

MATTHEW 26

50. But Jesus said to him, "Friend, for what *purpose* have you come?" Then they came *and* laid their hands on Jesus, and arrested Him.
51. And one of those with Jesus suddenly stretched out his hand, drew his sword, and struck the servant of the high priest, cutting off his ear.
52. Then Jesus said to him, "Put your sword back in its place; for all who take up *the* sword shall die by *the* sword.
53. Don't you realize that I have the power to call upon the Father at this time, and He will furnish Me with more than twelve legions of angels?
54. But how then shall the Scriptures be fulfilled? For this is ordained to be."
55. At that point Jesus said to the crowd, "Have you come out to take Me with swords and clubs, as against a robber? I sat day after day with you, teaching in the temple, and you did not arrest Me.

MARK 14

46. Then they laid their hands on Him and arrested Him.
47. But a certain one of those standing near drew out a sword and struck the servant of the high priest, cutting off his ear. [a]
48. And Jesus answered *and* said to them, "Have you come out to take Me with swords and clubs, as against a thief?
49. I was with you daily, teaching in the temple, and you did not arrest Me; but *this is done* so that the Scriptures may be fulfilled."

LUKE 22

49. And when those who were with Him saw what was about to happen, they said to Him, "Lord, shall we strike with *the* sword?"
50. Then a certain one of them struck the servant of the high priest and cut off his right ear.
51. But Jesus answered *and* said, "That is enough!" Then He touched his ear *and* healed him.
52. And Jesus said to those who had come out against Him, *the* chief priests and captains of the temple and elders, "Have you come out, as against a thief, with swords and clubs?
53. When I was with you daily in the temple, you did not stretch out *your* hands against Me; but this is your hour, and the power of darkness."

JOHN 18

10. Then Simon Peter, who had a sword, drew it out and struck the servant of the high priest, and cut off his right ear. And the servant's name was Malchus.
11. But Jesus said to Peter, "Put your sword into the sheath; shall I not drink the cup that the Father has given Me?"
12. Then the band and the chief captain and the officers of the Jews took hold of Jesus, and bound Him;

PASSOVER DAY NISAN 14 – WEDNESDAY MORNING, APRIL 5 – 30 AD
339. ALL WAS DONE TO FULFILL PROPHECY

MATTHEW 26	MARK 14
56. But all this has happened so that the Scriptures of the prophets might be fulfilled." Then all the disciples forsook Him and fled.	50. Then they all forsook Him and fled. 51. Now a certain young man was following Him, having a linen cloth wrapped around *his* naked *body*; and the young men seized him, 52. But he *escaped*, leaving the linen cloth behind, and ran from them naked.

340. JESUS IS LED AWAY TO THE PRIEST'S HOUSE

MATTHEW 26	MARK 14	LUKE 22	JOHN 18
57. But those who had arrested Jesus led *Him* away to Caiaphas the high priest, where the scribes and the elders were assembled.	53. Then they led Jesus away to the high priest. And all the chief priests and the elders and the scribes assembled with him.	54. And after arresting Him, they led *Him away* and brought Him into the house of the high priest...	13. And they led Him away to Annas first; for he was *the* father-in-law of Caiaphas, who was high priest that year. 14. Now it was Caiaphas who had given counsel to the Jews that it was profitable for one man to perish for the people.

341. PETER FOLLOWS THEM INTO THE COURTYARD

MATTHEW 26	MARK 14	LUKE 22	JOHN 18
58. And Peter followed Him from a distance, even to the court of the high priest; and after going inside, he sat down with the officers to see *what* the end *would be*.	54. Now Peter followed at a distance, all the way to the court of the high priest; and he was sitting inside with the officers and warming himself at the fire.	54. ...Now Peter was following at a distance. 55. And when they had kindled a fire in *the* middle of the court, and had sat down together, Peter sat among them.	15. But Simon Peter and the other disciple followed Jesus. And that disciple was known to the high priest, and entered with Jesus into the court of the high priest. 16. But Peter stood outside at the door. Then the other disciple, who was known to the high priest, went out and spoke to the doorkeeper, and brought Peter in.

PASSOVER DAY NISAN 14 – WEDNESDAY MORNING, APRIL 5 – 30 AD

Herod's Palace and Courtyard—Model City Jerusalem

JOHN 18

18. Now the servants and the officers had made a fire, for it was cold; and they were standing *there* warming themselves, and Peter was *also* standing and warming himself.

342. ANNAS QUESTIONS JESUS AND SENDS HIM TO CAIAPHAS
JOHN 18

19. Then the high priest questioned Jesus concerning His disciples and concerning His teachings.
20. Jesus answered him, "I spoke openly to the world; I always taught in the synagogue and in the temple, where the Jews always assemble, and I spoke nothing in secret.
21. Why do you question Me? Ask those who have heard what I spoke to them; behold, they know what I said."

APPROXIMATELY 2 AM
JOHN 18

22. But after He said these things, one of the officers who was standing by struck Jesus on the face, saying, "Do You answer the high priest in that way?"
23. Jesus answered him, "If I have spoken evil, testify of the evil; but if well, why do you strike Me?"
24. *Then* Annas sent Him bound to Caiaphas, the high priest.

PASSOVER DAY NISAN 14 – WEDNESDAY MORNING, APRIL 5 – 30 AD
343. THE CHIEF PRIESTS ILLEGALLY CONDEMN JESUS

MATTHEW 26	MARK 14	LUKE 22

MATTHEW 26

59. Now the chief priests and the elders and the whole Sanhedrin sought false evidence against Jesus, so that they might put Him to death;
60. But *they* did not find *any*. Although many false witnesses came forward, they did not find *any evidence*.
61. Then at *the* last, two false witnesses came forward *and* said, "This *man* said, 'I have the power to destroy the temple of God, and to rebuild it in three days.' "
62. And the high priest rose up *and* said to Him, "Have You no answer for what these are testifying against You?"
63. But Jesus was silent. And the high priest answered *and* said to Him, "I adjure You by the living God that You tell us if You are the Christ, the Son of God."
64. Jesus said to him, "You have said *it*. Moreover, I say to you, in the future you shall see the Son of man sitting at *the* right hand of power, and coming in the clouds of heaven."
65. Then the high priest ripped his *own* garments, saying, "He has blasphemed! Why do we need any more witnesses? Behold, you have just now heard His blasphemy. [a]
66. What do you think?" They answered *and* said, "He is deserving of death!"
67. Then they spit in His face and hit Him with their fists; and some struck *Him* with rods,
68. Saying, "Prophesy to us, Christ. Who is the one that struck You?"

MARK 14

55. And the chief priests and the whole Sanhedrin were trying to find testimony against Jesus, to put Him to death; but they did not find *any*.
56. For many bore false witness against Him, but their testimonies did not agree.
57. And some rose up and bore false witness against Him, saying,
58. "We heard Him say, 'I will destroy this temple made with hands, and in three days I will build another made without hands.' "
59. But neither did their testimonies agree with one another.
60. Then the high priest stood up in the center *and* questioned Jesus, saying, "Have You nothing to *say in* answer *to* what these are testifying against You?"
61. But He remained silent and answered nothing. Again the high priest questioned Him, and said to Him, "Are You the Christ, the Son of the Blessed?"
62. And Jesus said, "I AM. And you shall see the Son of man sitting at *the* right hand of power, and coming with the clouds of heaven." [a]
63. Then the high priest ripped his *own* garments *and* said, "What further need do we have of witnesses?
64. You have heard the blasphemy! What is your verdict?" And they all condemned Him to be deserving of death.
65. Then some began to spit on Him, and to cover His face and strike Him with their fists, saying to Him, "Prophesy!" And the officers struck Him with the palms of their hands.

LUKE 22

63. Then the men who were holding Jesus mocked Him *and* beat *Him*.
64. And after covering His *head*, they *repeatedly* struck His face and asked Him, saying, "Prophesy! Who is it that struck You?"
65. And many other things they blasphemously said against Him.

Kidron Valley

Hills Around Jerusalem

a - Psa. 110:1; Dan. 7:9-14

PASSOVER DAY NISAN 14 – WEDNESDAY MORNING, APRIL 5 – 30 AD

344. PETER DENIES JESUS THREE TIMES

MATTHEW 26	MARK 14	LUKE 22	JOHN 18

69. Now Peter was sitting outside in the court; and a maid came to him, saying, "You also were with Jesus the Galilean."
70. But he denied *it* before everyone, saying, "I don't know what you are talking about."
71. And after he went out into the porch, another *maid* saw him and said to those there, "This man was also with Jesus the Nazarean."
72. Then again he denied *it* with an oath, *saying*, "I do not know the man."
73. After a little *while*, those who were standing by came to Peter and said, "Truly, you also are one of them, for even your speech shows *that* you *are*."
74. Then he began to curse and to swear, *saying*, "I do not know the man." And immediately a cock crowed.

66. Now Peter was in the court below; *and* one of the maids of the high priest came,
67. And saw Peter warming himself; *and* after looking at him, she said, "Now you were with Jesus the Nazarene."
68. But he denied *it*, saying, "I do not know *Him* or even understand what you are saying." And he went out onto the porch, and a cock crowed.
69. Then the maid saw him again *and* began to say to those who were standing by, "This is *one* of them."
70. And again he denied *it*. And after a little while, those who were standing by again said to Peter, "Truly you are *one* of them, for you are indeed a Galilean, and your speech confirms *it*."
71. Then he began to curse and to swear, *saying*, "I do not know this man of Whom you are speaking."

56. And a certain maid saw him sitting by the light; and after looking at him intently, she said, "Now this one was with Him."
57. But he denied Him, saying, "Woman, I do not know Him."
58. And after a little *while*, another saw him *and* said, "You also are *one* of them." But Peter said, "Man, I am not."
59. Now after about an hour had passed, a certain other *man* strongly affirmed, saying, "In truth, this one also was with Him, for he is indeed a Galilean."
60. And Peter said, "Man, I do not know what you are talking about." And immediately, while he was yet speaking, the cock crowed.
61. Then the Lord turned *and* looked at Peter; and Peter remembered the word of the Lord, how He had said to him, "Before *the* cock crows, you shall deny Me three times."

17. Then the maid who was the doorkeeper said to Peter, "Are you not also a disciple of this man?" He said, "I am not."
25. Now as Simon Peter was standing and warming himself, they said to him, "Are you not also *one* of His disciples?" He denied *it*, and said, "I am not."
26. One of the servants of the high priest, being a kinsman *of the one* whose ear Peter had cut off, said, "Didn't I see you in the garden with Him?"
27. Then Peter again denied *it*; and immediately a cock crowed.

PASSOVER DAY NISAN 14 – WEDNESDAY MORNING, APRIL 5 – 30 AD
APPROXIMATELY 3:30 – 4:30 AM

MATTHEW 26	MARK 14	LUKE 22
75. And Peter remembered the words of Jesus, Who had said to him, "Before *the* cock crows, you yourself shall deny Me three times." And he went out and wept bitterly.	72. And the cock crowed the second time. Then Peter remembered the words that Jesus had spoken to him: "Before the cock crows twice, you shall deny Me three times." And when he thought about this, he wept.	62. And Peter went outside *and* wept bitterly.

APPROXIMATELY 5:30 – 6 AM
345. THE SANHEDRIN CONDEMNS JESUS AND SENDS HIM TO PILATE

MATTHEW 27	MARK 15	LUKE 22	JOHN 18
1. Now when morning came, all the chief priests and the elders of the people took counsel against Jesus, so that they might put Him to death. 2. And after binding Him, they led *Him* away and delivered Him up to Pontius Pilate, the governor.	1. Now as soon as it was morning, the chief priests took counsel with the elders and *the* scribes and the whole Sanhedrin; *and* after binding Jesus, they led *Him* away and delivered *Him* up to Pilate.	66. Now as soon as it was day, the elders of the people assembled together, *with* both *the* chief priests and *the* scribes, and they led Him into their Sanhedrin, saying, 67. "If You are the Christ, tell us." And He said to them, "If I should tell you, you would not believe *Me* at all; 68. And if I should also ask *you*, you would not answer Me at all, nor let *Me* go. 69. Hereafter shall the Son of man be sitting at *the* right hand of the power of God." [a] 70. And they all said, "Then You are the Son of God?" And He said to them, "I am that *one, as* you say." 71. Then they said, "What need do we have of any other witness? For we ourselves have heard from His *own* mouth."	28. Now then, they led Jesus from Caiaphas to the judgment hall, and it was early. But they did not go into the judgment hall, so that they would not be defiled, but that they might eat the Passover.

Old Jerusalem Wall

a - Psa. 110:1; Dan. 7:9-14

PASSOVER DAY NISAN 14 – WEDNESDAY MORNING, APRIL 5 – 30 AD

LUKE 23

1. And when the entire assembly of them arose, they led Him to Pilate.

346. JUDAS REPENTS AND HANGS HIMSELF—
THE CHIEF PRIESTS BUY POTTER'S FIELD

MATTHEW 27

3. Now when Judas, who had betrayed Him, saw that He was condemned, he changed his mind *and* returned the thirty pieces of silver to the chief priests and the elders, saying,

4. "I have sinned and have betrayed innocent blood." But they said, "What *is that* to us? You see *to it* yourself."

5. And after throwing down the pieces of silver in the temple, he went out and hanged himself.

6. But the chief priests took the pieces of silver *and* said, "It is not lawful to put them into the treasury, since it is *the* price of blood."

7. And after taking counsel, they bought a potter's field with the *pieces of silver*, for a burial ground for strangers.

8. Therefore that field is called The Field of Blood to this day.

9. Then was fulfilled that which was spoken by Jeremiah the prophet, saying, "And I took the thirty pieces of silver, the price of Him on Whom a price was set, Whom they of *the* sons of Israel set a price on, [b]

10. And gave them for the field of the potter, as *the* Lord had directed me." [b]

ACTS 1

15. And in those days, Peter stood up in *the* midst of the disciples (now *the* number of names together was about a hundred and twenty) *and* said,

16. "Men *and* brethren, it was necessary for this scripture to be fulfilled, which the Holy Spirit spoke before by *the* mouth of David concerning Judas, who became a guide to those who took Jesus; [a]

17. For he was numbered with us, and had obtained a part of this ministry.

18. (Now then, this *man* acquired a field with the reward of unrighteousness, and after falling headlong burst in *the* middle, and all his bowels gushed out.

19. And it became known to all those dwelling in Jerusalem, so that this field is called in their own language Aceldama that is, 'The field of blood.')

a - Psa. 41:9 b - Zech. 11:13

293

PASSOVER DAY NISAN 14 – WEDNESDAY MORNING, APRIL 5 – 30 AD
347. JESUS IS CONDEMNED BEFORE PILATE—
HE QUESTIONS JESUS

MATTHEW 27	MARK 15	LUKE 22	JOHN 18
11. Then Jesus stood before the governor; and the governor questioned Him, saying, "Are You the King of the Jews?" And Jesus said to him, "*It is as you said.*" 12. And when He was accused by the chief priests and the elders, He answered nothing. 13. Then Pilate said to Him, "Don't You hear how many things they testify against You?" 14. And He did not answer even one word to him, so that the governor was greatly amazed.	2. And Pilate asked Him, "Are You the King of the Jews?" And He answered *and* said to him, "*It is as* you say." 3. And the chief priests were vehemently accusing Him of many things; but He answered nothing. 4. Then Pilate asked Him again, saying, "Have You no answer? See how many things they are testifying against You." 5. But Jesus did not say anything at all, so that Pilate was astonished.	2. And they began to accuse Him, saying, "We found this *man* subverting the nation and forbidding to give tribute to Caesar, claiming *that He* Himself is Christ, a King." 3. But Pilate questioned Him, saying, "Are You the King of the Jews?" And He answered *and* said, "*It is as* you say." 4. Then Pilate said to the chief priests and the crowds, "I find nothing blameworthy in this man."	29. Therefore, Pilate came out to them and said, "What accusation do you bring against this man?" 30. They answered and said to him, "If He were not an evildoer, we would not have delivered Him up to you."

348. PILATE SENDS JESUS TO HEROD
LUKE 23

5. But they were insistent, saying, "He stirs up the people, teaching throughout all of Judea, beginning from Galilee even to here."

6. And when he heard Galilee *named*, Pilate asked whether the man were a Galilean;

7. And after determining that He was from Herod's jurisdiction, he sent Him to Herod, *since* he also was in Jerusalem in those days.

8. And when Herod saw Jesus, he rejoiced greatly; for he had long been desiring to see Him because he had heard many things about Him, and he was hoping to see a miracle done by Him.

9. And he questioned Him with many words; but He answered him nothing.

10. All the while, the chief priests and the scribes stood vehemently accusing Him.

11. Then Herod and his soldiers treated Him with contempt; and after mocking *Him*, he put a splendid robe on Him *and* sent Him back to Pilate.

12. And on that same day, Pilate and Herod became friends with each other, because before there was enmity between them.

PASSOVER DAY NISAN 14 – WEDNESDAY MORNING, APRIL 5 – 30 AD
349. PILATE FINDS JESUS INNOCENT

LUKE 23	JOHN 18

LUKE 23

13. And when Pilate had called together the chief priests and the rulers and the people,
14. He said to them, "You brought this man to me as one who was turning away the people; and behold, I have examined *Him* in your presence *and* have found nothing blameworthy in this man concerning *the* accusation which you bring against Him;
15. Nor even *has* Herod; for I sent you to him, and observe, nothing worthy of death was done by Him.

JOHN 18

31. Then Pilate said to them, "You take Him and judge Him according to your *own* law." But the Jews said to him, "It is not lawful for us to put anyone to death";
32. So that the saying of Jesus might be fulfilled, which He had spoken to signify by what death He was about to die.
33. Then Pilate returned to the judgment hall and called Jesus, and said to Him, "Are You the King of the Jews?"
34. Jesus answered him, "Do you ask this of yourself, or did others say *it* to you concerning Me?"
35. Pilate answered Him, "Am I a Jew? The chief priests and your own nation have delivered You up to me. What have You done?"
36. Jesus answered, "My kingdom is not of this world. If My kingdom were of this world, then would My servants fight, so that I might not be delivered up to the Jews. However, My kingdom is not of this world."
37. Pilate therefore answered Him, "Then You are a king?" Jesus answered, "*As* you say, I am a king. For this *purpose* I was born, and for this *reason* I came into the world, that I may bear witness to the truth. Everyone who is of the truth hears My voice."
38. Pilate said to Him, "What is truth?" And after saying this, he went out again to the Jews and said to them, "I do not find any fault in Him.

350. PILATE RELEASES BARABBAS AND CRUCIFIES JESUS – 8 AM

MATTHEW 27	MARK 15	LUKE 23	JOHN 18
15. Now at *the* feast, the governor was accustomed to release one prisoner to the multitude, whomever they wished. 16. And they had at that time a notorious prisoner called Barabbas.	6. Now at *the* feast he *customarily* released to them one prisoner, whomever they asked. 7. And there was one called Barabbas, who was bound *in chains* with those who had made insurrection *and* who had committed murder during the insurrection.	16. Therefore, after I chastise Him, I will release *Him*." 17. Now *of* necessity, he had to release one to them at *the* feast. 18. But they all cried out at once, saying, "Away with this *man*, and release Barabbas to us."	39. And it is a custom with you that I release one to you at the Passover. Do you then desire *that* I release the King of the Jews to you?" 40. But they all shouted again, saying, "Not this one, but Barabbas." Now Barabbas was a robber.

PASSOVER DAY NISAN 14 – WEDNESDAY MORNING, APRIL 5 – 30 AD

MATTHEW 27

17. Therefore, when they had gathered together, Pilate said to them, "Whom do you desire *that* I release to you? Barabbas, or Jesus Who is called Christ?"

18. For he understood that they had delivered Him up because of envy.

19. Now as he sat on the judgment seat, his wife sent *a message* to him, saying, "*Let there be* nothing between you and that righteous *man*, for I have suffered many things today in a dream because of Him."

20. But the chief priests and the elders persuaded the multitudes to demand Barabbas, and to destroy Jesus.

21. Then the governor answered *and* said to them, "Which of the two do you desire *that* I release to you?" And they said, "Barabbas."

22. Pilate said to them, "What then shall I do with Jesus Who is called Christ?" They all said to him, "Let *Him* be crucified!"

23. And the governor said, "Why? What evil did He commit?" But they shouted *all* the more, saying, "Let *Him* be crucified!"

MARK 15

8. Then the multitude began to shout aloud, urging *Pilate to do* as he had always done for them.

9. And Pilate answered them, saying, "Do you desire to have me release the King of the Jews to you?"

10. For he knew that the chief priests had delivered Him up because of envy.

11. But the chief priests stirred up the crowd *to ask* him to release Barabbas to them instead.

12. And again Pilate answered, saying to them, "What then would you have me do *with Him* Whom you call King of the Jews?"

13. And again they shouted, "Crucify Him!"

14. Then Pilate said to them, "What evil then did He commit?" But they shouted all the more, "Crucify Him!"

LUKE 23

19. *He was* the one who had been cast into prison on account of making a certain insurrection in the city and *committing* murder.

20. Therefore, Pilate again called to *them,* wishing to release Jesus.

21. But they kept crying out, saying, "Crucify *Him,* crucify Him!"

22. And a third *time* he said to them, "But what evil did this *man* commit? I have not found any cause *worthy* of death in Him. Therefore, after chastising Him, I will release *Him.*"

23. But they were urgent with loud voices, asking for Him to be crucified. And their voices, and *those* of the chief priests, prevailed.

PASSOVER DAY NISAN 14 – WEDNESDAY MORNING, APRIL 5 – 30 AD
351. PILATE WASHES HIS HANDS IN A SHOW OF INNOCENCY
MATTHEW 27

24. Now Pilate, seeing that he was accomplishing nothing, but *that* a riot was developing instead, took water *and* washed *his* hands before the multitude, saying, "I am guiltless of the blood of this righteous *man*. You see *to it*."
25. And all the people answered *and* said, "His blood *be* on us and on our children."

352. PILATE RELEASES BARABBAS –
JESUS IS BEATEN AND SCOURGED

MATTHEW 27	MARK 15	LUKE 22	JOHN 19
26. Then he released Barabbas to them; but after scourging Jesus, he delivered *Him* up so that He might be crucified.	15. So Pilate, willing to do whatever would satisfy the crowd, released Barabbas to them. And after he had scourged Jesus, he delivered Him up to be crucified.	24. Then Pilate decreed *that* their request be granted.	1. Then Pilate therefore took Jesus and scourged *Him*.
27. Then the governor's soldiers, after taking Jesus with *them* into the Praetorium, gathered the entire band against Him;	16. Then the soldiers led Him away into the court, which is *named the* Praetorium, and they called together the whole band.	25. And he released to them the one whom they had asked for, who on account of insurrection and murder had been cast into prison, but he delivered Jesus up to their will.	2. And after platting a crown of thorns, the soldiers put *it* on His head; and they threw a purple cloak over Him,
28. And they stripped Him *and* put a scarlet cloak around Him.	17. And they put a purple robe on Him; and after weaving a crown of thorns, *they* put *it* on Him;		3. And *kept on* saying, "Hail, King of the Jews!" And they struck Him with the palms of their hands.
29. And after platting a crown of thorns, they put *it* on His head, and a rod in His right hand; and bowing *on* their knees before Him, they mocked Him, and *kept on* saying, "Hail, King of the Jews!"	18. And they began to salute Him, and *kept on saying*, "Hail, King of the Jews!"		4. Then Pilate went out again and said to them, "Behold, I bring Him out to you, so that you may know that I do not find any fault in Him."
30. Then, after spitting on Him, they took the rod and struck *Him* on the head.	19. Then they struck His head with a rod, and spit on Him; and kneeling *down*, they bowed in worship to Him.		5. Then Jesus went out, wearing the crown of thorns and the purple cloak; and he said to them, "Behold the man!"
31. When they were done mocking Him, they took the cloak off Him; and they put His own garments on Him and led Him away to crucify Him.	20. And when they had *finished* mocking Him, they took the purple robe off Him and put His own garments on Him; and they led Him out to crucify Him.		

297

PASSOVER DAY NISAN 14 – WEDNESDAY MORNIG, APRIL 5 – 30 AD

353. PILATE HAS SECOND THOUGHTS ABOUT CRUCIFYING JESUS

JOHN 19

6. But when the chief priests and the officers saw Him, they cried aloud, saying, "Crucify *Him*, crucify *Him*!" Pilate said to them, "You take Him and crucify *Him* because I do not find any fault in Him."

7. The Jews answered him, "We have a law, and according to our law it is mandatory that He die, because He made Himself *the* Son of God."

8. Therefore, when Pilate heard this saying, he was even more afraid.

9. And he went into the judgment hall again, and said to Jesus, "Where have You come from?" But Jesus did not give him an answer.

10. Then Pilate said to Him, "Why don't You speak to me? Don't You know that I have authority to crucify You, and authority to release You?"

11. Jesus answered, "You would not have any authority against Me if it were not given to you from above. For this reason, the one who delivered Me to you has *the* greater sin."

12. Because of this *saying*, Pilate sought to release Him; but the Jews cried out, saying, "If you release this *man*, you are not a friend of Caesar. Everyone who makes himself a king speaks against Caesar."

13. Therefore, after hearing this saying, Pilate *had* Jesus led out, and sat down on the judgment seat at a place called *the* Pavement; but in Hebrew, Gabbatha.

14. (Now it was *the* preparation of the Passover, and about the sixth hour.) And he said to the Jews, "Behold your King!"

15. But they cried aloud, "Away, away *with Him*! Crucify Him!" Pilate said to them, "Shall I crucify your King?" The chief priests answered, "We have no king but Caesar."

Jerusalem Wall

Way of the Cross—Via Dolorosa—Jerusalem

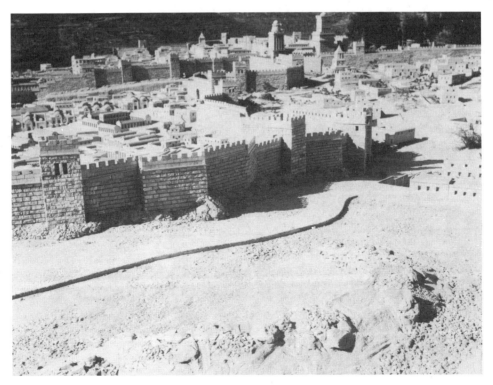

Golgotha—Model City Jerusalem

PASSOVER DAY NISAN 14 – WEDNESDAY MORNING, APRIL 5 – 30 AD
354. THE SOLDIERS LEAD JESUS AWAY TO BE CRUCIFIED, AND MAKE SIMON OF CYRENE CARRY HIS CROSS

MATTHEW 27	MARK 15	LUKE 23	JOHN 19

MATTHEW 27

32. Now as they came out, they found a Cyrenean man named Simon; *and* they compelled him to carry His cross.
33. And after coming to a place called Golgotha, which is called Place of a Skull,

MARK 15

21. Then they compelled one who was passing by coming from a field, Simon *the* Cyrenian, the father of Alexander and Rufus, to carry His cross.
22. And they brought Him to *the* place *named* Golgotha; which is, being interpreted, *"The* Place of a Skull."

LUKE 23

26. And as they led Him away, they laid hold on a certain Cyrenian *named* Simon, who was coming from a field; *and* they put the cross on him, that he might carry *it* behind Jesus.
27. And following Him was a great multitude of people with *many* women, who also were bewailing and lamenting Him.
28. But Jesus turned to them *and* said, "Daughters of Jerusalem, do not weep for Me, but weep for yourselves and for your children.
29. For behold, *the* days are coming in which they shall say, 'Blessed *are* the barren, and *the* wombs that did not bear, and *the* breasts that did not give suck.'
30. Then shall they begin to say to the mountains, 'Fall on us'; and to the hills, 'Cover us.' [a]
31. For if they do these things in the green tree, what shall take place in the dry?"

JOHN 19

16. Therefore, he then delivered Him up to them so that He might be crucified. And they took Jesus and led *Him* away.
17. And He went out bearing His own cross to the place called *The Place* of a Skull, which in Hebrew is called Golgotha.

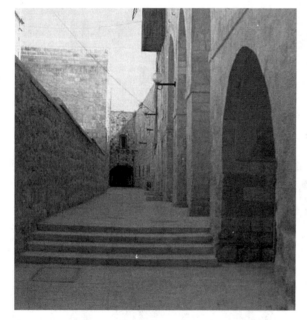

Street Scene from the Judgment Hall

a - Hos. 10:8; Isa. 2:10-12

PASSOVER DAY NISAN 14 – WEDNESDAY MORNING, APRIL 5 – 30 AD
APPROXIMATELY 9 AM – 12 NOON

355. JESUS REFUSES WINE AND MYRRH
(VINEGAR AND GALL)—THEY CRUCIFY HIM

MATTHEW 27	MARK 15
34. They gave Him vinegar mingled with gall to drink; but after tasting it, He would not drink. [a]	23. And they were attempting to give Him wine to drink, mixed with myrrh; but He did not take *it*.

a - Psa. 69:21

356. THE SOLDIERS CAST LOTS FOR HIS GARMENTS—
JESUS ASKS THE FATHER TO FORGIVE THEM FOR CRUCIFYING HIM

MATTHEW 27	MARK 15	LUKE 23	JOHN 19
35. And when they had crucified Him, they divided His garments *by* casting lots; so that it might be fulfilled which was spoken by the prophet, "They divided My garments among themselves, and for My vesture they cast lots." [a] 36. And they sat down there to keep guard over Him.	24. And when they had crucified Him, they divided His garments, casting lots [a] for them *to see* who would take what. 25. Now it was *the* third hour when they crucified Him.	34. Then Jesus said, "Father, forgive them, for they do not know what they are doing." And as they divided His garments, they cast lots. [a]	23. Now the soldiers, after they had crucified Jesus, took His garments and made four parts, a part for each soldier, and the coat *also*. But the coat was seamless, woven *in one piece* from the top all the way throughout. 24. For this reason, they said to one another, "Let us not tear it, but let us cast lots [a] for it *to determine* whose it shall be"; that the scripture might be fulfilled which says, "They divided My garments among them, and they cast lots for My vesture." The soldiers therefore did these things.

a - Psa. 22:18

357. PILATE HAS A TITLE AND ACCUSATION
WRITTEN AND PUT ON THE CROSS

MATTHEW 27	MARK 15	LUKE 23	JOHN 19
37. And they put up over His head His accusation, written, "This is Jesus, the King of the Jews."	26. And the inscription of His accusation was written, "The King of the Jews."	38. And there also was an inscription over Him written in Greek and Latin and Hebrew: "This is the King of the Jews."	19. And Pilate also wrote a title and put *it* on the cross; and it was written, "Jesus the Nazarean, the King of the Jews."

301

PASSOVER DAY NISAN 14 – WEDNESDAY MORNING, APRIL 5 – 30 AD

Western Wailing Wall

JOHN 19

20. As a result, many of the Jews read this title, for the place where Jesus was crucified was near the city; and it was written in Hebrew, in Greek *and* in Latin.
21. Then the chief priests of the Jews said to Pilate, "Do not write, 'The King of the Jews'; but that He said, 'I am King of the Jews.' "
22. Pilate answered, "What I have written, I have written."

358. TWO MALEFACTORS (THIEVES) CRUCIFIED WITH JESUS

MATTHEW 27	MARK 15	LUKE 23	JOHN 19
38. And two robbers were crucified with Him, one at *the* right hand and one at *the* left.	27. And with Him they crucified two robbers, one at *His* right hand and one at His left. 28. Then the scripture was fulfilled which says, "And He was numbered among lawbreakers." [a] a - Isa. 53:12	32. And two other malefactors were also led away with Him to be put to death. 33. And when they came to the place called *Place of* a Skull, there they crucified Him and the malefactors, one on *the* right and one on *the* left.	18. There they crucified Him, and with Him two others, *one* on this side and *one* on the other side, and Jesus in the middle.

359. THE PEOPLE, PRIESTS AND TWO THIEVES MOCK AND REVILE HIM. DARKNESS FROM THE SIXTH HOUR TO THE NINTH HOUR (APPROXIMATELY NOON TO 3 PM)

MATTHEW 27	MARK 15	LUKE 23
39. Then those who were passing by railed at Him, shaking their heads, 40. And saying, "You Who *would* destroy the temple and rebuild *it* in three days, save Yourself. If You are *the* Son of God, come down from the cross."	29. And those who were passing by railed at Him, shaking their heads, and saying, "Aha, You Who would destroy the temple and rebuild *it* in three days, 30. Save Yourself and come down from the cross."	35. Now the people stood *by* observing, and the rulers among them were also deriding *Him*, saying, "He saved others; let Him save Himself, if this is the Christ, the chosen of God."

PASSOVER DAY NISAN 14 – WEDNESDAY, APRIL 5 – 30 AD

MATTHEW 27

41. And in the same way also the chief priests were mocking, with the scribes and elders, saying,
42. "He saved others, *but* He does not have the power to save Himself. If He is the King of Israel, let Him come down now from the cross, and we will believe Him.
43. He trusted in God; let Him deliver Him now, if He will *have* Him. For He said, 'I am *the* Son of God.'"
44. And the two robbers who were crucified with Him also reproached Him with the same words.
45. Now from *the* sixth hour until *the* ninth hour, darkness was over all the land.

MARK 15

31. And in like manner the chief priests also were mocking with one another *and* with the scribes, saying, "He saved others, *but* He does not have the power to save Himself.
32. The Christ, the King of Israel! Let Him come down now from the cross so that we may see and believe." And *even* those who were crucified with Him reproached Him.
33. Now at *the* sixth hour, darkness came over all the land until *the* ninth hour;

LUKE 23

36. And the soldiers also mocked Him, coming near and offering Him vinegar,
37. And saying, "If You are the King of the Jews, save Yourself."
38. And there also was an inscription over Him written in Greek and Latin and Hebrew: "This is the King of the Jews."
39. Then one of the malefactors who was hanging *there* railed at Him, saying, "If You are the Christ, save Yourself and us."
40. But the other *one* answered *and* rebuked him, saying, "Do not even you fear God, you who are under the same condemnation?
41. And we indeed justly, for we are receiving due payment for what we did; but this *man* did nothing wrong."
42. Then he said to Jesus, "Remember me, Lord, when You come into Your kingdom."
43. And Jesus said to him, "Truly, I tell you today, you shall be with Me in paradise."
44. Now it was about *the* sixth hour, and darkness came over the whole land until *the* ninth hour.

360. JESUS MAKES JOHN RESPONSIBLE FOR HIS MOTHER, MARY

JOHN 19

25. And Jesus' mother stood by the cross, and His mother's sister, Mary the *wife* of Cleopas, and Mary Magdalene.
26. When Jesus saw *His* mother, and the disciple whom He loved standing by, He said to His mother, "Woman, behold your son."
27. Then He said to the disciple, "Behold your mother." And from that time, the disciple took her into his own *home*.

PASSOVER DAY NISAN 14 – WEDNESDAY AFTERNOON, APRIL 5 – 30 AD
APPROXIMATELY 3 PM

361. AT THE NINTH HOUR JESUS IS FORSAKEN
AND OFFERED VINEGAR—
A SPEAR IS THRUST INTO HIS SIDE AND HE DIES—
THE TEMPLE VEIL IS TORN IN TWO

MATTHEW 27	MARK 15	LUKE 23	JOHN 19
46. And about the ninth hour, Jesus cried out with a loud voice, saying, "Eli, Eli, lama sabachthani?" That is, "My God, My God, why have You forsaken Me?" [a] 47. And some of those who were standing there heard *and* said, "This *one* is calling for Elijah." 48. And immediately one of them ran and, taking a sponge, filled *it* with vinegar and put *it* on a stick, *and* gave *it to* Him to drink. [b] 49. But the rest said, "Let Him alone! Let us see if Elijah comes to save Him." *Then another took a spear and thrust it into His side, and out came water and blood.* * 50. And after crying out again with a loud voice, Jesus yielded up *His* spirit. [c] 51. And suddenly the veil of the temple was ripped in two from top to bottom...	34. And at the ninth hour, Jesus cried with a loud voice, saying, "Eloi, Eloi, lama sabachthani?" which is, being interpreted, "My God, My God, why have You forsaken Me?" [a] 35. And after hearing *it*, some of those who were standing by said, "Look, He is calling for Elijah." 36. Then one ran and filled a sponge with vinegar, [b] and after putting *it* on a stick gave *it* to Him to drink, saying, "Let *Him* be. Let us see if Elijah comes to take Him down." 37. And after crying out with a loud voice, Jesus expired. 38. And the veil of the temple was split in two from top to bottom.	45. And the sun was darkened, and the veil of the temple was split down *the* middle. 46. And after crying out with a loud voice, Jesus said, "Father, into Your hands I commit My spirit." [c] And when He had said these things, He expired.	28. After this, Jesus, knowing that all things had now been finished, so that the scripture might be fulfilled, said, "I thirst." 29. Now a vessel full of vinegar was sitting *there*. And after filling a sponge with vinegar and putting *it* on *a stick of* hyssop, they put it up to *His* mouth. [b] 30. And so, when Jesus had received the vinegar, He said, "It is finished." [d] And bowing His head, He yielded up *His* spirit. [c]

a - Psa. 22:1   b - Psa. 69:21   c - Psa. 31:5   d - Psa. 22:31

The latter half of this verse, which includes the words "...Then another took a spear and ...out came water and blood," has been omitted from the King James Version. However, some ancient manuscripts contain this part of the verse. The latter part of the verse is also found in other manuscripts that are designated by letter (L, T, Z) and by number (33, 49, 892 and 1241). Older translations which contain the complete verse are the Moffatt translation and the Fenton translation. Newer translations generally footnote this portion of Matthew 27:49 rather than including it in the text. The weight of evidence indicates that the latter half of the verse is an authentic part of the Greek text and should be included in translations of the New Testament. The veracity of this portion of Matthew 27:49 is substantiated by the records in John 19:34 and 20:27.

PASSOVER DAY NISAN 14 – WEDNESDAY AFTERNOON, APRIL 5 – 30 AD

362. AN EARTHQUAKE OPENS SOME GRAVES
FOR A RESURRECTION OF SOME OF THE SAINTS
TO ANOTHER PHYSICAL LIFE AS A SIGN AND A WITNESS

MATTHEW 27

51. ... the earth shook, and the rocks were split,
52. And the tombs were opened, and many bodies of the saints who had died arose.
53. And after His resurrection, they came out of the tombs *and* entered into the holy city, and appeared to many.

363. THE CENTURION ACKNOWLEDGES THAT
JESUS WAS THE SON OF GOD

MATTHEW 27	MARK 15	LUKE 23
54. Then the centurion and those with him who had been keeping guard over Jesus, after seeing the earthquake and the things that took place, were filled with fear, *and* said, "Truly this was the Son of God!"	39. Then the centurion who stood facing Him, witnessing *the words* that He cried out as He was dying, said, "Truly this man was the Son of God."	47. Now after seeing the things that took place, the centurion glorified God, saying, "Truly, this man was righteous."

364. THE JEWS WANT JESUS' BODY OFF THE CROSS
BEFORE THE HOLY DAY BEGINS AT SUNSET

JOHN 19

31. The Jews therefore, so that the bodies might not remain on the cross on the Sabbath, because it was a preparation *day* (for that Sabbath was a high day), requested of Pilate that their legs might be broken and *the bodies* be taken away.
32. Then the soldiers came and broke the legs of the first *one*, and *the legs* of the other who was crucified with Him.
33. But when they came to Jesus *and* saw that He was already dead, they did not break His legs;
34. But one of the soldiers had pierced His side with a spear, and immediately blood and water had come out.
35. And he who saw *this* has testified, and his testimony is true; and he knows that *what* he says *is* true, so that you may believe.
36. For these things took place so that the scripture might be fulfilled, "Not a bone of Him shall be broken." [a]
37. And again another scripture says, "They shall look upon Him Whom they pierced." [b]

a - Ex. 12:46; Num. 9:12; Psa. 34:20   b - Zech. 12:10; Rev. 1:7

PASSOVER DAY NISAN 14 – WEDNESDAY AFTERNOON, APRIL 5 – 30 AD
365. MANY OF THE WOMEN WATCH TO THE END

MATTHEW 27	MARK 15	LUKE 23
55. Now there were many women who were watching from a distance, who had followed Jesus from Galilee, ministering to Him; 56. With whom were Mary Magdalene, and Mary the mother of James and Joses, and the mother of the sons of Zebedee.	40. And there were also women who were watching from a distance, among whom was Mary Magdalene; and also Mary, the mother of James the younger and of Joses; and Salome; 41. Who also when He was in Galilee followed Him and ministered to Him; and many others who had come up with Him to Jerusalem.	48. And all the people who had gathered together to this sight, after seeing the things that took place, returned beating their breasts. 49. But all those who knew Him stood off at a distance observing these things, *the* women also who had accompanied Him from Galilee.

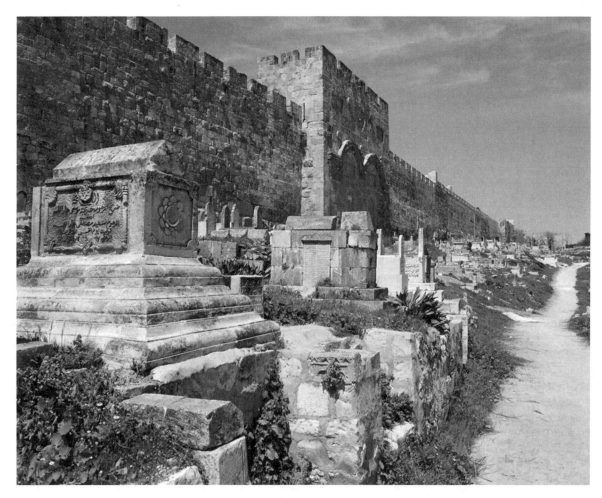

Graveyard Along Jerusalem Wall

306

PASSOVER DAY NISAN 14 – WEDNESDAY, APRIL 5 – 30 AD
APPROXIMATELY 4:30 – 6 PM

366. JUST BEFORE SUNSET, JOSEPH OF ARIMATHEA GETS THE BODY OF JESUS AND LAYS IT IN THE TOMB

MATTHEW 27	MARK 15	LUKE 23	JOHN 19

MATTHEW 27

57. And when evening was coming on, a rich man of Arimathea came, named Joseph, who was himself a disciple of Jesus.

58. After going to Pilate, he begged *to have* the body of Jesus. Then Pilate commanded the body to be given over *to him.*

59. And after taking the body, Joseph wrapped it in clean linen cloth,

60. And placed it in his new tomb, which he had hewn in the rock; and after rolling a great stone to the door of the tomb, he went away.

61. But sitting there opposite the sepulcher were Mary Magdalene and the other Mary.

MARK 15

42. Now evening was coming, *and* since it was *a* preparation (that is, *the day* before a Sabbath),

43. Joseph of Arimathea, *an* esteemed member of the council, who himself was waiting for the kingdom of God, came; and he went in to Pilate with boldness and requested the body of Jesus.

44. But Pilate wondered if He were already dead; and after calling the centurion, he questioned him, whether He had been dead long.

45. And when he knew it *by the report* from the centurion, he gave the body to Joseph.

46. Now he had bought fine linen cloth; and after taking Him down, he wrapped *Him* in the linen cloth and laid Him in a tomb which had been cut out of *the* rock. Then he rolled a stone to *cover* the entrance of the tomb.

47. And Mary Magdalene and Mary, *the mother* of Joses, saw where He was laid.

LUKE 23

50. And behold, *there came* a man named Joseph, a member of the council, a good and righteous man,

51. (He did not consent to the council and their deed.) from Arimathea, a city of the Jews, and who was also himself waiting for the kingdom of God.

52. He, after going to Pilate, begged *for* the body of Jesus.

53. And after taking it down, he wrapped it in linen cloth and placed it in a tomb hewn in a rock, in which no one had ever been laid.

54. Now it was *a* preparation day, and *a* Sabbath was coming on.

55. And *the* women also, who had come with Him from Galilee, followed *and* saw the tomb, and how His body was laid.

JOHN 19

38. Now after these things, Joseph (the one from Arimathea, being a disciple of Jesus, but having concealed it for fear of the Jews) asked Pilate that he might take Jesus' body away; and Pilate gave *him* permission. Then he came and took away the body of Jesus.

39. And Nicodemus, who had come to Jesus by night at *the* first, also came, bearing a mixture of myrrh and aloes, about a hundred pounds.

40. Then they took Jesus' body and wound it in linen cloths with the aromatics, as is the custom among the Jews to prepare for burial.

41. Now there was a garden in the place where He was crucified, and in the garden a new tomb, in which no one had ever been laid.

42. Because of the preparation of the Jews, they laid Jesus there; for the tomb was near.

THIS ENDS THE EVENTS OF THE PASSOVER DAY – NISAN 14
FROM SUNSET APRIL 4 TO SUNSET APRIL 5 – 30 AD
THE DAY GOD DIED!

PART VII

JESUS' THREE DAYS AND THREE NIGHTS
OF ENTOMBMENT
AND THE RESURRECTION

THE EXACT LENGTH OF TIME
THAT JESUS WAS IN THE TOMB

Many prophecies in the Old Testament foretold the death and resurrection of Jesus the Christ. The prophet Daniel foresaw that His life would be taken (Dan. 9:26), and both David and Isaiah described the suffering and humiliation that He would endure before His death (Psa. 22, Isa. 53). Other prophecies pointed to His resurrection to immortality (Psa. 16:10-11, Dan. 7:13-14, Isa. 9:6-7). However, there is no scripture in the Old Testament that foretold the length of time that the Messiah would be in the tomb before He was resurrected from the dead. This prophecy is found only in the Gospel accounts, spoken by Jesus Himself: "Then some of the scribes and Pharisees answered, saying, 'Master, we desire to see a sign from You.' And He answered *and* said to them, '**A wicked and adulterous generation seeks after a sign, but no sign shall be given to it except the sign of Jonah the prophet. For just as Jonah was in the belly of the whale three days and three nights, in like manner the Son of man shall be in the heart of the earth three days and three nights**' " (Matt. 12:38-40).

Jesus spoke these words because the scribes and Pharisees did not believe in Him, nor did they believe that His works of healing were done by the power of God. When they challenged Him to perform a miraculous sign in their presence, Jesus did not do so. Instead, the only sign He gave them was the sign of Jonah the prophet. The fulfillment of this sign was a testimony not only to that generation but to all future generations that He was the Messiah.

The vast majority of Christians today believe that Jesus was crucified and laid in the tomb on a Friday, and He was resurrected on Sunday morning. Thus, He was not in the tomb for three days and three nights, as He had prophesied, but for two nights and one full day. This traditional interpretation of Jesus' death and resurrection is completely contrary to the Gospel accounts.

Nearly all churches within Christendom have misinterpreted or rejected the scriptural record. In its place, they have adopted an ancient Babylonian religious tradition that predates the ministry, death and resurrection of Jesus the Christ by thousands of years.* Various theories have been advanced in an attempt to reconcile this ancient religious tradition with the scriptural accounts, but the error is clearly exposed by examining the accounts that have been accurately recorded and faithfully preserved in the Gospels of Matthew, Mark, Luke and John.

For historical evidence of the Babylonian practices, see The Two Babylons *by Alexander Hislop and* The Golden Bough *by Sir James George Frazer.*

The Gospel accounts do not support the traditional belief in a Good Friday crucifixion and an Easter Sunday resurrection. The facts that are recorded by the Gospel
writers reveal a profoundly different time frame for the death and resurrection of Jesus the Christ.

The Scriptural Definition of a Day

Some have claimed that Jesus was using an idiomatic expression when He declared that He would remain in the tomb for three days and three nights. They teach
that His words should be interpreted as referring to parts of days rather than to whole
days. But when the scriptural use of the term "day" is examined one finds that it is
very specific. The Scriptures of the Old Testament show that a day consists of an
evening and a morning (Gen. 1). An entire day has two portions: the night portion,
which begins at evening, or sunset; and the day portion, which begins at sunrise, or
morning. These two consecutive periods are identified as one complete day, reckoned
from sunset to sunset, or evening to evening (Lev. 23:32, *KJV*).

According to Scripture, each day has an average of twelve hours in the night portion and twelve hours in the day portion, making a complete day of twenty-four
hours. Jesus Himself verified that the day portion is about twelve hours long when
He said, "Are there not twelve hours in the day?" (John 11:9.) Jesus also spoke of the
three watches of the night, which extended from sunset to sunrise and were each four
hours long, making a total of twelve hours (Luke 12:36-38). There is no question that
Jesus included a full twelve hours of daylight and a full twelve hours of night in reckoning the length of each calendar day. This scriptural method of reckoning time had
been used by the Hebrews for centuries. Moreover, it is clear that Jesus and His disciples observed the Passover and the holy days of God each year according to the de-
termination of the Hebrew Calendar, as God had ordained. This is a key fact in understanding the exact length of time that Jesus was in the tomb.

When the four Gospel accounts are examined, it is clear that the Gospel writers
used the scriptural method of reckoning each day from sunset to sunset, or evening to
evening. Beginning six days before Jesus' last Passover until the day after His resurrection, the Gospel writers accurately recorded all the events day by day. They took
careful note of the mornings and evenings, making it possible to determine the beginning and end of each day. The fact that they meticulously noted the mornings and
evenings demonstrates that these days were whole days composed of twenty-four
hours. Nowhere do the scriptural records leave room for an interpretation of partial
days or partial nights.

An Analysis of the Phrase "Three Days and Three Nights" in the Book of Jonah

Jesus' prophecy that He would be in the grave for three days and three nights is a
direct reference to Jonah 1:17, which speaks of Jonah's symbolic entombment in the
belly of a great fish: "Now the LORD had prepared a great fish to swallow up Jonah.
And Jonah was in the belly of the fish three days and three nights" (*KJV*).

The word "days" in this verse is translated from the Hebrew *yom*, and the word
"night" is translated from the Hebrew *lailah*. Both of these words are preceded by

the cardinal number "three," which is translated from the Hebrew *shalosh*. This cardinal number is used as an adjective before the nouns "days" and "nights" to express a specific period of time. Other scriptural references confirm the use of cardinal numbers to record the exact duration of a condition or event:

Gen. 7:4	"seven days"
Gen. 7:12	"forty days and forty nights"
Ex. 10:23	"three days"
Ex. 24:18	"forty days and forty nights"
Lev. 12:4	"three and thirty days"
I Sam. 30:12	"three days and three nights"
I Kings 19:8	"forty days and forty nights"

The use of a cardinal number with the terms "days" and "nights" shows that these terms are being used in a very specific sense. The presence of the Hebrew *waw* (the conjunction "and") between "days" and "nights" makes the meaning of the text even more emphatic, limiting the duration of time to the exact number of days and nights that are specified. By the Scriptural method of reckoning time, it takes an "evening" and a "morning" to complete one full day (Gen. 1:5). Just as "the evening and the morning" in Genesis 1 denote a whole day of twenty-four hours, so the term "a day and a night" denotes a full day of twenty-four hours. In the same way also, the expression "three days and three nights" denotes three whole days of twenty-four hours each.

The Hebrew text leaves no room to interpret the expression "three days and three nights" in Jonah 1:17 in a broad or general sense. The use of this same Hebrew expression in I Samuel 30:12 demonstrates that it is a literal period of three 24-hour days: "... for he had eaten no bread, nor drunk water, three days and three nights" (*KJV*). The following verse in I Samuel 30 uses the expression "three days agone" in reference to the period of three days and three nights. These were the words of an Egyptian who was accustomed to reckoning days from sunrise to sunrise. The use of the expression "three days agone" by the Egyptian confirms that he had completed a full three days and three nights of fasting from sunrise on the first day until sunrise on the fourth day. The literal meaning of "three days" in I Samuel 30:13 is confirmed by the use of the same Hebrew expression in II Samuel 24:13 to describe a specific duration of time: "three days' pestilence."

The construction of the Hebrew text does not allow the expression "three days and three nights" in Jonah 1:17 to be interpreted in any manner except the literal sense of three 24-hour days. The Hebrew terminology cannot be interpreted as an idiomatic expression that is describing incomplete units of time, such as part of a day and part of a night. To denote incomplete units of time, the Hebrew text uses a word that means "to divide." This word is not found in the expression "three days and three nights," either in Jonah 1:17 or in I Samuel 30:12. However, this word is found in reference to a duration of time in Daniel 12:7: "... a time, times, and half a time." The word "half" is translated from the Hebrew word meaning "to divide." Since this word is not used to describe the duration of time in Jonah 1:17 and I Samuel 30:12, it is evident that the Hebrew text is describing complete units of time—three 12-hour days and three 12-hour nights. By testifying that Jonah was in the belly of the fish "three days and three nights," the Scriptures reveal that a full 72 hours had elapsed before Jonah was cast out on the shore.

The New Testament reveals that Jesus the Christ was the Lord God of the Old Testament before He became a man. He was the one Who caused the great fish to swallow Jonah and descend to the bottom of the sea for a period of time before swimming to the shore and depositing Jonah on the land. As the Lord God, He knew exactly how long Jonah had remained in the belly of the fish, and He inspired Jonah to record this duration of time, which was a foretelling of His future burial. There is no question concerning the length of time that passed as Jonah lay in the belly of the fish, because this fact is preserved in the Scriptures of the Old Testament. Since the Hebrew text cannot be interpreted in an idiomatic sense, but must be interpreted literally, it is clear that three whole days and three whole nights passed while Jonah lay in the fish's belly. Jesus was fully aware of this fact of Scripture when He declared to the Jews, "... **in like manner the Son of man shall be in the heart of the earth three days and three nights**" (Matt. 12:40).

Jesus Said That He Would Rise
Three Days After His Death

The Gospel writers record that Jesus made specific statements to His disciples concerning the length of time that He would be in the tomb and when He would be resurrected: "And He began to teach them that it was necessary for the Son of man to suffer many things, and to be rejected by the elders and chief priests and scribes, and **to be killed, but after three days to rise** *from the dead*" (Mark 8:31; see also Matt. 16:21 and Mark 9:31). Jesus proclaimed to His disciples that He would not rise from the dead until **three days after He had been killed**. Jesus' statement that **He would rise three days after He had died** is most significant. According to Jewish law, to be declared legally dead, a person had to be dead for more than three full days. If someone who appeared to be dead revived and came back to life prior to three full days, he or she was not legally deemed to have been dead. Therefore, if Jesus had risen from the dead before 3 PM on the afternoon of Nisan 17, a weekly Sabbath, He would not have been considered legally dead. As a result, His return to life would not have been considered a true resurrection from the dead.

Knowing this fact, one can understand why Jesus delayed going to Lazarus in the account in John 11. Jesus knew that Lazarus was sick unto death, but He deliberately remained where He was for two more days (John 11:6). He knew that Lazarus would not be considered legally dead until he had been dead for four days. When Lazarus was legally dead, Jesus went to resurrect him from the grave: "Jesus said, '**Take away the stone.' Martha, the sister of him who had died, said to Him, 'Lord, he already stinks, for it has been four days.'** Jesus said to her, 'Did I not say to you that if you will believe, you shall see the glory of God?' Then they removed the stone *from the tomb* where the dead man had been laid. And Jesus lifted *His* eyes upward and said, 'Father, I thank You that You have heard Me. And I know that You hear Me always; but because of the people who stand around I say *this*, so that they may believe that You did send Me.' And after He had spoken these things, He cried with a loud voice, **'Lazarus, come forth.' And he who had been dead came forth, his feet and hands bound with grave clothes, and his face bound up with a napkin**. Jesus said to them, 'Loose him and let *him* go' " (John 11:39-44).

Like Lazarus, Jesus had to remain dead for a minimum of three full days in order to be declared officially dead. If He had been crucified on a Friday and restored to

311

life on Sunday morning at sunrise, His death would not have been "valid" since only two nights and one day would have passed between Friday sunset and Sunday morning. In order for His death to be publicly recognized and acknowledged, it was necessary for Jesus to remain in the grave for three nights and three days before He was raised from the dead. The Scriptures reveal that Jesus died at the ninth hour, or 3 PM, on the Passover day, Nisan 14, which fell on Wednesday, April 5, in 30 AD (Matt. 27:46 and Mark 15:34), and He was placed in the tomb just before sunset at approximately 6 PM. The Gospel of Matthew describes His burial by Joseph of Arimathea: "And **when evening was coming on**, a rich man of Arimathea came, named Joseph, who was himself a disciple of Jesus. After going to Pilate, he begged *to have* the body of Jesus. Then Pilate commanded the body to be given over *to him.* And after taking the body, Joseph [with the help of Nicodemus (John 19:39)] wrapped it in clean linen cloth, and placed it in his new tomb, which he had hewn in the rock; and after rolling a great stone to the door of the tomb, he went away" (Matt. 27:57-60). Luke records that "a Sabbath was coming on" (Luke 23:54), which means that by the time they had closed the entrance of the tomb with a huge stone, the Sabbath was nearly upon them. Since all Sabbaths were reckoned from sunset to sunset, it is clear that the sun was about to set.

Both Matthew and Mark testify that Jesus died at the ninth hour, or 3 PM. Luke's account shows that they closed the entrance to the tomb with a huge stone just before sunset. Because the Passover is in the spring of the year when the days are twelve hours in length, we know that the tomb was closed at about 6 PM. Since He died about 3 PM, Jesus was dead for approximately 75 hours before He was resurrected. The total length of time included three days (from sunrise to sunset) and three nights (from sunset to sunrise) plus approximately three hours. Because He had been dead for more than three days, His death was legally established. When He appeared to His disciples three days after He had been placed in the tomb, the reality of His resurrection was beyond question.

Additional Statements of Jesus Confirm That He Was in the Tomb for Three Days and Three Nights

While Matthew and Mark record Jesus saying that He would be raised "after three days," Luke records that He would be raised "on the third day." Luke wrote: "For He shall be delivered up to the Gentiles, and shall be mocked and insulted and spit upon. And after scourging *Him*, they shall kill Him; **but on the third day, He shall rise again**" (Luke 18:32-33).

The apostle John records another statement by Jesus that He would be raised up "in three days." Jesus made this statement when the Jews confronted Him for casting the money exchangers out of the temple and driving out the animals they were selling: "... The Jews answered and said to Him, 'What sign do You show to us, seeing that You do these things?' Jesus answered and said to them, '**Destroy this temple, and in three days I will raise it up.**' Then the Jews said, 'This temple was forty-six years in building, and You will raise it up in three days?' **But He spoke concerning the temple of His body**. Therefore, when He was raised from *the* dead, His disciples remembered that He had said this to them; and they believed the Scriptures, and the word that Jesus had spoken" (John 2:18-22).

The phrase "in three days" contains the Greek preposition *en.* This Greek preposition, which is translated "in" in John 2:19-20, can also mean "within." At first glance, the statements "**in three days**" and "**on the third day**" appear to conflict with the statement that He would be raised "**after three days.**" How is it possible for all three of Jesus' statements to be correct?

When we understand Jesus' statements, we find that instead of being contradictory, they reveal the exact time that He was raised from the dead. Jesus made it clear that He would be raised after He had been dead for three days. The other statements, "**in three days**" and "**on the third day**," do not include the total time that He was dead but only the time that He was buried in the tomb. The Gospel accounts show that Joseph of Arimathea and Nicodemus closed the tomb just before sunset, three hours after Jesus died on the cross. Although He was in the tomb for exactly three days and three nights, He was dead for a longer period than that. Thus He rose from the dead "**after three days.**" The difference between this statement and the statements "**in three days**" and "**on the third day**" is that these two statements refer to His burial "**in the heart of the earth three days and three nights.**"

When one compares all of Jesus' statements, it is evident that they place specific limits on the time frame between His death and resurrection. Of itself, "**in three days**" could mean any time on the third day, even the first minute of the third day. "**On the third day**" could mean any time on the third day up to the last minute on the third day. But the statement that He would "**be in the heart of the earth three days and three nights**" shows that three whole days and three whole nights would pass while He lay in the tomb.

When all of Jesus' statements are taken into consideration, there is only one moment of time to which all can apply. Here is the explanation: The end of the third day is still "on" and "in" the third day. At the end of the third day, precisely at sunset, Jesus was resurrected. This was the only moment of time that could fulfill all of Jesus' prophecies concerning the time of His death, the length of time that He would be in the tomb, and the time of His resurrection.

The Gospels record that Jesus died on the Passover day, Nisan 14, which fell on a Wednesday in 30 AD. Joseph of Arimathea and Nicodemus placed Jesus' body in the tomb and closed the entrance with a huge stone when the sun was setting at approximately 6 PM, ending Nisan 14. Jesus was resurrected from the dead precisely three days and three nights later, when the sun was setting at the end of the weekly Sabbath, or Saturday, Nisan 17, 30 AD. As He had prophesied, He remained in the tomb for three full days and three full nights. **Jesus the Christ was raised from the dead at sunset on the weekly Sabbath, the seventh day of the week. He had already been resurrected when the sun rose on Sunday, the first day of the week**. *(Please see the chart on pages 320-321).*

Scriptural Evidence of Two Sabbaths During the Three Days and Three Nights

According to religious tradition, Jesus was crucified on a Friday. This religious tradition appears to be supported by the statement in John 19:31 that the day of His death "was the preparation." Most have assumed that this statement refers to the

313

Jews' preparation for the weekly Sabbath. They fail to realize that the Passover day, on which Jesus died, has always been a preparation day for the Feast of Unleavened Bread, which immediately follows (Lev. 23:4-6). The first day of this feast, Nisan 15, is observed as an annual holy day, or "high day." Like the Passover day, it may fall on different days of the week. Regardless of which day of the week it falls on, it is always observed as an annual Sabbath, and the day portion of the Passover is always used as a day of preparation. It is erroneous to interpret "the preparation" in John 19:31 as evidence that the day of the crucifixion was a Friday.

The mistaken belief in a Friday crucifixion is based on the assumption that there was only one Sabbath during the crucifixion week. However, the Scriptures clearly reveal that during that week there were two Sabbaths. The first Sabbath was an annual holy day, the first day of the Feast of Unleavened Bread. The second Sabbath was the weekly Sabbath, the seventh day of the week. Consequently, during the week of Jesus' crucifixion there were two preparation days. The day portion of Nisan 14, the Passover day, was the preparation day for the first day of the Feast of Unleavened Bread, the 15th, which was an annual Sabbath. The following day, the 16th, which was a Friday, was the preparation day for the weekly Sabbath.

When the Gospel of John is examined, it is evident that the Sabbath immediately following the day Jesus died was an annual Sabbath: "The Jews therefore, so that the bodies might not remain on the cross on the Sabbath, because it was **a preparation day (for that Sabbath was a high day)** ..." (John 19:31). The term "high day" was never used to refer to the weekly Sabbath, but only to annual Sabbaths. John's use of this term makes it clear that the Sabbath that was about to begin was the first day of the Feast of Unleavened Bread, Nisan 15. Mark's account makes reference to the coming of sunset, which would bring the end of the preparation and the beginning of the annual Sabbath, or high day: "**Now evening was coming, *and* since it was *a* preparation, (that is, *the day* before a Sabbath) ...**" (Mark 15:42).

As the Gospel of Luke shows, this Sabbath was about to begin when Jesus was put into the tomb: "Now it was *a* **preparation day, and *a* Sabbath was coming on**. And *the* women also, who had come with Him from Galilee, followed *and* saw the tomb, and how His body was laid" (Luke 23:54-55).

The Gospels record the events that followed Jesus' burial. On Nisan 15, the day after the crucifixion, the chief priests and the Pharisees went to Pilate to request that guards be assigned to watch Jesus' tomb. Because they were afraid that the disciples would come and steal away His body, they did not hesitate to take care of their business on the holy day (Matt. 27:62-66). While the priests and Pharisees went to Pilate, the women who followed Jesus were observing the annual Sabbath, as commanded by God. They could not buy spices on that day because all the businesses were closed in observance of the command to rest (Lev. 23:6-7). After the end of that Sabbath, or high day, they bought spices and aromatic oils to anoint Jesus. Mark relates this event: "**Now when the Sabbath had passed**, Mary Magdalene and Mary, the *mother* of James, and Salome bought aromatic oils, so that they might come and anoint Him" (Mark 16:1).

It is quite evident that the women could not have purchased the spices until after the high day, or annual Sabbath, had ended. The high day began when the Passover day, Nisan 14, ended at sunset. The observance of the high day, Nisan 15, lasted until the following sunset, which began Nisan 16. The women bought the spices "**when the Sabbath had passed**" and prepared them on the same day. When they had finished, they observed **a second Sabbath:** "And they returned *to the city, and* prepared spices and ointments, and *then* **rested on the Sabbath** according to the commandment" (Luke 23:56). The Gospel records concerning the buying and preparation of the spices by the women clearly reveal the observance of two Sabbaths during the crucifixion week.

Two Women View the Tomb
Late on the Weekly Sabbath

Before the weekly Sabbath came to an end, Matthew records that Mary Magdalene and the other Mary went to observe the tomb: "Now late on the Sabbath, as *the* first *day* of *the* weeks was drawing near, Mary Magdalene and the other Mary went to observe the sepulcher" (Matt. 28:1). Because it was still the Sabbath day, the women did not come to anoint His body with the spices they had prepared. Perhaps they went to observe the tomb because they remembered Jesus' words that after three days and three nights in the grave, He would rise from the dead.

After the two women viewed the tomb and saw that the stone covering the entrance was still in place with the soldiers standing guard, they returned home for the night. The next morning, as they were coming back to the tomb, they were wondering who might roll back the stone so that they could anoint Jesus' body: "And very early on the first *day* of the weeks, at the rising of the sun, they were coming to the tomb; and they were asking themselves, 'Who will roll away the stone for us from the entrance to the tomb?' " (Mark 16:2-3) But when the women arrived, they found that the stone had already been removed and the tomb was empty. The three days and three nights had ended at sunset on the weekly Sabbath, and Jesus had risen from the dead! (See Chart on pages 320-321 for The Three Days and Three Nights in the Tomb and the Resurrection After Three Days and Three Nights.)

"Today Is the Third Day Since These
Things Took Place"

Those who believe in a Sunday resurrection point to a statement in Luke 24:21 as evidence that Jesus rose from the dead at sunrise on the first day of the week. This statement was made by two of Jesus' disciples: "... today is the third day since these things were done." Because this statement was made on the first day of the week, many have assumed that Jesus rose from the dead early that morning. The King James Version reads:

"And, behold, two of them went that same day to a village called Emmaus, which was from Jerusalem *about* threescore furlongs. And they talked together of all these things which had happened. And it came to pass, that, while they communed *together* and reasoned, Jesus himself drew near, and went with them. But their eyes were holden that they should not know him.

"And he said unto them, 'What manner of communications *are* these that ye have one to another, as ye walk, and are sad?' And the one of them, whose name was Cleopas, answering said unto him, 'Art thou only a stranger in Jerusalem, and hast not known the things which are come to pass there in these days?' And he said unto them, 'What things?'

"And they said unto him, 'Concerning Jesus of Nazareth, which was a prophet mighty in deed and word before God and all the people: and how the chief priests and our rulers delivered him to be condemned to death, and have crucified him. But we trusted that it had been he which should have redeemed Israel: and **beside all this, today is the third day since these things were done**' " (Luke 24:13-21 KJV).

An Exegesis of Luke 24:21 Reveals the True Meaning of the "Third Day"

The translation of Luke 24:21 that appears in the King James Version has been used to support the teaching that the resurrection took place at sunrise on the first day of the week. However, the Gospel accounts clearly show that Jesus had already risen from the dead before the women came to the tomb at sunrise. There is no question that Jesus was in the tomb for "three days and three nights," beginning at sunset on Wednesday, Nisan 14, and ending at sunset on the weekly Sabbath, Nisan 17, in 30 AD. Jesus rose at the end of the three days and three nights, exactly as He had declared.

When one analyzes the phrasing that is used in the Greek text, one will see that the disciples were not talking about that day being the "third day" since Jesus was crucified. Let us examine this verse as translated in interlinear form by George Ricker Berry from the Stephens text of 1550, the same text that was used by the King James translators:

ημεις δε ηλπιζομεν οτι αυτος εστιν ο μελλω λυτρουσθαι τον Ισπαηλ.
But we were hoping he it is who is about to redeem Israel.
αλλα συν πασιν τουτιος <u>τριτην ταυτην ημεραν αγει</u> ηνερον <u>αφ ου</u>
but then with all these things third this day brings today since
ταυτα εγενετο.
these things came to pass.

In order to correctly interpret the meaning of the Greek text, we must examine the two expressions that are underlined:

1) <u>τριτην ταυτην ημεραν αγει</u> (*triten tauten hemeran agei*)

A. T. Robertson informs us that this expression is an idiom: "{Now the third day} (τριτην ταυτην ημεπαν αγει *triten tauten hemeran agei*). **A difficult idiom for the English**" (Robertson, *Word Pictures in the New Testament*, s.v. Luke 24:21). *Vincent's Word Studies* concurs that this is a difficult idiom to render into English.

Because τριτην ταυτην ημεπαν αγει *triten tauten hemeran agei* is an idiomatic expression, its true meaning cannot be understood by translating the Greek words literally, as the King James translators have done. The literal translation of this expression in the KJV (and many other translations) only serves to distort the true meaning of Luke's words in the Greek text. Edward Hobbs, a scholar who began teaching the Greek language over 50 years ago, recently wrote the following to another scholar regarding the translation of idioms: "But may I speak to the larger question of what are called '**IDIOMS**' in language-teaching….What older books almost always meant by an 'idiom' was **something which, when translated word-for-word into English either didn't make sense or made the wrong sense** … But the fact is, very little in other languages means the same thing when put word-for-word into English….**The semantic value of a word should always be evaluated contextually ... the good lexicons** [like Arndt and Gingrich] **already do this**, without singling such phrases for separate listing….**This principle applies equally to individual words and to strings of words which are semantically opaque (Idioms)**" (Bold emphasis added).

Hobbs concludes his remarks by stating, "One of the real reasons for studying ancient Greek is to learn how they thought about things, especially how they thought DIFFERENTLY about things, not simply what different thoughts they had about things….**We need to learn what translations cannot reveal: How the thinking itself was oriented differently**" (Edward Hobbs, EHOBBS@wellesley.edu, 12 Jul 1997, bold emphasis added).

Since the true meaning of Luke 24:21 depends on a proper understanding of the idiomatic expression that Luke used, we must examine the use of this expression by other writers of that era. When we examine their works, we find that τριτος *tritos* often appears in classical Greek literature as an expression of **completed time** (Liddell, Scott and Jones, *A Greek-English Lexicon*, s.v. "Tritos"). Notice Josephus' use of the word in this manner: "When the rigour of winter was over, Herod removed his army, and came near to Jerusalem, and pitched his camp hard by the city. Now this was the third [*tritos*] year since he had been made king at Rome …" (Josephus, *Ant.*, 14:15:14). As defined by classical Greek literature, Josephus' words indicate that Herod undertook the conquest of Jerusalem at the completion of his third regnal year; that is, after three full years—not at any time during the third year. As we will see, the additional use of αφ ου *aph hou* in conjunction with τριτος *tritos* makes the meaning of this idiom even more emphatic.

2) αφ ου *aph hou*

The function of this Greek expression is quite different from the idiomatic use of the first expression. Αφ ου *aph hou* is a linguistic formula and is very precise in meaning. It is used in classical Greek to delimit **a period of time that has been completed**. Arndt and Gingrich inform us that the translators of the Septuagint used αφ ου *aph hou* as a formula in Daniel 12:1, showing that this usage was common as early as the fourth century BC. Αφ ου *aph hou* was used in the same manner by the Levitical writers of the Maccabees nearly a century and a half later (see I Macc 9:29; 16:24; and 2 Macc 1:7 in the Septuagint). Arndt and Gingrich report that Josephus also used the expression in the same manner. The usage of this Greek formula by Josephus is of great value to our understanding, as he wrote within a short time after Luke wrote his Gospel. The English translation of Josephus' words is given below:

"(6)[78] Then it was that Miriam, the sister of Moses, came to her end, **having completed her fortieth year since** [αφ ου *aph' hou*] **she left Egypt**, on the first day of the lunar month Xanthicus."

The use of αφ ου *aph hou* in Josephus' works and the works of classical Greek writers enables us to understand the true meaning of Luke 24:21. As a formula, αφ ου *aph hou* specifically refers to completed time and cannot be construed as referring to time that is in progress. Thus Luke's use of αφ ου *aph hou* with τριτην *triten* must be interpreted as evidence **that the third day had already been completed**.

Thus it is erroneous to interpret Luke 24:21 as evidence that the first day of the week was "the third day since these things were done." The use of αφ ου *aph hou* with the idiomatic expression τριτην ταυτην ημεραν αγει *triten tauten hemeren agei* clearly conveys time that had already been completed and should be translated accordingly. When the disciples spoke of the "third day," the three days and three nights of Jesus' entombment had already been completed, although they did not yet know that Jesus had already been raised from the dead.

In addition, the use of τριτος *tritos* in the Gospel of Matthew clearly confirms that this Greek idiom refers to the completion of the three days: "Now on the next day, which followed the preparation *day*, the chief priests and the Pharisees came together to Pilate, saying, 'Sir, we remember that that deceiver said while *He was* living, "After three days I *will* rise." Therefore, command *that* the sepulcher be secured until **the third day** [της τριτης ημερας *tes trites emeras*]; lest His disciples come by night and steal Him away, and say to the people, "He is risen from the dead"; and the last deception shall be worse than the first' " (Matt. 27:62-64).

It is evident that the phrase "**the third day**" in Matthew 27:64 refers to the completion of the three-day period, as the chief priests and Pharisees were fully aware of Jesus' declaration that He would rise "**after three days**." It would make no sense to request a guard for the first and second days only, since He had declared that He would not rise before the third day; and this was the most likely day for an attempt to be made by the disciples if they had desired to steal His body.

As "**the third day**" in Matthew 27:64 refers to the end of Jesus' three days and three nights in the tomb, so "**the third day**" in Luke 24:21 refers to the end of the three days and three nights. As in every other reference to "**the third day**" that we find in the Gospel accounts, the focus in Luke 24:21 is on **the completion of Jesus' three days and three nights in the tomb.** Thus "the third day" did not include any part of the first day of the week. It is a mistake to apply this expression to the first day of the week when the records of Jesus' crucifixion and burial clearly show that His three days and three nights in the tomb began at sunset on Wednesday, Nisan 14. He remained in "the heart of the earth" from the beginning of Nisan 15, which was an annual Sabbath or "high day," until the end of Nisan 17, a weekly Sabbath. At the end of the weekly Sabbath, precisely as the sun was setting, He was resurrected from the dead. When the first day of the week arrived, the three days and three nights had been brought to completion.

The following translations of Luke 24:21 convey the true meaning of the phrasing that is used in the Greek text:

"… three days have already passed…." (Berkeley)
"… three days ago…." (Moffatt)

Both of these translations convey the idiomatic usage of τριτος *tritos* and the use of αφ ου *aph hou* as a formula to express a period of time that has been completed.

318

Based on this information, a precise translation of Luke 24:13-21, which conveys the true meaning of the Greek text, follows:

"And behold, on the same day, two of them were going to a village called Emmaus, which was about sixty furlongs from Jerusalem. And they were talking with one another about all the things that had taken place.

"And it came to pass, as they were talking and reasoning, that Jesus Himself drew near *and* went with them; but their eyes were restrained, *so that* they did not know Him. And He said to them, 'What *are* these words that you are exchanging with one another as you walk, and *why* are you downcast in countenance?' Then the one named Cleopas answered *and* said to Him, 'Are You only traveling through Jerusalem, and have not known of the things that have happened in these days?'

"And He said to them, 'What things?' And they said to Him, 'The things concerning Jesus the Nazarean, a man Who was a prophet, Who was mighty in deed and word before God and all the people; and how the chief priests and our rulers delivered Him up to *the* judgment of death, and crucified Him. And we were hoping that He was the one Who would redeem Israel. But besides all these things, **as of today, the third day has already passed since these things took place**' "(Luke 24:13-21).

When correctly translated, Luke 24:21 does not support the teaching that Jesus Christ was raised from the dead on the first day of the week at sunrise. Those who believe that He was resurrected at sunrise on Easter Sunday have been taught a falsehood! This religious myth rejects the sign of Jonah, which was the only sign that Jesus Christ gave as proof that He was the Messiah. Those who participate in the traditional observance of a Friday crucifixion and an Easter Sunday resurrection are observing traditions of men. Jesus said, "Well did Isaiah prophesy concerning you hypocrites, as it is written, 'This people honors Me with their lips, but their hearts are far away from Me.' But **in vain do they worship Me, teaching *for* doctrine the commandments of men....Full well do you reject the commandment of God, so that you may observe your *own* tradition**" (Mark 7:6-9).

The God of truth cannot be honored by practicing a lie. God the Father rejects that kind of vain worship. Rather, He is seeking those who will worship Him in spirit and in truth, as Jesus said: "But the hour is coming, and now is, when the true worshipers shall worship the Father in spirit and in truth; for the Father is indeed seeking those who worship Him in this manner. God *is* Spirit, and those who worship Him must worship in spirit and in truth" (John 4:23-24).

In order to worship God the Father and Jesus Christ in spirit and in truth, one must repent of his or her sins, accept the sacrifice of Jesus Christ for the forgiveness of sins, be baptized by full immersion in water, receive the Holy Spirit through the laying on of hands, and live from that time forward in the love and grace of God by keeping His commandments. These commandments include keeping the seventh-day Sabbath each week, and keeping the Christian Passover and the annual holy days of God at their appointed times each year. Only those who are under His grace, keeping all His commandments and living by His every word, are worshiping Him in spirit and in truth.

The Three Days and Three Nights In After Three Days

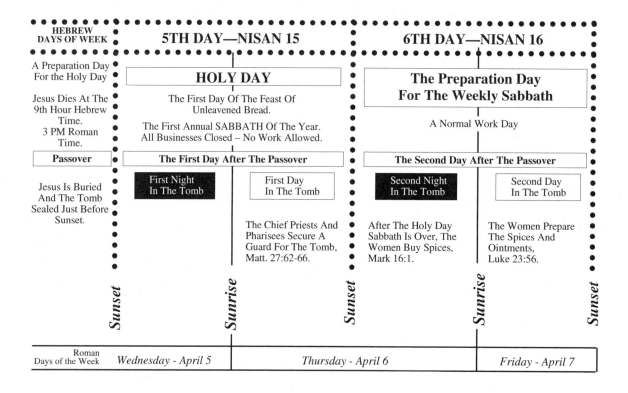

HEBREW DAYS OF WEEK	5TH DAY—NISAN 15	6TH DAY—NISAN 16

A Preparation Day For the Holy Day

HOLY DAY

The First Day Of The Feast Of Unleavened Bread.

Jesus Dies At The 9th Hour Hebrew Time. 3 PM Roman Time.

The First Annual SABBATH Of The Year. All Businesses Closed – No Work Allowed.

The Preparation Day For The Weekly Sabbath

A Normal Work Day

Passover

The First Day After The Passover

The Second Day After The Passover

| First Night In The Tomb | First Day In The Tomb | Second Night In The Tomb | Second Day In The Tomb |

Jesus Is Buried And The Tomb Sealed Just Before Sunset.

The Chief Priests And Pharisees Secure A Guard For The Tomb, Matt. 27:62-66.

After The Holy Day Sabbath Is Over, The Women Buy Spices, Mark 16:1.

The Women Prepare The Spices And Ointments, Luke 23:56.

Sunset *Sunrise* *Sunset* *Sunrise* *Sunset*

| Roman Days of the Week | *Wednesday - April 5* | *Thursday - April 6* | *Friday - April 7* |

The Key To The Time Period From The Burial To The Resurrection:
Jesus Said He Would Be In The Heart Of The Earth (The Tomb)
Three Days And Three Nights; A Complete 72-Hour Period.

Matt. 12:38-40; 27:63	John 2:18-22
Mark 8:31; 9:31	Acts 10:40
Luke 13:32; 18:33; 24:7, 46	1 Cor. 15:4

320

The Tomb and The Resurrection and Three Nights

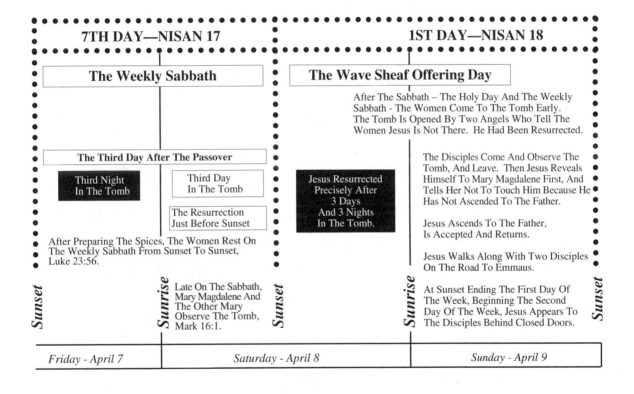

Knowledge of a Wednesday crucifixion was passed down for at least three centuries after the founding of the apostolic church. The *Didascalia*, which dates from the third century, offers historical evidence that the belief in a Friday crucifixion was a change from the original teaching. The following description of the day of Jesus' crucifixion appears in Book V of the *Apostolic Constitutions*, which contains the original words of the *Didascalia*: **"For they began to hold a council against the Lord on the second day of the week**, in the first month, which is Xanthicus; and the deliberation continued on the third day of the week; **but on the fourth day [Wednesday] they determined to take away His life by crucifixion"** (*Apostolic Constitutions—Didascalia Apostolorum*, book V, section I, paragraph xiv). A church historian explains the significance of this record in the *Didascalia*: "…the only reason can have been that **Jesus' passion began on a Wednesday, i.e., the day when He was arrested [and crucified]"** (Lietzmann, *A History of the Early Church*, p. 69).

Golgotha—The Place of the Skull

The Garden Tomb

THE FIRST DAY OF UNLEAVENED BREAD NISAN 15 – THURSDAY, APRIL 6 – 30 AD

367. ON THE HOLY DAY, GUARDS ARE PLACED AT THE TOMB

MATTHEW 27

62. Now on the next day, which followed the preparation *day*, the chief priests and the Pharisees came together to Pilate,

63. Saying, "Sir, we remember that that deceiver said while *He was* living, 'After three days I *will* rise.'

64. Therefore, command *that* the sepulcher be secured until the third day; lest His disciples come by night and steal Him away, and say to the people, 'He is risen from the dead'; and the last deception shall be worse than the first."

65. Then Pilate said to them, "You have a guard. Go, make *it as* secure as you know *how*."

66. And they went *and* made the sepulcher secure, sealing the stone *and* setting the guard.

THE PREPERATION DAY FOR THE WEEKLY SABBATH
NISAN 6 – FRIDAY, APRIL 7 – 30 AD

368. AFTER THE HOLY DAY IS OVER, THE WOMEN BUY AND PREPARE SPICES

MARK 16	LUKE 23
1. Now when the Sabbath had passed, Mary Magdalene and Mary, the *mother* of James, and Salome bought aromatic oils, so that they might come and anoint Him.	56. And they returned *to the city, and* prepared spices and ointments...

THE WEEKLY SABBATH NISAN 17 – SATURDAY, APRIL 8 – 30 AD

369. THE WOMEN REST ON THE WEEKLY SABBATH

LUKE 23

56. ...and *then* rested on the Sabbath according to the commandment.

370. TOWARD THE END OF THE WEEKLY SABBATH,
MARY MAGDALENE AND MARY GO TO OBSERVE THE TOMB

MATTHEW 28

1. Now late on the Sabbath, as *the* first *day* of *the* weeks was drawing near, Mary Magdalene and the other Mary came to observe the sepulcher.

A Sabbath Sunset   - American Stock Photos

PART VIII

THE EVENTS ON THE FIRST DAY OF THE WEEK— THE WAVE SHEAF DAY TO THE ASCENSION

The scriptural records and the calculations of the Hebrew calendar prove conclusively that Jesus was resurrected when the sun set at the end of the weekly Sabbath. The Gospel accounts do not directly reveal what Jesus did between the time that He was resurrected and the time that He was seen by Mary Magdalene the next morning. However, from the scriptural records we can piece together what Jesus did from the time that He was resurrected until He ascended to be accepted by God the Father in the morning as the true Wave Sheaf. The account in the Gospel of John gives us an understanding of what Jesus did first when He came back to life in the tomb: "Then Simon Peter came following him, and he went into the tomb and **saw the linen cloths lying, and the napkin that had been on His head, not lying with the linen cloths but folded up in a place by itself**" (John 20:6-7).

The record of John shows that when Jesus came back to life, He rose straight out of the burial wrappings without disturbing them. When Peter entered the tomb, he saw Jesus' burial wrappings still in the form of His body. This was absolute proof that Jesus had risen from the dead, and no one had taken His body. If someone had taken away His body, it would still have been wrapped with the linen burial cloths.

After rising out of the burial wrappings, Jesus took off the napkin that covered His head and neatly folded it and placed it close by, separate from the other burial cloths. This was an additional proof that He was alive. If anyone had taken His body, the napkin would have either remained on His head or fallen to the ground. It would not have been folded and placed neatly by itself. The apostle John, who was with Peter, saw these things and believed (verse 8).

After folding the napkin, Jesus undoubtedly offered a prayer of thanksgiving to God the Father for raising Him back to life. Perhaps Jesus thought of the prophecy of His resurrection in Psalm 16: "The LORD *is* the portion of mine inheritance and of my cup: *Thou* maintainest my lot. The lines are fallen unto me in pleasant *places*; yea, I have a goodly heritage....Therefore my heart is glad, and my glory rejoiceth: **my flesh also shall rest in hope. For Thou wilt not leave my soul in hell; neither wilt Thou suffer Thine Holy One to see corruption**. Thou wilt show me the path of life: in Thy presence is fullness of joy; at Thy right hand there are pleasures for evermore" (verses 5-6, 9-11, *KJV*).

After offering His prayer of thanksgiving, Jesus must have left the tomb. He did not need to have the stone removed from the entrance of the tomb because He was now spirit and had the ability to pass through matter. The Gospel of Luke confirms this fact. Luke records that approximately twenty-four hours after His resurrection, Jesus suddenly appeared in a closed room where the disciples were assembled. This took place late on the first day of the week, after He had walked with the two disciples to the village of Emmaus: "And they [the two disciples] rose up that very hour *and* returned to Jerusalem; and they found the eleven and those with them assembled together, saying, 'In truth, the Lord has risen! And He has appeared to Simon.' Then they related the things that had happened *to them* on the road, and how He was known to them in the breaking of the bread. Now as they were telling these things, **Jesus Himself stood in their midst** and said to them, 'Peace *be* to you' "(Luke 24:33-36).

The apostle John also wrote of Jesus' sudden appearance: "Afterwards, as evening was drawing near that day, the first *day* of the weeks, and **the doors were shut where the disciples had assembled for fear of the Jews, Jesus came and stood in the midst**, and said to them, 'Peace *be* to you.' And after saying this, He showed them His hands and His side. Then the disciples rejoiced, *because* they had seen the Lord" (John 20:19-20).

Because the resurrected Jesus had the ability to pass through matter, He was able to leave the tomb before the stone was rolled away from the entrance. It is certain that He left the tomb almost immediately after He was resurrected. Remember, Jesus had said, "...the Son of man shall be in the heart of the earth three days and three nights." If He had remained in the tomb for any length of time after His resurrection, He would have been in the heart of the earth for more than three days and three nights.

Where did Jesus go after He left the tomb? The Scriptures do not specify. However, it is probable that He went to a place on the Mount of Olives. Luke records that Jesus was accustomed to going there, where He had a special place of prayer. On the Passover night, after Jesus instituted the New Covenant ceremony, He and the disciples had gone to the Mount of Olives: "**Then He left** *the house and* **went, as He was accustomed, to the Mount of Olives**; and His disciples also followed Him. And when He arrived at the place, He said to them, 'Pray *that you* do not enter into temptation.' **And He withdrew from them about a stone's throw; and falling to** *His* **knees, He prayed**" (Luke 22:39-41).

In his account, Matthew identifies the place of prayer as Gethsemane: "Then Jesus came with them to a place called Gethsemane; and He said to His disciples, 'Sit here, while I go onward and pray' " (Matt. 26:36). This is the place where Jesus prayed for nearly three hours before He was arrested (verses 37-44).

Since Jesus did not ascend to the Father until the morning after His resurrection, it is very probable that He went to the Mount of Olives to His special place of prayer in the Garden of Gethsemane. Once there, Jesus most certainly would have offered up prayers of praise and thanksgiving to God the Father the entire night for having raised Him from the dead. We are able to get a glimpse of what Jesus might have prayed from the prophecies in the book of Psalms that foretold Jesus' death and resurrection.

Jesus Christ had complete faith that God the Father would raise Him from the dead. Psalm 108 reveals Jesus' faith for that deliverance: "O God, my heart is fixed; I will sing and give praise, even with my glory. Awake, psaltery and harp: I *myself* will awake early. **I will praise Thee, O LORD, among the people: and I will sing praises unto Thee among the nations**. For Thy mercy *is* great above the heavens: and Thy truth *reacheth* unto the clouds.

"Be Thou exalted, O God, above the heavens: and Thy glory above all the earth; that Thy beloved [Jesus Christ, the Father's beloved Son] **may be delivered**

325

[from the power of death]: **save *with* Thy right hand**, and answer me. God hath spoken in His holiness [to raise Jesus from the dead]; I will rejoice..." (Psa. 108:1-7, *KJV*).

Paul's epistle to the Hebrews confirms that while Jesus was still in the flesh, He cried out to the Father to save Him from death: "Who, in the days of His flesh, **offered up both prayers and supplications with strong crying and tears to Him Who was able to save Him from death, and was heard because *He* feared *God*.** Although He was a Son, *yet* He learned obedience from the things that He suffered; and having been perfected, He became *the* Author of eternal salvation to all those who obey Him..." (Heb. 5:7-9). During His life in the flesh, Jesus had prayed fervently to the Father for strength to resist temptation, so that He would not incur the death penalty for sin, but might lay down His life as the perfect sacrifice for the sins of the world. Since He prayed so fervently before He died, He must have been equally fervent in thanking and praising the Father for having raised Him from the dead.

We know that the words of Psalm 22 were uttered by Jesus as He was dying on the cross. Just before He died, He uttered the last words of Psalm 22, "It is finished," fulfilled in John 19:30. The following psalm, Psalm 23, has far more meaning when viewed in the context of His crucifixion and resurrection. Could He not also have uttered these words in His prayers to God the Father after He was resurrected?

"The LORD *is* my shepherd; I shall not want [lack any thing]. He maketh me to lie down in green pastures: He leadeth me beside the still waters. He restoreth my soul [by the resurrection]: he leadeth me in the paths of righteousness for His name's sake. Yea, though I walk through the valley of the shadow of death [the crucifixion], I will fear no evil: for *Thou art* with me; Thy rod and Thy staff *they* comfort me. Thou preparest a table before me in the presence of mine enemies: Thou anointest my head with oil; my cup runneth over. Surely goodness and mercy shall follow me all the days of my life: and I will dwell in the house of the LORD for ever [into the ages of eternity]" (Psa. 23:1-6, *KJV*).

The Events on the Morning After Jesus' Resurrection

The Gospel accounts show that as the sun was rising, early in the morning on the first day of the week, the women came bringing spices to anoint Jesus' body. Although Mary Magdalene left home while it was still dark, by the time she arrived at the tomb it was light enough for her to see that the stone had been removed (John 20:1). Apparently, just before she and the other women arrived, an angel had opened the tomb. If it had been opened for any length of time before the women arrived, the soldiers would not have been standing guard. "And *in the morning* suddenly there was a great earthquake; for an angel of *the* Lord descended from heaven, and came and rolled away the stone from the door, and sat upon it. Now his appearance was as lightning, and his raiment white as snow. And for fear of him, those who were keeping guard trembled, and became as dead *men*" (Matt. 28:2-4).

As the women were approaching the tomb, they were wondering who would roll away the huge stone from the entrance of the tomb in order for them to anoint Jesus' body with the spices. But when they arrived, they saw that the stone had already been removed and the tomb was open. Mark gives this account: "And very early on

326

the first *day* of the weeks, at the rising of the sun, they were coming to the tomb; and they were asking themselves, 'Who will roll away the stone for us from the entrance to the tomb?' For it was a massive *stone*. **But when they looked up, they saw that the stone had been rolled away**. And after entering the tomb, they saw a young man [the angel who had rolled away the stone] sitting on the right, clothed in a white robe; and they were very frightened. But he said to them, '**Do not be afraid. You are seeking Jesus the Nazarene, Who was crucified. He has risen; He is not here. Look, *there is* the place where they laid Him**. But go, tell His disciples and Peter that He goes before you into Galilee; there you shall see Him, as He said to you.' And they went out quickly and fled from the tomb, for trembling and astonishment had seized them; and they did not say anything to anyone because they were afraid" (Mark 16:2-8).

The Gospel accounts clearly record that the angel told the women, "**He is risen. He is not here.**" **Jesus was not in the tomb**! Jesus was not there because He had been resurrected from the dead as the weekly Sabbath ended over twelve hours earlier. He did not need the stone to be rolled away to leave the tomb, because He had the power to pass through matter. However, it was necessary for the stone to be removed in order for the women to see that He was not there. They found the tomb empty except for the grave cloths that had been wound around His body.

When the other women left to tell the disciples, Mary Magdalene went to tell Peter and John: "Then she ran and came to Simon Peter and to the other disciple whom Jesus loved, and said to them, 'They have taken away the Lord from the tomb, and we do not know where they have laid Him.' As a result, Peter and the other disciple went out and came to the tomb. Now the two ran together, but the other disciple ran faster than Peter and came to the tomb first; and he stooped down *and* saw the linen cloths lying *there*, but he did not enter.

"Then Simon Peter came following him, and he went into the tomb and saw the linen cloths lying, and the napkin that had been on His head, not lying with the linen cloths but folded up in a place by itself. Then the other disciple, who had come to the tomb first, also went in and saw *these things*; and he believed. For they did not yet understand the scripture *which decreed* that He must rise from *the* dead. Then the disciples went away again to their *home*" (John 20:2-10).

After Peter and John left, Mary Magdalene remained at the tomb because she thought that "they had taken away the Lord," and she did not know where He was. "But Mary stood outside the tomb weeping; and as she wept, she stooped down *and looked* into the tomb. And she saw two angels in white who were sitting, one at the head and the other at the feet, where the body of Jesus had been laid. And they said to her, 'Woman, why are you weeping?' She said to them, 'Because they have taken away my Lord, and I do not know where they have laid Him' " (John 20:11-13).

After all those things transpired, Jesus returned to the tomb and appeared to Mary Magdalene: "And after saying these things, she turned around and saw Jesus standing, but did not know that it was Jesus. Jesus said to her, 'Woman, why are you weeping? Whom are you seeking?' Thinking that He was the gardener, she said to Him, 'Sir, if you have carried Him off, tell me where you have laid Him, and I will take Him away.' Jesus said to her, 'Mary.' Turning around, she said to Him,

'Rabboni'; that is to say, 'Teacher.' Jesus said to her, 'Do not touch Me, because I have not yet ascended to My Father. But go to My brethren and tell them that I am ascending to My Father and your Father, and My God and your God.' Mary Magdalene came to the disciples, bringing word that she had seen the Lord, and that He had said these things to her" (verses 14-18).

Correcting the Misinterpretation of Mark 16:9

In the King James Version, Mark 16:9 reads as follows: "**Now when *Jesus* was risen early the first day of the week,** He appeared first to Mary Magdalene...." This translation makes it appear that Jesus was resurrected early in the morning on the first day of the week. However, the Gospel accounts show that Jesus was raised at the close of the weekly Sabbath, approximately twelve hours before the women came to the tomb. The erroneous impression that the KJV translation gives can be corrected simply by the addition of a comma in the proper place: "**Now when *Jesus* was risen,** early *the* first *day* of the week He appeared first to Mary Magdalene...." A more accurate translation, as well as the proper placement of the comma, clears up any misunderstanding or misinterpretation. It reads as follows: "**Now after Jesus had risen**, early *the* first *day* of the week He appeared first to Mary Magdalene...." With the proper translation and placement of the comma, this verse harmonizes with the rest of the scriptural facts as found in the other Gospel accounts.

Jesus Fulfilled the Wave Sheaf Offering

In John's Gospel we find this post-resurrection account: "Jesus said to her [Mary Magdalene], '**Do not touch Me, because I have not yet ascended to My Father**. But go to My brethren and **tell them that I am ascending to My Father and your Father, and My God and your God**' " (John 20:17).

When Jesus appeared to Mary Magdalene, He did not allow her to touch Him because He had not yet ascended to God the Father. The words that He spoke to her show that He was about to ascend. We can conclude that He ascended to the Father soon after she left to tell the disciples. When Jesus ascended, He fulfilled a very special temple ceremony that God had commanded for this day. This ceremony was the presentation of the wave sheaf offering of the first of the firstfruits of the grain harvest, which was performed at approximately 9 AM in the morning, after the morning burnt offering had been made. It was at this time that Jesus ascended to God the Father.

The wave sheaf was offered each year on the first day of the week during the Feast of Unleavened Bread. As the sacrifice of the Passover lamb was a foretype of the crucifixion and death of Jesus Christ, so the offering of the wave sheaf was a foretype of Jesus' ascension to the Father. This day was a special day, but not a holy day. At the temple, on the first day of the week during the Feast of Unleavened Bread, the priest would perform the wave sheaf ritual. We find God's command for the wave sheaf offering in the book of Leviticus: "And the LORD spake unto Moses, saying, 'Speak unto the children of Israel, and say unto them, When ye be come into the land which *I* give unto you, and shall reap the harvest thereof, then ye shall bring a sheaf of the firstfruits of your harvest unto the priest: and he shall wave the sheaf before the LORD, to be accepted for you: on the morrow after the sabbath [the first day of the week during the Feast of Unleavened Bread] the priest shall wave it' " (Lev. 23:9-11, *KJV*).

Messianic Rabbi Alfred Edersheim records the details of the harvesting of the wave sheaf in his book *The Life and Times of Jesus the Messiah:*

"This Passover-sheaf was reaped in public the evening before it was offered, and it was to witness this ceremony that the crowd had gathered around the elders. Already on the 14th [of] Nisan the spot whence the first sheaf was to be reaped had been marked out, by tying together in bundles, while still standing, the barley that was to be cut down, according to custom, in the sheltered Ashes-Valley across Kidron. When the time for cutting the sheaf had arrived—that is, on the evening of the 15th [of] Nisan [by Pharisaic reckoning], even though it were a Sabbath [the journey to harvest was undertaken before the end of the Sabbath, but was within the prescribed traditional "Sabbath day's journey"], just as the sun went down, three men, each with a sickle and basket, set to work.

"Clearly to bring out what was distinctive in the ceremony, they first asked of the bystanders three times each of these questions: 'HAS THE SUN GONE DOWN?' 'With this sickle?' 'Into this basket?' 'On this Sabbath? (or first Passover-day)'—and lastly, 'Shall I reap?' Having each time been answered in the affirmative, they cut down barley to the amount of one ephah, or about three pecks and three pints of our English measure" (*The Life and Times of Jesus the Messiah*, p. 619).

Note: There was a dispute between the Pharisees and the Sadducees as to which Sabbath this verse is designating. The Pharisees applied this command to the first holy day of the Feast of Unleavened Bread, which was the 15th day of the first month, or Nisan. In their view, the "morrow after the Sabbath"—the day for harvesting the wave sheaf—was always the 16th of Nisan. On the other hand, the Sadducees, who were in charge of the temple during the days of Jesus Christ, understood that God's command in Leviticus 23:11 was referring to the weekly Sabbath which occurred in conjunction with the Feast of Unleavened Bread. In years when the first day of the Feast of Unleavened Bread fell on the weekly Sabbath, both the Sadducees and the Pharisees would observe the 16th of Nisan as the day for the wave sheaf offering. Although the Sadducees and the Pharisees generally disagreed over the correct DAY for the wave sheaf offering, there was never any question about the correct TIME of the day for harvesting it.

After it was cut, the bundled sheaf was brought to the temple and placed alongside the altar of burnt offering. Then in the morning, after the daily burnt offering of a lamb, the priest would "wave" or elevate the sheaf to be accepted of the Lord. This was a special ceremonial sheaf. In The Shocken Bible, Volume I, The Five Books of Moses, Everett Fox translates Leviticus 23:10-11 in this manner: "Speak to the children of Israel and say to them; When you enter the land that I am giving you, and you harvest its harvest, you are to bring **the premier sheaf** of your harvest to the priest. He is to elevate the sheaf before the presence of YHWH for acceptance for you; on the morrow of the Sabbath the priest shall elevate it."

Note the key words in God's instructions for the wave sheaf offering: "for acceptance for you," meaning "on your behalf." When Jesus Christ ascended to the Father on the Wave Sheaf Day, as the first of the firstfruits, His sacrifice for our sins was accepted by the Father on our behalf. Jesus, as the Lamb of God, was accepted as the sin offering not only for our sins but for the sins of all mankind: "…The lamb of God, Who takes away the sin of the world" (John 1:29).

Jesus fulfilled the wave sheaf offering as the first of the firstfruits to be resurrected from the dead. The premier sheaf symbolized the risen Christ. When the priest elevated the sheaf to be accepted by the Lord, it represented Jesus Christ ascending to the Father to be accepted as the first of the firstfruits. The apostle Paul makes it clear that this premier sheaf of the firstfruits was a type of Jesus Christ after He rose from the dead and ascended into heaven to present Himself to God the Father: "But now Christ has been raised from *the* dead; **He has become the firstfruit of those who have fallen asleep**. For since by man *came* death, by man also *came the* resurrection of *the* dead. For as in Adam all die, so also in Christ shall all be made alive. But each one in his own order: **Christ *the* firstfruit;** then, those who are Christ's at His coming" (I Cor. 15:20-23).

Because Jesus is the first of many who will be resurrected from the dead as immortal children of God, He is also called "the firstborn from among the dead," as Paul writes to the Colossians: "Because by Him were all things created, the things in heaven and the things on earth, the visible and the invisible, whether *they be* thrones, or lordships, or principalities, or powers: all things were created by Him and for Him. And He is before all, and by Him all things subsist. **And He is the Head of the body, the church; Who is *the* beginning, *the* firstborn from among the dead, so that in all things He Himself might hold the preeminence**" (Col. 1:16-18).

In his epistle to the Romans, Paul makes it clear that many will be resurrected from the grave and be added to the Family of God as immortal brethren of Jesus Christ: "Because those whom He did foreknow, He also predestinated *to be* conformed to the image of His own Son, **that He might be *the* firstborn among many brethren**" (Rom. 8:29). Paul also tells the Corinthians that those who die in the faith will be resurrected at His coming. The resurrection of the saints of God to immortality and glory will mark the end of the firstfruits harvest, just as the resurrection of Jesus signaled its beginning. As He ascended to heaven in the clouds, so He will return, and all the transformed saints will rise into the air to meet Him. The entrance of the saints into the Family of God has been made possible through the sacrifice of Jesus Christ, which was accepted by God the Father on the Wave Sheaf Day.

Jesus Christ Accepted by God the Father

The ascension of Jesus to God the Father was an awesome event. Jesus Christ had finished the work that the Father had given Him to do. As God manifest in the flesh, He had lived a perfect, sinless life and had died by crucifixion to become the perfect sacrifice for the sins of all mankind. God the Father had raised Jesus back to life, and on the Wave Sheaf Day He was ready to ascend to the throne of God the Father to be accepted as the first of the firstfruits, the firstborn among many brethren, and the perfect sacrifice to propitiate the sins of the world.

As He was ascending to the Father, Jesus must have been filled with great joy and anticipation. He would see the Father face to face for the first time since He had become a pinpoint of life when He divested Himself of His power and glory as God to be born of the virgin Mary. Again, the Psalms help us comprehend some of the thoughts and feelings that Jesus might have experienced as He looked forward to being reunited with the Father: "**O God, *Thou art* my God**; early will I seek Thee: my soul thirsteth for Thee, my flesh longeth for Thee in a dry and thirsty land, where no water is; **to see Thy power and Thy glory, so** *as* **I have seen Thee in the sanctuary**. Because Thy lovingkindness is better than life, my lips shall praise Thee" (Psa. 63:1-3, *KJV*).

As previously noted, Psalm 23 foreshadowed the prayers of Jesus after He was resurrected from the dead. The psalm to follow, Psalm 24, is in prophetic sequence and depicts Jesus' ascension to be received of God the Father. When He arrived in heaven, the angels sang and shouted for joy. Perhaps this psalm was sung by the angels as they opened the everlasting doors and announced that the King of glory was entering into the presence of God the Father: "The earth is the LORD'S, and the fullness thereof; the world, and they that dwell therein. For *He* hath founded it upon the seas, and established it upon the floods. **Who shall ascend into the hill of the LORD? Or who shall stand in His holy place? He that hath clean hands, and a pure heart; who hath not lifted up his soul unto vanity, nor sworn deceitfully** [the perfect life of Jesus Christ]. **He shall receive the blessing from the LORD, and righteousness from the God of his salvation.**"

"Lift up your heads, O ye gates; and be ye lifted up, ye everlasting doors; and the King of glory shall come in. Who *is* **this King of glory? The LORD strong and mighty, the LORD mighty in battle** [He was victorious over human nature, sin, Satan the devil and death]. **Lift up your heads, O ye gates; even lift** *them* **up, ye everlasting doors; and the King of glory shall come in. Who is** *this* **King of glory? The LORD of hosts,** *He is* **the King of glory"** (Psa. 24:1-5, 7-10, *KJV*).

What a magnificent scene of splendor and glory Jesus would have seen when He entered through the everlasting gates of heaven! Standing on the sea of glass, He would have seen the resplendent glory and awesome majesty of God the Father seated on His throne with the heavenly host round about. The apostle John, the one whom Jesus loved, saw a vision of God's throne and recorded it in the book of Revelation. What John recorded is what Jesus would have seen when He ascended to the Father.

"After these things I looked, and behold, **a door opened in heaven**, and the first voice that I heard *was* as if a trumpet were speaking with me, saying, 'Come up here, and I will show you *the* things that must take place after these things.' And immediately I was in *the* Spirit; and **behold, a throne was set in heaven, and** *one was* **sitting on the throne**. And He Who *was* sitting was in appearance like a jasper stone and a sardius stone: and a rainbow *was* around the throne, like an emerald in its appearance.

"And around the throne *were* twenty-four thrones, and on the thrones I saw twenty-four elders sitting, clothed in white garments; and they had on their heads golden crowns. **And proceeding from the throne were lightnings and thunders and voices**; and seven lamps of fire, which are the seven Spirits of God, *were* burning before the throne. **And before the throne** *was* **a sea of glass, like crystal. And around the throne and over the throne** *were* **four living creatures, full of eyes before and behind**; and the first living creature *was* like a lion, and the second living creature *was* like a calf, and the third living creature had the face of a man, and the fourth living creature *was* like a flying eagle. And each of *the* four living creatures had six wings respectively; *and* around and within *they were* full of eyes; **and day**

and night they ceased not saying, 'Holy, holy, holy, Lord God Almighty, Who was, and Who is, and Who *is* to come.'

"And when the living creatures give glory and honor and thanksgiving to Him Who sits on the throne, Who lives into the ages of eternity, the twenty-four elders fall down before Him Who sits on the throne; and they worship Him Who lives into the ages of eternity, and cast their crowns before the throne, saying, '**Worthy are You, O Lord, to receive glory and honor and power because You did create all things, and for Your will they were created and exist**' " (Rev. 4:1-11).

This was the scene that Jesus would have seen as He walked forward to present Himself to the Father as the perfect sacrifice for sin. He was the first of the firstfruits and the firstborn from the dead. As He walked on the sea of glass toward the Father sitting on His throne, the angels, the twenty-four elders and God the Father would see on His body the scars of the lashes that He had received when He was beaten with the cat-of-nine-tails which tore open His flesh. They would see the scars in His hands and feet where the soldiers had nailed Him to the cross. When the Father's beloved Son greeted His Father, They must have opened their arms and embraced each other in profound love and tears of joy. Thus Jesus Christ, the Lamb of God, was accepted by God the Father on the Wave Sheaf Day.

After He was accepted of the Father, Jesus was selected to open the seven seals. He and He alone was qualified, because He had overcome all. The apostle John saw this tremendous scene in the vision and recorded it: "And in the right hand of Him Who sits on the throne I saw a book, written within and on *the* back, which had been sealed with seven seals. And I saw a strong angel proclaiming with a loud voice, '**Who is worthy to open the book and to loose its seals**?' But no one in heaven, or on the earth, or under the earth was able to open the book, or to look inside it. And I [John] was weeping greatly because no one was found worthy to open and to read the book, or to look into it.

"Then one of the elders said to me, 'Do not weep. Behold, the Lion Who is of the tribe of Judah, the Root of David, has overcome to open the book, and to loose its seven seals.' **Then I saw, and behold, before the throne and the four living creatures, and before the elders, *was* standing a Lamb as having been slain**, having seven horns and seven eyes, which are the seven Spirits of God that are sent into all the earth; and **He came and took the book out of the right hand of Him Who sits on the throne**.

"And when He took the book, the four living creatures and the twenty-four elders fell down before the Lamb, each having harps and golden bowls full of incense, which are the prayers of the saints. And they sang a new song, saying, '**Worthy are You to take the book, and to open its seals because You were slain, and did redeem us to God by Your own blood, out of every tribe and language and people and nation,** and did make us unto our God kings and priests; and we shall reign on the earth.'

"**And I saw, and I heard *the* voices of many angels around the throne, and *the* voices of the living creatures and the elders, and thousands of thousands, saying with a loud voice, 'Worthy is the Lamb Who was slain to receive power, and** riches, and wisdom, and strength, and honor, and glory and blessing.' And every creature that is in heaven, and on the earth, and under the earth, and those that are on the sea, and all the things in them, I heard saying, 'To Him Who sits on the throne, and to the Lamb, *be* blessing, and honor, and glory, and sovereignty into the ages of eternity.' And the four living creatures said, 'Amen.' And the twenty-four elders fell down and worshiped *Him Who* lives into the ages of eternity" (Rev. 5:1-12).

This is the glory and majesty that Jesus Christ received when He was accepted by God the Father as the Savior and Redeemer of mankind on the Wave Sheaf Day. Jesus had overcome sin in the flesh and gained complete victory over death, opening the way for the redemption and salvation of all mankind through faith in Him. Now He lives in eternal glory, as the first of many sons of God who will be resurrected at His second coming to share His eternal glory and immortality. Those who are Jesus Christ's are now being perfected through the love, grace and power of God the Father. They will be granted the identical spiritual existence that the Father and the Son have. They will be the sons and daughters of God the Father, and the brethren of Jesus Christ. Jesus shared human existence with mankind in order to become the sin offering for the world so that all who believe in Him may ultimately share His eternal existence and glory in the Family of God throughout the ages of eternity.

Sea of Galilee—"He Leads Me Beside Still Waters"

NISAN 18 – SUNDAY MORNING, APRIL 9 – 30 AD
371. EARLY THE FIRST DAY OF THE WEEK, JUST BEFORE WOMEN ARRIVE AT THE TOMB, AN ANGEL OPENS THE TOMB
MATTHEW 28

2. And *in the morning* suddenly there was a great earthquake; for an angel of *the* Lord descended from heaven, and came and rolled away the stone from the door, and sat upon it.
3. Now his appearance was as lightning, and his raiment white as snow.
4. And for fear of him, those who were keeping guard trembled, and became as dead *men*.

372. EARLY THE FIRST DAY OF THE WEEK, WOMEN COME TO THE TOMB, BUT JESUS HAS ALREADY BEEN RESURRECTED

MATTHEW 28	MARK 16	LUKE 24	JOHN 20
5. But the angel answered *and* said to the women, "Do not be afraid; for I know that you are seeking Jesus, Who was crucified.	2. And very early on the first *day* of the weeks*, at the rising of the sun, they were coming to the tomb;	1. Now on the first *day* of the weeks,* they came to the tomb at early dawn, bringing *the* spices that they had prepared; and certain *others came* with them.	1. Now on the first *day* of the weeks,* while it was still dark, Mary Magdalene came early to the tomb; and she saw *that* the stone had been taken away from the tomb.
6. He is not here; for He has risen, as He said. Come, see the place where the Lord Himself was lying.	3. And they were asking themselves, "Who will roll away the stone for us from the entrance to the tomb?"	2. But they found the stone rolled away from the tomb;	2. Then she ran and came to Simon Peter and to the other disciple whom Jesus loved, and said to them, "They have taken away the Lord from the tomb, and we do not know where they have laid Him."
7. And go quickly, *and* tell His disciples that He has risen from the dead. And behold, He goes before you into Galilee; there you shall see Him. Listen! I have told you."	4. For it was a massive *stone*. But when they looked up, they saw that the stone had been rolled away.	3. And when they entered *it*, they did not find the body of the Lord Jesus.	3. As a result, Peter and the other disciple went out and came to the tomb.
8. And they quickly left the tomb with fear and great joy, *and* ran to tell *it* to His disciples.	5. And after entering the tomb, they saw a young man sitting on the right, clothed in a white robe; and they were very frightened.	4. And it came to pass that while they were puzzling over this, suddenly two men in shining garments stood by them.	4. Now the two ran together, but the other disciple ran faster than Peter and came to the tomb first;
	6. But he said to them, "Do not be afraid. You are seeking Jesus the Nazarene, Who was crucified. He has risen; He is not here. Look, *there is* the place where they laid Him.	5. And *as* they bowed their faces to the ground, being filled with fear, they said to them, "Why are you seeking the living among the dead?	5. And he stooped down *and* saw the linen cloths lying *there*, but he did not enter.
	7. But go, tell His disciples and Peter that He goes before you into Galilee; there you shall see Him, as He said to you."	6. He is not here, but has risen: remember when He spoke to you *while He* was yet in Galilee,	6. Then Simon Peter came following him, and he went into the tomb and saw the linen cloths lying,

*This literal translation of the Greek words μια σαββατων *or* μια των σαββατων *shows that the day which followed the weekly Sabbath was the first day of the seven-week count to Pentecost, thus identifying this day as the Wave Sheaf Day (Lev. 23:10-11, 15-16). The ascension of Jesus Christ on that day fulfilled the offering of the wave sheaf for all time.*

NISAN 18 – SUNDAY MORNING, APRIL 9, 30 AD

MARK 16	LUKE 24	JOHN 20
8. And they went out quickly and fled from the tomb, for trembling and astonishment had seized them; and they did not say anything to anyone because they were afraid.	7. Saying, 'It is necessary for the Son of man to be delivered into *the* hands of sinful men, and to be crucified, and to arise the third day'?" 8. Then they remembered His words; 9. And after returning from the tomb, they related these things to the eleven and to all the rest. 10. Now it was Mary Magdalene and Joanna and Mary, *the mother* of James, and the others with them, who told these things to the apostles. 11. But their words appeared to them as idle talk, and they did not believe them. 12. Then Peter rose up *and* ran to the tomb; and stooping down, he saw the linen clothes lying alone; and he went home wondering about the things that had come to pass.	7. And the napkin that had been on His head, not lying with the linen cloths but folded up in a place by itself. 8. Then the other disciple, who had come to the tomb first, also went in and saw *these things*; and he believed. 9. For they did not yet understand the scripture *which decreed* that He must rise from *the* dead. 10. Then the disciples went away again to their *home*.

Jerusalem from Air

373. JESUS APPEARS FIRST TO MARY MAGDALENE

MARK 16

9. Now after *Jesus* had risen, early *the* first *day* of the weeks He appeared first to Mary Magdalene, from whom He had cast out seven demons.
10. She went *and* told *it* to those who had been with Him, *who* were grieving and weeping.
11. And when they heard that He was alive and had been seen by her, they did not believe *it*.

JOHN 20

11. But Mary stood outside the tomb weeping; and as she wept, she stooped down *and looked* into the tomb.
12. And she saw two angels in white who were sitting, one at the head and the other at the feet, where the body of Jesus had been laid.
13. And they said to her, "Woman, why are you weeping?" She said to them, "Because they have taken away my Lord, and I do not know where they have laid Him."
14. And after saying these things, she turned around and saw Jesus standing, but did not know that it was Jesus.

NISAN 18 – SUNDAY MORNING, APRIL 9, 30 AD

JOHN 20

15. Jesus said to her, "Woman, why are you weeping? Whom are you seeking?" Thinking that He was the gardener, she said to Him, "Sir, if you have carried Him off, tell me where you have laid Him, and I will take Him away."
16. Jesus said to her, "Mary." Turning around, she said to Him, "Rabboni"; that is to say, "Teacher."
17. Jesus said to her, "Do not touch Me, because I have not yet ascended to My Father. But go to My brethren and tell them that I am ascending to My Father and your Father, and My God and your God."
18. Mary Magdalene came to the disciples, bringing word that she had seen the Lord, and that He had said these things to her.

NISAN 18 – SUNDAY, APRIL 9, 30 AD

374. SOLDIERS BRIBED TO LIE

MATTHEW 28

11. And as they were going, behold, some of the guard went into the city *and* reported to the chief priests all the things that were done.
12. Then, after gathering together with the elders and taking counsel, they gave a large sum of money to the soldiers,
13. Saying, "Tell *everyone* that His disciples came by night and stole Him while you were sleeping.
14. And if the governor hears *of* this, we will persuade him to release you from responsibility."
15. And they took the money *and* did as they were instructed; and this report has been spread abroad among the Jews to this day.

375. JESUS APPEARS TO TWO DISCIPLES ON A JOURNEY TO EMMAUS

LUKE 24

13. And behold, on the same day, two of them were going to a village called Emmaus, which was about sixty furlongs from Jerusalem.
14. And they were talking with one another about all the things that had taken place.
15. And it came to pass, as they were talking and reasoning, that Jesus Himself drew near *and* went with them;
16. But their eyes were restrained, *so that* they did not know Him.
17. And He said to them, "What *are* these words that you are exchanging with one another as you walk, and *why* are you downcast in countenance?"
18. Then the one named Cleopas answered *and* said to Him, "Are You only traveling through Jerusalem, and have not known of the things that have happened in these days?"
19. And He said to them, "What things?" And they said to Him, "The things concerning Jesus the Nazarean, a man Who was a prophet, Who was mighty in deed and word before God and all the people;
20. And how the chief priests and our rulers delivered Him up to *the* judgment of death, and crucified Him.
21. And we were hoping that He was the one Who would redeem Israel. But besides all these things, as of today, the third day has already passed since these things took place.
22. And also, certain women from among us astonished us, after they went to the tomb early;

NISAN 18 – SUNDAY, APRIL 9, 30 AD

LUKE 24

23. For when they did not find His body, they came *to us*, declaring that they had indeed seen a vision of angels, who said, 'He is living.'
24. And some of those with us went to the tomb and found *it* exactly as the women had said, but they did not see Him."
25. Then He said to them, "O foolish and slow of heart to believe in all that the prophets have spoken!
26. Was it not necessary for the Christ to suffer these things, and to enter into His glory?"
27. And beginning with Moses, and from all the prophets, He interpreted to them the things concerning Himself in all the Scriptures.
28. And *as* they approached the village where they were going, He appeared to be going on farther.
29. But they constrained Him, saying, "Stay with us, for it is toward evening, and the day is declining." And He entered in *as if* to stay with them.
30. And it came to pass, as He sat *at the table* with them, He took the bread *and* blessed *it*; and after breaking *it*, He gave *it* to them.
31. Then their eyes were opened, and they knew Him; and He disappeared from them.
32. And they said to one another, "Did not our hearts burn within us as He was speaking to us on the road, while He was opening the Scriptures to us?"
33. And they rose up that very hour *and* returned to Jerusalem; and they found the eleven and those with them assembled together,
34. Saying, "In truth, the Lord has risen! And He has appeared to Simon."
35. Then they related the things that had happened *to them* on the road, and how He was known to them in the breaking of the bread.

MARK 16

12. Now after these things, He appeared in a different form to two of them as they were walking, going *away* into *the* country.
13. And they went and told *it* to the rest; *but* they did not believe them either.

Village of Emmaus

NISAN 18 – SUNDAY, APRIL 9, 30 AD

376. AT SUNSET, AS THE FIRST DAY OF THE WEEK IS ENDING, JESUS APPEARS TO THE DISCIPLES BEHIND CLOSED DOORS

JOHN 20

19. Afterwards, as evening was drawing near that day, the first *day* of the weeks, and the doors were shut where the disciples had assembled for fear of the Jews, Jesus came and stood in the midst, and said to them, "Peace *be* to you."
20. And after saying this, He showed them His hands and His side. Then the disciples rejoiced *because* they had seen the Lord.
21. Therefore, Jesus said to them again, "Peace *be* to you. As the Father sent Me, I am also sending you."
22. And after saying this, He breathed on *them* and said, "Receive *the* Holy Spirit.
23. Those whose sins you shall remit, they are remitted to them; *and* those whose sins you shall retain, they are retained."
24. But Thomas, called Didymus, one of the twelve, was not with them when Jesus came.
25. Then the other disciples said to him, "We have seen the Lord." But he said to them, "Unless I see the nail marks in His hands, and put my finger into the nail marks, and put my hand into His side, I will not believe at all."

MATTHEW 28

9. But as they were going to tell His disciples, all at once Jesus Himself met them, saying, "Hail!" And they came to *Him and* held His feet, and worshiped Him.
10. Then Jesus said to them, "Do not be afraid. Go, tell My brethren to go into Galilee, and there they shall see Me."

MARK 16

14. Afterwards, as they were sitting *to eat,* He appeared to the eleven and reproached *them for* their unbelief and hardness of heart, because they did not believe those who had seen Him after He had risen.

LUKE 24

36. Now as they were telling these things, Jesus Himself stood in their midst and said to them, "Peace *be* to you."
37. But they were terrified and filled with fear, thinking *that* they beheld a spirit.
38. Then He said to them, "Why are you troubled? And why do doubts come up in your hearts?
39. See My hands and My feet, that it is I. Touch Me and see *for yourselves;* for a spirit does not have flesh and bones, as you see Me having."
40. And after saying this, He showed them *His* hands and *His* feet.
41. But while they were still disbelieving and wondering for joy, He said to them, "Do you have anything here to eat?"
42. Then they gave Him part of a broiled fish and a *piece* of honeycomb.
43. And He took these *and* ate in their presence.

Caravan Inn—Model City Jerusalem

Mount Zion—Jerusalem

LUKE 24

44. And He said to them, "These *are* the words that I spoke to you when I was yet with you, that all *the* things which were written concerning Me in the Law of Moses and *in the* Prophets and *in the* Psalms must be fulfilled." [a]
45. Then He opened their minds to understand the Scriptures,
46. And said to them, "According as it is written, it was necessary for the Christ to suffer, and to rise from *the* dead the third day.
47. And in His name, repentance and remission of sins should be preached to all nations, beginning at Jerusalem.
48. For you are witnesses of these things.

377. EIGHT DAYS LATER, JESUS APPEARS TO HIS DISCIPLES AGAIN
JOHN 20

26. Now after eight days, His disciples again were within, and Thomas with them. Jesus came after the doors were shut, and stood in the midst and said, "Peace *be* to you."
27. Then He said to Thomas, "Put forth your finger, and see My hands; and reach *out* your hand, and put *it* into My side; and be not unbelieving, but believing."
28. And Thomas answered and said to Him, "My Lord and My God."
29. Jesus said to him, "Because you have seen Me, Thomas, you have believed; blessed are the ones who have not seen, but have believed."

378. JESUS DOES MANY MIRACLES IN THE PRESENCE OF THE DISCIPLES
JOHN 20

30. Now then, Jesus did many other miracles in *the* presence of His disciples, which are not written in this book.
31. But these have been written, so that you may believe that Jesus is the Christ, the Son of God; and that believing, you may have life through His name.

---

a - **Luke 24:44-48**: *By the time that Jesus had finished eating the fish and honeycomb, the sun had set, ending the first day of the week. Therefore, Jesus' teachings concerning prophecies about Him in the Law of Moses, the Prophets and the Psalms, did not occur on the first day of the week, but on the second day of the week. Undoubtedly, He did not finish His teachings for many hours. Because of the numerous Scriptures involved in these prophecies, it must have taken most of the night.*

379. SOME TIME LATER, JESUS IS SEEN BY 500 OF THE BRETHREN
1 CORINTHIANS 15

4. And that He was buried; and that He was raised the third day, according to the Scriptures;
5. And that He appeared to Cephas, *and* then to the twelve.
6. Then He appeared to over five hundred brethren at one time, of whom the greater part are alive until now, but some have fallen sleep.
7. Next He appeared to James; then to all the apostles;

380. JESUS MEETS THE APOSTLES AT THE APPOINTED MOUNTAIN
MATTHEW 28

16. Now the eleven disciples went into Galilee, to the mountain which Jesus had appointed *for* them *to meet Him.*
17. And when they saw Him, they worshiped Him; but some doubted.

381. LATER, JESUS APPEARS TO HIS DISCIPLES IN GALILEE
JOHN 21

1. After these things, Jesus again revealed Himself to the disciples at the Sea of Tiberias. And this *is how* He revealed *Himself*:
2. Simon Peter, and Thomas (called Didymus), and Nathanael from Cana of Galilee were there together, and the *sons* of Zebedee and two of His other disciples.
3. Simon Peter said to them, "I am going fishing." They said to him, "We also will come with you." They left immediately and got into the ship, but during that night they took nothing.
4. And when morning had now come, Jesus stood on the shore. However, none of the disciples realized that it was Jesus.
5. Then Jesus said to them, "Children, do you have any food?" They answered Him, "No."
6. And He said to them, "Cast the net to the right side of the ship, and you shall find *some.*" Then they cast *the net*, but they did not have the strength to draw *it in* because of the multitude of fish.
7. Then that disciple whom Jesus loved said to Peter, "It is the Lord." And after hearing that it was the Lord, Peter put on *his* outer garment, because he was naked, and threw himself into the sea.
8. But the other disciples came in a small ship, dragging the net *full* of fish; for they were not far from land, but about two hundred cubits *away.*
9. Now then, when they came up to the land, they saw a fire of coals spread, and fish lying on *it*, and bread.
10. Jesus said to them, "Bring some of the fish that you have just caught."
11. Simon Peter went up *to the shore* and drew the net to the land, full of large fish, one hundred *and* fifty-three; and *although* there were so many, the net was not torn.
12. Jesus said to them, "Come *and* dine." But none of the disciples dared to ask Him, "Who are You?" *For* they knew that it was the Lord.
13. Then Jesus came and took the bread, and gave *it* to them, and likewise the fish.
14. This *was* now the third time *that* Jesus revealed Himself to His disciples after being raised from *the* dead.

382. JESUS ASKS PETER IF HE LOVES HIM
AND COMMANDS HIM TO FEED AND SHEPHERD JESUS' SHEEP

JOHN 21

15. Therefore, when they had finished eating, Jesus said to Simon Peter, "Simon, *son* of Jonas, do you love Me more than these?" *And* he said to Him, "Yes, Lord. You know that I love You." He said to him, "Feed My lambs."

16. He said to him again a second time, "Simon, *son* of Jonas, do you love Me?" *And* he said to Him, "Yes, Lord. You know that I love You." He said to him, "Shepherd My sheep."

17. He said to him the third time, "Simon, *son* of Jonas, do you love Me?" Peter was grieved because He said to him the third time, "Do you love Me?" And he said to Him, "Lord, You know all things. You know that I love You." Jesus said to him, "Feed My sheep.

18. Truly, truly I say to you, since you were young, you have dressed yourself and walked wherever you have desired; but when you are old, you shall stretch out your hands, and another shall dress you and bring *you* where you do not desire *to go*."

19. Now He said this to signify by what death he would glorify God. And after saying this, He said to him, "Follow Me."

20. But when Peter turned, he saw the disciple whom Jesus loved following, who also had sat at the supper and *leaned* on His chest, and had said, "Lord, who is it that is betraying You?"

21. Seeing him, Peter said to Jesus, "Lord, what *shall happen* to this one?"

22. Jesus said to him, "If I desire that he remain alive until I come, what *is it* to you? You follow Me."

23. Then this saying went out among the brethren, that that disciple would not die. However, Jesus did not say to him that he would not die; but, "If I desire that he remain alive until I come, what *is it* to you?"

24. This is the disciple who testifies concerning these things and *who* wrote these things; and we know that his testimony is true.

383. JESUS CHRIST'S COMMISSION TO THE APOSTLES
BEFORE HIS FINAL ASCENSION TO HEAVEN

MATTHEW 28	MARK 16	LUKE 24	ACTS 1
18. And Jesus came *and* spoke to them, saying, "All authority in heaven and on earth has been given to Me. 19. Therefore, go *and* make disciples in all nations, baptizing them into the name of the Father, and of the Son, and of the Holy Spirit;	15. And He said to them, "Go into all the world and preach the gospel to the whole creation. 16. The one who believes and is baptized shall be saved, but the one who does not believe shall be condemned. 17. And these signs shall follow those who believe: in My name they shall cast out demons; they shall speak with new languages;	49. "And behold, I send the promise of My Father upon you; but remain in the city of Jerusalem until you have been clothed with power from on high." 50. Then He led them out as far as Bethany; and He lifted up His hands *and* blessed them.	1. The first account I indeed have written, O Theophilus, concerning all things that Jesus began both to do and to teach, 2. Until the day in which He was taken up, after giving command by *the* Holy Spirit to the apostles whom He had chosen;

MATTHEW 28	MARK 16	LUKE 24	ACTS 1
20. Teaching them to observe all things that I have commanded you. And lo, I am with you always, *even* until the completion of the age." Amen.	18. They shall remove serpents; and if they drink any deadly thing, it shall not hurt them in any way; they shall lay hands on *the* sick, and they shall recover." 19. After speaking to them, the Lord was indeed then taken up into heaven, and He sat down at *the* right hand of God. 20. And they went out and preached everywhere, the Lord working with *them* and confirming the Word by the signs that followed. Amen.	51. And it came to pass *that* as He was blessing them, He was separated from them and was carried up into heaven. 52. And after worshiping Him, they returned to Jerusalem with great joy, 53. And were continually in the temple, praising and blessing God. Amen.	3. To whom also, by many infallible proofs, He presented Himself alive after He had suffered, being seen by them for forty days, and speaking the things concerning the kingdom of God.

384. JESUS CHRIST DID FAR MORE THAN IS RECORDED
JOHN 21

25. But there are also many other things that Jesus did, which if they were written one by one, I do not suppose that even the world itself could contain the books that would be written. Amen.

"All Power and Authority In Heaven and Earth Has Been Delegated To Me"

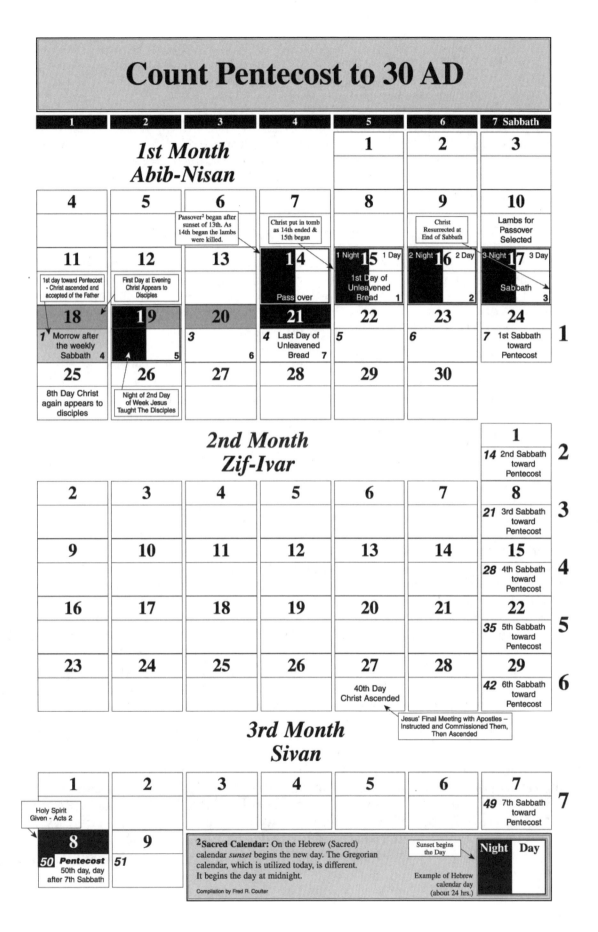

Count Pentecost to 30 AD

1	2	3	4	5	6	7 Sabbath

1st Month Abib-Nisan

1	2	3

4	5	6	7	8	9	10
		Passover² began after sunset of 13th. As 14th began the lambs were killed.	Christ put in tomb as 14th ended & 15th began		Christ Resurrected at End of Sabbath	Lambs for Passover Selected

11	12	13	14	1 Night 15 1 Day	2 Night 16 2 Day	3 Night 17 3 Day
1st day toward Pentecost - Christ ascended and accepted of the Father	First Day at Evening Christ Appears to Disciples		Passover	1st Day of Unleavened Bread 1	2	Sabbath 3

18	19	20	21	22	23	24	1
1 Morrow after the weekly Sabbath 4	2 5	3 6	4 Last Day of Unleavened Bread 7	5	6	7 1st Sabbath toward Pentecost	

25	26	27	28	29	30
8th Day Christ again appears to disciples	Night of 2nd Day of Week Jesus Taught The Disciples				

2nd Month Zif-Ivar

						1	2
						14 2nd Sabbath toward Pentecost	

2	3	4	5	6	7	8	3
						21 3rd Sabbath toward Pentecost	

9	10	11	12	13	14	15	4
						28 4th Sabbath toward Pentecost	

16	17	18	19	20	21	22	5
						35 5th Sabbath toward Pentecost	

23	24	25	26	27	28	29	6
				40th Day Christ Ascended		42 6th Sabbath toward Pentecost	

Jesus' Final Meeting with Apostles — Instructed and Commissioned Them, Then Ascended

3rd Month Sivan

1	2	3	4	5	6	7	7
						49 7th Sabbath toward Pentecost	

8	9
Holy Spirit Given - Acts 2	
50 **Pentecost** 50th day, day after 7th Sabbath	51

²**Sacred Calendar:** On the Hebrew (Sacred) calendar *sunset* begins the new day. The Gregorian calendar, which is utilized today, is different. It begins the day at midnight.

Compilation by Fred R. Coulter

Sunset begins the Day

Night	Day

Example of Hebrew calendar day (about 24 hrs.)

THE CONCLUSION

A Harmony of the Gospels in Modern English—The Life of Jesus Christ offers an entirely new perspective and depth of understanding of the life of Jesus Christ. The arrangement of this harmony is based on the Biblical holy days as determined by the Hebrew Calendar. These are the keys that help unlock the proper chronology of all the events recorded in the Gospels of Matthew, Mark, Luke and John. The events that the Gospel writers were inspired to record make it very clear that the prophecies of Jesus Christ's first coming were fulfilled on the holy days of God.

Jesus Christ's life, death and resurrection fulfilled scores of prophecies in the Old Testament. One of the most profound prophecies that He fulfilled is found in the book of Isaiah: "...He will magnify the law, and make it honorable" (Isa. 42:21). Jesus fulfilled this prophecy by revealing the full spirit and intent of God's laws in the Sermon on the Mount. The Scriptural records of His teachings in the Gospels clearly show that Christians are to keep the commandments of God not only in the letter but also in the spirit of the law. The commandments of God include observing His annual holy days and participating in the New Covenant Passover on Nisan 14. Partaking of the New Covenant Passover is done in remembrance of Jesus Christ's death for the forgiveness of sins. The epistle of Paul to the church in Corinth shows that Gentile believers as well as Jewish believers are commanded to keep the holy days and the Passover each year. Notice Paul's command to the Gentile believers at Corinth: "Therefore, purge out the old leaven, so that you may become a new lump, even as you are unleavened. **For Christ our Passover was sacrificed for us. For this reason, let us keep the feast, not with old leaven, neither with the leaven of malice and wickedness, but with unleavened *bread* of sincerity and truth**" (I Cor. 5:7-8).

Jesus Christ, Who was God manifest in the flesh, sacrificed His life on the Passover day, Nisan 14, as the true Passover Lamb to establish the New Covenant of eternal life. On the night of His last Passover, Jesus gave His apostles the instructions for the New Covenant Passover, which consists of the footwashing, partaking of the unleavened bread, and partaking of the wine. The footwashing symbolizes the true believer's attitude of love and humility toward Jesus Christ and toward other believers who are brethren. The broken unleavened bread and the wine symbolize the broken body and the blood of Jesus Christ, which sealed the New Covenant. By partaking of these symbols as Jesus commanded, the believer renews his or her commitment to live by Jesus Christ, Who dwells within each true believer and imparts the power to overcome sin and receive the gift of eternal life. Notice: "I am the living bread, which came down from heaven; if anyone eats of this bread, he shall live forever; and the bread that I will give is even My flesh, which I will give for the life of the world....**Truly, truly I say to you, unless you eat the flesh of the Son of man, and drink His blood, you do not have life in yourselves. The one who eats My flesh and drinks My blood has eternal life, and I will raise him up in the last day; for My flesh is truly food, and My blood is truly drink. The one who eats My flesh and drinks My blood is dwelling in Me, and I in him. As the living Father has sent Me, and I live by the Father; so also the one who eats Me shall live by Me**" (John 6:51-57).

Anyone who desires to live by Jesus Christ must do as Jesus taught: "*The* first of all the commandments *is*, 'Hear, O Israel [Substitute your name and ask yourself, "Am I doing as Jesus commanded?"]: *the* Lord our God is one Lord. And you shall love *the* Lord your God with all your heart, and with all your soul, and with all your mind, and with all your strength.' This *is the* first commandment. And *the* second *is* like this: 'You shall love your neighbor as yourself.' There is no other commandment greater than these" (Mark 12:29-31).

How does one love God as Jesus said? The apostle John, whom Jesus loved, was inspired to show true believers how to love God: "By this *standard* we know that we love the children of God: when we love God and keep His commandments. For this is the love of God, that we keep His commandments; and His commandments are not burdensome" (I John 5:2-3). True believers express their love for God by keeping His commandments. Jesus further clarified which commandments of God Christians are to obey: "Man shall not live by bread alone, but by every word that proceeds out of *the* mouth of God" (Matt. 4:4).

During His ministry, Jesus proclaimed that those who live by His words are building on a firm and lasting foundation. Notice Jesus' admonition: "Therefore, everyone who hears these words of Mine and practices them, I will compare him to a wise man, who built his house upon the rock; and the rain came down, and the floods came, and the winds blew, and beat upon that house; but it did not fall, for it was founded upon the rock" (Matt. 7:24-25). Jesus Christ is the Rock upon which all true Christians are being built up in the faith (I Cor. 10:4).

It is to this end and purpose that this book was written: to help you, the reader, to come into a close, intimate, personal relationship with your Creator and Savior, Jesus Christ, the Son of God; and to help you to grow in knowledge, understanding and faith in Him; so that you may ultimately be born of the resurrection into the Family of God, and thus fulfill the purpose of your existence. Jesus Christ, the Author of the New Covenant, offers you the gift of eternal life with Him as a glorified son or daughter of God. Through faith in Jesus Christ, repentance from sin, and baptism by immersion, you can receive the gift of the Holy Spirit and learn to live as Jesus taught, partaking of the Father's mercy, forgiveness, grace and love (Acts 2:38-39, Rom. 8:1-11). When the Spirit that empowered Jesus to live a sinless life is dwelling in you, you also will learn to overcome sin in the flesh. At the resurrection, that same Spirit, which raised Him from the dead to eternal power and glory, will also transform your body to immortal spirit. This is the promise to all who live by the teachings of Jesus Christ: "But as many as received Him, to them He gave authority to become the children of God, *even* to those who believe in His name; who were not begotten by bloodlines, nor by *the* will of *the* flesh, nor by *the* will of man; but *by the will* of God" (John 1:12-13).

Please direct any questions, comments or suggestions you may have to the author at the publisher's address: York Publishing Company; P.O. Box 1038; Hollister, CA 95024-1038.

DIAGRAM OF THE TEMPLE

1 Eben Shetiyyah

2 Candlestick

3 Altar of Incense

4 Table of Showbread

5, 6 Chamber of Knives

7 Attic of Abtinas

8 Chamber of the Pancake Makers

9 Chamber of Phinehas as the Vestment Keeper

10 Fifteen Semicircular Steps

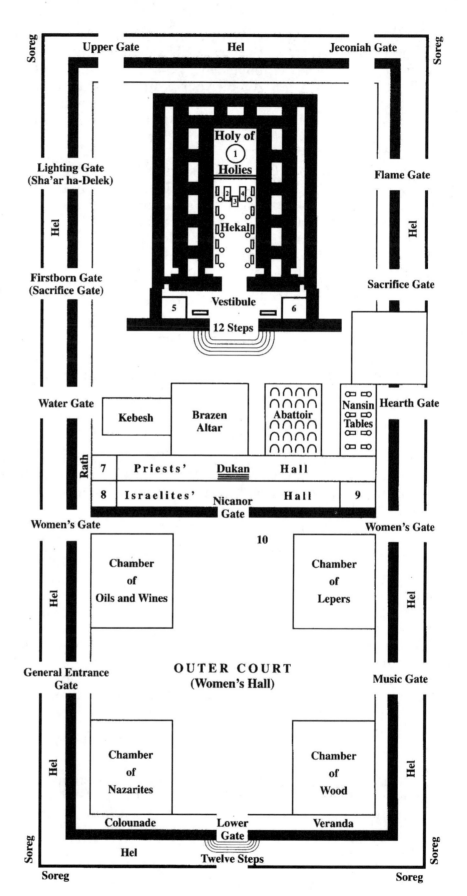

LIST OF ALL FEASTS DURING JESUS CHRIST'S LIFE

Year	Passover	Unleavened Bread (First)	Unleavened Bread (Last)	Pentecost	Feast of Trumpets	Day of Atonement	Feast of Tabernacles	Last Great Day
5 BC	MAR 22 WED	MAR 23 THU	MAR 29 WED	MAY 14 SUN	SEPT 2 SAB	SEPT 11 MON	SEPT 16 SAB	SEPT 23 SAB
4 BC	APR 11 WED	APR 12 THU	APR 18 WED	JUNE 3 SUN	SEPT 22 SAB	OCT 1 MON	OCT 6 SAB	OCT 13 SAB
3 BC	MAR 30 SAB	MAR 31 SUN	APR 6 SAB	MAY 19 SUN	SEPT 10 TUE	SEPT 19 THU	SEPT 24 TUE	OCT 1 TUE
2 BC	MAR 19 WED	MAR 20 THU	MAR 26 WED	MAY 11 SUN	AUG 30 SAB	SEPT 8 MON	SEPT 13 SAB	SEPT 20 SAB
1 BC	APR 7 WED	APR 8 THU	APR 14 WED	MAY 30 SUN	SEPT 18 SAB	SEPT 27 MON	OCT 2 SAB	OCT 9 SAB
1 AD	MAR 28 MON	MAR 29 TUE	APR 4 MON	MAY 22 SUN	SEPT 8 THU	SEPT 17 SAB	SEPT 22 THU	SEPT 29 THU
2 AD	APR 15 SAB	APR 16 SUN	APR 22 SAB	JUNE 4 SUN	SEPT 26 TUE	OCT 5 THU	OCT 10 TUE	OCT 17 TUE
3 AD	APR 4 WED	APR 5 THU	APR 11 WED	MAY 27 SUN	SEPT 15 SAB	SEPT 24 MON	SEPT 29 SAB	OCT 6 SAB
4 AD	MAR 24 MON	MAR 25 TUE	MAR 31 MON	MAY 18 SUN	SEPT 4 THU	SEPT 13 SAB	SEPT 18 THU	SEPT 25 THU
5 AD	APR 13 MON	APR 14 TUE	APR 20 MON	JUNE 7 SUN	SEPT 24 THU	OCT 3 SAB	OCT 8 THU	OCT 15 THU
6 AD	APR 2 FRI	APR 3 SAB	APR 9 FRI	MAY 23 SUN	SEPT 13 MON	SEPT 22 WED	SEPT 27 MON	OCT 4 MON
7 AD	MAR 21 MON	MAR 22 MON	MAR 28 MON	MAY 15 SUN	SEPT 1 THU	SEPT 10 SAB	SEPT 15 THU	SEPT 22 THU
8 AD	APR 9 MON	APR 10 TUE	APR 16 MON	JUNE 3 SUN	SEPT 20 THU	SEPT 29 SAB	OCT 4 THU	OCT 11 THU
9 AD	MAR 29 FRI	MAR 30 SAB	APR 5 FRI	MAY 19 SUN	SEPT 9 MON	SEPT 18 WED	SEPT 23 MON	SEPT 30 MON
10 AD	APR 16 WED	APR 17 THU	APR 23 WED	JUNE 8 SUN	SEPT 27 SAB	OCT 6 MON	OCT 11 SAB	OCT 18 SAB
11 AD	APR 6 MON	APR 7 TUE	APR 13 MON	MAY 31 SUN	SEPT 17 THU	SEPT 26 SAB	OCT 1 THU	OCT 8 THU
12 AD	MAR 25 FRI	MAR 26 SAB	APR 1 FRI	MAY 15 SUN	SEPT 5 MON	SEPT 14 WED	SEPT 19 MON	SEPT 26 MON
13 AD	APR 14 FRI	APR 15 SAB	APR 21 FRI	JUNE 4 SUN	SEPT 25 MON	OCT 4 WED	OCT 9 MON	OCT 16 MON
14 AD	APR 2 MON	APR 3 TUE	APR 9 MON	MAY 27 SUN	SEPT 13 THU	SEPT 22 SAB	SEPT 27 THU	OCT 4 THU
15 AD	MAR 22 FRI	MAR 23 SAB	MAR 29 FRI	MAY 12 SUN	SEPT 2 MON	SEPT 11 WED	SEPT 16 MON	SEPT 23 MON
16 AD	APR 10 FRI	APR 11 SAB	APR 17 FRI	MAY 31 SUN	SEPT 21 MON	SEPT 30 WED	OCT 5 MON	OCT 12 MON
17 AD	MAR 31 WED	APR 1 THU	APR 7 WED	MAY 23 SUN	SEPT 11 SAB	SEPT 20 MON	SEPT 25 SAB	OCT 2 SAB
18 AD	MAR 19 SAB	MAR 20 SUN	MAR 26 SAB	MAY 8 SUN	AUG 30 TUE	SEPT 9 THU	SEPT 13 TUE	SEPT 20 TUE
19 AD	APR 7 FRI	APR 8 SAB	APR 14 FRI	MAY 28 SUN	SEPT 18 MON	SEPT 27 WED	OCT 2 THU	OCT 9 THU
20 AD	MAR 27 WED	MAR 28 THU	APR 3 WED	MAY 19 SUN	SEPT 7 SAB	SEPT 16 MON	SEPT 21 SAB	SEPT 28 SAB
21 AD	APR 14 MON	APR 15 TUE	APR 21 MON	JUNE 8 SUN	SEPT 25 THU	OCT 4 SAB	OCT 9 THU	OCT 16 THU
22 AD	APR 4 SAB	APR 5 SUN	APR 11 SAB	MAY 24 SUN	SEPT 15 TUE	SEPT 24 THU	SEPT 29 TUE	OCT 6 TUE
23 AD	MAR 24 WED	MAR 25 THU	MAR 31 WED	MAY 16 SUN	SEPT 4 SAB	SEPT 13 MON	SEPT 18 SAB	SEPT 25 SAB
24 AD	APR 12 WED	APR 13 THU	APR 19 WED	JUNE 4 SUN	SEPT 23 SAB	OCT 2 MON	OCT 7 SAB	OCT 14 SAB
25 AD	APR 2 MON	APR 3 TUE	APR 9 MON	MAY 27 SUN	SEPT 13 THU	SEPT 22 SAB	SEPT 27 THU	OCT 4 THU
26 AD	MAR 22 FRI	MAR 23 SAB	MAR 29 FRI	MAY 12 SUN	SEPT 2 MON	SEPT 11 WED	SEPT 16 MON	SEPT 23 MON
27 AD	APR 9 WED	APR 10 THU	APR 16 WED	JUNE 1 SUN	SEPT 20 SAB	SEPT 29 MON	OCT 4 SAB	OCT 11 SAB
28 AD	MAR 29 MON	MAR 30 TUE	APR 5 MON	MAY 23 SUN	SEPT 9 THU	SEPT 18 SAB	SEPT 23 THU	SEPT 30 THU
29 AD	APR 16 SAB	APR 17 SUN	APR 23 SAB	JUNE 5 SUN	SEPT 27 TUE	OCT 6 THU	OCT 11 TUE	OCT 18 TU
30 AD	APR 5 WED	APR 6 THU	APR 12 WED	MAY 28 SUN	SEPT 16 SAB	SEPT 25 MON	SEPT 30 SAB	OCT 7 SAB
31 AD	MAR 26 MON	MAR 27 TUE	APR 2 MON	MAY 20 SUN	SEPT 6 THU	SEPT 15 SAB	SEPT 20 THU	SEPT 27 THU

Appendix A

A SYNCHRONIZED CHART OF
HISTORICAL AND SCRIPTURAL RECORDS
THAT ESTABLISH THE YEAR OF CHRIST'S BIRTH

The primary references that enable us to determine when Jesus Christ was born are those of Roman historians and of the Jewish historian Josephus, who lived from about 37 AD to 100 AD. These secular records can be used to establish the reign of Herod the Great, who attempted to kill the infant Jesus. Josephus records the names of the consuls who ruled in Rome at the time that Herod began his reign. Lists of all the consuls who ruled during the years from 509 BC to 337 AD have been preserved by Roman historians, giving us an exact time frame for dating the reign of Herod, which is essential to identifying the year of Christ's birth.

Josephus states that Herod received the kingdom in Rome in the 184th olympiad (*Antiquities*, 14:14:5). Each olympiad was four years in length, with the years being reckoned from July 1 through June 30. The 184th olympiad was from July 1, 44 BC, to June 30, 40 BC. Josephus also records that Herod began his reign when Calvinus and Pollio were consuls of Rome. Calvinus and Pollio were consuls from January 1, 40 BC, to December 31, 40 BC. Since the 184th olympiad ended on June 30, 40 BC, it is evident that the reign of Herod as king in Rome began sometime between January 1, 40 BC, and June 30, 40 BC.

According to Josephus, Herod reigned thirty-seven years from the time that he had been coronated in Rome (*Antiquities of the Jews*, 17:8:1; *Wars of the Jews*, 1:33:8). Consequently, the end of his reign occurred sometime between January 1, 4 BC, and June 30, 4 BC. Since Jesus was born during the final months of Herod's reign, all the historical facts limit the time of His birth to the period from June 30, 5 BC, to June 30, 4 BC. Because the Gospels place His birth during the fall festival season, the time is further limited to the year 5 BC. The historical and Scriptural records are presented in chart form on the following pages.

Greek Olympiad		Year of Rome	Year BC - AD	Hasmonian Rule	Reign of Herod	
					Roman Count	Jewish Count
179	1	691	63*	100		
	2	692	62	101		
	3	693	•61	102		
	4	694	60	103		
180	1	695	59	104		
	2	696	58	105		
	3	697	57	106		
	4	698	56	107		
181	1	699	55	108		
	2	700	54	109		
	3	701	53	110		
	4	702	52	111		
182	1	703	51	112		
	2	704	50	113		
	3	705	49	114		
	4	706	48	115		
183	1	707	47	116		
	2	708	46	117		
	3	709	45	118		
	4	710	44	119		
184	1	711	43	120		
	2	712	42	121		
	3	713	41	122		
	4	714	40•	123	1	
185	1	715	39	124	2	
	2	716	38	125	3	
	3	717	37†	126	4	1
	4	718	36		5	2
186	1	719	35		6	3
	2	720	34		7	4
	3	721	33		8	5
	4	722	32		9	6

* 63 BC   Jerusalem captured by Roman general Pompey during 179th olympiad. Antonius and Cicero are Roman consuls (Josephus, *Ant.*, 14:4:3).

• 40 BC   Herod receives kingdom in Rome during 184th olympiad. Calvinus and Pollio are Roman consuls (Josephus, *Ant.*, 14:14:5).

† 37 BC   Hasmoneans' 126-year rule of Jerusalem ends during 185th olympiad. Herod receives kingdom in Jerusalem. Agrippa and Gallus are Roman consuls (Josephus, *Ant.*, 14:16:4).

Greek Olympiad		Year of Rome	Year BC - AD	Life of Christ	Reign of Augustus	Reign of Herod		Temple Rebuilt
						Roman Count	Jewish Count	
187	1	723	31*		1	10	7	
	2	724	30		2	11	8	
	3	725	29		3	12	9	
	4	726	28		4	13	10	
188	1	727	27		5	14	11	
	2	728	26		6	15	12	
	3	729	25•		7	16	13	
	4	730	24		8	17	14	
189	1	731	23		9	18	15	
	2	732	22		10	19	16	
	3	733	21†		11	20	17	
	4	734	20§		12	21	18	1
190	1	735	19		13	22	19	2
	2	736	18		14	23	20	3
	3	737	17		15	24	21	4
	4	738	16		16	25	22	5
191	1	739	15		17	26	23	6
	2	740	14		18	27	24	7
	3	741	13		19	28	25	8
	4	742	12		20	29	26	9
192	1	743	11		21	30	27	10
	2	744	10		22	31	28	11
	3	745	9		23	32	29	12
	4	746	8		24	33	30	13
193	1	747	7		25	34	31	14
	2	748	6		26	35	32	15
Jesus Born	3	749	5★	0	27	36	33	16
	4	750	4Ω	1	28	37	34	17

* 31 BC   Battle of Actium, seventh year of Herod's reign, 187th olympiad (Josephus, *Ant.*, 15:5:1; 15:5:2).

• 25 BC   Two-year famine begins in Herod's thirteenth year (Josephus, *Ant.*, 15:9:1).

† 21 BC   Augustus visits Syria during seventeenth year of Herod's reign; Apuleius and Silvius are Roman consuls (*Dio's Roman History*, LIV:7:4-6; Josephus, *Ant.*, 15:10:3).

§ 20 BC   Construction of Herod's temple begins in Herod's eighteenth year (Josephus, *Ant.*, 15:11:1).

★ 5 BC   Jesus born during fall festival season—most likely on the Feast of Trumpets.

Ω 4 BC   Herod dies in thirty-seventh year of having received kingdom in Rome and thirty-fourth year of having received kingdom in Jerusalem (Josephus, *Ant.*, 17:8:1; *Wars*, 1:33:8).

Greek Olympiad		Year of Rome	Year BC - AD	Life of Christ	Reign of Augustus	Reign of Tiberius	Pilate Governs Judea	Temple Rebuilt
194	1	751	3	2	29			18
	2	752	2	3	30			19
	3	753	1 BC	4	31			20
		There is no year zero	There is no year zero	There is no year zero	There is no year zro		There is no year zero	
	4	754	1 AD	5	32			21
195	1	755	2	6	33			22
	2	756	3	7	34			23
	3	757	4	8	35			24
	4	758	5	9	36			25
196	1	759	6	10	37			26
	2	760	7	11	38			27
	3	761	8	12	39			28
	4	762	9	13	40			29
197	1	763	10	14	41			30
	2	764	11	15	42			31
	3	765	12	16	43	1		32
	4	766	13	17	44	2		33
198	1	767	14	18	45	3		344
	2	768	15	19		4		35
	3	769	16	20		5		36
	4	770	17	21		6		37
199	1	771	18	22		7		38
	2	772	19	23		8		39
	3	773	20	24		9		40
	4	774	21	25		10		41
200	1	775	22	26		11		42
	2	776	23	27		12		43
	3	777	24	28		13		44
	4	778	25	29		14		45
201	1	779	26*	30		15	1	46
	2	780	27	31		16	2	
	3	781	28	32		17	3	
	4	782	29	33		18	4	
202	1	783	30★	33½		19	5	
	2	784	31			20	6	
	3	785	32			21	7	
	4	786	33			22	8	

* 26 AD   Pontius Pilate assumes governance of Judea (Luke 3:1). Jesus begins ministry at about age thirty (Lk. 3:23). Herod's temple 46 years in building (John 2:20).

★ 30 AD Jesus crucified, Wednesday, April 5, 30 AD – The Passover Day, Nisan 14.

Greek Olympiad		Year of Rome	Year AD	Reign of Tiberius	Pilate Governs Judea
203	1	787	34	23	9
	2	788	35	24	10
	3	789	36	25	
	4	790	37	26	
204	1	791	38		
	2	792	39		
	3	793	40		
	4	794	41		
205	1	795	42		
	2	796	43		
	3	797	44		
	4	798	45		
206	1	799	46*		
	2	800	47		
	3	801	48		
	4	802	49		
207	1	803	50		
	2	804	51		
	3	805	52		
	4	806	53		
208	1	807	54		
	2	808	55		
	3	809	56		
	4	810	57		
209	1	811	58		
	2	812	59		
	3	813	60		
	4	814	61		
210	1	815	62		
	2	816	63		
	3	817	64		
	4	818	65		
211	1	819	66•		
	2	820	67		
	3	821	68		
	4	822	69		
212	1	823	70†		

* 46 AD   The apostle Paul begins his missionary journeys.
• 66 AD   Jewish wars begin.
† 70 AD   Destruction of temple occurs.

Appendix B

JESUS CHRIST WAS TAUGHT DIRECTLY BY GOD THE FATHER

JESUS DID NOT OBSERVE JEWISH TRADITION

The Gospels of Matthew and Luke record Jesus' physical genealogy and show that He was of the line of David, of the tribe of Judah. Although He was born of the virgin Mary and was human in every respect, nevertheless, He was the Savior of mankind, the Messiah of the world. Because He was divinely begotten by God the Father, Jesus was the Son of God. His education was different from that of other Jewish boys of the first century. We find no evidence in the Gospels that Jesus was educated by the rabbis in Jewish schools or synagogues, or that He was taught to observe the religion of Judaism and practice Jewish traditions. As the Son of God, there can be no doubt that His education was special.

In order to understand how and from whom Jesus received His education, one needs to examine His words and teachings, as well as what He did. First, Jesus Christ always kept the commandments of God. Second, He did not observe the commandments and traditions of Judaism, which are the commandments of men. Although Judaism claims that these traditional practices are based on the commandments of God, the truth is that they originated in the minds of men, not in the words of God. Third, **as the Lord God of the Old Testament, Jesus was the one Who had delivered the Ten Commandments**. He came to dwell on earth as the only begotten Son of God the Father, born of the virgin Mary. Since He was God in the flesh, Jesus kept the commands that came from God the Father. He did not keep the traditions that men had added to the commandments of God.

Some have assumed that Jesus was trained and brought up according to Jewish tradition. Those who have swallowed this false assumption believe that Jesus practiced the religion of Judaism and conformed to the traditions of the Jews. They claim that Jesus was thoroughly Jewish in habit, custom, tradition, religion and outlook. Some even claim that Jesus was a Pharisee, perhaps a Pharisaical rabbi, and therefore Jesus would certainly have kept the traditions of Judaism. NOTHING COULD BE FURTHER FROM THE TRUTH! Throughout the four Gospels, we find that Jesus strongly denounced the traditions of the Jews—ALL OF THEM! On many occasions, Jesus condemned the scribes and Pharisees for rejecting the commandments of God in order to keep their own traditions. He said, "... **Why do you also transgress the commandment of God for the sake of your tradition?** ... 'This people draw near to Me with their mouths, and with their lips they honor Me; but their hearts are far away from Me.' But they worship Me in vain, teaching *for* doctrine *the* commandments of men" (Matt. 15:3, 8-9).

A closer look at these words reveals that Jesus emphatically declared to the leaders of Judaism that in keeping their own traditions, they were **transgressing the commandments of God.** In short, such behavior is SIN. Worship that is based on the traditions of men is vain, empty and useless—sanctimonious pretense. Yes, with their mouths and lips they professed to serve God, but their hearts were far from Him!

Think for a moment! Knowing that the traditions of Judaism transgress the commandments of God, would Jesus ever have observed those traditions? ABSOLUTELY NOT! What did Jesus do? The Scriptures tell us that He kept the Father's commandments: "If you keep My commandments, you shall live in My love; just as **I have kept My Father's commandments and live in His love**" (John 15:10). Jesus went far beyond keeping only the letter of the law. Rather, He always kept the full spiritual intent of the law and did those things that pleased the Father: "And He Who sent Me is with Me. The Father has not left Me alone **because I ALWAYS do the things that please Him**" (John 8:29).

If Jesus had observed the traditional laws and commandments of Judaism, He would have been placing the traditions of men above the commandments of God. Instead, Jesus taught that to accept the traditions of men as the rule of law in place of obedience to the commandments of God, was sin. During a confrontation with the scribes and Pharisees, Jesus challenged them, "And because I speak the truth, you do not believe Me. **Which *one* of you can convict Me of sin**? But if I speak *the* truth, why don't you believe Me? " (John 8:45-46)

The Scriptures reveal that Jesus did not sin at any time. In II Corinthians 5:21, Paul expressly states, "**For He made Him Who knew no sin** *to be* sin for us, so that we might become *the* righteousness of God in Him." The apostle Peter also records that Jesus "COMMITTED NO SIN" (I Pet. 2:22).

JESUS' EDUCATION WAS NOT PHARISAIC

Jesus was twelve years old when He observed the Passover and Feast of Unleavened Bread with His parents in Jerusalem, as recorded in Luke 2:41-42. When the Feast ended, Joseph and Mary departed to go back to Nazareth, but Jesus remained. Having discovered that He was missing, they returned to find Jesus "... in the temple, sitting in *the* midst of the teachers, both hearing them and questioning them. And all those who were listening to Him were amazed at *His* understanding and His answers" (Luke 2:46-47).

How was it possible for Jesus to have such an extraordinary understanding of God's Word at such a young age? First, the Scriptures tell us that **Jesus had the Holy Spirit of God without measure**. John was inspired to say this about Jesus when he was questioned by the scribes and Pharisees: "**He Who comes from above is above all**. The one who is of the earth is earthy, and speaks of the earth. He Who comes from heaven is above all; and what He has seen and heard, this *is what* He testifies; but no one receives His testimony. The one who has received His testimony has set his seal that God is true; for He Whom God has sent [Jesus Christ] speaks the words of God; and **God gives not the Spirit by measure unto Him.** The Father loves the Son and has given all things into His hand" (John 3:31-35).

Second, the Scriptures show that **Jesus was taught directly by God the Father. Jesus was not taught by men, nor did He ever follow the traditions of men**. Here is what the Scriptures reveal about Jesus' education: "But then, about the middle of the feast, Jesus went up into the temple and was teaching. And the Jews were amazed, saying, 'How does this man know letters, **not having been schooled?**' " (John 7:14-15) The phrase "not having been schooled" means that **He was not taught in their schools**. He did not attend the rabbinical school of Hillel, as some have claimed. Jesus Himself tells us where He was educated: "Jesus answered them and said, '**My doctrine is not Mine, but His Who sent Me**' " (verse 16). Jesus' teachings were directly from God the Father, Who had personally taught Him. Jesus told the scribes and Pharisees, "I have many things to say and to judge concerning you; but He Who sent Me is true, and **what I have heard from Him, these things I speak to the world....I do nothing of Myself** [or of any man]. **But AS THE FATHER TAUGHT ME, these things I speak**" (John 8:26, 28).

Isaiah prophesied that Jesus would be educated directly by God the Father: "The Lord GOD hath given me the tongue of the learned, that I should know how to speak a word in season to *him that is* weary: **He wakeneth morning by morning, He wakeneth mine ear to hear as the learned**. The Lord GOD hath opened mine ear, and I was not rebellious, neither turned away back" (Isa. 50:4-5, *KJV*). As Isaiah foretold, Jesus was awakened early in the morning by His Father's voice and was personally taught by Him. With daily instruction directly from God the Father, Jesus did not need to be taught by men.

Jesus' education involved not only hearing the Father, but also seeing Him. So personal was His education from God the Father that Jesus actually saw the Father and what the Father did: "... Jesus answered and said to them, 'Truly, truly I say to you, the Son has no power to do anything of Himself [of His own will or the will of any man], but only what He sees the Father do. For whatever He does, these things the Son also does in the same manner. For the Father loves the Son, and **shows Him everything that He Himself is doing**.

And He will show Him greater works than these, so that you may be filled with wonder....I have no power to do anything of Myself; but as I hear, I judge; and My judgment is just because I do not seek My own will but the will of the Father, Who sent Me' " (John 5:19-20, 30). No one but Jesus could see the Father and what He was doing. This was a unique and special relationship between Jesus and God the Father.

Jesus' words in the Gospel of John confirm that He was not taught by rabbis or any other men who practiced the traditions of Judaism. Concerning their traditional education and schooling, the Jews distinctly said that He was unlettered—"not having been schooled," as recorded in John 7:15. As Jesus Himself testified, He was personally taught by God the Father.

Jesus had direct, instant communication with God the Father at all times. The Gospels record that this special relationship with the Father existed when Jesus was twelve years old, and it had undoubtedly existed from His birth. This is affirmed by Jesus' answer to Joseph and Mary when they found Him teaching the religious leaders at the temple: "And He said to them, 'Why *is it* that you were looking for Me? Don't you realize that I must be about My Father's *business*?' But they did not understand the words that He spoke to them" (Luke 2:49-50).

As the Son of God, sent to be the Savior of mankind, Jesus had to have a perfect and complete understanding of the Father's will. If He had failed even once to do the will of the Father, this sin would have brought Him under the death penalty, and we would have no Savior. In order to know the Father's will in everything, Jesus had to be taught directly by God the Father. No man—no scribe, no Pharisee, no learned sage or rabbi—could have imparted this divine knowledge to Jesus. It is critical for us to understand this fact so that we will not be deceived into believing that Jesus was taught by men and kept the traditions of the Jews.

Appendix C

EXEGESIS OF THE TRANSLATION OF "THE HOLY SPIRIT" AND ITS ANTECEDENTS IN JOHN 14, 15 AND 16

In this translation, the true scriptural understanding of the Holy Spirit is presented. The Greek New Testament reveals that the Holy Spirit is not a person. Rather, it is the power of God, which is imparted as the gift of God to everyone who repents of sin and accepts the sacrifice of Jesus Christ for the forgiveness of sin. Upon true repentance, baptism and the laying on of hands, God the Father puts the power of the Holy Spirit within each true Christian, thereby making him or her His begotten child. This process is called conversion. However, it is not until the resurrection, when Jesus Christ returns to the earth, that all those who have died in the faith, together with those truly converted Christians who are still alive, will be born again. They will be transformed from fleshly human beings to glorified children of God and will reign with Jesus Christ as kings and priests in the Kingdom of God.

In his account of the begettal and birth of Jesus Christ, Luke clearly describes the function of the Holy Spirit as the power of God. Note the angel Gabriel's message to the virgin Mary: " 'And behold, you shall conceive in *your* womb and give birth to a son; and you shall call His name Jesus. He shall be great, and shall be called *the* Son of *the* Highest; and *the* Lord God shall give Him the throne of David, His forefather; and He shall reign over the house of Jacob into the ages, and of His kingdom there shall be no end.' But Mary said to the angel, 'How shall this be, since I have not had sexual relations with a man?' And the angel answered *and* said to her, '**The** **Holy Spirit** [Greek πνευμα αγιον *pneuma agion*] **shall come upon you, and *the* power** [Greek δυναμις *dunamis*] **of *the* Highest shall overshadow you; and for this reason, the Holy One being begotten in you shall be** called *the* **Son of God**' " (Luke 1:31-35).

Just before Jesus Christ ascended into heaven, He told His disciples that they would receive power from the Father: "And while *they* were assembled with *Him*, He commanded them not to depart from Jerusalem but to 'await the promise of the Father, which,' *He said*, 'you have heard of Me. For John indeed baptized with water, but, you shall be baptized with *the* Holy Spirit [Greek πνευματι αγιω *pneumati agioo*] after not many days ... **But you yourselves shall receive power** [Greek δυναμις *dunamis*] **when the Holy Spirit** [Greek του αγιου πνευματος *tou hagiou pneumatos,* neuter gender] **has come upon you**, and you shall be My witnesses, both in Jerusalem and in all Judea and Samaria, and unto *the* ends of the earth' " (Acts 1:4-5, 8).

In the New Testament, the Greek noun *pneuma*, which is translated "spirit," is in the neuter gender. Likewise, the Greek noun phrases that are translated "the Spirit," "the Holy Spirit," and "the Holy Ghost" are always and only in the neuter gender. No masculine gender noun is used anywhere in the New Testament to designate the Holy Spirit, but only the Father and the Son. The use of the neuter gender in every scripture reveals that the Holy Spirit is not a person but the power that emanates from both the Father and the Son.

The forms of the noun *pneuma* that are found in the Greek text of the New Testament are as follows:

1) πνευμα *pneuma* spirit
2) το πνευμα *to pneuma* the spirit
3) το πνευματος *to pneumatos* the spirit
4) πνευμα αγιον *pneuma hagion* spirit holy
5) το αγιον πνευμα *to hagion pneuma* the holy spirit
6) το αγιον πνευματος *to hagion pneumatos* the holy spirit
7) το πνευμα το αγιον *to pneuma to hagion* the spirit the holy

Exegesis For the Translation of "The Holy Spirit"

The Greek noun *pneuma*, in all its various forms, is always and only neuter in gender. Likewise, all pronouns that refer to *pneuma* are always and only neuter in gender. If the Holy Spirit were a person, the nouns and pronouns in the Greek text would have to be written in the masculine gender, as are all the nouns and pronouns that refer to God the Father and Jesus Christ. However, nowhere in the Greek text of the New Testament is the Holy Spirit ever designated by a noun or pronoun in the masculine gender.

It is absolutely incorrect to translate any form or pronoun of πνευμα *pneuma* in the masculine gender. Unfortunately, because most translators believe in the doctrine of the trinity, they have mistakenly used the masculine gender when translating the neuter gender nouns and pronouns pertaining to the Holy Spirit. The following five key verses in the Gospel of John that have been incorrectly translated in the King James Version:

1) "*Even* **the Spirit of truth**; **whom** the world cannot receive, because it seeth **him** not, neither knoweth **him**: but ye know **him**; for **he** dwelleth with you, and shall be in you" (John 14:17, *KJV*).

"**The Spirit of truth**" is translated from the Greek phrase το πνευμα της αληθειας *to pneuma tees aleetheias*—literally, "the Spirit of the truth." This noun phrase is in the neuter gender. The pronoun "**whom**" is translated from the neuter relative pronoun ο, and should accordingly be translated "which." If the Greek text were expressing the masculine gender, the masculine relative pronoun ος would have been used instead of the neuter relative pronoun ο.

The three personal pronouns translated "**him**" are incorrectly translated into the masculine gender from the Greek neuter personal pronoun αυτο *auto*, which is properly translated "it." If "the Spirit" were a person rather than the power of God, the verse would read ο πνευματος, rather than the neuter το πνευμα. However, there is no such masculine noun anywhere in the Greek New Testament. If there were such a masculine gender noun, the masculine pronoun αυτος *autos* would be used instead of the neuter pronoun αυτο *auto*. Translators who know and understand the rules of Greek grammar do not mistake the neuter pronoun αυτο *auto* for the masculine pronoun αυτος. Thus the translation of the neuter pronoun αυτο in John 14:17 into the masculine personal pronoun "**him**" is completely incorrect. The neuter pronoun αυτο is used twice in this verse: "because it [the world] perceives **it** [αυτο *auto*] not, nor knows **it** [αυτο *auto*]."

The KJV translation of John 14:17 also violates another rule of Greek grammar. In the Greek text, a noun that serves as the subject of a verse often governs a number of verbs. In John 14:17, the noun phrase το πνευμα της αληθειας *to pneuma tees aleetheias*, meaning "the Spirit of the truth," is the subject. Since the noun *pneuma* is neuter in gender, the subjects of all verbs that it governs should be translated in the neuter gender. In John 14:17, two third person verbs are governed by this noun. In the first instance, the translators have incorrectly translated the third person verb μενει *memei* as "**he dwelleth**," rather than "**it dwelleth**." In the second instance, the subject of the verb εσται *estai*, "**[it] shall be**," was not translated, making it appear that "**he**" is the subject of both Greek verbs.

A correct translation of John 14:17 should read: "*Even* the Spirit of the truth, **which** [ο] the world cannot receive because it perceives **it** [αυτο *auto*] not, nor knows **it** [αυτο *auto*]; but you know **it** [αυτο *auto*] because **it dwells** [verb μενει *memei*] with you, and **shall be** [verb εσται *estai*] within you."

2) "But when **the Comforter** is come, **whom** I will send unto you from the Father, *even* **the Spirit of truth**, **which** proceedeth from the Father, **he** shall testify of me" (John 15:26, *KJV*).

The word "which," referring to "**the Spirit of truth**," is correctly translated from the neuter pronoun ο. In John 14:17, the translators of the KJV had incorrectly rendered this neuter pronoun as "whom." However, in this verse, they have correctly rendered the pronoun ο as "which."

The descriptive noun "**the Comforter**" is correctly translated from the masculine Greek noun ο παρακλητος *ho parakleetos*. While this masculine noun is used to describe a vital function of the Holy Spirit, it does not designate the Holy Spirit, or "**the Spirit of the truth**," as a person. A descriptive noun never changes the gender of the principal noun. For example: Jesus said that He is "the true vine" (John 15:1). The Greek word translated "vine" is the feminine noun η αμπιλος *he ampilos*. The use of this feminine noun to describe Jesus Christ does not make His gender feminine. In exactly the same way, the use of the masculine noun ο παρακλητος *ho parakleetos* to describe a function of the Holy Spirit does not alter the fact that the Holy Spirit is neuter. Because the Holy Spirit is neuter in gender—not masculine—there is no basis in the Greek text for interpreting the Holy Spirit as a person.

Although the Holy Spirit is not a person, it is in accord with Greek grammar to translate the pronoun ον *on* as "**whom**" because its antecedent is the masculine descriptive noun ο παρακλητος *ho parakleetos*, "**the Comforter**." However, it is misleading to translate the personal pronoun ον *on* as "whom" when the principal noun is το πνευμα της αληθειας *to pneuma tees aleetheias*, which is neuter in gender.

The last part of this verse has been translated: "... **he** shall testify of me." The use of the personal pronoun "**he**" once again gives the impression that the Holy Spirit is a person. However, that is not the meaning of the Greek text. The word "**he**" is translated from the Greek word εκεινος *ekeinos*, which means "that" or "that one." As with the pronoun ον *on*, the antecedent of εκεινος *ekeinos* is ο παρακλητος *ho parakleetos*, "the Comforter," which is a descriptive noun. Although it is masculine in gender, the principal noun is το πνευμα της αληθειας *to pneuma tees aleetheias*, which is neuter. The gender of the principal noun always takes precedence over the gender of the descriptive noun. Therefore, εκεινος *ekeinos* has been translated "... **that one** shall bear witness of Me" in order to reflect the true meaning of the Greek text.

The translation of John 15:26 should read: "But when the Comforter has come, **which** I will send to you from the Father, *even* **the Spirit of the truth, which** proceeds from the Father, **that one** shall bear witness of Me."

3) "But the Comforter, *which is* the Holy Ghost, **whom** the Father will send in my name, **he** shall teach you all things, and bring all things to your remembrance, whatsoever I have said unto you" (John 14:26, *KJV*).

As in John 15:26, the descriptive noun *ho parakleetos*, "the Comforter," is used with the principal noun *to pneuma*, "the Spirit." In the Greek text, the verse begins with these words: ο δε παρακλητος, το πνευμα το αγιον, ο ... *ho de parakleetos, to pneuma to hagion, o ...* The noun phrase το πνευμα το αγιον *to pneuma to hagion*, "the Holy Spirit," is the antecedent of the neuter pronoun ο, which has been incorrectly translated "whom" in the KJV. Since ο is a neuter pronoun, it should be translated "which." If the Greek text contained the masculine pronoun ος, it would be proper to translate it as "whom" to reflect the masculine gender. However, the Greek text uses the neuter form of the pronoun, not the masculine form.

The pronoun "**he**" in this verse is translated from the Greek εκεινος *ekeinos* and should be translated "**that one.**"

This translation of John 14:26 conveys the precise meaning of the Greek text: "But *when* the Comforter *comes*, *even* the Holy Spirit, **which** the Father will send in My name, **that one** shall teach you all things, and shall bring to your remembrance everything that I have told you."

The translators of the KJV have also used the masculine pronoun "he" in Verse 16 of this same chapter: "And I will pray the Father, and he shall give you another **Comforter**, that **he** may abide with you for ever" (John 14:16, *KJV*). As Verse 17 shows, "the Comforter" is describing the Holy Spirit, or "the Spirit of truth," which is translated from *to pneuma tees aleetheias*, the same noun phrase that is used in John 15:26. Since *pneuma* is the principal noun, the meaning of the pronoun is governed by its neuter gender, not by the masculine gender of *parakleetos*, or "Comforter," which is a descriptive noun. This translation of John 14:16 accurately conveys the meaning of the Greek text: "And I will ask the Father, and He shall give you another **Comforter**, that **it** may be with you throughout the age."

4) "Howbeit when **he**, the Spirit of truth, is come, **he** will guide you into all truth: for **he** shall not speak of himself; but whatsoever **he** shall hear, *that* shall **he** speak: and **he** will show you things to come" (John 16:13, *KJV*).

All six occurrences of the pronoun "**he**" in this verse refer to "the Spirit of truth," which is translated from το πνευμα της αληθειας *to pneuma tees aleetheias*. Since *pneuma* is neuter in gender, all six pronouns should accordingly be translated in the neuter gender. The first "**he**" is an incorrect rendering of the Greek εκεινος *ekeinos* and should be translated "that one." The remaining five occurrences of "**he**" are all subjects of verbs that are governed by the neuter noun *pneuma* and should be translated "**it.**"

The correct meaning of John 16:13 is reflected in this translation: "However, when **that one** has come, *even* the Spirit of the truth, **it will lead** [verb οδηγησει *odeegeesei*] you into all truth because **it shall** not **speak** [verb λαλησει *laleesei*] from itself, but whatever **it shall hear** [verb ακουση *akousee*] **it shall speak** [verb λαλησει *laleesei*]. And **it shall disclose** [verb αναγγελει *anaggelei*] to you the things to come."

5) "**He** shall glorify me: for **he shall receive** of mine, and **shall show** it unto you" (John 16:14, *KJV*).

As in John 16:13, the first "**he**" is translated from the Greek εκεινος *ekeinos*, meaning "that one." Since the antecedent of *ekeinos* is "the Spirit of truth" in Verse 13, both the noun and its pronoun are neuter in gender. The second "**he**," which is the subject of the verb "**shall receive**," is governed by "the Spirit of truth," or το πνευμα της αληθειας *to pneuma tees aleetheias*, and should also be translated in the neuter gender. The verb "**shall show**," which the translators of the KJV have rendered as a compound verb with "**shall receive**," is also governed by "the Spirit of truth," and should accordingly be translated in the neuter gender.

This translation of John 16:14 correctly follows the Greek text: "**That one** shall glorify Me because **it shall disclose** [verb αναγγελει *anaggelei*] to you *the things that* **it receives** [verb ληψεται *leepsetai*] from Me."

As the New Testament reveals, the Holy Spirit is not a person; rather it is the power of God. All references to the Holy Spirit in the Greek text are in the neuter gender. The use of the descriptive noun "the Comforter," which is masculine in gender, does not alter the neuter gender of the Holy Spirit. There is no basis in the New Testament for the claim that the Holy Spirit is a third person in a trinity.

Eminent Greek Scholar Refutes Personality of the Holy Spirit

The use of the pronoun εκεινος *ekeinos*, "that one," does not affirm that the Holy Spirit has personality or is a person. The arguments concerning *ekeinos,* attempting to make the Holy Spirit a third person in the Godhead, are only unsubstantiated theological theories that are not based on the true meaning of the Greek. In fact, there is no place in the New Testament where the Holy Spirit is designated as a third person of a trinity. These fallacious arguments begin with the premise that the Godhead is a so-called "trinity"—a word found nowhere in the New Testament. Rather than seeking the truth of the Scriptures, the proponents of this theory must resort to twisted interpretations of Scripture in order to give a plausible, but false, explanation. However, the Greek New Testament does not teach that the Holy Spirit is a person, nor a third member of a triune Godhead. Rather, it teaches that the Holy Spirit is the power of God that He uses to accomplish His will.

The advocates of attributing personality to the Holy Spirit use several key scriptures to attempt to prove their theory. One verse in question is John 15:26, which reads: "But when the Comforter has come, which I will send to you from the Father, *even* the Spirit of the truth, which proceeds from the Father, **that one** shall bear witness of Me."

In a detailed refutation of their claims, the eminent New Testament Greek scholar and syntax expert, Daniel B. Wallace wrote of this verse: "The use of εκεινος [a masculine pronoun, *that one*] here [in John 15:26] is frequently regarded by students of the NT to be an affirmation of the personality of the Spirit. Such an approach is based on the assumption that the antecedent of εκεινος [*that one*] is πνευμα [*spirit* a neuter noun]: [It is claimed], 'the masculine pronoun εκεινος [*that one*] is [also] used in John 14:26 and 16:13-14 to refer to the neuter noun πνευμα [*spirit*] to emphasize the personality of the Holy Spirit' " (Wallace, *Greek Grammar Beyond the Basics*, p. 331). In Footnote 42, Wallace noted: "The view is especially popular among theologians, not infrequently becoming the mainstay [the only basis] in their argument for the personality of the Spirit" (Ibid., p. 331).

"But this [conclusion] is erroneous. In all these Johannine passages, πνευμα [*spirit*] is appositional to a masculine noun. The gender of εκεινος [*that one*] thus has nothing to do with the natural [neuter] gender of πνευμα [*spirit*]. The antecedent of εκεινος, [*that one*] in each case, is παρακλητος [*comforter*, a masculine noun], not πνευμα [*spirit*, a neuter noun]. John 14:26 reads: ο παρακλητος, το πνευμα το αγιον, ο πεμψει ο πατηρ εν τω ονοματι μου, εκεινος υμας διδαξει παντα ... ('the Comforter, the Holy Spirit whom [which] the Father sends in my name, **that one** will teach you all things'). πνευμα [*spirit*] not only is appositional to παρακλητος [*comforter*] but the relative pronoun that follows it [πνευμα (*spirit*)] is neuter! This hardly assists the grammatical argument for the Spirit's personality. In John 16:13-14 the immediate context is deceptive: οταν δε ελθη εκεινος, το πνευμα της αληθειας, οδηγη σει υμας εν τη αληθεια παση .... εκεινος εμε δοξασει ... ('whenever **that one** comes—the Spirit of truth—he [*it*] will guide you in all truth....he [*that one*] will glorify me ...'). The εκεινος [*that one*] [in these verses] reaches back to v 7, where παρακλητος [*comforter*] is mentioned. Thus, since παρακλητος [*comforter*] is masculine, so is the pronoun [εκεινος "that one" is masculine]. Although one might argue that the Spirit's personality is in view in these passages, the view must be based on the nature of a παρακλητος [*comforter*] and the things said about the Comforter, not on any supposed grammatical subtleties [concerning το πνευμα το αγιον "the Spirit of the truth," which is neuter gender]. **Indeed, it is difficult to find *any* text** [in the New Testament] **in which** πνευμα [*spirit*] **is grammatically referred to with the masculine gender** [because there are not any]" (Wallace, *Greek Grammar Beyond the Basics*, pp. 331-332, some bold emphasis and all bracketed comments added).

Wallace added further comments in related footnotes. Concerning John 16:13, he wrote: "Although translations of v. 13 such as that of the NRSV may be misleading as to what the subject of the sentence is ('When the Spirit of truth comes, he will guide you...'), their objective is not to be a handbook for Greek students" (Ibid., *Footnote 43*, p. 332). To paraphrase, Wallace is saying that John 16:13 in the NRSV is an incorrect translation that does not follow the Greek text.

A correct translation of John 16:13-14 reads: "However, when **that one** has come, *even* the Spirit of the truth, it will lead you into all truth because it shall not speak from itself, but whatever it shall hear it shall speak. And it shall disclose to you the things to come. **That one** shall glorify Me because it shall disclose to you *the things that* it receives from Me."

Wallace further refuted the notion that personality of the Holy Spirit can be found in the Greek New Testament. In another extended footnote he wrote: "Besides the Johannine texts, three other passages are occasionally used for this: Eph 1:14; 2 Thess 2:6-7; and 1 John 5:7. All of these have problems. In Eph 1:14 ος εστιν αρραβων [*which is* the *earnest*] refers back to τω πνευματι [*the spirit*] (v 13), but the masculine relative pronoun [ος *he/which*] (*v.l.*) is easily explained without resorting to seeing the theological motifs [of attempting to prove personality of the Spirit] ... In 2 Thess 2:6-7 πνευμα [*spirit*] is nowhere mentioned; το κατεχον/ο κατεχων [*holding back/one Who is restraining*] are often assumed to both refer to the Holy Spirit. But in spite of the fact that there is much to commend this view, it certainly cannot use clear natural-gender passages in support [of personality for the Holy Spirit], nor can such a known *crux interpretum* [critical interpretation] become the basis for such a syntactical point. [In other words, such an interpretation is contrary to the Greek.] First John 5:7 is perhaps the most plausible of the passages enlisted. The masculine participle in τρεις εισιν οι μαρτυρουντες [*three that bear witness*] refers to το πνευμα και το υδωρ και το αιμα [*the Spirit and the water and the blood*] (v 8), all neuter nouns. Some see this as an oblique reference to the Spirit's personality ... but the fact that the author [John] has personified water and blood, turning them into witnesses along with the Spirit, may be enough to account for [the use of] the masculine gender [plural participle μαρτυρουντες— *bear witness*]. This interpretation also has in its behalf the allusion to Deut. 19:15 (the necessity of 'two or three witnesses'), for in the OT the testimony only of males was acceptable. Thus, the elder [the apostle John] may be subtly indicating (via the masculine participle) that the Spirit, water and blood are all valid witnesses" (Ibid., *Footnote 44*, p. 332, bracketed comments and some bold emphasis added).

When the context of I John 5:6-9 is included, it is clear that Wallace is quite correct: "This is He Who came by water and blood—Jesus the Christ; not by water only, but by water and blood. And it is the Spirit that **bears witness** [neuter singular participle] because the Spirit is the truth. For there are **three that bear witness** [masculine plural participle] on the earth: the Spirit, and the water, and the blood [all neuter nouns]; and these three *witness* unto the one *truth* [that Jesus was God manifested in the flesh and died for the sins of the world]. If we accept the witness of men, the witness of God is superior. For this is the witness of God, which He has witnessed [through the Spirit, the water and the blood] concerning His Son."

In verse 6 "the Spirit **that bears witness**" is translated from the neuter singular participle, μαρτυρουν *marturoun*. If John had intended to attribute personality to the Holy Spirit, he would have used a masculine participle, but he did not. Therefore, the shift to the masculine plural participle μαρτυρουντες *marturountes* in verse 7 does not by any means constitute attributing personality to the Spirit. Moreover, if the use of the masculine plural participle in verse 7 did, in fact, attribute personality to the Holy Spirit, then it would also have attributed personality to the water and the blood. However, no such argument has ever been made. Wallace's analysis of the three witnesses in verse 7 with John's use of the masculine participle is correct.

Proper analysis and exegesis of these critical verses clearly reveals that the Holy Spirit does not have personality. Therefore, the Holy Spirit cannot be a third person in a triune Godhead. The doctrine that the Godhead is a trinity of three persons is found nowhere in the Old or New Testaments.

Finally, the New Testament reveals that there are only two Persons in the Godhead— God the Father and Jesus Christ. The Holy Spirit is revealed to be the power by which God accomplishes His will. There is no basis in the New Testament for the claim that the Holy Spirit is the third person in a trinity.

Appendix D

BINDING AND LOOSING IN THE NEW TESTAMENT

Matthew 16:19 and 18:18

The Roman Catholic Church claims that Jesus gave to the apostle Peter and his future successors the powers of binding and loosing so that whatever they would bind or loose on earth, would be bound or loosed in heaven. They further contend that this authority grants an infallible pope the power to bind and loose contrary to the Word of God—thus making the Word of God void—and that this authority was given to Peter by Jesus Christ as recorded in Matthew 16:19 and 18:18. However, an exegetical study of the Greek does not support such claims.

In *Basics of Biblical Greek Grammar*, William D. Mounce gives a clear and insightful explanation of the underlying Greek text showing that what Jesus taught is entirely different from what many religious authorities assume, teach and practice. He writes, "In some translations of Matthew [16:19 and] 18:18, it sounds like Jesus promised his disciples that whatever they bound on earth would be bound in heaven, and whatever they loosed on earth would be loosed in heaven. In other words, they had the power to bind and loose, and Heaven (i.e. God) would simply back up their decrees. But the matter is not quite so simple; the actions described in heaven are future perfect passives—which could be translated 'will have already been bound in heaven ... will have already been loosed in heaven.' In other words, the heavenly decree confirming the earthly one is based on a prior verdict [God had already made—"For ever, O LORD, thy word is settled in heaven" (Psa. 119:89).]

"This is the language of the law court. Jewish legal issues were normally decided in Jesus' day by elders in the synagogue community (later by rabbis). Many Jewish people believed that the authority of Heaven stood behind the earthly judges when they decided cases based on a correct understanding of God's law. (This process came to be called 'binding and loosing.') Jesus' contemporaries often envisioned God's justice in terms of a heavenly court; by obeying God's laws, the earthly court simply ratified the decrees of the heavenly court" (p. 121, bracketed comments added).

Jesus **did not** give His apostles and disciples the authority to make binding decisions regarding anything on earth that had not already been decreed in heaven. Jesus specifically taught that He did not come to abolish the Law or the Prophets (Matt. 5:17). Therefore, whatever is bound or loosed cannot be contrary to the laws and commandments of God, the revelation of the prophets or the teachings of Jesus Christ. Jesus Christ **did not** give His apostles the authority to loose any of the Ten Commandments or any of God's laws that are not connected with the priesthood and temple ritual. However, Jesus **did** give His apostles the authority to loose the religious **traditions** of the Jews (Mark 7:1-13; Acts 10:28) as well as pagan religious traditions (I Pet. 1:18; Acts 14:8-18). New Testament teachings that were foreshadowed and prophesied in the Old Testament and "bound" or decreed in heaven before Jesus Christ came in the flesh are as follows: to love the Lord God with all one's heart, soul and might (Deut. 6:4-6; Matt. 22:37-40); for Jesus to magnify the law and make it honorable (Isa. 52:14; Matt. 5-7); for Christ to die for the sins of the world (Psa. 22; Isa. 53; John 1:36; Rev. 13:8); forgiveness of sin, upon repentance, without temple animal sacrifices (Psa. 32:1-2; 51:1-17; Rom. 3:20-24; Heb. 10:1-17); circumcision of the heart (Deut.10:16; Rom. 2:28-29; Col. 2:2-13); Sabbath and holy day keeping for uncircumcised Gentiles (Isa. 56:1-6), taught by Paul (Acts 13:42-44; Heb. 4:9; I Cor. 5:8); and many others.

Any Christian-professing ministry or church that promotes sin—the transgression of the law—in its binding or loosing decisions is operating contrary to the Word and will of God. Its decisions are simply **inventions of men** and do not have the authority of heaven behind them. Examples of these are: adding to or taking away from the Word of God (Deut. 12:30-32; Rev. 22:18-19); worshiping other gods or goddesses (Ex. 20:2-3; I Cor. 10:20-21); endorsing the making and worshiping of idols (Ex. 20:4-6; Isa. 42:8, 17; 44:9-20; I Cor. 10:14; 12:2; Rev. 9:20-21; 21:8); worshiping the dead "saints" (Isa. 8:19-20); exchanging the Sabbath and holy days of God for the pagan holidays of apostate Christendom such as Halloween, Christmas, New Years, Lent, Easter, etc., or any other so-called holy days of the religions of the world.

All binding and loosing decisions made by the ministry and brethren of Jesus Christ must be in complete accord with the Word of God and the teachings of Jesus Christ. These decisions are authoritative because they have "already been bound or loosed in heaven." As Jesus said, "**All authority in heaven and on earth has been given to Me**" (Matt. 28:18). All binding and loosing **must be based** on the authority of Jesus Christ and the Word of God.

INDICES

SCRIPTURAL INDEX

MATTHEW			MARK			MARK		
Chapter	Verse	Page	Chapter	Verse	Page	Chapter	Verse	Page
26	21-25	275	1	1	75	8	35-38	158
26	26	249	1	1-3	46	9	1-4	159
26	26	276	1	4-8	48	9	2-8	5
26	27-29	249	1	9-11	52	9	5-10	160
26	27-29	277	1	12-13	55	9	11-18	163
26	28	254	1	14-15	66	9	19-27	164
26	30	280	1	14-15	142	9	28-32	165
26	31-35	278	1	15	75	9	30-32	5
26	36-38	283	1	16-20	68	9	31	311
26	38	260	1	21-28	69	9	33-41	176
26	39-44	284	1	29-38	70	9	42-50	177
26	45-46	266	1	39	71	10	1	179
26	45-46	285	1	40-45	105	10	2-12	203
26	47-49	286	2	1-2	105	10	13-16	204
26	50-55	287	2	3-12	106	10	17-24	205
26	55	270	2	13-17	107	10	24-31	206
26	55-56	266	2	18-22	108	10	32-33	207
26	56-58	288	2	23-28	110	10	32-34	5
26	59-68	290	2	27	84	10	34-45	208
26	66	270	2	27	85	10	46-48	209
26	69-74	291	2	27-28	85	10	49-52	210
26	75	292	2	28	85	11	1-8	218
27	1-2	292	3	1-6	111	11	9-11	219
27	3-7	269	3	7-19	112	11	11	212
27	3-10	293	3	20-30	114	11	13-14	213
27	11-14	294	3	31-35	116	11	12-19	220
27	13-14	270	4	1-9	125	11	19	213
27	15-16	295	4	10-12	126	11	20	213
27	17-23	296	4	13-20	127	11	20-26	221
27	24-31	297	4	21-29	128	11	27-13:1	213
27	26-30	269	4	30-34	129	11	27-33	224
27	32-33	300	4	35-41	131	12	1-11	225
27	34-37	301	5	1-12	132	12	12	226
27	34	271	5	13-20	133	12	13-15	227
27	36	271	5	21-29	134	12	16-19	228
27	38-40	302	5	29-38	135	12	20-27	229
27	39-40	272	5	39-43	136	12	28-36	230
27	41-45	303	6	1-9	137	12	29-31	345
27	43-44	272	6	10-13	138	12	37-40	231
27	46	272	6	14	140	12	41-44	233
27	46-51	304	6	15-28	141	13	1-2	233
27	49	304	6	29	142	13	1-3	213
27	51-54	305	6	30-34	143	13	3-9	234
27	55-56	306	6	35-42	144	13	10-15	235
27	57-60	273	6	43-46	145	13	16-26	236
27	57-60	312	6	47-52	146	13	27-37	237
27	57-61	307	6	53-56	147	14	1	213
27	62-64	318	7	1-13	150	14	1-7	241
27	62-66	323	7	5-13	92	14	8-11	242
27	62-66	314	7	6-9	319	14	10-11	268
27	64	318	7	14-23	151	14	12-13	243
28	1	315	7	24-37	152	14	14-16	244
28	1	323	8	1-9	153	14	17	274
28	2-4	326	8	10-21	154	14	18-21	275
28	2-8	334	8	22-27	155	14	22	249
28	9-10	338	8	27-30	5	14	22	276
28	11-15	336	8	28-30	156	14	23-25	249
28	16-17	340	8	31	311	14	23-25	277
28	18-19	341	8	31-33	5	14	26	280
28	20	342	8	31-34	157	14	27-31	278

A Harmony of the Gospels in Modern English—The Life of Jesus Christ

ISAIAH

Chapter	Verse	Page
9	6-7	308
14	14-15	245
42	21	75
50	6	262
50	6	269
52	14	262
52	14	269
53		308
53	3-12	262
53	12	272
53	4-6	270
53	7	269
53	7	270
53	8-9	273
53	10-11	270
53	12	272
57	15	81

JEREMIAH

Chapter	Verse	Page
10	1-8	32

EZEKIEL

Chapter	Verse	Page
14	1-8	89
28	12-18	246

DANIEL

Chapter	Verse	Page
7	13-14	308
9	26	308
9	26	268
12	1	317
12	3	247
12	4	1
12	7	310

JONAH

Chapter	Verse	Page
1	17	310

ZECHARIAH

Chapter	Verse	Page
11	12	261
11	12	269
11	13	269
12	10	264
12	10	272
13	7	266
13	7	268

ACTS

Chapter	Verse	Page
1	1-2	341
1	3	342
1	15-19	293
2	38-39	345
4	8-12	15
4	11	156
5	27-31	15
6	1-4	17

ROMANS

Chapter	Verse	Page
1	16-18	9
1	19-25	12
2	28-29	81
3	9-19	74
3	23	246
5	12	245
5	21	90
6	23	246
7	14	74
8	1-11	345
8	2-3	265
8	29	330

I CORINTHIANS

Chapter	Verse	Page
3	16-17	81
5	7	255
5	7	269
5	7-8	88
5	7-8	344
9	13-14	83
10	4	156
10	4	347
10	7-9, 14	88
10	19-21	89
11	23-24	249
11	23-24	276
11	25-26	249
11	25-29	277
15	4-7	340
15	5-8	6
15	20	330
15	40-44	247
15	45-47	73

II CORINTHIANS

Chapter	Verse	Page
5	21	16

GALATIANS

Chapter	Verse	Page
3	1	17
3	7-8	247
3	14	247
3	16	247
3	17	250
4	4	32

EPHESIANS

Chapter	Verse	Page
1	22	156
2	1-10	16
2	11-19	86
2	18-22	81
2	20	156

PHILIPPIANS

Chapter	Verse	Page
2	5-8	250
2	5-11	15

COLOSSIANS

Chapter	Verse	Page
1	14-20	16
1	16-18	330
1	18	156
1	27	91
2	9-13	82

II THESSALONIANS

Chapter	Verse	Page
2	1-12	13

I TIMOTHY

Chapter	Verse	Page
3	16	14
3	16	245

II TIMOTHY

Chapter	Verse	Page
3	15	17

TITUS

Chapter	Verse	Page
2	13-14	14

HEBREWS

Chapter	Verse	Page
1	1-6	15
1	1-7	253
1	13-14	253
2	9-10	251
2	14	10
2	14-18	251
4	4-9	86
4	9	86
4	9	87
4	14-16	254
4	15	10
5	7-9	252
5	7-9	326
7	5-13	82
10	1-4	252
10	5-7	251
10	5-12	80
10	12-17	91
10	16-22	80
12	2	265

JAMES

Chapter	Verse	Page
2	8-12	77
4	11-12	93

I PETER

Chapter	Verse	Page
1	18-20	269
2	4-6	156
2	5	156
2	10	86
2	21-22	86
2	24	254

TOPICAL INDEX

Found – 2, 15, 18, 23, 28, 29, 39, 40, 42, 44, 46, 51, 53, 57, 66, 112, 113, 120, 133, 140, 150, 152, 160, 173, 179, 188, 195, 196, 199, 202, 207, 215, 218, 220, 221, 227, 244, 250, 263, 270, 284, 294, 295, 296, 300, 304, 308, 310, 315, 325, 328, 329, 333, 335, 338, 345, 356, 358, 361, 363, 364

Foxes – 131, 180

Fruit – 39, 48, 65, 103, 114, 125, 127, 128, 186, 188, 220, 221, 225, 245, 277, 280, 281

Fulfilled – 22, 31, 32, 38, 40, 41, 42, 45, 61, 66, 67, 70, 75, 76, 81, 83, 84, 85, 98, 112, 126, 129, 168, 179, 207, 218, 223, 236, 248, 249, 260, 261, 262, 263, 264, 266, 268, 269, 270, 271, 272, 273, 274, 275, 281, 285, 287, 288, 293, 295, 301, 302, 304, 305, 327, 329, 331, 335, 340, 345

Gabriel – 30, 31, 33, 34, 38, 39

Galilean – 69, 291, 294

Galilee – 5, 23, 39, 41, 45, 46, 47, 52, 53, 54, 61, 65, 66, 67, 68, 69, 71, 72, 83, 106, 112, 113, 122, 132, 133, 141, 142, 143, 144, 145, 149, 152, 153, 163, 164, 165, 168, 169, 176, 178, 179, 199, 219, 221, 272, 278, 294, 306, 307, 314, 328, 334, 335, 339, 341

Gehenna – 76, 98, 99, 139, 177, 185, 232

Generation – 9, 40, 83, 88, 115, 118, 154, 158, 163, 164, 183, 184, 197, 199, 232, 237, 247, 264, 273, 308

Glorified – 12, 60, 66, 106, 107, 116, 153, 159, 169, 189, 201, 213, 218, 221, 223, 247, 250, 264, 276, 279, 281, 284, 285, 358

Glorify – 97, 172, 213, 223, 250, 265, 276, 282, 284, 343

Glory – 11, 12, 14, 15, 41, 42, 47, 54, 55, 73, 84, 89, 91, 94, 100, 101, 102, 122, 158, 159, 160, 168, 172, 173, 186, 197, 199, 201, 202, 206, 208, 219, 223, 226, 236, 240, 246, 250, 251, 252, 253, 264, 265, 266, 284, 285, 311, 325, 326, 331, 332, 333

Gnashing – 113, 130, 190, 227, 238, 240

Goats – 240, 252

God – 13-18, 23, 28-32, 37-42, 46-48, 50, 52-53, 55-57, 60-62, 66, 68-71, 73-98, 101, 102, 106, 107, 110, 112, 114, 116, 117, 118, 121, 122, 126-130, 132, 133, 137, 139, 142, 143, 146-150, 153, 156, 157, 159, 165, 168, 171-173, 177, 180, 181, 183-186, 189, 190, 193-195, 197, 199, 200-206, 208-210, 213, 219, 220, 221, 224, 226-230, 232, 233, 236, 237, 245-255, 258-270, 272-274, 276-277, 279, 281, 282, 284, 290, 292, 298, 302-305, 307-309, 311, 314, 316, 319, 325, 326, 327, 329, 330-334, 337, 340, 342, 343, 345, 346, 354-358, 361, 362, 363, 364, 365

God is – 48, 61, 62, 147, 199, 229, 230, 319, 355

God the Father – 11, 12, 13, 14, 15, 16, 32, 60, 75, 78, 79, 80, 81, 83, 88, 89, 90, 91, 94, 96, 147, 156, 250, 253, 254, 255, 262, 263, 263, 264, 266, 319, 325, 326, 327, 329, 331, 332,, 333, 334, 354, 355, 356, 357, 358, 364

   Believe in – 16, 17, 47, 66, 75, 78, 96, 147, 165, 173, 177, 203, 223, 226, 265, 279, 282, 285, 308, 325, 335, 339, 343, 347, 359

   Christians are to become perfect as – 97-100

   Christians must worship Him in spirit and truth – 62, 89, 319

   Draws each Christian to Himself – 148

   Loves the Son – 61, 121, 355, 356

   Gave His only begotten Son – 17, 60, 254

   Has life inherent – 121

   Heavenly Father – 11, 101, 102, 151, 179

   Holy is His name – 40

   In heaven – 76, 80, 97, 100, 101, 103, 104, 116, 139, 156, 177, 178, 182, 221, 231

   In spirit – 62, 89, 319

   Jesus came in His name – 121

   Jesus did His will – 121, 148

   Loved the world – 17, 60, 254

   Works – 121

Gods – 192

Gold – 23, 44, 138, 206, 232

Gomorrah – 138

Good works – 14, 16, 97, 193

Gospel – 22, 27, 28, 29, 30, 31, 46, 49, 50, 51, 66, 67, 71, 75, 77, 82, 83, 86, 93, 117, 122, 136, 138, 212, 213, 224, 235, 242, 243, 250, 264, 308, 309, 311, 312, 313, 314, 315, 316, 317, 318, 325, 327, 328, 329, 342, 345, 356, 358

Grace – 14, 16, 39, 46, 47, 67, 90, 93, 94, 95, 250, 251, 252, 254, 266, 317, 321, 335, 347,

Grace of God – 16, 46, 90, 93, 95, 251, 266, 317, 321

Grave – 118, 156, 180, 197, 202, 254, 273, 309, 311, 312, 315, 329, 332

Grievous – 94

Hairs – 119, 139, 185, 236

Hated – 139, 210, 234, 235, 259, 260, 263, 265, 281, 285

Heal – 65, 67, 111, 112, 113, 126, 137, 138, 163, 180, 193, 209, 223

Healings

   Casting out a demon – 69

   Casting out deaf and dumb spirit – 163, 164

   Casting out legion of demons into herd of swine – 132-133

   Centurion's servant – 113

   Cut-off ear – 287

   Daughter of Canaanite woman – 152

   Dumb man possessed by demon – 136

   Of blind man – 155, 172, 209-210

   Of deaf man – 152

   Of man with dropsy – 193

   Of man with 38-year infirmity – 120

   Of many in Galilee – 153

   Of ten lepers – 199

   Of woman of 18-year infirmity – 189

   Jairus' daughter – 134-135

   Leper – 105

   Man with withered hand – 111

   Many – 70

   Multitudes – 112, 153

   Paralytic – 106

   Peter's mother-in-law – 70

   Lazarus raised from dead – 201

   Only son of widow raised from the dead – 116

   Sick healed by touching Jesus' clothes – 147

   Two blind men – 136

   Woman with 12-year hemorrhage – 134

Heart – 42, 46, 74, 75, 76, 77, 80, 81, 82, 89, 90, 97, 99, 101, 103, 115, 118, 126, 127, 150, 151, 179, 181, 187, 205, 206, 221, 230, 236, 238, 254, 261, 262, 263, 264, 270, 274, 279, 282, 308, 311, 313, 318, 325, 326, 332, 338, 339, 346, 365

Heart, All your – 181, 230

Heaven – 2, 3, 9, 10, 10, 15, 16, 41, 46, 52, 53, 60, 61, 67, 73, 74, 75, 76, 80, 81, 82, 83, 84, 85, 88, 90, 91, 97, 98, 99, 100, 101, 102, 103, 104, 113, 116, 117, 118, 125, 126, 128, 129, 130, 131, 138, 139, 144, 147, 148, 149, 152, 154, 156, 157, 176, 177, 178, 179, 180, 181, 182, 183, 187, 189, 195, 196, 197, 199, 200, 201, 204, 205, 207, 213, 217, 219, 221, 223, 224, 227, 229, 231, 232, 234, 236, 237, 239, 246, 258, 263, 264, 284, 290, 327, 331, 332, 333, 334, 335, 342, 343, 345, 355, 357, 364, 365

Heavenly – 11, 41, 60, 80, 82, 101, 102, 151, 179, 333

Hebrew Calendar-6 BC to 4 BC – 33-36

   Feasts During Jesus' Life – 348

Help – 18, 26, 68, 150, 152, 164, 182, 251, 254, 262, 263, 312, 333, 346, 347

Herod – 6, 22, 23, 24, 25, 26, 27, 28, 29, 35, 36, 37, 44, 45, 46, 65, 83, 122, 140, 141, 142, 154, 190, 294, 295, 317, 349, 350, 351

Herodians – 111, 227

Herodias – 65, 141

High priest – 6, 15, 25, 36, 80, 81, 82, 83, 110, 203, 241, 251, 253, 268, 287, 288, 289, 290, 291

Tears – 108, 119, 164, 252, 328, 334
Temple – 5, 6, 11, 13, 20, 25, 27, 29, 30, 31, 35, 37, 38, 42,
   44, 46, 55, 56, 57, 58, 66, 79, 80, 81, 82, 83, 109, 110, 120,
   140, 166, 217, 219, 220, 222, 223, 224, 230, 232, 233, 234,
   238, 242, 245, 266, 269, 272, 275, 287, 289, 290, 293, 302,
   304, 312, 329, 330, 343, 347, 351, 352, 353, 355, 356, 365
Tempt – 55, 56, 88, 170, 227
Temptation – 10, 56, 57, 63, 101, 182, 253, 254, 260, 283,
   284, 327, 328
Thanks – 144, 147, 153, 199, 276, 277
The day God died
   Commentary – 245-255
Thief – 144, 147, 153, 199, 276, 277
Thieves – 14, 101, 174, 181, 182, 220, 302
Third day – 53, 157, 165, 190, 207, 208, 216, 217, 312, 313,
   315, 316, 318, 319, 324, 336, 337, 340, 341
Thirst – 62, 97, 147, 163, 271
Thirty – 43, 99,86, 142, 146, 242, 248, 249, 261, 269, 293
Thirty pieces of silver – 242, 261, 269, 293
Three days – 46, 57, 115, 153, 157, 261, 272, 290, 302, 308,
   309, 310, 311, 312, 313, 315, 316, 318, 324, 326
Throne – 14, 39, 80, 99, 156, 206, 232, 240, 245, 254, 265,
   331, 332, 333, 334, 357
Tomb – 6, 142, 202, 218, 249, 250, 258, 261, 273, 307, 308,
   309, 311, 312, 313, 314, 315, 316, 318, 323, 324, 325, 326,
   327, 328, 329, 335, 336, 337, 338
Tombs – 132, 184, 232, 305
Tongue – 15, 40, 152, 198, 262, 357
Torment – 132, 197, 198
Tormented – 113, 164
Touched – 70, 105, 116, 134, 135, 136, 147, 152, 160, 210,
   287
Tradition – 5, 7, 8, 18, 22, 92, 93, 95, 150, 308, 313, 319, 354
Transgressors – 77, 262, 271, 272
Trespasses – 16, 82, 101, 198
Tribulation – 127, 235, 236, 260, 283
True – 1, 4, 5, 8, 9, 10, 12, 14, 17, 18, 22, 32, 46, 61, 62, 65,
   75, 78, 79, 80, 81, 82, 85, 86, 87, 88, 89, 90, 92, 94, 95, 96,
   97, 121, 147, 148, 159, 168, 170, 171, 174, 193, 197, 200,
   227, 246, 249, 255, 259, 264, 280, 284, 305, 311, 316, 317,
   318, 319, 325, 342, 345, 346, 355, 356, 357, 359, 360, 361
True God – 4, 264, 284
Truly – 14, 16, 17, 53, 57, 60, 62, 65, 67, 75, 77, 78, 83, 85,
   98, 100, 101, 113, 114, 117, 121, 126, 137, 138, 139, 140,
   146, 147, 148, 149, 154, 159, 163, 165, 168, 169, 171, 172,
   173, 174, 176, 177, 178, 187, 190, 204, 205, 206, 221, 224,
   232, 233, 237, 238, 239, 240, 242, 263, 264, 269, 274, 275,
   277, 278, 179, 282, 284, 291, 303, 305, 342, 245, 256, 257
Twenty-eight prophecies fulfilled in one day – 268-273

Unclean – 69, 112, 113, 114, 115, 132, 133, 137, 152, 164, 183
Unclean spirit – 69, 114, 115, 132, 152, 164, 183
Understand – 2, 4, 7, 9, 13, 46, 75, 78, 80, 85, 86, 106, 126,
   127, 146, 151, 154, 165, 171, 174, 179, 212, 218, 223, 235,
   243, 246, 250, 259, 266, 272, 274, 282, 291, 311, 313, 317,
   328, 336, 340, 354, 356, 358
Understanding – 10, 17, 18, 22, 46, 126, 151, 156, 203, 212,
   213, 230, 317, 325, 345, 346, 355, 357, 364
Understood – 1, 10, 12, 14, 17, 18, 37, 75, 82, 84, 89, 130,
   154, 163, 208, 245
Unpardonable sin – 114, 185, 239
Unprofitable – 198
Unquenchable – 49, 177

Vengeance – 200, 235

Vine – 7, 277, 280, 359
Vineyard – 188, 207, 224, 225
Vipers – 48, 115, 232
Virgin – 3, 5, 10, 29, 31, 34, 39, 40, 83, 250, 253, 331, 354,
   357

War – 195, 238, 245
Wars – 28, 234, 249, 251, 259
Wave sheaf offering – 325-335
Wedding – 66, 187, 194, 227, 237, 239
Week – 25, 26, 27, 29, 30, 31, 32, 35, 84, 85, 86, 87, 201,
   216, 313, 314, 315, 316, 318, 319, 325, 327, 329, 335, 336,
   337, 340
Wept – 202, 219, 292, 328, 336
Wheat – 49, 128, 197, 221, 278
Wicked – 26, 80, 94, 97, 100, 103, 115, 127, 129, 130, 154,
   179, 183, 210, 240, 252, 262, 265, 271, 273, 308
Wickedness – 227, 346
Widows – 67, 231
Wife – 25, 29, 30, 31, 37, 38, 40, 41, 43, 65, 99, 122, 141,
   178, 194, 197, 200, 202, 203, 204, 206, 228, 229, 296, 303
Wilderness – 5, 28, 46, 47, 48, 51, 55, 60, 86, 105, 117, 143,
   144, 147, 153, 195, 236
Will of God – 47, 84, 116, 254, 347
Willing – 22, 40, 117, 121, 177, 210, 242, 260, 269, 284, 297
Wine – 31, 38, 53, 54, 65, 66, 108, 118, 181, 249, 254, 258,
   274, 277, 301, 345
Wisdom – 4, 7, 8, 31, 38, 46, 95, 115, 118, 137, 183, 184, 235
Wise men – 35, 44, 232
With God – 13, 15, 16, 37, 39, 46, 73, 121, 206, 250, 253, 357
Witness – 46, 60, 173, 235, 289, 292
Witnesses – 6, 73, 121, 177, 270, 290, 340, 357, 363, 364
Words of God – 4, 10, 13, 18, 28, 47, 55, 61, 68, 82, 83, 91,
   92, 95, 116, 127, 150, 183, 192, 193, 246, 354, 355, 364, 365
Work – 14, 15, 16, 27, 29, 30, 33, 62, 70, 83, 84, 85, 91, 95,
   104, 114, 121, 140, 147, 168, 172, 173, 176, 189, 193, 217,
   224, 237, 241, 250, 264, 284, 330, 331
Workers of unrighteousness – 190
World – 1, 2, 3, 4, 5, 8, 9, 10, 11, 12, 13, 14, 15, 16, 17, 18, 27,
   32, 41, 46, 52, 55, 60, 65, 74, 75, 79, 80, 82, 83, 85, 88, 91,
   93, 94, 95, 96, 97, 129, 133, 145, 147, 148, 158, 165, 170,
   171, 172, 173, 174, 177, 184, 186, 193, 197, 201, 202, 213,
   216, 218, 221, 223, 226, 235, 236, 238, 240, 243, 242, 245,
   250, 251, 253, 254, 255, 259, 260, 264, 265, 266, 267, 268,
   269, 270, 279, 280, 281, 282, 283, 284, 285, 288, 289, 294,
   295, 327, 330, 331, 332, 334, 342, 343, 344, 345, 354, 356,
   358, 359, 363, 365, 375, 376, 377, 379, 380, 381
Worshiped – 3, 12, 23, 44, 62, 88, 105, 132, 134, 146, 152,
   174, 178, 334, 339,341
Worshiper – 173
Worshipers – 62, 80, 319

Your Father – 76, 97, 100, 101, 103, 139, 170, 171, 177, 182,
   221, 329, 337
Your God – 55, 56, 90, 172, 181, 182, 230, 329, 337, 346
Your Son – 264, 284
Your strength – 181, 230, 346
Your will – 80, 101, 182, 251, 260, 284, 333

Zabulon – 67
Zacharias, John the Baptist's father – 30, 31, 33, 37, 38, 39,
   40, 41, 42, 47
Zara – 43
Zeal – 57, 263
Zebedee – 68, 69, 112, 137, 208, 283, 306, 341

BIBLIOGRAPHY

Amadon, Grace. *"The Crucifixion Calendar,"* Journal of Biblical Literature, Vol. LXIII, pp. 188-189, 1944

Apostolic Constitutions—Didascalia Apostolorum, Book V.

Arndt and Gingrich. *A Greek-English Lexicon of the New Testament.* Chicago: The University of Chicago Press, 1952.

Berry, George Ricker. *The Interlinear Greek-English New Testament.* Grand Rapids: Zondervan Publishing House, 1979.

The Bible. A New Translation by James Moffatt. New York: Harper & Brothers Company, 1950.

Brenton, Sir Lancelot C. L. *The Septuagint With Apocrypha: Greek and English.* Peabody, MA: Hendrickson Publishers, 1999.

Chicago Tribune Magazine. 29 August 1993.

Dio's Roman History. Loeb edit. Book LVI: 29-30, Vol. 7.

Edersheim, Alfred. *The Life and Times of Jesus the Messiah.* Peabody, MA: Hendrickson Publishers, 1989.

Finegan, Jack. *Handbook of Biblical Chronology.* Peabody, MA: Hendrickson Publishers, 1998.

Fox, Everett, Trans. *The Schocken Bible, Volume I— The Five Books of Moses.* New York: Schocken Books, 1995.

Freedman, David Noel. *The Anchor Bible Dictionary.* New York: Doubleday, 1992.

Funk, Robert W., *Honest to Jesus: Jesus for a New Millennium* . San Francisco: HarperCollins, 1996.

Funk, Robert W. and the Jesus Seminar. *The Acts of Jesus: The Search for the Authentic Deeds of Jesus.* San Francisco: Harper Collins, 1998.

Funk, Robert W., and Roy W. Hoover, *The Five Gospels, The Search for the Authentic Words of Jesus:* New York: Scribner, 1993.

Geering, Lloyd. *The World to Come: From Christian Past to Global Future.* Polebridge Press, 1999.

Hobbs, Edwards. available at EHOBBS@wellesley.edu. Accessed 12 July 1997.

The Holy Bible. The Revised Berkeley Version in Modern English. Grand Rapids: Zondervan Publishing House, 1969.

Josephus, Flavius. *The Life and Works of, Seven Dissertations.* Translated by Willliam Whiston, A.M.

Kudlek, Manfred, and E. H. Mickler. *Solar and Lunar Eclipses of the Ancient Near East 3000 B.C. to 0 With Maps.* Neukirchen-Bluyn: Verlas Butson and Bercker Kevelaer, 1971.

Lietzmann, Hans. *A History of the Early Church.* Cleveland: The World Publishing Company, 1963.

Liddell, Henry George, Robert Scott and Henry Stuart Jones. *A Greek-English Lexicon.* Oxford: Clarendon Press, 1996.

Lust, K., Erik Eynikel, and Katrin Hauspie. *A Greek-English Lexicon of the Septuagint.* Stuttgart: Deutsche Bibelgesellschaft, 1996.

Luther, Martin. *Saemmtliche Schriften, Letter 99,* 1 August 1521. Translated by Erika Flores in The Wittenberg Project, The Wartburg Segment; published in Grace and Knowledge, Issue 8, September 2000.

Mounce, D. William. *Basics of Biblical Greek Grammar; 2nd Edition.* Grand Rapids, MI: Zondervan 2003

Robertson, A.T. *Word Pictures in the New Testament.* Nashville, TN: Broadman & Holman Publishers, 2000.

Rolfe, J. C. ed. *Seutonius: The Lives of the Caesars.* LCL, Vol. 1. Boston: Harvard University Press, 1998.

Tardo, Russell K. *Sunday Facts and Sabbath Fiction.* Arabi, LA: Faithful Word Publications, 1992.

Unger, Merril F. *Unger's Bible Dictionary.* Chicago: Moody Press, 1963.

Vincent's Word Studies in the New Testament. Peabody, MA: Hendrickson Publishers, 1984.

World Scripture—A Comparative Anthology of Sacred Texts. St. Paul, Minn.: Paragon House, 1995.

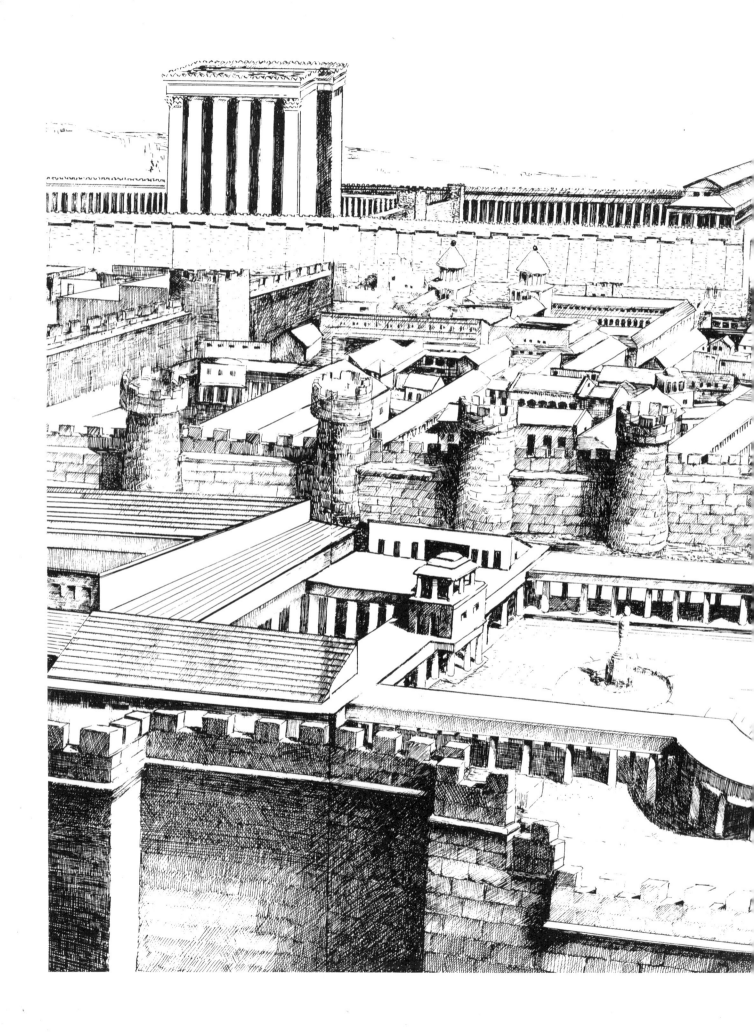